# RUSSELL'S IDEALIST APPRENTICESHIP

# Russell's Idealist Apprenticeship

NICHOLAS GRIFFIN

CLARENDON PRESS · OXFORD
1991

Oxford University Press, Walton Street, Oxford OX2 6DP
Oxford New York Toronto
Delhi Bombay Calcutta Madras Karachi
Petaling Jaya Singapore Hong Kong Tokyo
Nairobi Dar es Salaam Cape Town
Melbourne Auckland
and associated companies in
Berlin Ibadan

Oxford is a trade mark of Oxford University Press

Published in the United States
by Oxford University Press, New York

British Library Cataloguing in Publication Data
Griffin, Nicholas
Russell's idealist apprenticeship.
1. English philosophy. Russell, Bertrand
I. Title
192
ISBN 0-19-824453-3

Library of Congress Cataloging in Publication Data
Griffin, Nicholas.
Russell's idealist apprenticeship / Nicholas Griffin.
p. cm.
Includes bibliographical references.
1. Russell, Bertrand, 1872–1970. I. Title.
B1649.R94G75 1990 192—dc20 90-33417
ISBN 0-19-824453-3

Typeset by Hope Services (Abingdon) Ltd.
Printed and bound in
Great Britain by Bookcraft (Bath) Ltd,
Midsomer Norton, Avon

*To Richard*

# Preface

In his old age Russell always referred to his idealist apprenticeship with scorn. It was, he suggested, nothing but an incoherent muddle into which he had been led by teachers and friends and from which he extricated himself with difficulty after several entirely wasted years. His pride in having broken free from the neo-Hegelianism which dominated British philosophy at the end of the nineteenth century was well-earned, and the advance he made in breaking away from it was real enough. Yet Russell's neo-Hegelianism was by no means the unmitigated disaster most people nowadays assume.

It constituted (though often in outline only) a vast system of philosophy, encompassing a full philosophical analysis and reconstruction of the various sciences and their mutual relations. Although much of Russell's neo-Hegelian philosophy was left in programmatic form, parts of it were worked out with an attention to detail unparalleled among British philosophers of his day. Moreover, given Russell's initial assumptions, which were shared by most contemporary philosophers, the system had a high degree of logical coherence. Certainly, there are some scandalously invalid arguments (many of them borrowed from other authors), but these often concern points of detail and the overall system would stand without them. The major problems are much more subtle—though hindsight makes them easier to spot. In short, I believe that Russell's neo-Hegelian philosophy deserves rather more respect than it has received. By any standards, it is one of the most spectacular works by any philosopher in his early twenties.

Despite this, the tone of the central chapters of this book is unrelentingly critical. In part, this comes with the turf—philosophical books are rarely uncritical. In part, however, it comes from the specific historical focus of the book. For one of its main aims, beyond providing an accurate record of Russell's early philosophical development, is to show exactly why a radically new departure in philosophy was called for at the turn of the century. This can only be done when we know exactly what was wrong with the earlier views, and this is something which has not so far been adequately revealed by historical scholarship. The very detail with which Russell developed his neo-Hegelian philosophy makes it most suitable for this purpose, and also invites detailed criticism. One would not think of criticizing Bosanquet or Lotze, for example, because they failed to distinguish a dense series from a continuous one; nor Bradley because he could give no account of the difference between cardinal and ordinal arithmetic. That Russell's neo-Hegelianism is amenable to the sort of very detailed criticism provided here seems to me one of its virtues. Even as a neo-Hegelian, Russell sought (though he was not always able to achieve) the type of rigour that analytic philosophers have admired.

The criticisms are broadly of three types. There are those which point out the scandalously (and the not so scandalously) invalid arguments which Russell sometimes used. Others point out the respects in which Russell's scientific knowledge (the product of his education in the late nineteenth-century Cambridge Tripos system) was inadequate for his purposes. Finally, there are the problems, caused by unresolvable contradictions within his dialectic, upon which his neo-Hegelian project foundered. These problems were Russell's principal concern as a neo-Hegelian. It was by no means a minor achievement that he came to see that the main problems from each branch of the dialectic were all of just two forms, that all depended upon the same fundamental logical doctrines, and that these doctrines could be replaced.

Time has not been kind to Russell's neo-Hegelianism. The philosophical tradition to which it belonged is dead and unlikely to be resurrected. Not by this book, at any rate, for rehabilitating neo-Hegelianism in any form is not my intention. My chief purpose has been to fill a gap in the historical record. Most other parts of Russell's career are known—widely, if not well—through his own writings and (to some extent) those of others. But most of Russell's writings as a neo-Hegelian remain unpublished, and those which were published are no longer read, while the silence of the commentators has been deafening. Only Pujia (1977) has attempted an extended commentary on this period of Russell's work—with limited success, however (see Spadoni 1979).

The main topic of the book is Russell's dialectical encyclopaedia of the sciences and its dissolution. This occupies the whole of Chapters 4 through 8, and most of Chapter 3 as well. Chapters 1 and 2 and part of Chapter 3, by contrast, are concerned with Russell's intellectual development up to the time he became a neo-Hegelian—in particular, with his education at home (Chapter 1) and at Cambridge (Chapter 2). Some such account seems essential if one is to understand why his philosophical thought took the direction it did. By no means all of Russell's philosophical output before the turn of the century is considered. I have refrained from commenting on his study of Leibniz, despite the fact that his *Critical Exposition of the Philosophy of Leibniz* was one of his major achievements in the period. There is already a decent-sized tertiary literature dealing with Russell's view of Leibniz, and to have added to it would have taken me too far from my main concerns. Instead I have used the book where it threw light on Russell's own philosophical views, and discussed briefly (in § 8.4) the by no means straightforward question of what the development of those views owed to his study of Leibniz.

   Another major gap is that I have said nothing here about Russell's views on ethics, aesthetics, and politics, despite the fact that he wrote a considerable amount on these topics in the 1890s. His first book, *German Social Democracy*, was in this area; and his very first criticisms of neo-Hegelianism (in 1897*b*) were on moral grounds. Lack of space is my main excuse for neglecting these topics. But there are further extenuating grounds. Russell's views on aesthetics have already been examined as thoroughly as they are ever likely to be (Spadoni 1984). This is very far from true of his views on ethics or politics, both of which warrant further consideration. However, in neither case do they bear very directly on the dialectic of the sciences. And, since neither the author's nor the reader's patience is endless, they have had to be left out.

   Again largely for reasons of lack of space, I have tended to assume that the reader is familiar with at least the broad outlines of British neo-Hegelian philosophy, especially the work of Bradley and Bosanquet, and with the social and intellectual context in which the neo-Hegelian movement developed. These topics are better known now than they were a few years ago. But, at all events, I have had too little space to elaborate on them here. I am comforted by the thought that readers who are inconvenienced by this will be unlikely to complain too loudly at being thought to be better-informed than they are.

   I must confess that I have found Russell's neo-Hegelian writings to be much more interesting than I had expected. My initial reason for studying the period arose from my efforts to understand *The Principles of Mathematics*. Certain things Russell said there seemed completely incomprehensible, and I was led backwards through his earlier writings in the hope of understanding them. To this extent at least the present work is useful for the study of Russell's later philosophy, for a number of his neo-Hegelian ideas have left their mark on his later writings. More importantly, the change that occurred in Russell's philosophy in 1898–9 with which this book ends, is clearly one of the historically most important sources of analytic philosophy. A detailed study of this change and of the ideas which led up to it seems to me long overdue.

This book was originally intended as a joint work with Carl Spadoni (to be based in part on his doctoral thesis (1977)). As it developed, however, its basis in his thesis grew smaller. Moreover, other commitments and changing interests eventually led Spadoni to withdraw from the collaboration. I remain enormously grateful to him for allowing me to make use of the material we had worked on together (mainly in Chapters 1 and 2). Since then, this material has been worked over several times and revised and added to in ways which he has had no opportunity to approve. He is not, therefore, to be held responsible for what I say. I am grateful to him also for providing me with a great deal of bibliographic information concerning published and unpublished sources which made my work much easier. It is doubtful if the work would have been started without his initial co-operation.

Anyone who works very much on a thinker with interests as diverse as Russell's is likely soon to find their need for information in various fields outstripping their expertise. This makes them shameless in picking the brains of others. In this case Kenneth Blackwell, Albert C. Lewis, and John Passmore read almost the whole manuscript in an earlier draft and provided me with most helpful comments. Lewis has helped in many long discussions to keep me straight about the history of mathematics, and Blackwell provided a constant stream of information about the contents of obscure corners of the Russell Archives. Jed Z. Buchwald read Chapter 5 in draft and helped to make plain some of the intricacies of plenal physics. Ivor Grattan-Guinness and Gregory H. Moore helped with many particular points of enquiry. Finally, the students in my graduate Russell seminar had to tolerate the contents of this book when they were in an even more indigestible state than they are now. I, if not they, have benefited from their presence and from their insistence that I at least try to put things together properly.

A number of research assistants have helped at different times with the work. Chief among these is Ray Melkom who undertook the onerous chore of verifying my references. Alas, I have added some more since he checked, and if any are wrong they are probably these. In addition, it is a pleasure to thank Catherine Bölian-Johnson, Galib Khan, and Jill LeBlanc for their help. The typescript was prepared, through many different drafts, by Manon Ames and Patricia Goodall with unfailing kindness and astonishing accuracy. The copy I sent them would have tried the patience of a saint and the skills of a professional hieroglyphist.

I am grateful to Wolfson College, Oxford, where part of the book was written, for electing me to a Charter Fellowship for 1986. This enabled me to make use of sources which were only available in Britain. I am also grateful to the Social Sciences and Humanities Research Council of Canada for a grant which covered many of my research expenses.

This book is largely based upon unpublished material in the Bertrand Russell Archives at McMaster University. I am grateful to the Archives' Permissions Committee for permission to quote from this material. For permission to quote other copyright material I am grateful to the following: Bryn Mawr College (letters concerning Russell's 1896 lectures), Cambridge University Press (*An Essay on the Foundations of Geometry*), Cambridge University Library and Mr Timothy Moore (unpublished papers of G. E. Moore), Harry Ransom Humanities Research Centre, University of Texas at Austin (Russell's letters to Ottoline Morrell), Professor D. H. Mellor (minutes of the Cambridge Moral Sciences Club), Mrs Barbara Strachey-Halpern (letters of Alys Russell), and the Master and Fellows of Trinity College Cambridge (letter from Sidgwick to Ward).

Finally, my thanks to Cheryl Griffin, for tea and sympathy (in large quantities) over a long period and to Richard Griffin, for being who he is and for being (reasonably) patient even when he couldn't play Jumpman on the word processor.

Troy, Ontario
March 1990

N.G.

# Contents

# Note

The large number of references in this book has made an author/date system of citation necessary. Usually, the date given is the year in which the work was written or first published. The date of the edition actually used is given in the Bibliography. As has become common practice, Russell's main works (and those cited frequently) are referred to by means of an abbreviated title. A full list of these abbreviations is at the beginning of the Bibliography. Occasionally, it has been necessary to cite the editorial apparatus in the volumes of Russell's *Collected Papers*. Such references are handled in the way that they are in the *Collected Papers*. Thus '*Papers*, ii. T55: 16' refers to the textual note to page 55, line 16 in volume ii of the *Collected Papers*. Similarly '*Papers*, ii. A55: 16' would refer to annotation for the same passage. All unpublished material cited is in the Russell Archives at McMaster University unless otherwise stated. Where reference is made to Russell's reading the source is always his reading list 'What Shall I Read?' (*Papers*, i. 347–65), unless otherwise stated.

Pure mathematics . . . . seems to me a rock on which all idealism founders . . .

G. H. Hardy, *A Mathematician's Apology*

# 1

# 'First Efforts'[1]

Russell was born on 18 May 1872 to free-thinking and radical parents. His father, Viscount Amberley, had lost his briefly held seat in Parliament in 1868 as a consequence of his advocacy of birth control; Russell's mother became, under the influence of J. S. Mill, a feminist and advocate of women's suffrage. Neither parent was Christian, though both retained a vestigial deism which Amberley expressed in his posthumously published *Analysis of Religious Belief* (1876), characterized by his son as 'flat and dull' (*Amb.P.* ii, 573). Mill, who was a friend of Amberley and his wife, became the secular equivalent of godfather for Russell. Two years after his birth both Russell's mother and his sister, Rachel, caught diphtheria and died; two years after that his father died also, having lost the will to live, according to Russell. The loss of both parents before he was 4 years old shaped the circumstances of Russell's childhood in ways which affected him for the rest of his life.

Russell's parents had made legal provision for him to be brought up by two free-thinking guardians, but his father's family had the will overturned, with the result that Russell and his brother, Frank, were removed to Pembroke Lodge in Richmond Park to be looked after by his grandparents, Lord John Russell and his second wife. Lord John Russell was considerably older than his second wife, and was living in retirement after a distinguished, though erratic, political career. He died in 1878. As a result, the upbringing of Amberley's children fell almost entirely to their paternal grandmother. Frank Russell was some seven years older than Bertrand and was already so intractable that he had to be sent off to boarding school —the last defence of well-to-do British parents against the wrath of their children. This left Bertrand to bear alone the brunt of his grandmother's child-rearing techniques, which ran to blackmail and terrorism. Puritanical, inflexible and domineering, 'she retained', Russell records, 'something of the outlook of the Covenanters' (*Amb.P.* i, 30). Despite her predilection for unconventional ideas, she practised, and, worse, preached, the virtues of Victorian middle-class

[1] Russell's early biography is traced in Wood (1957), Clark (1975), and Russell, *Auto.* i. His family background can be studied in *Amb.P.*, Robson (1972), Trent (1966), and Prest (1972). Non-philosophical aspects of Russell's early intellectual development are studied extensively in early chapters of Willis (1982). See Brink (1979, 1989) for remarks on the psychological sequelae of Russell's upbringing. My chapter title comes from Russell, *MPD*.

morality. Here, however, we are concerned only with her intellectual influence.

Little is known about Russell's early education at the hands of a succession of tutors hired by his grandmother. We know that he absorbed a great deal of history, politics, and culture simply by being a member of the Russell household. Lord John's library was his primary source of intellectual material, although certain books were placed off limits as inappropriate for a young Victorian gentleman. This form of censorship only spurred Russell to read them. Unfortunately, with the exception of a few standard authors such as Shakespeare, Gibbon, Swift, Newton, Dante, and Machiavelli, and some eccentric curiosities, we do not know what the library contained.[2] Russell's reading aloud to his grandmother throughout the years of her guardianship contributed to his early knowledge of English and continental literature, as well as to his lifelong appreciation of prose and verse rhythms. He was a shy, sensitive, intelligent youth. Frank Russell (1923: 38) presents an unflattering but probably accurate portrait of his brother: 'Bertie, whom they caught younger and who was more amenable, did enjoy the full benefits of a home education in the atmosphere of love, with the result that till he went to Cambridge he was an unendurable little prig.' A few general essays which Russell wrote in 1889 (as trial essays for his Cambridge entrance examinations) are extant (*Papers*, i, 24–38) and show him to have been well-informed on the politics and policies of the day. We know also that he studied Greek and Latin, and that he could read French, German, and Italian fluently. But as regards his formal programme of study, little information has survived beyond a short set of 'Questions and Answers on English History', a sort of Whig catechism, dictated by his Aunt Agatha in 1878–9.

It is clear, however, that two subjects, mathematics and philosophy, became important to Russell at an early age. The record of his early training in mathematics is very scant, but in philosophy we have, in a large and heterogeneous collection of documents, a fairly continuous record of his thinking from the age of 16 onwards. His philosophical starting-point, not unexpectedly, was his grandmother's religious belief. Although dogmatically religious, as a late convert to Unitarianism she was not orthodox and indeed belonged to the more rationalist wing of the Christian church, rejecting such standard dogmas as the Trinity and vicarious atonement. Lady Russell ensured that her charge adhered to her position mainly by hurtfully ridiculing any of his attempts to break free. Russell accepted her teaching without question until he was 14, at which age, as he records, 'my grandmother's

---

[2] Russell records his early enthusiasm for Carlyle, Shakespeare, Swift, and Milton (*FF* 29–33) among the standard English authors, as well as for Buckle (1857) and Draper (1875) (*FF* 37). The eccentric curiosities are described briefly at *FF* 36–7. He also records reading Comte, but didn't like him (*Auto*. i, 41).

intellectual limitations became trying to me' (*Auto.*, i, 22). To escape her sarcasm, however, Russell kept his doubts to himself.

'My original interest in philosophy had two sources,' Russell wrote some seventy years after the event.

On the one hand, I was anxious to discover whether philosophy would provide any defence for anything that could be called religious belief, however vague; on the other hand, I wished to persuade myself that something could be known, in pure mathematics if not elsewhere. I thought about both these problems during adolescence, in solitude and with little help from books. As regards religion, I came to disbelieve first in free will, then in immortality, and finally in God. As regards the foundations of mathematics, I got nowhere.[3]

The first part of this endeavour is chronicled in two journals which Russell kept between 1888 and 1894. The first, headed 'Greek Exercises' (GE),[4] was transliterated into Greek letters with phonetic spelling 'for purposes of concealment' (*MPD* 28), and covers the period from March 1888 to April 1889. It was started, as the first entry implies, when one of Russell's tutors,[5] an agnostic with whom Russell could discuss ideas and religious doubts, was dismissed 'presumably because he was thought to be undermining my faith' (MMD 7). The 'Greek Exercises' reflect a brooding atmosphere of intense adolescent introspection (considerably watered down by Russell's later excerpting). This was heightened by the repressive environment of his Victorian upbringing which made the journal Russell's only means of free expression.

Apart from their biographical and social interest, Russell's 'Greek Exercises' are the starting-point for a consideration of his philosophical development. Certain passages are even indicative of his later style. One such example concerns a sermon on immortality delivered by his Unitarian minister. Reference was made in the sermon to the standard uses of the Christian doctrine of immortality to justify present injustice by appeal to an after life in which virtue would be rewarded and suffering recompensed. Russell's comment is delightful: 'Although he believed in immortality, he said, he thought these uses should not be made of the doctrine, though why not I don't know, being logical consequences of it, whose absurdity ought properly to condemn their ground, which is belief in immortality' (GE 13).

Certain attitudes are to be found in Russell's journal which he continued to express throughout his life. Chief among these is the attitude taken to

---

[3] *MPD* 11. For similar statements see *Auto*. i, 40; 1938: 31–3; *PFM* 14; 1927: 181–2; *SP*: p.[x].

[4] Extracts are printed, with a brief commentary, in *MPD* 28–34 and *Auto*. i, 47–55. The second journal (LD) to be discussed later, was kept occasionally between 1890 and 1894. It is printed in *Papers*, i, 43–67.

[5] J. F. Ewen, an acquaintance of Eleanor Marx, from whom Russell first heard of both Marx and non-Euclidean geometry. (Russell's note to a letter of Jan. 1890 from Ewen; RA 710.049836.)

4 'First Efforts'

'reason'. Reason, for Russell, implied the rejection of sentiment, the acceptance of scientific grounds in argument and consistency in belief. It was the one sure guide to truth. The role of reason in the conduct of his religious inquiry is displayed early in the 'Greek Exercises'. For example, in an early statement of intent he writes: 'in finding reasons for belief in God I shall only take account of scientific arguments' (GE 5) and, later: 'In all things I have made the vow to follow reason, not the instincts inherited partly from my ancestors and gained gradually by them owing to a process of natural selection, and partly due to my education. . . . I endeavour to go by reason as far as possible' (GE 10–11).

Although his view of what constitutes a scientific argument was subject to change, his view that scientific arguments were important and had to be accommodated by philosophy was not. The theme is repeated many times in Russell's subsequent works.[6] So, also, is its corollary that the cost of keeping this vow is high in terms of thwarted desires and the loss of consoling doctrines.[7] The unhappiness which accompanied Russell's gradual loss of religious belief was so great as to lead him to doubt the value of seeking truth and to consider suicide (GE 5, 10, 16–17, 19). It also brought domestic disadvantages. At first Russell tried to discuss his doubts with his family, but having told his grandmother that he was a utilitarian and having been 'covered . . . with ridicule' for his pains (Auto. i, 45), he kept his thoughts increasingly to himself. 'I perceived that she had no good grounds for rejecting utilitarianism, and that her opposition to it was not intellectually respectable' (Auto. i, 45).[8] However, the disadvantages of pursuing reason and science were somewhat equivocal, for in another entry in 'Greek Exercises', Russell reports that original thought 'is yet my chief stay and support in troubles' (GE 17).

The intellectual background for Russell's thoughts consists very largely of the theory of evolution. Almost every page bears reference to it, directly or indirectly.[9] As a boy Russell had been confronted with the choice between

[6] A survey of the prefaces to his epistemology books provides sample evidence: e.g. OKEW 7–8; A.Mind 5; SP: p.[ix]; HK: p. xi.

[7] For a comparable statement from the other end of his career see Auto. iii, 222. For commentary on this aspect of Russell's thought around the turn of the century see Griffin (1984). Similar distress is to be found in some of G. E. Moore's early unpublished papers (e.g. 1899c).

[8] His grandmother's attitude to philosophy is concisely expressed in a letter of 6 Feb. 1869 to her son, John, in which she proposed to publish 2 vols., one entitled 'The Philosophy of Twaddle', the other 'The Twaddle of Philosophy' (the 2nd was, among other things, to correct Mill); not surprisingly, neither appeared (Amb.P. ii, 258).

[9] It is not clear how much of the evolutionary literature Russell read at this time apart from Tennyson (1850), Argyll (1866), Spencer (1884), and probably Ritchie (1889) of which he received a presentation copy. The Duke of Argyll, though now largely forgotten, was at the time an influential and widely read contributor to the debate on Darwinism, which he combated on scientific as well as religious grounds. A highly flattering account of his amateur scientific

religion and science, which Darwinism had thrust into prominence, when a
tutor said to him: 'If you are a Darwinist, I pity you, for it is impossible to be
a Darwinist and a Christian at the same time.' (Russell 1935: 76). Russell,
however, was not concerned with the clear conflict between Darwinian
theory and the Christian creation myth, and the consequences this might be
thought to have for the question of God's existence. Russell, initially, was
content to 'prove' the existence of God, as Mill had done, by means of the
argument from design (GE 20–1). Admittedly the sort of God whose
existence is thereby 'proved' remains unclear. Nevertheless Russell was still
prepared to call himself a 'theist' (GE 5), and even went so far as to believe
in the impossibility of miracles on the grounds that a miracle would imply a
breach of a universal law and, therefore, an imperfection in the law itself and
thus in its divine maker. This is glossed over very quickly in his journal and
the discussion soon leads to the implications that evolution has for the theory
of human nature, in particular for free will and immortality.

These two topics, free will and immortality, are the central concern of the
'Greek Exercises'.[10] Russell's treatment of them, in the year covered by the
journal, falls into two distinct parts. In the first he uses the theory of
evolution to support the thesis that 'there is no clear dividing line between
man and the protozoon' (GE 6); then, by means of a slippery slope fallacy,
he obtains the conclusion that man can have no free will since the protozoon
has none. Subsequently, two further supporting arguments are given for this
conclusion: the first relies upon the tacit identification of motives with causes
(GE 7);[11] the second maintains that free will is incompatible with divine
omniscience. Russell, as a result of reading Argyll (1866 ch. 5), came to
reverse the slippery slope argument, admitting that the protozoon may be
'endowed with a germ . . . of free will' (GE 11).

Russell's most surprising conclusion from his discussion of free will is
briefly stated: 'And not having free will we cannot have immortality' (GE 7).

work is given by his wife in Argyll (1906: ch. 46); a more balanced, but still sympathetic, account
is given by Gillespie (1977). Argyll, as a Cabinet Minister in a succession of Liberal governments,
shared a political connection with Russell's grandfather, although he broke with Gladstone
over the Irish Land Bill of 1881 and maintained a strong opposition to any type of land reform
(cf. Mason 1978). In these respects also Argyll seems to have had an influence on Russell in the
1880s.

[10] Both were topics of vital concern to many late Victorian thinkers. The free will problem
had been stirred up a few years before by T. H. Huxley's enormously controversial lecture on
reflex actions in animals (Huxley 1874). The furore was not really laid to rest until the
emergence of more voluntaristic brands of psychology in the 1880s and 1890s supported by a
wide variety of experimental results. Binet's studies of micro-organisms (1888) are particularly
apposite for Russell's argument. Russell very likely knew of Huxley's work but presumably was
ignorant of the later developments. G. E. Moore, writing in 1894, was prepared to ascribe will
and consciousness to even the most primitive animal (cf. Moore 1894).

[11] Russell may have been influenced here by Mill (1843: vi, ii, 4) which he read and
abstracted about this time (cf. his unpaginated notes, RA 220.010360).

This is nowhere argued, but Russell seems to have in mind the view that whatever has a soul must have free will and that whatever has immortality must have a soul. It is clear that he takes all three attributes to stand or fall together. The 'consequences' of Russell's position are widely drawn, for example, in ethics (GE 7–8).[12] Man has become 'nothing more than a species of ingenious machine endowed with consciousness . . . a mere perishable chemical compound' (GE 7–8). '[T]ruth in biology', he ruefully concludes, 'lowers one's idea of man' (GE 16).

In his second treatment of free will and immortality in 'Greek Exercises', Russell clearly distinguishes the two issues: 'Now however I should not say . . . that without free will, immortality is impossible. Force and matter are most likely wanting in free will, yet they have immortality. So that argument is done for' (GE 17). Having separated the two problems, Russell finds that the problem of free will has become much clearer, while that of immortality 'remains wrapped in uncertainty' (GE 17). The slippery slope argument against free will has now disappeared without trace and with it all reference to evolution. The other two arguments remain, however, and the slippery slope argument is replaced by an argument from the reign of law; that is, the standard determinist argument that what happens does so according to fixed laws.

Russell's treatment of immortality in the next entry is much more equivocal. The theory of evolution and the slippery slope make a brief reappearance: he defines the soul as 'anything distinguishing man utterly from dead matter . . . [and which it is] impossible to suppose evolved from dead matter' (GE 19). Part of this he takes to be consciousness. Given this, Russell concludes, 'we see that man has a soul, for consciousness is undeniable, whatever else may be attacked' (GE 19). Russell's conclusion seems definite enough, but it is immediately attacked by a counter-argument based on the interdependence of the soul and the body, which 'tend[s] to make one imagine that the bond of body and soul is indissoluble, both living and both dying together. Of course the resurrection of the body gets one out of this, but is manifestly absurd, for we see it rot in the ground' (GE 20; also p. 13).

In later reminiscences Russell declared that during this early period he was trying unsuccessfully to combine 'seventeenth-century knowledge, eighteenth-century beliefs and nineteenth-century enthusiasms' (*MPD* 35). While Russell's assessment of his adolescent philosophy is not entirely accurate, it is none the less possible to discern elements of all three centuries in the 'Greek Exercises'. The desire to set knowledge on a new and rational foundation stems from the seventeenth century. Eighteenth-century elements

---

[12] Russell's ethical theory at this time was an unsophisticated utilitarianism (GE 9, 11). The only idiosyncratic touch was his use of the theory of evolution to account for conscience (GE 8–9).

are provided by the strict determinism and the doctrine of man as a machine. Apart from romanticism and the theory of evolution, the nineteenth century contributed to the 'Greek Exercises' mainly a sense of regret at the loss of religion. The rationalism Russell came to lacks the heroic and optimistic qualities of eighteenth-century rationalism, largely, one suspects, because the theory of evolution had lowered man's position in the universe as well as God's.

Faced with the lingering presence of doubt and the gradual loss of religious belief, Russell became susceptible to the consolations of 'poetic arguments' (GE 20). Prior to his sixteenth birthday and his going to the military crammer at Southgate, to which he was sent to prepare for his Cambridge scholarship exam, he had been reading Wordsworth's 'Ode: Intimations of Immortality from Recollections of Early Childhood'. On the question of the soul's relationship to the body he had rejected Wordsworth's explanation outright: 'Wordsworth's "Intimations" are humbug, for it is obvious how the soul grows with the body, not as he says, perfect from the first' (GE 12). At Southgate he found the atmosphere vulgar: 'No mind, no independent thought, no love of good books, nor of the higher refinements of morality' (GE 14). But in spite of this, he reported: 'I have become of a calmer, thoughtfuller, poeticaller nature than I was' (GE 14). He had developed an intense appreciation of the beauty of nature, and took to reading romantic poetry and literature (especially Wordsworth, Tennyson, and Carlyle). Russell would later refer to such writings as 'sentimental apologies for religion . . . [which] seemed to me very splendid, in spite of my thinking that at bottom they were nonsense' (MPD 35). Nevertheless, his last entry of 'Greek Exercises', written in April 1889, is a rhapsodic testimony to these influences. He states there that 'a new aspect of God burst in upon me' (GE 20). His former view of God as the First Cause was now replaced by a thoroughgoing pantheism. Even more important than Wordsworth was Shelley, whom he read after Tennyson. It was Shelley's lyrical and love poetry which first attracted him and it was only later that he became aware of Shelley's political rebellion: 'I liked his despair, his isolation, his imaginary landscapes that seemed as unreal as scenery in sunset clouds. He did not offend my intellectual taste by accepting conventional beliefs for which there seemed to be no good evidence' (FF 12).[13]

Russell's early pantheism didn't last long. But, even after he had abandoned it, he retained a deep appreciation of nature. In youth, he 'loved natural

---

[13] See also Leithauser (1984) for Russell's enthusiasm for Shelley. Lester (1968: 159) notes a difference between the earlier 19th-century mysticism in which mystical experience was sought as the revelation of a higher truth, and mysticism at the end of the century which sought mystical experience, not as revelatory, but as an end in itself, a purely subjective experience. Certainly Russell's mystical leanings fit well with the type Lester ascribes to the *fin de siècle*.

beauty with a wild passion' (*MPD* 35) and many years later declared that '[t]he sea, the stars, the night wind in waste places, mean more to me than even the human beings I love best' (*Auto*. ii, 38). But, regarded as doctrine rather than as emotion, Russell's pantheism was relatively short-lived, and he came quickly to see it as a momentary lapse from the rationalist standards of belief he set for himself. By 31 May 1890, as reported in his next journal, his rebellion against reason was in decline. On the recurring theme of immortality, he confessed that all the arguments in its favour 'seem to me to be of a vague poetic nature, such as that put forward in Wordsworth's ode, while the arguments on the other side, though scarcely convincing, are I am afraid far more scientific' (LD 47). Approximately two weeks later he attended a sermon on the reconciliation of faith with reason. Although Russell admitted his mind to be in 'a haze about fundamental axioms', his provisional position was 'that nothing is to be accepted which is incapable of experimental or inductive proof, except perhaps such laws of thought as no person could at first sight have any hesitation in accepting' (LD 52).

The conflict between faith and reason generated a pervasive *malaise* in late nineteenth-century Victorian England. Sams (1979) has argued persuasively that many of Russell's intellectual predecessors and contemporaries—William Hale White, Beatrice Webb, Havelock Ellis, J. M. Synge, to name a few— experienced similar mixed feelings of anxiety and optimism. The causes of this uneasy ambivalence were several: the social upheaval unleashed by the industrial revolution, the growth of liberalism and democracy, evolutionary theory and the decline in traditional religious values. The biblical creation story had clearly been undermined by Darwin's *Origin of Species* (1859), and historical criticism in *Essays and Reviews* (1860) and Renan's *The Life of Jesus* (1863) further challenged the Bible's authenticity. It was not just orthodox Christianity that was on the defensive. If man is but a product of mechanical laws and a descendent of supposedly 'lower' forms of life, then it appears that there is little room for *any* spiritual explanation of the purpose of human existence. And the traditional humanist view of man's special place in the universe is challenged. The resulting sense of gloom and alienation in nineteenth-century thought was almost inevitable and is reflected, for example, in the poetry of Arthur Clough and Matthew Arnold. The latter's 'Dover Beach', a classic in the Victorian crisis of faith genre, records the 'eternal note of sadness' ushered in by the 'melancholy, long, withdrawing roar' of '[t]he sea of faith'. Tennyson, rejected by Russell as sentimental, would not abide a purely scientific view and ends *In Memoriam*, another classic of the genre, optimistically with God directing the evolutionary process.

How Victorian intellectuals coped with this crisis of faith is too large a theme to discuss here, but it is of interest to note that Russell's father devoted his short life to proving that unbelief 'is consistent with a deep religious feeling, and with goodness and purity of life' (*Amb.P.* i. 340). Amberley embraced a stoic agnosticism in which Spencer's Unknowable is invoked to bridge the gulf between religion and science. When Russell first read his father's journals in December 1893, he related to his fiancée, Alys Pearsall Smith, that it was uncanny that his father's religious development had so closely parallelled his own.[14] Another relevant case is Amberley's mentor, J. S. Mill, who, as we shall see, strongly influenced Russell in this early period. Although Mill did not undergo a loss of Christian faith, he was faced by a similar crisis when, as a young man, he came to question the utilitarian faith with which his father had indoctrinated him. He took to reading Wordsworth's poetry for consolation and eventually came to the view that the intellect cannot with impunity be isolated from feeling. Russell's similar reading of Wordsworth prompted him to remark to Alys Pearsall Smith that Mill's *Autobiography* is 'at the bottom of a great deal in me'.[15] Wordsworthian pantheism, according to Willey (1952: 102), served as an important alternative to despair for many nineteenth-century intellectuals. Quite unexpectedly, Moore tried this route in an uncharacteristically rhapsodic paper 'Is Conversion Possible?' (Moore 1900*b*) in which he uses what he calls the 'literary method', epitomized by Wordsworth's 'Ode to Duty' and contrasted with the scientific or analytic method, to characterize moral conversion.

While it is possible to trace Russell's approach to philosophy through religion, it is not easy to make out the details of his other approach to philosophy, through mathematics. It seemed clear to him that if any science could lay claim to knowledge, mathematics could. Thus, in trying to discover whether anything could be known with certainty, it seemed natural for him to begin with mathematics. Moreover, Russell was captivated with the entire mathematical approach. To begin with, he found he possessed a high degree of technical competence; he took delight in proof procedure and in the knowledge that demonstrations are strict and certain. More important than this, however, was the role of mathematics in the sciences. Nature, he believed, operated by means of mathematical laws, and consequently, if sufficient skill and knowledge were at hand, everything in nature, past and present, could be determined and predicted. For the adolescent Russell, the importance of mathematics lay in its applications. Machines could be constructed to do away with arduous work, and the human condition improved.[16]

[14] B. R. to A. P. Smith, 19 Dec. 1893.  [15] B. R. to A. P. Smith, 8 July 1894.
[16] *MMD* 7; *MPD* 36; *FF* 42; 1948*a*: 143; *SP*: p. [ix]. Russell's early scientific knowledge came mainly from his uncle Rollo, a meteorologist who was also variously interested in diet and atmospheric pollution, and who published a substantial work on epidemics (1892). (See Parker

Despite the clearly privileged place mathematics held in Russell's thought, it was not immune to sceptical doubts. It may well be the case that if anything could be known, mathematics could be known. But could mathematics be known? This question was of paramount importance to Russell's philosophic work until at least 1913. With the advantages of hindsight it has been possible to find intimations of logicism in early childhood. There is the famous story[17] of Russell's introduction to Euclid at the age of 11. Russell's delight in the proofs was marred by the fact that the axioms could not be proved. Russell's brother, Frank, was responsible for these early lessons in Euclid, which took place during the summer of 1883 when Frank was down from Oxford. Frank, whose diary gives a fragmentary account of the lessons, does not record Russell's doubts about the axioms; but it is clear that they did not impede Russell's mastery of the material: 'I did the 12th prop. with Bertie to-night', Frank records, 'and so finished Hawtrey's book: he has gone thro them all with great success and seems to me to thoro'ly understand them: I am very proud of my pupil.'[18] Russell's early encounter with Euclid seems less important when, in 1890 at the age of eighteen, he excuses his failure to complete a geometry paper with the remark 'geometry never was my strong point' (LD 47). What is clear is that well before Russell went up to Cambridge he was intrigued by the question why mathematics was true. Instead of an answer to that question, a more disturbing question surfaced: that of *whether* mathematics was true.

Philosophic doubt about the truth of mathematics was, for Russell, assuaged, if not removed, by the philosophy of mathematics he found in Clifford's *Common Sense of the Exact Sciences* (1885) which he read at the age of 15 'with passionate interest and with an intoxicating delight in intellectual clarification'.[19] Nor was this an enthusiasm of his adolescence only. In a letter of 10 March 1912 to Ottoline Morrell, Russell described Clifford as 'an absolutely first-rate mathematician, [who] cared immensely about philosophy. . . . All his writing has the clearness and force that comes of white-hot intellectual passion.' There are many respects in which Clifford's thought would have been congenial to the young Russell, and even a number

1959: 113.) Rollo took Russell to meet the physicist Tyndall who was his neighbour. Tyndall gave Russell a copy of his book *The Forms of Water* (1878). (Cf. *Auto*. i, 24, 47.) It seems to have been Rollo who arranged for Russell to enter Trinity College, Cambridge (see V. H. Stanton to Rollo Russell, 25 Nov. 1886).

[17] Related in *Auto*. i, 36; MMD 7; *PFM* 14–16; Clark (1975: 31); Wood (1957: 21–2).

[18] F. Russell, Diary, 14 Sept. 1883 (RA 741.080043); Hawtrey (1874) is the book mentioned.

[19] Russell 1945: p. v, on Clifford 1885. See also *MPD* 36. The flyleaf of Russell's copy of Clifford's book is inscribed 'Bertrand Russell from his tutor J. Stuart. New Years Day 1888.' It is not annotated. We cannot be sure what other works of Clifford's Russell read at this time, but it seems likely he read at least some of his (1879), including perhaps Clifford (1873). The secondary literature on Clifford's philosophy is not extensive. The most comprehensive treatment is Smokler (1959), though Smokler (1966) is better on the philosophy of geometry.

of enduring similarities between their work. Clifford, like Russell, was very much concerned with certainty in knowledge and expected advances in scientific knowledge to aid in the solution, or at least the clarification, of philosophical problems. Like Russell too, Clifford placed a moral emphasis on the use of reason in the pursuit of truth. In one of his essays, Clifford had stated: 'it is wrong always, everywhere, and for any one, to believe anything upon insufficient evidence' (1877: 186). The young Russell adhered to this dictum. It was to be a permanent fixture in his philosophy.[20]

Clifford's skills as a popularizer, which Russell held in high esteem, may have served as a model in Russell's own popular writings. The clarity of Clifford's style, which excited Russell so much on first reading him, can certainly be found in Russell's later writings. So, too, can the fundamental obscurity of philosophical position which it sometimes masks. This strange combination of stylistic clarity with a deeper obscurity seems to have had similar origins in both philosophers. Both Clifford and Russell were systematic philosophers whose ideas and interests changed with such frequency that a final synthesis always eluded them. As a result positions were frequently abandoned before they could be worked out in explicit detail, and were often left in tantalizingly fragmentary form. In Clifford's case, his early death certainly contributed to the unsatisfactorily incomplete nature of his philosophical work. Both men advocated treating philosophical problems in scientific detail, yet usually confined themselves to broad programmatic hints. There are even, in Russell, continuations of certain key themes of Clifford's philosophy, for example, the problem of the external world was treated repeatedly by both men and from similar points of view. Russell wrote on the topic at greater length than Clifford, but just as Clifford could never demonstrate how external objects could be 'filled up' (in his own phrase)[21] from retinal images, Russell never managed to construct them out of sensibilia. It would be a mistake to suppose that Russell's later epistemology is a development out of Clifford's hints, just as it is a mistake to suppose that the general theory of relativity is (of which Clifford's (1870) is an inspired anticipation). But anyone who knows Russell's epistemology and style of argument and exposition will frequently be struck by an uncanny sense of familiarity in reading Clifford.

Russell's early enthusiasm for Clifford, however, focused upon two aspects of Clifford's thought: his philosophy of mathematics and his belief in the benefits to be gained from the application of science to social problems. In the latter, mathematics played a key role. Clifford (1885) sought not only

---

[20] Compare the passage from Clifford with the following from Russell (*SE* 9): 'it is undesirable to believe a proposition when there is no ground whatever for supposing it true'.

[21] Russell uses similar language when he talks of 'filling out' the sensational core with animal inference in perception (*HK* 146, 169).

to explain mathematical concepts but also the role of such concepts in the workings of the physical sciences. Clifford went about this task with the optimistic faith that mathematics, once properly understood, leads to social progress. Of this, Russell would later write:

In this beneficient process rational knowledge was to be the chief agent, and mathematics, as the most completely rational kind of knowledge, was to be in the van. This faith was Clifford's, and it was mine when I first read his book; in turning over its pages again, the ghosts of old hopes rise up to mock me. (1945: p. ix)

In the philosophy of mathematics Clifford's position was an amalgam of rationalist and empiricist principles. In geometry, for example, Clifford followed Kant in urging that the postulates of geometry were rules for ordering empirical data; yet, following Riemann and Helmholtz, he believed that their truth-values could be determined empirically.[22] In geometry, and in the philosophy of mathematics as a whole, Clifford was clearly torn between the empiricist and the rationalist approach, and it is doubtful that any fully coherent position can be reconstructed from his remarks. In arithmetic the physical operation of counting was central to Clifford's account, supplemented on the rationalist side by principles of organization which, as a result of evolutionary development (Clifford was not the only thinker to bring Darwin to the aid of Kant), had become part of the human mental apparatus. The principles of organization included a principle of the uniformity of nature, principles for the analysis of concepts to give definitions, and a principle in accordance with which sensory experience was arranged to yield distinct objects. Assuming that the notion of 'distinct object' was understood, then, as a result of the principle of the uniformity of nature, distinct objects could be expected to remain distinct throughout space and time and to be indifferent to the order in which they were enumerated. Through the operation of counting, numerals could be brought into one-to-one relation with standard sets of distinct objects, each set containing one more element than its predecessor. Finally, through the principle of definition, other arithmetic operations could be defined in terms of counting. As Smokler (1959: 109) comments, Clifford's 'general account of arithmetical propositions . . . is too obscure to be properly evaluated'. Some of its shortcomings, however, are readily apparent. Apart from the obvious impossibility of constructing transfinite arithmetic on this basis, less sophisticated number systems (e.g. signed integers and real numbers) are also beyond its scope.

---

[22] The influence of Clifford on Russell's early geometrical writings must remain a topic for speculation, for Russell made only a handful of incidental references to him. But as we shall see in Chapter 4, they shared a common concern in distinguishing the empirical from the a priori aspects of geometry—a concern which was rarer then than it is now. It is almost certain that Russell learnt of the Kantian approach to geometry (which he for a while adopted) from Clifford before he read Kant.

Clifford, indeed, recognized this and in his extremely sketchy remarks about real numbers (1873: 337) he claimed the need for quite different organizational principles in order to account for them—in fact, 'a hypothesis of continuity' which, one might expect, would have been quite incompatible with the 'hypothesis of the distinctness of things' which he required for the natural numbers. While Clifford's account may have allayed Russell's initial doubts about the truth of mathematics, he could not have remained satisfied for long, even though his own first efforts followed somewhat similar lines (see Chapter 6 below). But even after the shortcomings of Clifford's theory must have become apparent to him he had nothing better to serve as a replacement.

In the mean time, his acquisition of technical skill proceeded both at the crammer's and with a private tutor, H. C. Robson, who coached him in geometry and dynamics in the ten months between the award of his scholarship and his taking it up.[23] This brief period between December 1889 and October 1890 was an important one for Russell's intellectual development, largely because he read J. S. Mill. In referring to his subsequent conversion to neo-Hegelianism he called Mill 'my former pope' (MMD 10), and before going up to Cambridge he claimed (1930a: 525) to have read all of Mill except the *Examination of Sir William Hamilton's Philosophy*. Mill's *A System of Logic*, was, he declared, the first book, apart from Buckle's *History of Civilization*, he had read 'which seemed to me to possess intellectual integrity' (MPD 35). He made an 'elaborate abstract' of the *Logic* and of Mill's *Principles of Political Economy* (Auto. i, 41; MMD 8).[24]

Unfortunately, it is not clear exactly what impact Mill's *Logic* had on Russell's thinking. Most probably it was considerable, since it was the first technical philosophy book Russell had read and it warrants three separate references in *My Philosophical Development* (pp. 28, 35, 37). One thing is clear, namely that Mill's crudely empiricist account of arithmetic was never accepted by Russell. On this point, at least, Clifford's analysis, for all its failings, was more sophisticated and presumably saved Russell from copying some of Mill's errors. On Mill's empiricist theory of mathematics (cf. Mill 1843: III, xxiv, 5) Russell wrote:

I first read Mill's *Logic* at the age of eighteen, and at that time I had a very strong bias in his favour; but even then I could not believe that our acceptance of the

---

[23] Details of this period are provided in *Auto.* i, 42–7, *MPD* 28; Clark (1975: 31–5). Primary documentation is provided in Russell's occasional journal (LD) which contains frequent references to his work with Robson. Robson was a Cambridge man whose method as a mathematics teacher, according to *The Times*' obituary, 'was well adapted to the needs of all but the ablest men' (27 Jan. 1945, p. 6). As Russell's coach he used as texts Routh (1882) and (1884), then widely used at Cambridge.

[24] Only fragments of the former abstract survive (RA file 220.010360) all of which concern Book VI, 'On the Logic of the Moral Sciences' (viz. ch. vii, §§ 1–5; ch. ix, §§ 1–8, ch. xi, §§ 1–4). They contain only two brief comments of Russell's own, neither of much philosophical interest.

proposition 'two and two are four' was a generalization from experience. I was quite at a loss to say how we arrived at this knowledge, but it *felt* quite different from such a proposition as 'all swans are white', which experience might, and in fact did, confute. It did not seem to me that a fresh instance of two and two being four in any degree strengthened my belief. But it is only the modern development of mathematical logic which has enabled me to justify these early feelings and to fit mathematics and empirical knowledge into a single framework.[25]

What Russell derived from Mill was a recognition of the importance of induction:

I read Mill's *Logic*, and derived without complete agreement a view (not exactly like his) that induction is what is important, and that deduction is little more than an idle amusement of the Schoolmen. I began to give due weight to the obvious fact that deduction is powerless without major premisses, and that its major premisses must therefore have some independent source. I could not accept the theory that the necessary major premisses were supplied by a priori intuitions; but I was equally unable to believe Mill's contention that it is induction from experience which persuades us that two and two are four. This dilemma left me in a perplexity which lasted for many years (FF 44).

The other work of Mill's which Russell read at this time, and which had an even greater immediate influence on him, was the *Autobiography* (1873). It turned him into an agnostic by demolishing the argument from design on which his theism had hitherto rested. In a journal entry for 31 August 1890 Russell writes:

Alas! the only shred of faith I had left in me is, for the time at least, gone. I did believe in a Deity, . . . But now!—I have begun to feel that the reasoning which always convinced me before, for a long time so as to preclude even comprehension of doubt, has lost its cogency . . . I was finally overturned by some passages in Mill's *Autobiography*, in which he puts this argument very clearly . . . [A] necessary prime Cause and Law-giver . . . affords no explanation of the mystery but merely offers one permanent unchangeable Mystery in the place of the many which Science is now unable to answer. This argument Mill puts clearly in speaking of the education he got from his father: 'He told me that the question, Who made me? cannot be answered, because it immediately suggests the further question, Who made God?[26]

He did not, on account of this, become an atheist for he noted that 'the hypothesis of an Almighty First Cause affords a consistent explanation of the Universe' (LD 46). Nevertheless Mill's argument produced a pessimistic

[25] *PFM* 124–5. See also MMD 8; *FF* 44.
[26] LD 56; also MMD 8; *WNC* 15; *Auto*. i, 41 (where he mistakenly says rejection of the first cause argument led him to become an atheist). The passage cited comes from Mill (1873: 45). Russell's agnosticism did not, as yet, run deep enough completely to efface his earlier religious belief, as the extraordinary guilt-ridden prayer recorded in his diary 15 months later shows (LD 60).

agnosticism, for with the Almighty First Cause went the view that evolution embodied a necessarily progressive principle. (Russell had apparently not considered the possibility that the Almighty First Cause may not have had moral improvement in mind when setting up the process of evolution.) However, this initial despair did not long survive Russell's arrival at Cambridge, for in his next journal entry, the first at Cambridge (20 November 1890), he wrote: 'It is strange, on looking back to what I wrote on August 31, to see the pain with which I came to Agnosticism; for now I have become quite reconciled to it, and have even found some increase of repose in the feeling of having nothing to lose' (LD 57). 'Strange', he concluded, 'how completely I have changed in the last two years.'

# 2
# Cambridge (1890–1894)

## 2.1 MATHEMATICS AT CAMBRIDGE: 1890–1893

Russell went up to Cambridge in October 1890 on a minor scholarship to Trinity College. There was no strong connection between Russell's family and Cambridge. Russell's father had been there, but he had been sent down without taking a degree and Russell's brother had gone to Oxford. Russell was drawn to Cambridge by its reputation for mathematics. Since Newton's day, according to Ball (1921: 261), 'Cambridge has been regarded as . . . the home of English mathematicians'.[1] From Newton through to Cayley, Cambridge had indeed a distinguished record in the history of English mathematics. Its reputation in the natural sciences, given a similarly powerful start by Newton, and considerably revitalized in the nineteenth century by William Whewell, was comparably strong.

By the end of the nineteenth century, however, this Newtonian heritage weighed heavily on the University. The nineteenth century saw a major drive toward abstraction and rigour in mathematics as practised in continental Europe. But these developments largely passed Cambridge by. There, influenced by the Newtonian tradition, mathematics laboured under a heavy load of geometrical intuition and physical application. This situation was not due to ignorance or inadvertence. Abstract algebra, for example, had made inroads in Cambridge in the 1820s and 1830s, under the influence of George Peacock, Charles Babbage, and other members of the Analytical Society.

While a sound training in modern analysis was necessary if Cambridge was to produce good research mathematicians, this was not felt to be the primary function of the Mathematical Tripos. At Cambridge mathematics was a prerequisite for all honours students, and even when the Moral Sciences

[1] Further details of Russell's mathematical education can be found in Lewis and Griffin (1990). For a history of the Mathematical Tripos see Ball (1889: ch. 10; 1921: 259–311). For its defects at the end of the nineteenth century see Forsyth (1935). That the Tripos suited some students is demonstrated by Karl Pearson's acerbic reply to Forsyth (Pearson 1936). It is significant that Pearson's main interests were in applied mathematics, in contrast to Forsyth's in pure mathematics. The main emphasis of the Tripos was on the former. A swingeing attack on the Tripos system, even after the reforms of 1907, can be found in W. H. Young's unpublished report, written during the First World War, on university education in mathematics (now excerpted in Grattan-Guinness 1972a: esp. pp. 373–5). For an undergraduate view see 'The Cambridge Sphinx', *The Cambridge Observer*, 31 Jan. 1893, pp. 5–6. *The Cambridge Observer* was a student paper with which Russell was involved (see Blackwell 1981).

Tripos and Natural Sciences Tripos were added in 1851 it was still necessary for a student to complete the elementary part of the Mathematical Tripos before he could compete in the others. As a result, mathematics was taught to many students whose interests and abilities were not mathematical and for such students the rigours of analysis were both excessive and unnecessary. A decision had to be made as to whether mathematics at Cambridge was to provide specialized training for career mathematicians or to remain the central part of a liberal education intended to provide the national élite with the intellectual training it needed. The decision was made largely by William Whewell, whose position of influence at Cambridge after he became the autocratic Master of Trinity in 1841 was unassailable. Whewell had originally been among those who helped introduce analysis to Cambridge. But as his influence grew so did his conviction that the needs of a liberal education were paramount, and that these needs were best served by the old style of mathematics in which rigour and generality were sacrificed to physical application and intuitive appeal.[2] In practice this meant: back to Newton! Forsyth noted the results:

In patriotic duty bound, the Cambridge of Newton adhered to Newton's fluxions, to Newton's geometry, to the very text of Newton's *Principia*: in my own Tripos of 1881 we were expected to know any lemma in that great work by its number alone . . . Thus . . . Cambridge became a school that was self-satisfied, self-supporting, self-content, almost marooned in its limitations. (Forsyth 1935: 167.)

Russell's entry into Newton's Cambridge was eased by Alfred North Whitehead, eleven years his senior and then a fellow of Trinity and lecturer in mathematics at the University. At Russell's scholarship examination in December 1889, Russell's nervousness apparently affected his performance and another candidate got better marks. Whitehead, however, who was an examiner that year, was more impressed with Russell's essays and recommended Russell for the scholarship in preference to the other student (*Auto.* i, 57).[3] Moreover, Whitehead urged other bright undergraduates at Cambridge to look out for Russell, with the result that '[a]ll the people then in

---

[2] It is interesting to compare this situation in Cambridge with the one Glas (1982) describes in Germany, where mathematicians emphasized the abstract, pure nature of their subject— 'mathematical research exclusively for the benefit of mathematics itself'—in order to protect their academic freedom against state interference. This is not the place to go into the historical accuracy of this view, but it does connect directly with another claim (to be discussed below in §3.4), that Russell's thought is best understood against the background of a sharp contrast, along the lines indicated, between English and continental mathematics. The changing fortunes of analysis in Cambridge are fascinatingly surveyed by Becher (1980). For Whewell's educational thought see especially his (1845), among other works of this exceptionally prolific author.

[3] Russell says he was told that Whitehead burnt the marks. Lowe (1985: 222) suspects this may have been a 'dramatic embellishment' by Whitehead's wife.

residence who subsequently became my intimate friends called on me during the first week of term' (*Auto.* i, 56).[4]

At Cambridge Whitehead was regarded as an applied mathematician due to his fellowship dissertation on Maxwell's *Electricity and Magnetism* (1873*a*), and he lectured on applied mathematics throughout this year at Cambridge (Lowe 1985: 311–12). By the 1890s, however, his research interests had changed to abstract algebra, and lectures by him on non-commutative algebras—work which culminated in his *Universal Algebra* (1898*a*)—were scheduled for 1892 and 1893, though the latter may well have been cancelled.[5] It is unlikely that Russell attended Whitehead's lectures on pure mathematics, for they were irrelevant to his needs in the Mathematical Tripos. Moreover, Russell was still primarily interested in applied mathematics, believing, in his 'Victorian optimism', that 'applied mathematics . . . was more likely to further human welfare' (*MPD* 39). We do know, however, that he attended a course on statics given by Whitehead during Michaelmas Term 1890. Russell recalled: 'He told the class to study article 35 in the text-book. Then he turned to me and said "You needn't study it, because you know it already". I had quoted it by number in the scholarship examination ten months earlier. He won my heart by remembering this fact' (*Auto.* i, 127). Indeed, Whitehead must be exempted from the criticism with which Russell, in retrospect, assailed his mathematics teachers:

Whitehead was extraordinarily perfect as a teacher. He took a personal interest in those with whom he had to deal and knew both their strong and their weak points. He would elicit from a pupil the best of which the pupil was capable. He was never repressive, or sarcastic, or superior, or any of the things that inferior teachers like to be. I think that in all the abler young men with whom he came in contact he inspired, as he did in me, a very real and lasting affection. (*PFM* 99.)

Whitehead's teaching must have been a striking contrast to that to which Russell was regularly subjected. J. E. Littlewood (1953: 70) recalled Whitehead's course on the foundations of mechanics as one of only two he attended with any enthusiasm.

---

[4] In fact, this informal inspection of new undergraduates whose school records or scholarship examinations were intellectually distinguished, was part of the standard recruitment procedure of the Cambridge Apostles (cf. Spater and Parsons 1977: 28). That Whitehead, who was a member of the Apostles, had suggested Russell as a prospective member is confirmed by a letter of congratulations from McTaggart (17 May 1892) on Russell's election to the Apostles. The letter is published in *Auto.* i, 70, where it is misdated. The best source of information on Whitehead's early career is Lowe (1985), who paints an inexplicably cheery picture of mathematics at Cambridge.

[5] See *The Cambridge University Reporter*, 11 Jan. 1892, p. 386, and 6 Oct. 1892, p. 17. Whitehead's interest in abstract algebra went back at least to 1888 when he offered a course on Grassmann's *Ausdehnungslehre*, the first to be given at Cambridge on the topic (Lowe 1985: 150).

The Mathematical Tripos in Russell's day was governed by regulations enacted by the University in the 1880s which had split the Tripos into two parts, elementary and advanced, both highly competitive. The new arrangements were widely criticized within the university.[6] And even partisan defenders of the system like Ball (1921: 302) had to admit that the number of students studying mathematics at Cambridge suffered a serious decline until sweeping reforms, which for the most part had Russell's approval, were enacted in 1907. To some extent this was anticipated. The *Student's Guide* said that Part II was 'intended for those students who wish to make advances into the higher regions of Pure and Applied Mathematics, and it is not expected that many students will avail themselves of this opportunity of extending their studies' (Besant 1893: 1). Russell was among those who did not. He took only Part I of the Tripos in May and June of 1893, and was bracketed 7th wrangler. The range covered even by the papers of Part I was very wide, but students were warned against attempting 'too large a range of reading' and advised 'that any subject, or portion of a subject, which is undertaken, should be studied closely and thoroughly' (Besant 1893: 14). In fact, wide superficial knowledge was an endemic problem with the Mathematical Tripos where the average of marks obtained in all divisions determined the final mark.

Although the description provided by the Cambridge *Student's Guide* (Besant 1893) is quite detailed, very little is known specifically about Russell's mathematical career at Cambridge between 1890 and 1893. With one exception, his notes for this period are lost, as are most of his letters. He did refer much later to geometrical optics and spherical astronomy, 'two subjects of incredible dullness which I had to get up'.[7] 'What Shall I Read?', a notebook in which Russell recorded his reading, covers these years but does not list his reading in mathematics. Even his library is not much help since, after completing the Tripos, Russell sold all his mathematics books in disgust (*MPD* 38). The only significant document that survives from this period is a revision notebook, dating from May Term 1893, which was preserved among Dora Russell's papers. It contains brief notes on Tripos problems on a number of topics. It faithfully reflects the Tripos, and gives a clear idea of the sort of performance expected of a wrangler. But it is concerned exclusively with techniques for answering Tripos problems and tell us little directly about the scope or content of Russell's mathematical education.[8]

[6] Cf. Rothblatt (1976) for the development of the Tripos system and Winstanley (1947: 223–33) for attempts to reform it in the 1860s and 1880s.

[7] B. R. to Katharine Tait, 6 Dec. 1946.

[8] The notebook is now in the Russell Archives, Rec. Acq. 1027. It survived because two years later Russell used its blank versos to make notes on his reading on non-Euclidean geometry. The

Like all students, Russell had a college tutor who acted *in loco parentis* but was not usually directly involved in the tuition of the student. Russell's college tutor was A. H. F. Boughey, a classics and theology don. Formal university tuition was undertaken by lecturers. After the appointment of the first college lecturer in 1868, lectures were given increasingly on a college- or even a university-wide basis, so that by the 1890s, it would have been quite normal for Russell to have attended lectures outside Trinity.

Throughout the eighteenth and nineteenth centuries, however, the official system of college instruction was much less influential than the informal system of private tuition by coaches. These coaches were paid directly by their students of whom they often had considerable numbers. The coach was primarily responsible for directing his students' work and supervising their progress through the Tripos. This was achieved by lectures, often several times a week, to small groups of students and the setting and marking of large numbers of examples based on previous Tripos papers. Sample solutions to set problems would be given at the lectures or circulated among the students in manuscript. The best known, and by far the most successful, coach was J. E. Routh of Peterhouse, whose *Rigid Dynamics* (1882) and (1884) Russell had studied before going up to Cambridge. Between 1858 and 1888 Routh had coached over 600 students, most of whom had become wranglers, 27 of them senior wranglers.[9]

It is important to emphasize that this coaching system was entirely unofficial and private. Some coaches were not even members of the University. This long-standing anomaly had been called into existence by the extremely competitive nature of the Tripos examinations which required not so much imagination and understanding as simple mechanical speed at working through examples. All the students taking the Tripos were arranged in a strict order of merit to which the utmost importance was attached. The papers themselves were far longer than even the best students could hope to complete. In 1881, for example, out of a possible total of 33,541 points, the senior wrangler scored 16,368, the second wrangler 13,188, and the last wrangler 3,123 (Littlewood 1953: 25). Success demanded the long hours of practice that the coaches provided. Russell was bitterly critical of the results of this system, complaining, at the end of his first term, of the type of person 'brought to the fore by the cram system' (LD 60). Many years later he commented: 'The necessity for nice discrimination between the abilities of different examinees led to an emphasis on "problems" as opposed to

---

topics covered by the revision notes are: elementary and advanced optics, elementary astronomy, Newton, hydrostatics, elementary dynamics, elementary statics, trigonometry, elementary algebra, and rigid dynamics.

[9] For a detailed account of how Routh organized this massive production of wranglers, see Forsyth (1935: 173–5) who was one of them. For Routh see also Forsyth's obituary (1906).

"bookwork" . . . Indeed, the whole subject of mathematics was presented as a set of clever tricks by which to pile up marks in the Tripos' (*MPD* 38). In setting each examination, insight, utility, and general principles were ignored in favour of devising ever more ingenious twists and pitfalls in the problems set. The same material was set year after year, each time with changes only in the subtle details and the tricks designed to trap unwary undergraduates.[10]

In the final years of the nineteenth century, the coaching system was under attack. The students, after all, had paid fees to the University for tuition and were then expected to pay again for essential private help that the University didn't provide. The recent introduction of college and inter-collegiate lectures was 'intended to give a larger amount of help to undergraduate students, and to make the assistance of the private Tutor less a matter of necessity than hitherto has been the case' (Besant 1893: 20). But the remedy was far from effective, especially since the mathematics dons at Trinity in 1887 had declared themselves against giving an hour a week of personal supervision to honours students (Rothblatt 1968: 232). It was only the abolition of the order of merit in 1907 that brought the coaching system, and with it many of the evils of which Russell complained, to an end.

Russell, like most other students of his day, worked with a coach. Routh had retired from coaching in 1888, leaving no one of comparable stature to take his place. Russell's coach was Robert Rumsey Webb (1850–1936) of St John's College, who, with Routh's retirement, became 'the most famous mathematical coach of his time' (Anon. 1937: 273). He must have been successful since at one time he taught 60 hours a week (Venn 1954: vi, 388). Forsyth regarded him as the best of the younger coaches, 'a superb teacher' (Forsyth 1935: 168). Not surprisingly, in view of his teaching load, Webb's original contributions to mathematics were slight, though '[t]he breadth and exactness' of his knowledge were said to be 'a source of wonder to his pupils'[11]—but not, apparently, to Russell. It seems likely that Russell attended a course of his on hydrostatics and found it 'quite uninteresting' (*PFM* 59). Webb's obituary in *The Cambridge Review* diplomatically states: '[I]f Routh was mild, and Besant was courteous, Webb was impressive. Those who enjoyed his teaching, and endured his personalities, learnt from him much more than mathematics; slovenliness, sham and personal advertisement received a decisive reward, in words not easily forgotten. But his devotion to his pupils . . . shewed itself in a changed manner . . . in after life'. Webb lived most of his life in college, in his later years as a virtual recluse. According to

[10] 'Particles were made to describe arabesque paths under fantastic laws of force never imagined outside an examination paper' (Forsyth 1935: 170). Forsyth, who in 1907 was largely responsible for reforming the system through the radical step of abolishing the order of merit, summed up the old system in Pope's couplet: 'Tricks to show the stretch of human brain, | Mere curious pleasure or ingenious pain' (p. 176).

[11] 'Robert Rumsey Webb', *The Cambridge Review*, 16 October, 1936, p. 25.

Russell, 'He went mad, but none of his pupils noticed it. At last he had to be shut up' (*PFM* 57). It is difficult to see what influence, if any, this somewhat curmudgeonly product of the Tripos system had on Russell.[12]

Russell's lack of enthusiasm for Webb did not differ much from his lack of enthusiasm for the rest of his mathematical education at Cambridge. Despite the claims in the *Student's Guide* (Browne 1893: 26) that '[t]he Mathematical Honours Examination is widely celebrated, and has given to this University its character of the Mathematical University *par excellence*', mathematics at Cambridge was bad. Russell recalled that '[t]he "proofs" which were offered of mathematical theorems were an insult to the logical intelligence' and said that the overall effect of the system was to make him 'think mathematics disgusting' (*MPD* 38). And elsewhere he wrote:

My teachers offered me proofs which I felt to be fallacious and which, as I learnt later, had been recognized as fallacious. I did not know then, or for some time after I had left Cambridge, that better proofs had been found by German mathematicians . . . I was encouraged in my transition to philosophy by a certain disgust with mathematics, resulting from too much concentration and too much absorption in the sort of skill that is needed in examinations. The attempt to acquire examination techniques had led me to think of mathematics as consisting of artful dodges and ingenious devices and as altogether too much like a crossword puzzle. (*PFM* 15–16.)

Russell was not alone in his opinion. Forsyth, who graduated ten years before, observed: 'The proofs, such as were current about the Binomial Theorem, would stir the explosive contempt of any of the critical mathematicians of to-day' (Forsyth 1935: 170; see also Wood 1957: 26 and Howe 1942: i, 203). Grace Chisholm, Russell's contemporary in the Mathematical Tripos, wrote at greater length in her unpublished memoirs:

Mathematical science had reached the acme of perfection. Through the long future ages, no new methods, no new subjects were to appear. The edifice of mathematical science was complete, roof on and everything. All that remained to be done was to consolidate and repair the masonry, and to add and correct the ornamentation. This was the view in those days, and the atmosphere was stifling to the young mathematician . . . At Cambridge the pursuit of pure learning was impossible. There was no mathematician—or more properly no mathematical thinker—in the place. The depressing character of the intellectual atmosphere was due to the examination. Everything pointed to examinations, everything was judged by examination standards, progress stopped at the Tripos. There was no interchange of ideas, there was no encouragement, there was no generosity. (Grattan-Guinness 1972*b*: 115, 131.)

She went to Göttingen to work with Felix Klein.

---

[12] Russell's Tripos revision notebook (Rec. Acq. 1027), interestingly enough, does not contain notes from Webb, but from R. A. Herman. Herman later coached J. E. Littlewood, who described him as 'the last of the great coaches' (1953: 70), though he was generally compared unfavourably with both Routh and Webb. It seems likely that Russell copied the notes from a friend who coached with Herman.

By far the most important Cambridge mathematician in Russell's day was Arthur Cayley (1821–95), Sadleirian Professor of Mathematics, the inventor of matrices, and an important early contributor to projective geometry. But Cayley was already in his seventies when Russell went up and suffering from a long terminal illness which caused him to cancel lectures for a whole term in 1893.[13] Cayley's illustrious past did little to enhance his contribution in that later period. Chisholm describes him, perhaps a little unfairly, as a remote Buddha (Grattan-Guinness 1972*b*: 115). Cayley's work on projective geometry was known to Russell who refers to it in his *Essay on the Foundations of Geometry*. However, Russell's personal contact with Cayley must have been slight or non-existent. Russell makes no reference to any meetings with the great mathematician in any of his autobiographical writings. In general, contact between undergraduates and professors was very restricted. Forsyth recalled of his undergraduate years:

Between the great professors and our unfledged selves there was nothing in common, absolutely nothing . . . They did not teach us . . . We did not read their work: it was asserted, and was believed, to be of no help in the Tripos. Probably many of the students did not know the professors by sight. Such an odd situation . . . was due mainly, if not entirely, to the Tripos and its surroundings which . . . had settled into a position beyond the pale of accessible criticism. (Forsyth 1935: 166.)

Little had changed in this respect in the decade between Forsyth's and Russell's graduations. Under such conditions, the eminence of the senior mathematicians at Cambridge could matter little to undergraduates like Russell.

The Mathematical Tripos was better served by its physicists than by its pure mathematicians. In physics Cambridge boasted J. J. Thomson (1856–1940) who lectured widely at the Cavendish Laboratory on such topics as the properties of matter, electricity, and magnetism, and the kinetic theory of gases. He also gave one course of mathematics for physicists and another of physics experiments for mathematicians. The discovery of the electron, for which he is famous, occurred in 1897. Russell became interested in his experimental work, but only after taking the Tripos (*MPD* 39). Also at Cambridge at this time was Joseph Larmor (1857–1942), lecturing on both electromagnetism and optics. Although Russell later read Larmor's works, it seems unlikely that Larmor, who was a remote and autocratic figure, ever had much personal influence on Russell. Even more aloof, by reason of age, eminence, and temperament, was J. C. Adams (1819–92), nicknamed 'Father Neptune' by the undergraduates on account of his remoteness and his calculations which had led to the discovery of that planet (Forsyth 1935:

---

[13] *The Cambridge Review*, 16 Jan. 1893, p. 366.

163). In a similar position was Sir G. G. Stokes (1819–1903) who in earlier years had done important research on wave motion and optics.

Thomson, Larmor, Stokes, and Adams were undoubtedly the four most eminent applied mathematicians at Cambridge in Russell's day, but, with the possible exception of Thomson, it is unlikely that any of them had much personal influence on Russell. At the undergraduate level, A. E. H. Love (1863–1940) was likely to be a more important influence. Like Russell, Love had been one of Webb's pupils, and had been appointed as college lecturer in mathematics at Trinity in 1886. At this time he was primarily interested in the theory of elasticity (cf. his monumental (1892) of which Russell read the first volume in July 1897). He was also, however, widely involved in college lecturing: 'His lectures . . . were extremely popular with students for their clarity, intelligibility and real efforts to enter into the students' point of view' (Milne 1941: 72). In all his work he was concerned with organizing the material on a firm foundation and in his *Theoretical Mechanics* (1897) he attempted to provide a philosophical analysis of dynamics. Russell, who reviewed the book on its first appearance, thought well of it: 'The present work is undoubtedly, from the point of view of first principles, the best English book on Dynamics; its free sceptical discussions are a most refreshing contrast to the scornful dogmatism of most mathematicians' (1898a: 108). Love's philosophical contacts at Cambridge included G. F. Stout, who became one of Russell's teachers in the Moral Sciences Tripos, and who invited Russell to lunch with Love in 1895, since the two had common interests.[14] It seems likely that Russell already knew Love, and had possibly attended some of his classes, but exact details are not available.

The dominance of applied mathematics within the University was, like everything else, the product of the Tripos. This dominance was so great that even Cayley came under criticism for using differential equations of third order, on the grounds that only those of second order were required in natural philosophy (Forsyth 1935: 171). The ossified respect in which Newton was held had established a tradition which lasted throughout the eighteenth and nineteenth centuries. In the latter part of the nineteenth century the tradition was defended by Routh's immense reputation within the University. Routh's own work was entirely concerned with rational mechanics, and his thirty years of intense coaching had given him a status which was hard to challenge. Routh had reluctantly acceded to the Tripos reforms of the 1880s, but had blocked a proposal in 1900 to abolish the order of merit. Its abolition finally came in 1907 just before his death, and even then had to be carried over his strenuous protests. Since the entire mathematical life of the undergraduates was centred around the demands of the Tripos

[14] G. F. Stout to B. R. 17 Oct. 1895. It was Stout, as editor of *Mind*, who gave Love (1897) to Russell for review.

system, the bias towards applied mathematics in the syllabus ensured that few of them received adequate training in pure mathematics—and, since each generation of dons was recruited from among the wranglers of the previous generation, the bias was perpetuated.

## 2.2 THE MORAL SCIENCES TRIPOS: 1893–1894

It seems that, even before he went up to Cambridge, Russell had planned to study philosophy after he had completed Part I of the Mathematical Tripos. In a letter of 14 March 1894 he told Alys Pearsall Smith of a conversation he'd had before going up with Frank Costelloe, Alys's brother-in-law and a barrister with interests in idealist philosophy, who had criticized his plans to take the Moral Sciences Tripos in his fourth year on the ground that mathematics would unsuit his mind for philosophy. Russell, to my knowledge, makes no other reference to these plans. But there are a few signs during his three years as a mathematics student of his continuing interest in philosophy. In his second term, for example, he joined the Cambridge Moral Sciences Club, a society primarily intended for those who had taken or were taking the Moral Sciences Tripos. In 1891, he reread much of Mill's work, with the notable exception of the *Logic*. This suggests that he was still strongly interested in empiricism (and also political philosophy)—perhaps trying to arm himself against the idealist philosophy prevalent in Cambridge. That he did not bother to reread the *Logic* suggests that he continued to regard it as fundamentally mistaken.

Towards the end of 1892, Russell purchased a second-hand copy of Jowett's Plato, of which he wrote his Uncle Rollo: 'It is really delightful to get philosophy presented in an easy amusing conversational form and yet not feel as one does with most French books that the arguments are superficial—such a contrast to the lumbering Germans'.[15] Since reading for the Mathematical Tripos was widely regarded as a strain sufficient to undermine one's health it is remarkable that Russell should have found time for any philosophical reading. For a time, it would seem, his work in mathematics did deteriorate. In retrospect, however, Russell attributed this deterioration to an attack of influenza early in 1892 which destroyed his capacity for working on either mathematics or philosophy (*MPD* 37). Russell's mathematics tutors were concerned; and James Ward, who seems to have acted as an unofficial tutor guiding his philosophical reading, recommended that Russell postpone his work in philosophy until after he had finished the Tripos.

It is not known what Ward recommended Russell to read at this time, but

---

[15] B. R. to R. Russell, 4 Dec. 1892.

we do have a list of philosophical books recommended by Harold Joachim, an Oxford idealist philosopher with whom Russell, more than a decade later, waged a protracted debate on the nature of truth. Russell knew Joachim through his Uncle Rollo who had married Joachim's sister, and Russell at one time clearly asked his advice on what to read in philosophy. Joachim's reply has survived and it was this list of books which, Russell claimed years later, 'started me on philosophy'.[16]

Joachim's letter is not dated, but internal evidence makes it probable that it was written on 23 September 1892.[17] Joachim's recommendations are dominated by the great philosophical classics, but they reveal very clearly his neo-Hegelian predilections. He includes several of Plato's dialogues (a more tepid recommendation of Aristotle's *Ethics, Metaphysics*, and *Politics* is added in a postscript), the main works of Spinoza, together with Descartes and Leibniz. (The last, he confesses, he hasn't read himself.) With this done, Joachim recommends that Russell 'attack Hume' (the choice of words is instructive)—but only in Green and Grose's devastatingly critical edition (Hume 1874)—'and, I suppose, Locke', though, again, Joachim had 'hardly read [Locke] at all'. Of the empiricists, Joachim warms only to Berkeley, who is 'delightful reading'. After the rationalists and empiricists, Russell should 'tackle some Kant'. Joachim recommends all three critiques and the *Metaphysics of Morals*. There is not much secondary literature on Joachim's list, though he recommends Erdmann (1878: he complains of the English translation), Burnet (1892), and Ferrier (1866), the last, though 'elementary, [are] good as far as they go'. In a postscript he recommends, besides Aristotle, some works on logic: Mill (1843), though 'full of fallacies'; Lotze (1874); Jevons (1874), 'tho' this isn't really Logic'; Bradley (1883), which is 'First rate—but very hard'; and Bosanquet (1888), which is 'Good, but still harder'. In 1959 Russell recalled only two of the books on Joachim's list, both of which he described with fair accuracy: 'one was Bradley's *Logic* which, he said, was good but hard; the other was Bosanquet's *Logic* which, he said, was better but harder' (*MPD* 37).

It is widely believed that, in his fourth year at Cambridge, Russell turned to philosophy in order to try and make good by philosophical analysis the defective 'proofs' he had been offered as a mathematics student. This seems to be Ayer's view, for example: 'but his first love . . . was mathematics, and it was his desire to find some good reason to believe in the truth of mathematics that led him in his third[18] year at Cambridge to make philosophy his

---

[16] B. R. to B. Blanshard, 16 May 1942.

[17] I have published Joachim's letter and the grounds for so dating it in Griffin (1988). One consequence of this dating is that the influenza attack Russell mentions in *MPD* must have occurred early in 1893, and not in 1892 as he claims.

[18] *Sic.* Ayer corrects this trivial error in his (1972: 13–14).

principal study' (Ayer 1971: 5). But this explanation will not do. By 1893 Russell had left the Mathematical Tripos with the intention of never reading another mathematics book (*MPD* 38). This vow was soon broken, first of all when Russell became interested, during his moral science year, in non-Euclidean geometry. But at the time, Russell took the vow seriously enough to sell all his mathematics books. Moreover, had he been seriously interested in the philosophical analysis of mathematical reasoning he would surely have specialized in logic and methodology in the Moral Sciences Tripos. This area of specialization was certainly the closest offered at Cambridge to that particular group of problems. Part I of the Moral Sciences Tripos on logic and methodology was fairly traditional, covering syllogistic, induction, and the theory of terms and propositions with the help of mainly traditional texts. However, Part II dealt with such topics as symbolic logic, statistics, scientific method and probability theory, in addition to a deeper treatment of the topics of Part I, some of which required 'some knowledge of mathematics or physical science, as analysing the methods, or appealing to the notation of, those sciences' (Ward 1893*a*: 15). The reading list for Part II suggests Lotze (1874), Sigwart (1873), Bradley (1883), and Bosanquet (1888) for the then fashionable idealist logic, as well as Venn (1881), Boole (1854), and Jevons (1874) for symbolic logic. Interestingly enough the reading list for symbolic logic also recommended Schröder (1890: i), but only for its bibliography.[19]

That Russell did not work in this area indicates a significant, if temporary, change in his intellectual interests. The disgust he felt for mathematics in the summer of 1893 is probably sufficient to explain why he did not go on to read logic and methodology, but it scarcely explains the areas he did choose to study. We know of his long-standing interest in politics and in political economy (both of which were part of the Moral Sciences Tripos). As late as 1895 he was even considering leaving philosophy for economics. But in 1893 Russell decided to specialize in ethics, metaphysics, and history of philosophy. The ethics and metaphysics are easily explained: they were compulsory for students not doing advanced political economy (Ward 1893*a*: 2). Moreover, both were subjects in which Russell was deeply interested. Since the metaphysics syllabus also included a good deal of what would now be classed as epistemology (cf. Ward 1893*a*: 7–8) this naturally coincided with Russell's continuing search for certainty in human knowledge. His other choice, the history of philosophy, however, remains almost totally inexplicable. Each

[19] Cf. Ward (1893*a*: 5–6, 11–17). More elementary recommended texts on formal logic were Jevons (1870), Fowler (1866), and Keynes (1884). For scientific method Bacon (1620), Mill (1843), Whewell (1858), Jevons (1874), and Venn (1866, 1889) were recommended. Russell had already done some work in this area before he went up to Cambridge, for he told Jevons's son that when he was 18 he knew Jevons (1870) 'by heart' (B. R. to H. Stanley Jevons, 22 June 1955).

year some period in the history of philosophy was studied in detail. In 1892–3 it was the philosophy of Kant, which might have made sense for Russell in view of his fellowship work. But in 1893–4 it was philosophy of 1600–60 with special reference to Descartes, Bacon, and Hobbes (Ward 1893*a*: 35 n.). It is difficult to see what appeal this topic had for Russell in 1893.[20]

Whatever the reasons for his choice of specialization, Russell was not disappointed by the Moral Sciences Tripos. 'As soon as I was free to do so,' he wrote, 'I devoted myself to philosophy with great ardour' (*Auto*. i, 68). His study of philosophy gave him 'all the delight of a new landscape on emerging from a valley' (*PFM* 16). Soon after he'd started Sidgwick's course on ethics he wrote to his uncle: 'It is delightful doing work that I really like, as it was some time since I had ceased to care much for mathematics'.[21] Even the purely historical work was enjoyed, though possibly only for its curiosity value: 'Philosophy altogether seemed to me great fun, and I enjoyed the curious ways of conceiving the world that the great philosophers offer to the imagination' (*Auto*. i, 68). Surviving documents from the 1890s give the same impression. Russell's early letters to Alys Pearsall Smith, his future wife, contain many references to philosophical problems and discussions, despite occasional remarks about the absurdity of devoting one's life to such useless and arcane issues.[22] His complaints about the uselessness of philosophy need not be taken too seriously when, in the same correspondence, he resorts to philosophical arguments in support of his proposal that they get married. In the middle of his work for the Moral Sciences Tripos he writes: 'I have developed far more in every way in the last 6 months than the preceding three years'.[23] While Alys may have been expected to infer that part of this development was due to his love for her, the Moral Sciences Tripos deserves credit for a good deal of the rest.

Unlike the Mathematical Tripos, the Moral Sciences Tripos was largely reformed by the 1890s.[24] It had not been established until 1851, and for

---

[20] He did feel attracted to Descartes's reconstruction program in philosophy as a defence against scepticism (*PFM* 16), but it is not known whether this was before or after his formal study of Descartes.     [21] B. R. to R. Russell, 16 July 1893.

[22] Thus e.g. in a letter of 28 Feb. 1894: 'I have been reading controversies on the nature of the Self till I am quite sure it has no meaning and that I don't exist. Vastly pointless!' The controversies in question were likely those between Bradley and Ward. See also the letter of 28 Jan. 1894. A brief summary of the philosophic content of this correspondence is to be found in Spadoni (1978).

[23] B. R. to A. P. Smith, 8 Mar. 1894.

[24] In what follows I am indebted to Winstanley (1947) and especially to Rothblatt's excellent (1968). The social roots and some of the social consequences of the reform movement are discussed by Skidelsky (1983: 26–31). A useful account of philosophy at Cambridge by an insider is C. D. Broad (1957), although it deals primarily with a slightly later period. In particular it gives an account of some Cambridge philosophers (notably Venn, Johnson and J. N. Keynes) who appear to have had little or no influence on Russell. For an amusing memoir of pre-reform Cambridge see Stephen (1865).

many years it had been something of an also-ran at Cambridge (cf. Winstanley 1947: 185–9). Its independent status did not help to begin with, since it deprived philosophy students of prizes and scholarships which would have been available had philosophy remained part of the Classics Tripos. Unlike mathematics, where a good position in the Tripos list carried with it in some colleges a virtual guarantee of a fellowship, even the best student in the Moral Sciences Tripos was for many years not guaranteed a fellowship (Winstanley 1947: 189). By the 1860s the disadvantages of the order of merit, outdated syllabuses, the celibacy and subscription rules, the coaching system, and the remote and pedantic dons with life fellowships (awarded on the basis of their undergraduate performance in the Tripos) and little obligation either to teach or do research, were widely admitted.[25] But it wasn't until the 1870s that, prompted by Parliamentary enquiries and reforms and spearheaded from within by a new group of reforming dons, Cambridge began to reform, and the Moral Sciences Tripos came into its own.

The appointment of J. R. Seeley to the Regius Chair of History in 1869 was the first step in a long process of reform. Two years before his appointment Seeley had diagnosed the fundamental problem: the Tripos itself. 'Cambridge is like a country invaded by the Sphinx', he wrote, 'To answer the monster's conundrums has become the one absorbing occupation' (Rothblatt 1968: 181). One of Seeley's first attempts at reform was to propose the establishment of intercollegiate lectures in the hope of undermining the coaching system. He was the first of the Cambridge professors to emphasize his role as a teacher and to make undergraduate education his main concern. He was soon to be joined by a group of younger dons, including notably Sidgwick (in moral sciences), and Jebb, Currey, and Jackson (in classics). Around these innovative teachers a group of dons formed, sufficiently different from their predecessors to be labelled 'the new dons'. As Russell noted, 'The really fine flower of perfect don-ishness was already passing away when I was an undergraduate' (*PFM* 58), although he goes on to give some nice examples of surviving specimens.

Although the coaching system could never be overthrown while the Tripos order of merit existed, that was little excuse for the failures of the college tutors. The new dons sought to win back for the college some of the intellectual and moral influence with the students which had become the prerogative of the coaches. They attempted this firstly by concentrating upon their teaching, relating it more to the needs of their students and to the

---

[25] Not surprisingly the old dons of Oxford and Cambridge were frequent targets of literary satire, e.g. in Cuthbert Bede's *Verdant Green* (1853), Thackeray's *Book of Snobs* (1846), and Margaret Oliphant's *Chronicles of Carlingford* (1862). The most embittered attack—also the most famous—came somewhat later in Hardy's *Jude the Obscure* (1896).

concerns of the modern world. The mid-nineteenth-century idea that the students went to university primarily to learn from each other was rejected. In the 1880s the foundations of the present tutorial system were laid, at least at Trinity, which in 1889 set up the Tutorial System Committee, charged with improving teaching in the college and revitalizing the office of tutor. The educational impact of the new dons was felt not only in the formal instruction provided at Cambridge. Outside the classroom the new dons were equally active: they took part in undergraduate sports; founded and attended a variety of societies to which students contributed; gave parties for their students; and above all they were prepared to meet their students for discussions outside class hours. They were concerned to overcome the reputation for aloofness and isolation that the older dons had built up. G. L. Dickinson, with his intensely sensitive concern for his students' personal and intellectual problems, represents one type of new don; Oscar Browning, also of King's, a notorious snob and socialite, who took it upon himself to introduce his students into select social circles, was a caricature of another (cf. Russell 1959*b*: 277–8). On the whole, however, the new dons sought to develop the best aspects of a collegiate university with close relations between fellows and students.

The new dons achieved a large measure of success, and their influence was instrumental in producing a flowering of Cambridge talent in the late nineteenth century. Colleges varied greatly, however, and Trinity retained its reputation for unfriendliness. In part this was due to its sheer size. In 1890 when Russell went up, it was by far the largest of the Cambridge colleges with 639 students out of a total university population of 3,029 (Cambridge 1890: 816). In part, however, it was the result of Whewell's notorious remoteness and arrogance during his long period as Master (1841–66). In examining for scholarships, the dons' opinions were often suspect, either on the grounds that they would be biased in favour of their own students or else, in an attempt at fairness, be biased the other way; but no such doubts were ever held about Whewell's judgement, since he never knew which were his students and which were not.[26] After his death, however, Trinity became a stronghold for the new dons. Many of the younger dons at Trinity had suffered under Whewell's autocracy and were anxious to avoid continuing his alienating influence.[27] The Master in Russell's day, Montagu Butler, was much more approachable though somewhat ponderous (cf. *PFM* 62). Even mathematics at Trinity had some new dons, notably Whitehead, Love, and Glaisher. In the moral sciences the reform movement had triumphed by

[26] Cf. Ball (1921: 172–7) for this and other stories of Whewell's indifference toward his students and colleagues.

[27] Cf. Winstanley (1947: ch. 6). For Sidgwick's sense of emancipation after Whewell's demise see Sidgwick and Sidgwick (1906: 130–1, 147–8).

1893, and Russell's teachers were all new dons. Moreover, despite Whewell's faults, philosophy had been greatly strengthened by him at Trinity and throughout the university.

During his fourth year Russell attended lectures by Henry Sidgwick (1838–1900), James Ward (1843–1925), and G. F. Stout (1860–1944).[28] With Ward and Stout he kept in touch long after his graduation. Ward, in particular, inspired his affection, and it seems that at least part of the delight with which Russell turned to philosophy was due to the close relations he was able to establish with his teachers and which, with the exception of Whitehead, had been lacking with his mathematics tutors. He kept detailed notes of the philosophy lectures he attended, with the exception of Sidgwick's elements of philosophy.[29] There were certain things about Sidgwick's philosophy which might have been expected to appeal to Russell, notably his utilitarianism and his rejection of Mill's strong empiricism (especially in connection with inference). On the other hand, Sidgwick's fallibilism may well have seemed defeatist to Russell who had entered philosophy with a view to acquiring certain knowledge, especially when such certainty was widely proclaimed by the neo-Hegelians to be available.[30] Sidgwick's differences from classical utilitarianism, such as his refusal to define moral concepts in terms of non-moral ones and his insistence on common sense, were probably minimized by Russell, who referred to him (mistakenly) as 'the last survivor of the Benthamites' (*MPD* 38). With the neo-Hegelians as a contrast, Bentham and Sidgwick would seem much more alike.[31]

In fact, Russell, in common with the other young philosophers at Cambridge, 'did not give [Sidgwick] nearly as much respect as he deserved' (*MPD* 38). With the rise of Kant and Hegel in British universities, utilitarianism and common sense philosophy had been on the defensive, and 'Old Sidg', as he was called by Cambridge undergraduates, was considered philosophically out of date (*MPD* 38; MMD 10; *PFM* 63). The neglect of Sidgwick had as much to do with his style as his doctrines. Both resulted from his painstakingly scrupulous integrity, which was reclassified as diffidence as the issues over

[28] The lectures and the terms in which they started were: Sidgwick's ethics, Long Vacation 1893; Sidgwick's elements of philosophy, Michaelmas Term 1893; Ward's metaphysics, Michaelmas Term 1893, Ward's history of philosophy (Descartes, Locke, Malebranche, Spinoza, Leibniz, Berkeley, Hume, Kant, Reid, Mill, and Spencer), Lent term 1894; Stout's history of philosophy (Bacon, Descartes, Ramus, Digby, Temple, Hobbes, Galileo, Spinoza, Gassendi, Geulincx, and Malebranche), Michaelmas Term 1893.

[29] Cf. Russell's 'Lecture Notebooks' I and II (RA 220.010040, 50). Much later on Russell said that his attitude and that of most of his friends was that 'lectures were a pure waste of time' (*OE* 241). To judge by the very extensive notes he took, he must have wasted a lot of time.

[30] See Griffin (1989) for details of the respects in which Russell may have held out hopes that the neo-Hegelians might do better than Sidgwick.

[31] The best general study of Sidgwick and his place in moral philosophy is Schneewind (1977), but see also Broad (1930) and see Skidelsky (1983: ch. 2) for his role in Victorian culture. For his life see Sidgwick and Sidgwick (1906) or, more manageably, Blanshard (1984).

which he agonized came to appear less difficult. Thus, for example, Keynes's dismissive summary: 'He never did anything but wonder whether Christianity was true and prove that it wasn't and hope that it was' (Skidelsky 1983: 34). The writings of the then fashionable neo-Hegelians had a certain dash and elegance, which Sidgwick's entirely lacked. There was nothing, wrote C. D. Broad (1930: 114), 'to relieve the uniform dull dignity of his writing'. In labyrinthine Victorian sentences, heavily overloaded with dependent clauses and qualifications, Sidgwick pursued his argument, determined to leave no objection unanswered. His scrupulous attention to detail, which pursued his *Methods of Ethics* through seven editions of meticulous revision, made it difficult for his readers to follow his argument.

Some features of his writing transferred with unfortunate effects to his teaching. Although an earlier generation of undergraduates gave high praise to his teaching, even they noted the high degree of sustained attention that was necessary to follow his classes (cf. Sidgwick and Sidgwick 1906: 307, 312). In the early years of the Moral Sciences Tripos, Sidgwick's unpretentiousness, and the scrupulous care which he took in marking their essays and considering their opinions, endeared him to many students. In later years, however, some of this changed. The virtues which Sidgwick, as one of the first new dons, had exemplified almost uniquely became more common. Also the Moral Sciences Tripos itself became more popular and larger classes forced Sidgwick to give more formal lectures which he found uncongenial. Finally, as he got older he came to find teaching more and more burdensome (Sidgwick and Sidgwick 1906: 312). By the 1890s he was simply reading out his lectures, 'fit for publication as they stood' according to G. E. Moore (1942: 17), who added: 'I think I could have gained more by reading them to myself than by hearing him read them'.[32] This is almost certainly an opinion that Russell would have shared. Russell, much later, however, went out of his way to praise Sidgwick's intellectual honesty and the care and courtesy with which he commented on student essays (*UE* 214). Certainly, the latter was evident on Russell's own essays for Sidgwick (cf. *Papers* i, 419–22).

Although Sidgwick's interests were far from narrow (his teaching at Cambridge included classics, economics, literature, politics, and law, in addition to philosophy), his main contribution was to ethics and consists essentially of a single (great) book, *The Methods of Ethics* (1874). Indeed, his failure to achieve more was partly due to his failure to decide on a single line of activity. His vacillation between teaching, philosophy, parapsychology, and biblical studies (the last of which involved him in extensive work in Hebrew and Arabic) often undermined his efforts in any one area. In addition, he was plagued by personal problems and religious doubts which

---

[32] The ethics lectures Moore and Russell both attended were in fact published posthumously as Sidgwick (1902*a*) and the elements of philosophy lectures as Sidgwick (1902*b*).

took up his time and sapped his energy. In these areas especially he could not make quick decisions, and every move was preceded by an agonized period of self-interrogation. Once he had decided, however, he acted on his decision, sometimes in cases where action required courage, as when he resigned his fellowship in 1869 because he found he no longer subscribed to the Thirty-nine Articles. His public confrontation of this issue was instrumental in getting the subscription rules revoked.

Although Russell read *The Methods of Ethics*, in July 1893, there is little sign of its having had any major influence on him. The same can be said of Sidgwick's lectures. Russell, like Moore, found the latter dull and tiresome, as the notes he took illustrate. There was a marked contrast between Sidgwick's manner in the lecture-hall and his manner in private, where he was a congenial host and (despite a stammer) an unexpectedly good conversationalist. Moore noted the contrast in a letter to his mother (30 April 1895) after he'd had dinner with the Sidgwicks at Newnham College:

The professor is immensely interesting and amusing: he always has plenty to say, wandering on gently from topic to topic, with shrewd remarks and plenty of witty anecdotes; I wish it were the same with his lectures, but they generally seem three times as long as anybody else's, and are very difficult to follow. He is so familiar with his subject and all its side-issues, that he does not make its skeleton clear enough, being continually engaged in arguments on details (Quoted Levy 1979: 152.)

Russell's other teachers, Ward and Stout, have both secured minor places in the history of philosophy. The work of the two men was closely connected. Stout was Ward's pupil, and both were primarily interested in psychology and philosophy of mind (two subjects not easily distinguished at that time). Russell's serious concern with Stout's work dates from after the Tripos period. Thus, for example, in 1911 Russell wrote to Ottoline Morrell: 'Stout . . . is a delightful man—he was one of my teachers here, and I have kept up with him ever since'.[33] In fact, Stout gradually moved away from the idealism which was undoubtedly an influence on him in the 1890s toward realism and empiricism, a development which Russell, later on, would have found congenial. Indeed, in 1914 Russell and Stout were engaged in a dispute about Russell's theory of judgement (Stout 1914), and Stout's later letters to Russell show him concerned with the theory of descriptions and the Russell paradox. On the other hand, Russell did not keep up with Ward's work for long. Ward read chapter 3 of the manuscript of Russell's book on Leibniz and is thanked in the preface for 'several important criticisms' (*POL*: p. xv). But in 1912 Russell wrote to Morrell: 'I am very fond of Ward indeed, but as a philosopher he doesn't seem to me up to very much. He allows himself to remain puzzled by things that only want an effort to be

[33] B. R. to Morrell, 3 May 1911 (no. 51).

understood'.[34] In fact, most of Russell's references to Ward in his letters to
Morrell combine an appreciation of Ward's character on the one hand with a
complete rejection of his philosophy on the other: 'Talking with him is
difficult, because I respect him and greatly like him, and yet I feel his work
utterly futile, on wrong lines from the beginning, not even instructively
wrong. He no doubt realizes what I feel, and it is rather painful'.[35] By
contrast, Stout remained a philosopher with whom discussion was worthwhile.

When Russell was a student, however, things were very different, and
Russell's idealist efforts owe a good deal to Ward's thought, as we shall see.
It is not surprising that Stout's influence as a teacher failed to equal Ward's.
Stout was some seventeen years younger than Ward and, as the latter's student
with no major independent works to his name, must have appeared to Russell
in 1893 as the lesser of the two philosophers. His philosophical position was
notably eclectic, perhaps even more so than Ward's. As C. A. Mace (1945: 313)
put it, 'Most philosophers are distinctive in virtue of what they deny. Stout
was distinctive in the surprising range of his affirmations'. 'I have got them
all [idealism, rationalism, and empiricism] in my philosophy', he sometimes
boasted.[36] None the less, in 1892 Stout had succeeded Croom Robertson in the
influential position of editor of *Mind*, where he published some of Russell's
most important papers in the early years of this century (on Stout's editorship
see Passmore 1976). Stout's first important work (1896) was read by Russell as
soon as it came out.[37] The leading features of this work derive, with important
modifications, from Ward. Like Ward, Stout adopted an act-psychology,
although he disliked the term 'mental act' preferring to talk of 'attitudes of
consciousness' which relate a mind to an object. He laid more stress than
Ward upon Brentano's doctrine of the intentionality of consciousness,
although he left open the possibility of what he called 'anoetic sentience'
(consciousness without an object). He distinguished between the object, or
'objective reference', of consciousness, and the 'presentation' of this object,
which determines 'the direction of thought . . . to this or that special object in
preference to others' (1896: i, 122–3). This distinction, which parallels the
better-known distinction between 'object' and 'content' found in Twardowski
(1894) and Meinong (1899), is not to be found in either Ward or Brentano.[38]
Stout's position in his *Analytical Psychology* was developed and refined in

[34] B. R. to Morrell, 13 Nov. 1912 (no. 635).
[35] B. R. to Morrell, 30 Apr. 1913 (no. 759).
[36] Reported in Mace (1967: 23). Mace (1946: 51) places Stout in the British empiricist tradition.
[37] Soon after its publication, Stout left Cambridge for good to take up a position at Aberdeen. After a spell at Oxford he moved to St Andrews where he set up a psychology laboratory. For a good survey of Stout's psychological work see Mace (1954). For his philosophy see Passmore (1952).
[38] Stout discusses the differences between his position and Ward's in Stout (1926).

his subsequent writings, especially (1899) which for many years remained a standard psychology textbook in Britain.

Russell said little publicly about Stout as a teacher, though in a letter to John Wright (5 June 1948) he wrote: 'I enjoyed his lectures very much, and found him a stimulating teacher'. Moore attended Stout's lectures two years later and gives a similar account:

[W]e sat round a table in his rooms at St. John's, and Stout simply talked to us . . . [H]e was always interesting and exciting. It seems to me that Stout has a quite exceptional gift for seizing on some particular point of importance, involved in a confused philosophical controversy, and putting that point in the simplest and most conversational language: he is peculiarly direct, and utterly free from anything approaching pretentiousness or pomposity. (Moore 1942: 18.)

Stout was a small man with a very quiet voice, both disadvantages at large public lectures. Of one of his lectures it was said: 'Stout disappeared behind the lectern and was neither seen nor heard for an hour' (Mace 1945: 311). In the smaller, less formal setting of his classes these traits were not disadvantages, and Stout was excellent in private discussions.

It is very difficult to tell what, if any, influence Stout had on Russell during the latter's undergraduate years. Russell wrote to Alys that Stout 'has taken quite an affection for me apparently, as I have for him, tho' as McTaggart says he is an acquired taste'.[39] The only course Russell took with Stout was one on the history of philosophy concentrating mainly on the seventeenth century, in which Russell was the only student.[40] Bacon, Descartes, and Hobbes figure prominently in the course, and essays on all three by Russell have survived (*Papers*, i, 132–9, 156–94). In addition, a remarkable amount of time was spent on such minor sixteenth-century English figures as Everard Digby and William Temple, whose lack of contribution to philosophy was also discussed in Russell's essays (*Papers*, i, 163–5). Apart from demonstrating Russell's knowledge of these philosophers, and his capacity for concise summary, there is little in these essays which indicates any specific intellectual debt to Stout. Little of Stout's own views came across in the lectures. The one exception is the brief discussion of the ontological argument (1894c: 179) which had an important bearing on Russell's conversion to neo-Hegelianism (see § 3.2).

The case is quite different with James Ward, the most influential of Russell's three philosophy teachers.[41] Ward had come to philosophy comparatively late in life after he had abandoned, on conscientious grounds, a protracted

---

[39] B. R. to A. P. Smith, 16 May 1894.

[40] B. R. to John Wright, 5 June 1948 (Fisher Library, University of Toronto).

[41] The best source for Ward's life is the excellent memoir by his daughter (Campbell 1927). Unfortunately, the personal papers on which it was based seem to have been lost. For his philosophy see Murray (1937).

effort to be ordained as a minister. His loss of orthodox religious faith in his late twenties caused him immense spiritual anguish. His upbringing had been in a narrow, Calvinistic brand of Congregationalism. His father had written a tract reconciling science with the Bible, explaining the Flood, for example, by means of a sudden stopping of the earth's rotation (Campbell 1927: 6). Ward's letters to his family from the Congregational college at which he studied discuss, in tones of leaden piety, points of biblical interpretation as well as their father's business affairs. The latter caused great fluctuations in the family's fortunes, though the successes were never grand and the failures were on two occasions catastrophic. It was the final bankruptcy of his father's business in less than honorable circumstances that led to a final breach between father and son. This came shortly after James Ward had abandoned the family faith and entered Cambridge. His Puritanical upbringing, traumatic loss of faith, and the fact that he was in his thirties before his career was truly underway, all took their toll. He was, apparently, extremely moody, and prone to deep fits of depression. One of his favourite sayings was 'Das Denken ist schwer' (Campbell 1927: 54; Moore 1942: 16), and he seems frequently to have been overwhelmed by the feeling that philosophic thought, at any rate, was too hard for him.

Ward had made his debut in the field of psychology with a telling critique of associationism (Ward 1886), the central psychological doctrine of the empiricists, which, together with Bradley's earlier criticisms (1883), effectively put paid to the doctrine.[42] Bradley had criticized associationism chiefly for its atomism. Ward, on the other hand, attacked the passivity of the associationist conception of mind (an attack further developed by Stout 1896). Ward and Bradley soon departed company, however. In particular, Ward undertook a major critique of Bradley's theory of the self and, much later on, the doctrine of immediate experience.[43] In the 1890s, Ward was better known as a psychologist than as a philosopher. Boring (1929: 463) describes him as 'the senior psychologist in Great Britain' after Bain. His fellowship dissertation at Cambridge (1875) had been on 'The Relation of Physiology and Psych-

---

[42] Bain, in a generous (though needless to say critical) review, said that when Ward had fully developed his position he 'will have produced a work entitled to a place among the masterpieces of the philosophy of the human mind' (Bain 1886: 477). Ward did, after a long delay, produce the elaboration Bain called for (Ward 1918). But he waited too long and found himself outstripped by the development of psychology. The acclaim Bain anticipated never eventuated.

[43] The relevant papers are Bradley (1887, 1893b) and Ward (1887, 1893b, 1894). Ward summed up his criticism once Bradley was safely dead (Ward 1925). Ward's articles on Bradley's theory of the self remain the best treatment of the topic. They are much superior to Vander Veer's prolix (1970). See Wollheim (1959: 130–5) and Passmore (1957: 82) for comments. There is a letter in Bradley's *Nachlass* at Merton College, Oxford, written by Ward to Bradley's heirs, explaining how distressing he had found this dispute and how it had led to an estrangement that lasted until Bradley's death. Bradley was a notoriously sharp polemicist.

ology'; and in 1891, after fifteen years of trying, he had succeeded in getting £50 from the University with which to open a psychology laboratory (cf. Boring 1929: 489). Ward was responsible for bringing to England the continental psychological tradition which included Weber, Fechner, Stumpf, Müller, Lotze, Wundt, Brentano, and Meinong. In England he was followed by his student, Stout, and to a slight extent by William McDougall, but before long the tradition which had dominated psychology towards the end of the nineteenth century was overtaken by new movements, notably behaviourism and psychoanalysis, and came to seem something of an historical curiosity.

In later years, after he had been appointed to the new chair in Logic and Mental Philosophy at Cambridge in 1897, Ward's interests moved to metaphysics, on which he gave two series of Gifford lectures (Ward 1899, 1911). Here his differences from the absolute idealists in general, and Bradley in particular, became even more apparent. In broad outline, these differences can be inferred from Ward's act-psychology. The central thesis of Ward's psychology is that all experience involves volition on the part of a conscious subject attending to an object. From this it immediately follows, contra Bradley, that there is a self, that the self is distinct from the objects to which it attends, that monism is false, and that relations are real (in particular, even immediate experience is still of the subject–act–object form and thus cannot be pre-relational as Bradley thought). There were two respects in which Ward's metaphysics coincided with Bradley's. In the first place, Ward regarded conscious experience as continuous. Secondly, Ward regarded reality as entirely spiritual. This, coupled with his pluralism, resulted in a monadology owing something to Leibniz, but much more to Lotze.[44] Ward had travelled to Germany at the advice of a friend to learn something of Hegel, but it was Lotze, whose lectures at Göttingen he attended in 1870, who made the greatest impact. Ward's monads were like Lotze's, and unlike Leibniz's, in that they were not windowless—this was a necessary consequence of Ward's act-psychology. They were also like Lotze's monads in that it was through them that Ward sought to establish the compatibility, in all areas, of teleological and mechanistic explanation. What at one level appeared as matter subject only to mechanical explanation, at another level would appear as a congeries of monads susceptibie to explanation in terms of volitions. It was through the volitions of monads, he thought, that the

---

[44] Russell had a Lotzean phase in 1897–8, and attended McTaggart's lectures on Lotze given during Lent Term 1898. But Lotze seems to have exerted little influence on Russell before this, notwithstanding Ward's strong and obvious debts to Lotze. This may have been because Russell was acutely aware of the defects of Lotze's philosophy of geometry, which Russell excoriated in *EFG* 93–109, and which may have led him to ignore aspects of Lotze's metaphysics which would have been useful to him as an idealist.

dynamic nature of the world could be explained. It is no surprise, therefore, to find that he preferred history to physics as a model of global explanation.[45]

There was another respect in which Ward admired Lotze's work, and that was Lotze's concern for scientific fact. Lotze had studied physics and mathematics, taken a doctorate in medicine, and had made important contributions to psychology early in his career. He was anxious to incorporate the results of these disparate fields into a single system without short-changing any of them. These efforts gave Lotze's thought an eclecticism which Ward admired. Ward thought that philosophy should begin, not with a study of primitive epistemic data such as the empiricists proposed, nor with a final metaphysical system of the world such as appealed to the Hegelians, but in the realm of scientific fact. Philosophical psychology would push the analysis back to the empiricists' starting-point, while metaphysics would push it forward to that of the Hegelians. The results Ward expected to find at both places differed, of course, from those the empiricists and Hegelians had claimed, but the questions to be answered were the same. Ward's monadology, which received its definitive presentation in the first series of his Gifford lectures, *Naturalism and Agnosticism*, represented his fullest account of the realm of scientific fact. The lectures' aim, he modestly explained in the preface, was 'to discuss in a popular way certain assumptions of "modern science" which have led to a widespread, but more or less tacit, rejection of idealistic views of the world' and, of course, to show that that rejection was a mistake. He afterwards thought that the book might have been called 'The Realm of Nature', since his second series of Gifford lectures was called *The Realm of Ends*.

The trouble with Ward's metaphysics was that he couldn't leave well-enough alone. Having arrived at the monadology he still felt the need for some overarching unity, a sort of hunger for monism. His mentor, Lotze, had gone the same way. For both men, God was instrumental in pulling off the final synthesis and the result was, as Passmore (1957: 82) remarks, an awkward combination of 'individuality and God, diversity and the Absolute'. Ward's efforts towards the final synthesis are to be found in *The Realm of Ends* (subtitled, *Pluralism and Theism*), and his results were distinctly unhappy. It may have been this work which Russell had parti-cularly in mind when he complained of Ward's philosophy to Ottoline Morrell. He reviewed it critically but respectfully in *The Nation* (1912a) where he said it was 'a singularly careful, candid, and serious defence of

---

[45] There is much evidence in the notes that Russell took at his metaphysics lectures that Ward also sought a dynamic epistemology, a 'genetic epistemology' as he puts it at one point ('Lecture Notebooks', i, 134), which would account for an evolutionary growth in knowledge and understanding, in contrast to what he plainly regarded as the ossified strait-jacket of Kant's categories (ibid. 80, 123, 134, 136).

what is most vital in the Christian faith'. But to Ottoline Morrell he described it as 'dull and antiquated'.[46]

In the 1890s Russell probably had little intimation of this later development in Ward's thought. There are in Ward's metaphysics lectures many suggestions of the position he was to take in *Naturalism and Agnosticism* but virtually no hint of the monism of *The Realm of Ends*. Of those parts of Ward's doctrine which Russell knew in the 1890s, he took some elements and rejected others, though there was little stability in what was accepted and what rejected. For example, Russell was well aware of Ward's dispute with Bradley about the nature of the self (he alludes to it in (1849*a*)). But he was unable to decide which view to take. In February 1894 he confessed that he was unable to understand Bradley's position (EPIII 148)—a fact which reflects perhaps more on Bradley than Russell. But, late in the same year, he suggests it as a possible means of resolving ethical problems (1894*c*: 97–8). He still does not endorse it (though he obviously thinks he understands it), and simultaneously considers McTaggart's theory of the self an alternative means of solving the same problems.[47] On the theory of the self, he came apparently to no settled views until long afterwards.

Russell's pluralism owes much to Ward as well. Initially the pluralism he adopted in the autumn of 1893 was derived directly from McTaggart (see § 2.3 below). Then for most of 1894 he seems not to have taken a clear stand on the monism/pluralism question. In papers for both Ward and Stout from this year there are respectful accounts of Spinoza's monism (*Papers*, i, 141, 181), though there is no indication that Russell accepts Spinoza's position. By the end of the year, he admits the temptations of monism (1894*c*: 98), but again falls short of acceptance. There are few general metaphysical statements surviving from 1895–6, with the exception of (1895*b*). This work, despite the initial laudatory references to Bradley, is a pluralist work, as are *EFG* and various notes on physics from the same period (e:g. VN, 1896*e*). This pluralism is based on science—a relational theory of space and a point-atom theory of matter. In this it owes much more to Ward's monadology than it does to McTaggart. Indeed, Ward explicitly links his monads with point-atoms.[48]

---

[46] B. R. to O. Morrell, 13 Dec. 1911 (letter no. 284).

[47] Russell's reading McTaggart (1893*a*) at the beginning of his neo-Hegelian period would have inclined him towards Ward's view of the self, for McTaggart, like Ward and unlike Bradley, believed in a plurality of finite selves. Russell's understanding of Bradley's position may have been helped by his hearing J. S. MacKenzie read a paper (MacKenzie 1894) at the Cambridge Moral Science Club on 2 Mar. 1894. Not surprisingly, Stout and McTaggart dominated the discussion according to the Club minutes (Cambridge University, min. ix, 40, p. 168). See also Russell's letter to A. P. Smith, 28 Feb. 1894.

[48] Cf. Ward (1911: 255) and compare Russell VN 12; 1896*e*: 34. The idea, central to Russell's position in *EFG* that the concept of space presupposes that of movement is made in Ward's metaphysics lectures ('Lecture Notebook', i, 82).

Ward rejected the Hegelian approach of starting at the top with a grand metaphysical synthesis and working downwards. Ward maintained that one had to begin in the middle, with actual scientific results. With this, as we shall see, Russell was in complete agreement, even in his high a priori days. When this approach was abandoned it was for the sort of foundationalist approach to epistemology that Ward criticized in the empiricists: working entirely from the bottom up. In Russell's later epistemology this, too, was abandoned. Nowadays, when the twentieth-century epistemic foundationalism associated with Russell, Moore, Ayer, and the positivists has largely been played out, Ward's practice of beginning in the middle looks in principle more attractive. And even some of the results which the method achieved in Russell's hands, though definitely mistaken, were not misguided by the standards of the time. The besetting difficulty of this manner of proceeding when there is a tacit metaphysical agenda is that of adjusting the particular results achieved to the overall metaphysical scheme of things. Ward and Russell both suffered acutely from the problem, until Russell, in the end, dropped the metaphysical agenda.

It is curious that Russell repeatedly refers to Ward as a Kantian and Stout as a Hegelian (MMD 10; *MPD* 38). In Stout's case, Russell offered some explanation in his letter to Wright (already quoted). He was impressed, it seems, by Stout's remark that 'Bradley has done all that is humanly possible in ontology' and this led him to suppose that Stout was 'Hegelian to the extent that Bradley was'—which is considerably different from being Hegelian. That Stout's own views did not intrude into his lectures on the history of philosophy would have left this impression uncorrected. Both Stout and Ward owed something to Kant, but it was Ward who travelled to Germany to study Hegel, even though he ended up more influenced by Lotze. Ward, late in life, did write quite extensively on Kant (Ward 1922*a*, usefully précised in Ward 1922*b*), but what he had to say was almost entirely critical. The two clear points on which he thought Kant was right were that he based mathematics on intuition rather than entirely upon thought (1922*b*: 347), and that he held that all experience involves an active subject (though even here he felt that Kant had missed the fundamèntal point that experience involves conation, 1922*b*: 333). Such limited agreement hardly warrants calling Ward a Kantian. Nor, apparently, did Russell think of Ward as a Kantian when he was his student. Indeed, on one occasion he referred to him as an 'ultra-empiricist'.[49]

[49] B. R. to A. Russell, 9 Oct. 1895. Unfortunately, a paper on Kant which Russell wrote as an undergraduate is lost (see *Papers*, i, 119). However, other papers he wrote for Ward show him defending Kant against Ward's criticisms (see below, § 4.2). Moreover, the notes Russell took at Ward's lectures indicate that Ward made plenty of fundamental criticisms of Kant's philosophy in them (cf. 'Lecture Notebook', i, 80, 81, 83, 89–90, 93, 97–9, 133–4, 136). Indeed, the lecture notes anticipate several of the points Ward made later in (1922).

Ward was, by all accounts, an excellent teacher and his students frequently spoke well of him afterwards. Moore, who described him as 'the very finest kind of man', looked back on him 'with warmer feelings of admiration than on any other of my teachers . . . partly because of his extreme sincerity and conscientiousness, but partly also because of his melancholy' (Moore 1942: 18). His lectures were stimulating. Ward thought aloud to his class: 'We sat around a table in his rooms at Trinity, and Ward had a large notebook open on the table before him. But he did not read his lectures; he talked; and, while he talked, he was obviously thinking hard about the subject he was talking of and searching for the best way of putting what he wanted to convey.' (Moore 1942: 17). When F. C. Bartlett was his student the notes had dwindled to a half-sheet of paper and the delivery was apparently more fluent, but the lecture was just as good. Bartlett published this account of his first lecture from Ward:

He came slowly into the small room—there were only about eight or nine students—his long, spare form struggling into his gown, his very keen and penetrating eyes taking us all in . . . 'Well, I don't know why you come to me; I don't know what you expect to get out of me; but whatever it is I expect you'll be disappointed.' Then he sat down. Out came half a sheet of note-paper which he by no means needed, and for an hour he talked and we were literally held in spell. There was no hesitation, the right word seemed always to come, the illustrations were frequent, brilliant and human, the asides and reminiscences were full of fun. There was little formality. Nobody could do much in the way of taking notes (Bartlett 1925: 453.)

Unlike Bartlett, Russell found no difficulty in taking notes. They reveal that Ward was extraordinarily well informed and up to date about a wide range of philosophical work, as well as material on psychology and physics. Indeed, some of Ward's information on physics seems to have been more up to date than that routinely covered in the Mathematical Tripos (cf. Russell's notes on his lectures on matter, 'Lecture Notebook', i, 99 ff.). Some of the references Ward gave in class did turn out to be important for Russell's subsequent thinking. It was from Ward that, for example, Russell first heard of Meinong: students were recommended to read his *Hume Studien* ('Lecture Notebook', i, 85). Under Ward's direction, Russell was introduced to the writings of Poincaré, Lotze, Sigwart,[50] and Kant (MMD 10). Russell's reading of Kant was his 'first serious contact with the German learned world', and Kant inspired him with 'awed respect' (*PFM* 20).[51]

---

[50] 'I hope thee admired the neatness and ant-like industry betrayed by the abstr[act] of Sigwart. I have found him esp[ecially] very useful indeed, so far as he is intelligible' (B. R. to A. P. Smith, 29 Oct. 1894). 'Sigwart . . . is my favourite among German philosophers' (B. R. to A. P. Smith, 25 Mar. 1894).

[51] Russell read German editions of *Prolegomena to any Future Metaphysics* in Sept. 1893, *Foundations of the Metaphysics of Morals* in Oct. 1893, *Critique of Pure Reason* in Feb. 1896,

Ward had a special influence on Russell's early philosophical reading, starting before Russell completed his Mathematical Tripos, and continuing during Russell's year as a philosophy student:

During my fourth year I read most of the great philosophers as well as masses of books on the philosophy of mathematics. James Ward was always giving me fresh books on this subject, and each time I returned them, saying they were very bad books. I remember his disappointment, and his painstaking endeavours to find some book that would satisfy me. (*Auto.* i, 68.)

This practice continued long after Russell ceased to be Ward's student. For when Russell was a fellow, Ward gave him two books which, had he appreciated them, would have had a major impact on his thought. These were Frege (1879) and Cantor (1883).[52] Ward himself had read neither of them and did not suppose that they were of any value. Russell himself admitted that he didn't understand the Frege 'until I had myself independently discovered most of what it contained' (*Auto.* i, 68), and 'What Shall I Read?', which lists his reading up to March 1902, does not record it; although Russell said that he read it in 1901 (Russell 1955). The same source indicates that although he read part of the Cantor in French translation in March 1896, he did not read the complete German edition until July 1899. In 1896 he certainly failed to appreciate Cantor's thought (see below, § 6.2).

Russell's adherence to Ward's psychology is evident in an essay he wrote for Ward's metaphysics course. In this essay Russell distinguished between mental states (with which psychology was concerned) and their 'meaning' or 'objective reference' (which is the concern of physics). This, at least, is the case with 'normal states of consciousness' (1894a: 196). But Russell also admits the possibility of inferior states of 'pure sensation' (much like Stout's later anoetic sentience) in which there is no identifiable object. In these cases there is what Russell calls, following Bradley (1893b: 215), a 'vague mass of the felt'. Russell was inclined to modify Ward's basic position by the incorporation of elements derived from Bradley. (Though Russell did not accord such non-relational consciousness the fundamental role that Bradley did.) At the other extreme, Russell admits the possibility of 'states of mind where we are above the distinction of subject and object' (1894a: 196); these are mystical states of consciousness.

Having admitted the possibility of states of pure consciousness and of mystical consciousness, Russell does not develop either but proceeds to consider the 'normal states' which lie between the two extremes. His

and *Metaphysical Foundations of Natural Science* in Mar. 1896. Russell's abstract of the last is to be found in the first of the so-called 'Mit Gott' notebooks he kept at the time (RA 210.006550–F1).

[52] Russell's copy of the Cantor is dated 'June 1897'; the Frege is undated.

position here is orthodoxly Wardian. In such normal cases it is the objective reference of the mental state which is immediately given. The self and its states are known only indirectly: Berkeley and subjective idealism are criticized for the view that the mental states themselves were known more directly (and more certainly) than their objective references (1894a: 196). In actual experience a subjective idea and its objective reference are given as a single concrete whole, which thought splits into its constituents. It is the task of metaphysics to restore the unity to the concrete whole, and thus 'to bridge the chasm between physics and psychology' (1894a: 197–8). In the case of the analysis of desire, thought separates the psychological aspects (e.g. the aetiology of the desire) from the ethical aspects (i.e. the identification of the desired object with a personal good, and of the felt want with a contrast between the ideal and the actual). Again it is the task of metaphysics to unite the ideal with the actual (1894a: 197).

It appears that all particular disciplines are necessarily partial, and only metaphysics can combine their results into a higher unity. This at least is the doctrine of the first of three papers by Russell on epistemology, where particular sciences are admitted to be partial and it is said to be the task of epistemology to criticize them, and to correct their partiality so that 'the results of the different Sciences may be exhibited as consistent with each other and as parts of a whole of knowledge' (EPI 121). The sort of difficulty encountered in this programme of scientific unification is illustrated in the third of the epistemology papers where Russell compares the different advantages of the (mutually incompatible) vortex and centre of force theories of matter. Each gives problems which the other escapes, but each yields advantages not yielded by the other. In such cases, Russell says, it is 'very difficult to exclude contradictions' (EPIII 147); Russell's later attempts to do so are surveyed in Chapter 5.

Another prominent feature of the essays Russell wrote for Ward is the influence of Kant, which is present in almost all of them. His discussion of the problem of the external world centres around Kant's treatment (EPIII 149–50); his account of change begins with Kant (EPIII 147); as does his treatment of causality (EPIII 149). However, it is in his discussion of space and time that Kant's influence is the strongest, especially in the second paper (which will be discussed in § 4.2 since it is closely related to Russell's fellowship work on geometry). In the first epistemology paper (EPI 121–2) Russell applies a distinction between matter and form (which he gets from Wundt 1889: 228–9) to space and time. As a result space and time are seen as forms of perception, independent of their content and invariable. Russell accepts Kant's arguments for the apriority of space and time but restricts their application to the abstracted concepts of space and time—not to perceptual space and perceptual time. The latter 'are not infinitely divisible, time does not advance uniformly, etc. [Kant's] argument for their independence of experience as percepts a priori will therefore not hold' (EPI 122). He repeats the same point in connection with time a little later in the same essay, where he distinguishes perceptual time from 'objective', 'mathematical', or 'astronomical' time, 'an equi-crescent and one-dimensional continuum' (p. 123), which is derived by abstraction from perceptual time (cf. also EPII 125). The abstraction, for which Kant's account holds, lacks empirical status, being purely formal: '[E]qui-crescence is a pure convention: no meaning can be attached to it: mathematically it only amounts to saying that time is taken as the (or an) independent variable' (EPI 123). It is interesting to note that in the case of these abstractions Russell makes no suggestion that there is a need for metaphysics to re-establish a holistic unity by means of a dialectical transition, combining perceptual with abstract time. Nor is there any evidence of McTaggart's (already published) Hegelian critique of time (McTaggart 1893*b*) despite Russell's claim (doubtless tongue in cheek) that McTaggart had killed time 'in this month's "Mind" '.[53] It seems that, despite Russell's excitement over McTaggart's arguments he was never really happy with his conclusions about time, and there was a persistent tendency for Russell, when involved in idealist metaphysics, to place as little reliance on the unreality of time as possible.

Despite Russell's affection for Ward, his extensive early correspondence with Alys Pearsall Smith contains few references to Ward, apart from those to the papers Russell was writing for his courses, and to meetings with Ward around the time of the Tripos, when Russell was clearly worrying about his results. Thus he writes to Alys on 2 May 1894: '[T]omorrow I am going to Ward to have a paper on Kant [now lost] looked over, and I am very anxious to hear what he will say. I get more and more keen every day to do well in my exam; I want an outside proof of what I can do.' He also reports discussions with Stout who 'seemed pleased' with one of Russell's papers,[54] and of a discussion with Stout about his prospects in the Tripos: 'Stout . . . says he would be very much surprised if I did not get a good first, and not at all surprised if I got a mark of distinction'.[55] But it was Ward's opinion that he respected most: 'Ward is to be shown my paper on space and I shall be wildly eager to hear what he says about it. Short of love, his praise is about the most delightful thing in the world to me. I got none today, but enjoyed seeing him, he's such a delightful man'.[56] Ward shared Stout's high opinion of Russell's work. 'Ward used to be enchanted at my lucidity' Russell wrote.[57] Ward

[53] B. R. to A. P. Smith, 12 Oct. 1893. There is some later evidence (WDWR 95) that he was unsure as to how McTaggart's arguments might be refuted, but at the same time was unable to accept McTaggart's conclusion.

[54] B. R. to A. P. Smith, 2 May 1894.     [55] B. R. to A. P. Smith, 11 May 1894.

[56] B. R. to A. P. Smith, 3 Nov. 1894. The paper on space is now lost.

[57] B. R. to A. P. Smith, 22 Oct. 1894.

thought Russell's essay paper in the Tripos 'was the best; that he had never seen two better Essays done in three hours'. Russell apparently explained that some of it was due to luck, but Ward 'still seemed to think it a good paper and said my having done well in Essays augured well for the Fellowships'.[58] On 8 June 1894 Russell got the first with distinction that Stout expected of him.

## 2.3 THE CAMBRIDGE HIDDEN CURRICULUM

For all the failings of the Mathematical Tripos, Russell was, almost from the start, delighted with Cambridge. Beyond the coaching and cramming for the Tripos, there was a social and intellectual world of students and some of the younger dons whose company and thinking Russell found very sympathetic. They were a group of idealistic, intelligent, and highly privileged young men whose Victorian belief in progress was fortified by considerable self-confidence, a certain social myopia, and (as we shall see) neo-Hegelian metaphysics. Russell would look back on this sheltered setting with nostalgia, for he experienced his social life at Cambridge as an enormous liberation.

Entering Cambridge, Russell described himself as a 'shy prig'. Before Cambridge he had had few close friends, and had become completely cut off from his family in all that was most important to him. At Cambridge he was no longer isolated. 'From the moment that I went up,' he wrote, 'everything went well with me' (*Auto*. i. 56). Many of the young men he met during his first term became his lifelong friends. He had finally found a place where he could speak freely, without fear of ridicule, on subjects in which he was passionately interested.

I found myself suddenly and almost bewilderingly among people who spoke the sort of language that was natural to me. If I said anything that I really thought they neither stared at me as if I were a lunatic nor denounced me as if I were a criminal. . . [T]o find myself in a world where intelligence was valued and clear thinking was thought to be a good thing caused me an intoxicating delight . . . The environment . . . fitted me like a glove. (*PFM* 4.)

It is not surprising that Russell's writings at the time recall more of the bewilderment than the intoxication. To someone as rigidly brought up as Russell, the loss of priggishness could not be seen as unalloyed improvement. In a journal entry for 20 November, during his first term, 'I read no poetry or literature of any sort, I do no thinking, I can look with comparative indifference on natural beauty; . . . I have on the whole certainly deteriorated more than could at all have been expected, though to most outsiders I suppose I have seemed to improve' (LD 57). Against this could be counted a

---

[58] B. R. to A. P. Smith, 10 June 1894. The essays are lost. One of them, of which Russell thought highly, was on scepticism.

loss of shyness, which he hardly knew whether to count as gain or loss, and the fact that, as he noted with surprise, 'I actually find people willing to recognize my existence' (LD 57), which could hardly be other than gain. Nor did his future friends seem so appealing after less than two months' acquaintance:

The people I have hitherto met here are every one of them unsatisfactory [to which judgement the Llewellyn Davies's were granted a partial exemption] . . . The dons are sad specimens of wasted power . . . Among undergrads, there seems a large agnostic element [Russell by this time was supposed to be agnostic], characterized by a flippancy which entirely prevents my having any sympathy with them. In fact flippancy strikes me as *the* besetting sin of the whole place, perhaps of the whole country or of the whole world. (LD 57.)

He cautiously conceded, however, that 'short of the highest excellence', there were many at Cambridge whose company 'is rather pleasant than otherwise' and that 'perhaps the fault lies rather in me' (LD 57). This last opinion is confirmed by his next journal entry, on the last evening of his first term, where his acquaintances are credited with giving him a more healthy view of life (LD 57). By his fourth year, Russell would exhibit the same kind of flippant attitude for which he had criticized other undergraduates. Having become sympathetic once again to pantheism, Russell told his friends that he was God, at which they placed candles on either side of him and proceeded to acts of mock worship (*Auto*. i, 68). By 1893–4 he had ceased to be quiet and reserved, but his attachment to pantheism was possibly more serious than this story suggests.

Of all his approximate contemporaries at Cambridge between 1890 and 1894 none had greater immediate influence on Russell than J. M. E. McTaggart. McTaggart had entered Trinity College in 1885. He was renowned at Cambridge and in his earlier schools as a skilful debater, and eventually became President of the Union and fellow of Trinity in 1891.[59] Russell met McTaggart for the first time in 1890 barely two weeks after Russell arrived at Cambridge. Having heard from Whitehead of Russell's interest in philosophy, McTaggart paid him a visit. After knocking on the door and being invited in by Russell, McTaggart found he was too shy to enter and Russell that he was too shy to offer a further invitation. None the less the meeting was somehow effected (*Auto*. i, 63; 1938: 35). Russell dedicated his first philosophy book, *An Essay on the Foundations of Geometry*, to McTaggart, although it makes no detectable use of McTaggart's doctrines. Russell's adherence to these was strongest in the autumn of 1893, and early in 1894 Russell's correspondence already shows a gradual breaking away from McTaggart's position. After Russell's rebellion against neo-Hegelianism McTaggart's philosophical in-

---

[59] Cf. Russell (1938: 35; 1948*b*: 1); Dickinson (1931: 14–15).

fluence on Russell ended. Eventually political differences also separated them. McTaggart, though a radical at school, soon became a staunch conservative at Cambridge. If Hegel had found the closest earthly approximation to the Absolute in the Prussian state, McTaggart found it in the British Empire, as even the determinedly sympathetic Dickinson (1931: 106) was forced ruefully to admit. Ironically, for a philosopher whose ethics were based on friendship and whose politics were based on loyalty, McTaggart in 1916 took a leading role in getting Russell dismissed from his Cambridge position for his anti-war activities (Dickinson 1931: 116).

When they first met, McTaggart had published nothing of his distinctive brand of neo-Hegelianism—his first published contribution to philosophy (1893a), a privately printed pamphlet, was still three years away. Yet his reputation in metaphysics was already known to Russell who was in awe of him on account of it (*Auto.* i, 63). Russell called him 'the most noteworthy of younger graduates . . . His brilliance and enthusiasm as a philosopher were extraordinary' (1948b: 1). As an undergraduate Russell wondered, 'as an almost unattainable ideal', whether his own work would ever match McTaggart's in excellence (*Auto.* i, 127). At the time of their first meeting Russell was a utilitarian and had leanings towards empiricism (although he recognized the limitations of empiricism in mathematics). McTaggart declared utilitarianism 'dry' (Russell 1948b: 1) and empiricism 'crude' (MMD 10). A more sophisticated approach, McTaggart urged, was to be found in Hegel. McTaggart claimed that he had philosophical proofs of personal immortality and the goodness of the world. Such proofs, McTaggart admitted, were 'long and difficult', but nevertheless, they were possible. Their soundness could only be discerned after an extended study of philosophy, particularly of that of Hegel.[60] Given Russell's anxiety to know the truth on these issues one might have expected him to start work on Hegel immediately. Initially, this work must have been postponed because of the rigours of the Mathematical Tripos. But this cannot explain why it took him another three or four years to read Hegel after he had switched to philosophy in 1893. At least part of the answer must lie in the fact that Russell, during this period, was satisfied with the answers he was getting from the writings of Hegel's English followers.

What appeal did McTaggart have and exactly what influence did he exert on Russell? In Russell's adolescence the most notable characteristic of his philosophy was his adherence to reason. Yet, reason had created an uneasy tension in Russell's thinking since it had deprived him of 'metaphysical

---

[60] *MPD* 38. See also B. R. to O. Morrell, 28 Sept. 1911, no. 199: 'McTaggart, who was then young and enthusiastic, about 5 years older than I was, astonished me by announcing that he believed in immortality, which I supposed no intelligent people did. Moreover he said he could prove it by his philosophy . . . but no one could understand his proofs without mastering Hegelianism, which remained unintelligible.'

comfort'. Although Russell had rejected theological orthodoxy, he still wanted to provide a rational substitute for traditional dogmas.[61] Copleston (1966: 427 n.), for example, notes: 'Russell abandoned belief in God at the age of eighteen. But he continued to believe for some years that metaphysics could provide a theoretical justification of emotive attitudes of awe and reverence towards the universe.' Neo-Hegelianism promised the vindication of more definite consolatory doctrines such as immortality and the goodness of the universe, and a conviction 'that the universe and ourselves are implicitly in harmony' (McTaggart 1983*a*: 211).[62] Despite the fact that, in later years, Russell was to regard the desire to preserve consoling doctrines as a philosophical vice, such a desire was a motivating factor in his early philosophy; in fact, it was to linger on even after his rebellion against neo-Hegelianism (see Griffin 1984). It was this aspect of McTaggart's philosophy— the marriage of reason with metaphysical comfort—which greatly appealed to Russell.

McTaggart was in many ways ideally suited to be Russell's mentor. For one thing, his intellectual development closely parallelled Russell's. In 1885 when he came up to Cambridge, McTaggart was a materialist and atheist,[63] esteemed Mill 'as one of his divinities', and had read and accepted (for a while) Herbert Spencer (Dickinson 1931: 11, 12, 15, 21, 83, 110). All this he had in common with Russell, and it is not surprising that Russell, who was trying to escape from what he saw as the depressing consequences of these doctrines, should have followed McTaggart's lead in rejecting most of them on philosophical grounds. McTaggart also claimed that the 'poetic arguments' for immortality, which Russell had found in Tennyson and Wordsworth and which he had been so reluctant to abandon, were quite unnecessary. His way with such arguments was brusquer than Russell's. Of Tennyson's *In Memoriam* he wrote in a letter:

I don't think it's any good appealing, as he is rather fond of doing, to the heart on questions of truth. After all there is only one way of getting at the truth and that is by proving it. All that talk about the heart only comes to saying 'It must be true because we want it to be' which is both false and rather cowardly. (Dickinson 1931: 38–9.).

McTaggart, like Russell, felt an emotional need for mysticism, but, also like Russell, demanded intellectual rigour as well. 'A mysticism', he said, 'which ignores the claims of the understanding is doomed' (Dickinson 1931: 53). It

[61] *PFM* 16–18; MMD 11; 1946: 4–5; 1959: 755. See also: B. R. to Morrell, 28 Sept. 1911, no. 199: 'It was largely in hope of getting religion out of philosophy that led me to take it up. Even when I accepted Hegel, however, I found flaws in the most comfortable consequences.'

[62] This was not a view peculiar to McTaggart. Cf. e.g. Stirling (1865: p. xxii); Caird (1892: 191). In many ways neo-Hegelianism was well suited to deal with the Victorian crisis of faith in its various forms—at least for those unwilling to countenance social revolution to eliminate the underlying causes of the crisis. J. Bradley (1979) deals at length with this aspect of the movement.                     [63] He remained an atheist all his life.

is not difficult to see the intellectual appeal that such a person would have for Russell, especially when he also maintained that, for many comforting doctrines, proof was possible.

As presented by McTaggart, Hegel's philosophy seemed to Russell both 'charming and demonstrable' (*PFM* 17). McTaggart sought to justify his conclusions by logical deduction, a trait which distinguished him more and more from mainline neo-Hegelians as the initial appeals to dialectical reasoning in his early writings were dropped from his philosophy. On the other hand, the practical value of metaphysics lay for McTaggart in its success in demonstrating consoling doctrines:

The practical importance of philosophy consists . . . in the chance that it may answer the supreme question [whether the universe is good or bad] in a cheerful manner, that it may provide some solution which shall be a consolation and an encouragement. (McTaggart 1907: 151.)

The utility of metaphysics is to be found . . . in the comfort it can give us . . . (McTaggart 1899: 184.)

If metaphysics, for Bradley, was 'the finding of bad reasons for what we believe upon instinct' (1893*a*: p. xiv), for McTaggart it was the attempt to find *good* reasons for what we would like to believe. Philosophical problems may originate in our feelings about the universe, but feeling is not permitted to intrude in the solution of philosophical problems.

Russell later recalled that McTaggart's 'wit recommended his Hegelian philosophy' (MMD 10). But it seems to have been a good deal more than that. McTaggart was an inspiring teacher, at least in his early years. Maud Stawell, the Australian writer, attended his lectures in 1893 (at the height of his influence on Russell) and described him as a man 'who had found the secret of the universe and could have shown it to his generation . . . he made [his ideas] seem not only inspiring but *true*' (Dickinson 1931: 53, 55). This inspirational period seems to have been rather short-lived. Leonard Woolf recalled: 'When I came up to Trinity [in 1899], McTaggart, though regarded with respect and amused affection as an eccentric, had completely lost his intellectual and philosophical influence' (Woolf 1960: 133). Woolf doesn't elaborate on the reasons for this decline. But Woolf was a friend of Moore's in the Apostles, and McTaggart's eclipse may have been due to the rapid transmission within a small Cambridge circle of the new philosophy developed a year earlier by Russell and Moore (see below, § 7.4). Or it may have been that McTaggart's followers got tired of waiting for the long-heralded proofs of McTaggart's doctrines, while McTaggart himself had already apparently lost his way in the murky realms of Hegelian exegesis.[64]

---

[64] The later decline in McTaggart's teaching is hinted at in Dickinson's overly sympathetic study, e.g. in Dickinson's ambiguous compliment that McTaggart's introductory philosophy lectures were 'stimulating' though he couldn't remember whether he'd attended them (p. 62)!

Of McTaggart's doctrinal influence, Russell writes: '[McTaggart] had a great intellectual influence upon my generation, though in retrospect I do not think it was a very good one. For two or three years, under his influence, I was a Hegelian . . . After 1898 I no longer accepted McTaggart's philosophy' (*Auto*. i, 63). This passage contains two errors. The actual length of Russell's neo-Hegelian allegiance was roughly four to five years (1893–8) rather than two or three. Furthermore, Russell suggests that, throughout this period, it was McTaggart's version of neo-Hegelianism that he accepted. Yet, as we shall see in subsequent chapters, after McTaggart's initial impact, Russell adhered to his own brand of neo-Hegelianism in which the influence of Kant was prominent. Russell in fact accepted McTaggart's position for only a short period from August to October 1893; after this McTaggart's influence appears to have been general rather than specific.

McTaggart had incorporated his metaphysical doctrines in the privately printed pamphlet (1893*a*). Writing it, McTaggart said, was 'like turning one's heart inside out' and he felt 'almost ashamed' to have written it at all, although its favourable reception (by Caird and Bradley, among others) made him glad he had (quoted Dickinson 1931: 37). When Russell read this essay, in August 1893, it made a great impression on him, though he found it 'very stiff'.[65] For a short time, it induced him to believe in immortality: 'For a few months last autumn, after reading Green [1883] and McTaggart I believed in immortality—but Green's mistakes were soon evident to me, and since then I have had no solutions—I believe no other is possible' (B. R. to A. P. Smith, 29 October, 1894). Immortality of the self was a central doctrine in McTaggart's metaphysics. If Russell rejected this doctrine, he could hardly have been a disciple of McTaggart. During his fourth year at Cambridge, Russell made some attempt to resist McTaggart's influence;[66] towards the end of the academic year, however, he 'went over completely to a semi-Kantian, semi-Hegelian metaphysics' (*MPD* 38). The details of that conversion will be given in § 3.2. McTaggart's influence in Russell's first three years at Cambridge consisted mainly in preparing the way for it.

Russell's intellectual ability was generally recognized early in his stay at Cambridge, and resulted in his election, on 27 February 1892, to the Cambridge Conversazione Society, possibly the most prestigious—albeit unofficial—intellectual distinction available to an undergraduate. The Cambridge Conversazione Society—'The Society', better known as 'The Apostles'—was a highly exclusive, secret discussion club, intended officially

---

[65] B. R. to A. P. Smith, 19 Aug. 1893. On a second reading, however, he decided that 'all that is important is straightforward and all that is hard (except Hegel's definition of the Absolute Idea) is unimportant' (B. R. to A. P. Smith, 25 Aug. 1893).

[66] *MPD* 38. See also B. R. to O. Morrell, 28 Sept. 1911, no. 199: 'Throughout the greater part of the year [1894] I remained unconvinced of Hegelianism.'

to pursue the truth, however unorthodox, with fearless honesty. Its carefully preserved secrecy, which has ensured its widespread reputation and mystique, was initially an essential condition for its existence. It was founded in 1820 at a time when the subscription rules made public discussion of religious topics difficult.[67] In the 1890s the official justification for secrecy remained the same, though the topics discussed and positions taken (in so far as evidence is available) were no longer such as would lead to expulsion or punishment. The secrecy continued, one must assume, because of the members' desire to maintain a sense of their own exclusiveness and superiority. More creditably the secrecy also served to maintain an in-group sense of fun in the best traditions of schoolboy humour, and since admission was by invitation only the personal and intellectual compatibility of members was assured.

The sense of superiority was to some extent deserved—throughout the nineteenth century a large number of the most talented Cambridge undergraduates were members.[68] New members were elected as undergraduates, but remained members after graduation, sometimes coming back to Cambridge to give papers. The active membership was never large and consisted primarily of undergraduates. Russell was still involved in the affairs of the Society in 1912 and attended some of their annual dinners even in the 1950s, but there is no definite record of his having read a paper there after 1899 (but see Ryan 1986). The Apostles met every Saturday evening during term in the room of one of the members. One member would read a paper on which the others would comment in an order determined by lot. At the end of each meeting a vote was taken on some question arising from the discussion rather than the paper itself. The meeting would continue into the early hours, and often be continued in the streets and quadrangles of Cambridge. These meetings were important for Russell as an undergraduate, and even for a short time afterwards. After graduation, for example, he wrote to his future wife: 'The Society is a real passion to me—after thee, I know no greater joy'.[69] The joy was as much that of congenial companionship as of intellectual discovery. As Russell said in one of his papers to the Society,

[67] Details of the early years of the Society are given in Brookfield (1906) and Allen (1979). For later years we have to rely on memoirs; apart from Russell's own, see Dickinson (1973: 68–9), Keynes (1949: 78–103), Pollock (1933), Christie (1894), Sidgwick and Sidgwick (1906: 29–35), Woolf (1960: 129–56). The main secondary source is Levy (1979), but see also Skidelsky (1983: 116–32). There is a good analysis of the role of the Apostles in Cambridge society in Rothblatt (1974). More recently, the activities of the Apostles in the 1930s have attracted a good deal of attention, spawning an entire right-wing genre of remarkable inaccuracy, see Sinclair (1986) for a typically incoherent example.

[68] These included Tennyson, Maxwell, F. D. Maurice, Arthur Hallam, W. K. Clifford, F. W. Maitland, Sidgwick, Frederick Pollock, A. W. Verrall, Whitehead, Keynes, Russell, Moore, McTaggart, Lytton Strachey, Roger Fry. In 1912 Wittgenstein was elected but left after a single meeting. Levy (1979: 300–11) gives a list of members up to 1914. Toulmin (1980) gives a list of equally important non-members. Scientists, in particular, were not easily admitted.

[69] B. R. to A. P. Smith, 20 Oct. 1894.

'Personally I look forward to Saturday nights more as an occasion when I meet my friends in the pleasantest possible way than as an occasion for the intellectual exercise of following an argument and contributing to it. Indeed I believe much of my interest in the argument would cease if I were not interested in the arguers' (1894*b*: 88–9). On the other hand, by all accounts, the demand for intellectual honesty was admirably adhered to. Russell wrote to Alys that he found the society 'the very paradise of honesty',[70] and he wrote lyrically of it in his *Autobiography* (i. 69):

With rare exceptions, all the members at any one time were close personal friends. It was a principle in discussion that there were to be no *taboos*, no limitations, nothing considered shocking, no barriers to absolute freedom of speculation. We discussed all manner of things, no doubt with a certain immaturity, but with a detachment and interest scarcely possible in later life.

None the less, the manuscripts of some of the papers Russell read give evidence that certain things were of too personal a nature to bear discussion even before a group of close personal friends (cf. deletions from 1894*c*, *Papers*, i, T95: 19).[71]

In Russell's day the Apostles were a good deal less flippant than they subsequently became—a change which Russell (MMD 9) attributed to the baneful influence of Lytton Strachey who became a member in 1902. In Russell's recollection, members of the Society not only wanted 'to be clever and elegant, and to love the beautiful', but they also wanted 'above all to do "good"' (Harris 1971: 114–15), 'to contribute something of value' in a 'world which seemed hopeful and solid' (MMD 9). 'We took ourselves perhaps rather seriously, for we considered that the virtue of intellectual honesty was in our keeping' (*Auto*. i, 69). The seriousness is obvious, even to the point of absurdity, in some of Russell's Apostolic papers. However the earnestness did not prevent an amiable degree of self-parody. The proceedings of the Society by the 1890s had become highly and comically ritualized, with secret words and elaborate curses called down on miscreant members. With the election of McTaggart in 1886 the Apostles had fallen under the influence of the neo-Hegelians, and matters Apostolic had come to be referred to by means of neo-Hegelian categories. Thus the Society itself constituted Reality, while the outside world was appearance and non-members phenomena. Members were held not to be subject to space and

[70] B. R. to A. P. Smith, 29 Oct. 1894.

[71] In (1894*b*: 88), commenting on the difficulties likely to be caused to the Apostles by physical attraction between members were women to be admitted, Russell refers to the existing friendships between Apostles and adds the following guarded allusion: 'Nor is even a physical interest absent, for most of us care more or less about bodies, some of us care a great deal'. Even then the sentence was enclosed in square brackets very probably indicating that Russell omitted it when reading the paper—and this in a paper in which he maintained that women, if admitted, would have to be prepared to discuss 'unnatural vice' openly (p. 85).

time in accordance with the idealist doctrine that Reality lacked such constraints.

Not surprisingly, since neo-Hegelianism had worked its way so thoroughly into the vocabulary of the Society, philosophical questions had come to dominate Apostolic discussions (Trevelyan 1949: 14), though in earlier years, the emphasis had been religious, literary, or political. Technical questions in philosophy were, however, not addressed, and, indeed, in Russell's first papers, philosophical questions *tout court* were avoided. This is surprising only in the light of his subsequent career. Until mid-1893, he was a mathematics student with a taste for philosophy, and doubtless felt chary of discussing philosophical questions in front of an audience which included people like McTaggart with a university-wide reputation for both metaphysics and debate. By contrast, Russell's family background equipped him for debate on politics with the best of them, and thus his earliest Apostolic papers were on broadly political topics.

As an undergraduate Russell seems to have read only two papers to the Society, only the first of which has any real philosophic interest. The second (1894*b*) is a laboured examination of whether women should be admitted to the Society. Russell, of course, was in favour of the admission of women, as were his fellow Apostles when it came to the vote (only Dickinson voted against). None the less, the first woman was not elected until 1970 (Levy 1979: 128). Russell's lifelong political optimism seems not to have been unduly affected by this instance of the difficulty of bringing about social change even among the well-intentioned.[72]

Russell's first paper to the Society (1893*a*) was given on 18 November 1893. It represented yet another extension, in this case to political beliefs, of the scope of the destructive power of reason, which had first shown itself in the 'Greek Exercises'. His conclusion is that political position depends not upon reason but upon personal preference, and he supports it by a sceptical attack on a selection of methods for rational decision-making in politics. In connection with the paper Russell wrote to Alys Pearsall Smith: 'Ever since I came up I have been gradually discovering that Reason in most things if pushed too far refutes itself: so I don't see any ground for lamenting that one more subject should be abandoned to sentiment'.[73] The previous month he had been invited by Dickinson to participate in a discussion group on political theory. Russell looked forward to these discussions as both 'useful and interesting', especially since the participants 'would all have completely

---

[72] It was only in 1881 that women were permitted to sit Cambridge examinations, though they were not granted degrees until 1923. Russell for many years was involved in furthering the cause of women's education at Cambridge. In 1898 he donated £1000 to Newnham College and for many years sat on its governing council.

[73] B. R. to A. P. Smith, 21 Nov. 1893.

different views'. For himself, however, he confessed, 'I have at present little notion what theoretic basis (if any) my political opinions have or can have, and I believe we shall find that political differences depend ultimately on differences of temperament . . . '.[74]

The most easily discernible influence on the paper is Sidgwick, whose lectures on ethics Russell was then attending. Russell uses Sidgwick's *Methods of Ethics* as a quarry for arguments and specific points, and yet this influence is one of detail only, and is quite misleading as to the overall direction of Russell's thought. (The paper in fact opens with a gently sarcastic reference to Sidgwick.) The most important tendency in Russell's thinking illustrated by the paper is his increasing tendency to reject empiricist methods and positions. In this McTaggart's influence was paramount. There is also now a flat rejection of the crudely evolutionary views of Herbert Spencer and others, which Russell in GE was inclined to take seriously. Also noticeable is the tendency towards neo-Hegelianism. Russell makes it clear that his sceptical doubts would be allayed, given a thoroughly developed neo-Hegelian historicism. Moreover, failure to develop such a programme stems, apparently, not from any deep-seated theoretical difficulty, but from purely technical problems. (It is important to remember that, despite a degree of abstract philosophical argument, this paper concerns essentially *practical* decision-making in politics.) That Russell should point out the limits of Hegelian historicism, does not set him against the neo-Hegelians. McTaggart was in his audience and was on Russell's side.[75] Russell even leaves open the possibility that the historicist programme may eventually be completed. His sole point in this connection is that for *present, practical* purposes appeal to the dialectic is of no use. On the other hand, we may not conclude from this slender evidence that Russell was already a practising neo-Hegelian. If anything, he was fighting shy of having to confront McTaggart in debate on metaphysics.

It seems to have been Apostolic habit to make gentle fun of the ideas of whomever was dominant in the Society, and McTaggart certainly dominated it in the early 1890s. Thus in 1894 Russell's friend, C. P. Sanger, read a paper, 'Which Wagner?', which posed a choice between music and economics, or, more broadly, between art and social duty.[76] Russell thought the discussion very unsatisfactory:

McTaggart ran his Absolute, as usual, and we protested it was useless, and if not, worked the other way! but [Edward] Marsh, being new and not knowing the trick,

[74] B. R. to A. P. Smith, 9 Oct. 1893.

[75] B. R. to A. P. Smith, 21 Nov. 1893.

[76] The contrast in the title is between Richard Wagner, the composer, and Adolph Wagner, a liberal German economist and professor of economics at Berlin. Russell attended the operas of the former and the lectures of the latter.

was frightened at such an imposing machinery and was half converted to McTaggart. The odd thing about the Absolute is that it always goes against the [*Daily*] *Chronicle* whatever that paper may happen to say. Also that when anybody else uses it McTaggart says it can't be used.[77]

It would be a mistake to read too much into remarks such as these. Russell had never claimed to accept (or even to understand) the higher regions of McTaggart's metaphysics, nor his use of dialectic. McTaggart's frequent use of the full machinery of the Absolute to resolve commonplace or practical problems must have seemed (and no doubt was and probably was intended to be) rather ridiculous.

Russell's association with the Apostles had another important philosophical consequence, though its full effect was not to be felt for a few years. It was through the Society's meetings that Russell first got to know well the Trinity classics student, G. E. Moore, with whom, however incongruously, historians of philosophy would link him for the next fifty years.[78] Moore went up to Trinity to read classics in 1892, intending to teach classics at a public school, 'a prospect to which I looked forward with pleasure' (Moore 1942: 13). After gaining first class honours in the Classical Tripos, however, he switched to philosophy in which he graduated in 1896, again with first class honours. Russell got to know him in 1893 and was instrumental in getting him to take Moral Sciences (Moore 1942: 13), as well as nominating him for membership of the Apostles in 1894. Moore was in these years 'an ardent disciple of Lucretius' (*Auto.* i, 73) and his materialism was expressed in a paper to the Apostles which, according to Russell, began: 'In the beginning was matter, and matter begat the devil and the devil begat God'. Unfortunately, Russell seems to have improved on Moore's paper which (at least in manuscript) did not open as Russell remembered. It was, in fact, a rather mundane defence of psychological hedonism called 'What End?'[79]

Moore's initial impact seems to have been more due to his bearing and candour than his arguments. Moore himself in his characteristically modest autobiography (1942: 12) reports that he felt overawed by the discussions in the Society. Russell recalled their early acquaintance in lyrical terms: 'In my

[77] B. R. to A. P. Smith, 25 Feb. 1894. Similar evidence is to be found at the end of (1894*b*: 88), where McTaggart's Absolute is described as a Juggernaut, and in (1899: 113) where it is Moore, the Apostle's new leader, who is chaffed.

[78] On Moore the best published sources are his 'Autobiography' (1942) and Regan (1986), neither particularly good. At the opposite extreme to Moore (1942) is Levy's inaccurate hagiography (1979), on which see Griffin (1981). Moore's unpublished papers in the Cambridge University Library are much more revealing. Holroyd (1967: i, 173–6) is brief but perceptive; see also Skidelsky (1983: 133–47).

[79] See Levy (1979: 130–4) and Regan (1986: 70–1) for details of the paper. Moore's Apostolic essays are among his papers in the Cambridge University Library. By 1895 he had abandoned materialism for idealism, as shown by his paper 'What is Matter?' (see Levy 1979: 158–63) and Regan (1986: 70–8).

third year . . . I met G. E. Moore, who was then a freshman, and for some years he fulfilled my ideal of genius. He was in those days beautiful and slim, with a look almost of inspiration, and with an intellect as deeply passionate as Spinoza's. He had a kind of exquisite purity' (*PFM* 67–8). Moore was not a man of wide interests, or great humour, or ready conversation. His manner was quiet and reserved, but, on those questions which interested him, he pursued the truth 'with the tenacity of a bulldog and the integrity of a saint' (Woolf 1960: 134).

It was Moore's intense seriousness and honesty, combined with apparently guileless and almost childlike enthusiasm, which made its impact on the Apostles in the 1890s (and on Bloomsbury afterwards). Whatever he said was said with the full weight of passionate conviction. Russell said that the only time Moore ever told a lie was when Russell asked him if he always told the truth and he said 'No' (*PFM* 68). With his mind narrowly focused on some issue of philosophical concern he was a formidable opponent. 'What a brain the fellow has! I'm fagged to death', exclaimed Dickinson after a metaphysical discussion with him (Forster 1934: 110). Russell felt exhilarated rather than overwhelmed by him, as the following shows:

Yesterday Moore made his début in the Society and the scene was so perfectly wonderful and unprecedented that I would give anything to be able to describe it adequately. He spoke perfectly clearly and unhesitatingly, and at first with no sign whatever of nervousness . . . He looked like Newton and Satan rolled into one, each at the supreme moment of his life. I had said (we were discussing Cambridge education) that our training up here produced such profound scepticism about every thing that many of us are unfitted for practical life; Moore said that was the one great gain from education: at least, he said, we are not so unfitted as to be unable to earn our bread: we shall therefore spread scepticism until at last everybody knows that we can know absolutely nothing. At this point he was overcome by hysterical laughter (everybody else had been laughing a great deal all the time), and turned his back to the room and rested his forehead on the mantlepiece. When he had recovered, he went on, in the same attitude . . . All this he meant as earnestly as the most intense eagerness could make him: at one point he said: Scepticism cannot destroy enthusiasm, there is one which will always remain, and that is the enthusiasm for scepticism. And to see him say it no one could doubt his utter conviction of the truth of what he was saying. We all felt electrified by him, as if we had all slumbered hitherto and never realized what fearless intellect pure and unadulterated really means. If he does not die or go mad I cannot doubt that he will somehow mark himself out as a man of stupendous genius.[80]

[80] B. R. to A. P. Smith, 18 Feb. 1894. Russell was by no means alone in his enthusiasm for Moore: see also similar (though less over-blown) accounts by Woolf (1960: 137), Marsh (1939: 56), Harrod (1952: 76). For Moore's later impact on Bloomsbury see Holroyd (1967: i, 175 ff.), Rosenbaum (1987: 214–38), and Regan (1986). Moore's relations with the Apostles are described at great length by Levy (1979), whose account of Moore's relations with Russell, however, leaves much to be desired.

Russell presumably realized that he had overdone things, for his next letter is rather more restrained:

[Moore] has strong passions and emotions, but hardly those of a human being: they are all intellectual and critical. It is he who argued in the teeth of the wind. I find it impossible either to like or dislike him, because I have seen no trace of humanity in him yet . . . But enthusiasm for scepticism seems to me the most natural thing in the world: if you are of an enthusiastic disposition and believe in nothing, you *have* to be enthusiastic about disbelief.[81]

But neither Russell's inflated first estimate nor his rather more detached judgement three days later represented a settled opinion. His thoughts of Moore in this early period always carried something of the enthusiasm of his description of Moore's Apostolic debut. At the same time he felt, as he put it in another letter, that 'Moore is colossally ignorant of life',[82] though it is not clear how far he saw this as a defect.

Russell's admiration for Moore lasted, with some reservations, until a few years before the First World War. A number of factors were involved in the disillusion which set in then. Holroyd (1967: i, 128) reports that James Strachey thought that Russell resented Moore's greater influence over the bright young men of Cambridge. There is perhaps something in this. C. B. Martin told me of a time while he was Russell's student at Trinity in the 1940s when Russell asked Martin what people at Cambridge thought of him. Martin replied that they were unfairly critical. 'Yes,' Russell replied, 'they always did prefer Moore'.[83] None the less, James Strachey's suggestion that it was Moore's influence over his brother, Lytton, which Russell resented is preposterous. Slightly less so is Levy's view that Russell resented Moore's greater influence in the Apostles. If this had been the case, however, Russell's resentment would have appeared earlier, for he resigned active membership of the Apostles in February 1897. It is true that Russell liked to be at the centre of whatever he was involved in, and the fact that leadership in the Apostles passed from McTaggart to Moore might have been felt as a slight. But Russell could hardly have felt it to be a very important slight (he never mentions it, for example, in his confessional letters to Ottoline Morrell). Moreover, Russell must have realized very early that the Society was not an appropriate forum for the very technical philosophy that he was starting to do.[84] Moore shone in the Apostles because it was one of the few places

[81] B. R. to A. P. Smith, 21 Feb. 1894.　　[82] B. R. to A. P. Smith, 22 Feb. 1894.
[83] Russell's remark may well be untrue, depending upon whom he intended to refer to by 'they'. Moore, after all, did not get a fellowship on his first attempt in 1897 but had to resubmit his dissertation the following year. Nor, when his fellowship ended in 1904, did he get another Cambridge position until 1911.
[84] Witness the fiasco of the meeting in 1899 when Moore read a paper by G. H. Hardy on non-Euclidean geometry to an audience which consisted of Russell, and they voted opposite

where, surrounded by people he knew well, he felt completely at ease. Levy is, in fact, misled by his myopic concentration on the Apostles. They were, indeed, extremely important for Moore, but much less so for Russell (especially after his first years of membership). Purely Apostolic events of any kind could hardly have carried sufficient importance for Russell to affect his relationship with Moore.

Another suggestion of Levy's is that Russell was jealous of Moore's relations with Wittgenstein, whom Russell allegedly wanted to keep for himself (Levy 1979: 265 ff.). At least this gets the timing right, and Wittgenstein was certainly of sufficient importance to Russell to disrupt his relations with Moore. But there is no sign of even covert jealously in Russell's daily letters to Ottoline Morrell at the time, even though they make reference to Wittgenstein's friendship with Moore. Russell clearly did not feel jealous that Wittgenstein found Moore lovable—after all, almost everybody did, including Russell himself. There was even less basis for intellectual jealousy on Russell's part. Wittgenstein was much more involved with Russell's work in philosophy of logic than with Moore's, which was then concerned primarily with epistemology.[85] Indeed, by all accounts, Moore was having great difficulty understanding Wittgenstein. The one serious dispute between Moore and Russell which concerned Wittgenstein was occasioned by Moore's inexplicable withholding of notes he'd had from Wittgenstein (Wittgenstein 1914). Since the notes largely concerned Russell's philosophy of logic, Russell was understandably anxious to see them, and irritated by Moore's procrastination.[86] But this episode was a consequence of the deterioration of their relationship, rather than a cause.

It seems most likely that Russell became disillusioned with Moore only when the latter returned to Cambridge in 1911, and that the basic cause was intellectual. Russell had seen comparatively little of Moore between 1904 and 1911, but the memory of Moore's greatness had been kept alive by *Principia Ethica* and by an intermittent correspondence. When Moore returned, Russell came to feel that he had lost his inspiration.[87] In 1911 he

ways on the question 'Is space probably Euclidean?' (Levy 1979: 207). Russell, so far as is known, read only 7 papers to the Apostles during his 5 years of active membership, Keynes read 20 papers in 8 years (Skidelsky 1983: 33, 265), and Moore read 20 in 6 years (Levy 1979). Had Russell seriously wished to dominate the Society he would have tried harder. Coteries, however, were not his style.

[85] Wittgenstein was a severe critic of Russell's lectures (cf. B. R. to O. Morrell, 16 Mar. 1912, no. 385), but seems to have been no kinder to Moore's (Hayek 1953: fo. 14).

[86] See Levy (1979: 271–4), who puts quite a different construction on it. See also Wittgenstein (1974: R28, R30).

[87] This may well also have been the opinion of the generation of undergraduates then at Cambridge—the generation of Rupert Brooke—who were attracted to Fabianism and looked for intellectual leadership to Shaw, Wells, and the Webbs rather than to Moore. For Mrs

could still write to Ottoline Morrell that Moore, whom he had just observed in discussion, was 'full of the enjoyment of sheer mental power' (letter no. 240) and offer an extravagantly enthusiastic account of one of Moore's lectures (letter no. 211). But on reading the typescript of Moore's lectures on metaphysics he found them not nearly 'as good as they ought to be' and that 'Moore's intellect is not so good as it was' (letter no. 97); and like most of Moore's friends, he thought Moore's *Ethics* (1912) 'very poor' (letter no. 577). By this time, moreover, Moore had been supplanted by Wittgenstein as Russell's 'ideal of genius'. There was in the middle-aged Moore a lack of that passion and intensity which Russell found so attractive (and also so disturbing) in Wittgenstein. While Moore's patient, pedantic pursuit of unvarnished truth was, as we shall see, important in dispelling the pretensions of neo-Hegelianism, it produced less impressive results once the new philosophy was off the launching pad. Moore's famous remark (1942: 14) that he had never found philosophical problems in the world or the sciences, but only in what other philosophers had said about the world and the sciences, indicates the problem. When Russell and Moore were engaged in controverting the prevailing neo-Hegelian philosophy, Moore's critical common-sense approach was exactly what was called for; but when the task was to build up the new philosophy, Moore's inability to find philosophical problems in the subject-matter itself was a distinct handicap. At all events, Russell could only have been disappointed in Moore's attitude to philosophical problems.

Moore's attitude to Russell seems, from the start, to have been more equivocal. There is no denying Russell's early influence on Moore, in persuading him to take up philosophy and in converting him to neo-Hegelianism (although, in the latter, McTaggart was influential too). Moreover, in public statements throughout their lives they remained unfailingly respectful and appreciative of each other, each making often exaggerated acknowledgement to the influence of the other.[88] This has certainly fostered the impression of a close and constant friendship. The unpublished record modifies this picture more than a little. Moore, almost from the earliest days, felt some personal antipathy to Russell. For example, Moore went to considerable lengths to exclude Russell from his annual reading parties, and Russell noted that Moore avoided him and wasn't always very genial with him.[89] There is also the well-known occasion on which Russell said to Moore: 'You don't like

Webb's characteristically forthright estimation of Moore see Regan (1986: 278). The Apostles preserved their ethos by electing only one new member between 1909 and 1912 (Skidelsky 1983: 239–40).

[88] e.g. see Russell (*POL*: p. xv; *POM*: p. xviii; *POP*: p. [vii]; *MPD* 11–12, 42), Moore (1942: 14–16). See § 7.4 below for comment on Russell's early debts to Moore.

[89] B. P. to O. Morrell, 2 Sept. 1913 (no. 860) and 2 Oct. 1911 (no. 205).

me, Moore, do you?' Moore, after due reflection, said 'No' (Wood 1957: 76). The reasons were complex. There is little doubt that Moore felt uncomfortable with Russell's intellectual style, however much he might admire its results. Moore's own style was slow, meticulous, and absolutely literal. In discussion he sought first an absolutely clear understanding of what was being said. Sometimes he would spend as much effort getting clear about unimportant details as he would about the main point. Sometimes Russell was inclined to think he couldn't tell the two apart. At all events, Moore's efforts at clarity, conducted with painstaking slowness, taxed his concentration to the limit. Russell's style in discussion was the exact opposite. His arguments were delivered with machine-gun rapidity, focusing immediately on main points and rarely bothering with the careful exegesis that Moore took such pains over. He was not above scoring debating points, and his arguments could appear brilliant, flashy, or slick, depending on your point of view. Moore found that Russell's performances only impeded his own efforts at clarity. Worse, he was inclined to think Russell's methods dishonest, achieving victory by good debating technique rather than good arguments. There is no denying that Russell relished debate for its own sake and took a delight in the intellectual rough and tumble which resulted. With this Moore could have no sympathy whatsoever.

There were differences in background and personal values as well. It would be wrong to suggest that Moore, coming from a sheltered, middle-class, Quaker background, was in awe of Russell's aristocratic lineage. But such differences in background couldn't help but produce differences in the way the two men viewed the world. When they were undergraduates together both men were shy and puritanical. Yet Russell was at home in the 'great world' beyond the University in a way that Moore would never be. Russell apparently made some efforts to make Moore a teetotaller, which Moore resented (Wood 1957: 38). But Moore seems to have resented even more Russell's tendency, as an undergraduate, to play the man-of-the-world for Moore's benefit.[90] Moore, from the very earliest days of their relationship, had moral reservations about Russell. Russell, apparently, had no serious reservations about Moore in these early years, even Moore's foibles he took to be either amiable eccentricities or else symptoms of Moore's innocence and purity of nature. Only later, as we have seen, did Russell develop intellectual reservations about Moore. I think Levy grossly exaggerates the degree of antipathy that Russell felt toward Moore, and even exaggerates

---

[90] Witness the hilarious episode of their first walking holiday together when they fell in with a ribald who, with some prompting from Russell, managed deeply to offend Moore (*Auto.* i, 64). Russell's attempt to justify himself to his puritanical fiancée (B. R. to A. P. Smith, 20 May 1894) rivals the original escapade in absurdity, as Levy's overdone outrage rivals Moore's (Levy 1979: 135–7). It was a minor incident in which all three parties, except possibly the ribald, behaved with schoolboy silliness.

Moore's antipathy to Russell. They were not lifelong enemies. On the other hand, in the early years, Moore's reservations about Russell introduced a degree of tension into their relationship which prevented the sort of intimacy that the Apostles (and Bloomsbury) prized, no matter how fruitful their mutual intellectual influence was to be.

# 3

# Love and the Absolute

## 3.1 PERSONAL LIFE (1894–1897)[1]

Russell's years as a student at Cambridge came to seem to him years of liberation from the influence of his grandmother and the oppressive, high bourgeois atmosphere of Pembroke Lodge. Simply going up to Cambridge broke the spell cast upon him by his mausoleum-like family home. The frivolity of Cambridge, which had so shocked him on his arrival, always seemed to him unsatisfying but at least it lightened the burden of the stolidly respectable course his grandmother had mapped out for him. And philosophy took him completely off her map. At Oxford philosophy was widely read as a normal part of the training of future politicians and Civil Servants, at Cambridge things were different. Not many students read philosophy at Cambridge and those who did often intended to make a career of the subject, or at least to take up some form of academic career. This was obviously no starting-point for the boy whom Granny had brought up to be prime minister. Granny was seriously alarmed. In fact, she had good cause to be alarmed, and not just on account of the deleterious effects of a Cambridge education. For, as if on purpose to darken further her declining years, Bertie had fallen in love, and with such a woman as would, in his grandmother's eyes, by no means make a suitable wife for a prime minister. Indeed, the woman with whom he had fallen in love was the very reverse of what might have been desired for him. She was Alys Pearsall Smith, the younger of two daughters of Robert and Hannah Pearsall Smith, rich and well-known American Quakers. Their wealth had come from mines and factories in Philadelphia, their fame from evangelical crusades on both sides of the Atlantic. Unfortunately, Robert's crusading days were brought to an abrupt end when he became the centre of a full-blown, widely publicized sex scandal: the result, apparently, of too literal an interpretation of St Paul's injunction to 'salute one another with a holy kiss'. This was in 1875, when the family had to beat a strategic retreat to Philadelphia, in the face of adverse publicity in Britain. By the 1880s, however, the furore had died down

[1] The following account of Russell's personal life is based on Clark (1975: 35–70). Primary documentation is provided by Russell's diary (LD 61–7) and by his correspondence with Alys Pearsall Smith and members of his family. The best account of his engagement and first marriage is Strachey (1980). Russell's own account can be found in *Auto*. i, chs. 4 and 5. His wedding is described in Turcon (1983). The most accurate chronology for Russell's life in these years is that printed in *Papers*, i, pp. xxix–xxxiv, also due to Turcon.

enough for the Pearsall Smiths to return to Britain, where they settled at Friday's Hill, a large estate near Fernhurst in Sussex, and close to the house of Russell's Uncle Rollo at Hindhead in Surrey. There Russell was taken to meet them by his uncle in 1889. At this time Robert Pearsall Smith had thought better of evangelicalism and had entered a Quietist phase (oddly enough, he was somewhat drawn to Buddhism) very much under the thumb of his domineering wife, Hannah, who in later years led Russell to remark that 'mothers-in-law are a very stubborn part of the Mystery of Evil'.[2] Hannah, also, had abandoned the full-fledged Bible crusades of earlier days, turning instead to writing extremely popular religious tracts. These writings tended to warn against too great a reliance upon divine inspiration, a misinterpretation of which had led to her husband's downfall.

Hannah and Robert had three children living with them at Friday's Hill. Their son, Logan, was to become a literary connoisseur and stylist. The eldest, Mary, was, at the time Russell first met the family, apparently happily married to an Irish barrister, Frank Costelloe. By 1891, however, she had left Costelloe and was on her way to Italy to join Bernard Berenson, whom she married in 1900 on Costelloe's death. Alys, though the youngest, was still five years older than Russell; she was unattached and devoted to good works of various kinds, including temperance reform, feminism, and social work. Her seriousness and reticence, which contrasted with the flamboyance of her older sister, made a favourable impact on the priggish young Russell. The priggish young Russell was likewise welcomed by her parents who found an aristocratic suitor for their daughter greatly to their liking.

Although, by Russell's own account (*Auto.* i, 76), he fell in love at first sight in 1889, nothing much seems to have been done until the summer of 1893. The reason is not obscure: in May 1893 Russell turned 21. This brought him legal independence—he could now marry without his grandmother's consent—and also financial independence, for at 21 he received an inheritance of £20,000 from his father's estate. This translated into a yearly income of £600, a sum quite sufficient for a couple with modest needs to live on. No sooner was his majority achieved that Russell turned up at Friday's Hill to lay siege to Alys. Excited journal entries by Russell and tentative early letters (the first in June 1893) chronicle his efforts. It was by no means plain sailing. Alys, initially, seemed determined not to fall in love, and even when it was plain that her affections were aroused she struggled long and hard against marriage, maintaining that women should have an independence that was incompatible with marriage. Russell responded with whatever weapons came to hand. On 12 August 1893 he was planning to 'shew her some of the

---

[2] B. R. to O. Morrell, postmarked 20 July 1912 (no. 506).

more intelligible passages . . . about love in its philosophical aspect' in McTaggart's *Further Determination of the Absolute* (LD 62–3). A week later, her argument that independence was better for women than marriage was controverted on grounds drawn from political economy:

as a motive [independence] is of course a non-moral one & might be overcome as you said by the non-moral motive of falling in love. But as an ideal I am convinced it cannot stand a moment: in the practical regulation of one's life it occupies the same position in relation to the higher ideal that laissez-faire did in relation to Socialism; that the individualist philosophy of last century does to the modern, which regards the only reality as Spirit, & the whole universe as a unity of spirits connected as the members of the body are in working together for a common end.[3]

Russell had even composed for her a little essay (1898*b*) purporting to establish the perfectly general proposition that any two people in a situation similar to their own should get married both on general utilitarian grounds and for the continuation of the liberal tradition. 'How absurd . . . to have to argue and argue on a question of social ethics before acquiring the minutest right to speak of one's own feelings!' Russell wrote, with some justice, in his diary after he had given Alys the essay (LD 62).

   This somewhat curious manner of courtship paid off. 'All is accomplished', Russell wrote in triumph in his diary on 16 September (LD 63). Yet what had been accomplished was not their engagement, but merely that the question had been put. They were still talking of waiting years before getting married (LD 64). It was not until 31 May 1894 that their engagement was announced. Granny did not wait until this lamentable turn of events before she launched a counter-attack. Russell announced his proposal to his family when he returned from Friday's Hill in September 1893: '[T]hey reacted according to the stereotyped convention. They said she was no lady, a baby-snatcher, a low-class adventuress, a designing female taking advantage of my inexperience, a person incapable of all the finer feelings, a woman whose vulgarity would perpetually put me to shame' (*Auto.* i, 82). But Granny had more tricks up her sleeve than mere expression of opinion and abuse. Her first plan was to enlist the support of suitably instructed physicians to point out the strong strain of insanity present in the Russell family. Such a genetic inheritance, it was alleged, made marriage inadvisable since any children would almost certainly be insane. Such arguments threw Russell into deep despair. He did not challenge the claimed facts of the newly revealed family history, nor the genetic theory from which were drawn the implications of that history for his marriage to Alys.[4] He wrote gloomily in his diary of his family's

[3] B. R. to A. P. Smith, 19 Aug. 1893.
[4] Indeed, he set himself to study something of genetics. He read, and was apparently convinced by, Francis Galton's quirky (1892) and his even quirkier (1889). Some further details of Russell's interest in eugenics can be found in *Papers*, xii, 363–5.

solemn and reiterated warnings; the gradual discovery, one by one, of the tragedies, hopeless and unalleviated, which have made up the lives of most of my family; above all, the perpetual gloom which hangs like a fate over P[embroke) L[odge], and which, struggle as I will, invades my inmost soul whenever I go there, taking all joy even out of Alys's love; all these, combined with the fear of heredity, cannot but oppress my mind; they make me feel as though a doom lay on the family and I were vainly battling against it, to escape into the freedom which seems the natural birthright of others ... I am haunted by fear of the family ghost, which seems to seize on me with clammy invisible hands to avenge my desertion of its tradition of gloom— (LD 65–6).

No wonder he was impressed by Ibsen's *Ghosts*, in which the sins of the fathers are visited so chillingly upon the sons. But in the end, Russell rallied. Victorian faith in technical progress extricated him from his moral dilemma: if their children would be mad, then they should marry and take steps to ensure that they had no children. This was not the response Granny wanted to hear: the prospect of contraception was worse than that of mad children. She tried again.

Had she realized that it had been love at first sight in 1889 and had only reached the stage of proposals by 1893 she would have been less sanguine about the chances for success of her second plan. She hoped that an enforced separation of the two would cause their ardour to diminish. To this end she engineered a three-month appointment for Russell as an honorary attaché at the British Embassy in Paris (where Lord Dufferin, a former attaché of Lord John Russell's, was ambassador). The post occupied him from 10 September to 1 December 1894; his separation from Alys ran from 17 August to 17 November 1894. It was hoped that Lord Dufferin would take the young Russell under his wing and introduce him to the sophisticated pleasures of Paris, thereby inducing in him a distaste for Alys's Quaker plainness. There were dangers in this course, but on the whole it was better for the future prime minister to be a man-about-town than married to a vulgar, low-class, American adventuress. Russell and Alys stuck faithfully to their undertaking not to see one another for three months: in fact they stuck it to the day. But from Granny's point of view the scheme was an entire failure. Russell came to hate Paris and all things French. He priggishly refused all temptations set in his way by Lord Dufferin and others at the Embassy, and he abhorred the diplomatic service and despised all who worked within it.

While Russell was counting the days until his reunion with Alys, Granny was planning further, more permanent, diversions. Again using family connections, she cajoled John Morley, then Secretary of State for Ireland, into offering Russell a post as his private secretary when the exile in Paris was over. Russell's response was a firm refusal. By this time Granny had realized that a mere job wasn't going to prevent Russell's marriage to Alys.

Indeed, she pointed out to him that she had raised the question of his marriage to Morley 'and he answers that it is *not* an obstacle—he mentions that he believes he knows her, but without naming her or makg. any comment'.[5] Alys, of course, was the sort of person about whom the less said the better. The point of the position with Morley was to try and wean Russell away from Cambridge. For since Russell's graduation in the summer of 1894, Granny was fighting a war on two fronts: on the one hand she was trying to prevent his marriage to Alys, on the other she was trying to get him to start on a political career. In the letter just quoted she went on to sympathize with Russell's desire to pursue his studies at Cambridge, though she could not 'but strongly feel that for *you*, such employment as J. M. offers . . . would be better.' She also invoked the shades of his dead father and grandfather, who 'I *know* . . . wd. have felt as I do in this matter'. Russell's response remained a firm 'No'.

It might be thought from the above letter that Granny, with Bertie's stay in Paris coming to a close, had given up the fight against Alys. In fact, she was merely pursuing this battle by other means. Her latest tactic was to claim that Russell's obstinacy was undermining her health, an argument urged on her behalf by various members of Russell's family and backed by a major cancer scare which initially troubled Russell a good deal.[6] Not unnaturally, however, Russell had become exasperated with the year-long guerrilla war with his family: 'It is sad that my Grandmother should be so ill again', he wrote to Alys, 'but so long as we are able to marry December 14, I wish nothing better for her than a speedy death.'[7] Russell's life at Pembroke Lodge had come to seem to him a total nightmare. '[N]o one who knows anything of P[embroke] L[odge] wonders at anything but my having stood it so long.'[8] He had dug his heels in early over the separation, admitting that he wouldn't have minded so much 'if it were not an instance of my Grandmother's power so that it enhances the superstitious feeling of the power of my family and class' (ibid.). None the less, Granny didn't give up, and her campaign culminated in the following, astonishing performance just three days before the wedding took place: 'How thankfully I remember that all through your childhood & boyhood you would always give up your own wishes for those of others, never attempt an excuse when you had done wrong, never fail to receive warning or reproof as gratefully as praise. We trusted you, you justified our trust, & all was happiness & affection'.[9] It was the final shot in a war which was lost. Russell and Alys were married on 13 December. Granny and her entourage did not attend.

---

[5] Countess Russell to B. R., 13 Sept. 1894.
[6] See e.g. B. R. to A. P. Smith, 17 Aug. 1894; 22 Aug. 1894; 27 Aug. 1894.
[7] B. R. to A. P. Smith, 31 Oct. 1894 (10 a.m.).
[8] B. R. to A. P. Smith, 21 Aug. 1894.        [9] Countess Russell, 6 June 1894.

The few months after his graduation in the summer of 1894 set the seal on Russell's emancipation from the control of his family. The process had started when he went up to Cambridge, but it was only in the second half of 1894 that one could be sure that he had been successful in making himself independent of his family. In the first place, of course, he had married the woman of his choice against the concerted and formidable opposition of his family. Secondly, and no less importantly, he had decided not to pursue the career they had laid out for him. It was clear to Russell by the time he graduated that he would rather continue with academic work than enter politics.

The natural next step for him in such a career was a Trinity prize fellowship, for which he would have to submit a dissertation by the August following his graduation. Though Russell had set his sights on a fellowship he had not decided what the topic of his dissertation would be, or even in which discipline he should write it. He seriously considered leaving philosophy to write on economics. He even told his Uncle Rollo that he didn't 'wish to spend another two years on philosophy',[10] but this letter seems to have been written in the first flush of post-Tripos disenchantment. Shortly after his Tripos (before the results were out) he went to see Alfred Marshall, then not only the leading economist at Cambridge but the dominant figure in neo-classical economics, about his plans to study economics. Marshall gave him 'an enormous list of books to read' and asked him 'to come again in October and report progress'.[11] Although Russell read voraciously in economics for the next two or three years, he could not have gone far through Marshall's list before he decided that he would stick to philosophy.[12] An important consideration must have been his success in the Moral Sciences Tripos, the results of which were announced on 8 June 1894.

Two days after this Russell met with Ward to discuss his work and his future prospects. On the basis of his performance in the Tripos Ward thought that Russell was 'much more likely than not' to get a fellowship.[13] It was at this meeting that Russell not only decided to do a thesis in philosophy, but decided upon his thesis topic:

We discussed a lot of possible subjects and finally seemed to fix on the Epistemological Bearings of Metageometry, which sounds well at any rate. I then went on, at Ward's recommendation, to a somewhat younger member of the Society, named Whitehead, another Trinity don, who has worked at this subject from the mathematical side, and he instructed me in the Bibliography of the subject. I may write on the meaning and

[10] B. R. to Rollo Russell, 6 June 1894.     [11] B. R. to A. P. Smith, 5 June 1894.
[12] See *Papers*, i, pt. vii, for details of Russell's early economic work. Unfortunately Marshall's reading list has not survived, but a record of Russell's economic reading (with commentary) can be found in the second of the two so-called 'Mit Gott' notebooks he kept at this time (RA 210.006550-F1).
[13] B. R. to A. P. Smith, 10 June 1894.

validity of the differential calculus instead, but I think that would be harder and less exciting. In either case I shall be able to utilize both my Triposes, and so, I hope, make my dissertation unintelligible to all my examiners, in which case I shall be safe.[14]

Russell's choice of philosophy of geometry as a topic for his dissertation was undoubtedly influenced by the Kantian paper on geometry (EPII) he had written for Ward (see § 4.2 below). It could be argued that, from the point of view of his later work, the meaning and validity of the differential calculus would have been a better topic, since it would have brought him more quickly into contact with nineteenth-century European work in analysis, of which he was entirely ignorant. As it was he didn't get around to the calculus until 1896 (see § 6.2 below).

Even with his topic chosen, he did not give up his plan to work on economics. From Paris he wrote to Alys that he planned to do two dissertations—one on geometry and one on economics.[15] Alys, whose reforming zeal was even greater than Russell's, had always been in favour of his studying economics with a view to entering politics. But the two dissertations plan was not designed merely to placate her: Russell explained it to Sanger and, through him, also to Ward. His friends, especially the philosophers among them, were aghast,[16] while Ward cautioned that 'two moderate dissertations do not count as one good one'.[17] Despite these discouraging reactions, and the fact that a dissertation on whichever topic would have to be submitted by the following August, Russell immediately after his marriage went off to Germany for a honeymoon which would include a serious study of economics (attending lectures by Adolph Wagner at the University of Berlin) and of the German Social Democrat movement. It was in Berlin, however, that he started to write a draft of his dissertation on geometry—in the end, his only dissertation.

On leaving Germany in March 1895, Russell and Alys travelled to Italy to see Alys's sister, then living next door to Bernard Berenson at I Tatti. In April they returned to England, taking a small cottage near the Pearsall Smith household at Friday's Hill. There Russell undertook the serious work of finishing his fellowship dissertation. Writing the thesis was his 'first experience of serious original work. There were days of hope alternating with days of despair, but at last, when my dissertation was finished, I fully believed that I had solved all philosophical questions connected with the foundations of geometry' (*Auto.* i, 125). 'I had when I was younger', he explained, 'an almost unbelievable optimism as to the finality of my own theories' (*MPD* 41). The dissertation was submitted in August, and Russell learnt he had won a prize fellowship on 10 October. The fellowship was for

[14] B. R. to A. P. Smith, 10 June 1894.        [15] B. R. to A. P. Smith, 4 Nov. 1894.
[16] See especially the letters from Sanger and Marsh in *Auto.* i, 113 ff.
[17] C. P. Sanger to B. R. 19 Oct. 1894 (in *Auto.* i, 114).

six years, carried a small stipend (which Russell donated to the newly founded London School of Economics to establish a Russell Research Studentship), but involved virtually no duties; not even residence in Cambridge was required. Most of Russell's time as a prize fellow was spent away from Cambridge working on the philosophy of mathematics. Almost immediately after the award of the fellowship Russell and Alys both returned to Germany for further work on German Social Democracy. By this time they had definitely formed the plan of writing a book on the movement, and pursued their research assiduously, interviewing members at all levels in the party. The immediate outcome of this work was a series of lectures early in 1896; these were later published as *German Social Democracy*.

In the spring of 1896, the Russells returned to Fernhurst, this time taking a small workman's cottage, The Millhangar, on the edge of the Friday's Hill estate. The cottage was tiny, even after they added two bedrooms and a sitting-room, had no electricity, and relied upon well water. None the less, Russell said, 'In this cottage many of the happiest times of my life were passed' (*Auto.* i, 127). His love for Alys was undiminished; his troubles with his in-laws were still in the future. But, primarily, he was happy because his work was going well. His best-known work was produced later and elsewhere. But in terms of his personal intellectual development, the work he did at The Millhangar from 1896 to 1900 constitutes perhaps his greatest intellectual achievement. These years saw his transformation from a Cambridge student into a philosopher of importance. Throughout the period his thought was rarely static for more than a couple of months. He embarked upon an ambitious encyclopaedia of the sciences; reworked his ideas on geometry almost as soon as they had been published; and started a philosophical analysis of physics based on Boscovich's point-atom theory, only to change the basis half-way through to a plenal theory of matter, finally abandoning the whole effort in order to turn his attention to pure mathematics. These years saw the abandonment of his neo-Hegelianism, the adoption of a new and strikingly original metaphysics, the mastery of new techniques (first Peano's symbolic logic and then Cantorean set theory) and finally the emergence, after many drafts, of a book under the title 'Principles of Mathematics' which bore a strong resemblance to the volume that was eventually published under that title. In these five years Russell brought his mathematical knowledge up to date. In 1898 he abandoned for the first time the eighteenth-century view that mathematics was based primarily on the concept of quantity. This brought him mathematically into the early nineteenth century; relations now seemed to him of fundamental importance in mathematics (as Gauss had said they were in the 1820s); order rather than quantity became the fundamental concept (as W. R. Hamilton had said it was in the 1830s). Russell for the first time learnt of the rigour of early nineteenth-century

analysis—itself not very rigorous by the standards that were to follow—
which had been expunged from the Cambridge curriculum through the
efforts of Whewell. Having arrived at the 1840s by 1898, Russell took the
next three years to catch up with the rest of nineteenth-century mathematics:
studying Weierstrass, Dedekind, Cantor, Peano, Pieri, Pasch, Hilbert, and
at last, a couple of years later, Frege. The speed of his advance was
staggering, and it was not his fault that most of his effort had to be devoted to
catching-up. He had good reason for being happy at The Millhangar.

## 3.2 CONVERSION TO NEO-HEGELIANISM

In his later writings, Russell gave the overwhelming impression that he
became a neo-Hegelian primarily because he was indoctrinated with it at
Cambridge.[18] Not surprisingly, this version of events has been accepted by
commentators (e.g. Jager 1972: 47; McMahon 1972: 15–22; Ayer 1971: 3).
Yet the historical record belies it. 'I fought every inch of the way against
Idealism in Metaphysics and Ethics—and that is why I was forced to
understand it thoroughly before accepting it, and why when I came to write
it out, Ward used to be enchanted by my lucidity'.[19]

Philosophy for Russell was of no use if it failed to withstand the most
thorough-going critical attacks. Ward had told Russell 'that in reading a
philosophical book one should be as critical as possible and make all the
objections one can'.[20] It was advice Russell tried to follow. The only beliefs
worth holding, he thought, were those 'one has fought against . . . wrestled
with . . . and struggled to understand'.[21] His own method, so he declared in a
letter intended to convince Alys of the rigour of his mind, was

to consider a question as impartially as I can for as long as it needs or as I can spare it,
and then to decide as best I can, and by an act of will refuse to reconsider any decision
until new facts come up. For so sceptical a nature as mine it is only by such a process
that I can believe even a proposition of Euclid, much more than that one course of
action is right and another wrong.[22]

It is this scepticism, a constant feature of Russell's intellectual life, that
attracted him in particular to Bradley. Bradley today is remembered mainly
for his big metaphysical system. But what was notable about his approach to
philosophy in the 1890s was his use of *reductio* arguments intended to
establish sceptical conclusions. Bradley himself described *Appearance and*

[18] Extensive textual evidence is assembled by Spadoni (1977: 88). See e.g. Russell (1938: 33;
1948: 142; MMD 10; *PFM* 17; *MPD* 11; *Auto.* i, 134).
[19] B. R. to A. P. Smith, 22 Oct. 1894 (9.00 p.m.).
[20] B. R. to A. P. Smith, 25 Sept. 1893.          [21] Ibid.
[22] B. R. to A. P. Smith, 19 Dec. 1893. Russell continued to recommend this method: cf.
1930b: 47.

*Reality* as 'a sceptical study of first principles' that was 'satisfied to be negative' in the hope that it might help to 'produce a rational system of first principles' (1893*a*: p. xii). That such a corrosively sceptical approach to first principles might, none the less, leave intact a metaphysics still capable of yielding consolatory doctrines was no doubt an immense attraction to Russell.

Russell's conversion to neo-Hegelianism was chiefly (though not exclusively) the result of rational argument. In his student years Russell gradually came to accept various neo-Hegelian doctrines; no doubt, as he said, fighting every inch of the way, but none the less slowly succumbing. In Russellian autobiography, however, things rarely happen gradually. If his own accounts are to be believed, his life focused around a series of startling about-turns as surprising to Russell as to anyone else since they were all completely unheralded. One of these was his acceptance of neo-Hegelianism, of which he writes: 'I remember the exact moment during my fourth year when I became [a neo-Hegelian]' (*Auto.* i, 63). To make the account good, he has to minimize his adherence to neo-Hegelian doctrine before this moment. Thus he writes to Ottoline Morrell: 'Throughout the greater part of the year I remained quite unconvinced of Hegelianism'.[23] His account in *My Philosophical Development* is a bit less misleading in this respect: 'I stood out against [McTaggart's] influence with diminishing resistance until just before my Moral Sciences Tripos in 1894, when I went over completely to a semi-Kantian, semi-Hegelian metaphysic.' (*MPD* 38).[24] Russell's fullest account of this event, which like many of Russell's other 'conversions' contains elements of the bizarre, is in the letter to Morrell just quoted:

One day, a week before my last Tripos [21–4 May 1894], I ran out of tobacco while I was working, so I went out to get some. As I was coming back with a tin, I suddenly seemed to see truth in the ontological argument. I threw the tin in the air and exclaimed out loud 'Great God in boots, the ontological argument is sound'. (I can't imagine the reason for such an oath.) So I became a Hegelian . . .

Russell, however, never bothered to explain the connection between accepting the ontological argument and accepting a neo-Hegelian philosophy. Likewise, others have reported the incident but without comment, and it was only recently that the connection was explained.[25]

[23] B. R. to O. Morrell, 28 Sept. 1911 (no. 199).

[24] He was writing then after having recently reread his Moral Science papers. There is little explicit mention of them in *MPD*, but the manuscripts had been typed a few years earlier for Alan Wood's benefit (see *Papers*, i, 119), and Russell acquired the typescripts on Wood's death in 1957.

[25] Cf. Spadoni (1976) on which the present account is based. Other commentary on the episode is almost non-existent, but connoisseurs of the bizarre may enjoy Poots's reinterpretation of the role of the tobacco tin and its contents in this episode (1950: 16–17).

The ontological argument, as originally devised by St Anselm and used by others, is intended to prove God's existence. God, according to Anselm in the *Proslogion*, is that-than-which-nothing-greater-can-be-conceived. The possibility that God, so conceived, may not exist—may exist, as it were, in the mind but not in reality—is ruled out by Anselm on the ground that the conception of God as both existing in reality and in the mind is greater than the conception of him as existing merely in the mind. It follows by definition that necessarily he exists, for otherwise something greater than God can be conceived.

The classic objections to the ontological argument are those of Kant (1781: A592–602 = B620–30). It is convenient to distinguish two objections, which I shall call '*A*' and '*B*'. The *A*-objection concedes that the proposition 'A perfect being exists' is a (disguised) identical proposition (Kant's term), that is, one can't consistently admit the subject of the proposition and deny the predicate (since existence is conceded to be a perfection). None the less, we are not entitled to infer from such identical propositions that a perfect being exists for we may reject subject and predicate alike (1781: A594 = B622). The *B*-objection is the more famous and is usually presented as the slogan that 'exists' is not a predicate. Its upshot is to deny that a contradiction results from affirming the subject and denying the predicate of the identical proposition, since if existence is not a predicate there is no predicate to deny. This is not the place for Kant exegesis, but there seems to be little textual warrant for ascribing the 'exists'-is-not-a-predicate slogan to Kant. Kant seems to have held, rather, that 'exists' was not an ordinary predicate in that it could not be used to determine a subject conceptually. If 'exists' is a predicate, albeit of an unusual kind, then the *B*-objection as given will no longer hold. But an effective objection can still be mounted. For if 'exists' cannot conceptually determine the subject then either the subject of 'A perfect being exists' cannot be affirmed, or it can only be affirmed in a way which ensures that the proposition cannot be an identical proposition, since what is given in the predicate does not occur in the subject. It is worth distinguishing Kant's two objections since Russell uses the lesser-known *A*-objection.[26]

As we have seen from Chapter 1, Russell gave up his belief in God's existence at the age of 18. Despite religious feelings and an attraction to pantheism, he never returned to this belief. So Russell's acceptance of the ontological argument in the spring of 1894 is puzzling. The only clue in

---

[26] The distinction between the two types of objection is clearly made by Hick (1967: 539). Ontological arguments of all kinds are comprehensively criticized in Sylvan and Griffin (1989). It is shown there that they fail even if 'exists' is a predicate. For textual evidence that Kant thought 'exists' was a predicate, but one of an unusual type, see Routley (1980: 180–2). For Russell's own later objections see OD 54; *IMP* 203–4; *WNC* 141–2.

Russell's published reminiscences is to be found in *Portraits from Memory*: 'Hegel thought of the universe as a closely knit unity . . . The only reality was the Absolute, which was his name for God' (*PFM* 17). Although Hegel's discussion of the ontological argument is open to a latitude of interpretation, it is clear that he denied the force of Kant's objection (cf. 1817: §§ 50–1; 1832: iii, 347–67; 1836: iii, 62–7). Whether Russell was right in thinking that Hegel identified the Absolute with God is open to dispute, though Russell was not alone in thinking it. Hegel's version of the ontological argument appears to be as follows. The existence of any being (including our own) presupposes the existence of the Absolute (or God), which is the only true being as such. Hence the existence of the Absolute cannot be denied, once our own is granted. Hegel relied on two claims: first, that all predicates apply ultimately to the Absolute; second, that our existence requires the Absolute to support it. Hick (1967: 540) rightly comments that the conclusion of Hegel's argument is either trivial (as McTaggart, for one, thought, 1901: 56) or terribly unclear. Is the Absolute identical to the sum of finite beings, or is it a metaphysical entity over and above this sum? If the former, the argument is trivial; if the latter, it is not clear either what it adds or why this needs to be added.

Fortunately, Bradley's use of the ontological argument is somewhat clearer and provides the basis for Russell's appeal to the argument. Bradley's discussion begins with a 'puzzle': the idea of perfection is merely 'in my head', but in no way can it be divorced from reality since all ideas, no matter how preposterous, must refer to reality. The Absolute is thus qualified by perfection, as by every idea.

This general result at once bears upon the ontological proof. Evidently the proof must start with an idea referred to and qualifying Reality, and with Reality present also and determined by the content of the idea. And the principle of the argument is simply this, that, standing on one side of such a whole, you find yourself moved necessarily towards the other side. Mere thought, because incomplete, suggests logically the other element already implied in it; and that element is the Reality which appears in existence. (Bradley 1893*a*: 350.)

This observation however is soon challenged. According to Bradley's coherence theory of truth, the truth of a judgement is a matter of degree and not every predicate can be entirely true of reality 'as such'. Certain ideas possess more reality than others, and the greater an idea's degree of reality the more necessary becomes its existence. But what then are we to say of the idea of the Absolute itself? Bradley's reply is as follows:

But the ontological argument, it will be rightly said, makes no pretence of being applicable to every finite matter. It is used of the Absolute, and, if confined to that, will be surely legitimate. We are, I think, bound to admit this claim. The idea of the

Absolute, as an idea, is inconsistent with itself: and we find that, to complete itself, it is internally driven to take in existence. (1893*a*: 351.)

Russell's first encounter with the ontological argument was probably during Stout's course on the history of philosophy. He reported: 'I have been engaged in learning Descartes's three proofs of the existence of God and the fallacies they involve: an occupation admirably calculated to exterminate any lingering respect for the "Gottesbegriff" in any one who had it'.[27] In the Lent term of 1894, Descartes's philosophy was the major topic of Stout's lectures, with a smattering of Spinoza, Leibniz, Geulincx, and Malebranche. In Russell's lecture notes under the heading 'Ontological Proof', there is a fairly standard exposition of Descartes's argument, comparing it with Descartes's proof of his own existence, but in addition there are the following remarks: 'The mere existence of an idea involves reference to reality'; 'This true: whole of reality must exist, and must be completion of any fragment we happen to know: such fragment, *known as fragment*, is self'.[28] In fact, all the essentials of Bradley's argument (which Russell hadn't yet read) are present in Stout's lecture. Obviously, Russell was still fighting every inch of the way against neo-Hegelianism.

Much briefer references to the ontological argument are also contained in Ward's course on the history of philosophy. The first reference in Russell's lecture notes, for example, concerns whether the idea of God is innate and, if so, whether his existence can be inferred from this fact. Ward raises the question whether such an innate idea is one involving existence. Russell recorded in his notes: 'if lays stress on this[,] Kant's objection that can't treat existence as a quality I think becomes sound: though Bradley would challenge this'.[29] Ward's later opinion of the ontological argument (cited by Cock 1918: 363), that Kant 'has for all time exposed its fatal defects', was already clearly stated.

It seems clear that Stout favoured the neo-Hegelian use of the ontological argument, whereas Ward opposed it. Stout had in fact assigned a paper on Descartes which involved the following questions: 'Discuss the nature and logical validity of the ontological argument for the existence of God, as stated by Descartes. To what extent had it been anticipated by previous writers? In what form does it re-appear in Spinoza and Leibnitz?' (cf. *Papers*, i, 178). The date of Russell's response (1894*d*) to these questions— May 1894—corresponds with his recollection of having seen the validity of the ontological argument just before the Moral Science Tripos. His answers reveal why he accepted neo-Hegelian philosophy.

[27] B. R. to A. P. Smith, 7 Feb. 1894.
[28] 'Lecture Notebook', ii, 140, 142. It is difficult to date these remarks exactly, but internal evidence makes clear that they were written before 8 Mar. 1894.
[29] 'Lecture Notebook', ii, 25; cf. also p. 44.

Russell's brief discussion is extremely interesting. It includes a compressed account of Leibniz's version of the argument, and that of Anselm, who is held responsible (surprisingly) for the 'crude form of the ontological argument' (1894d: 179). The main concern, however, is Descartes. Russell outlines Descartes's argument as follows:

The idea of God, as the most perfect (or complete) being, says Descartes, involves *necessary* existence: for existence is a perfection. In answer to objections he says that every concept involves existence, but the concept of an all-complete being involves *necessary* existence. God, as that from which all existence we know derives its being, as the only independent reality, as *omnitudo realitatis*, is a concept in which necessary existence is part of the essence. Hence God exists. (1894d: 179.)

Russell's preference for formulating Descartes's argument in terms of the most complete being, rather than the most perfect, derives from Stout's lectures.[30] It connects with the neo-Hegelian view that only a complete, i.e. all-embracing, entity can exist independently.

Russell objects to this argument briefly and rather obscurely, but it seems he has in mind Kant's *A*-objection: 'if I deny the existence of the object of the concept, all the predicates are denied with it, and no contradiction can possibly arise' (1894d: 179; cf. Kant 1781: A594 = B622). He concludes that Descartes 'should have added (and I believe he does say somewhere) that we are compelled to think God' (p. 179).[31] A fair bit of this is at cross purposes, largely, I suspect, because two different ontological arguments are muddled up together. The first argues that 'An all-complete being does not exist' is self-contradictory, because it involves affirming the subject while denying the predicate which is contained in the subject. Kant's *A*-objection is that we don't have to affirm the subject at all. What Descartes, therefore, needs to make good his reply is evidence that we necessarily *affirm* the subject. But this is a good deal stronger than the claim Russell thinks he needs, namely that we necessarily *think* the subject. The second ontological argument starts from the premiss that if an all-complete being can be thought of then such a being exists. In order for Descartes to infer that an all-complete being exists from this premiss, it is necessary for him to have the premiss that such a being can be thought of. But this is a good deal weaker than the premiss Russell thinks he needs, namely that such a being is *necessarily* thought of.

There is, however, a third consideration to be dealt with, for as Russell formulates Descartes's argument the conclusion is not that an all-complete being exists, but that such a being *necessarily* exists. This suggests a third

[30] Cf. 'Lecture Notebook', ii, 140.

[31] In fact Descartes (1640: 182) says exactly the opposite. It is possible that Russell has in mind Descartes's view that the idea of God is innate (Descartes 1640: 170).

ontological argument. Suppose Descartes starts his argument from the *necessary* premiss that if an all-complete being is thought of then such a being exists. We can then derive the conclusion that *necessarily* such a being exists, only if we have the premiss that *necessarily* we think of such a being. (The argument has the form: $\Box(p \supset q)$, thus $\Box p \supset \Box q$, whence $\Box q$, provided $\Box p$.) If this is Descartes's argument, the required premiss is exactly that which Russell supplies. That we *can* or *do* think of the all-complete being is insufficient to make the argument valid, as the formalization readily reveals. The difficulty with this interpretation of Russell's argument is that it does not make it clear why he embarks on (what is on this view) a detour through Kant.

So much for Russell's thoughts on Descartes. The really important part of his paper, from our point of view, is his refurbishing of the ontological argument as an argument for the existence of the Absolute. He writes:

> But those who wish to maintain the ontological argument may reply that whatever we think we cannot get away from reality: if we judge at all, we must affirm some predicate of reality; even negative judgment is only possible owing to some positive incompatible ground, i.e. must be based on an affirmation; but if we try to deny reality as a whole, there is no positive ground left as basis of our denial. We *must* think the Absolute, and its essence involves existence; hence the ontological argument can, it would seem, only be met by complete scepticism, by abstaining from judgment altogether; which is a negligeable alternative. (1894*d*: 179.)[32]

The account of judgement given here is largely, but not wholly, Bradleian. Thus we find Bradley's existential theory of judgement (1883: i, 41–3), namely that all judgements, including negative judgements, refer to something real. So also we find Bradley's view that 'negation presupposes a positive ground' (1883: i, 114), and that this positive ground is some 'quality *x* in the subject which is incompatible with the suggested idea' (1883: i, 117). Yet Russell's view that negation 'must be based on affirmation' is explicitly denied by Bradley, who points out, very justly, that while the negative judgement presupposes the incompatible quality *x* this quality is not made explicit in the negative judgement (1883: i, 117)—'it is a mistake to say that an affirmative judgment is presupposed in denial' (p. 116). On this point, Bradley is certainly right and Russell wrong. None the less, the point does not much affect Russell's argument.

The whole argument is a transcendental deduction of the existence of the Absolute from the existence of judgement. Now there is a certain sense in which the argument, or at least one close to it, is valid. If a judgement is

---

[32] Cf. also 1897*a*: 102: 'The ultimate premiss of any subject should have an evidence which cannot be questioned. The premiss of Logic and Metaphysics is that truth is true of reality, and that some knowledge is true. This depends on the ontological argument, which again depends on the impossibility of total scepticism.'

made then it follows that something exists, namely the judgement.[33] But this is as trivial as McTaggart thought Hegel's ontological argument. Russell clearly wants a grander conclusion than this, and he clearly thought he could obtain one by means of Bradley's two principles that all judgement involves 'a reference to something beyond' and that this external reference must be to something actual (Bradley 1883: i, 41). This will take us a bit further, for we can now establish not only the existence of the judgement but the existence of its external reference.

Russell somewhat later clearly states this form of the ontological argument and attributes it to Bradley:

Its validity is indisputable if the existential theory of judgment be admitted. To maintain that there is no truth is self-contradictory, for if our contention were itself true, there would be truth. If, then, all truth consists in propositions about what exists, it is self-contradictory to maintain that nothing exists. Thus the existence of something is metaphysically necessary. This argument, which is set forth at length in Book I., Chaps. II.–IV. of Mr. Bradley's *Logic*, partakes of both the Ontological and Cosmological arguments. (*POL* 177.)

By this time, Russell had rejected the existential theory of judgement, for he distinguished among the terms that a proposition may be about between those which existed and those which merely had being (cf. AMR 168). This is a view to be found also in Moore (*POM*: p. xviii; cf. Moore 1899a).[34] Moore's influence shows up in the passage in other ways; for example, interestingly enough, in the reference to the liar paradox (cf. Moore 1897b: 555). Moore, in his fellowship dissertations, had used such considerations to show that scepticism is self-refuting (1898a: ch. 1: 25) and to argue that metaphysics must be based upon first principles which cannot be denied without self-refutation (1897a: Introduction, p. 5a;[35] 1898a: ch. 2: 33). In this respect Moore's new metaphysics and probably (at this time) Russell's also, represents a continuation of Bradley's programme by other means. For

[33] The connection here between the ontological argument, evident in Hegel's formulation, and Descartes's *cogito*, is a topic of one of Stout's lectures (cf. 'Lecture Notebook', ii, 140–1). It is to be noted that this is not a transcendental deduction from the *possibility* of judgement, but from its actuality. Judgement would still be *possible*, but non-actual, in a world in which *nothing* existed, as the appropriate semantic models show.

[34] See below, § 7.2 for a fuller discussion of Moore's possible influence. Moore rejected the ontological argument on similar grounds in (1898b: 178), although he does concede it was more convincing than the other arguments for the Absolute.

[35] In several places Moore's fellowship dissertations have unusual pagination. Chapters are paginated separately and often in different ways. In this case (and several others) the chapter is written on large sheets folded in two to form a signature of four pages. Of the four, Moore wrote only on the first and third, the rectos, leaving the versos for notes and later insertions. Only the first page of each signature is paginated. In giving page references, therefore, the page number gives the number of the signature, 'a' or 'b' indicates which recto is cited. If material from a verso is cited, the fact is indicated by a superscript 'v'. Thus, in the present instance, 5a refers to the first recto of the fifth signature; 5b to the second recto; 5aᵛ to the verso of the first recto; etc.

Bradley also hoped for a set of first principles immune to sceptical attack because to deny them would be self-contradictory. None the less, this continuity of method did not ensure similarity of results, since Russell and Moore now rejected the existential theory of judgement and the ontological argument which depends upon it.

All this, however, belongs to a later period of Russell's thought. Bradley defends the existential theory of judgement, and Russell in 1894 followed him. This, together with his view that negation presupposes a positive ground, gives him a valid ontological argument of sorts. But even on these assumptions it would seem impossible to extend the Absolute beyond the judgement, its positive ground, and whatever is implied thereby. Given the neo-Hegelian conception of the Absolute as a complete whole of mutually entailing parts, however, this would be sufficient to prove the existence of an Absolute worth having. For, supposedly, with sufficient logical dexterity and patience, it should be possible to deduce the existence of everything which exists from any given judgement and its positive ground.

That this was the crucial argument for persuading Russell that neo-Hegelianism should be accepted is confirmed by a letter written some fifteen years later to Ottoline Morrell:

Stout, who chiefly taught me, persuaded me that [neo-Hegelianism] all turned on the ontological argument. This argument, in the crude form invented by Archbishop Anselm . . . is: 'God is the subject of all perfections; existence is a perfection; therefore God exists'; or 'God is the most perfect Being; what exists is more perfect than what does not exist; therefore God exists'. The argument has been subtilized since, and now it proves the Absolute, not God.[36]

Russell's claims that his coming to think the ontological argument valid constituted a dramatic change in his philosophical position are certainly misleading. He had been accepting various neo-Hegelian doctrines for several years before May 1894, even though most of them had been resisted (as, indeed, the ontological argument was). Indeed, he could hardly have accepted the ontological argument as a proof of the existence of an Absolute worthy of the name unless he already accepted several key neo-Hegelian doctrines, in particular, holism. What he evidently lacked before the episode of the tobacco tin was any convincing logical reason for concluding that such an Absolute existed. This the ontological argument gave him. In particular, the 'conversion' episode indicates what he thought was really important about neo-Hegelianism at this time. It was not the anti-empiricism, or the idealism, or the doctrine of internal relations, but the question of the existence of the Absolute. Until he thought he had a valid argument for that, he was unable to regard himself as a neo-Hegelian.

[36] B. R. to O. Morrell, 28 Sept. 1911 (no. 199).

## 3.3 THE TIERGARTEN PROGRAMME

Russell's claimed 'conversion' to neo-Hegelianism in May 1894 did not produce a rapid change in the direction of his philosophical work. Immediately afterwards, of course, he was involved in the Moral Science examinations, and his next philosophical task was his fellowship dissertation. His decision to write on the philosophy of geometry seems not to have been influenced by his 'conversion'. It had little direct connection with metaphysics, or with any other topics about which the neo-Hegelians concerned themselves. Once the topic was chosen, his thoughts were taken up with it and with the family crises precipitated by his impending marriage. Once the marriage was accomplished, the honeymoon over, and Russell was safely removed to Berlin in order to study economics and write on geometry, he had time to take stock of where his 'conversion' had brought him, and to lay plans for his future life-work as a neo-Hegelian. The plans he laid were very ambitious indeed. For he decided he would redo Hegel's encyclopaedia of the sciences, using Kantian methods and (this time) getting the science right. Typically, he said the decision came to him suddenly:

I remember a cold, bright day in early spring [1895] when I walked by myself in the Tiergarten, and made projects of future work. I thought that I would write one series of books on the philosophy of the sciences from pure mathematics to physiology, and another series of books on social questions. I hoped that the two series might ultimately meet in a synthesis at once scientific and practical. My scheme was largely inspired by Hegelian ideas. Nevertheless, I have to some extent followed it in later years, as much at any rate as could have been expected. (*Auto.* i, 125; cf. also MMD 11.)

As Russell says, much of his subsequent output can be located within this plan for two series of books. What will concern us in the remainder of this book, however, are his efforts to fulfil this plan as a neo-Hegelian and the reasons why he abandoned them. In this section I shall outline Russell's intentions. He did indeed plan a comprehensive Hegelian dialectic of the sciences, complete with dialectical supersessions and culminating in a metaphysical science of the Absolute Spirit.

Although Russell credits Hegel with the inspiration for the Tiergarten programme, he made virtually no direct use of Hegel in carrying it out.[37] In fact, the most direct philosophical influences on Russell in the period 1895–8 were Kant (whom I shall discuss later), Bradley, and Ward. His debts to Bradley were chiefly in logic and epistemology. But he differed from Bradley both as regards metaphysics—he was a pluralist— and in his belief that the Absolute was knowable. In these two respects, he sided with Ward

---

[37] The same can be said of other early 19th-cent. dialectical systems, e.g. Schleiermacher's, which, in intention at any rate, was quite similar to Russell's.

and McTaggart. Unlike McTaggart, Russell did not propose to tackle the Absolute head-on by starting with metaphysics and moving on, when metaphysical issues were settled, to establish the basic postulates of the various sciences in conformity with metaphysical principle. Russell, as one might expect from his subsequent career, started with science. The investigation of the individual sciences would, if pressed far enough, reveal the nature of the Absolute and thereby determine (at least in part) the principles of metaphysics, which could be regarded as the general, or universal, science.

It was not, of course, that Russell had no idea of what sort of metaphysical conclusions he expected to arrive at. He was an idealist (*MPD* 32), and had been even before he thought he saw the validity of the ontological argument (1893b: 210). He clearly expected that the dialectic would bear him out, although comparatively little is said about this in the surviving notes from the period (but see § 5.3 below). On this much, of course, all neo-Hegelians agreed. What divided them was the question of monism versus pluralism. Bradley led the monists, McTaggart the pluralists. Ward started as a pluralist but later on slid towards monism. Russell's inclination towards monism late in 1894 seems to have lapsed for the next three years. There is not much direct evidence from this period, but as we shall see strong indirect evidence confirms that he was a pluralist (§ 4.6). In 1897 there is direct evidence of another flirtation with monism, which seems to have lasted until he abandoned neo-Hegelianism in 1898. Neither in 1894 nor in 1897–8, however, does Russell clearly espouse monism: he was inclined towards it, but never fully embraced it.

This explains, in a preliminary way, the aims of Russell's dialectic of the sciences. The methods to be used for their accomplishment, however, were Kantian. For Russell, each science was a composite of empirical and a priori parts. His first task was to separate the two. Once this was done the empirical part could be left to the scientist, while the philosopher concerned himself with the a priori component. It is significant that, in this respect, his neo-Hegelian approach to the sciences did not change even after Kant had been rejected. In a letter to Ottoline Morrell he says:

Most actual knowledge is a mixture of both [empirical and a priori knowledge]. The analysis of a piece of actual knowledge into pure sense and pure a priori is often very difficult, but almost always very important . . . As regards the *mathematical* element in science, *Principia Mathematica* does the extraction [of the a priori] very elaborately. But there are a number of other more elusive a priori elements in knowledge—such problems as causality and matter involve them. It is these I want to get hold of now . . . [38]

In a sense, then, his work after *Principia* can be regarded as continuous with the project he conceived in the Tiergarten. In a later letter to Morrell he

[38] B. R. to O. Morrell, no date (no. 616).

remarked how, sixteen years before, he had started work on the philosophy of matter. However, he had found after a year that 'there were a few preliminaries to be settled, which have taken all my time till now'.[39] The preliminaries encompassed all his work on pure mathematics which culminated in *Principia*. Now the preliminaries were dealt with, he proposed to return to the neglected philosophy of matter.

As a neo-Hegelian, Russell sought to establish the a priori parts of each of the sciences by means of a two-part transcendental deduction. The general approach is explained as follows:

We may start from the existence of our science as a fact, and analyse the reasoning employed with a view to discovering the fundamental postulate on which its logical possibility depends: in this case, the postulate, and all which follows from it alone, will be à priori. *Or* we may accept the existence of the subject-matter of our science as our basis of fact, and deduce dogmatically whatever principles we can from the essential nature of this subject matter. In this latter case, however, it is not the whole empirical nature of the subject-matter, as revealed by the subsequent researches of our science, which forms our ground; for if it were, the whole science would, of course, be à priori. Rather it is that element, in the subject-matter, which makes *possible* the branch of experience dealt with by the science in question.(1896c: 291–2 = EFG 5.)[40]

Aspects of this approach survived throughout Russell's career. The choice of axioms, in systems such as *Principia Mathematica*, was to be justified, not by their self-evidence, but by the fact that the true propositions of the science in question followed from them (cf. *PM* i: p. v; LA 163–4). He even kept (for a while) the Kantian phrase 'regressive method' to describe the process whereby the axioms were arrived at (cf. RMDP). Also little noticed is the fact, to which Paul Hager has drawn attention (Hager 1986) that Russell kept throughout his career the view that analysis proceeds in two strokes, the first backwards from the science as given to the premises and the second forwards from the premises to a reconstruction of the original science. Recognition of this has been hampered by the fact that Russell used the term 'analysis' to apply both to the whole process and to the first stroke alone. In the latter, more restrictive usage Russell follows the Euclidean distinction between analysis and synthesis. Russell's later treatment of the sciences differs from his treatment of them as a neo-Hegelian in his complete abandonment of Kant's transcendental methodology. This was a step he

[39] B. R. to O. Morrell, postmarked 8 Feb. 1913 (no. 695). Interestingly, Whitehead in one of his few personal statements, also claimed continuity for his work, from his dissertation on electromagnetism, through *Principia*, to the works on philosophy of science in his middle period (see Lowe 1975).
[40] Russell attributes both methods to Kant: the former, known as the 'analytic' or 'regressive' method to (1783), and the latter, known as the 'synthetic' or 'progressive' method to (1781). See Kemp Smith (1923: 44–50) for further discussion.

made in 1898 and probably reflects Moore's influence (see § 7.2). Until that time he worked within the framework of a (revised) Kantian system.

Russell applies the two methods together, so that the whole treatment is supposedly self-correcting. This is perhaps best indicated by the example of metrical geometry, where Russell's use of the technique is clearest. In the first move, various metrical geometries are analysed to determine the basic postulates common to all of them. These, on Russell's account, are the axiom of free mobility (or congruence), the axiom of dimensions, and the axiom of the straight line. These three axioms form general metrical geometry and constitute the a priori component of all metrical geometries. This result is then confirmed by the second stage of the argument, a transcendental deduction which starts from the (experiential) subject-matter of metrical geometry, namely the form of externality in so far as it admits of measurement. Since, Russell subsequently argues, all measurement involves a form of externality, general metrical geometry is that science which is necessary if measurement is to be possible. Obviously, both parts of the investigation, the analytic investigation from geometry to its axioms, and the synthetic investigation from the form of externality to the postulates which make it possible, are supposed to end in the same place, namely with the three axioms of general metrical geometry. Russell makes brave efforts to maintain that this is so (see § 4.6).

Russell's claim is that each of these two methods, when properly applied, will always produce the same result as the other: 'if reasoning in the science is impossible without some postulate, this postulate must be essential to experience of the subject-matter of the science' (*EFG* 5). The argument requires rather strong assumptions. It must be supposed (1) that there is a postulate, *P*, which is necessary for any possible theory about the subject-matter, *S*, and (2) that if *S* can be experienced then there is some possible theory about it. (1) looks implausible, given the radically different types of theory that might be constructed to handle any given subject-matter. Moreover, it would seem impossible in principle to prove that *P* was necessary for *every possible* theory about the subject-matter. (2) will hold if the possibility of experiencing *S* implies the possibility of articulating propositions (or making judgements) about it, and if every such set of propositions (or judgements) constitutes a theory about *S*. The first of these conditions may be granted: it amounts to the claim that experience is not ineffable. But the second condition imposes such weak constraints on what counts as a theory that (1) can no longer be satisfied. For if any set of propositions about *S* is to count as theory about *S* then there will be no postulate *P* necessary for every such theory. Remember that *P* is supposed to be arrived at by an internal analysis of theories, and thus *P* itself, by Russell's assumptions, must be among the propositions of any theory for which it is necessary. (This follows without Russell's assumptions if we require, as seems desirable, that every theory be closed under implication.) Thus the possibility of there being two disjoint sets of propositions about $S$ ensures that the first assumption cannot be met. (Russell may have held, on holist grounds, that no two such sets closed under implication were possible.) Short of these assumptions, however, there seems to be no way in which Russell can show that what is a necessary condition for the science will be a necessary condition for the experience of its subject-matter. For there would seem to be no a priori guarantee that what makes the subject-matter capable of being experienced will be the necessary postulates of the science. Of course, that the subject-matter can be experienced is a necessary condition of our knowing the science, so any necessary condition of experiencing the subject-matter will be a necessary condition of knowing the science. But there is no guarantee that the conditions necessary for knowing the science will be the axioms upon which the science is based. Knowing the axioms is sufficient for knowing the theory, but not necessary for knowing it (as Russell implicitly admits).

The defects of Russell's approach are those inherent in transcendental deductions of all kinds (see Körner 1967), but especially damaging to those transcendental deductions designed, as Russell's in part was, to counter scepticism. As far as the analytic part is concerned, it would seem possible to establish that the axioms chosen were *sufficient* for the science in question;[41] but not that they were *necessary*. For the possibility of alternative sufficient axiomatizations cannot be ruled out. The problem is a real one for Russell, for, as is well known, his three axioms of general metrical geometry are not necessary for every metrical geometry; in particular, metrical geometries for spaces of variable curvature are possible. Similar problems occur in the synthetic part of the programme, compounded there by the difficulty of knowing when the basic postulates are sufficient because of the inherently greater vagueness of the subject-matter. At least for the analytic deduction one has an articulated theory to deal with, which is more than can be said in the synthetic deduction where one has to determine the essential properties of such vague items as a form of externality. In short, Russell makes three claims: (*a*) that some postulate is necessary for the science; (*b*) that some postulate is necessary for the experience of the subject-matter; (*c*) that the postulate necessary for the science is that which is necessary for the experience

---

[41] Although even this is suspect in the case of an empirical science for which not all the empirical data is in. An axiom set sufficient for chemistry before the discovery of radioactivity, for example, could not be regarded as sufficient afterwards. But it should, at least in principle, be possible to establish the sufficiency of an axiom set for a particular scientific theory or, in certain cases, for a science at a given stage of its development.

of the subject-matter. It would seem impossible to show that any of these three claims is correct.

None of what has so far been said, of course, explains why Russell felt he needed a *dialectic* of the sciences. The transcendental deductions as so far described might simply be applied to each science in isolation. It is clear, as early as 1893, that Russell sought a *system* of the sciences, and that he conceived the task of producing one as the prime task of epistemology (EPI 121). That such a system should be dialectical in nature follows, Russell thought, from two points. First, each science is incomplete as a description of the world, leaving out, of course, all the features that are treated by other sciences. 'Every Science', Russell writes, 'deals necessarily with abstractions: its results must therefore be partial and one-sided expressions of truth' (EPI 121). The language is Bradley's, but the basic point seems undeniable. The second point which makes the dialectic necessary is more disputable, for Russell goes on, in typically Bradleian fashion, to claim that the incompleteness of each science involves it in contradiction. Bradley and many other of the neo-Hegelians did not distinguish clearly between contradiction and incompleteness, claiming that anything less than a fully comprehensive description of the Absolute involved contradictions.[42] In a later piece (1896*f*), which develops the thought of EPI, Russell does distinguish incompleteness and inconsistency, but he still refers to both as contradictions, and claims that both require a dialectical transition for their resolution.[43]

A dialectical transition, of either type, was a transition to a new science which would repair the defects of the old. It was only when metaphysics was reached that this process of successive replacement of sciences would stop. Metaphysics alone constituted 'independent and self-subsistent knowledge' (1896*f*: 5). The distinction between the two types of transition is not so clear in application as it seems in outline. In fact, although he mentions very many contradictions in the course of his work as a neo-Hegelian, he generally does not indicate to which category he thinks a particular contradiction belongs. He nowhere develops anything approaching a *theory* of contradictions. The purpose of the analysis of each individual science, according to Russell, is to reduce to an absolute minimum the number of contradictions it contains. Having uncovered its basic postulates and concepts with this aim in view, the task is 'to supply, to these postulates or ideas, such supplement as will abolish the special contradictions of the science in question, and thus pass to a new science, which may then be similarly treated' (1896*f*: 5).

[42] This kind of formulation persisted late among the idealists. See e.g. Oakeshott (1933: 328), who refers to 'the element of self-contradiction inherent in all abstraction'.

[43] Garciadiego (1987) has argued that Russell has implicit precise distinctions between paradoxes, antinomies, and contradictions. Although Garciadiego is concerned with a slightly later period (1899–1903), his evidence I think is weak for both periods.

Russell explains the point most fully in connection with geometry:

[W]e abstract the spatial qualities of things, not only from all other qualities, but also from the things themselves, leaving, as the matter of our Science, a subject totally devoid of what may be called Thinghood . . . So in Geometry: our study concerns itself with what fills or may fill Space from time to time. The set of relations among things, which in presentation are distinguished as spatial, are abstracted from the things and set in a continuum, called space, whose only function is to allow the creation, *ad lib.*, of these relations. (OSG 93–4.)

All abstraction is ultimately, from a metaphysical point of view, falsifying. None the less, it is legitimate and even necessary for each individual science: 'Of course such an abstraction cannot give us metaphysical truth—we know, all the while, that space would be meaningless if there were no things from which to abstract it—still, as the subject of a special Science, the abstraction is as legitimate as any other' (OSG 93). To remove the falsification which is inherent in geometry, it is necessary to make a dialectical transition to physics, which reintroduces those 'things' from which spatial relations are abstracted. Russell also mentions the need for a transition from physics to psychology, for physics abstracts matter from perception, though matter 'wholly apart from perception is an absurdity' (OSG 94; cf. also 1894*a*).

It is well known that Russell embarked on the Tiergarten programme with geometry. There is not much, I think, to be read into this fact. Russell was already working on geometry before his walk in the Tiergarten. Moreover, the *logical* order of the dialectic was arithmetic first, then geometry, then physics, and finally psychology and metaphysics. It is not easy to summarize the Tiergarten programme, since its details varied continuously as Russell worked on it. The following, however, is not too inaccurate a sketch of its logical structure. (The necessary qualifications will be introduced in the course of the more detailed study in subsequent chapters.) We start with mathematics of which number is the fundamental concept. The natural numbers presupposed a variety of discrete things which could be enumerated. The real numbers, by contrast, presupposed continuous quantity. The presupposed concepts do not belong to mathematics, so mathematics cannot be regarded as an entirely self-contained science. The required concepts of discrete things and continuous quantity fall, in fact, within the purview of geometry. The possibility of distinguishing a variety of qualitatively diverse items, according to Russell, depends upon projective geometry; while the possibility of measurement, the application of number to continuous quantity, depends upon metrical geometry. Thus the first dialectical transition in Russell's encyclopaedia of the sciences is that from pure mathematics to geometry. Projective geometry provides, without reference to quantity, the qualitatively distinguishable diverse items whose enumeration gives us the natural numbers. Metrical geometry, which is quantitative, deals with continuous (extensive) quantity as required for the real numbers.

But metrical geometry itself cannot be considered a self-contained science either. According to Russell it depends upon the possibility of moving figures without deformation through every part of space. Such figures cannot be provided by geometry itself, for space, on Russell's view, is purely relative, and if geometrical points and figures are defined by relation to other points and figures one can't talk of moving them from place to place. Accordingly a new dialectical transition is needed, this time to kinematics, in order to provide a concept of kinematic matter which is capable of being moved in the way metrical geometry requires. Within physics, there is a further transition, that from kinematics to dynamics. The transition cannot be made directly from geometry to dynamics, since dynamics introduces the concept of force, and forces, once admitted, might cause the deformation of material bodies, thereby vitiating their usefulness for geometrical purposes. The transition from kinematics to dynamics, about which Russell says little, seems to rely entirely upon the law of causality which Russell apparently treats as an a priori principle. If kinematic bodies are to move, there must be causes for their movements; these causes stem from the operation of forces. Thus kinematics itself is incomplete and requires dynamics.

Even a fully dynamic conception of matter, however, is not self-contained. The key problem here is that of absolute motion, which, in the days before Einstein, was thought by most to be required for dynamics. Yet, if space were relative, as Russell had argued at length in dealing with geometry, there could be no absolute position. This defect in physics was to be remedied, Russell hoped, by a transition to psychology, although he said virtually nothing about this transition. He did have hopes, however, that the introduction of the conscious subject would provide a basis for absolute position (rather as it does in Strawson 1959). He also hoped, rather more obscurely, that the concept of force could be replaced by the concept of conation. The resulting metaphysical picture would be some form of monadology, owing more to Lotze and Ward than to Leibniz. The details are the more obscure because, before Russell developed this view, he abandoned the point-atom theory on which his physics had hitherto been based, and attempted a plenal theory of matter. This position, in turn, was abandoned, along with neo-Hegelian metaphysics, before it was worked out in any detail.

The historical order in which Russell worked on his dialectic of the sciences differed from the logical order. Historically, Russell considered geometry first, followed by physics and psychology. His work on pure mathematics seems to have continued throughout the period, starting with investigations of continuous quantity in 1896.

It is worth listing at the outset some of the main features of Russell's dialectic, even though their exact nature and the role they play in his system will not become fully apparent until some of the detailed work is done. As a neo-Hegelian, Russell subscribed to the following interrelated doctrines: (1) each science is incomplete on its own; (2) to be is to have effects; (3) all relations are internal; (4) all aspects of reality are interrelated; (5) to be fully real is to be self-subsistent, i.e. to be capable of existing independently of anything else. The last two theses ensure that only the Absolute is fully real, where 'Absolute' is used in its etymological sense, to refer to that which is not relative. When other philosophers, such as McTaggart or even Bradley, use the term 'Absolute' they intend to refer to an item whose properties are adumbrated by their particular brand of neo-Hegelianism, an item, that is, with a quite definite nature. When Russell uses the term in developing his own philosophy, which is rarely, he uses it in the weaker, etymological sense.

Of all these doctrines, that of internal relations was in many ways the most crucial to Russell's dialectic of the sciences. Russell himself is rarely explicit about the doctrine until after he had abandoned it, and this lack of scrutiny is of some historical importance. For it was only late in his neo-Hegelian period that he realized how many of his troubles stemmed from this one thesis. Russell's doctrine of internal reactions had two parts, both of which Russell attributed to Bradley, though only one was really his. In the first place there was the view that every relation had to be in some way grounded upon the non-relational qualities of its terms. That is, if $a$ has the relation $R$ to $b$ then there must be non-relational features of $a$ and $b$ (i.e. features which can be expressed without reference to any other term) upon which the relation depends. This doctrine is stated by Bradley at least as regards specific cases (cf. 1883: i, 289n.), and is a consequence of his distinction between that aspect of a term which supports a relation and that which results from it (1893a: 26). The second part of Russell's doctrine of internal relations, however, is not to be found in Bradley. This is the view that relations are reducible to non-relational qualities either of their terms individually or of the composite which consists of both their terms taken together. Thus the fact that $a$ has the relation $R$ to $b$ can be expressed in terms of non-relational qualities either of $a$ and $b$ taken individually or of $a$ and $b$ taken together.

It is important to realize, if Russell's neo-Hegelian work is to be understood sympathetically, that when he embarked on his encyclopaedia of the sciences his view of internal relations was by no means so clear as we have made it here. It turns out, as will be shown in detail later, that all the antinomies on which the supersessions of his dialectic turn involve the doctrine of internal relations, and that, with the doctrine, there was no hope of entirely eliminating them. It was this discovery that led Russell to abandon both the doctrine of internal relations and the neo-Hegelianism of which it was an integral part. Nevertheless, the clarity which comes easily with hindsight was not available to Russell as he struggled with the morass of problems into which neo-Hegelianism had led him.

## 3.4 RUSSELL'S MATHEMATICAL DEVELOPMENT (1893–1900)

Russell's mathematical education at Cambridge had left him ill-equipped for research in the foundations of pure mathematics. In so far as the remainder of this book is a success story, it concerns his efforts to re-equip himself for this work. It did not take long for the limitations of his Cambridge education to become apparent, though what he called 'the conceited superiority of the insular Briton' made it a difficult lesson to learn. 'Against my will', he wrote, . . . the belief that everything worth knowing was known in Cambridge gradually wore off'. He came, in particular, 'to realize the superiority of Germany to England in almost all academic matters'—a remark which applied especially to mathematics (*Auto.* i, 133). Ironically enough, he attributed this realization to his visit to America in 1896, and not to his two trips to Germany in 1895 (*MPD* 38). In Germany he met mainly politicians, economists, and philosophers, and had little contact with mathematicians. It was in America that, for the first time, his ideas were exposed to mathematicians who had not been through the Cambridge system. It is not obvious why this experience should have turned him towards *German* mathematics, though Klein's recent lecture trip to the USA may have been influential.

A more direct influence, however, may have been exerted by those mathematicians that Russell met in America who had been through the Cambridge system. At least three of these can be identified, since they attended Russell's lectures on the foundations of geometry at Bryn Mawr in 1896[44] and Russell read some of their works when he got back to England. One was Frank Morley, a friend of Whitehead's. In Part I of his Tripos he had been eighth wrangler—a very respectable result, but one which profoundly disappointed him. When he missed a first in Part II, he had a nervous breakdown. On recovering, he took a job as a school teacher in Britain before moving to the United States where he had a distinguished career, ending up as professor of mathematics at the Johns Hopkins University. Thereafter, he had little time for Cambridge. He sent his sons to Oxford. (See Lowe 1985: 105.) In 1898 he published, along with another Cambridge expatriate, James Harkness, an *Introduction to the Theory of Analytic Functions*, which Russell read early in 1899. Russell never mentions it, but Littlewood (1953: 69–70) recalled reading it as a 'rare interlude' in two and

---

[44] For an account of these lectures see § 4.3 below, and *Papers*, i, 339–43.

a half years wasted on Tripos reading. It was, he complained, 'a bit woolly' on real numbers, but 'this was perhaps hardly avoidable in 1898; nothing my generation ever came across (at any rate in English) had the sharp bracing precision the student gets today.' Both Harkness and Morley attended Russell's lectures, and Russell may well have first heard of Weierstrass from them.[45] They present the theory of functions throughout from a Weierstrassian point of view. They also complain in their preface that current works in English 'show little or no trace' of recent discoveries about the number system (Harkness and Morley 1898: p. vi).

Another former Cambridge student who attended Russell's Bryn Mawr lectures was Charlotte Angas Scott, then professor of mathematics at Bryn Mawr. Her line of work was more closely related to Russell's in 1896, and in 1899, while he was working on the French edition of *EFG*, he read her text *Plane Analytical Geometry* (1894). Scott had taken the Tripos examinations in 1880 and had ranked equal to the eighth wrangler, though, as a woman, she had no official standing. In 1885, equipped with a bachelor's degree and a doctorate from the University of London, she went to Bryn Mawr to establish a mathematics department there (see Lehr 1971). For Russell, the significant point about her textbook was the emphasis she gave to duality principles by treating point and line coordinates simultaneously. Russell appreciated the importance of duality before reading her book in October 1899, but there is no evidence that he had done so before meeting her in 1896. Moreover, around 1899 duality took on an importance for Russell that it had not had previously. He reached this position somewhat before October, however, and his study of Scott's book is more likely to have been a consequence of his adopting it than a cause.

At least part of what Russell learnt from the Germans consisted of up-to-date techniques, especially in analysis. Clearly this was of some importance to him since he graduated from Cambridge knowing nothing of the ε–δ approach in the theory of limits, for example. But from this point of view he might have found French work equally enlightening, for he had graduated without knowing of Cauchy's treatment of limits either. Indeed, he mentions 'several French *Cours d'Analyse*' (a genre in which the French seem to have been especially prolific) among his post-Tripos mathematical reading (*MPD* 39). Clearly Russell had much to learn about nineteenth-century developments in pure mathematics, and the acquisition of this knowledge (largely between 1896 and 1900) was of the first importance for him. But some of it, at any rate, could be learnt at home, for a crucial step in Russell's understanding of the calculus came from reading De Morgan (see § 6.2).

The preponderance of German names on the list of major mathematicians

[45] He complains that he had never heard of Weierstrass until his trip to America (*OE* 242; *MMD* 11).

whose work Russell studied in the last two or three years of the nineteenth century confirms Russell's recollection that his mathematical knowledge was advanced primarily by studying German sources (at least up until 1900, when he discovered Peano and the Italian school). Moreover, his list of works read gives some idea of what he learnt, as far as new mathematical results and techniques were concerned, although, as we shall see in Chapter 6, a number of works were lost on him when he read them for the first time. In some cases, notably Cantor's work, he fought every inch of the way against the new mathematics, as he did with neo-Hegelianism.

Yet new techniques and results were not all that Russell seems to have learnt from his mathematical studies in the 1890s. There was, in addition, something rather harder to isolate, namely a new approach to mathematics. It had to do with the increasing generality, abstractness, and rigour of nineteenth-century pure mathematics. This trend was one Russell caught up with very rapidly during the second half of the decade under consideration, for his initial training at Cambridge did little to prepare him for it.

Joan Richards, on the basis of a study of nineteenth-century British algebra, has distinguished an insular British tradition in mathematics (1980; 1988). Her starting-point was the question why British algebra, despite a promising beginning in the nineteenth century at the hands of George Peacock, Augustus de Morgan, and others, never developed into a fully abstract system such as is found in modern algebra. Her answer was that the British algebraists were working within a conception of mathematics which inhibited the development of the modern, fully abstract, point of view. British mathematicians tended to view mathematics as similar to other sciences in that its purpose was to provide a correct theoretical description of a particular subject-matter. Thus, just as kinematics is the study of motion, arithmetic is the study of quantity, and geometry the study of space. The concept of truth is of special importance, in obvious ways, in this view of mathematics. Truth in mathematics, as in the other sciences, consists in correspondence with the facts of the subject-matter.

The subject-matter initially constrains the development of mathematical science, but with increasing generality the rules of the science yield results which are not readily interpretable on the original subject-matter. In such cases, the result is held by some mathematicians to be meaningless unless an interpretation can be provided, and by others to be devoid of interest. At all events, the situation was not to be tolerated if it could be avoided, for the algebraic results were only really understood when interpreted. Thus, new developments (and some old ones) tended to be treated cautiously until an interpretation was in prospect. (Chapter 6 is in part taken up with Russell's efforts to provide an interpretation in the notion of quantity for negative and imaginary numbers, which were generated by arithmetical algebra but not easily understood in terms of quantity.) Mathematicians, however, were not anxious to choke off abstraction altogether and often divided the various branches of mathematics into two parts: one concerned with the abstract application of rules, the other with the interpretation of the results on the subject-matter of the relevant branch of mathematics. Thus De Morgan (1837) spoke of the 'art' of algebra, which was concerned with the derivation of results from specified rules, and the 'science' of algebra which was concerned with interpretation (see Richards 1987). Whewell (1840: i, 150) drew a parallel distinction between 'synthesis' and 'analysis'. Russell's treatment of geometry included just such a distinction: between a (genuine) geometry which was synthetic a priori, and an algebra which was analytic (see §4.2). Both parts, however, were regarded as essential to mathematics.

This view of mathematics, which I shall call the descriptive approach, is quite different from the abstract point of view which is often taken to be that of modern mathematics, in which results are derived from an axiom system, often said to be in some sense 'arbitrary', with no regard for their possible interpretation. On the abstract view, the idea that mathematical theories are about some subject-matter is rejected. They are purely formal structures, having no content, and inviting a range of equally appropriate interpretations. In consequence the concept of truth has little or no role to play. Its place, as a major constraint on theory construction, is taken by the concepts of completeness and consistency. Theorems are said to be interesting, not in virtue of their applications, but essentially for aesthetic reasons such as 'depth', 'elegance', and 'power'. There is certainly something to be said for Richards's distinction between these two different views of mathematics. The sort of distinction she draws, though not necessarily the terms in which she draws it, is almost a commonplace even in mathematics textbooks. For example, a distinction is sometimes drawn between the traditional style of axiomatics, exemplified by Euclid, and the modern, exemplified by Hilbert. The defining features of each vary with the author, but the following is typical. In traditional axiomatics primitive terms are explained with a view to suggesting their meaning to the reader; all other terms are defined in terms of the primitives. Axioms are stated concerning the primitives, which, though unproved, are held to be true in virtue of the nature of the primitives as revealed by the preliminary explanation. Other propositions are derived from the axioms and are held to be true in virtue of being so derived. In modern axiomatics, by contrast, the primitive terms are not only undefined but unexplained. They get whatever meaning they have from the axioms. The axioms are taken simply as postulates: they are not asserted to be true, and are not assumed to have any intrinsic evidence in virtue of the primitive terms which occur in them. Rules are specified for the manipulation of symbols. All non-primitive symbols are defined. Other propositions are derived from the axioms by means of the rules.[46] This distinction between traditional and modern axiomatization has a clear relation to the distinction between the descriptive and the abstract traditions in mathematics.

The great attraction of the abstract approach was the wealth of important and powerful results it generated, especially results which unified apparently unrelated branches of mathematics. Throughout the nineteenth century these developments continuously threatened to overwhelm whatever interpretative base the descriptive approach might provide. Paying undue attention to matters of interpretation seemed likely to choke off the growth of mathematical knowledge, leaving the subject confined to its elementary branches and such higher concerns as might be of use to physicists and engineers. It was difficult for research mathematicians in the late nineteenth century to concern themselves overmuch with questions of interpretation. At the same time even those branches of mathematics which were a clear necessity for physicists and engineers, notably the calculus, posed interpretational problems which had defied the best mathematical and philosophical minds for centuries. Ironically, it was precisely here, in the foundations of analysis, where one might have expected the virtues of the descriptive approach to be most evident in providing a clear conceptualization, that the abstract point of view claimed some of its major victories. By pursuing a rigorous approach to the definition of concepts such as that of a limit, and eschewing all attempts at intuitive conceptualization, late nineteenth-century analysts were able finally to achieve a clarification of fundamental concepts that could be generally accepted as definitive.

Returning to the terms in which Richards draws the distinction, we have two contrasting views of mathematics: the descriptive and the abstract. The descriptive view regards each branch of mathematics as having a subject-matter, while the abstract view does not. Stemming from this difference is a difference in the concept of truth each employs: the former adopts a correspondence theory, and the latter a form of the coherence theory (or perhaps, in its more hard core varieties, denies that the concept of truth is applicable to mathematical propositions). Richards's chief concern is to relate the descriptive mathematical tradition to broader themes in British intellectual life in the nineteenth century: in particular, to show the influence of widely held philosophical beliefs on the way mathematics were conceived. Her account has a clear bearing on Cambridge mathematics. The great emphasis on applied mathematics in the Cambridge Tripos was partly for social and educational reasons. But these were reinforced by philosophical considerations of the sort that Richards adduces. There is indeed some

---

[46] Cf. the distinction between 'material' and 'formal' axiomatics in Eves and Newsom (1965: 15) and compare Richards (1979: 148–9).

question whether Richards's British tradition in nineteenth-century algebra wasn't just a *Cambridge* tradition. All the mathematicians she considers (Peacock, De Morgan, Whewell, and Herschel) were part of what Susan Cannon (1978) has called 'the Cambridge Network'. This fact alone would make it surprising if Russell's own attitude to mathematics had not been influenced by the descriptive tradition.

Richards has applied her account specifically to Russell's treatment of geometry in a subsequent paper (Richards 1984; 1988). Of all branches of pure mathematics, geometry seemed the most amenable to the descriptive approach. For it seemed intuitively obvious that geometry was the science of space. Euclid's definitions served to clarify and specify precisely certain pre-theoretical spatial notions (A typical view of definition was that it turned confused and vague 'notions' into clear and precise 'concepts'.) Euclid's axioms were basic true propositions about space, and the theorems to be derived from them were further true propositions about space. This attractive picture was seriously challenged by the development of non-Euclidean geometries. It seemed impossible that they could be regarded as alternative true descriptions of space. But if they were false descriptions of space they seemed entirely devoid of interest. There seemed to be as little point in studying false systems of geometry as in studying false systems of astronomy. Undoubtedly, this view helped keep non-Euclidean geometries in relative obscurity for several decades. Certainly it served to exclude them from the Cambridge syllabus until after Russell had taken the Tripos.

Richards places Russell more or less firmly in the descriptive tradition as far as geometry is concerned, in her view a resolutely British tradition. The only real exception to this that she admits belongs to the time in which Russell first discovered projective geometry. At this time, she believes, he came under abstract continental influences (notably Klein 1890; von Staudt 1847), which led to the position he took in the notes, 'Observations on Space and Geometry' (OSG), written between March and June 1895. In contrast, she claims *EFG* reverts to the British descriptive tradition. She sees significance in the fact that Russell started to write OSG while he was in Berlin. On his return to Britain, she says his allegiance to the British tradition became 'even more pronounced' (Richards 1984: 42–3). There is too much emphasis on geography here. Russell left Berlin soon after starting OSG (and probably before he got to projective geometry) and he seems not to have made contact with the German mathematical community while in Berlin. So whatever influence there was must have come from books and journals. The writings which influenced him towards abstraction were not exclusively German, as Richards concedes. For he was much influenced by Ball's theory of the content (Ball 1887) a work which broke (though not completely) with the descriptive tradition in projective geometry. Moreover, Richards seems to overestimate the degree of abstraction Russell was prepared to tolerate in 'Observations'.

None the less, Richards has hit on an important point, though one which is apt to be obscured by too close an association with regional influences. An understanding of the descriptive tradition in mathematics is essential for a sympathetic view of Russell's mathematical work, both before and after 1900. The problems with which he struggled during his neo-Hegelian period were often those which were bequeathed to him by the descriptive tradition; and those he struggled with later were often, from the point of view of the abstract approach, exacerbated by assumptions he brought with him from mid-nineteenth-century Cambridge. There is nothing unduly surprising in this. Indeed, it would have been extraordinary if he had been able to shrug off his Cambridge background completely, however much he might have come to despise it. At the same time I don't think that Russell's mathematical work, even as a neo-Hegelian, can be understood simply as part of the descriptive tradition. As so often happened in Russell's life and career he was drawn in more than one direction at once.

Between 1893 and 1900 and slightly beyond Russell was influenced both by the primarily descriptive view of mathematics he gained from Cambridge and by a view closer to that which Richards associates with continental abstraction. During that period the descriptive view gradually gave way to abstraction, though the process was not always smooth. Interpretation, for Russell, remained one of the central tasks of the *philosophy* of mathematics; though after 1899 he seems to have thought it not one of the tasks of mathematics itself. In addition to this change in the division of labour, there was also a change in emphasis. Early in the process, interpretation played a controlling role. In 1893 and for a few years afterwards, he was prepared to dismiss branches of mathematics, in typical nineteenth-century Cambridge fashion, as of no interest (or of merely 'algebraical' interest) on account of failures of interpretation. Subsequently, interpretation was dragged along behind the abstract development of the science. That a branch of mathematics, for example, real number theory, was not interpretable on the quantity interpretation of number, reflected adversely on the interpretation, not on the mathematics. The defect was to be made good by a more adequate philosophy of mathematics.[47]

All Russell's work in philosophy of mathematics was concerned with matters of interpretation, and the development of new areas of mathematics (outside logic) was not his concern. To modern mathematicians working firmly in the abstract, algebraic approach his work is frequently regarded as

[47] There was one respect, at least, in which Russell's development was a return to Newtonian Cambridge, and this was his adoption of an absolute theory of space after 1898 (cf. FIAM 270; 1900).

an irrelevance (witness, for example, the fulminations of the *Bourbakistes* against him). But it is important to realize that, in this, he is being criticized for not doing what he never attempted to do. Whether what he attempted was of importance depends upon what the proper tasks of a philosophy of mathematics are, and whether philosophy of mathematics in any form is worth doing. Russell, in his attitude to mathematics, as in his politics and epistemology, combined nineteenth- and twentieth-century strands of thought. This is hardly surprising since he was not born to twentieth-century thought, but was one of those who helped to create it. The tension created by these often conflicting elements in his intellectual make-up gave him the problems on which he worked, and his efforts to overcome them gave him his unique historical importance—few, if any, other thinkers have spanned the two centuries in quite so many different fields.

It is not so clear, however, that the issues which Richards uses to distinguish the British from the continental tradition are really those which were in the forefront of Russell's mind as he made the transition. What seems crucial from Russell's point of view is the question of the role of intuition in mathematics. This is not entirely separate from the issues Richards mentions, but it is not exactly the same either, and, whatever may be the case about the difference between British and continental mathematicians, so far as Russell was concerned the question of intuition was the one which drove his philosophy of mathematics forward. Seeing Russell's work in this way will help to explain why, during this period, he came to be so impressed by German mathematics, rather than German philosophy or German philosophy of mathematics. In fact, the changes in Russell's views on intuition can be linked (rather too simply, however) with a rejection of German philosophy inspired by newly acquired knowledge of German mathematics.

The role that intuition played in the philosophy of mathematics in the nineteenth century was one part of Kant's enormous legacy. According to Kant, the propositions of mathematics depend upon the existence of pure intuitions, pure forms of sensibility, which are given a priori in the mind. They are arrived at neither by empirical nor by logical means, but through the operation of our intuition. This was taken to explain the fact that they were not analytic, and yet were apodeictically certain. Mathematical propositions were (literally) intuitively certain. This was taken to include, for example, all the propositions of Euclidean geometry (for it was held to be intuitively certain that two straight lines could not enclose a space). Exactly what this intuitive certainty amounted to was never made quite clear, but generally, it was supposed that a proposition was intuitively certain if one could not conceive of, or imagine, or (in the case of space) visualize, its negation.

Throughout the nineteenth century, this doctrine received repeated shocks as mathematics developed. Historically the first shock, and the only one widely known to philosophers by the 1890s, was the development of non-Euclidean geometries. But perhaps even more important was Weierstrass's discovery of a continuous curve that was nowhere differentiable (Weierstrass 1872), thus refuting what was held to be intuitively obvious, that any continuous curve must have a tangent at most points, if not at every point. Another famous example was the Peano curve which filled a plane (Peano 1890).[48] These 'pathological cases', as they were often called, brought the concept of intuition into disrepute. By the end of the century James Pierpont could list eight intuitively obvious properties of a curve and produce a counter-example to each one (Pierpont 1899). Each counter-example was logically consistent but, by showing that a curve may consistently lack one or more of the features intuitively assigned to it, demonstrated that the intuitive concept of a curve was not coherently defined. The elaboration of such cases opened up a gap between intuition and formal logic. It had never been assumed that the deliverances of the two would be identical—in that case intuition would not have been necessary—but it had not been expected that logic would ever undermine what was supported by intuition.

The concept of intuition came under philosophical attack as well, for its epistemological status was anything but clear. If one took seriously Kant's remarks about pure intuition being given a priori in the mind, then it seemed that intuition was simply a matter of cognitive psychology. But the facts of psychology are certainly a contingent matter, and thus, if mathematics depends upon intuition in this sense, mathematical truths must themselves be contingent. On the other hand, if intuition is not merely a psychological fact, is it a matter of logic? But it was precisely the fact that mathematical propositions were thought not to be purely logical that occasioned the need for intuition in the first place. Either way, the doctrine seemed trapped.[49]

The consequence of these developments was that the concept of intuition fell into decline. Since it had led people so badly astray, it would have to be abandoned. In its place mathematicians began to insist that mathematics must depend only upon purely logical derivation. Initially, logic was not sufficiently developed to take on this task. But in its place arithmetic was taken to be reliable where geometrical intuition was not. This led to the

---

[48] Russell also noted that, when he read Peano's works in 1900, he liked the space-filling curve and also, significantly, that he liked Peano's treatment of geometry without the use of diagrams 'thus displaying the needlessness of Kant's *Anschauung*' (*MPD* 56). Russell probably had Peano (1888) in mind.

[49] Russell tried in *EFG* to find some middle way between these two approaches, and Moore convinced him a year or two later that he had failed (see below, § 4.4).

arithmetization of mathematics and ultimately, as logic itself developed, to logicism and formalism.[50]

This intuitional view of mathematics fits well with the descriptive view Richards outlines, though they are not the same. The intuitional approach is essentially through epistemology, whereas the descriptive view, being concerned with interpretation, is more semantic in orientation. The two marks of the descriptive view—the interpretation of mathematics on a subject-matter and the correspondence theory of truth—are not essential features of the intuitional view. For example, the intuitional view need not regard the appropriate pure intuitions as being the subject-matter of a mathematical theory, and thus the question of whether the propositions of the theory are true simply *because* they correspond to the intuition need not arise. (Conformity to intuition may be a necessary but not a sufficient condition for truth.) On the other hand, the two views are linked, for the doctrine of intuition constrains what can be admitted as an interpretation on the descriptive view.

My concern here is solely with Russell, however, and it seems to me that Russell's development during the 1890s is more clearly seen in terms of intuition than in terms of subject-matter, whatever may be the case with other mathematicians and philosophers of the period. In a paper of 1893 (EPII) to be discussed in § 4.2, Russell was prepared to embrace the whole Kantian doctrine of intuition as far as geometry was concerned. This committed him to the apodeictic certainty of Euclidean geometry. Non-Euclidean geometries, though recognized as logically consistent, were denied status as geometries and admitted merely as formal algebraic systems. In later writings, notably *EFG*, the intuitive restraints were relaxed somewhat to admit a (restricted) range of geometries as in accord with our space intuitions. Very typically what Russell took to be philosophically interesting in a science was that which depended upon intuition; the rest was of purely algebraic concern. As his work developed, however, Russell came to regard intuition as of less and less importance. Even early on Russell was somewhat ambivalent about intuition, as his occasional gestures in the direction of formalism show (e.g. EPII 126; *EFG* 44). Further evidence is provided by his early interest in Grassmann, whose scouting of intuition in his calculus of extension is praised by Nagel (1939) (although neither Russell nor Nagel

[50] The classic popular account of the decline of intuition is Hahn (1933). An excellent survey of its decline in geometry which stresses the role of projective geometry is Nagel (1939). The subsequent history of the concept is of some interest. Faced with its general rejection, Kant loyalists (notably Hintikka in an impressively long series of papers, but see his (1969) and (1972) to get started) have claimed that Kant's notion of intuition is much broader than usually supposed, amounting essentially to existential instantiation. Accordingly, Hintikka can claim that Kant's own position is not impugned by Hahn's crisis in intuition. More recently still, intuition (though no longer tied to the philosophy of Kant) has made something of a come-back, e.g. Volkert (1986), Kitcher (1983), Kline (1985).

seem to have recognized that in Grassmann's dialectic a priori sciences are balanced by empirical or intuitional ones). For Russell, however, these isolated features of his early work never really bore fruit until he read Whitehead (1898*a*). From this point of view, 'Observations on Space and Geometry' fits smoothly into Russell's development, contrary to what Richards suggests. As might be expected from a Kantian, he criticizes Riemann's treatment of space, despite its admitted mathematical brilliance, as 'very ill-fitted to settle what space-conception we require to fit our space-perceptions' and claims that it thus trades geometrical truth for logical self-consistency (OSG 67–8). Similarly he criticizes Helmholtz for ignoring 'the living *intuition*' required for the visual imaginability of non-Euclidean spaces (OSG 85). As regards projective geometry, Russell denies its philosophical significance in OSG, a position he reversed (apparently under Whitehead's guidance) in *EFG*. This change also depends upon intuition—Russell only later discovered an intuitive basis for projective geometry, in the Kantian notion of a form of externality (cf. § 4.5).

In 1897 and 1898 Russell was approaching arithmetic in much the same way: by attempting to answer the Kantian question, 'How is pure mathematics possible?' Little survives of his properly foundational work of 1897 on this question, but in 1898 he seems to have the intention of pursuing it by means of a transcendental deduction of parts of pure mathematics from the possibility of (various types of) judgements. In some respects, this was an anticipation of logicism, although the central claim of logicism, that pure mathematics is reducible to logic, had not yet made an appearance, and Russell's logic at the time was in any case too underdeveloped to support it. Moreover, the historical record is made more confused by Moore's complaints (Moore 1899*b*) that Russell's previous use of intuition and associated devices such as transcendental arguments were merely examples of a well-disguised psychologism. Russell took these criticisms to heart, as we shall see at the end of this volume, and they produced a striking realignment in his treatment of mathematics. But they did not result immediately in his conversion to logicism. Instead, just before embracing logicism, Russell in 1899–1900 seems to have embraced an extreme of formalism that might have put Hilbert to shame.[51] He propounded (in AOG) an abstract axiomatization of projective geometry which made absolutely no concessions to intuition—the axiomatization was faulty and its development dropped from the published version of the paper, but there is no doubt that in it Russell eschewed intuition with a hardihood that few at that time would equal.[52]

[51] Remember, in Hilbert (1899), his acknowledgement of intuition in § 1, his Kantian epigraph, and his claim in the introduction that his task was 'the logical analysis of our perception of space'.

[52] It is not surprising that this formalist outburst should have occurred in his work on

It is this formalism, rather than Russell's better known logicism, which represents the extreme antithesis of his earlier intuitional approach. It is still not a complete antithesis, but it is as far as Russell got from his Kantian origins, and not many others got much further. Russell repudiates intuition in both his main works of 1899: 'The Fundamental Ideas and Axioms of Mathematics' and the draft of *The Principles of Mathematics*. His treatment of the calculus in the latter work begins with an extended criticism of intuition, 'that lazy limbo of mystery'.[53] While in the theory of space and time there is '[n]o need of intuition any more than in arithmetic' (FIAM 270). The position Russell defends there will, he says, 'be completely destructive of Kant's intuitional a priori' (POM/D, Pt. VI, fo. 2). In Russell's logicism, at least in its early forms, the propositions of mathematics were again synthetic a priori truths, mathematics had a subject-matter in the realm of subsistent, abstract, logical objects, and intuition was reintroduced as the logical intuition of these abstract entities and their relations. The primitive concepts of mathematics, for example, were admitted to be indefinable, but were still the subject of a long propaedeutic discussion 'in order that the mind may have that kind of acquaintance with them which it has with redness or the taste of a pineapple' (POM: p. xv). These developments are beyond the scope of this book. But Russell's own crisis of intuition during the 1890s is an essential part of our story, although at times it underlies, rather than dominates, the action. His coming to learn of the work of German mathematicians, especially their construction of pathological examples, was the main driving force in the early stages of this development. Moore's criticism of the whole structure and foundations of Kant's philosophy later forced him to recognize that the situation could not be repaired by replacing one set of Kantian intuitions by another—which had earlier been his approach.

One of the things which makes Russell's development in the 1890s so interesting is that, within the space of seven years, he moves from a full-blooded Kantian position, such as might have been widely accepted at the beginning of the century, to a complete rejection of Kant, a position which was not common even among the advanced mathematicians of the time. In short Russell's intellectual development between 1893 and 1899 encapsulates the declining fortunes of Kantian intuition among nineteenth-century mathematicians. The course of this development will be traced in the ensuing chapters.

projective geometry, because for Russell, as for many rank and file formalists, the duality principles of projective geometry were an important source of inspiration.

[53] POM/D, Pt. V, fo. 1. The unpublished POM/D manuscript is foliated by part. See also POM/D, Pt. V, fo. 67; FIAM 270.

# 4

# Geometry

## 4.1 'YONDER SOPHISTICAL PHILISTINE'[1]

Apart from the lessons in Euclid he received from his brother, very little is known of Russell's education in geometry. The available facts can be summed up briefly. He seems to have exhibited no special interest in, nor aptitude for, geometry as a mathematics student. In 1890 he recorded in his diary that geometry was not his strong point (LD 47). Although he knew of non-Euclidean geometry by the time he was 14, he did not study it until he was working for the Moral Sciences Tripos (FF 42), even though the first question of one of his Mathematical Tripos papers was very obliquely on the topic. None the less, it is not difficult to see why he wrote his fellowship dissertation on the philosophy of geometry. It had been for many years a very important topic of philosophical discussion.

For several hundred years there had been epistemological interest in geometry, not so much because it yielded important epistemological problems, but rather because, in some ways, it was thought to be completely devoid of them; in particular it seemed devoid of those occasions for doubt that formed the basis of philosophical scepticism. Geometry, and the geometrical (or deductive) method was seen, by philosophers as different as Descartes, Spinoza, and Hobbes, as an important source of certainty. In the nineteenth century, however, this confidence was shaken by the development of non-Euclidean geometries. The development of the new geometries led to new philosophical debates on the logical and epistemic status of geometric propositions, and ultimately to important new insights into axiomatics and the philosophy of mathematics. These debates were exacerbated by the philosophical dominance of Kant, who had argued that the propositions of Euclidean geometry were synthetic a priori truths, a prerequisite for the mere possibility of external perception. This clash between the entrenched philosophy of Kant and the new developments in mathematics made geometry a major source of philosophical perplexity in the nineteenth century.

The philosophy of geometry at the time when Kant entered the debate was of major interest to both rationalists and empiricists. The propositions of geometry, although universally admitted, did not fit easily with either view. On the one hand, geometric relations seemed to be in some way

---

[1] Cantor's description of Kant (*Auto.* i, 217).

clearly exhibited by the spatial relations of physical objects, but, on the other, physical objects could not be identified with the objects studied in geometry which were said (misleadingly) to be 'ideal'. Again, while it seemed clear that geometrical propositions were not analytic (true by virtue of the meanings of the words employed in them), it was felt that the propositions of Euclidean geometry were epistemologically more certain and logically more necessary than inductive generalizations from experience. Kant's important contribution to the philosophy of geometry can be seen as an attempt to preserve what seemed correct in both positions.

In the 'Transcendental Aesthetic' Kant starts, in a manner not dissimilar to that of the empiricists, with the representation of physical objects in intuition. The empirical object of a sensory intuition Kant calls 'appearance'. He distinguishes between the matter and the form of appearance in quite a different way than empiricists who made this distinction: the matter is that 'which corresponds to sensation' whereas the form is 'that which so determines the manifold of appearance that it allows of being ordered in certain relations'.[2] While the matter is thus given a posteriori, the form concerns the structure of sensory intuition itself and constitutes a necessary condition for the possibility of sensory intuition and must, therefore, be found, Kant says, '*a priori* in the mind'. A cognitive state, or representation (*Vorstellung*), is said to be *pure* when it contains 'nothing that belongs to sensation' (A20 = B34). There are two pure forms of sensory intuition or sensibility: space and time (A22 = B36). Thus the form of appearance consists of the spatio-temporal relations between the elements (sometimes called 'sense-data', e.g. by Ward 1922*a*: 42; Copleston 1960: 32) of the manifold of sensory intuition or sensibility. Kant distinguishes an internal and an external sense: the external sense is that by which we 'represent to ourselves objects as outside us', and the internal sense is that by which 'the mind intuits itself or its inner state' (A22 = B37). Space is the form of the external sense, time of the internal sense. Since all representations belong to the inner state, time 'is the formal *a priori* condition of all appearances whatsoever' (A34 = B50), while space is the a priori condition of external appearances.

It is now not difficult to see how Kant will resolve the dilemmas with which we started. The propositions of geometry are a priori and certain because they concern a form of intuition which is given a priori in the mind. They are necessary in the sense that their truth is a formal precondition of experience. But they are not necessary in Kant's other use of the term, since they cannot be shown to be true by analysing the meanings of the words contained in them. They are, therefore, synthetic and a priori.

---

[2] Kant 1781: B34. In the 1st edn. the form of appearance is given differently as 'that which causes the manifold of appearance to be intuited as ordered in certain relations' (A20). The reasons for the switch are convincingly explained by Kemp Smith (1923: 85).

Kant seeks to demonstrate the necessity of his theory of space by means of a transcendental argument. In such arguments the necessity of a proposition is established by showing that it asserts a condition for the possibility of some established body of knowledge. Kant's theory of space is used, as we have seen, to answer the question, how is it possible that the propositions of geometry are synthetic a priori? Kant maintains (though the uniqueness claim is clearly suspect) that his 'explanation is thus the only explanation that makes intelligible the *possibility* of geometry, as a body of *a priori* synthetic knowledge' (B41). Thus the necessity of Kant's doctrine of space is (allegedly) established by appeal to the synthetic a priori nature of geometry. Moreover, the necessity of geometry is established by a further transcendental argument, since it is maintained that space is a precondition for the possibility of external sensory intuition, and thus for all knowledge about the external world. Consequently, the concept of space cannot be an empirical concept derived from the external world, and must be a priori and subjective. But what is a priori and subjective can be known with apodeictic certainty. Consequently, geometry, the science of space, is apodeictically certain. Russell describes Kant's position succinctly as follows: 'On the one hand, he says, Geometry is known to have apodeictic certainty: therefore space must be *a priori* and subjective. On the other hand, it follows, from grounds independent of Geometry, that space is subjective and *a priori*; therefore Geometry must have apodeictic certainty' (*EFG* 55–6; cf. also *EFG* 1, OSG/P 260).

Russell maintains (*EFG* 56) that, of the two arguments, the development of non-Euclidean geometry has undermined the argument from the apodeictic certainty of geometry, but that it has not undermined Kant's other argument, that (Euclidean) geometry is certain because space is subjective and *a priori*. Non-Euclidean geometry has shown only that Euclidean geometry is not *logically* necessary; it has not shown that it is not necessary in Kant's other sense. This concession, however, does Kant little good in Russell's eyes, for Russell denies both that space is subjective and that whatever is subjective and a priori must be known with apodeictic certainty (OSG/P 259).

In dealing with both arguments Russell clearly assumes that Kant thought that it was Euclidean geometry which had apodeictic certainty. But so far nothing has been said which commits Kant to this restriction. We may grant that the objects of external sensibility necessarily are intuited as having spatial relations, but it by no means follows that they necessarily are intuited as having Euclidean spatial relations.[3] Yet it seems clear that it was precisely

---

[3] This point was made by Helmholtz (1878: 213), who in many ways can be regarded as a neo-Kantian: '[T]he representation of all external objects in space-relations may be the only possible form in which we can represent the simultaneous existence of a number of discrete objects, though there is no necessity that a particular space-perception should co-exist with or

Kant's view that Euclidean geometry was apodeictically certain. He claims 'indisputably [to] prove that all external objects of our world of sense must necessarily coincide in the most rigorous way with the propositions of geometry' (1783: 31). And, again, more explicitly:

[T]he space of the geometer is exactly the form of sensuous intuition which we find *a priori* in us, and contains the ground of the possibility of all external appearances (according to their form); and the latter must necessarily and most precisely agree with the propositions of the geometer, which he draws not from any fictitious concept but from the subjective basis of all external appearance, viz., sensibility itself. In this and no other way can geometry be made secure as to the undoubted objective reality of its propositions . . . (1783: 32).

Historical context, if nothing else, makes it clear that by 'geometry' Kant means Euclidean geometry. Textual evidence which excludes non-Euclidean geometry occurs in the *Critique* (A716 = B744) where he refers to Euclid's 32nd proposition, the proof of which requires the parallel postulate. In so far as Euclidean geometry is treated by Kant as a necessary condition for the possibility of spatial representation, and thus for the possibility of empirical knowledge, it follows that non-Euclidean geometries are spatially inconceivable, and excluded by the mere possibility of empirical knowledge.

It is ironical that, as Kant was coming to this conclusion, mathematicians were coming to the view that non-Euclidean geometries were conceivable. Indeed, Saccheri (1733) had already considered a non-Euclidean geometry (in fact a fragment of Bolyai–Lobachevski geometry) in an attempt at an indirect proof of the parallel postulate; but Saccheri had come to orthodox Euclidean conclusions. It was only after Kant's death that full-fledged alternatives to Euclidean geometry were proposed in the works of Lobachevski (1829), Gauss (1828), and Bolyai (1832). Even then, this work did not become well-known until the publication of Gauss's correspondence (1860). That this publication should have coincided with the birth of the 'back to Kant' movement in German philosophy[4] compounds the irony. The conflict between the non-Euclidean geometers and the neo-Kantians, however, was only part of the philosophical debate about the nature and status of geometry which erupted in Germany in the 1870s. In this, Riemann's work was an important catalyst, especially when developed and, above all, popularized

follow upon certain others . . . By Kant, indeed, the proof that space is an *a priori* form is based essentially on the position that the axioms are synthetic propositions *a priori*. But even if this assertion with the dependent inference is dropt, the space-representation might still be the necessary *a priori* form in which every co-extended manifold is perceived. This is not surrendering any essential feature of the Kantian system.' In this view he seems to have had the support of Riemann (1854). See also Erdmann 1877: 105.

[4] For a history of the back-to-Kant movement see Willey (1978), which is, however, primarily concerned with its impact on social and political thought.

by Helmholtz and his student, Erdmann. German thinkers dominated the discussion in the 1870s and 1880s, but in the 1890s the debate moved to France. In 1897, when Russell published *EFG*, Britain was still not seriously involved. It was the German contribution which provided the stimulus for Russell, but it was in France that Russell's work was read with most interest.

Given the development of non-Euclidean geometry and its subsequent utilization in physics, it seems that Kant was simply mistaken in maintaining the a priori necessity of Euclidean geometry. However, by the time non-Euclidean geometries became well known to philosophers, neo-Kantianism was institutionally well entrenched, and the neo-Kantians were not prepared to give up any doctrine of their mentor without a struggle. Faced with this conflict there are three ways, short of simply abandoning Kant, in which a resolution may be attempted: the first is to maintain, appearances to the contrary notwithstanding, that Kant did not deny the possibility of non-Euclidean geometry. This is now the most commonly maintained Kantian line (cf. Buchdahl 1969: 609–15). The second line is perhaps the most interesting, for it involves modifying Kant's doctrine in such a way as to preserve many of its key features, and yet remove the clash with non-Euclidean geometries. This line has not been popular, but Russell's early work on geometry is probably the most extended attempt to bring it off (see below §§ 4.4–4.5). It is worth noting that Poincaré (1898) also attempted what can be naturally construed as such a repair of the Kantian position (a fact obliquely noted by Russell 1914: 53). Poincaré, however, in early work located the a priori element of geometry in the concept of an abstract group. He differed from Kant in maintaining that it was a product of the understanding and not a form of intuition (1898: 41–3). Later he turned his attention to topology and located the a priori in geometry there (1912: 42–4). The third and most futile approach is simply to deny the coherence, consistency, conceivability, or intelligibility of non-Euclidean geometries. Unfortunately, it was this third line which appealed most to the nineteenth-century neo-Kantians and on which Russell at first embarked in his study of the foundations of geometry (§ 4.2).

A number of texts might be appealed to by those who wish to maintain that Kant was not, after all, committed to the rejection of non-Euclidean geometry. It is true that in his early writings Kant espoused a relationist view of space, in which the structural properties of space are determined by the dynamic inter-reactions of particles (Kant 1746). Torretti (1978: 65) suggests that some of Lobachevski's speculations concerning the physical application of non-Euclidean geometries bear a marked similarity to these early speculations of Kant. However, the relationist theory of space was clearly and decisively rejected in the *Critique* and, even earlier, in the *Dissertation* (1770). Kant's critical philosophy cannot be defended by appeal to the earlier writings.

Alternatively, it may be pointed out that, while Kant maintained that Euclidean space is an a priori representation of the *human* mind, he does admit the possibility that other beings have different forms of intuition: 'For we cannot judge in regard to the intuitions of other thinking beings, whether they are bound by the same conditions as those which limit our intuition and which for us are universally valid' (A27 = B43). But what Kant is claiming here is not that the intuition of other thinking beings may be bound by non-Euclidean forms of intuition, but that they may not be bound by spatial conditions at all. None the less, it is an initially attractive, if ultimately unavailing, modification of Kant's view (which originated with Helmholtz, according to Beck 1967) to admit the possibility that other beings have non-Euclidean forms of intuition. This issue was raised in some of the nineteenth-century debates on the subject, and it appears briefly in one of Russell's earliest writings on non-Euclidean geometry (EPII 127; see § 4.2 below).

Kant's claim that the propositions of geometry are not analytic has given scope, in various ways, for the claim that his theory did not exclude non-Euclidean geometries. This is done by noting that, since the propositions of Euclidean geometry are not analytic and therefore not logically necessary, the propositions of non-Euclidean geometry are not logically impossible (cf. Buchdahl 1969: 611). Kant has at least two senses of 'analytic'. On the one hand, he maintains that analytic propositions are those which can be derived from the law of non-contradiction alone (e.g. A151 = B190); on the other, that analytic propositions are those in which the predicate is contained in the subject (e.g. A7 = B10).[5] On either view, the propositions of Euclidean geometry are clearly not analytic. Non-Euclidean geometries are thus (in one of Kant's senses) possible.[6] But in the other, and for present purposes more important, sense, namely that in which the possible is that which is consistent with the a priori requirements of knowledge, they are impossible.

[5] Russell was to criticize both accounts severely. On the one hand, he maintained that no proposition follows from the law of non-contradiction alone, 'except the proposition that there is truth, or that some proposition is true' (*POL* 22); on the other, that a proposition in which the subject contained the predicate either presupposed some non-analytic proposition (*POL*, 18) or else was a tautology and thus not a genuine proposition at all (*POL*, 17). Kant's second definition is, in any case, too restrictive as it stands, since many geometrical propositions are not of subject–predicate form. However, we may consider the account amended to the more generous claim that analytic propositions are true by virtue of the meanings of their constituent words.

[6] Saccheri (1733) had shown, albeit unintentionally, that the negation of the parallel postulate does not yield a contradiction in conjunction with the first 26 propositions of Euclid (the proofs of which do not depend upon the parallel postulate), and a fortiori does not yield a contradiction on its own. Saccheri had, in effect, provided an independence proof of the parallel postulate. Leonard Nelson (1927: 162–4) uses the possibility of independence proofs in mathematics and logic, as well as in geometry, to argue for the syntheticity of the whole of mathematics, thus claiming a striking vindication of Kant.

Russell distinguishes the two senses clearly (*EFG* 56).[7] The distinction is
crucial to his interpretation of Kant. It is interesting to note that J. H. Lambert,
a friend of Kant's who had done work similar to Saccheri's, dismissed the
alternative geometries, not on the ground that they were logically inconsistent,
but on the ground that they were incompatible with what he called 'the
representation of the subject-matter' (*Vorstellung der Sache*) (Lambert
1766). This was clearly a view somewhat similar to Kant's, namely that non-
Euclidean geometries are *logically* possible, but *objectively* impossible,
since they do not conform to the requirements of geometric representation.

It is only by ignoring the distinction between these two senses of 'possibility'
that Williamson is able to claim that 'the existence of non-Euclidean systems
is not only compatible with Kant's view that geometry is synthetic: his view
demands that there should be such systems' (Williamson 1968: 508; see also
Meinecke 1906). The same distinction also undermines the textual evidence
alleged to show that Kant was scrupulous in making allowance for non-
Euclidean geometry: for example, the following passage cited by Wiredu
(1970–6) and Martin (1955: 24), who share Williamson's view:

[T]here is no contradiction in the concept of a figure which is enclosed within two
straight lines, since the concepts of two straight lines and of their coming together
contain no negation of a figure. The impossibility arises not from the concept in itself,
but in connection with its construction in space, that is, from the conditions of space
and of its determination. And since these contain *a priori* in themselves the form of
experience in general, they have objective reality; that is, they apply to possible
things. (A220–1 = B268.)

A careful reading of this passage makes clear that Kant is admitting the
*logical* possibility of non-Euclidean geometries (which amounts to no more
than that the propositions of Euclidean geometry are not analytic), but at
the same time denying that such geometries are *objectively* possible. This,
again, is an important issue in the Kantian debates on geometry, including
Russell's first contribution to the controversy.

This last point relates to an issue of major importance in the nineteenth-
century debate about geometry. It was often argued (e.g. Land 1877) and
sometimes still is (e.g. Jones 1946) that there is no contest between Kant's
view of geometry and non-Euclidean geometries. Non-Euclidean geometries
must be accepted as logical possibilities, or as algebraic systems, or as a priori
deductive systems (formulations vary), yet they could not properly be regarded
as geometrical theories since they were incapable of spatial representation
by the mind. Thus it was maintained that mathematicians, in developing
non-Euclidean geometry, were not doing the impossible, they were merely
not doing geometry, since only Euclidean geometry was consistent with

---

[7] He cites B39 for support, though Kant draws the distinction more clearly in a note at
A596 = B624.

spatial intuition.[8] The geometers replied with an extended series of attempts to show that non-Euclidean geometries were indeed capable of spatial representation (one such attempt is discussed in more detail in § 4.2, below). Since these attempts characteristically involved a discussion of the spatial intuitions of hypothetical two-dimensional beings on non-Euclidean surfaces embedded in three-dimensional Euclidean spaces, the neo-Kantians had two possible replies. First they could maintain that the intuitions of such beings were quite compatible with Kant's doctrine, since his concept of objective possibility was concerned only with human intuition. Second they could maintain that, as Kant had said (1770: 404–5), such accounts required the notion of a Euclidean space for their very formulation, and thus non-Euclidean geometries could only receive an intuitive representation on the assumption that real space was Euclidean.

Ultimately, the no-contest view can be turned into a change of meaning thesis. The basis of the latter is the claim that the meanings of expressions used in deductive systems are given completely and exclusively by the axioms and postulates of the systems in question. Since Euclidean and non-Euclidean geometries have different postulate sets, the meanings of the expressions used in the formulation of both are different. In particular, the parallel postulate gives part of the meaning of the term 'straight line' as used in Euclidean geometry. Thus there is no contest between Euclidean and non-Euclidean geometries, and a fortiori between Kant's espousal of Euclidean geometry and non-Euclidean geometries.[9] The grounds for this view are not very strong, but in any case, even if the change of meaning thesis is granted, Kant's position is not materially aided. For on the change of meaning thesis the *meaning* of key theoretic terms is given entirely by the axioms of the system. From this it would follow that the theorems are analytically true, which was not Kant's view. Thus Kant may not consistently adopt the change of meaning thesis.[10]

[8] For an accurate exegesis of these debates (which is not my purpose here) it is necessary to distinguish various alternative policies on the neo-Kantian side (e.g. the strong claim that non-Euclidean geometries were not geometries at all from the weaker claim that they were geometries but not objectively possible ones).

[9] There is something of this view in Wiredu 1970. (Ibid. 11, he maintains that his position is 'essentially equivalent' to that of Russell's *EFG*, though the claim is somewhat doubtful.) The change of meaning thesis has more recently been urged by Carnap (1937: p. xv) against alternatives to classical logic. Cf. Prior (1960, 1964) for criticism of the view that the meanings of logical primitives can be given by the axioms and rules of inference; and Putnam (1957, 1969) for the view that the rivalry is genuine because primitives common to more than one system share a substantial overlap of meaning. It is clear that the term 'straight line' (or 'geodesic') shares a core meaning in both Euclidean and non-Euclidean systems, as Lobachevski (1840: 11–12) was at pains to point out.

[10] The inconsistency of Kant's position with the change of meaning thesis can be seen immediately by comparing Kant 1781: A716 = B744 with S. F. Barker's account of the change of meaning thesis (Barker 1964: 51).

In the final analysis, therefore, there seems little to justify the view that Kant allowed for the objective possibility of non-Euclidean geometries. Thus the first kind of neo-Kantian response to non-Euclidean geometry should be written off as a failure. The second kind of response, as Russell developed it, will occupy us for most of this chapter. The third response, which was to reject non-Euclidean geometry, can be briefly dismissed, although it proved the most popular response by nineteenth-century Kantians. Their views often depended upon gross misunderstandings. The German neo-Kantian, Wilhelm Tobias (1875), attributed to Riemann the absurd view that at an unspecified distance from earth the ordinary Euclidean space of experience gave place to a different space embodying a different geometry and possibly a different number of dimensions. Charles Renouvier (1891: 64) feared that if the objective foundation of Euclidean geometry were challenged so, too, might be the objective foundation of the moral law.[11]

Lotze's mathematical criticisms of non-Euclidean geometry, though a great improvement on Tobias's and Renouvier's, are similarly ill-considered (Lotze 1879: ii, ch. 2; *EFG* 99–108, for careful and effective criticism). But Lotze's writings on geometry have an additional interest on account of his philosophical position, which represents an important change on Kant's. Kant had maintained that space is a subjective form of externality, things-in-themselves do not have spatial relations. Lotze, however, maintained that it was this subjectivist account that had fostered the whole development of non-Euclidean geometry, which he regarded as 'one huge coherent error' (1879: 276). Lotze argued that the subjectivity of space, so far from establishing the universal validity of Euclidean geometry, as Kant supposed, established Euclidean geometry only after empirical investigation as to the nature of spatial intuition. Moreover, it allows the possibility that different types of being have different spatial intuitions, i.e. that for some (presumably non-human) subjects spatial intuition may take non-Euclidean forms. Lotze (1879: 276–314) sought to show that this was an empty possibility, about which it was impossible to have any information. Unlike Kant, Lotze maintained that subjective or presented space has an objective counterpart consisting of relations between monads which experience the relations as modifications of their internal states. From this Lotze argued that either all monads experienced these objective spatial relations in the same way, or, if they did not, we could not know how they experienced them. Either way, non-Euclidean geometries could be excluded, either as impossible or as unknowable. As Russell pointed out (*EFG* 95), if Lotze's argument for the

---

[11] Renouvier's style of objection was not unique. Given Euclidean geometry's former status as the one sure source of indubitable knowledge, the rise of non-Euclidean geometries produced a scepticism which was liable to spread beyond geometry and science into areas such as ethics and theology. For a survey of this little noted phenomenon, see Toth 1982.

objective space-counterpart were valid and it were possible for monads to experience this counterpart, it would be possible to infer that it must meet the requirements for any manifold of experience. This would provide some information about the nature of the space intuitions of other types of being, but it would not limit those intuitions to Euclidean ones. For Russell claimed that relativity of position did not limit subjective space to a Euclidean structure, though it did limit it to a structure of constant curvature. The cogency of this latter claim will be considered in § 4.5 below. In any case, it is an ironical reversal of history for Lotze to claim that Kant's views on the subjectivity of space promoted the development of non-Euclidean geometries, the more so since the early non-Euclidean geometers (with the arguable exception of Riemann) held more or less naïvely realistic views about the nature of space.

## 4.2 DEFENDING KANT AGAINST METAGEOMETRY AND WARD

Ward's lectures on metaphysics were important both for Russell's knowledge of Kant and for his knowledge of non-Euclidean geometry (or metageometry as it was then often known). Ward was concerned with non-Euclidean geometry primarily for its bearing on Kant's philosophy of geometry. Russell's lecture notes record that he criticized Kant's position on grounds drawn from psychology and geometry.

The psychological criticisms, which concern us less, are quite various. Ward maintains that the homogeneity of space cannot be established psychologically by attending to our external perceptions, since places are perceptually distinguished by their qualities rather than their relations to other places. Similarly, the three-dimensionality of space emerges only by reflection and comparison, and is not given directly by the visual field. Again, space is not perceived as either bounded or unbounded, and the idea that space is infinite is supplied only by the imagination.[12] His conclusion is again a strongly anti-empirical one: 'In space perception [we] get no ground for an exact Science or for any general statements' ('Lecture Notebook', i, 89).

This important and fundamental type of criticism of Kant's position has since been pursued by others: e.g. by Poincaré (1898: 1–6) who argued that space as empirically given was neither infinite, unbounded, homogeneous, nor isotropic; and by Klein (1925: 193) who argued that the axiom of parallels could not have been given in intuition. Interestingly, before Kant, Thomas Reid (1764: 142–53) in investigating the structure of the visual field

---

[12] It is not clear from Russell's notes whether Ward distinguished the unboundedness of space from its infinity.

had come to the conclusion that it was spherical, and not a Euclidean plane. Reid's common-sense ontology, however, led him to suppose that such a surface existed in a three-dimensional space which he assumed to be Euclidean.[13]

Exactly how these complaints affect Kant's position depends upon a feature of Kant's account which has not so far been considered. Kant regarded space not only as a form of intuition but as a formal intuition or an a priori percept. (The distinction is clearly made—though hardly made clear—in the second edition, cf. B 41, B160; see Kemp Smith (1923: 88–98) for commentary). On the view that space is a formal intuition, that the concept of space is suggested by, constructed from, or abstracted out of, external experience, there would seem to be no reason to regard it as an infinitely extended, three-dimensional, Euclidean continuum, for none of these properties seem adequately suggested by the relevant experience. On the other hand, if we regard space as a form of intuition, given a priori in the mind independently of all experience, then the arguments of Ward, Poincaré, Klein, and Reid about the nature of space-perceptions lose some of their force. On this view, Euclidean geometry may be seen as a structural limitation on human thought (the familiar Kantian spectacles) ensuring that the only way the relations between the elements of the manifold of experience can be conceived are as Euclidean spatial relations. But, although this is a possible explanation, it is hardly good enough, for why exactly these limitations and not others are given a priori in the mind remains deeply mysterious. The synthetic a priori character of Euclidean geometry is explained by an unsupported assertion about the nature of our minds. Only if this assertion can be supported by the empirical facts about spatial perception, only if space as a form of intuition can be made to coincide with space as a formal intuition, does Kant have a position which looks both plausible and interesting. The coincidence of the two notions of space, however, is exactly what Ward's psychological criticism tends to undermine.

Ward's geometrical criticism is briefly stated: we know that other three-dimensional geometries than Euclid's are (logically) possible; we have no guarantee that one of them is not applicable to the real world; nor have we any guarantee that Euclid's geometry does not embody certain physical assumptions which we have not recognized. Evidence against the two last claims from the fact that bodies can move freely without change of shape, for example, is challenged by Ward on the ground that no actual body is

[13] For this reason I reject the claim in Daniels (1972) that Reid discovered a non-Euclidean geometry. His geometry of visibles was simply the geometry of a spherical surface in a three-dimensional Euclidean space. But Helmholtz (1868) did arrive at genuine non-Euclidean geometries as a result of work on the visual field. For an interesting modern account of visual space in terms of a geometry of variable curvature see French 1987.

completely rigid and thus we have no reason to suppose that bodies do move freely without changing their shape ('Lecture Notebook', i, 90). Ward's arguments from metageometry were hardly original, yet they seem to have awakened Russell from his dogmatic slumbers. For, in his second essay for Ward's course (EPII), he attempted 'to defend Kant against Metageometry and Ward'.[14] Ward's psychological criticism of Kant is not directly addressed in this essay, Russell had already attended to it in an earlier essay written for Ward (EPI). There he had defended Kant by means of a distinction between space and time in conception and space and time in perception. Ward's criticisms are admitted against the latter, but not against the former (EPI 122). Russell's position, however, unless supplemented, leaves the Euclidean character of the concept of space essentially unexplained.

In the second essay, Russell develops a markedly Kantian view of space. The Euclidean axioms, he states, 'are held to derive their validity from the impossibility of picturing a case in which they fail'. Non-Euclidean geometry, by contrast, postulates its axioms 'arbitrarily', with the result that non-Euclidean geometry is purely algebraical, requiring translation 'by a sort of dictionary . . . into the language of geometry' (EPII 126). Alternatively we can proceed analytically from the intuitive principle of constancy of curvature to non-Euclidean geometries. But, ultimately, the non-Euclidean systems must be ruled out:

In analytical geometry, the letters employed are symbols, not, as in algebra, of *any* kind of quantity, but of spatial quantities only; and as such, if they are to retain their *meaning* as symbols, they must remain subject to certain restrictions which would not be imposed on them in algebra. When we remove these restrictions, or substitute others for them, there is no *primâ facie* reason for supposing the symbols to be capable of geometrical interpretation. (EPII 126.)

Russell is here arguing for a strong 'no contest' view; namely that the hegemony of Euclidean geometry is not challenged by non-Euclidean systems since the latter are only admissible as algebraic systems and not as genuine geometries.

---

[14] B. R. to A. P. Smith, 2–3 Dec. 1893. The readings on non-Euclidean geometry Ward suggested for this essay are of interest. Russell took down the references as follows (some important names he was clearly hearing for the first time): 'On Metageometry *vide Erdmann's* Axioms of Geometry [Erdmann 1877] two articles by Helmholtz one in Mind Vol. 1 [Helmholtz 1876] then Criticism [Land 1877] then reply [Helmholtz 1878], in first three volumes. Some papers by Colignon in *Revue Philosophique* vol. 28 [Calinon 1889, 1891, 1893; 'vol. 28' is clearly erroneous], and by La Schalas in next volume [Lechalas 1890*a*, 1890*b*] by Point Carré (?) in *Nature* vol. 45 [Poincaré 1891]. Criticisms in *Lotze* [1887] and in Sigwart's Logik [Sigwart 1873], *vide Mind* Vol. III, p. 551 [Land 1878]' ('Lecture Notebook', i, 90). Russell read most of these works eventually (cf. the bibliography in *EFG* 114 n.), but the essay he wrote for Ward shows only that he read the two papers by Helmholtz.

The formalism of Russell's account is quite striking. It is true that in the above passage he explicitly denies that geometry is an uninterpreted calculus—a geometry, as he makes clear, requires a spatial interpretation. None the less, he must explicitly concede that some calculi which have been called 'geometries' preclude such interpretation. It would be quite natural to re-express his position either as the claim that geometries were just uninterpreted calculi only one of which was capable of an intuitively satisfactory spatial interpretation, or else as the claim that 'intuitive' or 'physical' geometries were capable of such an interpretation while 'abstract' or 'mathematical' geometries were not, being merely uninterpreted calculi. The modern distinction between pure and applied geometry, in which this line of thought culminates, did not appear in a fully developed form until after the work of Pasch, Hilbert, and the Italian school had been assimilated. In 1893, however, it is more likely that Russell had in mind a vaguer and more traditional distinction, sometimes made by British mathematicians, between mathematics as an art and mathematics as a science: non-Euclidean geometries were part of the art, only Euclidean geometry was a science (see Richards 1980).

Whether we grant Russell's premiss that in analytical geometry the symbols are subject to certain (geometric) restrictions which, if removed, would render the purely formal system incapable of geometric interpretation, will depend upon what we mean by a 'geometrical interpretation'. To be convincing, Russell's argument needs to be supplemented by a much more detailed account of what such an interpretation is. I will return to this shortly. However, it is clear that, even if we grant Russell's premiss, his conclusion—that only Euclidean analytic geometry is capable of geometric interpretation—does not follow. For, from the fact that certain geometric restrictions are imposed, it does not follow that *Euclidean* restrictions are imposed, without the question-begging Kantian assumption that the only admissible geometrical interpretations are Euclidean ones.

Before Hilbert (1899), geometrical axiomatics were not in a state where a clear answer could be given to the question of what constitutes a specifically geometrical interpretation of a formal system. However, in the nineteenth-century debates on geometry the essential issue had been raised in a different guise, and various intuitive or experiential criteria had been suggested. The question whether non-Euclidean systems were genuinely geometrical had boiled down to that of whether non-Euclidean spaces were 'imaginable'. And one highly restrictive account of what was meant by 'imaginable', strong enough to satisfy even the Kantians, was the empiricist view that whether or not a space was 'imaginable' was to be decided by whether it could be visually represented. While it was clearly too much to claim that only what was visually representable was imaginable, it was none the less entirely reasonable to claim that if non-Euclidean spaces could be visually represented then Kant was wrong in supposing that Euclidean geometry was a necessary condition for any visual (or other external) representation. So the question was: were non-Euclidean spaces capable of visual representation?

Russell was entering into this dispute rather late in the day, and on the losing side, since much work had already been done (notably by Helmholtz 1866, 1868, 1876, 1878) in providing visual representations of non-Euclidean geometries.[15] Russell, therefore, had to find a refutation of Helmholtz's arguments. Helmholtz's attempt (1868: 637–8) to represent a pseudospherical space, by means of what Russell calls 'an elaborate analogy with the space inside a sphere' is rejected by Russell on the grounds that

this analogy has been obtained . . . by giving to the symbols a new meaning, so that all the algebraical results have two interpretations, one for the one space and one for the other. But when the question at issue is whether the first of these meanings can be given to the symbols, it does not seem a good way of deciding it to give them another. (EPII 126.)

Russell's point is a shrewd one, even though his argument is not completely effective. Moreover, if it were effective it would apply against any of the various attempts to demonstrate that non-Euclidean systems are genuine geometries by the construction of visualizable analogies. Russell's point is the following. The non-Euclidean geometers take a purely algebraic theory and seek to show that it is capable of a genuinely geometrical, though non-Euclidean, interpretation, $I_1$. To do this to the satisfaction of the Kantians they have to show that $I_1$ is visualizable. To establish this last, they construct a visualizable analogy for the original algebraic theory. But, Russell claims, this analogy simply amounts to a second interpretation, $I_2$, of the original theory, and from the fact that $I_2$ can be visualized it doesn't follow that $I_1$ can be. The trouble with Russell's argument is that $I_2$ already involves the violation of Euclidean principles; and thus to concede that it is visualizable is to concede the point at issue, namely that Euclidean visualizations are not a priori necessities of thought. The usual reply to this is that $I_2$ holds only within an embedding Euclidean space, for example, that Helmholtz's sphere is a non-Euclidean two-dimensional space embedded in a Euclidean three-dimensional one. But this overlooks the fact that the embedding space is not

---

[15] Helmholtz was not the only author engaged in work of this kind. Others, of whom Russell was aware, included Clifford (1885) and (more whimsically) Abbott (1884). For the importance of Helmholtz, cf. Torretti 1978: 154–71. Russell gives a much fuller critique of Helmholtz's philosophy of geometry, especially his empiricism, in *EFG* 70–81, but makes no mention of Helmholtz's efforts to show that non-Euclidean geometries are *visualizable*, being content to dismiss them as 'fairy-tale analogies of doubtful value' (*EFG* 101).

essential for the interpretation. Counter-charges that $I_2$ can be visualized only if the embedding space is assumed (cf. Land 1877) seem doubtful.

If Russell's critique of Helmholtz is to be effective, it requires a more direct attack on the issue of visualizability. This Russell attempts. He claims, without obvious justification, that Helmholtz leaves out all that is epistemologically essential.

To take spherical space: how can I picture a three-dimensional space in which two straight lines enclose a space, or in which the line of sight, if unimpeded, ends on the back of my head? The analogy of flat-fish living on the surface of a sphere seems irrelevant, if only because we are not flat-fish;[16] and I do not see why the line of sight of such a flat-fish should not be just as much a Euclidean straight line as ours. (EPII 127.)

These are hardly strong considerations, and go the way of most attempts to argue limits on the imagination. Those who claim that what others imagine is unimaginable are not unfairly accused of being unimaginative. Some of Russell's specific remarks seem uncharacteristically obtuse: for example, the world of the flat-fish cannot be Euclidean because they inhabit a *two*-dimensional spherical space (not a two-dimensional surface in a three-dimensional Euclidean space), a point which Russell apparently overlooks. Beyond the enumeration of such problems, the entire approach Russell uses is radically defective. There is little point in arguing to-and-fro about what can be pictured, visualized, or imagined. Even if such questions were open to clear-cut answers (which typically they are not), the answers would tell us about human psychology rather than about the nature of space. What is needed is some precise specification of what is to count as a *geometrical* interpretation of a given formal system. It would seem highly plausible to take as a clearly sufficient (though plainly not necessary) condition that it was possible to specify the metric properties of extended figures in the space given by the interpretation. The geometries with which Russell was dealing all clearly meet this requirement. Of course, on this account the efforts of Helmholtz and others to make non-Euclidean geometry visualizable are not of fundamental importance for its acceptability—though the heuristic importance of such efforts remains.

Russell is on firmer ground when he maintains 'I do not see how any experience could force us either to reject the first axiom [of Euclid] or to alter our view of the nature of space' (EPII 129; see also OSG/P 262 n.). As is now well known, accommodation of any experimental result to Euclidean geometry can be achieved by, for example, postulating universal forces which deform extended bodies. None the less, this is a considerably weaker conclusion

---

[16] This point, though Russell does not elaborate it, suggests one neo-Kantian gambit, namely, that non-humans may have non-Euclidean space intuitions.

than Kant's. It may have been suggested by Poincaré's conventionalism (Poincaré 1891), though Russell was later to attack conventionalism (in AOG).

Despite the fact that positivists have claimed Helmholtz as 'the source of modern philosophical knowledge of space' (Reichenbach 1928: 36; see also Milne 1952: 82) and the clearly empiricist tenor of much of what he says about geometry, Helmholtz was strongly influenced by Kant and has good claim to be regarded as a neo-Kantian. He states (1878: 213) that it was not his aim to refute Kant's view that the notion of space was an a priori transcendental intuition. But it is clear that the Kantianism which is consistent with his position is very much chastened. Helmholtz made some concession to Kant by maintaining that the principle of the free mobility of rigid bodies 'might . . . be conceived as transcendental' (Helmholtz 1876: 119–20). Clearly the principle is not purely empirical, since actual rigid bodies are not to be found. Moreover, the free mobility principle, Helmholtz believes, is necessary if dynamics is to be possible. Given the principle of free mobility, possible spaces are limited to those of constant curvature. The general geometry which studies such spaces may thus be regarded as transcendental. However, Helmholtz removes himself further from Kant by maintaining that the propositions of such a geometry are not synthetic, but result from an analysis of the concept of a rigid body. On the other hand, he maintains that determining which among the three types of space of constant curvature is actual is possible only by empirical investigation.

This position is reasonably clear. However, in his reply to the Dutch neo-Kantian, J. P. N. Land (1877) Helmholtz (1878: 217–25) makes different concessions to Kant and adds considerably to the obscurity of his position. He distinguishes again between a geometry based upon transcendental intuition and one based on empirical measurement. This time, instead of the principle of free mobility, he adopts the principle of causality—that all perceptions occur according to fixed laws, so that different perceptions have different causes, and the same perceptions the same causes—as a synthetic a priori principle, justified transcendentally by the possibility of science. One of Land's persistent criticisms had been that Helmholtz had ignored Kant's distinction between noumena and phenomena and, writing as a scientist, had adopted a scientific realism which conflicted with Kant's doctrine of the unknowability of the noumenal (Land 1877). Helmholtz is careful to avoid any such realism in reformulating his position. He uses the principle of causality in the following way: since we think that we perceive objects occupying particular spatial positions, there must, by the principle of causality, be some set of causes which determine 'at what particular place in space an object shall appear to us'. To avoid 'misleading associations' he calls these 'topogenous moments'; they amount to no more than the 'circumstances determining space-perception' whose nature is unknown (Helmholtz 1878: 223). While nothing of the nature of topogenous moments may be known, their structural relationships may be determined from sense experience, via the principle of causality. However, Helmholtz still does not rule out the possibility of a transcendental geometry (or even of a transcendentally established Euclidean geometry), if it were the case that humans immediately intuited (Euclidean) spatial relations as a result of the operation of topogenous moments upon their minds. However, he does go on to call this an unproved, unnecessary, and irrelevant hypothesis (1878: 225). Whether this transcendental geometry coincided with the actual physical geometry of the topogenous moments themselves would depend, he says, 'on a pre-established harmony between intuition and the real world' (1878: 225).

Russell is surely right in maintaining that this concession to Kant is no concession at all. It does concede the unknowability of the noumenal, but apart from that Kant would have to maintain that the transcendental and physical geometries are necessarily 'one and the same' (EPII 127). For if the transcendental geometry were a necessity of thought then the actual relations of topogenous moments would remain unknowable and unthinkable, if the physical geometry were different from the transcendental. But if a geometry is to be regarded as a *theory* of space, i.e. the result of human intellectual activity, this amounts to the claim that there is no such thing as a physical geometry distinct from the transcendental geometry.

Russell's two conclusions in the geometry section of his paper are: '[t]hat other space than ours can be intuited does not seem to me to be proved by meta-geometry: and this seems to be all that Kantians need maintain against it' (EPII 129), and its corollary from a Kantian point of view, that 'the speculations of meta-geometry have no epistemological importance' (EPII 127). Yet Russell's own allegiance to Kant is not clear-cut. At one stage he writes: 'I am not here concerned to defend Kant's argument, but only to attack Helmholtz's attack on it' (EPII 128). Unfortunately, Russell does not elaborate and the context of this remark makes it unclear whether what he doesn't wish to defend is Kant's position on geometry or merely Kant's view that the noumenal is unknowable. It does seem most likely that it was the latter, since his paper goes well beyond a criticism of Helmholtz's attacks on Kant's theory of geometry. Moreover, as a neo-Hegelian influenced by McTaggart and writing for Ward, Russell would hardly have wished so easily to commit himself to Kant's view that the reality beyond appearance was completely unknowable.

Russell's defence of the apriority of Euclidean geometry was neither conclusive nor particularly original, though we cannot assume that he was familiar with much of the previous literature. It is clear that he had read Helmholtz's reply to Land, but it is not clear whether he had read Land himself. Russell had read Helmholtz's articles, not in their original publication in *Mind* where Land's criticism was published, but in German in Helmholtz (1882). (The relevant papers in Russell's copy of this work are extensively annotated.) Russell's essay makes no reference to Land and his arguments bear only very general similarities to those of Land. The main tenor of Land's remarks, that there is a strict separation between the concerns of science and philosophy since the latter calls into question the nature and existence of a real world beyond that of appearance, was unlikely to be sympathetically received by Russell. In any case, it is clear that Russell had grasped one important strand in the nineteenth-century debates about the philosophy of geometry, and had correctly identified the important issues in the neo-Kantian debates.

## 4.3 RUSSELL'S FELLOWSHIP DISSERTATION AND OTHER LOST WORKS

Russell's second epistemology paper for Ward gains importance only in retrospect. Although it was the paper in which he most emphatically took issue with his tutor it did not represent, at the time it was written, a firm commitment to research on the foundations of geometry. In fact, Russell graduated from the Moral Sciences Tripos without clear plans for the thesis that would be required if he were to gain a Trinity fellowship.It was only in June 1894 that Russell decided to write on the philosophy of geometry (see § 3.1). Once the topic was chosen, however, he started work on it straightaway. In late July and early August, before he left for Paris, he went to stay with Alys Pearsall Smith's family at their home, largely in order to be able to work in peace. Among the works he studied at this time were Frischauf (1872), Killing (1885), Klein (1890), Lotze (1879), Wundt (1889), and Kant (1781). While there he also started writing on the topic. Although these writings are lost, we know at least some of the topics on which he worked, for a few days after he left he wrote asking Alys to send him '[t]he few loose sheets of manuscript headed *Geometrical Axioms*, and those headed *Absolute Position* (1 page) and *Congruence* (3 pages)' which he had left on his desk at Friday's Hill.[17] The manuscripts on geometrical axioms and congruence, at least, represent a clear continuity of topic with the central concerns of his first published geometrical writings (1896*b*, 1896*c*, *EFG*).[18]

[17] B. R. to A. P. Smith, 24 Aug. 1894.
[18] The same *could* be true of the MS on absolute position, for one of Russell's main arguments against the possibility of spaces of variable curvature is that they involve absolute position (cf. 1896*b*: 269–70, 272; 1896*c*: 294–6; *EFG* 150–2). On the other hand, Russell was also concerned about the problem of absolute position in dynamics, e.g. in connection with his review (1895*a*) of Heymans (1890), and later in connection with his work on the philosophy of dynamics (see 1896*e* and VN 11–19 *passim* for the relevant fragments).

He continued to work on both topics while he was away in Paris. On 29 September 1894 he wrote to C. P. Sanger about Euclid's method of establishing congruence for three-dimensional figures, since the method of superposition used for plane figures was clearly inapplicable. By late October 1894, he was hard at work on a full-fledged paper on geometry (which required the help of the second volume of James (1890)). The paper gave him considerable trouble,[19] but on 28 October he reported that he had been inspired to write 'several fairly good pages, embodying an entirely original and very bold idea, which I got during the month at F[riday]'s H[ill] . . . It is *so* bold that it almost terrifies me. I shall be interested to see what they think of it at Cambridge.' The following day he reported that he had finished the paper 'to my great relief'. Although the bold idea which he had got at Friday's Hill had not previously been mentioned in his correspondence with Alys, he continued to be enormously excited by it: 'it differs so much from most of the books that I'm alarmed and feel as if I must be on the wrong track'. He thought the paper as a whole 'much too hard to be understood when read aloud, and the crux of the argument, the psychological part, has been treated much too sketchily, for want of the necessary knowledge: but there seems to me to be a good deal of good reasoning and solid thinking in it'.[20] The paper in fact was written for the Cambridge Moral Sciences Club where it was read, under the title 'Geometrical Axioms', by Sanger in Russell's absence on 9 November. According to the minutes, it 'led to a very mathematical discussion'.[21] Unfortunately, the minutes do not say anything about the paper's contents, for the paper itself is lost and with it the 'entirely original and very bold' idea it contained.

Also lost is Russell's dissertation itself. Here, however, with the help of a surviving partial draft together with some correspondence on the topic, we can gain a fairly good idea of its scope and with the help of Russell's subsequent publications on geometry (1896b, 1896c, and *EFG*) we can establish at least one of the main theses Russell defended in it. Russell's *EFG* was, in Russell's own phrase, an 'elaboration' of his fellowship dissertation (*MPD* 31). As we shall see, however, it was an elaboration which involved a very great deal of alteration, including the addition and deletion of whole chapters.

OSG, the draft from which it started, was written between March and 6 June 1895 (cf. *Papers*, i, 256–7). The two longest of its six sections, a critique

---

[19] See letters to A. P. Smith, 22 and 25 Oct. 1894.
[20] B. R. to A. P. Smith, 29 Oct. 1894.
[21] Cambridge University Library, Min. IX. 41, p. 2. This paper was the first Russell gave to the Moral Sciences Club of which he had been a member since 27 Feb. 1891. He had attended his first meeting as a guest in Nov. 1890. For Russell's connection with the Moral Sciences Club see Pitt 1981.

of Lotze and a 'Mathematical History of Meta-geometry', are first drafts of parts of *EFG*. Both were considerably revised for publication. A comparison of the two texts shows quite a remarkable number of stylistic changes. While a number of these can be traced to a desire to improve clarity and style, some (which would otherwise imply an uncharacteristically pedantic tinkering with words) suggest that Russell found it easier to rewrite some sentences than to copy them. The published version of the history of metageometry, in particular, is considerably expanded and several passages in the notebook version have been replaced by completely new material in the published book. An intermediate version doubtless appeared in his dissertation. The revisions made to the material on Lotze are much less extensive. The remaining sections of OSG did not appear in *EFG*. One, a criticism of Erhardt's neo-Kantian attack on non-Euclidean geometry, (Erhardt 1894) was dropped, presumably because Erhardt's criticisms essentially replicate those of Lotze (1887). The others, a note on apriority and two versions of an introduction, were both replaced in *EFG*.[22]

The changes which took place in Russell's account of the history of non-Euclidean geometry between 1895 and late 1896 (when *EFG* was finished) reveal the development of his knowledge of the subject. The overall format remains the same, with the development of non-Euclidean geometry divided into three phases (following Klein 1890). The first phase, dominated by Bolyai and Lobachevski, was concerned primarily with the independence of Euclid's parallel postulate, and thus essentially used non-Euclidean geometries as tools for investigating the nature of Euclidean geometry, which still dominated the field. In the second period, mainly the work of Riemann and Helmholtz (although Russell also mentions Gauss), the independence of the parallel postulate had become a minor issue. The study of geometry was placed on a new mathematical and philosophical foundation by Riemann's application of the concept of a manifold, of which space was just one instance (Riemann 1854). The metrical properties of different spatial manifolds depend upon the manifold's measure of curvature, with no priority assigned to a zero (Euclidean) measure of curvature. Thus the study of non-Euclidean systems (with non-zero measure of curvature) became independent of the study of Euclidean geometry, and the contending metrical geometries could be regarded as equals from the mathematical point of view for the first time. The third period saw the development of projective geometry by Cayley and Klein. Cayley in his early work saw projective geometry as a new way of formulating Euclidean geometry, but Klein, especially in his *Erlanger Programme* (1871), using group-theoretic techniques conceived of projective geometry as a means of unifying the study of geometry by showing that

[22] Parts of OSG not appearing in *EFG* are printed in *Papers*, i, 258–65, and are cited as OSG/P. All other references are to the MS.

competing geometrical systems could be obtained from projective geometry by means of changes in the definition of the distance function. By the time Russell came to include this history in the *EFG* there is much evidence of further reading, e.g. of Veronese (1891), but especially of a much deeper understanding of Klein (1890). Russell's treatment of Lie (1888), however, though expanded, remains extremely sketchy (despite copious note taking).

The most important change between the two versions lies in Russell's recognition of the *philosophical*, as distinct from the purely mathematical, importance of projective geometry.[23] In OSG the third period is claimed to have yielded 'few fresh philosophical ideas' (p. 103) and the projective elimination of metrical notions is said to be 'irrelevant for philosophical purposes' (p. 104; rearranged). In *EFG*, by contrast, while it is regretted that projective geometry has 'found no exponent so philosophical as Riemann or Helmholtz' (p. 28), 'the underlying philosophical ideas' are said to differ radically from those of the second period (p. 27), and 'almost every important proposition [of projective geometry], though misleading in its obvious interpretation, has nevertheless, when rightly interpreted, a wide philosophical bearing' (p. 28). Russell's concern with philosophy was paramount throughout *EFG*, a fact which helps explain some otherwise extraordinary judgements. At one point, for example, he complains of Beltrami (1868*b*) that its main 'results sink . . . to the level of mere mathematical constructions' (*EFG* 27). This is an instance of Russell's early preference for geometrical intuition over 'algebraic' abstraction (see § 3.4). Russell's recognition of the philosophical significance of projective geometry was clearly a central factor in his extended treatment of it in *EFG*, and was very likely part of the reason for his more detailed study of Klein (1890), a book he had read in 1894 but read again (twice) in 1895 after OSG was written. It seems most likely that his transcendental deduction of projective geometry was included, in some form, in the dissertation.

None the less, there is evidence that in his dissertation as submitted the status assigned to the axioms of metrical geometry was not very different from that assigned to them in *EFG*, although certain of the arguments were new in the latter work. The dissertation was submitted in August 1895. It was read by Whitehead who assessed its mathematical content, and initially by Sidgwick. Whether Sidgwick was intended to assess its philosophical content, or merely acted as a clearing house for incoming theses is not clear. In any case, he made only a preliminary report on it and passed it on to Ward explaining that it was 'many years since I interested myself in psychological and epistemological controversies relating to space' and making a full report would take him more time than he had to give. Sidgwick did tell Ward that

---

[23] Whitehead's help in this is acknowledged in the preface to *EFG*.

both he and Whitehead thought the dissertation 'decidedly able, and deserving a careful estimate'.[24]

This, however, was not the impression Russell was given when he went to see Whitehead on the day before the results of the fellowship competition were announced:

He says he and Ward (who are both ultra-empiricists) disagreed with almost every view I advocated; Ward also found my metaphysic and Psychology rather thin—like my chances, I thought when Whitehead told me. So I don't think I shall be elected tomorrow, and I suspect I am not much good at Philosophy.[25]

Russell was, in fact, elected to the fellowship the next day,[26] but he had been so discouraged by Whitehead's remarks that he was not present to hear the announcement, but instead watched the proceedings from his room. Alys gave a vivid description of the event:

I must tell you that Bertie has really got his Fellowship. It was announced to-day, just after I came up, and we watched it all from Bertie's window. The Master & Examining Fellows wrangled about it for three hours and a quarter—then they marched across the Court in the rain, old Sidgwick running after, . . . to the Chapel, and went in thro' the old doors. There the Holy Spirits revealed the names of the four Fellows, and these were announced to an expectant crowd waiting in the drizzling mist outside. Of course, we could only see the excitement, not hear anything, but Bertie's friends soon came rushing over to tell him.[27]

From a variety of scattered remarks we can form a good idea of the dissertation's structure. From Sidgwick's letter to Ward we learn that, like *EFG*, the dissertation had four chapters. The first half of the dissertation was 'primarily mathematical . . . it falls *mainly* within the competence of Whitehead'. It was on the philosophical part, chapters 3 and 4, that Ward

[24] H. Sidgwick to J. Ward, 6 Sept. 1895 (Trinity College Library, Cambridge). Unfortunately, Sidgwick's preliminary report, referred to in his letter, has not survived. Nor have the reports by Whitehead and Ward.

[25] B. R. to A. Russell, 9 Oct. 1895. Russell's later account (*Auto.* i, 126) is somewhat different. After noting that Whitehead 'criticized it rather severely, though quite justly' so that Russell 'came to the conclusion that it was worthless', Russell says he went, 'as a matter of politeness' to see Ward 'who said exactly the opposite, and praised it to the skies'. There is no indication in Russell's letter of 9 Oct. that he had been to see Ward, and in his *Autobiography* he may have been confusing a subsequent meeting with Ward. In *PFM* 95, Russell says that Whitehead's wife took Whitehead to task for the severity with which he had criticized Russell's dissertation. Whitehead defended himself by saying that it was the last time he would be able to speak to Russell as a pupil. The danger of failure was real: it was hard to get a fellowship on a first attempt.

[26] Trinity fellowships under title (α), 'Prize Fellowships', to which Russell was elected, ran for six years without obligation of teaching, research, or residence. Russell donated the stipend the fellowship carried to the London School of Economics to establish a Research Studentship there.

[27] A. Russell to Mary Mackall Gwinn, 10 Oct. 1895 (Bryn Mawr College Archives).

was particularly asked to report.[28] Clearly one or both of the mathematical chapters were devoted to the history of non-Euclidean geometry drafted in OSG and polished in chapter 1 of *EFG*. There is also good evidence that 'The Logic of Geometry' (1896*b*) formed part of a chapter of the dissertation.[29] At their meeting before the election Whitehead had told Russell that 'certain parts [of the dissertation], more or less as they stood, were well worth publishing'.[30] Russell seems to have taken him up on this almost immediately, for (1896*b*) was published in the January 1896 issue of *Mind*.[31] Alys told Mary Gwinn that this paper 'was a part of [Russell's] dissertation',[32] and to confirm it there is an internal, uncorrected reference to 'our chapter' in the published version (*Papers* i, T285: 20).

There was also a chapter on the 'Psychological Origin of Space-relations',[33] which must have been either chapter 3 or chapter 4. We have seen that Russell was interested in the psychology of space-intuition as early as the Moral Sciences Club paper on 'Geometrical Axioms', and he read James (1890) and Stumpf (1873) at that time in connection with his work on the topic.[34] Russell was discontented with the psychological argument presented in 'Geometrical Axioms' and it is clear he worked the material up into a chapter for the dissertation. But, as Alys explains, the chapter 'was severely criticized, and Ward felt very strongly that it was not necessary for the logically complete treatment of the subject'.[35] The chapter was dropped from *EFG* and no trace of it remains.[36]

This accounts for about half the material in *EFG*. Of the remaining two chapters, the first part of chapter 4 (§§ 180–93) can be dated with fair certainty as 1896.[37] So, too, can the bulk of chapter 2, which is a semi-

---

[28] H. Sidgwick to J. Ward, 6 Sept. 1895 (Trinity College Library).

[29] 1896*b* does not correspond to any chapter in *EFG*, though much of it is included in one form or another in ch. 3. See *Papers*, i, 486–91, for a detailed collation.

[30] B. R. to A. Russell, 9 Oct. 1895.

[31] Russell was correcting proofs for the article early in Nov. 1895 (cf. A. Russell to R. P. Smith, 4 Nov. 1895).

[32] A. Russell to M. Gwinn, 20 Jan. 1896 (Bryn Mawr College Archives).

[33] A. Russell to C. Thomas, 1 Feb. 1896 (M. Carey Thomas Papers, Bryn Mawr College Archives).

[34] The topic was, in fact, quite fashionable both for philosophers and psychologists in the late 19th century, stemming in part from the influence of Kant and Helmholtz. There is an excellent survey of German work on the topic in Sully 1878.

[35] A. Russell to C. Thomas, 1 Feb. 1896 (M. Carey Thomas Papers, Bryn Mawr College Archives).

[36] There remain in *EFG* a number of approving references to William James's treatment of space-intuition (*EFG* Preface, pp. 158, 170–1, 197) and to Stumpf (*EFG* 158, 181, 193–4, 196; see also OSG/P 260, 262). But it is impossible to construct a full psychological theory from these and other scattered remarks. Indeed, at one point (*EFG* 196) Russell sharply distinguishes his own epistemological concerns from Stumpf's psychological ones.

[37] The remainder of ch. 4, §§ 194–209 is impossible to date with accuracy. None of it appears in earlier writings and there are no references to its content in contemporary correspondence.

historical account of the philosophy of geometry in the nineteenth century (paralleling his history of mathematical developments in chapter 1). Alys reported on the philosophical history that Russell 'did nothing of that part of the subject in his Dissertation for lack of time'.[38] In fact, the material on Lotze was present in the dissertation, but as an appendix,[39] and some of that on Helmholtz occurred in the chapter of the dissertation which became 'The Logic of Geometry' (cf. 1896*b*: 266).

The idea of publishing a book on geometry seems originally to have come from Ward, who wrote to congratulate Russell on the fellowship: 'I think you might make an excellent monograph of ch[apters] i, ii, and the Appendix on Lotze'.[40] Russell, at this time, was working to complete *German Social Democracy*, his first book, and he seems to have confined his early attempts to publish on geometry to the hasty revision of (1896*b*) for *Mind*. The work on *German Social Democracy* went on into early 1896, with Russell becoming increasingly impatient to be done with it and get back to what Alys called 'his dear dull space'.[41]

Writing plans for *EFG* rapidly became entangled with another writing project. Even before the fellowship was announced the Russells had been making plans to visit the United States, primarily to visit Alys's relations in Pennsylvania. It was hoped, also, that Russell would be able to give a series of lectures at Bryn Mawr college where Carey Thomas, a cousin of Alys's, was the (apparently autocratic) president.[42] The original plan had been for a series of lectures on logic, and hopes were high after the fellowship that this could be arranged in the spring of 1896. However, with a book on geometry to work on Russell had to put off the idea of visiting before the autumn, and even then he doubted that he could get up a lecture course on logic in the time available. It came as something of a relief, therefore, when Carey Thomas proposed that he should lecture on geometry.[43] A syllabus for the lectures was quickly dispatched (*Papers*, i, 339–40), and Alys explained in a covering letter that 'Bertie had entirely given up the thought of lecturing at Bryn Mawr, because he felt he had not enough time to get up Logic or any other subject, and it never occurred to him that anyone would wish to hear lectures on his own subject.'[44]

The MS of *EFG* was probably more or less complete early in Aug. 1896, for on 4 Aug. 1896 Alys wrote to Carey Thomas to say it had been accepted by Cambridge University Press and they hoped to have it in proof before they left for the USA on 26 Sept.

[38] A. Russell to C. Thomas, 1 Feb. 1896 (M. Carey Thomas Papers, Bryn Mawr College Archives).

[39] J. Ward to B. R., 10 Oct. 1895; also OSG 73.
[40] J. Ward to B. R., 10 Oct. 1895.      [41] A. Russell to M. M. Gwinn, 20 Jan. 1896.
[42] For some amusing, and none too flattering, stories about C. Thomas see *Auto* i, 131–2. For a more respectful account see Finch 1947.
[43] C. Thomas to A. Russell, 12 Jan. 1896.
[44] A. Russell to C. Thomas, 1 Feb. 1896 (Thomas Papers, Bryn Mawr College Archives).

The syllabus outlined six lectures, following closely the structure of *EFG*. The first two lectures were to be on the history of non-Euclidean geometry (corresponding to chapter 1 of *EFG*), the first covering metric geometry and the second projective geometry. Lectures 3 and 4 together Russell headed 'Critical account of some previous philosophical theories of geometry' (the title of chapter 2 of *EFG*). Lecture 3 dealt with Kant, Herbart, Riemann, Helmholtz, and Erdmann, and lecture 4 with Lotze and recent French philosophers of geometry. Lecture 5 was to provide the transcendental deduction of projective geometry, and lecture 6 that of general metrical geometry.[45] It was lectures 3 and 4 of the syllabus which, as Alys explained, had still to be written and which would thus make it impossible to deliver the lectures in the spring of 1896.

Alys was not without misgivings. She thought that the faculty at Bryn Mawr might find the lectures 'too deadly' for the students, that there would not be enough psychology in the lectures, or that they would be too obscure. (Although, on this last point, she did promise that the lectures 'would, of course, be given more clearly than that article in *Mind* [1896*b*] I sent thee'.)[46] She was also concerned about Russell's abilities as a lecturer: 'I must tell thee one thing, that I don't believe Bertie will have a good manner in lecturing. He is fearfully nervous & shy about it, and he thinks he will have to read the lectures. But of course he will have had some practise this Spring, which will undoubtedly improve him.'[47] Her fears, however, did not prevent the smooth development of their plans. The mathematicians at Bryn Mawr were not daunted by the obscurity of 'The Logic of Geometry'. '[O]ur mathematicians,' Carey Thomas wrote, 'are delighted with Bertie's paper. They say it is brilliant, original, acute, that his propositions, radical as they are, are maintained, and many other ecstatic things'.[48] They were even prepared to rearrange their classes so that their students could attend

[45] The lectures, as actually given, were somewhat different from the syllabus. (The lectures themselves have not survived, but brief accounts of all but the second and sixth were published in the Philadelphia *Public Ledger and Daily Transcript* during Nov. 1896. These reports are printed in *Papers*, i, 340–3.) Lectures 1 and 3 (and presumably also 2) were given according to the syllabus. But Russell devoted the fourth and fifth to metrical and projective geometry, respectively. The final lecture covered material in ch. 4 of *EFG* §§180–93, which, it is almost certain, had not been worked out by the time the syllabus was prepared. (Information on the final lecture comes from E. N. Martin (1897), printed in *Papers*, i, 343.)

[46] A. Russell to C. Thomas, 1 Feb. 1896 (Thomas Papers, Bryn Mawr College Archives).

[47] Ibid. The practice was to come from giving six lectures on German social democracy (the basis for *GSD*) at the London School of Economics between 6 Feb. and 13 Mar. 1896; and a public lecture (1896*g*) to the 'Fabian Society on 14 Feb. Russell was nervous on the latter occasion also (see Wood 1957: 35).

[48] C. Thomas to A. Russell, 13 Apr. 1896. It was the syllabus, now, that was giving trouble. '[O]ur mathematicians thought it very difficult' and there were fears the lectures might be 'too technical' for philosophers: 'Both Mamie [Mary Gwinn] and I found ourselves so completely baffled by his syllabus that we have the vanity to believe that if we cannot understand them philosophers cannot' (C. Thomas to A. Russell, 14 July 1896).

Russell's lectures, which were now firmly scheduled for November. There was also talk of getting him to give a paper to the conference of the American Mathematical Society in New York in November, but nothing seems to have come of that.

One set of additional plans which did come to fruition was the idea that Russell should go on to give the same series of lectures at the Johns Hopkins University in Baltimore. Here they ran into more difficulties, despite the fact that Carey Thomas's father was Chairman of the Executive Committee of Trustees for the university. James Thomas was clearly a man to be reckoned with and organized effective support for Russell against the indifference and occasional opposition of the local mathematicians. Warm references were secured from Ward, Sidgwick, and Montagu Butler, the Master of Trinity. Ward wrote:

I know of no one in England so competent to deal with [the philosophy of geometry] as Mr. Russell is. I have never heard him lecture but I have read most of the things that he has written and regard his style as masterly in respect of order, clearness, and awareness. In all probability he would publish his lectures and I feel sure they would bring honour to the Johns Hopkins University.[49]

Sidgwick also said that he could think of no better person for the task than Russell, 'a man of remarkable promise' whose dissertation was 'a masterly piece of work'.[50] Butler, having dwelt on Russell's aristocratic connections, described him as 'a young man of altogether exceptional ability, [who] has devoted himself mainly to Metaphysics, Moral Philosophy and grave social questions . . . [F]or thoroughness of knowledge, acute analysis, and (I will add) charm of character you will not find many to equal him'.[51]

The American mathematicians whom Gilman approached for their opinion of Russell were less than enthusiastic. H. B. Fine, of Princeton, found that 'on examining myself that I have no definite knowledge of him whatsoever'.[52] Simon Newcomb, the astronomer shortly to be appointed to the Johns Hopkins faculty, was hardly more helpful: 'I never heard of Mr. Bertrand Russell.' But he did offer the opinion that there was nothing 'of real value in the theme that cannot be developed in two lectures, at the outside'.[53] But by far the most curious response, in two rambling letters, was from Thomas

[49] J. Ward to D. C. Gilman, President of Johns Hopkins, 7 July 1896. The documents together with some background information relating to Russell's invitation from Johns Hopkins are printed in Armstrong 1969. (A truncated account without accompanying documentation is given in Feinberg and Kasrils 1973: i, 20–1.) Ward's letter is given in full in Armstrong, p. 31. The originals of the documents are in the Daniel Coit Gilman papers, Johns Hopkins University.

[50] H. Sidgwick to D. C. Gilman, 11 July 1896. Printed in Armstrong 1969: 31–2.

[51] H. M. Butler to D. C. Gilman, 11 July 1896. Armstrong 1969: 32.

[52] H. B. Fine to D. C. Gilman, 5 Aug. 1896. Armstrong 1969: 33.

[53] S. Newcomb to D. C. Gilman, 26 Aug. 1896. Armstrong 1969: 34.

Craig, then professor at Johns Hopkins and editor of the *American Journal of Mathematics*. Unlike the others, Craig had 'known of Mr. Russell for a number of years owing to my habit of going over all the mathematical journals as soon as they are received'. On the basis of confusing Russell with someone else, Craig found that there was 'nothing particular to say' about him—'I question if there are a dozen mathematicians outside of Cambridge who have ever heard his name'. He did admit that the lecture course was 'certainly very attractive . . . and would be valuable . . . if given by a *very able* man' but that there was not 'the slightest use for it here at present'. Part of his objection was due to the lack of students adequately prepared for the course: 'There is no student here now . . . who could profit by such a course' which would be 'a sort of dilettante affair at best'. Craig also mistook the purpose of Russell's visit, thinking that Russell was seeking permanent employment at Johns Hopkins. On this basis he concluded that Russell's strong recommendations from Cambridge were 'due to the fact that his friends want to find him a position'.[54] Later the same day Craig wrote again to correct the latter confusion (but not the former). This time his objection to Russell shifted somewhat. The 'very attractive' lecture course Russell proposed was now unnecessary at Johns Hopkins, not because there were no students capable of appreciating it, but because 'two or three lectures of the same kind that Mr. R. announces' were regularly given at Johns Hopkins by none other than Craig himself. And, far from falling on deaf ears, Craig knew they 'do good' (presumably because Craig was the sort of '*very able* man' required to make such lectures valuable).[55] Indeed, Craig pursues the syllabuses and virtues of his special lectures at such length that one might think he was seeking promotion. It is not known whether Gilman also sought the opinion of philosophers and that that was more favourable (it was from the philosophy department, after all, that the invitation was expected to come), or whether James Thomas's position on the Trustees' committee was sufficient to carry all opposition before it. In any case, reluctant mathematicians notwithstanding, the invitation was issued and Russell gave the lectures at Johns Hopkins in December.[56]

Russell himself seems to have been aware that he would have little of significance to say to mathematicians who were not interested in the

---

[54] All preceding quotations from Craig: T. Craig to D. C. Gilman, 31 Aug. 1896 (1st letter). Armstrong 1969: 34–5.

[55] T. Craig to D. C. Gilman, 31 Aug. 1896 (2nd letter). Armstrong 1969: 35–6. These two letters are well worth reading in their entirety both as curiosities and for the sharp, if somewhat skewed, light they throw on forms of life in American cultural institutions at the turn of the century.

[56] Alys noted after the Johns Hopkins lectures that the audiences, though large, were not as sympathetic as the Bryn Mawr audiences. (A. Russell to C. Thomas, 4 Dec. 1896).

philosophy of geometry. On 28 July he wrote to Carey Thomas in the hope of dispelling some of the misconceptions about his work:

This book [*EFG*] is mainly occupied with an epistemological problem, and requires, I fear, as much philosophy as mathematics, if not more. I have not done any original *mathematical* work, but have only studied the mathematics of the subject with a view to philosophical questions. Some knowledge of Kant and a modern logic (Lotze's, Bradley's, Sigwart's or Bosanquet's) would, I think be necessary for a comprehension of most of the original parts of my work.

For the same reason he turned down an invitation to give a paper to a mathematics conference in Chicago.

Carey Thomas was willing to write letters of introduction for the Russells to other US colleges and universities, but they did not take her up on this. Alys explained that Russell was 'not keen on going to other Colleges, because he feels that the Johns Hopkins and Bryn Mawr are the best'.[57] It is questionable whether this was more than tact. It may have been that Russell did not want lecturing to interfere with the main object of the visit, which was to meet Alys's relatives. Or that he was unwilling to risk rejection outside the helpful influence of Alys's family connections. On the other hand, Alys's comments to Carey Thomas reveal that he was beginning to feel isolated at Cambridge: 'What he wants is to find a few young people who will take an interest in the subject, and with whom he can discuss it. Except Ward and Whitehead and one or two Oxford people, nobody cares about the subject here, & nobody wants to listen to him!'[58] It seems clear, and there is much other evidence to support the conclusion, that the Apostles, which served Moore as a satisfactory platform for so many years, already had drawbacks as an audience for the sort of technical philosophy Russell was doing. The intellectual limitations of Cambridge were increasingly noted by Russell as he came into contact with a wider academic world. In this his American lectures were very useful to him. He also seems to have enjoyed himself, taking a close interest in the presidential election then in progress (*Auto.* i, 139–41). He reported to his Uncle Rollo: 'I have had an extraordinary number of people at [my lectures]—about thirty, I think—many of them teachers and professors, from this and neighbouring colleges'. He was also favourably impressed by Bryn Mawr: 'it seems to me much better than Girton and Newnham, especially in the greater freedom it allows to the girls. Also those girls that I have met seem to have more independence of mind, more spirit and more originality, than most of the girls at Cambridge'.[59]

While arrangements for the lectures were being made Russell was working,

[57] A. Russell to C. Thomas, 1 Feb. 1896 (Thomas Papers, Bryn Mawr College Archives).
[58] A. Russell to C. Thomas, 1 Feb. 1896 (Thomas Papers, Bryn Mawr College Archives).
[59] B. R. to R. Russell, 20 Nov. 1896 (both quotations). Feinberg and Kasrils 1973 i, 24.

apparently obsessively, on the *EFG*: 'it haunts him night and day', Alys reported.[60] A number of important ideas were added during the summer's work. There was, of course, the major expansion of the material in the dissertation on alternative philosophical theories of geometry to form the long chapter 2. Of more direct concern here, however, are the developments made in Russell's own philosophy of geometry. The chief of these was the completion of his transcendental deduction of the axioms of geometry, turning it into a two-part argument: down from geometrical theory, and up from spatial intuition. The development can be clearly seen in examining the advance that 'The *A Priori* in Geometry' (1896c) makes on 'The Logic of Geometry' (1896b).[61] In the latter Russell argues that three axioms—the axiom of congruence (or free mobility), the axiom of dimensions, and the axiom of distance—are necessary for any form of metrical geometry, and thus are a priori. This result is achieved by an internal analysis of the logic of geometry. None the less, the argument is genuinely transcendental, resulting from an inquiry into the conditions under which spatial measurement is possible. The result of the investigation is that the three axioms mentioned— the axioms of general metrical geometry—are such necessary conditions.

In 'The *A Priori* in Geometry' these arguments are restated more briefly but are supplemented by the second wing of Russell's transcendental deduction, an argument upwards from the form of externality itself. Russell's aim is to show that the same three axioms of general metrical geometry are necessary conditions for any form of externality.[62] The required link between the axioms and the form of externality is provided in 'The *A Priori* of Geometry' by the principle of relativity of position which, though it occurs in 'The Logic of Geometry', is given much greater prominence in the later paper. Since Russell claims that the upwards transcendental argument is 'more convincing for exposition' (1896c: 292) it is unlikely that he would have omitted it from 'The Logic of Geometry' if he had already worked it out in his dissertation. Moreover, it is the second part of the argument which received the most extensive revisions in *EFG*, indicating that Russell's thought about it was still in the formative stage early in 1896.

[60] A. Russell to C. Thomas, 20 Jan. 1896 (Thomas Papers, Bryn Mawr College Archives).

[61] In both of these papers Russell speaks only of 'geometry', but his characterization of the discipline makes it clear he has metrical geometry in mind. It is only in *EFG* that the transcendental deduction of the axioms of projective geometry makes its public appearance, although it must have been included in some form in the dissertation since it is scheduled at an early date for inclusion in the Bryn Mawr lectures with no suggestion that it required further extensive work. As already noted, 1896b was part of the dissertation, probably in much the form we have it today. 1896c was given to the Aristotelian Society on 30 Mar. 1896, and was written by 1 Mar. (B. R. to A. Russell, 1 Mar. 1896).

[62] Both wings of the argument are given in *EFG*. The parts of 1896b omitted in 1896c were restored with a few minor changes. A full collation of 1896b, 1896c, and *EFG* is given in *Papers*, i, 486–95.

When Russell came to include both transcendental arguments in *EFG* he transferred the second from general metrical to projective geometry. This opens up a gap in his overall argument because he nowhere attempts to show that the possibility of spatial measurement is a necessary condition for any form of externality. One gap in the argumentation of 'The *A Priori* in Geometry' which Russell did try to close in *EFG* is that between experience itself and a form of externality. His earlier distinction between internal and external experience (OSG/P 261) would lead one to suppose that a form of externality was not a necessary condition for experience *per se*, because not for *internal* experience. Later he tries to show that a form of externality is essential for any external experience and thus for knowledge itself (1896c: 302). But his argument is perfunctory and taken over fairly directly from Kant. This part of the argument is developed much more thoroughly in *EFG* (§§ 180–93, which were almost certainly written during the summer of 1896). Russell's entire transcendental deduction of geometry, a much more detailed, thorough, sophisticated, and rigorous attempt than any previous one in the entire field, if successful, would be an event of major importance in the philosophy of geometry. The question of its cogency will be investigated in §§ 4.5, 4.6.

## 4.4 *AN ESSAY ON THE FOUNDATIONS OF GEOMETRY*[63]

Russell's *EFG* consists of four main chapters: two historical and two philosophical. The first presents an historical survey of the development of non-Euclidean geometry; and the second surveys the history of the philosophy of geometry from Kant to the end of the nineteenth century. Philosophers included are Kant, Riemann, Helmholtz, Erdmann, Lotze, Delbœuf, and very briefly Calinon, Renouvier, Lechalas, and Poincaré (the last deserving much fuller treatment). Russell's treatment throughout is extremely critical, but since his main criticisms (apart from a point by point refutation of Lotze) derive directly from his own account of geometry they will not be considered independently here. In chapter 3 Russell presents his transcendental deduction of projective and general metrical geometry (see below, §§ 4.5, 4.6). In the final chapter Russell seeks to complete his transcendental deduction by

[63] I am indebted to Blackwell 1972 for basic 'bio-bibliographical' background information, and Radner 1972 for a useful name index to *EFG*. Secondary literature is not extensive, but see Torretti 1978: 301–19; Richards 1984; Kilmister 1984: 6–35; and Bontafini 1970. Dambska 1974 is not very helpful. Contemporary commentary was more extensive, especially in France. See e.g. Lechalas's massive and enthusiastic summary (1898a) and his reply (1898b) to Couturat 1898a. In Britain, E. T. Dixon was highly critical. His 1898a, though idiosyncratic and at points unreliable, deserves to be rescued from the total oblivion into which it fell. It contains, e.g., some very good remarks about dimension which seem to have been completely ignored then and since. Despite its age, Poincaré 1899 is still probably the best published criticism of *EFG*.

showing how the possibility of knowledge depends upon a science of pure externality, which is what he conceived projective geometry to be (see § 4.6). He also seeks to show that geometry involves antimonies which can only be overcome by a dialectical transition to a new science (see § 4.8). These chapters are preceded by a brief introduction, concerned mainly with the concept of apriority, and a preface.

In his preface, Russell acknowledges the influence of Klein (1890) (a work whose two volumes he had read three times in the course of preparing his book) in his treatment of the mathematical aspects of non-Euclidean geometry.[64] In philosophy, especially logic, he acknowledges Bradley, Sigwart, and Bosanquet in that order; and in psychology James's *Principles of Psychology* (*EFG*: p. [x]). Stout and Whitehead are mentioned for their help in reading proofs and making 'many useful criticisms' (*EFG*: p. [x]). But, curiously, Ward is not acknowledged at all. It seems possible, in view of this, that Ward's comments on the dissertation were very largely confined to the psychology chapter which was omitted in the book. The dedication is to McTaggart, 'to whose discourse and friendship is owing the existence of this book' (*EFG*: p. [xi]), although McTaggart's name is never mentioned in the text and there is little in the book's doctrine that can be traced to him.

The introduction of *EFG*, like the early sections of 'Observations', is concerned with trying to clarify a number of logical and epistemological concepts, notably subjectivity and apriority, which will be of importance in the subsequent discussion. Mercifully, the attempt is rather more successful in *EFG* than in 'Observations'. Both discussions take off from an account of sensation. Unexpectedly enough, Russell at this time is a direct realist as regards perception. For Russell, sensations are those mental states whose immediate cause lies in the external world (*EFG* 2; OSG/P 258). Russell makes it clear that he is using 'external' in a non-spatial sense to mean that which is not part of the self (OSG/P 261; *EFG* 2). This is obviously essential, since Russell's central concern is the logical reconstruction of spatial concepts. He also makes it clear that the notion of a pure sensation is an abstraction, since 'we are never wholly passive under the action of an external stimulus' (*EFG* 2).[65]

In OSG Russell uses his account of sensation to define 'a priori': 'A priori is that, and that alone which is neither part of sensation nor assumed for the

----

[64] In OSG, 121 Russell recommends Klein's book 'as one of the very best text-books I have ever come across, being at once sound, lively, interesting and exhaustive.' Russell's collotype edition of Klein (1890), transcribed from Klein's lectures of 1889–90, is completely different to the work posthumously published under almost the same title (Klein 1928). The collotype edn. is cited here.

[65] The point is defended at greater length in OSG/P 258. In this, he seems to have retreated from the position he expressed in 1894*a*: 196, where pure sensations were admitted as possible, though not very common. The change can probably be attributed to the influence of Ward.

sole purpose of explaining sensations'; it 'must be presupposed to make experience possible' (OSG/P 261). In *EFG* a similar account is given: the phrase 'a priori' 'applies to any piece of knowledge which, though perhaps elicited by experience, is *logically* presupposed in experience' (*EFG* 2). But since the a priori is presupposed by experience, it can't be given in experience. It would seem, then, that only logic is thus presupposed (OSG/P 261) and, of the sciences, only arithmetic is wholly a priori (OSG/P 259). At the same time Russell agrees with Kant that space is given in intuition, thus the knowledge of space that geometry gives 'can be derived only by psychology, primarily introspective and always empirical' (OSG/P 259). Thus Kant cannot be said to have established the apodeictic certainty of geometry (OSG/P 259, 261); nor even in fact that geometry is true (though Russell doesn't state this conclusion).

In OSG Russell seems to have thought that the difficulty might be avoided by a distinction among the postulates of geometry between those which are genuinely a priori and those which arise from spatial intuition and which are merely subjective (OSG/P 259). This distinction would be comparable to a distinction traditionally made in the study of Euclidean geometry between the genuinely geometrical axioms (i.e. those which involve essential reference to geometrical concepts such as point and line) and the arithmetical axioms or common notions (e.g. that equals added to equals yield equals).[66] In his published work on geometry, however, Russell rejects the traditional distinction (1896*b*: 267, 275; 1896*c*: 293–4).

In *EFG* Russell's treatment of the problem is less stark. He asserts, clearly enough, that his use of 'a priori' will be 'purely logical' and 'without any psychological implication', since to suppose that the a priori will always be subjective leaves it 'at the mercy of empirical psychology'. 'My test of apriority', he writes, 'will be purely logical: Would experience be impossible, if a certain axiom or postulate were denied?' (*EFG* 3). Elsewhere he distinguishes the a priori from the empirical by the fact that 'what is merely intuitional [i.e. the empirical content or matter of knowledge] can change, without upsetting the laws of thought, without making knowledge formally [i.e. logically] impossible: but what is purely intellectual [i.e. a priori] cannot change, unless the laws of thought should change, and all our knowledge simultaneously collapse' (*EFG* 135). Russell's use of the phrase 'purely intellectual' to characterize the a priori component of knowledge is certainly unfortunate in view of his own effort to separate the a priori from the psychological (as Moore 1899*b*: 400 pointed out). The most charitable gloss to put on it is perhaps that it was supplied by the context of discussion, namely a discussion of Grassmann's attempts (1844) to found a pure science

[66] See Heath 1908: i, 154–5; cp. Kant 1781: B16–17.

of mathematics whose subject-matter would be entirely the creation of the intellect, with no intuitional element provided. Russell can hardly have had in mind that a priori principles were intellectual creations, as Grassmann conceived them, any more than he could have taken quite literally the then-current phrase 'laws of thought'.

Separation of the a priori from the psychological was of considerable importance to Russell. It simply wouldn't do for him to establish that the propositions of geometry depended upon psychological facts about the nature of the (human) mind. For those facts were merely contingent and consequently any deductions based upon them would also be merely contingent, a conclusion clearly inadequate for Russell's purposes. Nor was Russell in the least inclined to accept an account of logic which would reduce it to psychology. Russell had, in any case, already published his own criticism of psychologism (1895a: 251–2), and there was little in his intellectual environment in the 1890s that would have led him to reconsider his position. Russell was quite clear that Kant's interpretation of apriority was psychologistic, and therefore inadequate (*EFG* 180). This was, and indeed remains, the standard interpretation of Kant especially among the early neo-Kantians (e.g. Lange and Zeller). None the less it had some critics among the later German neo-Kantians, notably Hermann Cohen and others of the Marburg school (cf. Willey 1978). The attempt to de-psychologize Kant was not, however, limited to Marburg. Windelband, for example, gave this account: '*A priori* is, with Kant, not psychological, but a purely epistemological mark; it means not a chronological priority to experience, but a *universality and necessity of validity in principles of reason which really transcends all experience, and is not capable of being proved by any experience*'. (Windelband 1892: 534). Some modern commentators (e.g. Allison 1983) have been moved in similar directions. But it was probably harder for Russell, in the 1890s, to see how to define an autonomous field for epistemology since the relations between epistemology and the then emerging discipline of psychology were the topic of much, confused, controversy.[67] Russell's attempt to revise transcendental arguments, setting them upon a logical rather than a psychological foundation, was no minor undertaking and the question remains as to whether he was successful.[68]

[67] See e.g. Robertson 1883; Dewey 1886; Stewart 1876; and Russell's own 1894a. Witness also Moore's apparent identification of the epistemic with the psychological in 1899a. Russell refers to the problem of separation as 'one of the cardinal problems for any reflective philosophical thinker' (EAE 333).
[68] There is little doubt that Russell's attempts to separate the psychological from the a priori owe something to Ward's criticism of Kant's psychologism, (cf. Ward 1922a: 88 ff. and a note added to the 2nd and subsequent editions of 1899: ii, 287). The same point is very briefly made in Ward's metaphysics lectures (cf. Russell's 'Lecture Notebook', i, 97, 136). The major source for Russell's psychologistic interpretation of Kant, however, seems to have been Vaihinger

G. E. Moore, for one, thought that he wasn't. In the course of a severely critical review (1899*b*), Moore argued that Russell's position was largely undermined by repeated confusions on just this point. In some cases, Moore's criticism seems to be a rather unthinking reaction to some of Russell's (perhaps injudiciously) psychologistic terminology: e.g. Russell's use of 'cognition', 'mind', and 'intellectual' (*EFG* 60, 179, and 135 respectively): all criticized by Moore (1899*b*: 400). It seems likely that Russell's use of such expressions was merely a terminological hang-over from the psychologistic tradition he was attempting to replace. Conceptual breaks are rarely terminologically clear-cut, and Moore's own early work suffered in this respect as well.

One of Moore's arguments, however, is more difficult to dispose of. Russell tries to establish the truth of projective geometry by means of a transcendental deduction, that is by trying to show that some branch of experience would be impossible if projective geometry were false. Against this Moore argues, first, that in showing that some branch of experience is impossible all that is done is to show that the judgements which concern that branch of experience could not be known; and, second, that this 'cannot imply that the judgments in question cannot be true' (Moore 1899*a*: 400). Now there is a degree of confusion in Moore's argument, concerning which judgements he means by 'the judgments in question'. In order to clarify matters, let us consider a particular example. Suppose that Russell is trying to establish the truth of a judgement $P$ of projective geometry by seeking to show that if it were false, judgement $E$, concerning some branch of experience, would be incapable of being known. Moore's argument is intended to show that Russell's conclusion (that $P$ is true) doesn't follow from his premiss (that $E$ is knowable). Now Moore is quite correct to say that from the fact that a proposition is unknowable it doesn't follow that it is false. (In fact, it is provable that there are true propositions which are unknowable: see Routley 1981.) But Russell's argument does not involve him in denying this.

To see that this is the case, consider which judgements Moore intends to refer to by the phrase 'the judgments in question'. Suppose that he means $E$. Now it is true that Russell is considering a circumstance, namely the falsity of $P$, which would make $E$ unknowable, and Moore is right in saying that this is not sufficient to show that $E$ is false. But Russell is not concerned with trying to establish the truth or falsity of $E$. Indeed, he is taking the knowability, and hence the truth of the $E$, for granted in an argument designed to establish the truth of $P$. Thus if Moore means $E$ by 'the judgments in question', he is attacking a conclusion that Russell does not want to draw. On the other hand, suppose Moore means $P$. It is true that Russell is trying

1881. Russell read Cohen (1883) in Mar. 1898, but otherwise seems to have been ignorant of the work of the Marburg school.

to establish the truth of *P*. But Moore would be mistaken in thinking that Russell derives this conclusion from the 'unknowable' implies 'false' thesis. Russell in this argument makes no claim about the knowability or otherwise of *P*. Thus if Moore is referring to *P* by 'the judgments in question', he is attacking a premiss which Russell doesn't use.

None the less, though Moore may lose this battle, he seems unlikely to lose the war. For one thing, Russell is committed to the claim that *P* is not merely true, but necessary. And this certainly cannot be inferred from any purely contingent claim as to what we do or can know. Moreover, though Russell does not need to claim that from the fact that a given proposition is universally (or even necessarily) believed we can infer that it is true, he does need to claim that it is legitimate to infer that some other judgement is (necessarily) true. Of course, the truth of all the analytic consequences of the fact that *E* is a necessity of thought (say) may be legitimately inferred. But it is not *these* consequences that Russell is after, for they do not need a transcendental argument. Transcendental arguments are supposed to gain new ground, beyond what can be achieved by drawing merely analytic consequences.

But now we see that Russell's project of utilizing purely logical transcendental arguments is caught in a dilemma. In so far as non-logical matters are excluded it would seem inevitable that the transcendental argument will be recast as a purely deductive argument, perhaps not even a valid one. As a result the special territory that transcendental arguments were supposed to carve out between the logically necessary and the merely contingent will be eroded. In particular, it would seem that such a reconstruction will leave no room for the special type of necessity (noted in § 4.1) which Kant accorded geometry. This was certainly the direction that Russell's thought was to take, with those propositions which had previously been regarded as synthetic a priori being re-classified as either empirical and contingent or as logical and analytic. He had already taken the first steps along this road in his attempt to de-psychologize Kant, and it seems likely that Moore's criticism persuaded him to go further.[69] Whether this is an inevitable fate for transcendental arguments, once psychologism is rejected, is a broader issue than can be tackled here.

---

[69] Russell seems to have accepted Moore's criticisms when they were published. Cf. B. R. to G. E. Moore (18 July 1899): 'I had not written to you about your review, because on all important points I agreed with it'. In EAE, written at almost exactly the same time, Russell excludes psychologism more rigorously, abandoning a transcendental proof of the apriority of the axioms of geometry and concerning himself instead with their necessity (EAE 333). By this time he had abandoned his earlier Kantian approach.

## 4.5 GEOMETRY AND THE A PRIORI: PROJECTIVE GEOMETRY

It was entirely natural that Russell in 1897 should have sought a transcendental deduction of projective geometry. It was widely agreed by those sympathetic to the new geometries that Kant had gone wrong in drawing too specific a conclusion from his transcendental deduction, in assuming (in effect) that the curvature of space must be exactly zero. With the development of non-Euclidean geometry, it became evident that Kant had claimed too much—if only because a very small negative or positive curvature in actual space would produce a non-Euclidean geometry not empirically distinguishable from Euclidean geometry. Thus there could be nothing in our spatial intuitions which would serve to distinguish Euclidean geometry from one of these alternatives, and it could hardly be maintained that the possibility of spatial intuition depended upon space being exactly Euclidean. It became plausible, in fact, once the possibility of non-Euclidean geometries was admitted, to maintain that the actual metric of space was a matter for empirical determination within the limits of observational accuracy. For no a priori reason had been discovered for assuming that spatial curvature was zero (apart from the exploded view that alternative values did not yield consistent geometries). By the same token, it became plausible to think that if transcendental arguments were able to establish anything in geometry it would be in projective geometry where metrical considerations were entirely absent. Moreover, Klein had shown that the various metrical geometries could be obtained from projective geometry by the addition of an appropriately defined distance function, and this gave to projective geometry a generality not possessed by any other geometry at that time.

It was the absence of metrical considerations in pure projective geometry that aroused Russell's hopes for a transcendental deduction. Not only because subsequent metricization yielded the differing metric geometries, but because he saw a purely qualitative science as necessarily prior to any quantitative science. Any quantitative comparison, he argues (*EFG* 129), 'depends on a recognized qualitative identity' which is thereby 'presupposed in every judgment of quantity' (see also *EFG* 83 and RNQ). Thus spatial figures which differ only in quantity must have an identity of quality which is recognizable without reference to quantity. Identity of quality in spatial figures is given, Russell thought, by projective equivalence, and projective geometry thus provides the 'qualitative substrata of the metrical superstructure' (*EFG* 119), and forms a purely 'qualitative science of abstract externality' (*EFG* 120). Once this is understood it is easy to see why Russell was so insistent upon showing that projective geometry requires no metrical conditions whatsoever.

Russell's early interest in projective geometry can certainly be related to his concern with spatial intuition, though different views can be taken of the connection between the two. Nagel, in an influential paper (1939), has argued that projective geometry made an important contribution to the development of abstract formalism in geometry by introducing items of which no spatial intuition was possible. Against this, Richards (1979, 1986) has argued that Nagel's account is historically inaccurate, at least as regards the reception of projective geometry in England. She argues that in England at any rate, projective geometry, imaginary points and points at infinity notwithstanding, was seen (especially by Cayley 1859, 1883) as a way of rehabilitating spatial intuition in geometry. In this, she sees it as a conservative defence against the more radical claims of differential geometry, which Riemann had sought to establish on the basis of the more abstract notion of magnitude. Certainly Russell initially was concerned primarily with the intuitive aspects of projective geometry. Whether in this he was swimming with, or against, the current is a wider issue in the history of ideas which cannot be decided here.

The transcendental deduction of projective geometry was, in many ways, so obvious a project for Kantian philosophers that it is surprising that Russell was alone in attempting it.[70] This must be attributed, in part, to the ignorance of the philosophers who, as Russell frequently remarks, were not generally aware of projective geometry, and to the indifference of the mathematicians to Kant's programme. In part, however, it was due to the difficulty of the undertaking. Obviously, no transcendental argument could establish a geometry proposition by proposition. The deduction had to be used to establish the axioms, on the grounds that the deductive consequences of a priori propositions are themselves a priori (*EFG* 3, 60). This made the task more manageable, but still not easy.

Russell, however, eschewed, at least in *EFG*, rigorous axiomatization. Projective geometry had been rigorously axiomatized by Pasch (1882), nearly twenty years before the first rigorous axiomatization of Euclidean geometry in 1899 (Hilbert 1899). According to Freudenthal (1962: 617, 619), it was Pasch, 'the father of rigor in geometry', who first taught mathematicians how to formulate axioms. Russell, however, makes only one reference to Pasch (*EFG* 50), and that merely to excuse his not having said anything about Pasch's work. It is not clear how far Russell was acquainted with Pasch's work; it is probable that he knew of it only from other authors (he was certainly acquainted with it through Veronese (1891)

---

[70] An alternative target, and in many ways a better one, would have been topology. However, the crucial notion of a topological space wasn't sufficiently developed at the time Russell wrote. (Riemann's topological insights in (1854) had been largely overlooked.) Poincaré, who made important contributions to topology, regarded it, and not projective geometry, in the later part of his career, as a purely qualitative science of the type Russell sought (see Poincaré 1899).

which he frequently cites). He came close to reading it as early as May 1895, when he made a list in his revision notebook (RA, Rec. Acq. 1027) of works to be read on non-Euclidean geometry. The list includes Cayley (1859), Gauss (1828), Beltrami (1868a, 1868b), Lie (1890), and Pasch (1882). The ensuing pages of the notebook duly contain notes on all these works except Pasch. The notebook gives no indication of why Russell stopped where he did, but it does seem clear he didn't read Pasch before November 1900, when he used it in writing chapter 45 of *POM*. He may well have been encouraged to read it by a favourable reference in Peano (1889) which he read in September 1900. Veronese, by contrast, was critical of Pasch's work (e.g. of his treatment of congruence), though Russell would certainly have rejected some of his complaints (e.g. that Pasch, in omitting metrical considerations, had failed to develop a genuine geometry). At any rate, Russell could hardly have studied Pasch's axiomatization closely before October 1899, for he would surely have referred to it in his dispute that year with Poincaré, which in part centred on Russell's axiom set for projective geometry in *EFG* (see Poincaré 1899, 1900). The formalistic axiom set Russell provided in his reply (AOG) was inspired by Cremona (1893), not Pasch.

Although he is not explicit on the point, it is likely that Russell would in any case have rejected Pasch's work on philosophical grounds. He complains that the axioms of projective geometry had not been formulated 'philosophically' (*EFG* 118), by which he apparently means that covertly metrical concepts had not been entirely excluded. This stricture would certainly apply to Pasch's axiomatization, in which ten congruence axioms are introduced in order to permit the assignment of coordinates to points in projective space. These axioms introduce what amounts to a notion of measurement into Pasch's system, and at precisely the point where Russell complains it is normally introduced: in assigning coordinates. Despite this, however, there is no indication that Russell had Pasch specifically in mind on this point.[71]

There are further reasons why Russell would not have been impressed with Pasch's axiomatizations: Pasch's work was unabashedly empirical and Russell might well have thought it entirely inappropriate to his own Kantian approach. Pasch based his axiomatization on certain fundamental undefined concepts (viz. point, straight segment, flat surface) based on the shape, size, and mutual position of physical objects. The axioms of projective geometry state relations between the fundamental concepts (Pasch 1882: 3–17). Now it is quite clear that Russell, who was attempting to show that projective geometry was a necessary condition for the possibility of experience, could not embrace an axiomatization which was itself heavily dependent upon

---

[71] A few pages later (*EFG* 122 n.), he explicitly cites Cremona (1983: 50) as responsible for a metric definition of anharmonic ratio.

empirical data. Veronese's references to Pasch's empirical interpretation of his axioms were marked by Russell in his copy of Veronese (1891: 655), which indicates that he was aware of Pasch's empiricism early on. Later, when praising Pasch's work, Russell is at pains to distance himself from Pasch's empiricism.

Instead, Russell appeals to an older tradition: to Cayley's theory of distance (Cayley 1859) and von Staudt's quadrilateral construction (von Staudt 1847). In projective geometry the notions of spatial quantity, distance, and size, which figure prominently in metric geometry, are abandoned. Given a projective (re)definition of distance, the various competing metric geometries can be obtained from projective geometry by apparently inessential changes in the conventions used to define metrical relations in projective space. Cayley (1859: 61) sought to establish the notion of distance 'upon purely descriptive principles', but his success was questionable since he defined distance as a function of the coordinates but did not explain how the coordinates could be introduced without a prior conception of distance. Klein, who first recognized the way in which the various metrical geometries could be obtained from Cayley's theory of distance (Klein 1890: i, chs. 1, 2), also discovered that the projective coordinates could be assigned without reference to measurement by means of von Staudt's quadrilateral construction (Klein 1890: i, 338–54).[72]

Projective geometry studies those properties of spatial figures which are invariant under projective transformations. Since two collinear projective points do not uniquely determine a third, which at most may be any point collinear to the given two, there is no projective invariant involving fewer than four points. The projective invariant for four collinear points, *A, B, C, D*, is their anharmonic (or cross) ratio. This is arrived at as follows.[73] By means of the quadrilateral construction it is possible to find, given any three collinear points, *A, B, D*, a unique fourth point *C*, the harmonic conjugate of *A*, on the same line as *A, B, D* and projectively interchangeable with *A*. Choose any two points, *E* and *F*, collinear with *A* but not with *B* and *D*. Construct the points at which *DE* intersects with *BF* and *DF* intersects with *BE*. The line through these intersection points cuts *AD* at *C*. Given a point outside the plane *ADF*, the uniqueness of *C* can be demonstrated. This can be done without any appeal to numbers or measurement. Since *C* is unique it

[72] In fact, there is a defect in Klein's account to which Russell subsequently alludes (AOG 409 n; *POM* 389–90). For only rational coordinates can be assigned by Klein's methods. This, of course, destroys the continuity of the projective line, since the missing points cannot be assigned coordinates defined in terms of the rational coordinates, for reasons Russell explains in *POM*. In 1896–7, however, Russell was in no position to appreciate these subtleties, as will be seen in Ch. 6 below.
[73] The order of presentation here follows that of *EFG/F*, rather than *EFG*, for reasons of clarity.

is possible to assign it a unique coordinate number. Thus points can be distinguished from each other by means of numbers, as with the coordinates of metric geometry, but in the case of projective geometry the numbers have purely conventional significance and do not rely on distance, as the coordinates of metric geometry do. With numbers now assigned to points we can define the key projective invariant, anharmonic ratio:

$$[A,B;C,D] \ = \ \frac{(AC)(BD)}{(AD)(BC)}$$

Any set of four points is thus projectively equivalent to any other set of four points with the same anharmonic ratio. Since $C$ is the harmonic conjugate of $A$, we have

$$[A,B;C,D] \ = \ [C,B;A,D]$$

By means of appropriate conventions in assigning numbers to points of projective space, the space may be metricized without special numerical transformations (as Klein had shown); but this is purely a matter of convenience and does not affect the conventionality of the numbers assigned to the points.

But anharmonic ratio and the quadrilateral construction are scarcely more promising targets for a transcendental deduction than Pasch's 23 axioms. As Russell notes, however, both depend upon simpler principles of projective equivalence based in two dimensions on the following:

To project the points $A$, $B$, $C$, $D$ . . . from a centre $O$, is to construct the straight lines $OA$, $OB$, $OC$, $OD$ . . . (D1)

To cut a number of straight lines $a$, $b$, $c$, $d$ . . . by a transversal $s$, is to construct the points $sa$, $sb$, $sc$, $sd$ . . .[74] (D2)

Projective transformations, in two dimensions, are effected through the application of D1 and D2. Applying D1 and then D2 transforms a figure of points into another figure of points projectively equivalent to the first. Applying D2 and then D1 transforms a figure of lines into a projectively equivalent figure of lines (*EFG* 126–7). Russell hoped to show that these principles of projective transformation were the basis for all qualitative judgements about the contents of intuitional manifolds, and thus were a priori principles of any form of externality. In so far as this could be done, and two-dimensional projective geometry could be derived from the two principles of projective transformation, two-dimensional projective geometry could be shown to be entirely a priori.

[74] *EFG* 126; adapted from Cremona 1893: 2. D1–2 provide the essential conditions for the definition of the projective plane. Russell restricts his argument on projective geometry entirely to two dimensions for reasons of mathematical simplicity (*EFG* 122).

These claims have now to be made good. Russell has to show, in particular, that qualitatively equivalent figures are projectively equivalent figures. The argument proceeds as follows:[75] Russell characterizes points as 'the terms of spatial relations', while, so far as geometry is concerned, whatever is not a point is 'a relation between points' (*EFG* 128). Since he takes extension to be relational, he concludes that points have no extension. On either characterization, points have no intrinsic qualities and, since different points are distinguished, they must be distinguished by their relations (*EFG* 129). The relation between any two points is the straight line on which they lie. But, in the absence of quantity, two points are qualitatively identical to any other two on the same line (*EFG* 130). The two pairs can, Russell admits, be distinguished perceptually (*EFG* 131), but since the aim of the broader enterprise is to determine the conditions under which external perception is possible, thereby identifying its a priori presuppositions, this fact is not relevant here. For Russell the (philosophical) aim of projective geometry, as the study of projectively equivalent figures, is 'the determination of qualitative spatial similarity, . . . the determination, that is, of all the figures which, when any one figure is given, can be distinguished from the given figure, so long as quantity is excluded, only by the mere fact that they are external to it' (*EFG* 133).

Any pair of points on a line is thus qualitatively identical to any other pair of points on the line. But since the first pair can also be projected on to any other pair, the thesis that qualitatively identical figures are projectively equivalent figures is not falsified. Indeed, it is easy to see intuitively that the thesis is verified, not only in this case, but in all others. For, in practical terms, in projective geometry one can do whatever can be done using only an ungraduated straight-edge. The ungraduated straight-edge, however, corresponds exactly to the conceptual resources Russell allows for his purely qualitative science: the non-quantitative relation between two points, which is the straight line joining them. Consequently, it is not surprising to find that what can be achieved by the one can be achieved by the other.

Having demonstrated to his own satisfaction both that projective geometry is purely qualitative and that whatever is both spatial and purely qualitative can be treated by projective geometry, Russell's next task is to discover what properties space must have if purely qualitative spatial equivalence is to be possible (*EFG* 132–3). The expectation, of course, is that these properties will be sufficient to establish the principles of projective transformation (based on D1 and D2) on which projective geometry is said to rest. This

---

[75] Russell throughout takes points as basic, but, since in two dimensions points and lines are projective duals, this is merely conventional (*EFG* 128). This duality is important in overcoming the apparently metrical basis of Russell's account of points, namely as items with zero extension (cf. *EFG* 128 n.).

point at least helps to make clear, even if it fails to justify, Russell's choice of axioms for projective geometry. The axioms he gives are the following (*EFG* 132):

> We can distinguish different parts of space, but all parts are qualitatively similar, and are distinguished only by the immediate fact that they lie outside one another. (PGI)

> Space is continuous and infinitely divisible; the result of infinite division, the zero of extension, is called a *point*. (PG II)

> Any two points determine a unique figure, called a straight line,[76] any three in general determine a unique figure, the plane. Any four determine a corresponding figure of three dimensions, . . . But this process comes to an end, sooner or later, with some number of points which determine the whole of space. (PGIII)

It is easy to mock Russell's calling these 'axioms of projective geometry'. But, as Freudenthal (1962: 617) has pointed out, mathematicians then were not used to stating axioms in anything like the rigorous way that would now be considered appropriate. Indeed, for many (Freudenthal cites Klein as a prominent example), axioms, though often referred to, were rarely stated at all. While Russell was not up to the most advanced standards of his day, he was not noticeably behind the common practice.

It is easy enough to see in outline why Russell thought these three axioms were required for his projective transformation principles. To consider the axioms, briefly, in reverse order: That, in the two-dimensional case, any two points determine a line is necessary if projecting a point $A$ through a centre $O$ is to construct the line $AO$, as required by D1. Similarly, the continuity of space (PGII), in particular the continuity of line segments, is required in order to ensure that two lines always intersect in a point, as required for projective section D2. The first axiom, the requirement of spatial homogeneity, is necessary to ensure that the results of projective transformation are qualitatively identical to the original. Given a figure of lines (or points), successive operations of section and projection (or projection and section) will transform the figure into a figure in a different position. The two figures are, by definition, projectively equivalent, but if they are also to be qualitatively identical it is necessary that their intrinsic properties are not affected by mere difference of position. That this is the case, Russell argues (*EFG* 133–4), is assured by PGI.

---

[76] There is a potential problem for Russell's attempt to give a purely qualitative account of projective geometry owing to his use of the concept of a straight line. For a straight line is normally defined metrically as the *shortest* distance between two points. In early work Russell had used this to argue that projective coordinates could not be assigned without appeal to metrical considerations (1896b: 284). However, the relevant sentence was dropped when Russell incorporated the surrounding material into *EFG* 175 (cf. *Papers*, i, T284: 22–3). In 1899, he considered eliminating the concept of a straight line (defining it in terms of addition of distances), but to no avail (FIAM 297).

Russell, in different places, puts this last point in three different ways:

1. PGI is a requirement of spatial homogeneity: all positions in space are qualitatively similar (*EFG* 133, 137, 144). If they were not so, a spatial figure would take on different (intrinsic) qualities depending upon its position.

2. PGI is a requirement of pure relativity of position: all positions are distinguished merely in their external relations (*EFG* 134, 137, 143). External relations, by definition, do not affect intrinsic properties. Thus pure relativity of position implies the homogeneity of space. (And vice-versa, since if all positions are qualitatively similar they can only differ in external relations.)

3. PGI is a requirement that space is entirely passive: space itself does not affect the qualities of the figures which occupy positions in it (*EFG* 133, 140, 144). If this were not the case, we could not be sure, in projecting a figure from one position to another, that space itself had not effected some change in its (intrinsic) qualities.

If any one of these requirements failed, figures that are projectively equivalent might yet differ in intrinsic qualities. But Russell has already argued that projectively equivalent figures are qualitatively identical, from which it follows that all three requirements hold. Russell, in fact, treats all three requirements as equivalent, and does not always distinguish between them. His grounds for this are less than conclusive, as we will see shortly.

It can hardly be denied that Russell's presentation of the axioms PGI–III leaves much to be desired. Indeed, Russell himself says that they are only 'roughly stated' and are not intended to have 'any exclusive precision'—by which he means, apparently, that they may 'be enunciated in many ways' (*EFG* 132). But before discussing defects in formulation, we should note that Russell makes no attempt to prove that these three axioms are sufficient for projective geometry. In fact, it is clear that they are insufficient. He has shown that projective geometry requires anharmonic ratio, which depends upon the quadrilateral construction, which in turn depends on the projective principles D1 and D2, which in turn require PGI–III. Thus, if his argument is so far satisfactory, he has shown that projective geometry requires that projective space have the properties ascribed to it by PGI–III. He will go on to argue that these properties are required also by any form of externality. It is immediately obvious that his transcendental deduction of projective geometry from the possibility of a form of externality will fail unless PGI–III can be shown to be, not only necessary, but sufficient for projective geometry. It is true (assuming all the individual parts of his overall argument to be valid) that he will have shown that *parts* of projective geometry are a priori, namely those parts which follow from PGI–III. But he will have done nothing to show that the whole science is a priori, unless he can show that PGI–III are sufficient for the whole of projective geometry. But this he cannot do. His only hope, therefore, if his transcendental deduction is to be saved, is that those principles of projective geometry which cannot be derived from PGI–III are of a clearly logical or arithmetic nature, and could thus be assumed to be a priori without special proof. In ascertaining whether this was in fact the case, Russell was obviously hampered by his lack of knowledge of axiomatic projective geometry.

Torretti (1978: 303–4), in a hostile analysis, complains that Russell does not distinguish between real projective space and complex projective space when stating his three axioms, although in his earlier historical discussion of meta-geometry he had made the distinction (*EFG* 28). Torretti (1978: 303) quotes Russell as saying that projective geometry deals 'only with the properties common to all spaces' (*EFG* 118)—a view which is plainly mistaken, since real and complex projective spaces have different properties. But what Russell actually says is this: 'Projective Geometry, *in so far as* it deals only with the properties common to all spaces, will be found . . . to be wholly *a priori*' (emphasis added). Indeed, a similar passage on the previous page sets the context for the discussion of the axioms of projective geometry: 'The properties dealt with by projective Geometry . . . in so far as these are obtained without the use of imaginaries, are properties common to all spaces' (*EFG* 117). This explicitly makes the distinction Torretti claims is missing. Torretti's criticism is, in fact, even wider of the mark than this indicates, for it ignores Russell's arguments for thinking that the use of complex numbers for coordinates fails to specify any true geometrical points not already specified by the use of real numbers. For Russell, points whose Cartesian coordinates are imaginary are merely convenient algebraic fictions without any genuinely spatial import (*EFG* 43–6). Accordingly, Russell considers himself justified in ignoring complex projective geometry in his transcendental deduction.

The issue is not merely one of how much Russell knew about projective geometry, it involves once more his view of what was geometrically admissible. Cayley (1883: 8–9; cited *EFG* 42) had raised the question of the interpretation of imaginary points in geometry as one of key importance. Russell comes close, as Richards (1986: 324) has pointed out, to dismissing the problem along formalist lines. While admitting that any set of coordinates, if they determine a point at all, determine it uniquely, he denies that every set of coordinates determines a point. 'As well might a postman assume that, because every house in a street is uniquely determined by its number, therefore there must be a house for every imaginable number' (*EFG* 44). This is rather an impressive move for someone in Russell's position; he seems about to embrace a much more abstract approach to mathematics, bringing him well in line with advanced contemporary thinking. Yet he draws back from this radical conclusion, using his old distinction between geometry and algebra:

For all the fruitful uses of imaginaries, in Geometry, are those which begin and end with real quantities, and use imaginaries only for the intermediate steps. Now in all such cases, we have a real spatial interpretation at the beginning and the end of our argument, where alone the spatial interpretation is important: in the intermediate links, we are dealing in a purely algebraical manner with purely algebraical quantities, and may perform any operations which are algebraically permissible. If the quantities with which we end are capable of spatial interpretation, then, and only then, our result may be regarded as geometrical (*EFG* 45.)

In other cases, geometrical language is only 'a convenient help to the imagination'. The circular points in projective geometry 'are not to be found in space' but are 'a mere *memoria technica* for purely algebraic properties' (*EFG* 45). The claims of intuition here prevent Russell from making a significant advance in his treatment of geometry. In his comments on Russell's treatment of complex projective geometry, Torretti not only gets things wrong, but misses what is of most importance.

Poincaré (1899) is closer to the mark when he complains that PGIII is insufficient to specify the projective straight line unless further properties are given.[77] Russell admitted the problem and in 'On the Axioms of Geometry' (AOG) produced a new set of six axioms for projective geometry. Although they are still insufficient (he gives no axioms of order, only axioms of incidence), this time they are presented with more mathematical rigour, and a serious effort to prove their sufficiency for the quadrilateral construction is made.

Russell's next problem is to provide a transcendental deduction of his three axioms. His deduction, as already noted, proceeds in two steps. The first, is to show that the axioms are required for any form of externality and thus for any possible space. The second, to be considered later (§ 4.6), consists in showing that a form of externality is required if knowledge is to be possible. Our first need, therefore, is to clarify the concept of a form of externality.

A form of externality, Russell says, is a 'principle of differentiation', that is 'an element, taken in isolation and abstracted from the content which it differentiates, by which the things presented are distinguished as various' (*EFG* 136; rearranged). The form of externality is not concerned with the diversity of actual material contents, but with 'the bare possibility of such diversity', which is what is left 'when we abstract from any sense-perception all that is distinctive of its particular matter' (*EFG* 136). A form of externality is thus

---

[77] Cp. the eight axioms for points and lines given by Pasch 1882: 5–7; or Coxeter's seven axioms of incidence 1942: 20.

something like a display rack on which diverse items may be simultaneously presented. The existence or diversity of the items does not depend upon the rack, but the possibility of their being *simultaneously presented* does. Three further issues, which Russell puts off for later study, are involved in proving the necessity of such a form. (i) Russell maintains that such a principle of differentiation is required '[i]n any world in which perception presents us with . . . discriminated and differentiated contents' (*EFG* 136). To establish the *existence* of such a form requires the unexceptionable claim that experience in the actual world is of this type; but to establish the *necessity* of such a form requires a transcendental argument for the claim that all possible experience must be of this type. (ii) Russell also needs to show that the *form* of externality, rather than, for example, merely differentiated objects, is required for differentiation. (iii) Finally, Russell needs to show that what is left over from the differentiated things presented to us when their material content is abstracted is the bare possibility of diversity or form of externality, and not something else. These issues are shelved for the time being, as Russell concentrates on the relation of geometry to the form of externality. He writes: '[S]ince space, as dealt with by Geometry, is certainly a form of this kind, we have . . . to ask: What properties must such a form, when studied in abstraction, necessarily possess?' (*EFG* 136).

The first property Russell ascribes to the form of externality is relativity: 'externality is an essentially relative conception—nothing can be external to itself. To be external to something is to be another with some relation to that thing' (*EFG* 136). Now it is curious to see Russell invoking difference in a definition of externality, for the use to which he wants to put the form of externality is as a ground for difference (not vice-versa): the form is that by which presentations are distinguished as various. Thus we might have expected that he would define '*x* is diverse from *y*' or '*x* is not *y*' in terms of '*x* is external to *y*'. Quite apart from this, Russell's point, on one rather natural reading, seems to amount to no more than the claim that 'is external to' is a relation. But he uses it to support a further conclusion: that position is purely relative. Now if we take '*x* is external to *y*' as a judgement of externality and abstract it from all material content, then presumably what are left to be related by 'is external to' are bare unoccupied positions. And what Russell means by saying that position is purely relative is that positions have no *internal* relations or qualities. And this we can grant, since we have arrived at positions by abstracting out the material content of a judgement of externality, i.e. precisely by the removal of all intrinsic qualities from the terms of the judgement. Since the form of externality requires that positions be distinguished and they cannot be distinguished by their intrinsic qualities, it follows that they are distinguished by external relations, and thus are purely relative. Thus the form of externality satisfies PGI: its parts are qualitatively alike and distinguishable from one another only by the fact that some are wholly external to others.

Russell backs up this argument with one far less satisfactory: namely, that the form of externality has neither elements nor a whole, because (i) these are material features that get abstracted out in framing the conception of the form, and (ii) elements and wholes are not external to themselves and thus cannot be pure externality. 'Hence arise', concludes Russell, 'infinite divisibility, with the self-contradictory notion of the point, in the search for elements, and unbounded extension, with the contradiction of an infinite regress or a vicious circle, in the search for a completed whole' (*EFG* 137). The first part of this argument looks somewhat worse than it is. To understand it we need to take Russell's doctrine of internal relations into account. For Russell, as will become clear in the sequel, holds that only elements with diverse intrinsic qualities may be combined into wholes, while spatial positions have been shown to lack such qualities. The second part of the argument, however, is certainly incoherent. Why should externality have to be external to itself? and why should a *relation* be more likely to have this weird property than an element or a whole? The root problem here seems to be the sort of paralogism frequently encountered in the Platonic dialogues: the Form of Exernality (or as Russell has it, pure externality) contains nothing that is not external. Consequently, it must be external to itself. But nothing is external to itself. Once the first premiss is accepted, the conclusion is not blocked, whether externality is a relation or no. But even without this difficulty Russell's argument is inconclusive for it presupposes that what has neither elements nor whole must be purely relational. But it is not clear why. The doctrine of internal relations doesn't help, since it shows, at best, that what is purely relational cannot have elements or a whole, not the converse.

The second feature of the form of externality which Russell seeks to derive is its homogeneity. For this he offers two arguments. In the first he treats homogeneity as a consequence of the relativity of position: 'For any quality in one position, by which it was marked out from another, would be necessarily more or less intrinsic, and would contradict pure relativity. Hence all positions are qualitatively alike, i.e. the form is homogeneous throughout' (*EFG* 137). Russell has indeed ensured that positions within the form of externality lack intrinsic qualities, so space could not be heterogeneous on account of any intrinsic quality of some position not shared by all the others. However, this gives no reason to suppose that some positions are not singled out by virtue of their relations to other positions. Of course, each position is distinct precisely on account of the relations it alone has to other positions, but Russell's principle of homogeneity does not require that each position have the same relations to other positions as all the others. That would be clearly impossible. What homogeneity does rule out is the possibility that certain positions have relations of a different type to others, or that positions differ in their higher-order relations. What homogeneity should exclude are situations in which some positions are singled out within the form, such as when one position is equidistant from all the others. Alternatively, since this involves metrical notions, we should want to exclude a form of externality in which some positions were distinguished by not being between two others (i.e. the end points of a closed interval). It seems Russell has done nothing to exclude such possible forms of externality, and thus homogeneity may not be taken as an immediate consequence of relativity.

Russell's other argument for homogeneity is the following: 'The diversity of content, which was possible only within the form of externality, has been abstracted from, leaving nothing but the bare possibility of diversity, the bare principle of differentiation, itself uniform and undifferentiated. For if diversity presupposes such a form, the form cannot, unless it were contained in a fresh form, be itself diverse or differentiated' (*EFG* 137). This argument seems to embody the opposite fallacy to that involved in the previous argument concerning pure externality. Here it is argued that pure diversity, since it is the presupposition of diversity, cannot itself be diverse, and must therefore be homogeneous. By parity of reasoning, one might have concluded, as Russell did not, that pure externality, as the presupposition of things external, was not itself external. But claims of the sort Russell appeals to, that externality is external and that diversity is not diverse, are best treated as nonsignificant (not, as Russell would later have it, on grounds of self-reference, but because they involve category mistakes).

Using the twin properties of relativity and homogeneity Russell seeks to show that the form of externality is infinitely divisible: 'that the relation of externality between any two things is infinitely divisible, and may be regarded, consequently, as made up of an infinite number of the would-be elements of our form, or again as the sum of two relations of externality' (*EFG* 137–8). Russell's claim that relations may be divided is, at first sight, another category mistake. But Russell (following William James 1890: ii, 148–53) identifies the spatial relation between two points as the line which joins them (1896b: 282–3; 1896c: 299–300; *EFG* 170–1). James's disastrous account of relations was a potent source of difficulty for Russell (see below, § 4.6, and Dixon 1898: 8–9). In particular, if the straight line simply is the relation between two points, the notion of collinearity becomes incoherent. For if *A, B, C* are collinear, but distinct, points, the relation between *A* and *B* cannot be identical to that between *A* and *C* (as Russell belatedly noticed, COS: 317). Given James's account, however, since lines are divisible, spatial relations in the James-Russell sense can also be regarded as divisible. However, our problems are not at an end here because Russell needs to prove that the line must be infinitely divisible, not to assume that it is in a proof that the form of externality is also infinitely divisible.

Russell attempts to provide the required argument, working from the premiss that the form of externality must be homogeneous. The argument runs as follows: since the form of externality is homogeneous, 'the relation . . . of externality between two or more things must . . . be capable of continuous alteration. . . . Hence it follows, that every relation of externality may be regarded for scientific purposes, as an infinite congeries of elements, though philosophically, the relations alone are valid, and the elements are a self-contradictory result of hypostasizing the form of externality' (*EFG* 138). But here it is difficult to see why the relation of externality must be capable of continuous alteration, just because the form of externality is homogeneous. For suppose that space were composed of a finite number of discrete positions or regions. Each position may surely be qualitatively identical to every other. Space is then homogeneous, but spatial relations are not capable of continuous variation.

There seems, however, to be a somewhat better (though still not flawless) argument for infinite divisibility available to Russell, based essentially on arguments he uses to establish the relativity and homogeneity of the form of externality. Suppose that the form of externality is incapable of infinite division. Then there would be some limit to its degree of divisibility, and thus some discrete components of the form which were incapable of further division. These components would be diverse from each other. But since all content has been abstracted from the form, they could not be diverse by virtue of their qualities and thus would have to be diverse by virtue of their (external) relations (i.e. they are purely relative). But such diversity requires a form of externality. Thus either there is another form of externality and we are led into an infinite regress; or else the form of externality itself cannot have purely relative components. Thus the form of externality must be infinitely divisible.

There are two difficulties with this argument. Firstly, the case has been ignored in which the indivisible component of the form of externality is not a proper part of the form, but consists of the entire form. In other words, nothing has been done to exclude the possibility that the form of externality itself is indivisible. It would seem that the form of externality ought to be declared either infinitely divisible or not divisible at all. The latter option would be more in keeping with a monistic metaphysics, but there are passages in *EFG* (pp. 182–7) that indicate Russell would have ruled it out on the grounds that it would have rendered impossible the diversity necessary for knowledge (see § 4.6).

The other difficulty is one which Russell explicitly confronted in *EFG*. According to PGII the result of infinite division is the point, the zero of extension. Now if it is true that infinite division yields points, then it would seem that exactly the same argument that Russell has mounted against finite divisibility could be used against infinite divisibility which tends to points. That is, we should be able to argue that the different points yielded by infinite division were all qualitatively identical, and thus distinguished only by their external relations, and thus that some other form of externality was required to distinguish them, and finally that, since no such form was available, the result of infinite division could not be such points. Russell is aware of this consequence and labels it the antinomy of points: for he regards points as inconsistent items which result from hypostasizing the form of externality (see § 4.8). But, from the point of view of the present argument, there would seem to be nothing to choose between infinite divisibility which results in points which are both diverse and homogeneous, and finite divisibility which results in (finite) elements which are diverse and homogeneous. Accordingly, the present argument for infinite divisibility cannot be regarded as satisfactory.

The argument for the apriority of PGIII is, by contrast, quite simple. If positions are to be defined by means of their relations to other positions then there must be some finite, integral number of relations which suffices to define them.[78] 'Every relation thus necessary for definition we call a dimension. Hence we obtain the proposition: *Any form of externality must have a finite integral number of dimensions*' (*EFG* 140). Torretti (1978: 306) claims there is a technical difficulty in Russell's argument. For if $k$ be the Peano curve which fills the Euclidean plane, and $P$ its origin, then every point $Q$ on the Euclidean plane is, according to Torretti, 'unambiguously determined' by the arc of $k$ joining $P$ to $Q$. Thus, on Russell's account of dimension, the Euclidean plane would be one-dimensional. There is, indeed, an important technical difficulty in Russell's account, but not the one Torretti alludes to. It is rather surprising that Torretti claims the Peano curve as a counter-example to Russell's traditional, coordinate view of dimensionality. For the Peano curve is not a one–one mapping; some points of the plane are covered twice or four times by the curve. Thus the arc of $k$ from $P$ to $Q$ cannot unambiguously determine any point $Q$ on the plane. Peano himself (1890: 147) uses this fact to argue that his curve does not disturb the then-prevalent view that dimensionality was invariant under continuous one–one mappings.

[78] The idea of infinite dimensional spaces was available at the time Russell wrote and in sources with which he was familiar (Riemann 1854: 59). A few years later the possibility of fractional dimensions was mooted also (see Fréchet 1910). Even here Russell may have had a hint since he mentions (*EFG* 162 n. that Delbœuf 1893: 450) refers to geometries of $m/n$ dimensions. But Russell was unable to follow up this lead, since Delbœuf gives no references. Both kinds of spaces have since found application in physics: infinite dimensional spaces in quantum mechanics and fractional dimensional spaces in the theory of fractals (see Mandelbrot 1975).

The real difficulty with Russell's view of dimensionality had come earlier, with Cantor's demonstration that there was a one–one mapping from a unit square to a unit line segment, and, more generally, from a unit cube of $n$-dimensions (even where $n$ is denumerably infinite) to a unit line segment.[79] It was Cantor, and not Peano, who had put paid to the traditional concept of dimensionality which Russell was using, the idea that the dimension number of a space was simply the number of coordinates needed to specify uniquely a point of the space. This view of dimensionality had been widely held by geometers before Russell (Cantor mentions Gauss, Riemann, and Helmholtz; Russell, OSG 61, cites Riemann). Cantor himself immediately realized that his mapping from the $n$-dimensional cube to the line segment destroyed the traditional view.[80] In the face of this, the only way to retain the traditional view would be to maintain that dimensionality was not invariant under one–one mappings. But this was almost impossible to accept, and a much more plausible conclusion to draw was that coordinate number and dimension number were distinct concepts. This renounced the traditional theory, but left hopes that the concept of dimension could be redefined in some way so as to preserve dimensionality under one–one mappings. The problem of redefining dimensionality and proving its invariance remained unsolved until work by Poincaré (1903, 1912) and Brouwer (1911, 1913). By that time it had become clear that dimension was a topological concept (see Johnson 1979, 1981).

Russell, of course, couldn't have been expected to have a satisfactory account of dimensionality in 1897. But he could have been expected to be aware of the difficulties of the account he was using. Cantor's proof had provoked an immediate controversy. Moreover, Cantor's paper was republished in French in a special issue of *Acta Mathematica* in 1883 which Russell had read in 1896. In fact Russell had recognized the dimensionality argument as 'the kernel of [Cantor's] article' (*Papers*, ii, 466). But at this time Russell thought that the argument, like most of Cantor's work, was fallacious. In particular, he objected to Cantor's theorem that, if $e_1, e_2, \ldots e_n$ were $n$ independent variables taking all irrational values between 0 and 1 and $d$ a single variable taking all irrational values between 0 and 1, each value of $e_1, e_2, \ldots e_n$ could be mapped onto a unique value of $d$. 'The Proposition', he complained, 'seems absurd, for $d$ runs through exactly the same series of values as any $e$, and not $n$ times as many' (*Papers*, ii, 467): a complaint which simply ignores Cantor's proof to the contrary. In slightly later writings Russell came to regard dimension as an 'essentially projective

[79] Cantor 1878. The Cantor mappings are all discontinuous, which prompted the speculation by Dedekind, Netto, and others that dimensionality is invariant under continuous one–one mappings.

[80] See his letter to Dedekind, 25 June 1877 (Cantor and Dedekind 1937: 33).

notion (COS 319), a view elaborated to some extent in working notes of the same period (NOG 377–9). He seems to have thought, for a while, that this would evade Cantor's difficulty. For he mentions Cantor's argument, but denies that it undermines his account of dimension, on the grounds that Cantor is concerned with what Russell terms 'series by correlation', whereas for Russell all series by correlation depend upon self-sufficient series (AOG 413). The relevance of this distinction is hardly clear and Russell's subsequent remarks are too brief to reveal what he had in mind. In *The Principles of Mathematics* he still lacks an adequate theory of dimension. There he takes Cantor to have shown that, for $n \leqslant \omega$, every $n$-dimensional series is also a one-dimensional series, i.e. that dimension number simply is not invariant under one-one mappings (*POM* 374–5).

With PGIII demonstrated to his satisfaction, Russell's transcendental deduction of the three axioms of projective geometry is essentially complete.[81] The conclusion he hopes to have established is that projective geometry is the science of the form of externality, and can be deduced from the a priori properties of all such forms. Thus he maintains that projective geometry is itself a priori. That the form itself cannot be regarded as a real object independent of the material content from which it is abstracted, Russell freely admits. Projective geometry, like all sciences, deals with ideal abstractions from concrete experience.

Russell's entire enterprise begins to look somewhat less old-fashioned once it is realized what precisely is achieved by means of his appeal to anharmonic ratio and the quadrilateral construction. More recent philosophers (e.g. Strawson 1959) who have been tempted by a Kantian approach to such questions as 'What features must any conceptual scheme have?' have not infrequently suggested that any conceptual scheme must provide at least the resources for determining the identity conditions for objects in its ontology, and for securing unique reference to them. These are exactly the resources supplied by anharmonic ratio and the quadrilateral construction to Russell's purely qualitative science, which is itself the a priori precondition of any form of externality. Any single point in projective space can be projectively mapped onto any other point; similarly, any pair of points can be mapped onto any other pair. Any three collinear points may be mapped onto any other three collinear points. But four collinear points can be mapped onto four other collinear points only if both sets of points have the same anharmonic ratio. Since projective mapping determines projective equivalence, figures which can be mapped onto one another being regarded as projectively identical, anharmonic ratio gives for projective geometry one of the two canvassed requirements for any conceptual scheme: criteria whereby identity

---

[81] Some further details and replies to possible objections are also given (*EFG* 140–6).

and distinctness claims can be assessed. The quadrilateral construction gives the other: the requirement that unique reference must be possible. The quadrilateral construction, as we have seen, enables a fourth point to be identified uniquely, given three others. If criteria for identity and unique reference are essential features of any form of externality, then Russell has shown that projective geometry at least provides these two required features.

The limitations of Russell's approach, however, are evident enough—some of them it shares with more recent ventures in similar directions (including Strawson's). Russell's attempts to show that projective geometry is wholly a priori fall into two parts. In the first, analytic, part, projective geometry is analysed to reveal its fundamental postulates, PGI–III. In the second, synthetic, part, the concept of a form of externality is analysed to reveal its fundamental properties. Russell attempts to show that the fundamental properties of a form of externality are those properties which are ascribed to projective space by the 'axioms' PGI–III. It then follows, or so Russell maintains, that projective geometry must be true if a form of externality is to be possible, i.e. that projective geometry is a priori true. Even if we ignore all the difficulties of detail in this enterprise (a number of them have been discussed, but several more bear consideration), it is plain that there are two large gaps in Russell's argument, gaps which he makes no attempt to fill. In consequence, even if all were well with the case he presents, it would not be sufficient to establish the conclusion he claims.

In the first place, although Russell does present arguments to show that PGI–III are *necessary* for projective geometry, he nowhere even attempts to show that they are *sufficient*. Moreover, as critics from Poincaré to Torretti have shown, it is pretty obvious that they are not sufficient. Secondly, although Russell presents arguments to show that PGI–III assign properties to projective space which are *sufficient* for a form of externality, he does not attempt to show that they assign properties which are *necessary*. Yet, if projective geometry is to be shown to be a priori, it is plain that this situation must be reversed. For if it is to be shown that projective geometry is necessary for a form of externality, then it needs to be shown that a set of axioms *sufficient* for projective geometry assigns a set of properties *necessary* for a form of externality. As things stand, Russell has done nothing to show that the properties assigned by PGI–III are necessary for a form of externality, and thus that a form of externality might not be founded upon some other basis than projective geometry. Moreover, it would seem *impossible* in this, as in other transcendental arguments, to show that the properties in question are necessary (cf. Körner 1967). On the other hand, the fact that PGI–III are not sufficient for projective geometry leaves open the possibility that parts of projective geometry (those parts not derivable from PGI–III) are not a priori. The final verdict on Russell's transcendental deduction of projective geometry must be that, even if all the arguments he presents are valid, they are not sufficient to establish the conclusion he wants.

## 4.6 GEOMETRY AND THE A PRIORI: GENERAL METRIC GEOMETRY[82]

Russell takes projective geometry to give the conditions for any form of externality that is, for the experience of a 'consistent multiplicity of different but interrelated things' (*EFG* 167). He takes general metric geometry to give the conditions for spatial measurement, i.e. for any quantitatively determinable form of externality (*EFG* 146–7). Now Russell nowhere argues that spatial measurement is essential for any form of externality (indeed, to do so would undermine his claim that projective geometry is *the* science of any form of externality). In consequence, his claim that general metric geometry is a priori cannot be interpreted in quite the same sense as his claim that projective geometry is a priori. For projective geometry is a priori in the wide sense of being a necessary condition for knowledge. (Russell has an argument, to be considered later, to show that a form of externality is a necessary condition for knowledge.) General metric geometry, by contrast, is a priori in a more restricted sense (noted by Russell, *EFG* 3), in that it is a necessary condition only for those experiences which involve spatial measurement, and spatial measurement is not itself a necessary condition for knowledge. However, this restricted sense of apriority can be widened somewhat, because Russell argues elsewhere that spatial measurement is a necessary condition for measurement of any kind (see § 6.1). Thus general metric geometry is a presupposition of any quantitative science.

For Russell, quantitative judgements are always judgements of comparison, and quantitative comparison always presupposes qualitative identity on the part of the things compared (cf. SDCQ, RNQ). Projective geometry, as we have seen, is the science of qualitative spatial comparison, consequently it is presupposed by general metrical geometry, which is the science of quantitative spatial comparison. The a priori component of general metrical geometry, therefore, must include projective geometry. But general metrical geometry has further a priori features introduced by the new idea of quantity. In addition to the concept of quantity itself, we need another new concept, namely motion, for Russell will argue that 'an ideal motion of [geometrical] figures through space' (*EFG* 149) is necessary for spatial measurement.[83]

---

[82] 'General metric geometry' will be used here, as Russell uses it, as a generic term encompassing metric geometries for all spaces of constant curvature.

[83] The view that geometry presupposes motion, although rejected by Kant 1781: A41 = B58, was not an uncommon one. Russell had it from Ward (cf. 'Lecture Notebook', i, 89). It raises questions, on which Russell vacillated, about the relation between geometry and kinematics in Russell's dialectic (see § 5.1).

Strictly, there will be a dialectical transition from projective to general metrical geometry, though Russell hardly mentions it in *EFG* beyond an extremely oblique footnote (p. 128 n). This transition, like the others, is driven by a contradiction, in this case one engendered by the covertly metrical distinction between lines and points. The contradictions in metrical geometry are different and stem from the necessary hypostatization of space (VN 20). Projective geometry, by contrast, Russell suggests, does not necessarily hypostatize space—though some of the arguments Russell puts forward for the necessity of hypostatizing space in metrical geometry would seem to apply equally to projective geometry. This, at least, is Russell's early position (VN 20). Later, he thought that the distinction between the two geometries could be made by means of the part–whole relation (*EFG/F* 165 n), which by 1899 had come to play a major role in his philosophy of mathematics (cf. FIAM, POM/D). The part–whole relation would permit comparison as to size, but not measurement. Russell's views of what this shows about the relations between projective and metrical geometry fluctuate. On occasion, he takes it to show that projective geometry is still dependent upon metrical considerations, though not upon quantitative ones (NOO 344, 352). Elsewhere, he hints that it marks an intermediate stage between projective and metrical geometry (COS 319).

General metric geometry is defined by the following axioms, said to hold for all spaces of constant curvature:[84]

> *Axiom of Free Mobility (or Congruence)*. Spatial magnitudes can be moved from place to place without distortion: *or, as it may be put*, Shapes do not in any way depend upon absolute position in space. (*EFG* 150.)                    (MGI)

> *Axioms of Dimensions*. Space must have a finite integral number of Dimensions. (*EFG* 161).                    (MGII)

> *Axiom of Distance*. [T]wo points must determine a unique spatial quantity, distance. (*EFG* 164).                    (MGIII)

Of these three axioms, the second need not detain us since we have already considered it in connection with projective geometry. The other two, however, are the subject of long and complex arguments. The third is by far the most problematic for Russell.

The main purpose of the axiom of free mobility was to permit the development of a concept of spatial quantity, or extension, in general metric geometry. Russell's account of spatial quantity in *EFG* is based upon a definition of quantitative spatial equality. When this is given, spatial quantity

---

[84] In this presentation Russell was mainly influenced by Riemann (1854) and Helmholtz (1866 and 1868), although he had important criticisms of both (cf. *EFG* 14–25). Vuillemin, in an intriguing but to my mind unconvincing article (1969), claims that Kant anticipated them all in this choice of axioms.

itself can be defined, for we can compare two spatial quantities by counting the number of equal spatial quantities contained in each (*EFG* 149–50).[85]

The procedure is what would now be called a definition by abstraction, and Russell, as a neo-Hegelian, found definition by abstraction problematic—as he did later on, for different reasons. As a neo-Hegelian the difficulty was that definition by abstraction is a special case of a definition of an item by means of its relations to something else. Such definitions run counter to an intuitive feeling that definition should somehow articulate the intrinsic nature of the item defined. In Russell's case, as we shall see more fully later, this intuition was supported by the doctrine of internal relations to which he subscribed as a neo-Hegelian. Later on Russell preserved the intuition, while admitting relational definitions, by distinguishing between philosophical definitions (which dealt only with the intrinsic nature of the item defined) and mathematical definitions which were relational (see AOG 410–12; *POM* 111). His later (and better known) objection to definition by abstraction was that it offered no guarantee that the definiendum was uniquely defined (*POM* 114–15).

For spatial equality Russell uses Euclid's definition: 'Magnitudes which exactly coincide are equal'. But for this definition to be useful it must be applicable to distinct spatial figures, as well as those which spatially coincide, and this requires that such figures can be brought into coincidence with one another. Moreover, if to bring them into coincidence is to determine uniquely their relative magnitudes then the result of bringing them into coincidence must be unaffected by the route by means of which they are brought into coincidence. And this requires the axiom of free mobility.

Russell's argument hovers ambiguously between a physical and a purely mathematical interpretation. On a physical interpretation (like that used by Helmholtz 1868, 1876, and rejected by Russell, *EFG* 75–8) we assume that a rigid body $B$ occupying a region $R$ of space, has marks $a$ and $b$ on it which coincide with points $p$ and $q$ of $R$. Then points $p'$ and $q'$ in a different region $R'$ will be the same distance apart as points $p$ and $q$ in $R$ iff $a$ and $b$ can be brought to occupy $p'$ and $q'$ when $B$ is moved to $R'$. Now such a procedure is only possible if there are ways of knowing that $B$ is moved from $R$ to $R'$ without deformation due to the action of forces or changes of temperature etc., or, what amounts to the same thing, if there are ways of knowing that $B$ is in fact a rigid body. Moreover, whatever means we have for determining

---

[85] Russell seems to think that infinite divisibility is required here to ensure that any degree of accuracy may be attained. But if space is a finite, discrete manifold (e.g. if space were quantized) then, although this would place a finite, lower limit on spatial magnitudes which could be used as units of measurement, it would also place the same limit on what magnitudes spatial figures could have. Thus there would be no loss of exactitude. Curiously, in view of the difficulties he had with infinite divisibility and the like (see Ch. 6), Russell does not seem to have taken the idea of discontinuous space very seriously.

that *B* really is rigid must not involve any reference to the measurement of spatial quantities. Our knowledge of the rigidity of physical bodies must precede, and not depend upon, geometry. But, as Russell argues in sharp criticism of Helmholtz:

> We are . . . concerned with the changes of spatial configuration to which material systems are liable: the description and explanation of these changes is the proper subject-matter of all Dynamics. But in order that such a science may exist, it is obviously ncessary that spatial configuration should be already measurable. If this were not the case, motion, acceleration and force would remain perfectly indeterminate. Geometry, therefore, must already exist before Dynamics becomes possible. (*EFG* 79.)

But even apart from this, resting spatial measurement upon the actual existence of rigid bodies (even if rigidity could be determined without appeal to geometry) would be insufficient for an argument to the a priori nature of the basic postulates of spatial measurement, unless some further transcendental argument could be given for the existence of rigid bodies. Not only is there no such argument for the necessity of rigid bodies, but whether they actually exist is very doubtful. Accordingly the physical interpretation must be ruled out.

The mathematical interpretation, by contrast, construes bringing different figures into coincidence as a spatial transformation of the figures which preserves distances. Such an interpretation has two desirable features from the point of view of Russell's transcendental argument: (i) it does not rely upon empirical facts such as the existence of rigid physical objects; (ii) it does presuppose a metric which is preserved under the transformation. Unfortunately, it is too general to do all the work Russell intends. For spatial transformations, such as those used in Weyl's infinitesimal geometry, may be specified, in which whether or not points $p'$ and $q'$ in $R'$ can be brought into coincidence with points $p$ and $q$ in $R$ depends upon the path chosen from $R$ to $R'$. For Russell's enterprise we would need some a priori ground for excluding such transformations. This Russell claims to give, but it is achieved in *EFG* by the axiom of free mobility, so it cannot be appealed to in establishing the axiom.

Russell's own interpretation is a curious amalgam of the physical with the mathematical.[86] Russell utilizes Land's distinction (Land 1877) between physical and geometrical rigidity, supposing physical objects abstracted from all dynamical properties. While actual physical objects cannot be supposed to be rigid because of the possible connection between their shape and their physical properties, the 'geometrical matter' which results from

---

[86] Russell is clearer about this in the French edn. of *EFG*. There he adds a note (*EFG/F* 261–2) which makes a distinction between two senses of 'congruent' which is essentially equivalent to the distinction noted here. He also adds a passage (*EFG/F*, 198) which makes a further, equivalent, distinction between the empirical and the a priori components of congruence.

the abstraction of dynamical properties, must be rigid because such matter is 'devoid, *ex hypothesi*, of causal properties' so 'there remains nothing, in mere empty space, which is capable of changing the configuration of any geometrical system' (*EFG* 79). We shall return to Russell's concept of 'geometrical matter' later, in dealing with his treatment of kinematics (§ 5.1).

Russell seeks to show that the rejection of the axiom of free mobility 'would involve logical and philosophical absurdities', and that without it metric geometry could not establish the notion of spatial magnitude (*EFG* 150–1). To this end he has a philosophical and a geometrical argument. The philosophical argument (*EFG* 151–2) involves two related points. First, if the axiom did not hold, then spatial magnitudes would vary as their position in space varied. And this would mean that certain marked points in space could be picked out (e.g. those points at which the magnitude was at a maximum or a minimum) and these points could then be used for assigning absolute positions to any body in space. This, Russell holds, conflicts with all forms of externality, which allow only relative and not absolute position. This argument is insufficient as it stands, for we have only Russell's word that forms of externality cannot allow absolute position. It is true we cannot allow absolute position in a form of externality to be determined by contents arranged in the form for the form is abstracted from all contents.[87] But absolute position as envisaged above does not involve contents at all, and it is defined purely geometrically. There seems no reason why a form of externality which permitted absolute position in this way should not be admitted.

The second point which Russell makes under the heading of the philosophical argument is that if spatial magnitudes varied with position, then we would have to assume space itself operated causally on spatial magnitudes. (Since every other feature has been abstracted out to leave only the form, any causal interaction would have to be between the space itself and the geometric figures in it.) This, of course, rules out the passivity of space, though again it is arguable whether the form of externality requires space to be causally passive. In defence of the passivity of space Russell ties this point up with the earlier one about absolute position: for it space acts causally on geometrical figures, position can be absolutely assigned by means of these causal effects. But this merely shifts the onus back on to proving that absolute position is not permitted within a form of externality.

The geometrical argument is more interesting, and consists in an attempted

---

[87] This would preclude such constructions as Strawson's spatio-temporal framework (Strawson 1959: 24–6), in which absolute position may be determined by the position of the subject, from counting as forms of externality in Russell's sense. See, however, Russell's earlier suggestion along exactly these lines (*VN* 16).

refutation of any geometry in which free mobility is denied. 'Suppose', Russell writes of such a geometry, 'the length of an infinitesimal arc in some standard position were $ds$; then in any other position $p$ its length would be $ds.f(p)$, where the form of the function $f(p)$ must be supposed known. But how are we to determine the position $p$?' (*EFG* 152). Russell argues that we require $p$'s coordinates, that is, 'some measurement of distance from the origin', but that this entails knowing what the function $f(p)$ is (*EFG* 152). For it will be impossible to measure the distance from the origin to $p$ unless it is known how distance depends upon position. Let us call this the argument from empiricism.

The differential geometries which Russell is here trying to refute had been around for some time: they were studied by Gauss (1828) and Riemann (1854). That Russell virtually ignores them was not due to ignorance, as he later maintained (see below), but indicates in part his emphasis on geometrical intuition. Surfaces of variable curvature he, of course, accepted since the curvature could be measured by means of radii of curvature in the embedding space. But if space itself were curved such considerations would be ruled out. Russell, in discussing the issue, draws an important distinction between space and the general conception of a manifold, on which Riemann based himself, where higher-dimensional manifolds were not ruled out as violating the conditions of spatial intuition (*EFG* 20). Manifolds of variable curvature could be admitted because of the possibility of embedding manifolds of higher-dimensionality. This did not, however, apply to space or to forms of externality which were subject to additional constraints of spatial intuition. The neglect of differential geometry also indicates the influence that group-theoretic considerations were having on Russell at this time. Differential geometries did not lend themselves easily to the sort of group-theoretic treatment of geometry that had been pioneered by Klein and Lie. (It was only in the twentieth century that Elie Cartan was able to bring the two approaches together, using the concept of connectivity.) Despite Russell's rather sketchy remarks on Lie (*EFG* 46–50), he was, as we have seen, strongly influenced by Klein and quite likely thought that differential geometry, which could not be assimilated to Klein's approach, was probably not of very great significance.

Russell's use of infinitesimals in the argument from empiricism is really quite incidental, but not in Russell's second argument against differential geometry:

The geometry of non-congruent surfaces is *only* possible by the use of infinitesimals, and in the infinitesimal all surfaces become plane. The fundamental formula, that for the length of an infinitesimal arc, is only obtained on the assumption that such an arc may be treated as a straight line, and that Euclidean Plane Geometry may be applied in the immediate neighbourhood of any point. If we had not our Euclidean measure, which could be moved without distortion, we should have no method of comparing small arcs in different places, and the Geometry of non-congruent surfaces would break down. Thus the axiom of Free Mobility, as regards three-dimensional space, is necessarily implied and presupposed in the Geometry of non-congruent surfaces; the possibility of the latter, therefore, is a dependent and derivative possibility, and can form no argument against the *a priori* necessity of congruence as the test of equality. (*EFG* 159.)

At first, it seems as if Russell is here arguing that since differential geometry requires infinitesimals, and since infinitesimals are incoherent (as he argues elsewhere: VN 14 n, 17; SDCQ 50), so differential geometry can be rejected. This argument would be unsound, for appeal to infinitesimals could be eliminated by the then-available techniques of analysis, with which, however, Russell was only just becoming acquainted. However, as the argument develops it becomes clear that this is not Russell's point. The main thrust of his argument is to show that differential geometries presuppose Euclidean geometry. There was good point to this claim at the time Russell wrote, for differential geometries could only be treated then by assuming that locally they approximated Euclidean geometry. Infinitesimals could be avoided even in 1897, but the global treatment of differential geometries did not become possible, except by appeal to their local properties, until the topological concept of a differentiable manifold was developed in the years after 1925.

Russell's argument was not new (cf. Jevons 1871), but its status is puzzling: if it is any good, it will surely render the argument from empiricism superfluous. Yet Russell's main attack on differential geometry is by the argument from empiricism, and his second argument is accorded only a subordinate status. In fact, it is presented as part of a discussion of surfaces of non-constant curvature in a higher-dimensional embedding space—though it will surely apply equally to *spaces* of non-constant curvature without the consideration of an embedding space. Russell, of course, has to explain how such surfaces are possible in Euclidean embedding space when he has ruled out *spaces* of non-constant curvature on a priori grounds. His answer is that such surfaces presuppose the Euclidean line element of the embedding space. But, once this is said, his argument is immediately seen to lose its force against *spaces* of variable curvature. For if *surfaces* of non-constant curvature are admissible provided a Euclidean line element is available, there would seem to be no ground for dismissing *spaces* of non-constant curvature. A geometry of constant curvature could be given a priori along with a form of externality. This would then give the formula for the line element, and with it all the conceptual apparatus required for a differential geometry. Whether physical space is of constant or variable curvature could then be left to empirical determination. Of course, this account opens up a gap between the geometry given a priori as the form of intuition, and the geometry of physical space. Such a gap might be regarded as unfortunate (though why is not entirely clear), but there would seem to be nothing to show that it was impossible. This, however, brings us back to the argument from empiricism. For if that argument is valid, it shows that, even assuming the line element to be given a priori, the question of whether or not physical space is of constant or non-constant curvature cannot be decided empirically, because the nature of the function $f(p)$ cannot be determined empirically.

The required function, of course, could be known if the metric structure of space were given a priori, that is, if the value of the line element $ds$ in each region could be known a priori. One of Russell's main conclusions in his discussion of geometry in *EFG* is that the metric structure of space can only be determined empirically, but here he seems to be assuming that this is the case. Russell might have in mind an argument from the passivity of space, for if length depended upon position in space, then space would have causal effects upon geometrical figures. Yet this argument seems hardly conclusive, for it supposes that such a dependence of length on position must be causal and that all causal connections are dynamical. Suppose that the metric structure of space could known a priori, then length would depend in knowable ways upon position. Either the effect of spatial position on geometrical figures could be regarded as a non-causal relation (in this case the causal passivity of space could be maintained); or else space could be admitted to have a causal effect on geometrical figures and thereby a new type of non-dynamical causal relation could be admitted (in this case the abstraction of all dynamical properties from space and geometrical figures could still be maintained). It does seem as though Russell simply assumes that the metric structure of space cannot be known a priori. The assumption is an easy one to make, and not implausible either. For not only is there no account as to how the metric structure of space could be determined a priori, but knowledge of its structure would be a quite different kind of a priori knowledge to the kinds usually canvassed: quantitative details of particulars (e.g. particular regions of space) are seldom touted as fit subjects for a priori knowledge.

Russell does have an argument to show that such features could not be determined by direct empirical means (*EFG* 152–3). If the curvature of space varies in different positions this fact could not be detected by moving measuring rods with geometrical figures from one part of space to another, for the measuring rods will themselves change size proportionately to the change in the size of the figures that they are moved with. Russell presses home this objection by claiming that talk of change of magnitude in such circumstances would be 'logically absurd'. Torretti (1978: 316) says that this argument uses the discredited verification criterion of meaning, but in fact it does no such thing. To begin with it makes no reference to meaning, but merely claims 'logical absurdity' in talking about undetectable changes of magnitude. But further, Russell protects himself from any charge of verificationism by claiming at the outset that judgements of magnitude are always judgements of comparison, 'in unmeasured quantity, comparison as to the mere more or less, but in measured magnitude, comparison as to the precise how many times' (*EFG* 153–4). It is because of this specific fact about judgements of magnitude, and not because of any general theory of meaning or of logical absurdity, that Russell draws the conclusion that '[t]o speak of differences of magnitude . . . in any case where comparison cannot reveal them, is logically absurd' (*EFG* 154).

The defect with the argument as stated is not that it relies upon an inadequate theory of meaning, but that Russell jumps too hastily to the conclusion that changes in spatial magnitude with position in space could not be detected. Admittedly, direct methods of measurement, such as that with measuring rods, would be ineffective. But other methods are not ruled out. For example, in space of positive curvature the ratio between the circumference and diameter of a circle differs from $\pi$, the degree of difference depending upon the measure of curvature. In such a space in which the measure of curvature varied with position, the variation could be detected by sufficiently accurate comparison of the circumference and diameter of circles at different positions. In a similar manner, the angles of a triangle in hyperbolic space add up to less than 180°, the amount depending again upon the curvature of the space. Careful comparison of triangles could thus, within limits, show changes in spatial magnitudes at different points in the space.[88] But this criticism, as we shall see, remains superficial.

Ever since the advent of Einstein's general theory of relativity it has been widely recognized that spaces of the sort Russell rules out, in which the measure of distance depends on position, are possible. Moreover, despite what Russell said in retrospect (*MPD* 40), this development was not something that had simply never crossed his mind before. Russell was aware in the 1890s both of the existence of differential geometry (he read Riemann (1854) in February 1894, and Gauss (1828) in May 1895)[89] and the possibility of its physical application.[90] As early as 1746, Kant had speculated that the

[88] Such experiments had been proposed long before Russell wrote. The most famous experiment, Gauss's triangulation of three peaks in Hanover, however, may not have been intended as a test of the curvature of space (see Miller 1972). Russell himself proposes such an experiment in a later paper (EAE 326).

[89] Russell made notes on both. His study of Riemann was particularly careful. He made a set of notes on the entire article, including a partial translation (despite the availability of Clifford's translation, of which he must have known).

[90] In *MPD* 40 he wrote: 'The theory of tensors . . . would have been useful to me, but I never heard of it until [Einstein] used it'. But this, also, is false. One of his notebooks (RA 210.006550–F1) from the 1890s contains notes on Bianchi (1896), ch. 2, following a list of

properties of space might depend upon the disposition of forces (1746: 29), and Lobachevski (1829) had made much more sophisticated proposals for the geometrical representation of forces. It is not clear whether Russell knew of these proposals at the time he wrote *EFG* (he did read the Lobachevski in October 1899). It is clear, however, that he was aware of similar suggestions by W. K. Clifford (1885: 223 n.) to the effect that the expansion of bodies due to increasing temperature might be interpreted in terms of a change in the curvature of space with change in temperature (see EPII 127). It is clear, therefore, that Russell did not ignore such possibilities because they hadn't occurred to him, rather he felt that all such suggestions could be excluded on a priori grounds.

In all such cases, distance depends upon position in a way which Russell declares to be inadmissible. But the difficulty which Russell finds in such cases, of knowing how distance is related to position, is circumvented by making both a function of the distribution of some other physical quality (temperature in Clifford's case, matter in Einstein's). Since the distribution of the latter is to be determined empirically, the function which relates distance and position is also a matter for empirical determination. Even though Russell was prepared to agree that the space metric could only be determined empirically, he was unwilling to admit the possibility that space was of non-constant curvature. To understand why, it is necessary to consider his broader dialectic of the sciences. Russell regarded geometry as an a priori necessity for any theory of physics, and, in particular, as we have seen, that metric geometry was necessary for any science which involves measurement, since all measurement presupposes the concept of spatial distance. Accordingly, in investigating a priori metric geometry no use could be made of measurement, for measurement presupposes metrical geometry and thus could not be appealed to in establishing the latter. It is now clear what, in Russell's view, would have been wrong with proposals like Clifford's and Einstein's: they both appealed, in determining the metrical nature of space, to measurement, e.g. of temperature or of density, but in Russell's view temperatures and densities could only be measured if either the local metrical nature of space had already been determined or space was of constant curvature. Such proposals, therefore, if accepted, do more than merely local damage to Russell's apriorism, for they would refute Russell's claim that metric geometry was logically prior to physics. On the other hand, it does seem to me that Russell's reasoning is sufficiently tight to show that, if metric geometry is a necessary condition for the possibility of measurement,

'Important Works in Theory of Curvature' which includes Ricci 1884, 1888; Christoffel 1869, and Beltrami 1868c (RA 210.006550–F1). These notes were written in 1896, presumably in the course of writing *EFG*. Apart from the Bianchi, it is not clear which of the listed works he studied.

then there are prima facie grounds for ruling out hypotheses like those of Clifford and Einstein.

Russell's 'proof' of the axiom of distance is rather more difficult. It involves demonstrating the following four propositions (*EFG* 164):

That if distance, as a quantity completely determined by two points, did not exist, spatial magnitude would not be measurable. (1)

That distance can only be determined by two points, if there is a [unique] actual curve in space determined by those two points.[91] (2)

That the existence of such a curve can be deduced from the conception of a form of externality. (3)

That the application of quantity to such a curve necessarily leads to a certain magnitude, namely distance, uniquely determined by any two points which determine the curve. (*EFG* 164.) (4)

Consider first the 'proof' of (1). We can immediately concede that if distance did not exist, spatial magnitude would not be measurable. What is at issue is Russell's characterization of distance as a quantity completely determined by two points. Is such a quantity necessary for the measurement of spatial magnitude? Russell argues for (1) as follows. Any two points must have some relation between them. From the axiom of free mobility it follows that given any two points in relation it is possible to construct another pair of points in another part of space congruent with the original pair. '[I]t follows that the relation is quantitatively the same for both figures, since congruence is the test of spatial equality. Hence the two points have a quantitative relation' which is not affected by motion (*EFG* 165). And this ensures also that the relation between the two points does not depend upon any third point, because if it did, any change in position of the original point-pair would change their relation to the third point, and thus to each other. 'Hence the relation between the two points, being unaltered, must be an intrinsic relation, a relation involving no other point or figure in space; and this intrinsic relation we call distance' (*EFG* 165).

What this argument shows is that, assuming the axiom of free mobility, any two points have between them a quantitative relation which is not dependent upon any other point.[92] What is missing is an argument to show

[91] Russell states this proposition without the parenthetical insertion, but it is clear from his subsequent discussion (*EFG* 168–70) that this insertion is assumed.

[92] It may be doubted whether the argument establishes even this much. Torretti (1978: 311) claims it involves a circularity since it assumes congruence (a quantitative relation) in proving that the two points determine a quantitative relation. (Russell himself is concerned to rebut a similar charge of circularity, *EFG* 165–6.) I'm inclined to think, however, that the apparent circularity disappears when the conditional nature of (1) is taken into account. For Russell has already argued that congruence is necessary for spatial measurement, and (1) asserts that if spatial measurement is possible then the two points determine a quantitative relationship. In establishing this conditional, therefore, it would seem that congruence may be assumed.

that this relation not only can but *must* be used to define distance. In fact, Russell's case for (1) has broken down in two parts with no connection between them. On the one hand, it is easily admitted that distance is necessary for the measurement of spatial magnitude; on the other, that, given congruence, any two points determine a quantitative relation. What has not been demonstrated is that this quantitative relation is necessary for the measurement of spatial magnitude.

Another objection with which Russell attempts to deal concerns the uniqueness of the distance assigned to the two points. No reason has so far been given why the two points should not have more than one mutual quantitative relation. Russell argues for uniqueness on the ground that points, having no intrinsic qualities, are defined entirely by their relations. He claims that, given two points and a single relation $R$ between them, 'no fresh relations [between them] are possible, since the point defined has no qualities from which such relations could flow' (*EFG* 166). But this reply is entirely ineffective, since the points have between them one relation, $R$, which did not require that they had qualities from which it could flow, and there seems, as yet, no reason why there should not be other relations, like $R$ but distinct from it, which do not depend upon the points having qualities either. There is no basis in Russell's reply for an argument that $R$ must be unique. Russell's argument is caught up with the antinomy of the point and the doctrine of internal relations. But even when these are fully taken into account, it would seem that Russell could have no basis for thinking that a single relation was admissible whenever two or more were not.

Having established to his satisfaction that between any two points there is a unique distance-relation, Russell seeks to demonstrate (2), that this relation depends upon a curve in space which links the two points. His argument for (2) is that both the idea of moving the point-pair through space and that of constructing another point-pair, congruent with the first, elsewhere in space, involve such a curve. 'For without some such curve, the two point-pairs cannot be known as congruent, nor can we have any test by which to discover when a point pair is moving as a single figure' (*EFG* 166–7). Russell's intention is to link the curve whose existence he seeks to demonstrate with the concept of distance via the concept of congruence. Since congruence is essential for measurement, if he can show that the curve is essential for congruence he can show it is essential for measurement. Torretti's criticisms (1978: 312) here are pertinent. First, Russell simply assumes that the curve used to test whether the point-pair moves as a single figure must be used to measure the distance between them. Second, given two point-pairs $(P, Q)$ and $(P', Q')$, Russell assumes that in order to show that they are congruent we have to show that the curve $k$ which joins the first pair is congruent with the curve $k'$ which joins the second pair. But in order to prove the congruence of the curves we have to bring *P* into coincidence with *P'* and *Q* with *Q'*, so that congruence between the curves presupposes congruence between the point-pairs. Consequently, the congruence of the point-pairs cannot be said to depend upon the curves joining the points. This problem is illustrative of a type of problem which pervades Russell's dialectic. The problem of absolute motion is the best known example, and Russell devotes a good deal of discussion to it. But he does not notice the similar problem in his 'proof' of (2).

Russell also considers a difficulty in spherical space, where any two antipodal points are linked by an infinite number of lines of equal length. Thus there is no unique line determined by the two antipodes. Russell admits the exception, maintaining, rather obscurely, that '*in general*, two points still determine a unique straight line . . . and exceptional cases [i.e. cases in which the points are antipodes] can be treated . . . by the usual methods for limits' with the help of the axiom of distance (*EFG* 169; rearranged). But even when the two points are not antipodal, two lines of different length join them (since they cut the great circle on which they lie into two unequal arcs). Russell's only reference to this matter in *EFG* is his remark that distance in spherical space is a periodic function (*EFG* 169–70). Later, in defence of his position, he said that the shorter of the two arcs must be specified as the distance (EAE 331). From the point of view of *EFG* this is circular: the *shortest* line is to be specified before *distance* can be defined. In EAE, however, Russell may have hoped that the circularity could be avoided by means of the part–whole relation though he offers no definite suggestions.

As regards antipodal points, his position in EAE is more radical, namely that 'antipodal points coincide necessarily' and that the difference between elliptical and spherical spaces is a 'difference of notation' only (EAE 331). In *EFG*, he confesses, 'I had not the courage to condemn spherical geometry' (EAE 331). It is perhaps surprising that Russell did not consider such a possibility in *EFG*, since it was known to him (through Klein 1871) and would seem to provide a resolution of the problem of antipodes. As regards the more general problem, Russell offers further considerations in *EFG*. In particular, he argues that a unique distance between any two points may be defined for spherical space by reference to the circumference of the space itself (*EFG* 170). But this offers nothing for the axiom of distance. It shows, if anything, that distance can be defined in ways not countenanced by the axiom.

The unsatisfactory state in which (2) is left could be remedied if Russell's arguments for (3) are sound. For (3) asserts that it can be deduced from the concept of a form of externality that there exists a unique curve determined by two points. The demonstration of (3) would, at worst, rule spherical spaces out as a form of externality. More positively, it is conceivable that such an argument could suggest some way of selecting one of the infinitely many lines linking antipodal points in spherical space as being that uniquely determined by the points. It doesn't matter which one is selected so long as one is uniquely selected.

Unfortunately, our expectations in this regard are disappointed. Russell's argument for (3) relies essentially upon his erroneous Jamesian identification of the relation between two points with the line on which they lie. He argues for the uniqueness of the relation between them:

Since position is relative . . . any two points must have *some* relation to each other: since our form of externality is homogeneous, this relation can be kept unchanged while the two points move in the form, i.e., change their relations to other points: hence their relation to each other is an intrinsic relation, independent of their relations to other points. (*EFG* 170–1.)

But this offers no reason to suppose that there is only one intrinsic relation between the two points, and the example of spherical geometry should suggest otherwise. He then argues that since the form is given, and consists entirely of relations, the relation between the two points must be given with the form. Then, since the relation is to be identified with a line, he concludes that the unique curve between the two points is also given. Russell's argument for (3) thus stumbles on the uniqueness claim just as his argument for (2) did.

Russell's argument for (4) is comparably brief. In projective geometry the figure formed by any two points is indiscernible from that formed by any other two points on the same line. Since projective geometry deals with the qualitative properties of figures, the difference between the two point-pairs cannot be qualitative difference. For example, if one of the points remains fixed while the other moves the change may be real, but can not be qualitative (since all points are qualitatively identical). Thus the change must be a change of quantity. 'If two points . . . determine a unique figure, there must exist, for the distinction between the various other points of this figure, a unique quantitative relation between the two determining points, and therefore, since these points are arbitrary, between [any][93] two points. This relation is *distance*' (*EFG* 172). In this argument we have omitted, without loss to the argument itself, Russell's references to unique lines joining the two points. These are not only superfluous, but encumber the argument with the (unjustifiable) assumption that two points do not determine a figure unless there is a line joining them. Without this assumption, and with the additional assumption that if a relation is not qualitative it must be quantitative, Russell's argument is valid.

[93] *EFG* has 'only' here, but 'any' is clearly intended.

This concludes Russell's arguments for the axiom of distance, and with it his case for the apriority of general metrical geometry. Russell's a priori admissible metric geometries are restricted to those with a constant measure of curvature, thus excluding those of variable curvature such as are required by general relativity. The theory of relativity was subsequently cited by Russell as the most crushing refutation of the position he took in *EFG*: 'Einstein's revolution swept away everything at all resembling this point of view. . . . Apart from details, I do not think there is anything valid in this early book' (*MPD* 40).

In § 4.5 we saw how Russell sought to show that projective geometry was a necessary condition for a form of externality. In this section we have seen how he sought to show that general metric geometry was necessary for spatial measurement, and thus for all measurement. He is therefore in a position to conclude that general metric geometry is a necessary condition for measurement of any kind, or for any kind of judgement as to magnitude.[94]

The final issue which demands our attention in this section is Russell's argument that a form of externality is a necessary condition for any possible knowledge. The first step is to clarify the general concept ('general class-conception', *EFG* 178) of a form of externality. The concept of a form of externality is a general concept under which must fall 'every logically possible *intuition* which can fulfil the function actually fulfilled by space', that is to make 'possible experience of diverse but interrelated things' (*EFG* 179); or, as he later puts it, to reveal 'simultaneously presented things as mutually external' (*EFG* 181).[95] Now Russell has already argued, in his discussion of projective geometry, that some intuition falling under the general concept of a form of externality as he describes it is necessary for the perception of things as mutually external. The remaining task of the deduction to be considered here is to show that, without the perception of things as mutually external, there could be no knowledge at all. Or, as Russell puts it, 'if there were not, in sense-perception, some form of externality the existence of diverse but interrelated things [would] be unknowable' (*EFG* 182; rearranged). Russell's argument starts with the premiss taken from Bradley, that all judgement involves identity-in-difference,

[94] The dependence of time-measurement on space-measurement is asserted in various writings between 1893 and 1896: cf. *Papers*, i, 124, 273–4, 295–6; *EFG* 157. The general case, however, is argued in SDCQ 55–6, RNQ 78–9.

[95] Russell rejects Kant's view that space also serves to reveal presented things as external to the self for this, apart from raising 'the whole question of the nature and limits of the Ego', requires that the self be regarded 'as a phenomenon presented to sense-perception' (since externality to the self cannot be derived from spatial presentation unless the self has a position in space, and things can have position in space only if they can be presented in sense-perception), and this 'reduces externality to the self to externality to the body'. Since the body is a presented object like any other, externality to the body is simply 'a special case of the mutual externality of presented things' (*EFG* 182; see also p. 61).

and thus that all knowledge requires that diversity which, allegedly, only space makes possible (*EFG* 184).[96] The inference from Bradley's theory of judgement is fairly direct. The only problem seems to be that Bradley's theory of judgement is most naturally interpreted in terms of conceptual difference (difference of *whatness*) united in referential identity (different properties predicated of one and the same item; cf. Bradley 1883: i, 27). Russell, by contrast, assumes that what is required is referential difference united in referential identity (*EFG* 183, 141 n.). The use Russell makes of this assumption will appear shortly, but it is not entirely clear why he should think the assumption essential, for the argument he bases on it is not crucial to his case, as we shall see.[97]

What remains to be proven is that the diversity required for judgement does, in fact, depend upon a form of externality as claimed. Russell considers the possibility that the 'mental object' of a judgement could provide the diversity even if the object about which the judgement is made is simple. In this case, no form of externality would be required to provide the diversity on which the judgement depends, the diversity would be entirely internal. Russell argues against this by means of a dilemma: 'either we could have no knowledge except of our present perception,[98] or else we must be able to contrast and compare it with some other perception' (*EFG* 184). The first case he dismisses summarily by appeal to the identity-in-difference theory of judgement. Now this move initially seems question-begging, given the position which the dilemma is intended to refute. For might not a simple perceived object be responsible for a complex mental representation of it, which provides the diversity necessary for knowledge? It must be assumed, I think, that Russell would hold that in this case the knowledge obtained would be knowledge of the mental object, and not of the object perceived, and thus that simple objects would remain unknowable. On the second horn of the dilemma Russell argues that 'the other perception, with which we compare our first, must have occurred at some other time, and with time, we have at once a form of externality' (*EFG* 184).[99] 'Time at least, therefore, is essential to that identity in difference, which all knowledge postulates' (*EFG* 185).

[96] The argument is briefly summarized in EAE 334. See also a passage deleted from SDCQ, *Papers*, ii. T53: 34 where he states that what is simple is unthinkable because it is 'mere pure Being'.
[97] Russell does argue for the assumption in COR 145, but on grounds that were not available to him when he wrote *EFG*. The assumption was criticized in Moore 1899*b*: 400.
[98] By 'present perception' he means 'the object presently perceived'. He stricts consideration to perception on the ground that 'knowledge must start from perception' (*EFG* 184).
[99] Russell's classifying time as a form of externality contrasts sharply with Kant's view. Russell's reasons are not explained but it may be due to his attempts to depsychologize Kant's notion of the a priori and the related tendency to regard time as a one-dimensional manifold akin in many ways to space (cf. WDWR).

The next problem is whether we need anything more than time in order to ensure the possibility of knowledge: in other words, do we need a form of externality of more than one dimension? Against this possibility Russell brings four arguments. First, if time were the only form of externality only one thing could be given at any one moment, and this thing must constitute the whole of the world. Secondly, he argues that such a form of monism would not yield the identity-in-difference required for judgement:

> The object of past perception must—since our one thing has nothing external to it, by which it could be created or destroyed—be regarded as the same thing in a different state. The complexity, therefore, will lie only in the changing states of our one thing—it will be adjectival, not substantival [i.e. the difference will be in the *what*ness of the object, not its *that*ness].(*EFG* 185.)

This argument of course depends upon the view that judgement requires referential and not merely conceptual difference. But, in any case, Russell's reasoning is obscure. For it is assumed that the one object which constitutes the world can change its states without external help, but that it cannot be created or destroyed without external help. The grounds for this distinction (unless some conservation principle is presupposed) are obscure. Russell's third argument is that this one thing must be the self. Indeed, if there is only one thing in the universe and the self is in the universe then the self must be the only thing in the universe. This fits with Kant's account of time as the form of inner presentation. Russell's fourth argument reverts to our criticism of his second argument. In such a world, he argues, causality could not be applied, since there was nothing external to the one existent object which could cause it to change its state. Now if the principle of external causality ('All changes of state follow from external causes') is granted, the view that the one existent object can change its state has to be rejected. Thus there could be no change in such a world, and a fortiori no adjectival change. Thus there could be no possibility of diversity of any kind—no differences of *what*ness or of *that*ness—in such a one-dimensional world. On this view Russell gets a much stronger argument for the impossibility of judgement in such a world—since any judgement requires diversity of some kind. Thus Russell's strengthening of Bradley's requirements on judgement (by adding the claim that differences of *that*ness are also essential) is no longer needed for this part of the argument.

Russell's whole line of argument can be applied exactly, without change, to Bradley's form of Absolute Monism. For Bradley does, indeed, maintain that Reality is a single indivisible whole. Thus there can, by the principle of external causality, be no changes in the Absolute (there being nothing outside to cause such changes). And Bradley is prepared to admit that change is illusory (1893a: 38–44). Now Bradley does concede that the

Absolute presents itself to us with differing contents, but if, as Russell seems to maintain, referential differences as well as conceptual differences are required for judgement, it would follow that judgement is impossible on Bradley's ontology. For there are no differing *objects* of reference which could be united in judgement, only conceptual differences attached to the Absolute. Since Russell maintains both the principle of external causality and the view that referential differences are required for judgement, he could not subscribe at this time to Bradley's absolute monism without self-defeatingly denying the possibility of judgement. This is the strongest evidence available to us for concluding that Russell, even as a neo-Hegelian, was a pluralist.

The arguments just considered deal primarily with time as a one-dimensional form of externality, and many of the arguments cannot be redeployed against one-dimensional forms of externality in general. For example, the arguments involving causality, which Russell thinks form 'the chief difficulty' (*EFG* 185), cannot be used against a one-dimensional but non-temporal form of externality. However, Russell has other arguments against this broader claim. He argues, successfully I believe, against the claim that items arranged along a one-dimensional continuum could change their order. In order for them to do so, they would have to pass through each other, and this, Russell argues, is impossible 'since a form of externality is the mere expression of diversity among things, from which it follows that things cannot occupy the same position in a form, unless there is another form by which to differentiate them' (*EFG* 141). This, indeed, seems inescapable, but Russell's conclusion, that a one-dimensional form 'could not, by itself, allow that change of the relations of externality, by which alone a varied world of interrelated things can be brought into consciousness' (*EFG* 142), does not yet follow. There seems no reason why, just because relations of order among presented items cannot change in a one-dimensional form, the items arranged in such a form cannot be interrelated. It is, of course, true of the world as actually presented that its contents may change the order in which they are presented, but what we are seeking now is not this merely contingent fact about the world, but a feature which characterizes any world in which knowledge is possible.

However, at this point we may adapt Russell's argument against solipsism in a one-dimensional temporal continuum. If we consider items $a_1$, $a_2$, etc., arranged one-dimensionally along a line, we can indeed consider their inter-relations (e.g. that $a_1$ is next but one to $a_3$, and so on). But for the purposes of a form of externality we have to consider these items as presented to the mind. Now, either the self is arranged among the items on the line or it is not. If it is not, then the self is conceived of as outside the line, the line is presented as external to the self and at once we require an extra dimension to accommodate this fact.[100] If, on the other hand, the self is on the line, then not all the items on the line can be presented to the self (without interpenetration). As Russell puts it: 'In a one-dimensional space . . . only a single object, which must appear as a point, or two objects at most, one in front and one behind, could ever be perceived' (*EFG* 142). This, of course, certainly reduces the number of possible worlds in which knowledge is possible, but it does not eliminate judgement altogether. For there is still diversity, and though the judgements which might be made by such a perceiver in such a world would be restricted, judgement would not be altogether impossible. Thus the possibility of a one-dimensional form of externality is not entirely ruled out. And, indeed, this possibility is not strictly ruled out by the axioms of dimensions in projective and general metrical geometry, although in projective geometry at least three dimensions are required for the definition of harmonic range. The most that would be ruled out by the axioms of dimension would be the possibility that the single dimension was temporal and not spatial. For a single, temporal dimension would not permit direct simultaneous presentation of diverse items. But again, we have no firm grounds for denying that judgement would be impossible even in a one-dimensional temporal continuum. For the felt succession of distinct, locationless events would, presumably, constitute a basis for the identity-in-difference required for judgement. It is only if Russell can make good his claim that both the simultaneous and the successive presentation of distinct items were impossible in a one-dimensional form of externality, that he can make good his claim that the form of externality must be of more than one dimension.

## 4.7 THE STATUS OF EUCLIDEAN GEOMETRY

Though Russell thought that general metrical geometry was an a priori necessity, he held that the determination of which among the admissible metrical geometries was correct for physical space was an entirely empirical matter. There are infinitely many possibilities to choose from, since the main constraint imposed by the axiom of free mobility on the a priori admissibility of a geometry is that the space should be of constant curvature. This means that the measure of curvature, $k$, for the space takes the same value at every point of the space, and $k$ may take a continuum of values, negative and positive, depending on the degree to which space is curved. Negative values hold for hyperbolic spaces, positive for spherical spaces. In the case in which

---

[100] An alternative, which avoids this conclusion, might be to identify the self with the line itself. This possibility was pointed out to me by Albert Lewis.

$k = 0$, space is Euclidean.[101] The value $k$ takes for physical space is, Russell thought, a matter to be determined empirically. Not surprisingly, Russell, in common with most thinkers of his time, thought that the most likely value was 0, that the geometry of physical space was most probably Euclidean. The limits of experimental accuracy, however, ensured that $k = 0$ could never be empirically established with absolute certainty, because small deviations from this value would be incapable of experimental detection. Large deviations, however, might well be detectable, so it might be possible by experimental means to show that physical space was not Euclidean. In fact, however, Russell thought that the available empirical evidence did not support any large divergence of $k$ from 0: 'The observed truth of physical science . . . constitutes overwhelming empirical evidence that [Euclidean geometry] is very approximately correct, even if not rigidly true' (*EFG* 6 n.; see also EAE 326–7).

If $k = 0$, the axioms of three-dimensional Euclidean geometry are, on Russell's view, contingent truths. These axioms are the following:

> *The axiom of parallels.* Through a point external to a line, $L$, it is possible to draw only one line parallel to $L$.     (EGI)
>
> *Axiom of dimensions.* Space has three dimensions.     (EGII)
>
> *Axiom of the Euclidean straight line.* Two straight lines cannot enclose a space.     (EGIII)

Alternative geometries, which deny one or more of these axioms, are equally viable logically, and can only be excluded as the geometry of physical space by empirical considerations. This might be denied in one of three ways, carefully listed by Russell (AOG 394–5) in a reply to Poincaré:

> It might be argued that the truth or falsity of Euclidean geometry was known *a priori*.     (1)
>
> It might be argued that, although Euclidean geometry was true or false, it was impossible empirically to determine which.     (2)
>
> It might be argued that the truth or falsity of Euclidean geometry could not be determined empirically because Euclidean geometry was neither true nor false.     (3)

Russell's position was attacked in the first way by Couturat (1898) and in the third by Poincaré (1899). He replied to each of them in separate articles in

---

[101] In *EFG* 17–21 Russell uses 'measure of curvature' synonymously with 'space-constant'. In EAE, however, he introduces a new sense in which the measure of curvature is the square of the reciprocal of the space-constant (EAE 328 n.). Unfortunately, he never adapted to the new terminology, and used 'space-constant' repeatedly through EAE in both senses (see *Papers*, ii, A327: 20–9). Russell distinguishes the two senses in a note in *EFG/F* 262. In what follows the term 'space-constant' will be avoided, and measure of curvature' will be used for what is now usually called the Gaussian curvature.

the *Revue de métaphysique* (EAE, AOG). In both, his case is strong; it is his case against (2) that is weakest. Needless to say, much of his argumentation concerns the possibility of empirically determining the measure of curvature of physical space.

Only the axiom of three dimensions falls outside the discussion of the measure of curvature, and constitutes, in many ways, a special problem. In the first place, of course, since the measure of curvature can take a continuum of values, its exact determination will not be possible by empirical means. In the case of dimensionality, however, as Russell notes, 'small errors are . . . impossible' and the axiom 'though empirical, will be declared . . . exactly and certainly true of our actual world' (*EFG* 6). But this certainty constitutes no grounds for its apriority, since experience would be rendered possible by spaces of different dimensionality. A second respect in which the axiom of dimensionality differs from the others, according to Russell, is its immutability: 'if space has three dimensions, . . . it has always had, and must always have the same number of dimensions' (EAE 336). Russell gives no argument for this claim, and it is not clear what argument would be available to him. The claim is not, apparently, analytic, nor does he try to show that it is a priori necessary.

In reply to Couturat's claim that the whole of Euclidean geometry might be a priori Russell, doubtless influenced by Moore's criticism of the lingering psychologism of *EFG*, ignores the question of apriority and seeks to show that EGI–III are not necessary. Now the simplest such argument is the following: since non-Euclidean geometries, which involve the rejection of one or more of the Euclidean axioms, are not impossible it follows that Euclidean geometry is not necessary. The consistency of non-Euclidean geometries had gradually come to be accepted as efforts to prove inconsistency, from Saccheri (1733) onwards, had foundered. The relative consistency of non-Euclidean geometries *vis-à-vis* Euclidean geometry had been established in works Russell had read, e.g. Beltrami (1868*a*), Klein (1871), as a result of the so-called Euclidean models of non-Euclidean geometries. (The proof of the consistency of Euclidean geometry itself had to wait until Hilbert's axiomatizaton (1899).) However, this line of argument is not one which appealed to Russell, for it ignores the Kantian distinction between the two types of possibility, logical and objective, drawn in § 4.1. That non-Euclidean geometries are logically possible cannot be used to show that Euclidean geometry is not objectively necessary. Yet it is the objective necessity of Euclidean geometry which has to be rejected, if we are to show that Euclidean geometry is empirical. Russell is well aware of the situation. He notes that non-Euclidean geometries 'do not seem to be [objectively] impossible', but continues that he does not know how they can be proved to be possible 'once it is admitted—as it must be—that the contrary of a necessary proposition can fail to be contradictory', a proviso which admits the distinction between the two types of possibility (EAE 335). There remains, however, a deeper doubt about the admissibility of this distinction in Russell's theory of geometry. For Russell had abandoned Kant's transcendental psychology, on which Kant's distinction between the two types of necessity was based, in favour of what he has billed as a purely logical approach. It remains questionable whether the purely logical approach allows him to distinguish objective from logical possibility.

Given the distinction, however, Russell has to make do with various persuasive considerations to establish the empirical nature of Euclidean geometry. He points out that non-Euclidean geometry has shown that the Euclidean axioms 'are logically independent of all the other axioms of Geometry' (EAE 337), i.e. that they cannot be derived from either projective geometry or general metrical geometry. And he claims also to have shown in chapter 4 of *EFG* that the Euclidean axioms are also 'independent of those general philosophical functions that space and time fulfil' (EAE 337). Now the general philosophical functions of space and time are, first, to make possible the apprehension of diverse but related items and, second, to make measurement possible. Since Russell has already argued that projective and general metrical geometry were necessary to fulfil these functions, the independence of the Euclidean axioms from projective and general metrical geometry is a corollary of their independence from the general functions of space and time. Moreover, if Russell really *has* shown what he *says* he has shown, that the Euclidean axioms are independent of the general functions of space and time and thus that they are not necessary for measurement or the apprehension of diverse but related items, then he has shown that the Euclidean axioms are not a priori. For a geometrical proposition is a priori if it is necessary for (a certain type of) experience, and it is necessary for (a certain type of) experience if it is true of any intuition which fulfils the 'general philosophical functions' of space. The Euclidean axioms are false of some such intuitions, and therefore are not a priori. The fact that Russell did not avail himself of this argument suggests that he was no longer confident that he had exhaustively specified the general functions of space and time. If there were further such functions, beyond the two outlined above, then there would be further a priori constraints on the choice of geometry, and Euclidean geometry might, after all, turn out to be a priori. (It is possible that Russell thought that physics would impose such further constraints, and that Euclidean geometry would turn out to be the only geometry which made physics possible.)

In his article, Couturat (1898*a*: 373–4) raises a new type of consideration designed to show that Euclidean geometry is a priori. While Russell had concerned himself with congruence in establishing the a priori character of general metrical geometry, Couturat argues that geometrical similarity is what is important. More explicitly, he argues that any a priori possible space must be such that the size of any figure can be changed without changing its shape (e.g., that the sides of a triangle can be increased or decreased in constant proportion without changing its angles).[102] This is a property which only Euclidean geometry has. If Delbœuf-homogeneity can be established as an a priori condition on space, then the apriority of Euclidean geometry is established. Couturat does not claim Delbœuf-homogeneity to be the result of fresh aprioristic considerations of the sort discussed in the previous paragraph. Instead he argues that its apriority follows from considerations already admitted by Russell. Couturat argues that space cannot be regarded as purely passive if the interior angles of a figure depend upon the length of its sides. In other words, that a space which is not Delbœuf-homogeneous violates Russell's a priori requirement of the passivity of space.

Russell does not attack this argument directly, although it is very hard to see exactly why Couturat should have thought the passivity requirement was violated. Russell's reply (EAE 328) is that if Delbœuf-homogeneity is an a priori feature of space, then so, too, should be its dual: that is, it should be possible to increase or decrease the interior angles of a geometrical figure without changing the lengths of its sides. Since this is impossible in all geometries, he concludes that Delbœuf-homogeneity cannot be an a priori feature of any possible geometry. This argument, though ingenious, is not entirely satisfactory. The very fact that some geometries are Delbœuf-homogeneous, while no geometry has the dual property, would seem to tell against Russell's assumption that Delbœuf-homogeneity and its dual have the same status as regards apriority. What Russell requires is some argument to show that while the two may differ as regards possibility and impossibility, they may not differ as regards apriority. But he makes no attempt to supply the needed argument, and (given the expected close linkages between modality and apriority) it is difficult to see how he could.

Perhaps a better line of defence for Russell, though he does not explicitly use it, would be to argue that the fact that in any space it was impossible to change the interior angles of a figure without changing the lengths of its sides showed that this impossibility was consistent with the passivity of space, and thus, by analogy, that the impossibility in some spaces of changing the linear measurements of a figure without changing its interior angles was also consistent with the passivity of space. In other words, he could argue that Delbœuf-homogeneity with respect to linear measurements was not a consequence of the passivity of space, since Delbœuf-homogeneity with

[102] Couturat calls this property 'homogeneity' after Delbœuf 1894. Russell, for his reply (EAE 327), adopts Delbœuf's terminology, abandoning his own usage in *EFG*. In what follows I shall speak of 'Delbœuf-homogeneity'.

respect to angles was not. A reply to this line of reasoning would then have to show that angular measurements differed from linear ones in some respect relevant to the passivity of space.

It would now be generally conceded that, on the issue of the apriority of Euclidean geometry, Russell was right and Couturat wrong. On the issue which separated Russell and Poincaré, whether choice of geometry is an empirical matter, opinion remains divided. According to Poincaré (1899) the choice of geometry is conventional and Euclidean geometry, though it could not be established by empirical or a priori means, was yet to be preferred as the most convenient. Poincaré made much of the fact that any physical phenomena which could be explained on the basis of Euclidean geometry could also be explained using non-Euclidean geometry. For example, the motion of bodies could be explained either by assuming the operation of forces in a Euclidean space, or by assuming a non-Euclidean space without the operation of forces. Poincaré's own example (1899: 265) concerns the possibility of finding a star with a negative parallax. Such a result could be explained either by introducing a non-Euclidean geometry, or by keeping Euclidean geometry and assuming that light rays do not travel rectilinearly. All this, of course, supports the (by now) familiar thesis of the underdetermination of theory by evidence. Russell was well aware of it, having used such considerations in attacking Lotze (*EFG* 100).

But are considerations of this kind sufficient to establish that choice of geometry is conventional? Russell, quite wisely, thought not. Hence his initial distinction between (2) and the position he correctly attributes to Poincaré, namely (3). As Russell points out, the sort of considerations that are used to establish the underdetermination of theory by evidence are not sufficient to support (3). Indeed, it is not at all clear what would establish (3). Nor, for that matter, is it altogether clear in Poincaré's 1899 article what it means to say that choice of geometry is conventional. Russell seems implicitly to assume that if the choice is conventional it must be arbitrary, though this is usually denied by conventionalists, who appeal to features other than truth or falsity, such as simplicity or convenience, to 'guide' the choice, though never to 'force' it. In his later writings Poincaré was inclined to cash out convenience in evolutionary terms, claiming that certain geometrical choices offered evolutionary advantage over certain others. (At the same time, he came to feel that 'convenience' wasn't a sufficiently forceful term to convey the advantages offered: 1912: 38.) Simplicity, for Poincaré, usually meant mathematical simplicity coupled with the usual, rather vague, aesthetic connotations. He often used the example of choice of coordinate systems to illustrate what he meant, some coordinate systems being simpler to use (for some problems) than others. Experience also played a role in his account of choice of geometry, but only a loose one. The whole amalgam of physical theory plus chosen geometry had to conform to experience. But the role of experience in choosing a geometry seems to have been mainly confined to setting the parameters within which the simplicity criterion could operate. The absence of any clear account of simplicity (or, for that matter, convenience) leaves Poincaré's position regrettably vague (and, by the same token, difficult to refute).

Russell, in his reply to Poincaré, is very largely concerned to show that measurement is not entirely arbitrary, and that the empirical facts rule out certain, a priori admissible, values for the curvature constant $k$.[103] Restricting the debate to purely metrical considerations makes things somewhat easier for the conventionalist. For there, at any rate, he has the advantage of a clear metaphor: the choice of a metric geometry is like the choice of a system of units of measurement. Just as a length can be measured in feet or in metres, so can the metrical properties of physical space be given by Euclidean or non-Euclidean geometry. In neither case can we say one method of proceeding is true and the other false. How good are Russell's grounds for rejecting such an account?

Russell argues that if Poincaré is correct about the conventionality of metrical propositions then such propositions do not state 'what is the case as regards actual parts of space, but merely what result we shall obtain by measurement . . . he must hold that measurement does not give the size of figures in space, but merely shows what results measurement gives' (AOG 395–6). But in this case, Russell argues, why bother with measurement at all, any other operation will do as well. Russell's argument is hardly clear. It bears on a point where both men were subject to confusion at this time: the relation between pure and applied geometry. There is a good sense in which Poincaré can be said to have confused the undeniable truth that different pure metric geometries were inter-translatable, which warrants the view that choice of notation for pure geometry is conventional, with the claim that the choice of applied geometry is also conventional (cf. Nagel 1961: 261–3). As not infrequently happens in philosophy, Poincaré's position is left attractively ambiguous between a truism and a stronger claim which is difficult to defend. It is difficult to determine, however, whether Russell's objection hits this weak spot in Poincaré's position. On the one hand, it seems as though Russell is relying (in part at least) on the mistaken view that what is conventionally chosen must be arbitrary. For it looks as though he's claiming that the methods and results of measurement on Poincaré's view are

---

[103] Russell assumed that Poincaré would admit that the axiom of three dimensions (EGII) was not conventional (AOG 395), a claim which Poincaré denied in his response (1900: 73). It has been suggested (e.g. Torretti 1978: 413 n. 15) that Poincaré had second thoughts about it later on (see Poincaré 1912, of which Torretti cites the last sentence). It seems to me that there is some evidence in (1912) that Poincaré had become uncomfortable with the position he had adopted, but not that he had changed it (cf. Johnson 1981: 110).

entirely arbitrary, that *any* methods and *any* results would do as well. If this is
his claim, it rests upon a fairly widespread misconception of conventionalism.
None the less, Poincaré is committed to the view that the results of
measurement are conventionally chosen, while Russell is committed to the
view that they are determined (at least in part) by the actual size of spatial
figures. Here is a genuine conflict, but one which requires care in its
adjudication. Certainly Poincaré cannot accept Russell's view, since Poincaré
denies that spatial figures have any actual size. But it is not so clear what
Poincaré's position amounts to. Poincaré may claim that the choice of pure
metric geometry is conventional (arguing from the admitted fact that
different pure metric geometries are inter-translatable). Against this, Russell
can correctly argue that even when a pure metric geometry is chosen in this
way, the methods and results of measurement are left entirely undetermined on
the conventionalist position. But this is a result which is unlikely to worry
Poincaré, who will merely reply that further conventions are needed before
measurement becomes definite. On this view, the key conventional element
is not the choice of pure metric geometry, but the choice of a definition
of distance. But once the definition of distance is chosen, the results
of measurement no longer remain undetermined, and Russell's criticism
collapses. The dispute at this stage, becomes one of counter-assertion.
Russell continues to maintain that spatial figures have actual size, Poincaré
to dispute this.[104]

Russell, therefore, develops an attack on Poincaré's definition of 'distance'.
Against Russell's view that two points determine a distance (*EFG* 164),
Poincaré urges that distance is a relation between two pairs of points, *A, B*
and *C, D*, such that *AB* is greater than, equal to, or less than *CD* (1899: 262).
Suppose that *A* is a point in Paris and *B* a point in London, and that *C* and *D*
are the end-points of the standard metre. Poincaré must maintain that it is a
matter of convention whether we say that *AB* is greater than, equal to, or
less than *CD*. This Russell regards as quite bad enough, but he recognizes
that it is a conclusion that Poincaré will not shirk. (Poincaré embraces it,
1900: 80–1.)

Russell, therefore, tries to press home his case with two additional claims
which, he argues, follow from Poincaré's theory of distance, neither of
which, he hopes, will be acceptable to Poincaré. First, he argues that
Poincaré's account entails that '[d]istance itself must be created by the
conventional rules' (*EAE* 396). If there were any actual distance between

---

[104] Similar remarks apply to Russell's more limited treatment of Poincaré in *EFG* 30–6.
There Russell assumed that Poincaré's conventionalism depended entirely upon the various
possible definitions of distance in projective geometry. Russell maintained, on the contrary,
that projective geometry lacked the concept of distance, replacing it by an analogue involving
four points rather than two (viz. anharmonic ratio).

two points in physical space, e.g. that between London and Paris, then measurements would have to be accepted or rejected according as they gave a true or false value for this distance, and the measurement could not be conventional.

[I]f distances are to be measured, they must be there before measurement. . . . It seems to be thought that, since measurement is required to *discover* equality and inequality, there cannot *be* equality or inequality without measurement. The true inference is exactly the opposite. What can be discovered by an operation must exist apart from the operation: . . . two quantities of the same kind must *be* equal or unequal before measurement. (AOG 396.)

On this point, Russell is on firm ground, but things go wrong when he develops it to make his second point, namely that if distance is not there to be measured 'equality and inequality are words destitute of meaning' (AOG 397). Here Russell is the victim of his overly referential view of meaning (cf. POM 47), and he ignores the possibility that 'equality' and 'inequality' may be defined, as Poincaré would define them, by means of operations.

How do these issues relate to the question of whether Euclidean geometry is true or false? In Poincaré's view it is only physical objects that are measured, and only with respect to such measurements is it possible to talk about distances. Thus while it makes sense to compare the sizes of physical objects, it makes no sense to compare the size of purely geometrical figures. Geometrical figures lack shape and size. Russell, by contrast, insists that measurement gives (at least approximately) the shape and size of the geometrical figures of bodies. This being so, physical space must have a geometry which makes possible geometrical figures of the shape and size that physical objects are found by measurement to have. Thus we have to admit, as a matter of contingent fact, that 'the volume of a body may be as great as one cubic millimetre, which would show that space is not very elliptic' (AOG 395). Russell does not maintain that the measure of curvature can be determined exactly, merely that it can be determined within limits. For this to be done by experiment, it is not necessary that lines be absolutely straight nor that bodies be absolutely rigid.

In his reply to Couturat Russell has suggested a very simple and inaccurate experiment for determining the measure of curvature, at least within broad limits of experimental accuracy.[105] Take a coin with a point marked on its edge, and make it turn a complete revolution along a geodesic in order to measure its circumference. Then measure its diameter and calculate the ratio of the two. If the value is as close to $\pi$ as observational accuracy

---

[105] The experiment has been suggested to him by Whitehead in a letter of 13 Feb. 1895. See also Whitehead 1898*b*.

permits, we can conclude that space is approximately Euclidean, and may definitely rule out geometries in which the measure of curvature takes a large positive or negative value (EAE 326). Philosophical arguments are rarely so simple, and this one is no exception. It was Poincaré who pointed out its difficulties in a letter to Couturat in which he noted that the experiment was really one on the nature of solid bodies and 'is therefore liable to the same objections as all similar experiments'.[106] The objections are by now familiar: any hypothesis as to the nature of space can be made consistent with the results of such an experiment provided compensating hypotheses are adopted with regard to the properties of solid bodies.

Russell's reply (AOG 398–9) is commonsensical and rather good, but not decisive. Russell admits that all such experiments illustrate both 'the behaviour of bodies with regard to rigidity, and the nature of space'. A single experiment can therefore determine either one of these only if the other is previously known. In fact, however, we can perform a large number of such experiments of many different types. In interpreting the results of a series of such experiments we are constrained in imputing behaviour to material bodies by the a priori requirement that material bodies behave according to dynamical laws of some kind.[107] Only some among the logically possible dynamical laws will be a priori admissible and only a single set of such laws can be used for the interpretation of all experiments. Within these constraints, it may be hoped that a series of experiments 'will . . . leave possible only one hypothesis as to the nature of space and one as to the nature of bodies' (AOG 400). These hypotheses cannot be said to be established with certainty, but they have received the best support that is possible in the empirical sciences and 'according to the usual procedure of the inductive sciences, are to be accepted as empirically proved (AOG 400). Russell clearly expects that, within the framework of dynamics, experiments such as the one with the coin will show that space is approximately Euclidean.

Poincaré's arguments are important, and have played a major role in the subsequent development of the philosophy of geometry. But they do not establish his thesis that the axioms of Euclidean geometry are merely conventional and lack truth-values. The validity of each of his arguments could be admitted even though conventionalism was denied. It could well be that the axioms of Euclidean geometry have a truth-value but, for the reasons Poincaré has given, it is impossible to determine which truth-value they have. Russell clearly did not expect to be able to establish that they were true, because of the impossibility of verifying $k = 0$ with absolute precision. But he did think that experiment might establish that they were

[106] H. Poincaré to L. Couturat, 1 June 1899 (cf. Poincaré 1896: 124–5). Couturat sent the letter on to Russell.
[107] For this a priori requirement see VN, 15. See Ch. 5 below for comment.

false, since $k$ might deviate from 0 sufficiently to be detected. The only concession he found it necessary to make to Poincaré was that even this could not be established with certainty. For one might still be able to match the experimental data by setting $k = 0$ and making appropriate adjustments in dynamics. But this, so far from showing that the axioms of the various metrical geometries were not empirical truths or falsehoods, was exactly the sort of uncertainty that one expected in the empirical sciences.

## 4.8 ON THE PARADOXES WHICH LIE AT THE FOUNDATION OF GEOMETRY

It was not Russell's expectation, when he undertook his analysis of geometry, that he would find it to be an entirely consistent and self-contained science. According to Russell, 'every Science may be regarded as an attempt to construct a universe out of none but its own ideas' (1896*f*: 5). In this attempt, each science must be considered a failure, since each required its own stock of basic ideas to be supplemented by ideas drawn from another science. The need for this supplementation was shown by the existence of fundamental contradictions within the science in question.

Within geometry, Russell finds two types of 'inevitable' and 'fundamental' contradictions. There are those which are 'inherent in the notion of the continuum'; Russell cites Zeno's paradoxes as examples. And there are those which 'spring from the fact that space, while it must, to be knowable, be pure relativity, must also, it would seem, since it is immediately experienced,[108] be something more than mere relations' (*EFG* 188). Russell doubts, however, whether the two types of contradiction are really distinct, for 'any continuum . . . in which the elements are not data, but intellectual constructions resulting from analysis, can be shown to have the same relational and yet not wholly relational character as belongs to space' (*EFG* 188). At all events, Russell's discussion does little to keep them distinct. Both types of contradiction seem to depend entirely upon the relational character of space, and both, Russell hopes, will be resolved by a transition from geometry to physics. In the sequel, contradictions of both types will constantly recur. Ultimately they will all be found to have their roots in Russell's theory of relations.

Before proceeding we need to be clear about the differences between relational and absolute view of space. Russell's clearest statement on the topic comes slightly later in a well-known passage in his book on Leibniz

---

[108] This phrase requires some qualification, for elsewhere Russell says that, unlike Kant (1781) and Stumpf (1873), he regards space itself as 'wholly conceptual'. It turns out to be spatial relations which are given in experience: 'Space is given only as spatial order' (*EFG* 194; see also p. 197). The puzzling claim which results, that spatial relations to be given must be more than mere relations, was no oversight, as will emerge. The distinction between (empty) space itself (or pure externality) and spatial relations is of considerable importance (see below and n. 111).

where he says that they arise from 'emphasizing one or other of the following pair of ideas':

If we take two points $A$ and $B$, they have (1) a distance, which is simply a relation between the two, (2) an actual length, consisting of so much space, and stretching from $A$ to $B$. If we insist on the former as the essence of space, we get a relational theory; the terms $A$ and $B$, whose distance is spatial, must themselves be non-spatial, since they are not relations. If we insist on the latter, the actual intervening length, we find it divisible into an infinite number of points each like the end points $A$ and $B$. This alternative gives the Newtonian theory of absolute space, consisting, not in an assemblage of possible relations, but in an infinite collection of actual points. (*POL* 112–13.)

It is reasonable to ask why Russell thought geometry required a relational view of space, since, on present showing, a non-relational view might have rendered geometry consistent. In *EFG* Russell derives the relational theory of space from the axiom of free mobility or, more directly, from the passivity of space. For Russell, to be a substance or an entity is to have effects. This is a principle which follows from neo-Hegelian metaphysics, where everything that exists is internally related to everything else which comprises the Absolute. Thus in existing an item has effects throughout the Absolute.[109] Since space is passive, it cannot be an entity or substance. As Russell put it elsewhere '[T]hose axioms, which alone make a knowledge of space possible, can only be true on condition that space is a mere adjective' (VN 14).

At first sight, it seems not surprising that Russell should find that the relational nature of space lands geometry in contradictions. For Bradley had maintained with a brisk vehemence that space was riddled with contradiction and was to be dismissed as mere appearance (cf. Bradley 1893*a*: 30–3). The trouble with space, for Bradley, was that it depended upon relations, and the rejection of relations was the pivotal point of his entire metaphysics. But Russell's discovery of contradictions in geometry did not arise from his simply taking over Bradley's theory of relations, nor did it result in his rejecting space as mere appearance as Bradley had done. Any account of Russell's early treatment of relations requires special care, for a number of reasons. His remarks on relations are spread over a number of works written at different times and often on different subjects; moreover, a great deal of what he thought seems never to have been made explicit, and may have been taken over without much reflection from others. There is a serious danger, therefore, that his early views on relations never formed a coherent theory. He seems not to have been aware of the extent to which his entire dialectic

---

[109] There are even passages (VN 12) which suggest he held a stronger view, derived from McTaggart and Spinoza, that to exist involved self-assertion, but Russell's language on this point is somewhat tinged with scepticism, and it would be rash to attribute this position to him as a settled opinion.

hinged upon problems stemming from his views about relations until 1898, and only then does he attempt consciously to formulate a fully fledged theory of relations.

Although Russell agreed with Bradley that all relations involve identity-in-difference it is not clear that he regarded them as inconsistent on that account. There is already a very typically Russellian confusion arising out of the distinction between grammatical and logical form. Although it was Russell who made this distinction famous, such a distinction (though not so described) is to be found in Bradley; indeed, it is forced on Bradley by (among other things) his rejection of relations, since, from the point of view of overt grammar, some judgements are undeniably relational. Such judgements have to be reformulated in a way which eliminates the relation. Russell has his own ways for doing this, and they will be discussed later. But there is an underlying unclarity in Russell's account as to whether when a putatively relational judgement *J* is reformulated into a judgement *J'* which makes no apparent use of the relation, we have replaced one judgement with another, or whether a single judgement is merely given two formulations. On the first view, grammatically relational judgements are regarded as defective and eliminated; on the second, grammatically relational judgements are admitted since they are legitimated as merely notational variants of admissible non-relational judgements. Russell on different occasions states his position in both ways, a fact which can give the impression of a serious inconsistency. As it turns out, not all grammatical relations can be eliminated by the methods Russell suggests, and the contradictions on which Russell's dialectic hinges depend precisely upon relations for which the elimination fails. Russell seems to have discovered this more or less by induction, once a fair number of contradictions had been assembled. Moreover, he was in no position to diagnose the real problem until he had come to distinguish the different types of grammatical relation. As he wrote *EFG*, however, this was still two years off. The insights which now seem almost trivial were hard won by Russell in the 1890s. That they do seem trivial now is an important part of Russell's legacy as a philosopher.

It will not do, therefore, simply to assume that Russell followed Bradley in finding contradictions in geometry, nor that he simply consigned space to a phantom realm of appearance. Some of Bradley's more specific objections to space can hardly have impressed Russell either. Consider the following passage, which bears some initial similarities to Russell's antinomy of the point:

[W]hen taken itself as a unit, [space] passes away into the search for an illusory whole. . . . As a whole it *is*, briefly, the relation of itself to a non-existent other. For take space as large and as complete as you possibly can. Still, if it has not definite boundaries, it is not space; and to make it end in a cloud, or in nothing, is mere blindness and *our* mere failure to perceive. A space limited, and yet without space that is outside, is a self-contradiction. . . . Space, to be space, must have space outside itself. (Bradley 1893*a*: 32.)

Sympathetic as Russell may have been to Bradley, he can hardly have been sympathetic to this tangle of naïveties. Russell was well aware of non-Euclidean spaces which were finite and yet required no external embedding space. Nor, for that matter, is there any need to suppose that finite Euclidean spaces must have further spaces beyond them. Bradley's claim that space must have boundaries is similarly unsupported. In the first place, Bradley ignores the possibility of finite but unbounded spaces. Secondly, Bradley seems to have misconstrued what is involved in taking space as 'a unit' or a 'whole', assuming apparently that space must be finite in order to be considered as a whole or as a unit. Yet there is no warrant for this assumption, and even if there were it would hardly show that space is illusory. Only on this last point is there any evidence that Bradley would have had Russell's support. For Russell in 1896 regarded space and all extensive continua as involving illusory wholes (cf. SDCQ 58–9, discussed below, § 6.3).

It is not the fact that space involves relations which makes geometry inconsistent for Russell; it is the fact that space is *nothing but* relations, that it is 'pure relativity' or abstract externality. Around this point contradictions form at many levels. At the most superficial, the pure relativity of space, on which assumption alone geometry is possible, ensures that space cannot be substantival. Yet geometry, in making space an object of study, requires that it be more than mere relativity (*EFG* 190). At another level, geometry requires that space can be considered as a whole—since geometry ascribes properties to the whole of space—yet the pure relativity of the constituents of space ensures that it is incapable of forming a whole. The antinomies of geometry all depend, so it will turn out, upon a falsifying reification of space or spatial figures. Elements of this position are to be found in Bosanquet. However, there is, in Bosanquet, a suggestion that space and time are beyond the scope of human knowledge on account of their relativity: '[T]hough no human knowledge is free from relativity, i.e. from the reference to what falls outside it; yet on the other hand no actual human knowledge is, like the abstract infinities [space, time and the real number line], mere relativity and nothing more' (1988: i, 187). It seems most likely that Bosanquet means that space and time as, in some sense, infinite wholes, cannot be objects of human knowledge. It could hardly be the case that Bosanquet was maintaining that geometric knowledge, for example, was impossible. Geometry, though involving relativity, was at some level correct. The abstract infinities, as nothing more than relativity, were at every level illusory. At all events, it could not have been Russell's view that the pure relativity of space made it unknowable. Quite the reverse, in fact, since he had argued in his transcendental deduction that if knowledge of space (i.e. geometry) was to be possible space must be pure relativity.

Russell's own distinction between relativity and relations is somewhat clearer. Relativity, Russell says, is 'itself not a relation, it gives the bare possibility of relations between diverse things' (*EFG* 190; cf. also p. 138). What this means becomes clear later in Russell's discussion, where the issue of pure relativity is resumed under the guise of externality. Externality, Russell explains, 'gives only the element of diversity required for a relation': 'Every relation, we may say, involves a diversity between the related terms, but also some unity. Mere diversity does not give a ground for that interaction, and that interdependence, which a relation requires. Mere unity leaves the terms identical, and thus destroys the reference of one to another required for a relation' (*EFG* 198). Externality is relational only in the sense that it gives the diversity which is 'a necessary aspect or element in every relation (*EFG* 198). It is thus not itself a relation, since it 'does not give that indivisible whole of which any actual relation must consist, and is thus, when regarded abstractly, not subject to the restrictions of ordinary relations' (*EFG* 198). Externality, while not itself a relation, is rather a necessary condition for relations. Exactly similar remarks apply to identity. Since neither identity nor diversity are to be regarded as genuine relations, but merely as necessary conditions for relations, I shall call them 'proto-relations'. They will appear again in Chapters 7 and 8.[110]

What, then, are the contradictions which Russell thinks are to be found in geometry on account of the pure relativity of space? Russell lists three though it is not clear that each is to be regarded as quite distinct from the others, and some of them are given in more than one form.

1. *The antinomy of the point*: The simplest formulation is quoted from Veronese (1891: 266): 'There are different points. All points are identical'. Less baldly stated the antinomy runs:

Though the parts of space are intuitively distinguished, no conception is adequate to differentiate them. Hence arises a vain search for elements, by which the differentiation could be accomplished, and for a whole, of which the parts of space are to be components. Thus we get the point, or zero extension, as the spatial element, and an infinite regress or a vicious circle in the search for a whole. (*EFG* 188; cf. also p. 137.)

A number of issues seem to be involved here. Russell's talk of the 'parts' and 'elements' of space suggests that he is referring to an antinomy which was thought to arise on the absolute, or substantival, theory of space, that of explaining how any number of points of zero extension could be combined to

[110] Traces of this view appear even in 1903 (cf. *POM* 172).

form a finitely extended line (cf. *POL*, 120). This objection was plainly put by philosophers with whose work Russell was familiar. Thus, for example, Bradley:

[A]ny space must consist of parts; and, if the parts are not spaces, the whole is not space. Take then in a space any parts. These . . . are obviously extended. If extended, however, they will themselves consist of parts, and these again of further parts, and so on without end. . . . Anything extended is a collection, a relation of extendeds, which again are relations of extendeds, and so on indefinitely. The terms are essential to the relation, and the terms do not exist. . . . Space is essentially a relation of what vanishes into relations, which seek in vain for their terms. (Bradley 1893*a*: 31–2.)

Sigwart is clearer still:

[N]o space-idea which is in the least extended can really be brought into consciousness by one indivisible act; there is always presupposed the comprehension of a continuous manifoldness, distinguishable into parts, a comprehension moreover which cannot take place merely as a repetition of the simple, of the point, since points can never give rise to a line. (Sigwart 1873: ii. 49.)

Russell apparently thinks his own account of space, even though it is a relational account, is open to the same objections: 'We saw, in discussing projective Geometry, that straight lines and planes must be regarded, on the one hand, as relations between points, and on the other hand as made up of points' (*EFG* 189). The reason lies in the fact that, according to Russell, in order to do geometry it is necessary to hypostatize space. But then 'the mind imperatively demands' spatial elements (*EFG* 189). This opens the way to the Bradley–Sigwart antinomy. Russell, however, derives another antinomy as well. For the spatial elements of necessity have contradictory properties. They must be genuinely spatial, but at the same time they must 'contain no space' (*EFG* 189), because if they did so they would be capable of further analysis, and thus not genuinely elemental. 'Such a conception', Russell concludes in heroic Bradleian style, 'is a palpable contradiction, only rendered tolerable by its necessity and familiarity' (*EFG* 189).

The problems so far discussed arise fairly directly from the false hypostatization of space, which naturally brings upon Russell's theory all the problems of the absolute theory. A wider science avoids the antinomies by avoiding the hypostatization. None the less, there is more to the antinomy of the point than has so far been revealed. The main problem with points is revealed in an argument from Bosanquet, which looks very similar to the one just quoted from Bradley, but which is, in fact, subtly and importantly different. Bosanquet described points as 'absolutely homogeneous' parts, that is, parts 'whose repetition has no tendency to generate a whole. The idea of infinite space is the idea of the endless synthesis of such parts, which must always present to us the appearance of an unsolved problem' (1888: i. 186).

That Bosanquet's argument starts with the fact that points are absolutely homogeneous is crucial. It is not that points cannot combine to form lines because they lack extension, but that they can't function as relata of spatial relations because they are homogeneous. The doctrine of internal relations is what is important here. Spatial relations, like all others, are internal. Thus they cannot hold between spatial points because points lack the intrinsic features on which alone internal relations can be founded (cf. *EFG* 166). The upshot is, as Bradley expressed it, 'you can not have a relation between points that are not different in quality' (1883, i, 289 n). Now this can be expressed as an objection to either the absolute theory or the relational theory. It is an objection to the relational theory, even without false hypostatization, because spatial relations require relata, and, since all relations are internal, relations cannot hold between relata which are devoid of intrinsic qualities. But it is also an objection against the absolute theory, because the absolute theory regards spatial figures as wholes composed of points. Now, any whole consists of parts in relation. But, by the doctrine of internal relations, parts cannot be related if they are devoid of intrinsic qualities, and thus points cannot be related to form spatial figures.

Russell's resolution of the paradox of the point makes ingenious use of his distinction between space itself as pure relativity and spatial figures as actual relations among points of 'geometrical matter' which he calls atoms. Spatial figures must be allowed to vary continuously (*EFG* 191), and the point is derived from 'geometrical matter' as the 'unit of differentiation' (*EFG* 192). This, of course, raises its own problems, the atom as unit of differentiation is little better than the point as zero of extension. But the atom as relatum of spatial relations does mark an advance. The atom is simple and contains within it no spatial relations, and thus 'it cannot appear as a spatial figure; for every spatial figure involves some diversity of matter. But our atom must have spatial relations with other atoms, since to supply terms for these relations is its only function. It is also capable of having these relations, since it is differentiated from other atoms.'(*EFG* 192). The upshot is that spatial points become redundant once atoms of geometrical matter are introduced as terms for spatial relations.

So long as we sought [such terms] without reference to anything more than space, the self-contradictory notion of the point was the only outcome of our search; but now that we allow a reference to matter differentiated by space, we find at once the term which was needed, namely, a non-spatial simple element, with spatial relations to other elements. To Geometry such a term will appear, owing to its spatial relations, as a point; but the contradiction of the point, as we now see, is a result only of the undue abstraction with which Geometry deals. (*EFG* 192.)

Spatial points are thus falsifying abstractions of unextended material atoms. Viewed from a purely geometric point of view the atoms appear as points. There will be more to say about atoms of geometrical matter in Chapter 5. The sense in which the antinomy of the point arises from the false hypostatization of space will be considered below under (3).

2. *The circle in the definition of straight lines and planes*. The problem here is this: 'All positions being relative, positions can only be defined by their relations, i.e. by the straight lines or planes through them; but straight lines and planes, being all qualitatively similar, can only be defined by the positions they relate. Hence . . . we get a vicious circle' (*EFG* 188–9, cf. also pp. 120, 127). Again, Russell makes use of material atoms to help him escape the dilemma, claiming that where material atoms have replaced points 'the duality of points and lines . . . has disappeared, and the straight line may be defined as the spatial relation between two unextended atoms' (*EFG* 193).

3. *Space is at once relational and more than relational*. This paradox derives from one of Bradley's: '[O]n the one hand, space has parts, and is therefore not mere relations, while on the other hand, when we try to say what these parts are, we find them after all to be mere relations' (*EFG* 194; cf. Bradley 1893*a*: 31–2). The problem, according to Russell, arises from the reification of 'empty space'. 'For only when space is regarded as possessed of some thinghood, can a whole or a true element be demanded. . . . When space is regarded . . . as only spatial order,[111] unbounded extension and infinite divisibility both disappear' (*EFG* 196). Divisibility is a feature of matter, and in the case of matter (unlike that of space), the divisibility in question is not infinite divisibility. As far as the question of infinite divisibility is concerned, what Russell seems to have in mind is that spatial figures are determined by configurations of unextended atoms. This becomes apparent in his account of what 'division' of spatial relations amounts to. Suppose that a set of geometrical atoms is given. As Russell notes, 'other atoms may be imagined, differently localized . . . on the straight line joining two of the original atoms, this straight line appears as divided by them' (*EFG* 197). But this appearance is an illusion, what has happened is that the original relation (straight line) has been replaced by two or more jointly equivalent relations. The situation, Russell explains, is similar to that in which 'two compounded relations of father and son may replace the equivalent relation of grandfather and grandson' (*EFG* 197). The 'infinite divisibility' of spatial relations is now

---

[111] Russell here appeals to a distinction of Stumpf's (1873: 15) between relations or order and an underlying ('absolute') content which is ordered. This generates two senses in which 'space' may be used: to denote spatial order or to denote empty space, the underlying content (cf. *EFG* 193–4).

to be interpreted as that fact that infinitely many pairs of spatial relations may be substituted for any given spatial relation (*POL*, 113).

This move makes full use of the distinction between spatial order and empty space which Russell drew from Stumpf. The account just given construes space as spatial order. From the point of view of empty space, an alternative account of infinite divisibility can be developed. On this account a spatial relation 'appears as a complex thing, necessarily composed of elements, which elements, however, nowhere emerge until we analyze the pseudo-thing down to nothing, and arrive at the point. In this sense, the divisibility of spatial relations is an unavoidable illusion' (*EFG* 197). On the second account, it is clear that there is, on Russell's view, a false hypostatization of the spatial relation. Empty space is an 'inevitable illusion' (*EFG* 198). If this false hypostatization is eschewed, the second account becomes, Russell claims, equivalent to the first. This is as far as Russell goes towards an account of space itself. But it is not immediately obvious that the account he gives is incoherent.

What seems open to question is the role of material (unextended) atoms in this theory. Two questions concerning their role arise: whether they are necessary for avoiding the third paradox, and whether they are sufficient for avoiding the first and second. The problem is that the atoms of geometrical matter are just too much like points of space. In looking over Russell's argument as presented in the last two paragraphs, it would seem quite possible to replace the word 'atom' by the word 'point' at every occurrence without upsetting the argument. Why, then, are material atoms necessary? For two reasons: Firstly, because on such a view space would consist of a scattering, as it were, of spatial points linked by spatial relations and there would be no reason why the spatial points had the spatial relations they did, nor any way of telling whether they had different ones. Worse, there is a real difficulty in making intelligible the claim that such points have spatial relations. The second reason material points are necessary is because the upshot of Russell's transcendental deduction was that empty space is pure externality, the bare possibility of spatial relations. However, as soon as one needs to speak of particular spatial relations, one needs terms between which the relations can hold, and such terms must in some sense be things or substances. Points of empty space are inadequate for this role, since they (and space itself) are completely non-substantival (*EFG* 199).

It is the second question—whether material atoms are sufficient to avoid the first and second paradoxes—that seems more pressing. Both paradoxes are problems of identification. In the first, points have to be distinguished but there is nothing by which to distinguish them. In the second, points can be distinguished by means of the lines which join them, but lines can only be identified by means of the points they join. With the introduction of material atoms, however, points can be distinguished by means of their relations to atoms, which, in turn, provides an identificatory grounding for lines and other geometric figures. Whether material atoms provide a satisfactory resolution of the paradoxes in geometry requires further consideration. It will be an important concern in the next chapter where I deal with Russell's attempts to extend his dialectic to include physics.

# 5

# Physics

## 5.1 THE POINT-ATOM THEORY

It is easy to see why physics was next on Russell's agenda when he had completed *An Essay on the Foundations of Geometry*. In fact, he had already begun sketching out his ideas on physics in 1896 and an outline of a new book on the philosophy of matter was drawn up early in 1897 following an organizational plan similar to that used in *EFG*: historical surveys of dynamics and philosophy of dynamics followed by a rational reconstruction of dynamical theory (cf. 1897*d*). In the case of physics, however, Russell never got beyond the stage of drawing up plans and writing down notes. First, his thinking about the fundamental nature of matter underwent a major change in 1897 which invalidated much of his earlier work. Then philosophical problems in pure mathematics pushed the philosophy of physics into the background. Many years later, when his work on *Principia Mathematica* was over, he turned again to the philosophy of matter, claiming that he had long been diverted from it by necessary preliminaries.[1]

Not all the geometrical antinomies discussed in § 4.8 were of significance for Russell's analysis of physics. The point/line circularity, for example, was not of direct consequence, and much of what Russell said about the third antinomy, that space must be both relational and more than relational, concerns the metaphysics of space rather than physics. Moreover, there is one problem implicit in the axiom of free mobility which Russell does not discuss in the final chapter of *EFG*, but which is none the less of great importance for his treatment of physics. In dealing with Russell's physics, therefore, it is helpful to state at the outset the geometrical antinomies which are most relevant. They are the following three:

The antinomy of the point: all points are alike, yet each is distinct. (1)

The antinomy of pure relativity: if space is composed entirely of relations, there is nothing for them to relate. (2)

The antinomy of free mobility: if spatial figures are individuated solely by their relations to other figures, it makes no sense to talk of the same figure being moved from one position to another. (3)

---

[1] B. R. to O. Morrell, postmarked 8 Feb. 1913 (letter no. 695).

The way in which matter was introduced in order to resolve the first and second antinomies has already been discussed in § 4.8. But the question remained of whether the introduction of matter genuinely solved the antinomies or merely replicated them in a somewhat different form. To answer this, one needs to know more about the nature of matter. As became clear in § 4.8, Russell knew that if matter was to solve the geometrical antinomies, it must be atomic, and the atoms must be unextended. This already commits Russell to a point-atom theory of matter. Another feature can now be added. It is plain, when Russell's discussion of the geometric antinomies is added to his critique of Helmholtz's philosophy of geometry (which based the axiom of free mobility upon the existence of actually rigid, or very nearly rigid, bodies), that the matter required is kinematic rather than dynamic. For, if the claims of the axiom of free mobility are to be met, it must be possible to move material bodies about in space without deformation. If the material bodies in question were dynamical in nature then one could not exclude the possibility that they were deformed in the course of their movement by the operation of forces. I'm not here concerned so much with the question of whether it would be possible in any way at all to support the axiom of free mobility on the basis of the motions of such bodies (perhaps by means of arguments such as Russell had used against Poincaré in connection with the empirical determination of lengths) as with the fact that Russell in *EFG* had maintained, in his critique of Helmholtz, that it would not. He was compelled, therefore, by the logic of his own position, to assert that the transition from geometry to physics was specifically a transition from geometry to kinematics where considerations of the operation of forces would not arise. Kinematics would provide the concept of force free matter in which geometry was deficient.

In fact, Russell was far from clear about the division between geometry and kinematics. In 1896 he seems to have thought that kinematics was a clearly distinct science in which the notion of kinematical matter was introduced for the first time. By 1897 this distinction is denied (1897c: 87), and he now includes the relevant concept of matter in metrical geometry (as well he might, since the axiom of free mobility clearly requires it). He distinguishes the two sciences by the fact that kinematics is concerned with the *process* of motion while geometry isn't (VN 21). Implicit here is a tricky problem about how to distinguish the various sciences in the dialectical arch. Metric geometry involves matter and motion only on account of the axiom of free mobility. We can either regard metric geometry as lacking these concepts and being internally incoherent as a result, requiring a transition to a new science (kinematics); or we can admit the concepts as part of metric geometry and remove the antinomies. But if we can do this for metric geometry we can surely do it for all sciences; the divisions between the various sciences in the dialectic then break down. But demarcation disputes of this kind are not of great importance. And given the high degree of unity the neo-Hegelian world-view sought, a certain amount of arbitrariness in the division of the various sciences is to be expected.

More interesting is a false start that Russell made in his treatment of physics in 1896. As the situation is presented in *EFG*, it is clear that the transition should be from geometry to kinematics, where matter and motion can be considered apart from the operation of forces. However, in his very first treatment of physics Russell attempted a transition from geometry directly to dynamics (VN 11–12). He thought that this transition was forced on him by traditional views that defined matter either by extension (as in Descartes) or by force (as in Leibniz). Alternative accounts, in terms of mass or impenetrability, were ignored by Russell because, as he explains elsewhere, they depend upon the more fundamental notion of force (1896a: 39). For Russell, matter not only could not be *defined* by extension, it could not be *extended*. In 1896 this left him with a conception of matter essentially tied to the notion of force. Thus, it seemed, any attempt to introduce matter in the dialectic of the sciences in order to remedy the antinomies of geometry would inevitably take him from geometry to dynamics.

The role that dynamical matter was to play is clearly indicated in an early note of 1896 where Russell addresses the problems of the pure relativity of space: 'Matter, as atom, punctual carrier (*Träger*) of relations which constitute space: but in order that it may appear, in space, as preferable to other points, must have some super-spatial property. This supplied, on mechanical view of nature, by *force*, i.e. by causal relations between atoms' (VN 11–12). This leads him to speculate that force might be identified with distance, or else exhibited as a function of distance. This last, he thinks, is one of the a priori conditions of dynamics, because force must not only be an intrinsic relation between two particles (i.e. a relation which doesn't depend upon other particles), but if it is to be measurable, it must be a function of a 'measurable intrinsic relation, i.e. *distance*' (VN 12).

Russell did not pursue the transition to dynamics for very long. In his next note on physics in the 'Various Notes' series, also written in 1896 and probably not too long after the first, he turns his attention to kinematics as an essential preliminary to dynamics.[2] He distinguishes three definitions of matter:

---

[2] There are even hints of an intermediate kinematical transition toward the end of his first note, although the paragraph in question may have been added some time after the note was written (VN 12; see T12: 32–41). The priority of kinematics to dynamics was well entrenched in Cambridge scientific culture at this time, largely owing to the influence of Whewell. In Whewell's terms, every aetiological science, like dynamics, must be preceded by a phenomenal science, like kinematics (cf. Whewell 1840 ii, 109).

*General definition*. Matter is that, in the data of outer sense, which can be regarded with less contradiction than any other sensational datum, as logical subject, or as *substance*.

*Kinematical definition*. Matter is that of which spatial relations are adjectives.

*Dynamical Definition*. Matter is not only the moveable, but the mover: two pieces of matter are capable of causally affecting one another in such a way as to change their spatial relations. (VN 14, 15.)

The general definition is elaborated upon in a paper of the following year, where Russell draws out some of its consequences: that matter is not a pure category but requires schematization under the concept *space*; that it is the 'logical subject' of all assertions concerning immediate data given under the form of space, and thus of all assertions concerning immediate data which are not mental. Matter in general may be defined as 'substance in so far as it apears in space' (1897c: 86).

The kinematical definition given above is clearly directed toward the second of the three antinomies of geometry. Russell goes on almost immediately to address the third antinomy, that of free mobility, by noting that the only other property required of kinematical matter by geometry is 'that of being susceptible of varying spatial adjectives without loss of identity' (VN 14).[3] This last, however, isn't quite correct, for Russell also argues that the ultimate constituents of kinematical matter must be unextended, and this for largely geometrical reasons. Russell's basic argument is quite brief: since space consists of relations between elements of kinematical matter, these elements themselves cannot contain any space (VN 14; 1897c: 87). This basic argument is supplemented by a more extended discussion in a footnote. There Russell contrasts three different views of kinematical matter.[4]

The first is the plenal view that kinematic matter fills the whole of space. Such a view comes in two forms, depending on whether the kinematic plenum is homogeneous or heterogeneous. On either version Russell rejects it. If the plenum is homogeneous it will be 'indistinguishable' from space, and incapable of motion for the same reason that space is.[5] So the problem of absolute motion

---

[3] Both requirements are stated as part of the definition of kinematical matter in a later note (VN 21).

[4] The argument in this footnote repeats, but also elaborates upon, the argument of a footnote to the first note (VN 11 n.). The continuity of argumentation between this first note and later ones indicates that, although Russell abandoned the attempt to jump straight from geometry to dynamics, he did not abandon much of the detail of the earlier note. The same options, expressed in slightly different terms, are presented in (1897c) and in *POL* 90–1, where Leibniz's failure to choose between the three alternatives is said to have 'made his Dynamics a mass of confusions'.

[5] Locke had long before argued that a material plenum was impossible since matter required empty space to give it room to move (1690: II, xiii, 22). This was not Russell's argument. In fact Russell thought Locke's objections could be easily disposed of by considerations from fluid mechanics which enabled motion to take place in a fluid by the displacement of matter. Russell

is merely replicated at the kinematic level on this view of matter. There are logical problems as well, which leave the problem of pure relativity unsolved. For '[h]omogeneity is synonymous with complete relativity' and thus a homogeneous kinematic plenum 'suffers all the incapacity of space for thinghood'—in short it cannot provide the relata for spatial relations (VN iii, 14 n.; see also Stallo 1881: 74; Ward 1899: i, 132–3, 136). While Russell's identification of homogeneity with relativity may be questioned, it will be the case that a genuine homogeneous plenum will not contain elements between which spatial relations could hold. I shall return to this point in § 5.2.

On the other hand, if the plenum is heterogeneous then it must contain elements or quanta 'of which denser portions contain more'. It is true that kinematic matter as Russell conceives it offers little by which such quanta could be discriminated. But Russell's first argument against quanta is obscure to say the least: 'The Plenum has nothing from which to form a quantum except *extension*, which makes it necessarily homogeneous'. Neither part of this claim seems convincing. In the first place, nothing has been done to show that the plenum *cannot* have some property by means of which different regions may be differentiated. Secondly, while Russell has shown to his own satisfaction that space must be homogeneous there seems no warrant for concluding from this that all extension must be homogeneous. Russell has argued that the homogeneity of spatial extension is necessary for spatial measurement. But this function of space is not jeopardized if some other heterogeneous extension, such as a kinematic plenum, is superimposed on space. Russell has, however, a second argument against the possibility of elements in the plenum, namely that they would resurrect all the difficulties of geometrical points. Such problems are avoided on his own preferred kinematic theory which involves point-atoms which are not taken to compose a plenum.

The second view of matter which Russell rejects is the common view that kinematic matter consists of extended atoms with empty space between them. Against this Russell argues, first, that such extended atoms are internally 'on a level with the Plenum'. Apparently, he thinks that they will thus resurrect the difficulties he has already criticized in the plenal theory, though it is far from clear that this is the case. It is true that, on the view that the inside of an extended atom is a heterogeneous plenum, there remains the problem of identifying the elements which account for its heterogeneity. The possibility that atoms had an internal structure was one that physicists in the 1890s were beginning to broach, primarily in response to experimental data (e.g. from

(*POL* 93 n.) approvingly cites Leibniz's argument against Locke on this point (Leibniz 1704: 53–4). Russell's argument against motion in a homogeneous plenum is, in fact, closer to the one Leibniz himself gives (1714: § 8).

spectroscopy) rather than theoretical requirements.[6] It is not too surprising, perhaps, that Russell should either have been unaware of these developments or not have taken them seriously enough. But while Russell is right in thinking that for all heterogeneous plena there is the problem of identifying the elements (or qualities) which make them heterogeneous, there is no reason to have supposed (even in 1896) that the problem was insuperable for extended atoms, nor even (as Russell in 1897 came to admit) for an all-pervading material plenum. There would seem to be even less warrant for his claim that extended, homogeneous atoms replicate internally the problems of a homogeneous material plenum. The chief problem of the latter, for Russell, was that of defining motion within it. Such a problem doesn't arise in the case of extended atoms separated by empty space. Motions, both internal and external, may be referred either to other atoms or to the boundary which separates the atom from the rest of the world. Nor would there seem to be any reason to suppose that the inside of a homogeneous, extended atom would be indistinguishable from the space it occupied. Russell seems to have moved too swiftly to his conclusion from his dubious dictum that homogeneity is synonymous with complete relativity. Local homogeneity, at any rate, is not—as the case of extended, homogeneous atoms shows. Russell's first criticism of extended atoms is shallow and inconclusive.

His second criticism, however, though not without its embarrassing moments, takes him into a major controversy in the physics of his day. He argues briefly that since the atoms are extended they must have parts and must, therefore, be analysable into further atoms. These in turn, if they are extended, will be further analysable into new atoms, and so on indefinitely. Thus, as he puts it elsewhere, the extended atom 'cannot . . . afford a metaphysical solution of the composition of matter' (*POL* 92). Russell is not wholly explicit in his conclusion. He is not in a position to infer that each atom is composed of real, physically distinct, sub-atomic particles. But the infinite divisibility of space does warrant his concluding that extended atoms may be regarded as spatially divisible *ad infinitum*. He supplements this first, a priori argument with two more derived from physics. In the first of these he

[6] Ironically enough, in 1896, at the time Russell was writing, J. J. Thomson at the Cavendish Laboratory in Cambridge, where Russell was to spend a few unproductive weeks at the beginning of 1898 performing routine experiments on electricity and magnetism, was performing the experiments on cathode rays which revealed the existence of electrons (see J. J. Thomson 1897). Shortly afterwards W. Thomson (by this time Lord Kelvin) proposed a new model of the atom which would seem to satisfy Russell's requirements for a heterogeneous extended atom. On the new model, atoms were conceived as spheres of uniform, positive electrification within which discrete negative charges (electrons) were distributed. (See W. Thomson 1902, 1904*a*, 1905.) Russell's records of his experiments at the Cavendish Laboratory are preserved in a notebook among the Morrell papers at Austin. The nature of the work can be gauged from the text he used, Glazebrook and Shaw (1894).

claims that the fact that we can use the calculus to determine, say, the centre of gravity of an extended body indicates that such bodies must have 'internal elements since [the] infinitesimal calculus [is] really only possible where we have indivisibles and finite differences' (VN 15 n.). This argument depends upon Russell's disastrously anachronistic interpretation of the calculus in terms of finite indivisibles (see below, § 6.2). The argument is best ignored (Russell himself soon rejected it, see *Papers*, ii, A15: 33–4). On the one hand, it is redundant given his a priori argument that any finitely extended body contains finitely extended sub-regions. On the other, it does nothing to substantiate a claim that extended atoms contain physically distinct, sub-atomic particles. For the indivisibles supposedly required for the infinitesimal calculus are not themselves physical elements, but arbitrary, quantitative sub-divisions.

The second supplementary argument is much better. He points out that the 'only advantage' of extended atoms is that they allow contact action (VN 15 n.). But, against this, he notes, first, that this does not obviate the need for action at a distance, since gravitation cannot be explained by contact; and, second, that even contact action 'is wholly inexplicable' for extended atoms. To uninstructed common-sense (or, for that matter, the mind instructed in general relativity) it is action at a distance which seems inexplicable, while action by impact appears easily intelligible. As Russell puts it, we think contact action 'self-evident because we have played billiards' (VN 15 n.). By contrast, there seems something deeply mysterious in the idea that matter can transmit action across vast stretches of empty space. Newton himself, after all, was a by no means confident advocate of action at a distance. For the working physicist, however, contact action had mysteries of its own. Newton had originally supposed that atoms must be absolutely hard if they were not to 'wear out' through repeated impacts. At the same time it was realized, by Newton and others, that energy was lost in every impact between hard bodies. Thus, the law of conservation of matter seemed to require that the ultimate particles of the universe were hard, while the law of conservation of energy required that they were not. Russell refers to this as the antinomy of 'the elasticity of perfectly hard atoms' (1896*a*: 39; see also *POL* 92). Moreover, both views gave rise to puzzling singularities. In the case of hard bodies, infinite forces are generated at the moment of impact. In the case of elastic bodies, at the moment of rebound an equally puzzling instantaneous reversal of direction of motion takes place. From the middle of the seventeenth century to the middle of the nineteenth, physicists, philosophers, and engineers were embroiled in an extraordinary debate on these matters.[7] Eventually elasticity and the conservation of energy won and

---

[7] The debate is fascinatingly chronicled by Scott 1970; Russell refers to it briefly in *POL* 77. The story is replete with dead-ends and cross purposes, disputes about words confused with

hard atoms were either abandoned entirely (as in W. Thomson's vortex atom theory) or else they disappeared inside elastic molecules (as in Maxwell's theory).

For philosophical reasons, Russell in 1896 was unable to accept this outcome. In this, his a priori argument was the crucial one. He could not accept that the ultimate constituents of matter were elastic (or otherwise deformable) atoms, because if they were deformable they must have parts, and if they had parts they could not be ultimate. Russell referred to this as the antinomy of the 'divisible indivisible' or as the paradox that the number of atoms must be both finite and infinite (1896a: 39; *POL* 105). At the same time he could not ignore what physicists had known for two centuries: that impact could not be explained in terms of hard atoms. For, in an impact between hard bodies, either motion was lost (and the conservation of energy violated) or else it was transmitted internally (in which case the hard atom must itself have parts, and so could not be an ultimate constituent of matter). As Russell put it: 'the whole of molar impact depends upon deformation' (*NV*, 15 n.). Faced with this dilemma Russell adopted in quick succession the two main alternatives under consideration by physicists in the nineteenth century. In 1896 he held the point-atom theory; the following year he abandoned that and turned to a vortex atom theory set within a plenal theory of matter. Russell claimed that these were the only viable alternatives for logical reasons: 'It is to be observed that if there is any empty space, or any action at a distance, we are driven to material points, while if there is anything except material points in matter, we are driven to the Plenum. The extreme views seem necessary alternatives, and all middle positions seem untenable' (*VN* 22). As early as 1894 Russell had considered both theories, and come to the conclusion that neither was wholly satisfactory (*EPIII* 147–8).

The point-atom theory had been developed by Boscovich (1758), in an attempt to solve the problem of impact, although part of its philosophical inspiration lay in Leibniz's monadology.[8] Boscovich's point-atoms (or *puncta*)

---

substantive issues, and just about every kind of confusion that may attend a *bona fide* scientific dispute. Unfortunately, Scott does not consider the extent to which confusion was caused by a misunderstanding of the notion of continuity—which would certainly have been a factor in Russell's case.

[8] Russell discusses Leibniz's dynamics in *POL* 75–99; and the relation between Leibniz and Boscovich at p. 91. Boscovich acknowledges Leibniz in 1758: 13. Boscovich, following the stylistic canons of his day, presents his theory in that work in a strictly logical order—a fact which obscures both the development of his thought and the problem situations which gave rise to it. For these it is necessary to consult two earlier works (Boscovich 1745 and 1755; extracts from which are reprinted as Supplements III and IV of 1758). These early works reveal, what would not be apparent from 1758, that Boscovich's theory developed out of his early work on the theory of impact. English work on Boscovich is not extensive, but cf. Gill 1941 and Whyte 1961. His influence on Russell is discussed further in Lewis 1989.

were like Leibniz's monads in that they were unextended and endowed with a surrogate for Newtonian inertia. But Leibniz rejected action at a distance, whereas for Boscovich all action was at a distance, for no two point atoms could ever be in contact. A second important but less obvious difference, which Russell may have missed at first, is that action for Leibniz involves force (*vis viva*) as a principle of change or activity, whereas action for Boscovich is purely kinematic, a propensity of point pairs to approach or recede from one another. Boscovich makes no attempt to explain the origin of this propensity, unlike Leibniz who located action in the activity of monads.[9] Leibniz's theory is thus a form of dynamism, while Boscovich's is purely kinematic. Russell only later makes the distinction between Boscovich's position and dynamism explicit (1898a: 103). It is not easy to distinguish the two views linguistically: Leibniz and Boscovich both used the same word (*vis*), for which Boscovich's translator uses 'force'. In what follows I shall put 'force' in quotation marks when it means kinematic action.

The distinction between force and kinematic action was an important one for Russell, because the structure of his dialectic of the sciences required precisely an initial elimination of dynamical concepts in the transition from geometry. Boscovich's theory was therefore a more appropriate starting place than Leibniz's. However, Russell had already adopted the point-atom theory (on the grounds that all alternatives were flawed) when he was thinking of a transition directly from geometry to dynamics. In this early note action between point-atoms is construed in terms of force, and given its full Leibnizian dress with 'causal relations', active principles, and even 'self-assertion' (VN 12). Russell's later point-atom theory takes on a less Leibnizian flavour.

Force, in Newtonian mechanics, is correlated with mass. Boscovich's point-atoms, however, have no mass in the sense intended by Newton, since they are unextended. (Endowing any point-atom with mass would result in an infinite density, which Boscovich rigorously eschewed.) It follows that Boscovich's *puncta* could not be centres of force in the usual sense of the word. It follows also that Boscovich's theory is based upon only two dimensional magnitudes (length and time) rather than the more familiar three (mass, length, and time) of Newtonian physics.[10] The mass of an extended body on Boscovich's theory was a dimensionless number, namely the number of point-atoms it contained. The mutual acceleration of two bodies, which in Newton's theory is a function of their mass, is in Boscovich's a function of the number of particles they contain.

---

[9] Boscovich 1758: §§ 9, 516. Boscovich emphasizes the difference between his own theory and Leibniz's at § 293.

[10] Some equations by Russell designed to transform the Newtonian magnitudes into Boscovichian ones have survived from this period on the verso of one of Russell's MSS (see *Papers*, ii, 488).

Boscovich uses the mutual action between two particles to explain both gravitation and impact. At sensible distances apart two point-atoms attract each other, their mutual action diminishing indefinitely with *approximately* the square of their distance. At sensible distances, therefore, Boscovich's theory mimics Newton's. At smaller distances, however, the attractive 'force' begins rapidly to diminish to zero, thereafter becoming a 'force' of repulsion. In fact, on Boscovich's theory, the 'force' oscillates 'many times over' between attraction and repulsion (1758: 10). Eventually, however, as the distance between the point-atoms continues to decrease, the 'force' between them becomes finally repulsive and continues to increase indefinitely (1758: §§ 63–80).[11] Thus what Boscovich calls 'mathematical contact' between point-atoms is avoided, since the fact that the 'force' of repulsion gets larger as the atoms approach ensures that the repulsive 'force' will be 'capable of destroying any velocity, no matter how large it might be' (1758: § 77). 'Physical' contact, however, which is what normally passes for contact, occurs when two points are so close together that the 'force' of repulsion prevents their being brought closer together by the normal, everyday forces available. But two point-atoms can never be made to coincide, nor made contiguous—between any two, however close, a third may always be inserted. The cohesion of extended material bodies is explained by the fact that at the points where the repulsive 'force' changes to attraction configurations of point-atoms will be stable, requiring the exertion of force to either compress or dilate them.

Space and time, for Boscovich, consisted of relations between point-atoms. He distinguished between real or existing points of space and time and those which were merely possible. The former were those points actually occupied by point-atoms and were finite in number; the latter were those which a point-atom might have occupied, and were infinite in number. Possible points arise because between any two point-atoms it is always possible to insert a third. This 'endless "insertability" of real points', as Boscovich puts it, is responsible for the infinity and continuity of space, but only of 'imaginary space', not of real space (1758: 198). There are two ways of conceiving such a continuous imaginary space. In the first, it comprises all positions that might be occupied by material point-atoms. In the second, it comprises all positions that a given point-atom might occupy. As a result,

---

[11] Russell did some calculations on these Boscovichian oscillations (1896*d*) but apparently using a simpler 'force' function than the one usually attributed to Boscovich (cf. Rosenberger 1887: iii, 539–40). Earlier (Mar. 1896) he had questioned the need for repulsive forces in a marginal note to Hannequin 1895: 100. Although Russell had adopted the point-atom theory in notes written before this, it is difficult to see how the theory would have worked without repulsive forces. The many oscillations of the 'force' were needed to explain what was known of atomic behaviour, and they became steadily more complex as more was learnt. The apparently *ad hoc* nature of the Boscovichian 'force' function was one of the major defects of the theory.

Boscovich maintains that each material point contains within it the whole of imaginary space (1758: 199).[12] In so far as space and time can be known empirically, however, they are purely relative: absolute space and time and absolute motion are completely rejected (1758: 203–5).

It is not hard to see why such a theory was attractive to Russell. In the first place, Boscovich's theory of space fitted well with Russell's own (cf. VN 15). Second, Boscovich's kinematical approach fitted well with Russell's perception that the dialectical transition from geometry should take one to kinematics rather than dynamics. Third, Boscovich's point-atoms were exactly the sort of things whose relative motions could provide a practical basis for geometrical judgements of congruence. Fourth, the point-atoms were completely unextended, and thus devoid of parts or further constituents. They could thus be regarded as the ultimate constituents of matter without introducing the antinomy of the divisible indivisible. Fifth, Boscovich's theory neatly avoided the problems of impact which beset theories involving extended atoms by the simple expedient of abolishing impact. That all action was, as a result, action at a distance did not, in Russell's view in 1896, pose any fresh theoretical difficulties. For Russell, apparently, did not envisage (what some physicists of the day were already searching for) a theory of gravitation which did not involve action at a distance.[13] If action at a distance must be accepted for gravitation, why not for other actions as well (VN 15 n.)? Sixth, all this was achieved without threatening the durability of the basic constituents of matter, which was the consideration which had originally led Newton to suppose that atoms were extended and hard. Boscovich's theory made it possible to preserve both the conservation of matter and the conservation of *vis viva*.[14] Seventh, since there were no impacts in Boscovich's theory there were none of the singularities which had attended the various classical theories of impact. Indeed, Boscovich professed to derive his theory from the law of continuity which required that transitions from one magnitude to another take place through intermediate magnitudes (1758: §§ 17–72). This would have been particularly important for Russell, who at this time thought that any attempt to appeal to physical quantities that were either infinitely large or infinitesimally small would result in contradictions (see below, § 6.2). At the same time, Boscovich was able to preserve the

---

[12] This position has some similarity to Russell's theory of perspectival spaces in *OKEW* 93 ff. Both stem from Leibniz's monadology (cf. *POL* 122, 124).

[13] Cf. 1896a: 40. In notes on Kant (1786), however, written about the same time (RA 210.006550–F1), Russell did suggest that Le Sage's attempt to explain gravitation in terms of the impact of a random shower of particles might undermine Kant's dynamism. He would have learnt of Le Sage's ideas from Maxwell (1875).

[14] It is doubtful, on theological grounds, whether Boscovich himself wanted to conserve *vis viva* (cf. Scott 1970: 66). None the less, it is a natural consequence of his theory (see Hankins 1965).

infinite divisibility of space—which was for Russell an a priori requirement of geometry.

Russell subsequently spoke highly of Boscovich's theory, referring to it as the most thorough and consistent presentation of Newtonian mechanics.[15] Yet at the time that his own thought most closely resembled Boscovich's, Russell's knowledge of Boscovich was almost certainly second-hand. Boscovich's *Theoria* wasn't translated into English until 1922 and although Russell acquired in June 1897 a copy of the first Venetian edition of 1763 in Latin, it came too late to influence his own point-atom theory. He does cite it in his *Leibniz* (*POL* 91), but it is not recorded in his list of books read during this period, which means that he almost certainly did not read the whole work. Boscovichian ideas, however, were in fairly wide currency during the nineteenth century, though his theory as a whole continued to have few confirmed adherents. Not untypical of reactions to Boscovich in the nineteenth century were the vacillations of Faraday and William Thomson, both of whom tentatively accepted the point-atom theory at some stage(s) of their careers and rejected it at others.[16] Others who acknowledged Boscovich's influence included Joseph Priestley, Dugald Stewart, Kant, Herbart, Cauchy, Lotze, Liebig, Fechner, and Tyndall.[17]

None the less, the existence of this quasi-Boscovichian tradition is hardly sufficient to explain the conceptual similarities between Russell's point-atomism and Boscovich's. For while it was common for nineteenth-century scientists and philosophers to acknowledge debts to Boscovich, the views they attributed to him were not always his. Firstly, it was not common in the nineteenth-century to distinguish Boscovich's theory of kinematic action from dynamism. Secondly, it was often assumed that Boscovich had simply abandoned the Newtonian dualism of mass and force characterizing matter by force alone. Harman (1982*a*: 82–3; 1982*b*: 77) attributes this to the influence of Joseph Priestley who ascribed some of his own views to Boscovich in works which were widely read and frequently reprinted between 1780 and 1830. Boscovich's position here was rather subtle. He did not abandon mass *per se*, but he did abandon the Newtonian conception of mass as quantity of matter in favour of a view of mass (of an extended

---

[15] e.g. *A Matter* 13–14. Russell was here thinking of Newton's *Principia* and not the more speculative *Opticks* which contained elements quite opposed to Boscovich's position. See also 1898*a*: 103 where Boscovich's theory is said to be the 'natural result of Newtonian philosophy'.

[16] Thomson's changes of heart were particularly frequent, and his opinions (on both sides) strongly stated, as the documentary sequence provided by his biographer shows: S. P. Thompson 1910: 888, 889, 893, 1033, 1056, 1077 n.

[17] Some of these were philosophers in whom Russell was taking an especial interest at this time. At least some of the sources from which Russell got his knowledge of Boscovich's point-atom theory (or related dynamicist views) can be identified. They include: Kant 1786 (of which Russell wrote out a substantial abstract, RA210.006550–F1, pp. 45–53); Hannequin 1895; Maxwell 1875 and 1873*b*; Stallo 1881; and Lasswitz 1878.

material object) as number of *puncta*. At least some of the texts Russell used were confused on this point, e.g. Hannequin (1895: 100–1), who claimed that dynamism should be rejected because it necessarily involved giving up the concept of mass. Russell in his review was quite clear that this was not the case. He noted that the dynamist might reply that dynamism 'alone realizes force to be the only necessary correlate of mass' while its critics 'regard extension also as necessary' (1896a: 39).

It seems extremely unlikely that Russell got such information from a close study of Boscovich himself; nor could he have got it from Boscovich's nineteenth-century protagonists who were less than reliable on these points. It can't be excluded that Russell did have some source of reliable, second-hand information about Boscovich, but again, in the absence of any evidence, this seems unlikely. Most probably Russell's knowledge of what Boscovich had actually maintained was as vague and inaccurate as everybody else's. The likely explanation of the remarkable agreement between Russell's position and Boscovich's, even on points on which the latter was not well understood, is that Russell developed his own theory more or less independently, but through its own internal logic it turned out to be much closer to Boscovich's actual position than the positions commonly attributed to him. Thus when the distinction between kinematics and dynamics became important for his own work on the dialectic of the sciences Russell distinguished Boscovich's theory from dynamism (though not before). Similarly, since one of his concerns was to link an independently determinable concept of mass to the concept of force, he was able to appreciate that dynamism required neither the abandonment of the concept of mass nor a commitment to infinite densities.

Russell defends dynamism in his review of Hannequin (1896a: 39–40) a work that was written early in 1896 when Russell's own point-atom theory was dynamical. The advantages he claims for dynamism are that it avoids two physical antinomies, namely the elasticity of perfectly hard atoms and the divisible indivisible. That dynamism had not been more widely accepted he puts down to the fact that scientists find action at a distance inconceivable. On this last point, as we have seen, the theory of extended atoms was no improvement in Russell's day. Russell, however, makes only oblique reference in his review (1896a: 39) to the remaining antinomy which he thought was to be found in dynamism, that of absolute motion, doubtless because he was far from clear as to how to handle it.

Russell had noted a circularity in the dynamist conception of matter in his very first discussion of it in 1894: 'Force is usually defined in Dynamics as that which produces or tends to produce a change of motion: it is an essentially relative notion, and presupposes something moveable, so that to make this something moveable merely a centre of force seems to involve us in a circle' (EPIII 148). This was in the days before the Tiergarten programme was thought of, and Russell was inclined to take this circle as decisive evidence against the point-atom theory. He considers the possibility of adding some other feature besides force to the point-atom, but quickly dismisses it. On the one hand, it seems difficult to add the envisaged feature unless the atoms were extended; while, on the other hand, if the atoms are extended they are subject to the crop of difficulties discussed above. Accordingly, in 1894 Russell found himself unable to accept the point-atom theory—though he had no alternative to put in its place. By the time the Tiergarten programme was under way in 1896, the circle no longer seemed so damaging. In the first note of the 'Various Notes' series, Russell in fact sees it as an advantage for the theory. 'We have, here, a mainly relative conception of matter, which is desirable: a conception, moreover, whose relativity involves contradictions if matter [is] taken as ultimate category' (VN 11). By this time Russell had come to the conclusion (which he may not have had so clearly in 1894) that the real was mental and that a purely material world was inconsistent. That the account of matter provided by the point-atom theory was circular was exactly the sort of result he expected, and a welcome sign he was on the right track.

In fact, as the Tiergarten programme developed, Russell's thinking on the circularity in the definition of matter changed. When the transition from geometry to dynamics was replaced by a double transition—from geometry to kinematics to dynamics—the circularity in the definition of matter divided also. The kinematic circle was the following. To make sense of geometry it is necessary to have motion. For motion it is necessary to have something movable, i.e. kinematic matter. But kinematic matter has no property other than kinematic action, and kinematic action is nothing other than the propensity of two or more kinematic point-atoms to approach or recede from each other, i.e. a propensity for relative motion. The way out of the circle is clear: some other feature of matter in addition to kinematic action must be found. Russell had suggested as much in 1894 (in EPIII), but his efforts then had come to grief on account of the confusion of kinematic and dynamic features. For what is necessary is to add dynamical features to kinematic matter, thus moving from kinematics to dynamics. The import of the kinematic circle is to show that kinematics cannot be a completely self-contained science, equivalently that kinematic matter cannot be an 'ultimate category'.

Dynamics arises from 'the consideration of the non-spatial adjectives to be ascribed to matter' (VN 21). The kinematic circle shows that matter must have some such adjectives. The two contenders are force and substance, which Russell says are 'interchangeable' (VN 12). Presumably he means that dynamics could start with either of them. Presumably, also, he would consider a formulation of dynamics in which mass was primitive to be a variant of the substance approach. Russell himself starts with force, conceived as a function of distance (VN 12, 15). Force, therefore, for Russell could be said to confer individuality upon the point-atoms, as it did for Leibniz upon the monads (cf. Leibniz 1695: 478; 1698: 512–13). Leibniz's case for this position derived from the identity of indiscernibles and the mutual independence of monads (neither of which would have attracted Russell). Russell's general preference for Leibnizian over Cartesian dynamics, rather than Leibniz's specific arguments, seems to have been the influence here. Russell then introduces mass as a constant of proportionality between force and distance which, he says, 'assumes mass . . . [is] constant for the same particle at all times and places, which follows from the conception of matter as substance' (VN 16). Substance is necessarily conserved.

From a more philosophical point of view, forces are introduced to satisfy the requirements of the law of causality (to which Russell apparently appeals as an a priori principle). All that is given by kinematics are the point-atoms and their relative motions. These changes in the relative positions of point-atoms are events which, by the law of causality, must have causes. Forces are then introduced as the causes of the changes in relative position of the point-atoms. Thus while kinematic matter is that which is moved, dynamical matter is that which is both moved and mover (VN 15, 18).

The transition to dynamics, however, still leaves an antinomy, the companion to the kinematic circle just discussed, namely, the antinomy of absolute motion. The problem was not new. It is easy now to sneer at Newton's doctrine of absolute motion. It is easy also to assume that *the* problem of absolute motion was a problem of verification, a violation of the physicists' professed maxim (expressed by Newton himself) to avoid claims which could not be empirically tested. After all, the doctrine was given its definitive critique by Mach and its definitive resolution by Einstein, both from a verificationist point of view. It is important, if Russell's concerns are to be understood, to realize that the doctrine is problematic on other grounds than verification. In fact, Newton thought he had, in the bucket experiment, an experimental verification of absolute motion. Before 1911 no one knew how to reply satisfactorily to this argument.[18] Moreover, the earliest objections to absolute motion, e.g. those of Leibniz, were on metaphysical rather than verificationist grounds, namely that Newton misconceived the nature of space and time.

Russell puts the antinomy of absolute motion in different ways at different

---

[18] Mach's own proposed solution, that the water in the bucket rotated relative to the stars, 'savour[ed] of astrology', as Russell later put it in a memorable phrase (*A. Matter* 17). Russell's account of the problem of absolute motion in *A. Matter* (pp. 14–18) is rather good, certainly a useful corrective to the smugness of many post-relativity popularizers.

times. The most easily recognized is that presented in the first of a series of four short notes on the topic. There, in a clear analogue of Newton's bucket experiment, he considers the question of whether, if the stars were not visible, the rotation of the earth could be inferred from such facts as the direction of the trade winds and that bodies are lighter at the equator (1896*e*: 30–1). He continues:

Absolute space seems here a necessity, and is indeed already introduced by the first law of motion. For if a motion were purely relative, we could give our centre of gravity any irregular curvilinear motion we liked, and unimpeded particles would still describe straight lines relative to it. But this the first law does not allow us to do; on the contrary, it imposes on the centre of gravity rest or rectilinear motion. (1896*e*: 31.)

It is very important to realize that this is *not* a verificationist argument against absolute motion.[19] Russell was at this time, and remained, strongly critical of verificationism and associated doctrines. For example, he attacks the view (held by Mach and other positivists) that the function of a scientific theory is the economical description of phenomena (1898*a*: 100).[20] If this view of science is rejected it is hardly possible to maintain that theoretical statements which are incapable of verification are nonsense. In the case in point, however, Russell is not so much worried that absolute motion might be unverifiable, but that it is in some cases all too verifiable—in the bucket experiment, for example. Russell finds this troubling for metaphysical reasons, since his analysis of geometry has led him to conclude on a priori grounds that space is purely relative. There was thus a clash between a priori philosophical requirements and the empirical evidence of dynamics. More-over, force had been introduced by Russell precisely in order to break out of the relativity that infected completely homogeneous point-atoms. It was essential, therefore, for philosophical as well as physical reasons, that force not be merely relative. Yet the relativity of space made it apparently impossible to satisfy this requirement. Russell was a lot clearer about this problem when he discussed its occurrence in Leibniz's philosophy (cf. *POL* 84–7). 'Dynamics, at the present day,' he wrote, 'is still unable to reconcile the relativity of motion with the absoluteness of force' (*POL* 84). But by this time he had abandoned his relational view of space, so the philosophical aspects of the problem, at any rate, should have been capable of resolution.

It is easy, in view of the subsequent development of physics, to misread some of Russell's claims. For example: 'if there were no matter outside the

---

[19] The more so since Torretti (1978: 316) has already claimed (mistakenly) to find verificationist arguments in *EFG*.

[20] Whitehead may have been an influence here, cf. his letter to Russell of 13 Feb. 1895. The occasion of the letter seems to have been a request from Russell for information about absolute direction.

earth, it [the earth] would not be either rotating or not rotating, for there would be no axis to which we could refer its motion . . . Apart from such relation, rotation is nonsense' (1896e: 30). Russell is not claiming that the rotation is nonsense because it cannot be verified without reference to external matter. The rotation is nonsense because, on Russell's theory of space, there is no space given for the planet to rotate in. Russell is considering the dynamics which would be developed by the inhabitants of a rotating sphere if they were confined to its surface. For such creatures there would be no space external to the sphere within which it could rotate. The reason for this is the relational character of space, as Russell explains: '[I]f there were only two material points in the world, there would *be* no space except the line joining them: this distance could grow and diminish, and we should get a complete *one*-dimensional Geometry out of its possible values. But there would be no space perpendicular to it, just as now there is not a fourth dimension' (1896e: 30). Space arises for Russell, as it did for Boscovich, out of the possible positions of point-atoms. That space is relative is not a matter of what can be verified, but an a priori requirement imposed by the fact that space is a form of externality. Russell's antinomy of absolute motion is rooted far more in the seventeenth- and eighteenth-century rationalism of Leibniz, Boscovich, and Kant than it is in the nineteenth-century positivism of Mach, whose 'anti-metaphysical dogmatism' Russell elsewhere deplores (1898a: 100).

The clash between the a priori requirement that space be relative, and the apparent empirically based requirement of dynamics that it be absolute, was made more dramatic by the fact that matter had been introduced in order to make geometry possible. The theory of matter now seemed to be undermining the very science it was supposed to save. Faced with this clash, Russell called for major changes in dynamics. The laws of motion, especially the first law which required absolute space for its invidious distinction between uniform and non-uniform motion, would have to be 'formulated entirely afresh' (1896e: 30). But Russell's own efforts to this end were not satisfactory.

If all motions were relative then, as Russell noted, it would be possible to change a motion from (say) a rectilinear to a curvilinear one by a change of reference system. But, as Russell puts it, a change of reference system is a change of geometrical rather than of causal (i.e. dynamical) relations. 'How then can it make any difference?' (1896e: 31). Russell's approach is crude but perceptive. By the law of causality, there is a cause for any real change. A change of reference system is not a real change. It needs no cause and can make no difference. A change from rest or rectilinear motion to curvilinear motion, however, is a real change, it needs a cause and makes an observable difference (as the bucket experiment shows). Yet if *all* motions were relative, such a change could be effected by a change of reference system.

The 'only hope', Russell thought, for a solution to this dilemma was 'to establish a more intimate relation between distances and force, and thus *make* geometrical relations causal' (1896e: 31). Russell's suggestion is vague, but its import is clear. If geometrical changes can always be linked with causal changes (i.e. changes of operative force), then *any* change of reference system will involve a change in the dynamical situation, and the unwelcome distinction between inertial and non-inertial reference systems can be avoided. There is no way of telling to what extent Russell's line of thought here was pointing in the direction that Einstein eventually took. It depends on which was to be the dominant partner in Russell's proposed 'more intimate relation' between distance and force. The classical distinction between inertial and non-inertial reference systems was based on the operation of forces in the latter which were absent in the former. The distinction could be abolished in two different ways: by assuming the same forces in both or by denying forces in either. Einstein took the second route. It seems that Russell may have been proposing the first, but the text is just too vague here to be sure.

There are, in any case, important reasons, apart from lack of technical expertise in the appropriate areas, which would have prevented Russell at this time from pursuing Einstein's line of thought. Russell wished to abolish the distinction between inertial and non-inertial systems in order to save his theory of geometry. But his theory of geometry required that space be not only relative but homogeneous. Indeed, Russell went so far as to say that these two requirements were synonymous (VN 14 n.). Einstein's general theory of relativity, however, got rid of absolute motion only by assuming that space was of variable curvature. This outcome would have been completely unsatisfactory to Russell in 1896–7. Indeed it would have been self-defeating: geometry demands changes in dynamics which are only possible if the very principles of geometry which required them are abandoned. Yet the fact that Russell was prepared to consider the possibility that geometrical relations might be causal suggests that he was prepared to look critically at the passivity of space (a third supposed equivalent of homogeneity and relativity).

Russell made only a few perfunctory efforts to pursue these ideas. He realized that the law of gravitation would have to be reformulated, offering $F = f(r)$ where $r$ is mutual distance, as a general schema (1896e: 31; cf. also VN 11–12, 15). But then the approach was abandoned, and he went on to attempt a solution of the problem of absolute motion by means of a drastic change in the account he gave of matter. The new theory of matter, with which § 5.2 is concerned, was adopted for other reasons, but once adopted it threw the problem of absolute motion into a new light (or so Russell thought). To see how this came about it is necessary to see how he reformulated the problem of absolute motion within the point-atom theroy. The problem is not essentially changed in being reformulated, but to modern eyes the reformulations tend to obscure the issues which now seem pertinent.

The motions of matter, if they are to be useful for resolving the antinomies of geometry, must be perceptible. And if they are to be perceptible, they must be relative to some system of reference axes which is itself perceptible, and therefore material. The problem of absolute motion then arises as follows: 'If the axes be at rest or moving uniformly, they suffice for Dynamics, and no difficulty occurs. But if they have any acceleration, angular or linear, [the] equations [of motion] break down. Therefore motion must, for the laws of motion, be relative to axes not themselves under the action of any forces (1896e:33).

The problem then—familiar enough in Newtonian physics—is to find such axes. For practical purposes, of course, we can always find material axes sufficiently remote from the influence of other matter to qualify. Relative to such axes the classical equations of motion will be accurate enough for practical purposes (1898a: 104). But their exact theoretical truth remains elusive, and necessarily so as Russell points out:

Motion can . . . only be defined by relation to matter. But it is essential to the laws of motion that this matter should have no *dynamical* (i.e. causal) relation to the matter whose motion is considered or, indeed, to *any* matter. If it *has* such a relation, the laws of motion become inapplicable, and our equations become untrue. But the laws of motion lead to Gravitation, and if this be universal, there is *no* matter without any dynamical relation to any given matter. Hence arises an antinomy: For dynamics, it is *geometrically* necessary that our axes should be material, and *dynamically* necessary that they should be *immaterial*. (VN 16; cf. VN 18, and 1898a: p. 104.)

The advantage, from Russell's point of view, of this formulation of the antinomy over other formulations is that it brings out the connection of the antinomy to the full system of the sciences. In the other formulations, the antinomy appeared more as a deep problem *within* dynamics. Its connections to geometry were in danger of being lost. It now appears more clearly as an antinomy stemming from the relationship between geometry and dynamics, to be solved by a science which transcends both.

Yet another formulation, perhaps the definitive one, renders the antinomy more perspicuous in other ways. Motion, i.e. change of spatial relation between material bodies, can only be measured by comparison to an unchanging spatial relation between other material bodies. Only material bodies which are free from dynamical relations have unchanging spatial relations. But there are no such bodies, for matter is by definition that which is subject to dynamical relations (VN 18–19). From this Russell concludes that neither matter, motion, nor force can be measured, that dynamics 'is rendered dialectically untenable' on account of the 'essential relativity of matter' and that '[m]atter and motion cannot form a self-consistent world, and cannot constitute Reality' (VN 19).

Thus we see that the old kinematic antinomy of the relativity of matter reappears in the form of the antinomy of absolute motion. In the end it was Russell's theory of space that gave way. Towards the end of the century he abandoned the relational theory as the only way to solve the antinomy of absolute motion (*POM* p. xvii). Not surprisingly he didn't come to this reversal easily. He sought possible solutions, none too optimistically, in a transition to psychology (§ 5.3), and in a radically new theory of matter, the plenal theory, which replaced the point-atom theory in 1897.

## 5.2 THE PLENAL THEORY

It might seem plausible to explain Russell's switch to the plenal theory on metaphysical grounds, as another example of the sort of hankering after monism which can be found in Ward's later philosophy. Such an explanation might seem to be confirmed by the fact that Russell's adherence to the plenal theory coincided with his renewed flirtation with Bradleian monism (VN 21–2). But this explanation is naïve, and Russell's flirtation with monism is the consequence of, rather than the basis for, his plenal theory of matter. In the first place, the explanation underestimates the independence and power of the pluralist strand within neo-Hegelianism, assuming that all neo-Hegelian positions gravitate naturally towards monism. Second, it fails to recognize that Russell's theory of matter, whether punctual or plenal, was only one stage in his overall dialectic. He could well have combined a tendency towards metaphysical monism with the punctual theory of matter by means of a dialectical transition from physics to psychology. It is important to realize that for Russell as a neo-Hegelian the theory of matter did not give the final truth about the nature of the world. The point-atom theory in physics, therefore, did not exclude metaphysical monism.

Russell adopted the plenal theory for physical, not metaphysical, reasons. He explicitly denies that there is any a priori ground for a plenum (FIAM 270). In a passage written when he was considering it seriously for the first time, he wrote: 'But can we conceive matter after the fashion of Spinoza's God, i.e. as an infinite substance not consisting of elements at all? This seems harder than Monadism, but if tenable, would fit much better with modern Science' (VN 21). The difficulties, to present day eyes, are perhaps obvious enough, but what was it about the science of the late nineteenth century that made Russell think it fitted much better with a plenal theory of matter? Russell

suggests an answer in *My Philosophical Development* where he says that he
was won over to the plenal view by Whitehead and implies that Whitehead
favoured it on account of Maxwell's theory of electromagnetism (*MPD* 43).
We know very little about Whitehead's early work on Maxwell; in fact we
know that his fellowship dissertation was on Maxwell's *Treatise on Electricity
and Magnetism* (Maxwell 1873*a*) only because Russell said so (see Lowe
1985: 107). As a result there is little to be learnt from Whitehead about the
reasons for Russell's switch to a plenal theory. None the less the clue about
Maxwell is useful.[21]

It is possible that Russell was influenced by Maxwell's article on atoms in
the ninth edition of the *Encyclopedia Britannica* (Maxwell 1875). For
Russell's claim that a plenal theory of matter, although difficult, 'would fit
much better with modern Science' is exactly the impression conveyed by
Maxwell's article. Yet Russell read the article in April 1896, a year before he
became persuaded of the plenal theory.[22] In the article Maxwell is extremely
critical of the point-atom theory, accusing it, for example, of manufacturing
new forces to explain every new phenomenon (Maxwell 1875: 45). The
impression Maxwell gives is that, by the nineteenth century, the point-atom
theory was clearly outmoded, not least by the growing body of evidence
(surveyed by Maxwell) that atoms were finitely extended. Such evidence
could be accounted for on the point-atom theory, but only by the *ad hoc*
variations of the force function of which Maxwell complained. Given
Russell's conviction that the choice among theories of matter was between
the point-atom theory and the plenal theory, Maxwell's criticism of the
point-atom theory might in itself have been sufficient to lead Russell to think
that the plenal theory 'would fit much better with modern Science'.

In addition to the critique of the point-atom theory, Maxwell goes on to
give a much more sympathetic account of the vortex atom theory, a plenal
theory of matter proposed by William Thomson. Utilizing work by Helmholtz
on the behaviour of vortices in perfect fluids, Thomson had proposed that
material atoms could be regarded as permanent vortex rings in a perfectly
fluid ether (Thomson 1867, 1891). On this theory, space is pervaded by
material substance, a continuous fluid ether, while the extended atoms of

---

[21]  James Ward at the beginning of his fifth Gifford lecture (Ward 1899: i, 122–9) presents the
history of the theory of matter as a transition from the punctual theory of Boscovich (which he
mistakenly presents as a form of dynamism) to the plenal theory of Thomson. Russell read the
first six of Ward's Gifford lectures, prior to publication, in Feb. 1898. Ward's influence,
however, was certainly secondary to Whitehead's. Ward was in any case critical of the plenal
theory. None the less, it is interesting that Ward took for granted what, to Russell, was a new
discovery. Russell read neither Faraday nor Maxwell until after his Tripos (*FF* 41).

[22]  Russell's earliest advocacy of the plenal theory was in VN, Note XII, probably written
between Apr. and July 1897 (see *Papers*, ii, 7). The previous note in the VN series, though it
doesn't directly advocate the plenal theory, is clearly sympathetic to it and was probably written
about the same time.

gross matter are represented by distinctive patterns of motion within small regions of the ether. Maxwell said of the vortex atom that it 'satisfies more of the conditions [required of an atom] than any atom hitherto imagined' and went on to note that while the 'difficulties of this method are enormous . . . the glory of surmounting them would be unique' (1875: 45).

Yet Maxwell was not himself an advocate of the vortex theory. Even in his article he mentions two problems it faced: that of explaining inertia and that of explaining gravity. He devotes a remarkable amount of space to an ingenious (but fantastic) attempt to explain gravity in terms consistent with the vortex theory, based on earlier speculations by Le Sage. But since no one at that time had come close to a satisfactory explanation of gravity in any terms other than action at a distance, it would seem uncharitable to condemn the vortex theory for failure in this regard.

There were other problems as well. By 1884 Thomson himself had abandoned the vortex atom theory in the face of Maxwell's electromagnetic theory of light (curiously, Maxwell doesn't mention this difficulty). The problem was that the electromagnetic theory of light required that light consist of *transverse* waves in the electromagnetic ether. This in turn required that the ether be an elastic solid, rather than a fluid. But a solid ether would rule out the possibility of vortex atoms (see Thomson 1884).[23] The theory was kept going, however, even in the face of this objection, by means of a good deal of ingenuity by Larmor (1893 and 1900; both of which Russell read). The reason was not an irrational conservatism, but the fact that there was no theory available at the time which could do much better than the vortex atom theory. In particular, solid ether theories faced difficulties no less perplexing than fluid ether theories. Pending the revolution in physics at the turn of the century, fundamental research into the nature of the physical world had reached an impasse.

The classic problem for the vortex atom and one to which Maxwell alludes in his atoms article, was that of explaining inertia. Here the theory did seem to be at a disadvantage in comparison with its classical competitors (although, after general relativity, even the Newtonian explanation of inertia came to

[23] Russell says nothing about the relative merits of fluid compared to solid ethers, but he does make it clear that he assumes that the plenum is a fluid (see 1897e: 89; *POL* 93 n.). In his atomist days, however, Russell had cited the apparent need for several different ethers (one for the transmission of light, another for electromagnetism, and a third, as yet completely mysterious, for gravity) as a reason against plenal theories (1896a: 40). It is true that no one model of the ether seemed capable of fulfilling all the many different roles the ether was called upon to play in the 19th cent. This resulted in a proliferation of ethers as embarrassing to ether theorists as the arbitrary nature of the force function was to advocates of the point-atom theory. The variety of ether models available in the late 19th century and the variety of tasks for which they were proposed helps pull together Russell's apparently heterogeneous reading on physics in 1897 and 1898, which included, in addition to mainline works on mechanics and electricity, works on heat and elasticity. See *Papers*, i, 358–60.

seem shallow). For if material atoms were not substantially distinguished from the surrounding ether it was hard to see how they could have the property of inertia. Inertia could surely not be a property of a mere mode of motion (Maxwell 1875: 45).

The defence of the vortex atom, however, was not Maxwell's main concern. In fact, the problem of the relation between the ether and 'gross' matter tended to be ignored, not only by Maxwell, but by his entire school, which dominated British physics in the 1870s and 1880s (cf. Buchwald 1985). It is true that Maxwell had in his time suggested a variety of mechanical models of the ether (e.g. Maxwell 1856, 1861, 1865). And even in his *Treatise* he had maintained that electromagnetic theory would not be complete until a physical representation of the reality underlying electromagnetic phenomena could be established (1873a: ii. 202), and that this would involve a representation of the ether itself (1873a: ii. 438). But in the *Treatise* itself he was not at all concerned with doing this. There Maxwell pursued a purely mathematical representation of the electromagnetic field using the formalism of Lagrangian dynamics, and emphasized that any attempt to provide a specific mechanical representation of the ether was 'no more than . . . a demonstration that mechanism may be imagined capable of producing a connexion mechanically equivalent to the actual connexion of the parts of the electromagnetic field' (1873a: ii, 416–17; cf. also ii. 184–5).

This lack of concern, on the part of the Maxwellians, with the mechanical representation of reality and with the problem of the relations between ether and 'gross' matter (which was tied up with it), should not disguise the fact that the Maxwellians viewed physical reality as a continuum. The atomic constitution of matter was of less interest to them, not because they denied the existence of atoms, but because they thought that atomic phenomena were less fundamental. The atomic structure of matter was ultimately to be explained in terms of the continuum. How it was to be explained did not seem to them to be a profitable topic of speculation given the current state of the science. The main task on their agenda was, therefore, the mathematical characterization of the continuum (in particular, the electromagnetic field) by a set of field equations, the values of whose variables were defined at every point (cf. Buchwald 1985: ch. 3).

This view of physical reality seems to have been a peculiarly British phenomenon as far as physicists were concerned, and on occasion it was difficult for continental physicists to appreciate what their British colleagues were up to. Its intellectual origins have received some attention from historians of ideas. Wynne (1979), in a rather speculative piece, has suggested that it was linked to the late nineteenth-century interest in psychical research, which also had strong roots in Cambridge. Wynne sees both movements as an upper-class, idealist reaction to the progressive intellectual movements of empiricism and materialism. There are several difficulties with Wynne's account, including some sloppy class-analysis and too great an insistence on the progressive nature of empiricism and materialism. Without better documentation it seems difficult to sustain the view that psychical research was a serious influence on the physicists. But it would perhaps be worth investigating whether the physicists were influenced by monistic forms of neo-Hegelian philosophy. There seems to be no evidence whatever that philosophers like Bradley were influenced by contemporary science, but an influence the other way seems possible.

As things stand, however, these suggested links between physics and wider intellectual trends are largely speculative. Within physics itself, however, the provenance of Maxwell's continuum physics is clear: it stemmed from more speculative work by Faraday in the middle of the nineteenth century. Faraday's speculations had developed in a way which has curious similarities to the development of Russell's thinking on the nature of matter. Faraday had initiated the modern field theory of magnetic and electrical forces, and had speculated that gravitation, too, could be represented by means of a field. From a mathematical point of view this had already been done by means of the gravitational potential. The gravitational force at any point in space could be expressed as the force that would be exerted on a unit mass at that point. Borrowing techniques from fluid mechanics, where every point of a continuous fluid is assigned some velocity, thereby generating a field of velocities, a gravitational field could be described by assigning a gravitational potential $V$ to each point in space, satisfying Poisson's equation:

$$\frac{\partial^2 V}{\partial x^2} + \frac{\partial^2 V}{\partial y^2} + \frac{\partial^2 V}{\partial z^2} = -4\pi\rho$$

where $\rho$ is the mass density at the point in question. This approach was immediately seen to be a sophisticated reformulation of action at a distance, and the reason isn't hard to find. Unlike the case of the velocity field in fluid mechanics, where an actual velocity is assigned to each point of an actual continuous fluid, in the case of gravitation the force assigned to each point is merely *potential*: the force which *would be* exerted on a unit point-mass *if* one were present. This difference was felt to characterize the difference between the case in which a genuine field was present and that in which the field was spurious, a mere mathematical fiction. If a genuine field were present it was deemed essential that it should show itself in some way independently of the field potential. Various specific criteria for the existence of fields were proposed and many efforts were made to show that they were satisfied by the various phenomena which were capable of mathematical treatment as fields (cf. Hesse 1961: 196–8, 203–6). With the exception of gravitation, the various known forces, together with other phenomena such as the transmission of radiant heat, were shown to satisfy one or more of the criteria and this was taken as an indication that the field represented some underlying substantial medium by means of which the force was transmitted. Faraday (1852) treated these issues systematically, but he was not prepared to concede that gravitation was a genuine exception. Accordingly, he thought that (ultimately, at any rate) all forces could be accorded an explanation in terms of real fields.

This bold speculation about the nature of gravity led him to an even bolder one concerning the nature of matter. Traditionally, as was mentioned in § 5.1, matter was thought to be defined by force or extension. Faraday, like Russell,' preferred the former, and it led him, on occasion, to pursue a point-atom theory. But the traditional point-atom theory of Boscovich, in which effects were transmitted at a distance without an intervening medium, did not fit with Faraday's insistence on fields of force. In an audacious (but confused) flight of thought Faraday resolved the dilemma as follows. If forces were the characterizing feature of matter, then forces must in some sense be part of matter. But if forces permeated the whole of space, as on the field theory they were required to, then surely matter permeated the whole of space. The alternative, he thought, was to suppose that space itself was causally active in the transmission of force. This he regarded as impossible since, like Russell, he maintained that space must be causally passive. Faraday stated this view of matter concisely:

The view now stated of the constitution of matter would seem to involve necessarily the conclusion that matter fills all space, or, at least, all space to which gravitation extends (including the sun and its system); for gravitation is a property of matter dependent on a certain force, and it is this force which constitutes the matter. In that view matter is not merely mutually penetrable, but each atom extends, so to say, throughout the whole of the solar system, yet always retaining its own centre of force. This, at first sight, seems to fall in very harmoniously with . . . the old adage, 'matter cannot act where it is not'. (Faraday 1844: 293.)

Faraday's views did not receive widespread support and Faraday himself was unable to give them much theoretical elaboration. His theory of matter was exactly what he called it, a speculation, and on occasion he was quite apologetic about it (e.g. 1846: 452). It was, however, a view which Russell might have found more sympathetic than the vortex atom theory. For, in the first place, it preserved the centres of force of Russell's point-atom theory; and in the second, it avoided treating extension as the defining characteristic of matter. There is no evidence, however, that Russell read Faraday (1844)—he certainly made no attempt to salvage centres of force in the way Faraday suggested. In any case, the lack of formal articulation of Faraday

(1844) would have made it less useful for Russell's purposes than the more elaborate work of the Maxwellians. It was in the work of the latter group that Russell immersed himself in the middle of 1897.[24]

There is an irony in the fact that Russell took up the Maxwellian theory in 1897, for by then, despite Whitehead's recommendation, it was beginning to show its age. The chief theoretical problem it faced was that of explaining conductivity. Heaviside had shown in the early 1890s that no explanation of conductivity was possible within the framework of a Maxwellian theory (Buchwald 1985: ch. 7). In 1894 Larmor introduced the electron as a theoretical entity necessary for the explanation of conduction, and abandoned the continuum approach to electromagnetism that had dominated British physics for the previous twenty years (Buchwald 1985: chs. 19, 20). In 1897 J. J. Thomson published the first experimental confirmation of the existence of electrons; and by 1898 'few British papers . . . attempted to do without microscopic [i.e. discrete] considerations' (Buchwald 1985: 172). It is not clear how far Russell was aware of this work. He made brief notes on Larmor (1893) (RA230.030000–F1) but the difficulties of Larmor's style, the complexities of his paper, and the unfamiliarity of his point of view may have prevented Russell's grasping its implications.[25]

Russell's point-atom theory, as we saw, fitted quite nicely with the theory of space which emerged from *An Essay on the Foundations of Geometry*. Indeed Russell's point-atom theory seems to have been developed more in response to geometrical than physical requirements. But those very features of Russell's philosophy of geometry which made the point-atom theory attractive constituted difficulties for the plenal theory. Russell's first task in defending the plenal theory was to reverse all those arguments he had previously used against it.

Russell's philosophy of geometry required matter for two reasons: (i) to provide relata for spatial relations; (ii) to provide something movable in space. For both purposes it was essential that matter be substantial, at least that it be more substantial than the (purely relational) elements of space. Russell at this time adhered to a substance–attribute ontology, something he was later to excoriate as a prime example of bad metaphysics. Moreover, he did not in 1896 distinguish, among attributes between adjectives (or properties)

[24] In July and Aug. 1897 he read Maxwell (1873a), the *locus classicus* of the Maxwellians, and J. J. Thomson (1893), a state of the art account of British electromagnetic theory in the early 1890s (Buchwald 1985: 123–4).

[25] Even J. J. Thomson confessed he had 'in many places a great difficulty in grasping the author's meaning' (Buchwald 1985: 172). Larmor's lengthy paper was published in several parts, complete with additions and appendices. It was written over several years during which Larmor's thinking about fundamental issues in electromagnetic theory changed, often under the influence of criticism from the paper's referees. Buchwald (1985: chs. 19, 20) gives a blow-by-blow account of its composition.

and relations. Hence, matter must be substance rather than attribute. From this Russell derived, though not by any valid argument, the conclusion that matter could not be extended, since extension was relational and whatever was relational could not be substantial.[26] From all this we have three reasons why matter could not be a plenum:

A plenum extends through the whole of space. Thus it has exactly the same form of relativity that space does, and so the introduction of plenal matter does not advance the dialectic. (*a*)

There can be only one plenum, containing no substantial elements. Thus the plenum cannot provide the relata for spatial relations, since a plurality of such relata is required. (*b*)

If the plenum pervades the whole of space it cannot move in space. Thus it cannot provide the movable substance required by the axiom of free mobility. (*c*)

The best way for Russell to have dealt with the first objection would have been to undo the argument on which it was based, for it certainly involves some fairly gross blunders. The argument is the following: all extension is relational; thus, if matter is extended, matter is relational. There are a number of ways to diagnose what has gone wrong here, but perhaps the most straightforward is that Russell has confused the 'is' of predication with the 'is' of identity.[27] Granting (what might legitimately be questioned) that all extension is relational, it would follow that matter is relational only if it could be shown that matter is extension. But this is not at all the same thing as showing that matter is extended. The former is an identity statement, the latter is predicational. Russell's first argument against the plenum would be sound only if the plenal theory asserted the former. What it in fact asserts is the latter.

Unfortunately, Russell doesn't use anything like this approach to help clear the way for the plenal theory. Instead, he introduces fresh confusions to get around the old ones. He denies, in effect, that the plenum can

[26] The picture is made a bit more complicated by the fact that Russell did find, in view of the antinomies of dynamics (especially the antinomy of absolute motion), that matter was at least partly relational. While this was sufficient to show that matter could not be wholly substantial, and thus that reality could not be purely material, it did not invalidate matter's role in escaping the antinomies of geometry, so long as the relativity of matter did not derive from extension. If that had been the case, the geometric antinomies would simply be resurrected in physics, and no progress would have been made. The dialectic was required to spiral upwards, not spin in circles.

[27] For historical reasons this confusion is likely to be the culprit, for the distinction between the 'is' of identity and the 'is' of predication was not commonly marked at the time, and in any case tended to be blurred by the neo-Hegelian theory of predication as identity-in-diversity. Russell himself later warned of the difficulties of avoiding this confusion and that it is endemic in Hegelian philosophy (*POM* 64 n.; *OKEW* 48 n.).

properly be regarded as extended, 'the same matter . . . is present in every point of space, and is not, in the ordinary sense, extended, but *contains* all extension. . . . [I]n a sense, the whole Universe is present in every point of space, as well as every point of time' (VN 23). In the case of matter, this is said to result from the fact that a thing is where it acts and 'matter acts everywhere'. But this justification is dubious to say the least. For if we don't know what it means to say that matter *has* a spatial location, we can hardly be said to know what it means to say that matter *acts* at a spatial location. Elsewhere in the same discussion, however, Russell puts the point differently: matter 'is not properly extended: Space is in it, not it in space' (VN 23). The apparent options are these: either matter is in space or space is in matter. In fact, Russell does not see these as alternatives, but as two (probably misleading) ways of expressing the same point. Space may be said to be in matter, since space is derived by abstraction from matter: space is a 'mere aspect' of the differentiation, of matter (VN 23). Matter may be said to be in space since 'all space is matter's adjective', so 'matter will in some sense be everywhere' (VN 23). The underlying argument here seems to be that, since 'all space' (or equivalently, 'everywhere') is an adjective of matter then matter is everywhere; just as Socrates is mortal, if 'mortality' is an adjective of Socrates. There seems to be another consideration as well: 'space' is an adjective of matter, and adjectives are part of (or, in some sense, contained in) the substance in which they inhere, so space is (in some sense, contained) in matter. This seems to be about as clear as we are likely to get on the subject. Russell's arguments illustrate the difficulties of avoiding nonsense without a satisfactory theory of quantification.

The other two problems can be treated together. (Russell, in fact, gives no explicit treatment of the second problem.) To deal with them, Russell reconsiders his earlier position on heterogeneous plena. He still maintains, as he had the previous year, that motion would be meaningless in a homogeneous plenum (VN 21). The earlier objection to heterogeneous plena was that they would require elements (or quanta) but such quanta were both impossible and undesirable. They were impossible because different regions of the plenum would have to be distinguished by the different numbers of such quanta they contained, yet there was nothing in the plenum, which would support such differences of density. The only property available was extension, and extension, by Russell's a priori argument in *EFG*, was necessarily homogeneous. Moreover, quanta were undesirable, because they would resurrect all the problems of geometrical points; among others, the problems of composing a genuine continuum out of discontinuous elements.

In 1897 Russell evaded this objection by the fairly obvious expedient of abandoning the (untenable) claim that a heterogeneous plenum, requires (substantial) quanta. Different regions of the plenum could, he now maintains, be distinguished by purely adjectival means:

[M]atter must have differentiation, not individuation. . . . [T]he differentiation must be purely adjectival: differences of position, e.g., must not imply difference of substance. . . . All differentiations of matter must be different adjectives of the one substance, different factors in its essence, not differences of essence between different substances. Differentiations must be related as different thoughts of one person, not as two distinct persons. (VN 21–2.)

At the time Russell wrote this he was still uncertain as to whether the plenal theory would work. At about the same time (and still in the same state of uncertainty) Russell attacked the problem of motion in a little fragment entitled 'Motion in a Plenum' (1897e). There he supposes that the plenum has some adjective $A$ with a spatial distribution such that the degree $a$ of $A$ is a function of position. Motion occurs when this distribution changes. Thus 'Motion is not a change of spatial relation between two matters: it is a change in the correlation of spatial and non-spatial adjectives' (1897e: 89). He illustrates the point with a rainbow where there is a spatial distribution of colour. Motion in the rainbow occurs when the distribution of colours changes. None of this, of course, supposes that there is any substantial body moving within the rainbow.

So far, so good. Difficulties arise, however, in attempting to develop the physics of such a plenum. Russell is quite clear as to what is wanted: 'The science of motion in a plenum would be complete if we could specify the [non-spatial] adjective $A$, the laws of its distribution, and the laws of its change' (1897e: 89). Russell thinks, optimistically, that what the adjective is 'would probably emerge from Hydrodynamics' (1897e: 89). It would seem, rather, that hydrodynamics could give the laws by which $A$ changed, rather than identify the property $A$ represented. But concerning the other parts of his programme for the science of motion in a plenum Russell is not at all sanguine: 'If we are to work a plenum, it will be necessary to reconstruct entirely the Science of Kinematics. It seems questionable whether, on our present view, even the equation of continuity[28] can stand' (1897e: 89). Russell's project meshes quite neatly with the work of contemporary British physicists, especially those pursuing a vortex atom theory. The task was to define a material vector field on the continuum and to correlate this with a scalar field obeying the equation of continuity. Assuming that the continuum is an incompressible fluid, a vortex atom theory can be developed from these

[28] The equation of continuity was central to hydrodynamic theories of matter of the sort Russell was attempting to develop. W. M. Hicks in an address to the British Association in 1895 had maintained that with the triumph of the plenal theory 'the study of dynamics [will be] replaced by the study of the equation of continuity' (quoted by Ward 1899: i, 130). It supplied, Russell thought, the 'complete answer' to the problem of motion on a plenum (*POL* 93 n.).

conditions.[29] The particular difficulty for Russell was to develop such a theory rigorously from a priori principles.

Russell considers the problem of defining mass or density on the plenal view. On the point-atom theory, mass was determined either by the number of point-atoms or geometrically by means of operative forces and resulting accelerations. Such an account is not possible on the plenal theory. Russell maintained, at this time, that judgements as to number and quantity were essentially comparative (see § 6.4), thus on the plenal view, '[m]atter, as the one substance, has no number or quantity itself' (1897e: 89). Whatever properties can be ascribed to matter have to be derived from the relation between spatial position and the non-spatial adjective $A$, or rather its degree or intensity, $a$, at given spatial points. Given a volume $V$, Russell points out that we can define its density as $\int\int\int a\,dx dy dr / V$. But this presupposes that $a$ is a measurable quantity which in turn presupposes that it can be correlated with a spatial quantity. Now $a$ is, in fact, correlated with position. But if $a$ is to be capable of motion, i.e. of change of position, its quantitative determination cannot depend upon its position. Nor can $a$ be identified with quantity of motion, for motion is meaningless unless $a$ is defined. 'It seems very difficult' Russell concludes, 'under these circumstances, to see how $A$ can be susceptible of quantity, but perhaps some way can be found' (1897e: 90). The truth is that Russell has too few independent variables in his system. On the point-atom theory, with distance and number of point-atoms, he could do some genuine physics. On the plenal theory, he is stuck unless he can provide some independent numerical determination of $a$. As he notes 'I don't see how to go further without discovering what $a$ is' (1897e: 90).

Russell does not elaborate on the problem posed for the equation of continuity, but it is not hard to guess what he had in mind. The equation states that for an incompressible fluid the quantity of fluid glowing into a given volume must be balanced by an equal amount flowing out. The equation is based upon the law of conservation for mass which ensures that, since mass cannot be created or destroyed in the region under consideration, any inflow must be balanced by an outflow. In Russell's plenal physics, by contrast, mass could not be said to be transferred across a boundary. Moreover, Russell would need to reformulate the equation of continuity as the requirement that the quantity, $a$, of his non-spatial adjective, $A$, flowing into a given region was balanced by an equal outflow. But, first, there was the problem just discussed of the quantitative determination of $a$; and, second, the equation of continuity could not be established in the usual way, unless $a$ was conserved. While conservation laws for substance were easy to assume and apparently commonsensical, conservation laws for properties

---

[29] I'm grateful to Jed Z. Buchwald for information on this point.

were exactly the opposite. Yet it is essential for Russell's heterogeneous plenum that *a* be a property and not a substance.

Russell recognizes that *a* must be conserved 'if we are to rescue the indestructibility of mass, and the equation of continuity' (1897*e*: 89–90), though he does not at this early stage seem confident that this can be achieved. In a slightly later note on plenal physics (VN 23) he asserts the conservation of matter, without linking it to the conservation of the non-spatial adjective. Indeed, little is said now about the non-spatial adjective: 'There may be . . . some adjective with a distribution over points of space, giving discrete points peculiar properties' (VN 22–3). Presumably this silence must be due to the primarily metaphysical emphasis of this note, for the nature of, and laws governing, the non-spatial adjective remain essential to the physical development of the theory. Indeed, Russell's assumption of the conservation of mass seems questionable unless the conservation of the non-spatial adjective can be established. Yet the conservation of mass is now expected to provide the basis for the whole of dynamics: 'The laws of matter will have to result somehow from the immutability of the Whole' (VN 23); 'Our principles of motion, now, will lie in the permanence of the Whole' (ibid.). It is significant that Maxwellian electrodynamics raised exactly the same problem in connection with the equation of continuity. The philosophical fall-out from the problem was the same, too: can energy be regarded as a substance or thing? For, if it cannot, it becomes problematic whether it makes sense to talk of energy being transferred from one place to another, or even of its being localized in a place (cf. Buchwald 1985: 33, 41–3). Russell's non-spatial adjective *A* is simply a general, abstract version of a problem that had become pressing in attempts to treat electromagnetic phenomena by means of continuum mechanics. Conservation and continuity requirements seemed to depend on substantial, discrete elements.

It seems doubtful that Russell was ever able to solve, even to his own satisfaction, the problems associated with the equation of continuity. Most likely, the problem simply disappeared when Russell's physics returned to a form of atomism (though not to the earlier point-atomism) at the turn of the century. The crucial problem, which Russell cites as having thwarted his efforts in dynamics, was neither the problem of absolute motion nor the difficulty of the equation of continuity, but a problem to do with the composition of forces. This was, in fact, the only difficulty in dynamics which he cites in *The Principles of Mathematics* in his brief retrospective of the book's history. In dealing with dynamics, he writes, 'I was met by the difficulty that, when a particle is subject to several forces, no one of the component accelerations actually occurs, but only the resultant acceleration, of which they are not parts' (*POM*: pp. xvi–xvii). Little of Russell's thinking on this topic has survived, but a brief note of 1898 was devoted to the problem

(1886*b*). There is correspondingly little secondary material, but see Winchester (1984). The problem is not unlike that of absolute motion: both recognize that no material body is isolated from dynamical interactions with other material bodies, even though the laws of physics have to be formulated as if there were such isolated bodies. In the case of the composition of forces, the problem depends upon the principle of the mutual independence of forces, namely, that when a number of forces act upon a body, each acts exactly as it would if it had acted singly (cf. Thomson and Tait 1867: §§ 254–6; Russell 1896*b*: 108). As a result, Russell claims, the laws of dynamics are either hypothetical (statements of what the resultant would have been, had such and such forces acted in isolation) or else approximate. It seems, therefore, that dynamics rests upon a false abstraction (cf. *POM* 474, 477). Like the previous false abstractions, this one involves a circularity for the action of a force is defined by the effect it produces, yet we cannot say, when several forces act on a body, that each produces the same effect that it would if the others were absent. For, as the parallelogram law shows, no force produces that effect when others are present: 'The effects of . . . two forces cannot, like the sensations of colour and shape for instance, be simply laid side by side as separate elements of a complex content' (1896*b*: 108). Russell viewed the difference as one between ways in which terms may be combined, a contrast between logical combination, where the separate identities of the combined terms are preserved, and mathematical combination, where they are not. And this, in turn derives from a difference in the nature of the terms combined: those combined mathematically arise from intuition, those combined logically are contents (1898*b*: 109). In this way the problem of composition of forces leads directly to issues in the philosophy of pure mathematics, though it is difficult to see exactly what effect they had there. (Although there is plenty of discussion in the latter of different modes of combination, this seems largely to have been the result of Grassmann's and Whitehead's influences, rather than the influence of Russell's work in dynamics, although the latter was no doubt never far from his mind.) The more immediate result of Russell's consideration of the composition of forces, was that it cast doubt, as he put it, on the 'causation of particulars by particulars' (*POM*: p. xvii; *POL* 98). In *POM* he cites this as an apparent violation of the law of gravitation and takes it to undermine the concept of force (*POM* 474). The problem seems to be that, in Russell's dialectic, forces were required to give independent reality to matter, yet it seemed hard to sustain them in this role when they lost their own independent reality whenever they acted in combination with others (*POL* 98). Beyond this, it proves impossible to reconstruct Russell's thinking on these issues. We know from *POM* that the problem was an important one for him, and we can infer from this that he probably wrote a good deal on the topic. But, apart from the note of 1898, the other manuscripts are lost. In *POM* the problem is resolved by a radical revision of the concept of causality (pp. 478–9).

One physical advantage which Russell claims for the plenal theory, though again without full conviction, is a solution to the antinomy of absolute motion: 'It seems just possible that this view would solve the antinomy of absolute motion, for there is now no matter except the one whole, and this is eternally[30] under no forces. But matter under no forces was precisely what we required to solve the antinomy (VN 23). This is a Pyrrhic victory, however. The antinomy of absolute motion arose from the attempt to define mass by means of forces and motions. The antinomy may have disappeared, but so too has the characterization of mass, which on the plenal theory seems to be a largely ineffable quiddity.

It is natural, at this stage, to wonder what has become of Russell's relational theory of space. While Russell was exploring the plenal theory in these notes, *EFG* was with the publishers (it appeared on 20 May 1897). Some, at least, of what Russell had said about the relational nature of space in *EFG* is incompatible with his plenal theory of matter. On the latter theory, spatial relations cannot be regarded as holding between points of kinematic matter as was claimed in *EFG*. Yet in broader terms the relational theory of space is not abandoned. The main change needed is that of abandoning the requirement in that the relata of spatial relations be substantial. On the plenal theory spatial relations may hold between the values, or degrees of intensity, of the non-spatial adjective *A* at particular points. The spatial distribution of these values must be considered directly given, and the values themselves must be considered adjectives. Spatial relations thus hold between adjectives, but the adjectives are adjectives of a substance, so the whole system is ultimately grounded in substance, which is Russell's main requirement.

But there is another area in which the plenal theory clashes with Russell's views in *EFG*. At one point Russell writes of the plenal theory that it 'would, I think, almost necessarily imply Spinozism in Metaphysics, i.e. a denial of substantial diversity in the Absolute' (VN 22). It is not at all clear why he should have thought this would be so, unless he was assuming that the material plenum simply was the Absolute (a point to which I will turn shortly). For otherwise the diversity lost in the material realm might be regained in the mental. Nor is it clear whether this was a considered opinion or merely a tentative remark. But if it was a considered opinion it clashes with the theory of judgement which Russell put forward in the *EFG*, according to which judgement required *substantial* diversity. As was argued in § 4.6 there seems to have been no good reason why Russell insisted on substantial diversity for judgement. Bradley's theory of judgement, after which Russell

---

[30] Russell wrote 'eternally' unambiguously in the MS, but context leads one to wonder whether he didn't intend 'externally'.

modelled his own, could make do with adjectival diversity, or diversity of content. But at any rate it is clear that, if we are to take Russell's comments on the plenal theory at face value, the position expressed in *EFG* will have to be amended, both to allow adjectives to be the relata of spatial relations and to allow judgements to combine a diversity of adjectives in a unity of substance.

This second change to Russell's position in *EFG* would not strictly be called for *unless* Russell was assuming that the Absolute was in fact material. It would be surprising to find him coming to this conclusion, though the passage just quoted does suggest it. Moreover, there is no argument anywhere in his writings to show that the Absolute consisted of the material plenum and nothing else. If other substantial items were added then there would be substantial diversity in the Absolute and judgement would be possible (even on Russell's theory in *EFG*). It could be maintained that, even if diverse mental substances were admitted alongside a material plenum, they would not provide the sort of diversity required by Russell's theory in *EFG*. For *EFG* requires spatially located substances, and mental substances have no spatial location. But this still leaves us with substantial diversity in the Absolute, contrary to Russell's claim. Moreover, it shows, contrary to what he maintained in *EFG*, that diversity is possible without spatial diversity, and thus that judgement does not depend upon a form of externality. A key part of Russell's transcendental argument for geometry is thereby lost.

None the less, with the emergence of the material plenum Russell's dialectic has taken a surprising turn, though not necessarily one which lands Russell with a material Absolute. With the hoped-for solution of the antinomy of absolute motion, plenal matter will lose its element of relativity. It thus becomes self-subsistent and no longer stands in need of anything external to render its existence possible. By the same token, plenal physics does not need a transition to a wider science to render it consistent. The dialectic has nowhere else to go. This was an unexpected result, since Russell had always anticipated that the dialectic would reveal the mental nature of reality. He seems to have continued to think that some further transition was called for, or at least was possible, but had little idea of how to go forward: 'how to continue this process beyond Dynamics I do not know' (VN 23). The problem was not that Russell thought he might have shown that the Absolute was material, when he wanted to show that it was mental. He was, it seems to me, more strongly committed to a single, coherent, all-embracing system of the world, than he was to either the view that materialism or that idealism was correct. The dialectic which ended with the material plenum was a dialectic dealing with the data of the outer sense; there was still to be considered the data of inner sense, which would, of course, be mental.

The trouble was rather that there seemed no way to bring these two realms into a single unified system. It was as if the dialectic of the outer sense produced a material Absolute, and the dialectic of the inner sense a mental one, without any possibility of linking them. Whether this would have proved an insuperable obstacle we shall never know, for Russell's treatment of matter broke off at this point while he considered the philosophical problems of pure mathematics. By the time the antinomies of pure mathematics had been solved to his (temporary) satisfaction it was 1910 and his neo-Hegelian period was long over. What brief hints he left of how to pass from physics to psychology all stem from his punctual matter theory of 1896.

## 5.3 HINTS OF A TRANSITION TO PSYCHOLOGY

It is clear from his surviving notes that Russell never really had a clear idea as to how the transition from physics to psychology was to be made. The structure of psychology, then and now, was not conducive to the sort of analysis Russell had been able to make of geometry and physics, although in the late nineteenth century hopes for turning psychology into a rigorous science were high. Experimental psychology had recently got under way, and preliminary moves in the mathematical treatment of psychological phenomena had been made. Russell's knowledge of psychology, however, was limited. The fate of the chapter on psychology in his fellowship dissertation (see above, § 4.3) is indicative. Moreover, Russell's reading in psychology at this time was limited to Ward (1886), James (1890), Stout (1896), Stumpf (1873), and, slightly later, Meinong (1896). Undoubtedly, had his dialectic of the sciences ever got as far as a serious treatment of psychology his reading on the topic would have been more extensive. But as things were Russell was never in a position to do more than hint at how the transition to psychology should be made. The hints he left are few enough and all of them concern a transition from the point-atom theory of 1896. As noted at the end of the last section, with the plenal theory of matter he felt he had reached a dead end. The plenum left no loose ends to which a theory of psychology could be attached.

The antinomies in the point-atom theory that a transition to psychology was required to resolve were those resulting from the relativity of matter. This showed that matter could not be self-subsistent substance. The Absolute itself, however, could not suffer from such relativity—there was nothing for it to be related to. The most important such antinomy for Russell was the antinomy of absolute motion: all matter has dynamical relations to other matter; dynamical relations involve the change of spatial relations between the pieces of matter in question; change of spatial relations between pieces of matter can only be understood in terms of unchanging spatial relations between pieces of matter (VN 18–19). The circle could be broken if there was a way of specifying some position in space independently of other positions and pieces of matter. This would give us an absolute position with respect to which spatial relations could be determined. Alternatively, the circle could be broken if dynamical relations (i.e. forces) could be specified independently of spatial relations between pieces of matter. Russell in 1896 tentatively suggested the possibility of making these breaks by psychological means: '*Perhaps* there may be hope in restoring the pre-eminence of the *here*, as a source of absolute position; *perhaps* we may replace force by conation, and pass on into psychology' (VN 16).

Russell was yet in no position to be certain as to how this would work—hence his italicized 'perhaps'. Presumably, *here* is to be introduced as the psychological subject's position.[31] But whether it would enable the determination of spatial relations without reference to other positions or pieces of matter seems doubtful. As Russell had repeatedly remarked, it takes two pieces of matter to form even a one-dimensional space. It might be hoped, I suppose, that a variety of psychologically based *heres* might be introduced, depending upon the positions of a plurality of monads. But wouldn't this, in turn, reintroduce at the psychological level exactly the sort of relativity that had proved problematic at the physical level of the dialectic, and thereby prompt some further transition beyond psychology? Presumably, the science introduced beyond psychology would face the same problem, leading to an endless regress. On this point Russell gives no clue as to how things are to proceed.

On the question of replacing force by conation, he is equally inexplicit. At first sight, the suggestion seems better than the suggestion about absolute position because force itself is relational on the point-atom theory, and thus its elimination in favour of conation holds out the hope of reducing the relativity to be found in physics. But it is not clear that these hopes are well founded. In the first place a conation account of force generates special problems for the principle of the mutual independence of forces (as Russell notes, *POL* 98–9), and thus for the parallelogram law. But, further, if conation is to replace force, it is clear it must be capable of quantitative determination. Moreover, it must be directly given in experience, and thus be an intensive quantity. But such quantities, Russell had already argued at length, can only be measured by correlation with spatial quantities (see §§6.2, 6.3). Thus it would seem that, in order to give conation enough content to make it a realistic replacement for force, it will be necessary to

---

[31] Ward had suggested this point in his metaphysics lectures which Russell attended in 1893–4. Ward had said that all space refers originally to the self. See Russell, 'Lecture Notebook', i, 89.

make it dependent upon spatial measurement and thus to return us to the circle from which we were seeking an escape.

When Russell contrasted the monism of the plenal theory with the monadism of the point-atom theory, he was not using the term 'monad' loosely. It seems clear that Russell, in keeping with his idealist position, conceived of the point-atoms as genuine monads, i.e. point centres of will and consciousness as well as of 'force'. He spoke, for example, of the 'self-assertion required for the real' (VN 12), an idea which comes from McTaggart (1893a: 246). But he admitted that this was 'vague' and little is said elsewhere about this approach. The most extended treatment is the following, again directed to the problem of absolute motion:

Distance $AB$ is a relation, involving adjectives $\alpha_b$ and $\beta_a$ in $A$ and $B$. In a relative motion these adjectives change, say to $\alpha'_b$ and $\beta'_a$. There may be, further, an adjective of each monad due to the change, a sense of change in fact: let these adjectives be $c_{\alpha\beta}$ and $c_{\beta\alpha}$. Then $c_{\alpha\beta} = f(\alpha_b - \alpha'_b)$, $c_{\beta\alpha} = f(\beta_a - \beta'_a)$. Now if $A$ and $B$ have different natures in any respect, $c_{\alpha\beta}$ may differ from $c_{\beta\alpha}$. From this difference, a way of escape may be found from the perfect reciprocity of motion: but the way of escape is through the Psychology of monads. For example, in a relative motion of our bodies, we sometimes have muscular sensations, sometimes only ocular sensations: and according largely to this difference, we decide whether the motion is ours or the object's. (1896e: 34.)

The attempt now seems to be to break the antinomy of absolute motion by postulating that absolute motion itself can be directly given, rather than by supposing that it can be derived from a directly given absolute position. In the first place, it is clear that only absolute accelerations could be given in this way by the psychology of monads (at least, unless the psychology of monads is very different from our own). For it is well known that uniform rectilinear motions are not revealed by muscular and ocular sensations.

Essentially, however, the problems mentioned earlier remain. If Russell's move is to be sufficient to establish even the rudiments of physics, it is necessary that the changing adjectives of the monads be capable of quantitative determination, and this will require that spatial measurement is possible. Spatial measurement, however, is only possible when the motion of matter can be determined, and this, on the present account, can only be determined by a quantitative determination of the changing adjectives of monads. The circle is thus enlarged, but it is not removed. Relativity is introduced also in the fact that the sense of change which a given monad has will depend upon another monad. It is true that this sense of change does not depend upon the *sense of change* that the other monad has. We might have the sense of change in one monad correlated with the physical position of the other, and vice-versa. But even so, the sense of change remains a relational feature of monads; and thus not purely adjectival as required. I suppose the advantage of the present approach from Russell's point of view is that the sense of change may be supposed to be directly given to the monad in question. But this brings its own difficulties.

Normally, mental states of this perceptual sort involve the possibility of error. That is, it would normally be supposed possible that a monad could be in motion without being aware that it is, i.e. without having the required sense of change, and vice-versa. For Russell's dialectical purposes this possibility would have to be excluded. For every change in the monad's actual state of motion, there would have to be a corresponding change in its psychological state, so that the former could be exhibited as a function of the latter. If this is so, one wonders by what right one calls the internal state of the monad 'psychological'. It would seem that the monad is simply equipped with some absolute motion detector: there is no reason given to suppose that the detector must be mental. Calling it 'psychological' simply serves to mask its arbitrary introduction, working on the principle, beloved of empiricists, that all manner of theoretical entities may be introduced so long as they are mental and not physical. The advantage of a mental over a physical motion detector is that the deliverances of the former can be supposed to be 'directly given'. But the fatal disadvantage is that what is thus directly given is not correlated in the way Russell requires with what is actually the case. For we cannot, without argument, assume that monads are not subject to illusions of motion.

One important requirement for Russell's dialectic is shown up, however, by his attempts to found a theory of motion on the psychology of monads, namely the requirement that there be some psychological feature of monads capable of quantitative determination. Russell called such psychological quantities 'intensive' quantities (see § 6.2). It is clear that Russell's attempts to link physics with psychology would be hopeless without some such quantity with which to link at least one dynamical variable. It might be assumed, also, since dynamical variables were supposed to vary continuously, that the necessary intensive quantities would also have to be capable of continuous variation. By 1896 Russell was already considering both the nature of intensive quantity and the question of continuous quantity. His initial results (in SDCQ) were not particularly encouraging, for they led him both to abandon the notion of continuous variation (as employed in the calculus) and to suppose that intensive quantity was parasitic upon extensive quantity. With this, however, the needs of his dialectic had taken him away from physics and into pure mathematics. The problems he encountered there occupied his serious attention, to the exclusion of almost everything else, for many years. They showed also that his neo-Hegelian approach to the sciences was fundamentally wrong.

# 6

# Pure Mathematics

## 6.1 THE QUANTITY VIEW OF MATHEMATICS

Until well into the nineteenth century the pat definition of mathematics was 'the science of continuous and discrete quantity' (see Euler 1774: § 2, for an authoritative statement). This view of the nature of mathematics I shall call the quantity view. Russell came to it late, and never held the full version of the doctrine. He was aware, as we have seen, that projective geometry was a branch of mathematics which did not involve the notion of quantity. None the less until 1898 he held that quantity was one of the fundamental concepts of mathematics and that many branches of mathematics—in particular, all those based on arithmetic—were concerned primarily with the study of quantity in one form or another. It is this more restricted doctrine that I shall refer to as Russell's quantity view. He held it until he came to think that order was the more fundamental concept in mathematics.

This change arose from his recognition in 1898 of the importance of relations, upon which the concept of order depended. It is obvious nowadays that no satisfactory account can be given of order unless relations are admitted as a special logical category, yet the special nature of relations was quite generally overlooked by philosophers before Russell. The stages by which Russell came to recognize the importance of relations will be traced in Chapter 8. Russell's work on the theory of relations (which culminated in his well-known early paper, LOR, though it started, as we shall see, much earlier) was one of his most important and original contributions to philosophy and logic, a contribution of the same order of importance as Frege's work on quantification. Today his results seem so obvious that their originality and the difficulty of achieving them are apt to be overlooked.

Before 1898, Russell was primarily concerned with geometry and his writings on pure mathematics consisted for the most part of a variety of short pieces, mostly unpublished. Only one longer work found its way into print in this period, 'On the Relations of Number and Quantity' (RNQ). In these writings Russell is concerned mainly with the problem of continuity, in particular, with the relation between number and continuous quantity. Russell seems to have first considered the problem in February 1896 when reading Hannequin (1895), a work which had a considerable influence on him. Probably around this time he wrote a brief note on the relation of number and quantity (VN 13). In June of the same year he returned to the topic, attempting this time a major paper, 'On Some Difficulties of Continuous Quantity' (SDCQ) which he hoped to publish in *Mind*.[1] The paper, however, despite a major round of revisions and a further short note on continua (VN 17–18), was never completed and in 1897 Russell abandoned it for another, RNQ, which was published in *Mind*. Between these two efforts Russell read and reviewed for *Mind* Couturat's *De l'infini mathématique* (Russell 1897f), and probably wrote two more short, unpublished notes on continuous quantity (VN 19–20). Early in 1898 his efforts at an account of mathematics as the science of quantity culminated in plans for a book to be called 'On Quantity and Allied Conceptions: An Enquiry into the Subject-Matter of Mathematics' (VN 25–6). Some, at least, of this book was written (see OQ). It is clear that he abandoned this work, and the line of thought it represents, after reading Whitehead's *Universal Algebra* in March 1898, having made some perfunctory efforts to assimilate Whitehead's position to his quantity view (see OQ 134–5). Whitehead himself explicitly rejected the quantity view (1898a: pp. vii–viii). He defined mathematics as the study of 'all types of formal, necessary, deductive reasoning' (1898a: p. vi), a remark which provides a pointer to the title of Russell's next work, 'An Analysis of Mathematical Reasoning' (AMR), the manuscript of which was finished in July 1898. Parts of three different drafts of this work survive. But it, too, was abandoned. And by October 1898 Russell was planning yet another book, this one to be called 'An Inquiry into the Mathematical Categories' (VN 26–7), though it is not known whether anything of this was written. Before the year was out, yet another work was planned, 'The A Priori Concepts of Mathematics' (VN 27–8). Nothing of this work seems to have survived beyond the plan, and it is difficult to be sure whether it was intended to be a book (possibly an alternative to 'An Inquiry into the Mathematical Categories') or an article. The title suggests something on the scale of a book, but the actual summary of its contents suggests that an article may have been long enough for the points he intended to deal with.[2] Late in 1898 he started work on a new book, 'On the Principles of Arithmetic' (PA), two chapters of which survive.

In this chapter I shall look at the problems which beset Russell's quantity theory. The most difficult of these centre around the uses of number in measurement, that is, its application to continuous quantity; though, sur-

[1] B. R. to A. Russell, 3 June 1896. A summary of some of the results of SDCQ was published in 1896c: 301.
[2] It is possible that he intended it to be an article outlining the work he was thinking of doing in 'An Inquiry into the Mathematical Categories'. The plan has some important similarities to 'The Classification of Relations' (COR) which he read to the Moral Sciences Club in Jan. 1899. This prompts the conjecture that he might originally have planned to read 'The A Priori Concepts of Mathematics' to the Moral Sciences Club, but later substituted COR which has a more general philosophical bearing.

prisingly enough, it was not these problems which led him to abandon the quantity view. For the early Russell the use of numbers in counting was primary: '[C]ounting creates numbers', he maintained (VN 20), by means of a process described in the following passages:

Number primarily derived from instances of a concept: purely intellectual from the start.[3] Abstracts from concept of which they are instances, and pays attention merely to the iteration. . . . Wherever we have *discrete* things, they are numerable, for *some* concept will contain them all. . . . Only whole numbers are really numbers . . . (VN 13.)

*Number*, throughout the following discussion will only be used of discreta; it will be taken as always the result . . . of acts of synthesis (or analysis) of things whose qualitative or quantitative differences are disregarded. . . . Such an operation can only give rise to the natural numbers, the series of positive integers. (SDCQ 46 = RNQ 71.)

Having conceived numbers in this roughly Kantian way at the outset, Russell is hard pressed to explain how they could be used for the measurement of continuous quantities—a topic to which he devoted several painful pages in 1896 (see § 6.2).

In fact the main problem for Russell at this time was to show how numbers other than the counting numbers could be arrived at from this process of abstract synthesis of unities. This was a standard problem in the philosophy of mathematics up to this time. It was generally agreed that the natural numbers could be arrived at relatively straightforwardly, but that any extension beyond them required justification and was likely to lead to problems. In fact, every extension of the concept of number had been fiercely opposed, and each achieved general acceptance only, on the one hand, because it was required for algebraic purposes (e.g. to ensure that every equation of the form $ax^2 + bx + c = 0$ has roots) and, on the other, because it could be provided with some quantitiative interpretation which made it seem reasonable.

Even for the natural or counting numbers the process of synthesis is not entirely free from difficulty. There is a peculiarly Russellian problem, alluded to on one or two occasions in the early manuscripts, of the one and the many. Any collection is both one, a single collection, and many, its several members.

We have strictly, in number, two unities, one a complex whole, containing several of the smaller unity. But the unity of the whole is very loose, in that it is merely formal: it is supposed to derive, from its being a whole, no quality but that of formal unity.

---

[3] The process is *purely* intellectual because, for Russell as for Bradley, not even the discrete things on which it depends are given by immediate sense-experience. They depend upon conceptualization which itself precedes the abstraction process involved in counting (see SDCQ 46).

The simpler unities are regarded apart from all qualitative differences, in fact, qua unities in number, they *have* no qualitative differences. But they are discrete, and the unity is prescribed, not arbitrary.[4]

It is not difficult to present the basic point as an apparent paradox. For if an $n$-membered collection is both one and $n$, then it would seem to have inconsistent numerical attributes. For surely the collection itself is one, while none of its members can be regarded as $n$.

The problem depends upon treating cardinal numbers as properties of collections, and Russell evades it, in his early writings, by treating numbers as ratios. In the case of counting, the number of elements in a set expresses the ratio between a single element and the whole set. In the case of measurement, the number expresses the ratio between the quantity measured and the unit of measurement. The two processes are thus very similar, differing only in the extent to which the unit of reference (the element of the set or the unit of measurement) was given naturally or prescribed. Russell sometimes distinguished between units and (natural) unities (e.g. VN 20; 1897$f$: 63). The latter were the discrete instances of a concept upon which counting depended, while the former were arbitrarily chosen magnitudes used for measurement. The distinction was not hard and fast, at least when it came to empirical data, for Russell believed, on Bradleian grounds, that no instances of a concept were actually given as discrete. On the ratio theory of number the one–many problem cannot occur, for it is simply a mistake to think of one or $n$ as properties of an $n$-membered set. The ratio theory also helps explain why Russell insisted that all the elements of a set to be counted must be instances of some one concept. In counting the members one was, as it were, measuring the set by iterations of a single element. If the elements were not all instances of one concept, the result would be as arbitrary as that of measuring would be if a single unit of measurement had not been prescribed. Fortunately, the process of abstraction ensured that there was always a concept of sufficiently abstract generality to ensure that any set which could in fact be counted, could be counted in accordance with the requirements of the theory.[5]

---

[4] VN 13; see also 1897$f$: 60–1; AMR 203; AMR/TS 227–8; FIAM 277. In PM i, 72 n. the same argument appears as an argument against the reality of classes. Variants of this problem concerning the unity of a complex whole and the diversity of its various parts were to haunt Russell, in one way or another, for many years after he ceased to be a neo-Hegelian. (It was a problem on which Wittgenstein, for one, fastened in his early criticism of Russell). The neo-Hegelians dealt niftily with it by means of the doctrines of unity-in-diversity and internal relations. Without this solution Russell was left with a perennial difficulty—to which we shall return in Ch. 8.

[5] The ratio theory was not original to Russell. The most thorough-going defence of it at the time Russell was writing was Dewey and McLellan (1895), who claimed for it respectable antecedents in Euler and Newton. Although the elementary parts of Russell's ratio theory bear a marked similarity to Dewey and McLellan's theory, it seems unlikely that their book

It is clear how the ratio theory can account for the natural numbers and, by measurement, for the rational fractions. But plainly zero and infinity are going to pose a problem for the ratio theory, since neither can be expressed as a ratio without committing some absurdity. Russell draws the appropriate conclusion and denies that zero and infinity are numbers. As he puts it, 'the former [is a] denial of units, [the] latter of [the] whole in which they are collected. Neither is a number, i.e. neither contains a whole of unities' (VN 13). Russell puts this point succinctly elsewhere: 'all number is a synthesis of parts into a whole, and infinity denies the whole, as zero denies the parts (SDCQ 50). Russell's problems do not end here, however. For the ratio theory does not offer an obvious account even of negative numbers, let alone irrational and imaginary numbers.

In SDCQ Russell offered a classification of different types of number which was repeated the following year in RNQ. The first and most important classificatory distinction is between *pure* numbers and *qualified* numbers (SDCQ 46 = RNQ 71).[6] The pure numbers are the natural numbers, arrived at by counting abstracted unities. The qualified numbers, which include fractions, negative numbers, and complex numbers, all, according to Russell, have 'some more explicit reference to the specific qualities of the unit'. Qualified numbers 'absorb, into an apparently numerical expression, some properties which the unit does not share with all thinkable contents' (SDCQ 46 = RNQ 71). Thus, for example, a fraction, $m/n$, depends upon the chosen unit's being divisible into $n$ smaller units, and is meaningless when applied to units which are not so divisible (SDCQ 46–7 = RNQ 71; 1897*f*: 61).[7] In all these 'extensions of number', however,

the truly numerical element is nothing but the positive integers—everything else arises from abandoning that complete indifference to the properties of the unit in which pure number consists. So far, however, the properties implied remain perfectly abstract, and our object, being still posited exclusively by thought, is still subject to the laws of thought alone. (SDCQ 47 = RNQ 72.)

influenced him. There is no evidence that he even knew of its existence. The general idea, however, is not hard to find in other mathematics texts of the time. Traces of it can be found, e.g. in Russell's geometry text (Potts 1845: 159–60).

[6] Beyond pure and qualified numbers there is a third type, *applied* number, in which there is an explicit reference to a definite unit. '[T]he applied number is always to be regarded as the product of the corresponding pure number with the unit in question' (SDCQ 47 = RNQ 78). In what follows applied number will not concern us.

[7] Russell cites Ehrenfels (1891) for this view. Russell's position probably owed something also to Clifford (1873), see esp. p. 240. Russell in fact made some notes about this time on parts of Clifford's lectures, but only on the sections to do with geometry (see RA 210–006550–F4). Russell's distinction between pure and qualified number bears a superficial resemblance to Helmholtz's distinction between pure and concrete number (1887) though Russell did not read the latter until 1900.

This procedure leaves no room for the irrationals and thus is incapable of generating a genuine number continuum. Russell's account remained constant through 1896 and 1897 despite the fact that he read Couturat (1896) and Dedekind (1872) in the interim. Couturat (1896: 54) describes both Dedekind's definition of irrationals in terms of cuts and Cantor's in terms of either the limit of an infinite sequence or the sum of an infinite series of rational numbers (see Dedekind 1872 and Cantor 1883*a*: § 9). Russell's response to Dedekind cuts (the definition Couturat preferred) was that that they didn't define a number but showed 'the mere absence of a number of any of the former kinds [i.e. rational numbers] at certain points of the scale'. They thus showed that there is a gap 'which can only be filled in by a symbol expressing the absence of a rational number at the point in question' (1897*f*: 61). He would have rejected Cantor's alternative definition because it involved infinity. His thinking on this topic didn't progress much beyond this for some time.

What is most important for our present concerns is Russell's account of fractions. For from it he derives 'the important result, that the graduated infinite series of fractions, called the number continuum, has meaning only when applied to matter divisible *ad lib.*' (SDCQ 46–7 = RNQ 71). It is fractions, therefore, which bring us to the relation between number and continuous quantity. But the absence of the irrationals ensures that Russell's 'number continuum' is no real continuum. None the less, Russell continues to refer to it as one well into 1898, apparently thinking that a dense series (i.e., a series in which there is a third term between any two)[8] must be a continuous series, in as good a sense of 'continuous' as any that was legitimate.

## 6.2 NUMBER AND QUANTITY

Russell's very first problems in the philosophy of arithmetic can be said to have arisen from the fact that numbers are used both for counting and for measuring. The problem was to show how, when numbers were derived from an abstract counting process, they could be used for the measurement of *continuous* quantity.[9] On occasion he goes so far as to say that the measurement of continuous quantity is the chief use of number; certainly he thought that number was required for an adequate treatment of quantity.[10] The problem for Russell in 1896 was to find the elements out of which continua were composed. Such elements would provide a natural unit for

---

[8] Russell always used the word 'compact' for such series. See *POM* 193, 296–303; ONC; *PM* *270.

[9] Following Russell (RNQ 70), I shall henceforth use 'quantity' exclusively for continuous quantity.

[10] Cf. VN 13, 20; 1896*a*: 36–7; SDCQ 53; 1897*f*: 63.

counting which would then permit the measurement of continua by means of the natural numbers. The task was hopeless, as Russell realized from the outset:

To make numeration [of the continuum] as accurate as possible, make unit as small as possible, but still get no accuracy. Get no whole, either, of any real sort. Hence arises necessity for zero and infinity, former denial of units, latter of whole in which they are collected. Neither is a number, i.e. neither contains a whole of unities. (VN 13.)

This passage makes it look as though the reason for introducing zero and infinity was simply the need to try and get absolutely accurate measurements of continuous quantities. It also makes it appear that the need for infinite numbers arises from the need to represent the magnitude of finite continuous quantities as the sum of infinitely many units of zero magnitude. The first argument is far too weak to support Russell's conclusion: why not simply abandon, as we must in practice do in the end, the hope of exact measurement of continuous quantities? The second argument involves twin absurdities: on the one hand a unit of zero magnitude, on the other the supposition that finite magnitudes can be represented as infinite sums of such units. It was not, of course, that Russell was committing himself to these absurdities. He was pointing them out. But he was also suggesting that anyone committed to the numerical treatment of continua was committed to them, and in this he was plainly mistaken.

The problem of the relation between number and continua was most acute in the foundations of the calculus (the topic on which Russell had once considered writing his fellowship dissertation). Intuitively, one can approximate the area of an irregular figure, for example, by the ancient method of exhaustion, that is by counting the number of regular figures of known area it would take to fill (or exhaust) the given area. The approximation gets better as the regular figures get smaller. This 'inner' approximation gives a lower bound to the area sought, a similar 'outer' approximation gives an upper bound. The exact area of the irregular figure can then be thought of as the limit to which the inner and outer approximations tend as the area of the regular figures approaches zero. The integral calculus provided rules by which such limits can be calculated. Similarly, the differential calculus provides rules by which the rate of change of one quantity $x$ with respect to another $y$ can be calculated. The change, $\Delta x$, in $x$ is calculated for a small change, $\Delta y$, in $y$, to give the value $\Delta x/\Delta y$, and the instantaneous rate of change (the derivative of $x$ with respect to $y$, $dx/dy$) is the limit to which $\Delta x/\Delta y$ tends as $y$ approaches zero.

The techniques of the calculus of course worked very well and were indispensable for physics. But as to why they worked or how they were to be understood the situation was far less satisfactory. If $\Delta y$ were actually zero, the ratio $\Delta x/\Delta y$ would be meaningless. If the small regular figures which were supposed to exhaust the irregular figure were actually of zero area then no sum of them would yield the area being calculated. Leibniz had attempted to avoid these problems by an appeal to infinitesimals. But infinitesimals were problematic quantities, to say the least, and appeal to them was more like renaming the problem than solving it. Newton had eschewed infinitesimals and spoke instead of quantities which vary with time, and are therefore to be contrasted in calculations with constant quantities. Apart from the fact that time was not directly involved in many uses of the calculus, Newton's manœuvre masked the problem rather than solved it. For what were essential to Newton's account were what he called prime and ultimate ratios, the values that the ratio of these varying quantities took at the moment when they vanish, and these values shared the problems of Leibniz's infinitesimals. These foundational problems in the calculus were thrown into sharp relief by Berkeley's brilliant polemic *The Analyst* (1734), but little was done to solve them until Cauchy's work in the early nineteenth century started the move towards a more rigorous definition of a limit. Cauchy's work, though it did not solve the problems, was one of the first important contributions to the subject of mathematical analysis which had begun to emerge in the late eighteenth century and which, in the work of Weierstrass and Dedekind towards the end of the century, would result in a rigorous and philosophically perspicuous account of the foundations of the calculus.[11]

Russell had been familiar with the calculus well before he went up to Cambridge, but thanks to the mathematics education he received there, which stressed facility in applying the calculus to practical problems without concern for foundational issues, he emerged from Cambridge in total ignorance of nineteenth-century developments in analysis. His knowledge of the foundations of the calculus did not stretch very much beyond the late eighteenth century, and his attitude towards foundational issues was, not unreasonably, similar to Berkeley's. In various places Russell considered both traditional attempts to explain differentials—the theory of infinitesimals which stemmed from Leibniz, and the theory of limits which emerged from Newton's work.

On infinitesimals Russell follows Hannequin (1895: 40 ff.) with approval: 'The infinitesimals cannot...be absolute zero; for otherwise their integration could not give a finite sum, and their ratio could not give a determinate differential coefficient. Every time we use the method of infinitesimals, in fact, we postulate elements which are not zero, but only unassignably

[11] A good early history of the calculus and its pressing foundational problems is Boyer (1949), more recent accounts can be found in Grattan-Guinness (1980). Both books take the story up to the early years of the 20th century. In its later development, infinitesimals were rehabilitated by Abraham Robinson's non-standard analysis.

small'.[12] Russell was certainly right to abandon infinitesimals which, despite being ultimately retrieved from oblivion, were at the time an extremely unpromising line of research. His account of limits, however, left much to be desired:

[E]ither our increments, in the last stage, in which the limit is supposed reached, are still finite, or they are absolute zero. In the first case, we still have the method of indivisibles; in the second, the limit becomes unmeaning. Absolute zero is absolute negation: it is not a quantity, but the bare denial that there is quantity; the ratio of two absolute zeroes, therefore, is the ratio of two quantities which have no property except that of not being quantities. Such a limit, obviously, will give no result whatever.

But mathematical zero—so every mathematician would retort—is not this bare logical zero, but a quantity smaller than any we can assign. . . . To this there are two retorts: first, that we cannot assign a quantity smaller than any assignable quantity . . . and second, that the use of infinity, which is commonly resorted to in these discussions, involves precisely the same fallacies as the use of zero. For *absolute* infinity is merely the negation of possible synthesis, and thus the negation of number. . . . *Mathematical* infinity, on the other hand, is a quantity larger than any assignable quantity. (SDCQ 50.)

The remarks which Russell added later to this passage, in particular three remarks pointing out errors in his treatment of limits, will constitute a sufficient commentary for our purposes. Against the words 'in the last stage' Russell wrote 'Illegitimate phrase'; above 'we cannot assign a quantity smaller than any assignable quantity' he wrote 'We can assign a quantity smaller than any *assigned* quantity'; and in the previous sentence he enclosed the word 'can' in square brackets to indicate that it was a mistake (see *Papers*, ii. A50: 17–18, A50: 28–9, A50: 26). That these corrections had to be made indicates how rudimentary Russell's knowledge of the concept of a limit was when he started to write the paper. The corrections hardly bring him up to the $\epsilon$-$\delta$ style of analysis introduced by Weierstrass and Dedekind, but they do at least bring him into the nineteenth century. In fact, we know that he derived his new information from reading De Morgan's calculus text (1842) to which Russell refers in his corrections (see *Papers*, ii, A50: 28–9). De Morgan explicitly tackles the very point at issue: 'When we speak of a

---

[12] 1896a: 37. See also VN 17: 'in the differential calculus, $dx$ is of the same kind as $x$ and is a quantum, but yet $= 0$. This is nonsense: the only way to give sense to $dx$ is to suppose it small but finite, and thus abandon continuity'. Russell here alludes to a dimensionality argument used in the Leibnizian tradition of the calculus. On this argument, $d$ is regarded as a dimension-preserving operator on $x$. $dx$ is regarded as an infinitesimally small increment of the variable $x$: e.g. if $x$ is a line, $dx$ is a short line. The law $a + dx = a$ is then understood as a law for discarding infinitesimals, from which $dx = 0$ does not follow, since $dx$ is a short line, while $0$ is a point. Russell later replaced the dimensional theory by one even more bizarre, in which the differential is a special kind of zero even though $x$ and $x + dx$ are 'strictly equal magnitudes' (AMR/TS 237).

magnitude increasing without limit', he says, 'we do not mean that it actually increases so as to be above every limit which could be named, for that is impossible; but that we can make it greater than any quantity that we actually do name'.[13] In fact, Russell in his original draft had been talking about the limit quantities represented by differentials as if they were infinitesimals, with all the contradictory properties usually ascribed to infinitesimals (for example, that they were assigned quantities smaller than any assignable quantities). And this, in turn, seems to have stemmed from his talking about limits as points actually reached, not merely approached as closely as one cared to specify—as his 'illegitimate phrase', 'in the last stage', reveals. Reading De Morgan at least put Russell in a position where he would be able to appreciate more modern work on limits.

Given Russell's rejection of both infinitesimals and limits, it is hardly surprising to find him harking back to a pre-Newtonian tradition in the calculus, the method of indivisibles advocated by Cavalieri in the seventeenth century (SDCQ 49). According to Cavalieri continuous $n$-dimensional figures could be regarded as collections of elements of $n-1$ dimensions. Thus a three-dimensional solid was regarded as formed by a 'stack' of two-dimensional surfaces; a two-dimensional surface as formed from a series of one-dimensional lines laid side by side. Cavalieri himself seems to have wavered on the question of whether the lines had any breadth or the surfaces any thickness (see Boyer 1949: 117–23). Either way, problems ensued. For if the lines lacked breadth then no number of them laid side by side would exhaust a surface; while if they do have breadth there is no guarantee that any integral number of them will exactly exhaust a given surface. Faced with this dilemma Russell firmly embraced the second horn. The indivisible elements which compose a continuum must be finite in extent (VN 13, 17; SDCQ 49), for the alternatives lead to contradiction in ways we have already considered. But Russell was fully aware that this is, as he puts it, 'simply a renunciation of the attempt to deal with continua' (SDCQ 49). It is this which leads him to what otherwise would seem the extraordinary statement that the 'infinitesimal calculus [is] really only possible where we have indivisibles and finite differences' (VN 15 n.).[14] The upshot of Russell's first attempts to base a numerical treatment of continua on the calculus is that on

---

[13] De Morgan 1842: 27. Russell copied this passage out and transcribed De Morgan's definition of a limit which comes close to that of Weierstrass without Weierstrass's formalism (De Morgan 1842: 9), on a sheet headed 'De Morgan's Definition of a Limit' (RA 220.010680). The same sheet contains the following remark: '[Whitehead regards 0 and ∞ as names for processes rather than for quantities]'. Aficionados of Whitehead's later philosophy may make of this what they can. But, for Russell, the last part of the remark is of importance, for a large part of Russell's difficulties with zero and infinity stemmed from his attempts to construe them as quantities.

[14] This passage bears (not surprisingly) a later retraction (see *Papers*, ii, A15: 34–5). See also VN 13: 'Differential calculus really atomistic'.

the only viable interpretation of the calculus, the theory of finite indivisibles, continuous quantities (if there are any, a matter to be broached in the next section) cannot be treated at all.

Russell, in these early writings, considers one more attempt at a numerical treatment of continua, Cantor's set theory. In view of the fact that Russell was not yet in a position to appreciate Weierstrass's definition of a limit, it is hardly surprising that his first attempts to tackle Cantor ended in disaster. Russell first came across Cantor's work as a result of reading Hannequin (1895).[15] As a result of Hannequin's references, Russell was led to read French translations of a number of Cantor's articles published by Mittag-Leffler in a special issue of *Acta Mathematica* (Cantor 1883*b*).[16] By Russell's later admission, he did not understand Cantor on first reading:

While I was lecturing at the [London] School of Economics, my wife and I lived in a flat at 90 Ashley Gardens, but I could not work there because the noise of the lift disturbed me, so I used to walk every day to her parents' house in Grosvenor Road, where I spent the time reading Georg Cantor, and copying out the gist of him into a notebook. At that time I falsely supposed all his arguments to be fallacious, but I nevertheless went through them all in the minutest detail. This stood me in good stead when later on I discovered that all the fallacies were mine. (*Auto.* i, 127.)

This work took place in March 1896, and the fruits (such as they were) of what must have been a considerable labour appeared in 'Some Difficulties' and in the review of Hannequin.[17] Since Russell's study of Cantor was prompted by reading Hannequin's very critical account of his work, it is rather surprising that Russell should have devoted so much effort to Cantor only to come to conclusions which, in large part, duplicate Hannequin's.

[15] B. R. to P. Jourdain, 11 Sept. 1917 (Grattan-Guinness 1977: 143–4).
[16] The following articles were translated in Cantor 1883*b*: Cantor 1871, 1872, 1874, 1878, 1879, 1880, 1882, 1883*c*, together with parts of 1883*a*. In addition, a new paper, 1883*d*, was published for the first time in the same issue of *Acta Mathematica*. The fact that Russell read only a partial translation of 1883*a* may have had important consequences for his understanding of Cantor. Among the parts omitted from the translation were § 9, which gave Cantor's definitions of the rationals and irrationals, and §§ 5–7, which were devoted to the history of the concept of infinity. It is possible that had he read these historical sections, which relate Cantor's work to earlier work with which Russell would have been more at home, Russell might have gained a clearer impression of Cantor's position.
[17] In another passage, similar to that quoted from *Auto.* Russell gives the impression that he came to see that Cantor was right as soon as he had finished transcribing him 'almost word for word' into a notebook (*PFM* 20–1). But this impression is misleading. Russell remained critical of Cantor long after this first reading. (Cantor's transfinite arithmetic is attacked even in POM/ D.) Nor did Russell engage in a second bout of Cantor-transcription. For, although he read more Cantor in July 1899, and Aug. and Nov. 1900, he did not live in London again until Sept. 1902. (I'm grateful to Sheila Turcon for information on this point.) Alan Wood (1957: 39) tells the story in almost exactly the same terms as Russell in *PFM*. The notebook Russell kept on Cantor has been preserved among Dora Russell's papers. His notes are printed in *Papers*, ii, 463–81. The comments he subsequently added indicate the use he later made of the notes in his study of Cantor.

That Russell's first reaction was negative, however, should come as no surprise at all. Cantor's work was extraordinarily original, and Russell was not the only mathematician of the time to reject it. Even Dedekind did not see the need for Cantor's higher number classes (Dedekind 1872: 3). For a philosopher who, like Russell, was attempting to base numbers of all kinds on the concept of quantity, Cantor's claims for transfinite arithmetic must have seemed outrageous. One might, perhaps, have expected Russell's criticisms to be more scornful. That they were not is probably due to the fact that he wasn't quite sure of his ground with respect to the quantity theory. It is interesting that he never uses the quantity theory to refute Cantor, but tries to show that Cantor's theory is inadequate on its own grounds.[18] Moreover, it is not too difficult to detect, beneath the surface, some (justified) unease on Russell's part as to whether he had got Cantor right. Only some of these early criticisms of Cantor were published by Russell (in 1896a). A somewhat more extended and independent treatment in 'Some Difficulties' was left unpublished along with his criticisms of the concept of a limit in the calculus (though his treatment of Cantor in that paper, unlike his treatment of limits, does not carry any later self-critical commentary).

Russell's published criticisms of Cantor are brief and largely derived from Hannequin. In his copy of Hannequin's book Russell wrote at the end of Hannequin's critical discussion of Cantor (Hannequin 1895: 69): 'This criticism of Cantor seems to me sound and good'. In his review (1896a: 37) Russell cites criticism Hannequin derives from Kerry on the cardinality of infinite sets. Thus Hannequin (1895: 65) reproduces Kerry's argument (1885: 228) concerning two concentric circles. On Cantor's theory the sets of points which comprise the two circles have the same cardinality. Kerry argues against this on the ground that the outer circle is larger and thus has more points on its circumference. Few things reveal the inadequacy of the quantity view in dealing with transfinite numbers as well or as simply as Kerry's argument about the circles. From the quantity point of view there can be little question that Kerry is right. The circumference of the outer circle is a greater quantity than that of the inner one: it is longer. But if one applies the modern concept of cardinality originating with Cantor whereby two sets have the same cardinality if their members can be placed in one–one

---

[18] It is worth noting that in this reaction to Cantor Russell exhibits two traits which characterized a great deal of his philosophical career. In the first place, as a philosophical disputant Russell had an agreeable penchant for attempting to refute an opponent on his own terms. Other examples come easily to mind, e.g. his later criticisms of idealism and pragmatism. The second feature, noted also by Kilmister (1984: 77), was that Russell rarely felt confident of a position until he had taken its development a very long way. *PM* is the outstanding example of this tendency. In the 1890s we see it in his advocacy of the quantity theory. He could not feel quite confident of the theory until its ramifications had been worked out in considerable detail. In this I think he contrasts rather favourably with the modishness of much contemporary philosophy.

correspondence with each other the situation is very different. For it is clearly possible to assign a point on the inner circle to each point on the outer circle and vice-versa. (From each point on the circumference of the outer circle draw a radius to the centre. Each radius will cut the inner circle at a different point.) The sets of points which comprise the two circles are equinumerous. Russell could hardly have seen the errors in Kerry's argument while he retained the quantity paradigm.

In his review, Russell claims that Cantor's theory is 'open to even severer strictures' than those passed on it by Hannequin and Kerry. His argument is brief (and misguided): 'Cantor's second class of numbers, by which he hopes to exhaust continua, begins with the first number larger than any of the first class; but as the first class (the ordinary natural numbers) has no upper limit, it is hard to see how the second class is ever to begin' (1896a: 37; see also SDCQ 52). Cantor was obviously well aware that the sequence of natural numbers did not come to an end, but recognized that this did not prevent him from defining the second class of numbers (see Cantor 1883b: 383–4). In particular, there is no contradiction in thinking of the first number greater than any natural number. For this number Cantor introduced the notation $\omega$.[19] Indeed, one is forced to think about such a number if one thinks about the order-type of linearly ordered sets of natural numbers. If any such set has an order-type then the set of natural numbers itself, linearly ordered by magnitude, has an order-type and this is given by $\omega$, the first transfinite ordinal. The essential point is easily put even in Russell's quantity theory. For Russell each natural number is a synthesis of units and every collection of units can be synthesized to form a number. There is thus a number which synthesizes the collection of natural numbers. This is in effect the first number of Cantor's second number class. And once $\omega$ is introduced the (first) principle of generation which produces the first number class by successive additions will produce further transfinite ordinals:

$$\omega, \omega + 1, \omega + 2, \ldots, \omega + n, \ldots$$

This sequence itself is a linearly ordered set whose order-type is given by $2\omega$. Whereupon the first principle of generation takes over again to produce the sequence

$$2\omega, 2\omega + 1, 2\omega + 2, \ldots, 2\omega + n, \ldots$$

to be followed by $3\omega$, and so on up to $\omega^2$, $\omega^3$ and beyond. In this way the second number class is filled up (Cantor 1883b: 385–6).[20]

[19] In fact, '$\omega$' appeared for the first time in the French translations (1883b) of his writings. Previously he had used '$\infty$'. See Dauben 1979: 328 n. 14. Cantor changed the notation in order to distinguish the transfinite ordinals represented by $\omega$ as actual infinities from the potential or false infinite traditionally represented by $\infty$ (Dauben 1979: 99).

[20] In fact, Cantor subjected the second class to a cardinality restriction, his principle of limitation or *Hemmungsprinzip*, designed to produce natural breaks in the sequence of transfinite numbers (Cantor 1883b: 383, 388). We need not concern ourselves with it here.

It is clear that Russell's criticism was beside the point. Yet, given his own theory of number, it is easy to see why he thought as he did. If one regards the collection of natural numbers as a false totality (as is inevitable if one takes the psychological process of synthesis at all seriously), one is hardly in a position to appreciate how Cantor gets beyond the natural numbers to $\omega$. Russell's failure to understand limits at this time didn't help. He seems to have thought that if limits were to be philosophically defensible, limit values of a set would have to be members of that set in order to be actually assigned. The question of limits was connected to Cantor's second number class, as Cantor acknowledged when he referred to $\omega$ as the limit to which the sequence of natural numbers approached (Cantor 1883*b*: 385). Cantor brings out the relevant point in his definition of the second principle of generation, the principle which enabled him to introduce $\omega$, $2\omega$, etc.: 'Given any definite succession of defined actual[21] whole numbers, among which there is none larger than all the others, one sets up, relying on this second principle of generation, a new number which one regards as the limit of the first numbers, i.e., which is defined as the next number greater than all of them' (1883*b*: 386). Russell's objection to Cantor's second number class resembles his objections to limits: we can no more assign a limit, a value less than any assignable value, than we can posit $\omega$, a number greater than any number that can be posited. There is a certain irony in this, for it was not the flight from reality of neo-Hegelian metaphysics that was keeping Russell from a satisfactory philosophy of mathematics, but his own too robust sense of reality, which required physical quantities for numbers to measure, and concrete psychological processes by means of which numbers could be created.

In his more extended response to Cantor in SDCQ, Russell raises fresh objections. There is a chaotic objection based on Russell's failure to understand Cantor's concept of denumerability (SDCQ 51). It becomes apparent from this argument that Russell had not begun to appreciate the basic principles of Cantor's transfinite arithmetic. If he had, he could not have argued that the union of two sets of points, $\{1, 1-1/2, 1-1/3, \ldots 1-1/n \ldots\}$ and $\{2, 2-1/2, 2-1/3, \ldots, 2-1/n \ldots\}$, contained twice as many points as there were natural numbers. Only one thing in Russell's early critique raises issues of genuine concern for Cantor and that concerns the vexed issue of the cardinality of the continuum. To put the question in Russell's terms: were there enough numbers in the second number class to exhaust the continuum? Cantor had proved in (1874) that the set of real numbers was

---

[21] In 1883*a* Cantor distinguished between *reellen Zahlen* and *realen Zahlen*. The former were the real numbers as contrasted with complex numbers. The latter were real in the sense of actual or concrete: real as opposed to potential. The French translation of 1883*a* does not mark this distinction. In the passage quoted the German word is 'realen' which will be rendered throughout discussions of Cantor as 'actual'.

non-denumerable, i.e. could not be put into one–one correspondence with the natural numbers, using for the first time (a complicated version of) the diagonal argument. In (1878), in which he demonstrated that the points of a plane could be brought into one–one correspondence with the points of the linear continuum (see § 4.5 above), he formulated for the first time his continuum hypothesis, that the cardinality of the continuum is the next highest cardinal to that of denumerable sets. In (1883a: § 12) he proved that the second number class was of greater cardinality than the first, which is denumerable; and in § 13 he proved that the cardinal of the second number class is the next cardinal after the cardinal of the first number class. But the crucial step still eluded him: he was unable to show that the cardinality of the continuum was that of the second class of numbers. In (1883b: 404) he expressed the hope that he would soon be able to prove this, but, as Russell noted, 'the proof is not as yet forthcoming' (SDCQ 52).[22]

In rejecting infinitesimals, limits, and Cantor's set theory Russell had rejected the main means available to mathematicians for the numerical treatment of continua. One might have expected that Russell would have inferred from this that they were not amenable to numerical treatment at all. But Russell was unwilling to make such a claim without an a priori argument to back it up. Accordingly, he sought to show that the numerical treatment of continua is impossible. Of course, if his a priori argument is any good the criticisms of Cantor and the calculus are beside the point, for if the a priori argument is correct we will know that the calculus and Cantor's set theory are defective as numerical treatments of continua. Russell's procedure of pursuing both technical objections to particular scientific theories and a priori philosophical objections to the entire enterprise is highly characteristic of his work at this time. It is reminiscent of his two-pronged treatment of geometry: first, an analysis of the scientific theories results in contradictions, then the philosophical analysis reveals these contradictions to be inherent in the abstracted subject-matter with which the theories deal.

Russell's a priori argument against the numeration of continua depends at key points upon a distinction he drew in 1896 (and kept redrawing in subsequent writings over the next two years) between extensive and intensive continua. The distinction first appears in an early 'Note on continua' (VN 17–18), almost certainly written shortly before SDCQ, as a fundamental distinction between continua which are '[p]resented as wholes, in which the intellect seeks elements'[23] and those which are 'intellectually constructed as

---

[22] Cantor's hopes were repeated in 1884: 488, but, despite intense efforts, he was never able to prove his continuum hypothesis. The issue was resolved only by Cohen (1963) who showed that the continuum hypothesis was independent of Cantorean set theory.

[23] To avoid an obvious difficulty, he subsequently amended this to continua 'presented in a finite [i.e. bounded] extent', noting also that the elements are not presented (SDCQ 53).

wholes out of elements sensationally given' (VN 17). The first class comprises *extensive* continua, and the second *intensive*. It is the distinction between extensive and intensive continua, drawn in this way, which Russell treats as fundamental in SDCQ.[24]

According to Russell, for number to be applicable to a continuum the continuum must be homogeneous (SDCQ 48). Now, Russell had argued at length in *EFG* that homogeneity is a necessary condition for measurement. What that argument showed was that if measure is to be possible *space* must be homogeneous. But in SDCQ he argues, quite inadequately, on the basis of his account of measurement, for the stronger claim that only homogeneous continua can be measured (cf. also 1986c: 301). Measurement, the application of number to continuous quantity, requires units which can be enumerated. The unit is arbitrarily chosen, but all units must be assumed to be qualitatively identical, and this, Russell claims, necessitates the homogeneity of the continuum. It is indeed true that for the purposes of measurement the qualitative differences of different portions of the continuum must be disregarded but this does not imply that they do not exist. In fact, the need to ignore these qualitative differences is no different from the need to abstract out the qualitative differences of the various discrete unities to which pure number is applied. There is no more reason to assume that the continuum is homogeneous if it is to be measured than to assume that men are all qualitatively identical if they are to be counted. All that is necessary is the weaker condition that the continuum be capable of being considered as (treated as if it were) homogeneous.[25] At the same time, Russell rejects the type of homogeneity which is to be found in a series of similar objects, for in such a series 'the objects would provide a natural unit for numeration' and thus destroy the continuity of the series (SDCQ 48). Yet the continuum 'must contain or be susceptible of some kind of differentiation, otherwise it could not afford the differences which numeration, though it disregards them, finds indispensable' (SDCQ 48). The differentiations, whether given in sense or intellectually constructed, 'serve as marks for the *quantum* of the

---

[24] It is interesting that Russell comes to his distinction after rejecting as not fundamental a distinction between homogeneous and heterogeneous continua which arose, fairly naturally, out of his work on geometry (VN 17). In his first draft of SDCQ Russell had treated as fundamental a classification of continua according as they were substantival or adjectival (cf. *Papers*, ii, T53: 34). This distinction, which is made dependent upon the extensive/intensive distinction in later revisions of the paper, is none the less used by Russell as part of his critique of continua. Cf. e.g. the statement of his conclusion (SDCQ 57–8).

[25] This is the conclusion Russell actually states on some occasions (e.g. SDCQ 48, ll. 20–2, 33, 42–3). But elsewhere he claims that the continuum must *be* homogeneous, and not merely regarded as such (see p. 48, ll. 23–4, and, more importantly, p. 53, ll. 1–2, where he starts to apply this conclusion). The problem is a familiar one: Russell has arguments which support the weak conclusion, but he takes them to support the stronger one which he needs.

continuum, which *quantum* itself is regarded as homogeneous throughout'
(SDCQ 48; see also VN 17).

As regards measurement there is an important difference between extensive
and intensive continua, for intensive quantities 'cannot be directly measured,
but can only have numbers assigned to them by means of extensive (spatial)
correlates' (SDCQ 54). Temperature, which is an intensive quantity, can
only be measured by a correlation with spatial extension, for instance in a
mercury thermometer which correlates temperature to the height of a
column of mercury (SDCQ 55; the example comes from Sigwart 1873: ii,
71–2). Russell's argument for this claim is extremely obscure. He points out,
first, that since measurement is the application of number to (continuous)
quantity, and since number consists of a whole of qualitatively similar units,
it follows that for quantity to be measurable it must be a whole divisible into
qualitatively similar parts. This seems to rely upon a mistaken view of how
number is applied to quantity. Russell's next claim seems totally unsupported.
He urges that the quantity regarded as a whole is intensive, while regarded
as a collection of qualitatively similar parts it is extensive. Intensive quantity
is entirely lacking in the second aspect. Since both are required for measurement, it follows that intensive quantities cannot be directly measured
(SDCQ 54; cf. also 1896c: 301). Not only does Russell's principle, that a
quantity considered as a whole is intensive and that it is extensive when
considered as a collection, lack support or even intuitive plausibility, but, it
would seem, Russell's argument could be directed equally against extensive
quantities. For if the possibility of measurement requires that a quantity
have two aspects, extensive and intensive, and if intensive quantity is not
directly measurable because it lacks the extensive aspect, it would seem, by
parity of reasoning, that extensive quantity is not directly measurable
because it lacks the intensive aspect.

The point is not lost on Russell, who restates the difficult part of his
argument, in very much the same words, in *EFG*. There, however, he
continues: 'A purely intensive quantity, therefore, is not numerable—a
purely extensive quantity, if any such could be imagined, would not be a
single quantity at all, since it would have to consist of wholly unsynthesized
particulars' (*EFG* 176). But this masks the difficulty rather than solves it.
In the first place, why should it be assumed that there can be *purely* intensive
quantities but not *purely* extensive quantities? Moreover, Russell is now
comparing oranges with apples. His initial intention was to show that
intensive quantities were not directly measurable. What he now claims to
have shown is that *purely* intensive quantities are not measurable, an
importantly different result. Impurely intensive quantites, it would seem,
like impurely extensive quantities, remain directly measurable: while neither
purely intensive nor purely extensive quantities can be measured. The

dependence of intensive upon extensive quantity as far as measurement is concerned has not been demonstrated.[26]

Russell's argument is the more puzzling because, if his argument that a continuum must be homogeneous to be measurable were any good, the non-measurability of intensive continua would follow immediately. For he already has the result that all intensive continua are heterogeneous (VN 17). In fact, however, his argument that measurable continua are homogeneous is not sound. The best he can establish is that measurable continua must be capable of being regarded as homogeneous. This, in itself, might suffice for present argument, *if* intensive quantities could be shown to be incapable of being regarded as homogeneous. If Russell has some ground for this, he does not give it. But if he did hold it, then it *might* explain the sense in which he claims that intensive quantities lack the extensive aspect needed for measurement. This already pushes the identification of homogeneous with extensive quantities further than Russell has given warrant for. Moreover, even with this identification, Russell's argument is not satisfactory unless he can show that homogeneous quantities (unlike heterogeneous ones) were capable of being regarded both extensively and intensively. And it would seem difficult to supply any argument which would show that one of them had this property but not the other.

In the end, however, Russell's claim that intensive quantities can only be measured by means of their spatial correlates is more important to his discussion of geometry, where the apriority of general metrical geometry depends upon it, than it is to his discussion of continuous quantity. For Russell has further arguments to show that *no* genuinely continuous quantity, whether extensive or intensive, can be measured.

In measuring a quantity the quantity measured must be some whole multiple of the unit chosen to measure it. Fractions are ultimately inadmissible because, as we have seen, they simply involve a change of units. Since the continuum is infinitely divisible, 'there must be no limit to the smallness of our unit' (SDCQ 53). But the unit must always be finite, and to suppose a finite unit capable of measuring a genuinely continuous quantity is a mistake. For if the quantity is continuous the unit must be further divisible.

[26] It remains true, and interesting, however, that intensive quantities are generally measured by means of their extensive correlates (temperature by the height of a mercury column, weight by the extension of a spring, etc.) Whether the distinction between extensive and intensive quantity is the important one in this respect is doubtful, since Russell held that even measurement of time (itself an extensive quantity) was performed by means of space (1896*b*: 273–4; 1896*c*: 295–6). It would seem that *space* is in a unique position as far as measurement is concerned, as Russell had argued in his account of general metric geometry. (At least, this was so in the days before atomic clocks.) What Russell has not got, so far as I can tell, is any valid a priori reason why it should be so. Whether there are any intensive quantities which *are* measured without reference to extensive quantity, or whether there are any which could be, are questions I shall leave to the reader to decide.

In his review of Hannequin, Russell states this as 'the necessary divisibility of the indivisible element', one of the fundamental contradictions in the atomistic analysis of continua (1896*a*: 37). Accordingly we are left with a dilemma: 'either the object of our investigation is not infinitely divisible [and thus not a continuum], or number is inapplicable to it, and the whole mathematical treatment—the only possible treatment for a homogeneous continuum—is impossible' (SDCQ 53). Thus Russell comes to the conclusion that 'whatever we treat as a continuum must really, if it is to be intelligible, be discrete' (SDCQ 53).

One task now remains for Russell's early theory of continuity, and that is to show that the concept of a continuum is itself incoherent. He has demonstrated so far, at least to his own satisfaction, that continua cannot be made intelligible by means of number. It remains to be shown that they cannot be made intelligible in any other way. Russell's arguments for this will be our concern in the next section.

## 6.3 THE CONTRADICTIONS OF CONTINUITY

In SDCQ Russell is concerned to show the concept of continuity is intrinsically contradictory, and thus to be rejected in favour of an atomistic view of quantity. Despite the fact that Russell claims to have shown 'that if extensive continua are found to be logically contradictory, this conclusion will hold also of intensive continua' (SDCQ 55), he treats the two types of continua separately, attempting to find independent objections to each. This is prudent, for what he has established (at best) is not the claim just quoted, but the weaker claim that the measurement of intensive quantities depends upon the measurement of extensive quantities. He does maintain that the stronger claim follows from the weaker, but it will do so only when the latter is supplemented by some bridging theses which are far from self-evident and which Russell, in any case, leaves unstated. More surprising is the fact that, despite the alleged dependence of intensive on extensive continua, Russell criticized intensive continua at much greater length than extensive. His critique of intensive continua takes the from of a progression of steadily more severe criticisms.

In the first place, he notes that intensive continua may more easily be regarded as discrete than extensive continua (SDCQ 54). This is because the elements of an intensive continuum are given in sense, and therefore can never be smaller than a certain threshold size, but at the same time, as elements, must be regarded as indivisible. That successive elements differ infinitesimally is, therefore, inferred from the fact that 'a fresh element seems to correspond to every fresh quantity, and no limit appears to the minuteness of the possible difference between two elements' (SDCQ 54).

This, in turn, relies upon the correlation of intensive with extensive quantities. That we have a continuum of graduated intensive quantities is thus inferred ultimately from the fact that we have a continuum of graduated extensive quantities correlated to them. From this, Russell concludes (1) that collections of intensive quantities 'can never be known to be true continua':

> For a difference between two intensive quantities can only be found correlated with a difference between two extensive quantities, if the difference of intensive quantity is accessible to direct observation. But an observable difference cannot be infinitesimal. Hence we can never discover, by unaided experience, that intensive quantities are continuously variable. (SDCQ 55.)

This argument seems to trade on two confusions. In the first place, from the fact that the elements of intensive quantities are given in sense and cannot therefore be infinitesimal, it doesn't follow that the *difference* between any two such elements must be given in sense and cannot therefore be infinitesimal. Of course, it will follow that infinitesimal differences cannot be known 'by unaided experience', but from this it doesn't follow that they can't be known. Not even (1), however, warrants Russell's overall conclusion: (2) 'It is *unmeaning* to say, an intensive quantity has changed, unless we perceive the change; but we can only perceive the change if it is finite. Hence an infinitesimal change in an intensive continuum is meaningless, and our continuum must be regarded as discrete' (SDCQ 56; my italics). Yet plainly he needs (2), if his case against intensive continua is to be complete.

Russell is aware of the gap in his argument for (1), for he goes on to consider whether there could be any a priori ways in which the continuity of intensive quantities could be known. A brief discussion convinces him that there are not (SDCQ 55–6). Which leaves the correlation of intensive with extensive quantities as the only means still open for establishing intensive continuity and this, in turn, will be closed when Russell comes to treat extensive continua at the end of his paper. Russell's first confusion thus concerns (1) and the epistemic status of intensive continuity. His second, however, concerns the nature of intensive quantities themselves, and is thus more directly relevant to (2).

It seems, at first sight, that there is a pervasive confusion in Russell's use of the word 'element'. On the one hand it is the elements of intensive continua which are supposed to be given in sense, thus ensuring that they are finite in size. On the other hand, it often appears that Russell understands the elements of a continuum to be its ultimate, and therefore smallest, constitutents: hence the elements are said to be indivisible. This would be a particularly gross confusion and it seems charitable to suppose that Russell has a rather different picture in mind. The indivisibility of finitely large intensive quantities stems not from the fact that there are no smaller intensive quantities, but from the logical structure of intensive quantities which Russell doesn't really make explicit until RNQ, namely that intensive quantities, unlike extensive ones, are not subject to arithmetical operations like addition and division. Given a finite intensive quantity, such as a temperature, dividing it in two will not give two smaller temperatures.

The view of intensive quantities just outlined seems to be necessary for Russell's main objection to intensive quantities. 'An intensive quantity', he complains, 'is a whole which cannot be divided into parts. Such a notion . . . is a gross contradiction, since nothing can be a whole except in so far as it has parts' (SDCQ 56). Russell's argument seems to trade upon another terminological confusion. If all wholes have parts and intensive quantities do not have parts, then intensive quantities are not wholes. What has gone wrong is not anything necessarily to do with intensive quantities, rather with Russell's misleading characterization of them as wholes. Russell's objection is rather more subtle than this, however. As we shall see more fully in § 8.1 when his doctrine of internal relations is discussed, the difficulty he has in mind is the following. For anything to be a whole, it must have parts related together. But the doctrine of internal relations, the part–whole relation must be grounded upon the different intrinsic properties of its terms. But the elements of an intensive quantity are homogeneous, each is exactly like all the others as far as intrinsic properties are concerned. Thus the elements of an intensive quantity cannot be related, and thus cannot form a whole.

Originally, Russell had claimed that in order for number to apply to a continuous quantity the quantity must have both an extensive and an intensive aspect, since the number was itself a unity (requiring the intensive aspect) of diverse units (requiring the extensive aspect). He had maintained, however, that an extensive quantity which lacked an intensive aspect could not properly be regarded as a quantity at all (*EFG* 176). It now looks as though he is maintaining, reasonably enough, that an intensive quantity which lacks an extensive aspect (i.e. which 'cannot be divided into parts') cannot be regarded as a quantity either. These results, Russell seems to suggest, apply not just to measurable quantities but to any quantities whatsoever. Yet the argument which led up to them applies only to measurable quantities, since it depends solely upon the a priori features of number. Thus the more general conclusion would seem so far unwarranted. Moreover, if Russell is to insist that all quantities (whether measurable or not) have both an intensive and an extensive aspect, one must wonder what has become of his original distinction between extensive and intensive quantities. There are not, it would seem, extensive and intensive *quantities*, but extensive and intensive *aspects* of quantities. If this is so, it becomes even more obscure why intensive quantities must be regarded as wholes.

The result so far arrived at is that if the continuity of intensive quantity is to be established at all, it can only be by means of a correlation with extensive quantity. In effect, this provides a way of reducing the problem of continuity to the more manageable problem of the continuity of extensive quantity. Unless the continuity of extensive quantity can be established, there will be no reason for supposing that any quantities are continuous, and the way will be open for the atomistic views in favour of which Russell has been influenced by Hannequin. Russell's next step, therefore, is to demonstrate that extensive continuity itself involves irresolvable contradictions.

Russell argues surprisingly briefly for this conclusion at the end of SDCQ.[27] His argument takes the form of a dilemma. Either an extensive continuum is a thing (or has a This, as Russell puts it in Bradleian language) or it is merely a collection of adjectives or relations. But it cannot be the latter, since extensive quantities can be divided, while relations and adjectives cannot (SDCQ 57–8). Suppose, therefore, that extensive continua are substantival. This is suggested by the fact that extensive continua can be made independent objects of investigation, and by the fact that they may be given in sense (SDCQ 57). But this supposition, too, leads to contradictions. For the continuum, as we have seen, contains no parts. One might suppose, therefore, that the extensive continuum is simple. But, as Russell remarked in the first draft of SDCQ (a passage deleted in revision, see *Papers*, ii, T53: 34), what is simple is unthinkable, since it lacks the unity-in-diversity necessary for thought. Thus if the continuum were simple it could not be an independent object of investigation. The unthinkability of the simple, which is a fundamental Bradleian principle of Russell's epistemology at the time (*EFG* 182–4), gives us a clue as to why Russell thinks the necessity of construing the extensive continuum as a whole of parts stems from the nature of the extensive continuum itself and not just from attempts to apply number to it. For a whole comprised of parts is the only sort of thing which could be thought. (Russell's later view that propositions are complex wholes originates in part from this.) Thus, if the continuum is not such a whole, it must be unthinkable. Yet, if it is a whole of parts, it must be inconsistent. For its infinite divisibility ensures that we may never reach the parts, while the need for infinitely many parts in any finite quantity ensures that we can never fabricate the whole. 'Hence', Russell concludes, 'we stand before a dilemma: Either the extensive continuum has a This, in which case the absence of a whole and of elements renders it self-contradictory; or else it is a mere collection of adjectives or relations, i.e. an intensive continuum, in which case, as we saw above, it is no continuum at all' (SDCQ 58).

---

[27] The sheets containing the argument were in fact added to the MS when Russell revised it. However, the new argument must have replaced an earlier argument to the same effect, because Russell's overall conclusion is largely restated in the revised version (*Papers*, ii, T57: 6).

The difficulties of understanding continua, which after all were not new with Russell, suggest that it might be worthwhile to reconsider the reasons which made them appear necessary. Russell in SDCQ, rather surprisingly, gives only two: both mentioned in the concluding paragraph. The first is that they are convenient in dealing with mathematical topics. An example which Russell acknowledged in his review of Hannequin is the description of motion in dynamics (1896a: 36). But Russell, as his review makes clear, was very much less impressed by this reason than Hannequin was. Moreover, since Russell was prepared to treat the calculus in terms of finite indivisibles, an atomist account of motion would in any case have been necessary.

The other reason Russell mentions in SDCQ is that continua are suggested by sense, though they 'are not forced on us by experience' (SDCQ 58). The same view is implicit in a note written at the beginning of 1898 (VN 24) where Russell hopes that by means of the concept of the continuum it will be possible to achieve 'a chemical union between categories and sense'. In fact, it was Russell's view that all sense-perception involved putative continua: 'The matter to which number is to be applied, wherever this consists of sense-data[28] as opposed to conceptions, contains no ready-made divisions, but has to be divided artificially in order to manufacture a unit. Any portion of such a matter is called a *quantity* . . . the matter itself is a *continuum*' (SDCQ 48). Evidently, this position owes much to Bradley's account of sense-experience (cf. Bradley 1883: i, 98), although there is nothing in Russell's account to suggest that what is given in sense-experience is devoid of relations (as was Bradley's immediate experience). It is clear, however, that Russell did not regard the discrete things on which pure number depends as given in experience either, but as intellectual constructions. It was conceptualization which permitted the discrimination of discrete entities as so many $F$s, so many items falling under the sortal concept $F$. Judgements to the effect that there are so many $F$s did not, for Russell, result simply from the application of number to what was given in sense-experience, but required prior intellectual work in determining what, of all that was given, was to constitute a single $F$.

Now we have already seen that Russell does not think that putative continua given in sense-experience were *given as continua*. Rather he is arguing that sense-perception suggests the continuity of phenomena, which is a subsequent intellectual construction. But, again, it is hard to see why this reason in favour of continuity should seem so persuasive. After all, while it

---

[28] It is usually assumed that Russell (or Moore) introduced the term 'sense-data' 1910–12. However, even with this use in 1896, Russell was not introducing the term. He was adopting it from James (1890: ii, 146, 184, 620) or possibly from Fraser (1894: i, 108). The earliest use seems to be Royce (1885: 321), but there is no evidence that Russell saw it there. See Hall (1964).

would doubtless be impossible to embody the results of sense-experience in a science which made no reference to elements smaller than the *minimum sensible*, it should be possible to do so without reference to any which were less than finitely large.

What is curious about Russell's treatment in SDCQ is that he nowhere mentions his strongest arguments in favour of continuous quantity, namely those that derive from geometry. In Russell's transcendental deduction of geometry, continuity turns out to be an a priori necessary feature of space. This is true both of those possible metric spaces treated by general metric geometry, and of projective space, too, if Russell's transcendental deduction in *EFG* is to work. Although, later, Russell denied that projective space must be continuous (AOG 403), it seems likely that by this time Russell's definition of 'continuity' had changed. At the time he wrote SDCQ he thought that any dense sequence of points was continuous. In 1899, taking his first lesson from Cantor, he notes that a sequence that is merely dense does not give all the points on a line (AOG 409 n.). As he used the term in 1896, he had a priori grounds for thinking that space was a continuous quantity. Moreover, nowhere in *EFG* does he consider the possibility that an atomistic view of space was possible (unless we count those passages which deal with the antinomy of the point). It seems strange, therefore, that in SDCQ Russell makes no reference at all to these results.

Since at least two sentences of SDCQ found their way into *EFG* (see *Papers*, ii, A54: 33–7) we can be reasonably sure that at least some of those passages which deal with continuity in *EFG* were written or revised around the time he wrote SDCQ. It might be conjectured, therefore, that Russell had not arrived at the view that geometry required the continuity of space as an a priori necessity at the time he wrote SDCQ. This is prima facie implausible since the continuity of space was such a widely held doctrine that we could only admit that Russell rejected it if there were clear evidence to that effect. Moreover, in the geometry papers Russell published before *EFG*, continuity, though not prominent, is certainly presupposed. In (1896b: 285 n.) he goes so far as to note that he has 'freely used the postulate of Infinite Divisibility' which, he says, 'has sometimes been supposed to involve difficulties, though I have never been able to feel their force'. And in (1896c: 301), which comes closest to SDCQ, the antinomies of continuous quantity are not mentioned.

Russell, when he wrote SDCQ, must have been aware that his treatment there of continuous quantities as inherently contradictory and in need of replacement was inconsistent with the conclusions he had come to in his analysis of geometry, where the continuity of space was an a priori necessity. This sort of contradiction, however, is to be expected in a dialectical system. In *EFG* the problems arise, it is alleged, because geometry treats space as a thing, and are to be avoided, it is suggested, by an adjectival treatment. In

SDCQ, by contrast, this avenue is explicitly explored and rejected on the grounds that it reduces an extensive continuum (space) to a purely adjectival and therefore intensive one, which intensive continua are logically dependent upon extensive ones. The suggestion in SDCQ is that the antinomies are to be avoided by a transition to atomism, which would destroy the continuity on which, according to *EFG*, geometry depends. The dialectical tension is evident, but there is not the slightest hint as to how it is to be resolved. It seems possible that Russell did not cite geometry as one of the reasons for supposing the existence of continua in SDCQ because he was not in a position then to treat such evidence as unequivocal.[29] It is clear both from *EFG* and SDCQ, that he had no idea how to deal with the problem in 1896.

## 6.4 THE ANTINOMY OF QUANTITY

In the middle of 1896 when he was writing SDCQ, Russell's thinking about continuity was in a chaotic state. Almost every aspect of that paper gave him difficulty. He was uncertain, at the outset, how to classify continua; his arguments are weak and indecisive; and his knowledge of the mathematics of continuity was hopelessly inadequate. Altogether it was a paper he was wise to leave unpublished. His next paper in the area, RNQ, which he read to the Aristotelian Society in April 1897 and published in *Mind* in July, was much more sure-footed. Moore may well have 'despised it', as Russell reported, and said that it 'was so muddled that it was impossible to show that I was wrong, because no one could discover what I meant'.[30] But compared to SDCQ it was a model of clarity. Russell's later verdict on the paper, which he called 'unadulterated Hegel' and 'unmitigated rubbish' (*MPD* 40–1), was equally harsh. But Couturat liked it even though he disagreed, and wrote a long review in which he called it a 'little masterpiece of subtle dialectic' (Couturat 1898*b*: 432). Taking the paper on its own terms, I think Couturat was nearer to the mark than Moore or Russell.

Between the two papers Russell had learnt more about the mathematical treatment of continua (having read De Morgan 1842, Dedekind 1872, and Couturat 1896 in the interim) but still not enough for him to make a satisfactory evaluation. He surely recognized by 1897 that the matter was much more complicated than he had supposed when he wrote SDCQ. And in RNQ he neatly circumvented the difficulties posed by the calculus and Cantor by adopting what he called a purely logical approach. If it could be shown that the notion of continuous quantity was logically incoherent without reference to attempts to apply number to it then it would not be

---

[29] It is significant that in his published discussion (1896*a*) he is far more tentative in his condemnation of continua than in the unpublished SDCQ.

[30] B. R. to A. Russell, 6 Apr. 1897.

necessary, as Russell cannily noted at the outset, 'to deal with mathematical considerations here' (RNQ 70). The curious result is that 'On the Relations of Number and Quantity', despite its title, is much less concerned with the relations of number and quantity than was SDCQ. But this was not all, Russell, in RNQ skirted the problems of continuity almost entirely, in mathematical or any other guise. It is true that his stated purpose in the paper is to reveal a contradiction in the concept of continuous quantity, but the arguments he used make little or no direct appeal to the concept of continuity. It is the concept of quantity that is his main target.

In RNQ the distinction between intensive and extensive continua is drawn in terms of the nature of change. In extensive quantity a change in quantity is itself a quantity of the same kind as that changed; in intensive quantity it is not (RNQ 75). This is closer to the sort of view that Russell seems to have been groping for at the end of SDCQ as a replacement for the official SDCQ distinction in terms of whether the whole or the parts of the continuum were given. In SDCQ this skewed Kantian approach turned out to be not only problematic but largely beside the point. One consequence Russell draws from the new definitions is that extensive quantities are divisible while intensive ones are not. This was a claim made in SDCQ but not clearly supported by the definitions of intensive and extensive quantity given there. The basis for the claim is that extensive quantities are substantival while intensive ones are not. This, again, is a claim from SDCQ. The important new move in RNQ is to adopt from *EFG* the claim that extensive quantities are *false hypostatizations* of relations or adjectives, and that their contradictory nature stems from this fact. This opens the way for a reduction of extensive to intensive quantity (where relations and adjectives are not falsely hypostatized). The latter need not be regarded as continuous on Russell's account. In SDCQ Russell had given only weak arguments for intensive continua, and ultimately had found the concept of continuity was inconsistent and in need of replacement. But this, in itself, is not a problem for Russell before the adoption of his plenal matter theory. In fact, it fits very well with his finite differences interpretation of the calculus, and with his punctual theory of matter of 1896 and early 1897. What turned it into a problem was the fact that in SDCQ Russell had argued that intensive quantity must be reduced to extensive. The antinomies of extensive quantity suggested a transition to intensive quantity; but the logical dependence of intensive upon extensive quantity returned him to the beginning of an inescapable circle.

Russell's initial assumption in RNQ, which in the course of the paper he comes to reject, is that quantity is what all quantities have in common, as generosity is what all generous acts have in common. In its place he proposes a purely relational view of quantity, judgements of quantity being judgements of comparison between one quantity and another. Russell considers two ways in which it might be maintained that quantity is an intrinsic property common to all quantitative things. The first is the view he takes from Couturat (1896) that quantity is an independent category, not reducible to anything else. On this no-reduction view, quantities could have an intrinsic nature, though one not explicable in other than quantitative terms. Russell himself came to hold the no-reduction view (AMR 214), shortly before abandoning the quantity view of mathematics. The second is the view that quantity is given in sense-experience, a view he elsewhere (1897*f*: 60) attributes to Mill.

Russell deals with the second attempt briefly and decisively. He has two arguments against it. First, that if quantities are simply given in sense then they are 'purely psychical, non-measurable, indivisible intensit[ies]', they are thus not amenable to mathematical treatment and the connection of quantity to measurement is lost (RNQ 78). The second argument is even stronger. It is a familiar transitivity argument derived from Poincaré (1893: 29) and shows, as Russell puts it, that even if quantities are given in sense, quantity is not. Suppose that three quantities, $A$, $B$, and $C$, are given in sense such that $A$ is perceptually indistinguishable from $B$ and $B$ from $C$, but that $A$ is perceptually distinguishable from $C$. If quantity itself is given entirely by sense we would have $A = B$, $B = C$, but $A \neq C$, which is impossible. We have, therefore, to distinguish between quantitative equality and inequality, on the one hand, and the perceptual discernibility or indiscernibility of quantities on the other. This we cannot do if quantity is entirely perceptual.[31]

Russell's arguments against the no-reduction position are much more complex. It is here that Moore's charges of unintelligibility have some validity. Russell, in his review of Couturat, had already criticized some technical aspects of Couturat's attempt to found quantity independently of number (1897*f*: 64–5). For example, Russell attacks, on familiar grounds, Couturat's axiom of the modulus (Couturat 1896: 399), which postulates a zero quantity. But Russell's other criticisms in his review seem hardly persuasive, amounting often merely to counter-assertion. In RNQ, by contrast, Russell seeks for more general objections which will refute, not only Couturat's, but any no-reduction theory. Couturat's task, at least as Russell conceives it, is to find a characterization of the nature of quantity which does not reduce it to something else, while at the same time recognizing that every judgement about quantity is comparative by nature, for 'apart from comparison, there is nothing to be said about quantity except that it is quantitative' (RNQ 75). This last condition, however, might well be thought to beg the question. Russell has his own reasons for supposing that all

[31] It might seem incredible that anyone should have failed to distinguish the two, but, indeed, Mill's account of quantity does not leave room for the distinction (see Mill 1843: I. iii. 5).

quantitative judgements are comparative, but these grounds might be rejected by those who, like Couturat, maintain that quantity is an irreducibly independent concept. Russell's position, in fact, stems from his account of attempts to treat quantity numerically, but Couturat's theory implies that number and quantity are independent of one another. In introducing quantity as an irreducible concept Couturat could have supposed it equipped with its own category of judgements which were both non-comparative and irreducible to judgements of any other type.

Putting this difficulty to one side, however, what can Russell say against no-reduction theories? In his review, Russell had already suggested that Couturat's axioms of quantity held only for extensive quantities and not for intensive (1897*f*: 64). A case in point is Couturat's first axiom for the addition of quantities: the sum of two quantities of a given kind is a quantity of the same kind (Couturat 1896: 389). This holds for extensive quantities, for the sum of two lengths is a length, but not, Russell claims, for intensive quantities, for the 'sum of two temperatures . . . is meaningless'. I am hard pressed to see the plausibility of this view. It is plausible for some intensive quantities (e.g. for colours and for the composition of forces with which Russell was struggling in physics), but surely not for others. It is true that if you take two 'lengths', e.g. two metre rods, and lay them end to end you get a new 'length', whereas there is no way in which two hot bodies may be combined to form a body with a temperature equal to the sum of the original temperatures.[32] But such considerations seem hardly relevant to the issue at hand, for one can raise the temperature of a body to a new temperature by increasing its original temperature by so many degrees (just as you can 'lengthen' an elastic band). Moreover, though quantity of heat is not equivalent to temperature, it is surely equally intensive, and yet bringing together two bodies with the same quantity of heat results in twice as much heat as one had before.

Be that as it may, Russell's charge against Couturat's axioms is made a good deal more plausible by his new definition of intensive quantity, which implies (or is intended to imply) that intensive quantities cannot be divided. In fact, on the new definition, arithmetic operations in general make little sense as far as intensive quantities are concerned. Russell's subsequent argument against Couturat falls into two parts: the first deals with extensive quantities and the second with intensive quantities, to which extensive quantities are now reduced.

The antinomy in extensive quantity is that extensive quantity must be both a mere adjective or relation and yet more than a mere adjective or relation.

---

[32] Considerations such as these may have influenced Green's criticism of utilitarianism, to which Russell on occasion alludes (RNQ 78), that the sum of two pleasures (which are intensive quantities) is not itself a pleasure (Green 1883: § 221).

This is a generalization of the old problem of the hypostatization of space. Russell's argument for the general antinomy depends upon the nature of change, on which the definition of extensive quantity now depends. According to the definition of extensive quantity, a change of extensive quantity is a quantity of the same type as the quantity changed. Suppose, now, an extensive quantity $A$ undergoes a change $C$ and becomes a new extensive quantity $B$. In any case of change, Russell maintains, the object changed retains its identity throughout the change, which is thus a mere adjective of the original object. Thus $C$ is a mere adjective of $A$, which is supposed to be preserved through the change. Thus $A$ must be more than a mere adjective. For otherwise $A$ would, absurdly, be merely adjectival quantity which remained the same quantity while being changed into a different quantity. But $A$, $C$, and $B$ are all alike extensive quantities of the same type, so $A$, like $C$, must be a mere adjective. Hence, extensive magnitudes are both mere adjectives and more than mere adjectives (RNQ 75–6).

The fallacy in this argument lies in Russell's definition of extensive quantity, for it is a category mistake to say that a change of quantity is itself a quantity of the same type as that changed. Certainly, this is the case if 'change' is used in the sense in which a change can be seen as an adjective of a thing which retains its identity through the change. If a rubber band is stretched its length changes, and this change may be regarded as an adjective of the band. But to say that the stretching is a length is simply nonsense. On the other hand, in any sense in which one might want to say that the change was a length (a rather odd use of 'change', no doubt), then it would simply be false to describe such a 'change' as an adjective of the *quantity* changed. Put differently, in any sense in which the change can be described as an adjective, it is an adjective of the band, not of the length of the band.

If we refuse to hypostatize a relation in the way Russell alleges was done in extensive quantity we are left with intensive quantity. But intensive quantity is in no better condition, as Russell goes on to argue. Having noted, again, the inapplicability of number to intensive quantity, he argues that, given two intensive quantities of the same kind, $A$ and $B$, both, considered as quantities, are 'conceptually identical' and differ solely in that one is greater or less than the other. But this, he says, 'would seem to reduce intensive quantity to a relation between two terms', contrary to the original supposition that quantity was not to be explained in relational terms (RNQ 78).

This argument could hardly, I think, show that quantity was not an irreducible concept, but merely that it could not be the subject of quantitative judgements if it were. Those who held that quantity was an irreducible concept would be committed, at worst, to the ineffability of quantity. Moreover, this conclusion would follow quite generally for extensive and intensive quantity alike, without some of the detours through which Russell has taken us. For, on the one hand, the irreducibility claim is taken to imply that quantity has a non-relational nature, which can either be expressed in non-relational judgements or not at all. On the other hand, it is maintained that all judgements about quantities are relational, comparing one quantity with another. Thus there are no non-relational judgements about quantity and so quantity remains ineffable. But what is wanted here is the very distinction between quantity and quantities which Russell draws elsewhere. For it is judgements about *quantities* which are always relational, and there seems to be no reason to infer from this that judgements about *quantity* are also always relational. The antinomy of *quantities*, with which we started, that quantities have an intrinsic nature which consists wholly in difference from something else, is preserved, but a parallel antinomy of quantity which Russell uses to confute the no-reduction view is blocked.

Having rejected both empiricist and no-reduction theories of quantity, Russell returns to reconsider his initial assumption, that quantity is an intrinsic common property of quantities. This he now finds himself forced to reject in the face of the antinomy of quantities. 'Quantity is not a common property of quantitative things, any more than similarity is a common property of similar things. Quantity is a conception of relation, of comparison; it expresses the possibility of a certain kind of comparison with other things. . . . A quantity is any content whatever, so soon as this content is capable of a certain kind of comparison with other contents' (RNQ 79; a view he attributes to Bosanquet 1888: i, 116). In consequence 'quantity becomes essentially measure—using this word to mean any sort of quantitative comparison' (RNQ 79). The antinomy of quantities is immediately resolved, for it is now admitted that quantities have no intrinsic nature, but are purely relational. Russell also finds confirmation for his view of extensive quantity in the new account: for the terms of quantitative judgements (quantities) are purely relational and thus differences between such terms, being also relational, are of the same type as the terms themselves. This is the defining feature of extensive quantities (RNQ 80).

In so far as quantities are considered as contents without comparison they will be, presumably, intensive quantities. Thus the distinction between extensive and intensive quantities which had previously bulked so large is almost eroded away, for any quantitative thing may now be regarded as involving either intensive or extensive quantity. Again, this is a view that Russell was groping towards in SDCQ. It seems in many ways a natural conclusion from his position there, but not one that he explicitly states (see above, pp. 245, 249). Regarded in isolation quantity is adjectival, intensive, and unmeasurable; regarded in comparison with other quantities it is relational, extensive, and measurable (RNQ 80–1). 'The reduction of extensive to intensive quantities', Russell says, 'still holds good' but 'the two do not differ logically, but only in the manner in which they are given' (RNQ 80). The distinction, it seems, between adjectives and relations is not a large one. The present account also explains, quite nicely, why measurement of quantity always reduces to measurement of extensive quantity; first, measurement is purely comparative and therefore relational, and second, arithmetic operations such as division and addition, which are essential for numerical treatment, cannot be defined on intensive quantities. By contrast, a range of extensive quantities is closed under addition and division—a point which Russell made more of in the following year (see § 6.5).

It would seem that Russell's latest account resolves the problems that afflicted his earlier account of quantity. Certainly the chaotic nature of SDCQ is replaced by a relatively straightforward and clear account. But, as often happens in such systems, the contradictions which might seem to have been avoided have, in fact, been merely transferred. In closing RNQ Russell claims that the contradictions previously found in quantity are now to be found in the concept of measurement. The contradictions which now emerge turn out to precursors of the important contradictions of relativity which marked the last stages of Russell's dialectical work (see § 8.1).

In RNQ the antinomy of quantity, considered now as *measured* quantity, makes its appearance for the first time. Russell can arrive at it by a fairly direct argument as follows: (1) 'two things which differ quantitatively do not differ conceptually in anything except quantity'; (2) 'quantity is not an inherent conceptual property of quantitative things'; therefore (3) 'two things which only differ quantitatively do not differ in the conceptions applicable to them'; so (4) in a quantitative judgement 'we have a conception of difference without a difference of conception' (RNQ 81).[33] Russell regards (4) as a paradoxical conclusion, since he holds that two things which are conceptually identical must be exactly alike. There is a tendency in Russell's statement of the argument to muddle 'conceptual' with 'intrinsic', and it is important not to muddle them if the nature of the contradiction is to be clear. Many things (e.g. quantity itself) are conceptual for Russell, even though they are relational. So when Russell says that in difference of quantity we have a 'conception of difference without a difference of conception' we might suppose him merely mistaken, for we have difference of quantity which is conceptual and thus we have difference of conception. In fact, however, Russell is using 'conceptual' in a narrower way, to cover only those concepts under which the item in question, *taken on its own* and not in relation, falls. These concepts represent its intrinsic properties.

We can now reconstruct Russell's argument. Suppose we have two different quantities of the same kind, *A* and *B*, e.g. two lengths. *Qua*

[33] See also the similar statements of the 'quantitative contradiction' in VN 24–5.

quantities they are exactly alike, except in so far as they differ in quantity. But quantity itself is not an intrinsic property of quantities. To establish this proposition was one of the main tasks of Russell's paper. Thus the difference in quantity between *A* and *B* does not provide an intrinsic property that the one of them has and the other has not. Thus there is no (intrinsic) conceptual difference between *A* and *B*. But still the two differ, since they differ in quantity, and quantity is a concept, though not a concept intrinsic to either *A* or *B*. Thus on the one hand we have a conception of the difference of *A* and *B*, while on the other we have no difference in the intrinsic concepts which apply to either of them. We have, clearly, yet another analogue of the paradox of the point. The result seems innocuous, because what it amounts to is that we have two things which are similar in all intrinsic properties but differ in their relations. It becomes paradoxical only because of Russell's neo-Hegelian assumption that two different things must differ in their intrinsic, or internal, properties and not merely in relations. This assumption is the doctrine of internal relations as Russell held it during his neo-Hegelian period. It was in the course of trying to resolve the quantitative paradox, and its analogues, that Russell came to abandon the doctrine of internal relations. Once that has gone it becomes immediately apparent that there is no contradiction in supposing that things (such as points) which are similar as far as their internal properties are concerned may yet differ as regards their external relations.

## 6.5 'ON QUANTITY'

The antinomy of quantity with which Russell concluded RNQ was joined in 1898 by a companion, the antinomy of quality, which Russell described as follows:

In *quality* . . . we have a difference of conception without a conception of difference. This is best seen by taking quality pure, as it occurs in the categories. The content of two categories differs, and the whole difference is a difference of content. Nevertheless, the difference is not itself content: no conception exists by which the difference can be described. Suppose, e.g., that *all* the categories have been discovered; they all differ *inter se*, and the difference between any two is different from that between any other two. Nevertheless no category remains by which this difference can be described. (VN 24–5.)[34]

The neat symmetry of his dual antinomies suggested to Russell, however vaguely, a neo-Hegelian way out of the impasse. Quantity and quality were two sides of a dialectical whole. 'A world of pure categories involves a

---

[34] In the preceding note, dated 1 Jan. 1898, Russell had given the antinomy of quantity as 'the only unavoidable contradiction' in his dialectic (VN 24).

contradiction which is the precise counterpart of that involved in a world of pure quantities' (VN 25). The two must therefore be combined in the real which, as always, must be perfectly consistent. How this was to be achieved Russell wasn't sure. 'Can we say: Quality is mediacy immediately given, while quantity is mediated immediacy?' he suggested vaguely (VN 25). He took the matter little further than this, except for some sketchy mathematical notes (based on Whitehead's concept of a positional manifold) on the quantitative treatment of qualitative differences (OQ 134–5).

The antinomy of quality was part of logic.[35] The antinomy of quantity pervaded the rest of mathematics. He thought at first that arithmetic might be exempt (VN 25), but this hope proved illusory once signed numbers were considered. The antinomy of quantity was an important insight for Russell in organizing that part of his dialectic of the sciences which dealt with pure mathematics. With the antinomy of quantity in hand he felt he was in a position to embark on a major reconstruction of the philosophy of mathematics. His initial plans for this took the form of a book to be called 'On Quantity and Allied Conceptions: An Enquiry into the Subject-Matter of Mathematics', of which he left an outline (VN 25–6), plus two chapters, and a few rough notes and fragments (collected together as OQ). The outline is taken up with two lists of mathematical ideas. In the longer of the two, the ideas are classified as ideas of number, quantity, or quality of differing types. The other list gives the ideas which philosophical analysis reveals to be fundamental to mathematics. The extent to which Russell's thinking at this time was organized by the dual antinomies of quantity and quality is revealed in the longer list. Although Russell says that this list is drawn 'from the mathematical side', the four types of quantity and two types of quality into which he classifies mathematical concepts clearly owe more to the antinomies than they do to mathematical practice. None the less, Russell gives no indication in the outline as to how the antinomies are to be resolved.

More revealing is the list from the philosophical side. Russell there identifies the manifold and the continuum as the two fundamental ideas of pure mathematics. Significantly, these two were generally regarded as the fundamental ideas of the quantity view. The former, he says, is to be found throughout mathematics while the latter arises first in the calculus. Significantly, he considered the concepts of series and order to be '[s]ubordinate ideas of importance': their importance increased as his work progressed, especially after OQ had been abandoned. Again it is significant that, at this stage, these two concepts were treated independently. In identifying the manifold and the continuum as the two fundamental concepts, Russell reveals some development in his thought about the philosophy of pure

---

[35] See VN 25. Interestingly, Russell already regarded 'the logical Calculus' (by which he meant the Boolean algebra of Whitehead 1898*a*) as part of mathematics.

mathematics over SDCQ and RNQ. Between RNQ and OQ there is little evidence of Russell's thinking on pure mathematics; if any intermediate papers were written, they have not survived. None the less, it is not difficult to infer how his thought developed.

The concept of a manifold had long figured in Russell's philosophy of geometry, in particular as a term for collections of whatever was given in intuition. In this role its use stemmed from Kant and Riemann. In OQ, however, it takes on a somewhat different role, derived more from Grassmann and Whitehead. (Cantor's role in this development was probably minimal.) In 1898 Russell came to see both numbers and quantities as constituting manifolds on which algebraic operations could be defined. These manifolds, which form the subject-matter of mathematics, have to be of a special kind, in that they have to admit the possibility of an operation which Russell variously calls addition or synthesis. The requirement is that any number of terms in the manifold must be capable of being combined to form a new term of the same manifold (VN 26). Such manifolds had been called positional manifolds by Whitehead (1898*a*: 30). It is clear from the conclusions of the previous section that Russell thought that the manifold of extensive quantities is a positional manifold while that of intensive quantities is not. It seems therefore that pure mathematics, at least as far as arithmetical algebra was concerned, could be regarded as the science of positional manifolds.[36] For other branches of pure mathematics (e.g. the logical calculus) different kinds of manifold were needed. It seems unlikely that Russell thought mathematics was the science of manifolds, for the continuum plays an independent role in Russell's account of mathematics. Whereas nowadays we would regard continua as special types of manifold, it seems that Russell held that all manifolds were discrete.

That Russell should have regarded the concept of the continuum as the second main concept of mathematics suggests rather more of a turnabout in his thinking. In SDCQ we have seen Russell as an advocate of atomism at every level. He then regarded continua as inherently contradictory, and intelligible only when assumed to be discrete. Moreover, he thought then that there was a fundamental incompatibility between the concept of number, which was discrete, and that of continuity. On first reading RNQ seems to offer little change of position. He continues to argue that the concept of quantity is contradictory, and 'quantity' for Russell always designates continuous quantity. However, as we have seen, the arguments against quantity in RNQ have little or nothing to do with continuity. This fact is not advertised in RNQ, and one may wonder whether Russell really

---

[36] Russell says little in OQ about kinds of arithmetic operations other than addition. Presumably he intended to show how the other operations could be defined on a manifold closed under addition.

appreciated it when he wrote the paper. For it belies the paper's opening paragraph in which Russell maintains that his main concern will be the concept of continuity. It is possible he thought that in showing quantity to be inconsistent he had thereby shown continuity to be inconsistent, without realizing that he had established the former without any reference to continuity. Moreover, there is no reason to suppose that when Russell wrote RNQ, early in 1897, he was any more sympathetic to continua than he had been in 1896. By 1898, however, he simply accepted the continuum as a fundamental concept of mathematics without giving any indication that it might be a source of antinomies. The parts of OQ in which he dealt with the number continuum have not survived, so we cannot be quite sure that the concept did not lead to fresh antinomies. But we can be sure that, even if it did, they must have been antinomies that were resolvable within the treatment of the number continuum itself, for they are not referred to in later parts of the book. (Unlike the antinomy of quantity which is constantly appealed to.) But even if Russell did not regard the continuum as contradictory, he could hardly have regarded it as unproblematic. Unfortunately, the loss of the relevant manuscripts makes it impossible to tell how he might have dealt with, for example, Zeno's paradoxes or the foundations of the calculus. Yet it is clear from references in the surviving parts of the book that Russell no longer felt that these problems were the most fundamental in mathematics.

It is tempting to suppose that Russell's new attitude to continuity was the result of his reading Dedekind (1872)[37] and Couturat (1896) between writing SDCQ and OQ, and, perhaps, of a reconsideration of his earlier reading of Cantor (1883*b*). But, as we shall see, Russell, to judge from the surviving parts of OQ, seems to have learnt depressingly little from this reading. It is true there are no longer the gross errors about derivatives and limits that disgraced SDCQ, but he still has no account to offer of irrationals and, in fact, has not yet acquired the modern notion of mathematical continuity. He was not helped by the fact that Couturat, who was his main source of information, had made an important mistake in his definition of continuity (Couturat 1896: 416) which Russell had correctly criticized in his review (1897*f*: 64–5). On 4 May 1898, shortly after Russell had written OQ, Couturat had written to Russell with a correction. Russell remained doubtful, though he did admit he had 'not yet had the leisure to examine [the] question'.[38] All this suggests that his changed attitude toward continua was not the result of a greater appreciation of recent advances in the mathematical treatment of continuity, but stemmed from his change of physical theory in 1897 (see § 5.2). When Russell adopted the plenal theory of matter in 1897, it was clear his attitude to continua would have to change. Whether Russell

---

[37] He also read Dedekind (1878) in Apr. 1898. But this was probably after he wrote OQ.
[38] B. R. to L. Couturat, 12 May 1898. See *Papers*, ii, A64: 31–6.

had grounds in 1898 for thinking continua were less problematic than he had
previously supposed them is something of which we cannot be sure. It is
possible that in the missing parts of OQ he found some way of resolving the
problems. But it seems more likely that he simply ignored the difficulties
while he got on with other things. In this, his manner of proceeding would
not have been unlike that of earlier mathematicians who continued to use
the calculus before modern analysis had resolved its foundational difficulties. It
seems puzzling at first sight why Russell, having dismissed Cantor's work so
scathingly in 1896, should none the less have returned to it three years later
and discovered what a remarkable advance it was. The answer lies, rather
unexpectedly, in his physics, which suggested in 1897 that continuity was not
a concept that could be easily abandoned, whatever its difficulties.

It is difficult to know exactly what view Russell took of what he called the
number continuum in OQ, for the parts of the book that dealt with these
topics have been lost. We have only a few backward references to go by. But
there are sufficient to reveal some curious changes in his position and some
respects (equally curious) in which his position had not changed, despite
what appear now to be glaring inadequacies. It is especially unfortunate that
Russell's treatment of number is missing from OQ and that his position has
to be inferred from scattered, ambiguous, and inconclusive remarks. For
these remarks reveal that Russell was no longer entirely happy with the ratio
theory of number. Russell continued to accept the ratio theory for a wide
range of cases which involved counting and fractions. Such numbers continued
to be relational, to give a ratio between the unit and the collection. But even
here, as occasional remarks in OQ reveal, he found a range of exceptions to
the ratio theory, cases where the cardinal number of a class did not represent
a relation, namely those in which there was a 'natural unit' which could be
used for counting. In such cases, where the collection is a collection of so
many natural units, the number is an 'intrinsic adjective' of the collection,
and not a 'mere relation' (OQ 129). In 'An Analysis of Mathematical
Reasoning' later the same year, the use of such adjectival cardinal numbers
is confined to cases where the thing taken as unit is indivisible (AMR 211).[39]
But there were other uses of numbers, which Russell was beginning to
consider only in 1898, which forced a further restriction of the ratio theory.
These were cases in which numbers were ordered according to magnitude.
In this, the numbers themselves were terms of relations. The ratio view
would have to regard them in this case as hypostatized relations. But this
view was unacceptable to Russell in 'An Analysis of Mathematical Reasoning'

---

[39] It is possible, though I believe doubtful, that in OQ Russell used 'natural unit' to apply
only to things which were indivisible. At all events, the pages in which he explained his
terminology are missing. The admission of natural units of any kind represents a retreat from
the Bradleian position that had informed his earlier work.

as a result of much broader changes in his philosophy (see § 7.3). As a result he came to view the ordinal numbers as unanalysable adjectival terms or contents. (Again, details of the new view are missing.) It seems quite clear, however, that by the middle of 1898 Russell had come to recognize two kinds of number, adjectival and relational, and that these two classes corresponded roughly to the ordinal and cardinal numbers.

The rational fractions are generated in OQ in much the same way as in SDCQ and RNQ. We choose a unit, $A$, and form by addition a series of multiples of this unit, $A, 2A, 3A, \ldots nA, \ldots$ Any such multiple of $A$ would serve equally well as a unit, so a new unit $B = nA$ can be introduced. Thus we obtain the fractions $A = (1/n)B, 2A = (2/n)B$, etc. Between any two such fractions we can define any number of fractions, since the numerator and denominator may be made as large as we like (OQ 117–18). This apparently constitutes the continuity of the number continuum so far as Russell was concerned. Of course, it still leaves no room for the irrational numbers and Russell's thinking on mathematical continuity seems not to have progressed very far from what he had written on the topic in 1896 and 1897.

Russell, of course, was well aware of the problem of irrationals, but regarded it as arising entirely out of the treatment of quantity (especially in geometry). Originally in 1896 he regarded the sequence of numbers as discrete, since quantity itself was discrete, different quantities being distinguished by finite differences. There was thus no need in the mathematical treatment of quantity for a dense sequence of numbers. Any attempt to provide one would involve philosophically inadmissible infinitesimals. By 1898 he realized that the sequence of rational fractions can be dense without appeal to infinitesimals. The sequence of rational fractions he now calls the number continuum. But as Euclid's proof of the irrationality of $\sqrt{2}$ had shown, there were quantities to which no rational number corresponded. Russell in 1898 still takes this proof to show that there is *no number* which corresponds to such quantities. Pushed no doubt by his plenal theory of matter, Russell now admits the existence of such quantities and thus that quantities form a continuum in a stronger sense than numbers. Hence his remark that scalar quantity involves continuity 'more completely than in the number continuum' (VN 25). In view of his position on the number continuum this remark looks like a valuable insight, even though what is still needed is a realization that the continuum of scalar quantities can be treated purely arithmetically, that irrational numbers could in fact be defined by arithmetic means. But it is not an insight which bears much fruit in the extant discussion of scalar quantity. In the end Russell seems content to admit as elements of a quantitative manifold all and *only* quantities $nA$, where $A$ is a unit and $n$ a rational number (OQ 119). What then becomes of quantities which correspond to $\sqrt{2}$, for example, is left unexamined.

The dense sequence of rational numbers which Russell calls the number continuum is, however, achieved without appeal to either infinitesimal elements or infinite division. That new fractions can be inserted between any two given fractions is established by appeal to the fact that the units can be made arbitrarily small, rather than infinitesimal. This, at least, was an advance and one derived from his improved understanding of limits. Moreover, although Russell doesn't appeal to quantity of any kind in the definition of the rationals, he does correlate the sequence of rationals with an intensive continuum. For an intensive continuum, he now maintains, can be defined by the fact 'that its terms can be arranged in a definite order, and that between any two of these terms it is always possible to insert as many more as we please' (OQ 118). Thus the number continuum is an intensive continuum (cf. VN 25). This fits well with the position that suggested itself in RNQ, namely that the contradictions of extensive quantity could be avoided by refusing falsely to hypostatize relations and adjectives, thereby dealing only with intensive quantities. What blocked this move was the dependence of intensive upon extensive quantity if measurement was to be possible. As things stand in OQ intensive quantities themselves are directly amenable to numerical treatment. (I shall discuss how shortly.) This in turn fits well with the requirement of Russell's transition from physics to psychology which (as we saw in § 5.3) required that intensive quantities be capable of measurement without reference to extensive quantities. What it doesn't fit with is the claim in *EFG* that a metricizable space (i.e. an extensive continuum) is necessary if measurement is to be possible.

The number continuum, developed this way, makes use only of the arithmetic feature of addition, that any two elements in a manifold can be combined to form a third of the same manifold. It is this very feature, Russell argues (OQ 118–19), which makes the number continuum so construed useless for measurement unless the concept of quantity is added. For if we take each unit used for counting as an element of the manifold then the synthesis of any two will result in a third equally valid for counting. All we have so far is a collection of elements, $a_1$, $a_2$, etc., all of which have the property $M$, the defining property of the manifold (e.g. the property of being a region of space) in common. We have, therefore, using modern functional notation, $M(a_1)$, $M(a_2)$, etc. But the arithmetic feature of addition ensures that if $M(a_i)$ and $M(a_k)$ then $M(a_i + a_k)$, where '$a_i + a_k$' represents the synthesis or addition of $a_i$ and $a_k$. (For example, the synthesis of any two regions of space is itself a region of space.) Since on Russell's account so far anything which is $M$ may count equally as a unit, it is obvious that the present account provides no basis for measurement (for 'region of space' is not an adequate basis for counting). What is needed is to introduce a new property $A$ which only some elements in the manifold share, intuitively the property of having a certain quantity, or being a quantity of a certain magnitude (cf. OQ 123). Those and only those elements which are $A$ can then count as units, and $A(a_i)$ and $A(a_k)$ will not in general imply $A(a_i + a_k)$. Selecting $A$ introduces the concept of quantitative equality which, Russell says, must be added to that of the number continuum in order to be able to measure quantity (OQ 117).

Russell argues briefly that $A$ must be a quantity and has a further argument to show that the antinomy of quantity is not avoided if quantity is introduced in this way (OQ 120–1). The latter argument runs as follows. Given a manifold containing an element $a$, pick out from the manifold all those elements which are equal to $a$. The resulting submanifold comprises those terms which have in common the quantity $A$, which then becomes the defining property of the submanifold. But our choice of $a$ as unit was arbitrary, so alternative choices, say of $b$, are possible. Starting from $b$ gives a different submanifold comprising all elements which are equal to $b$, i.e. those which have the quantity $B$. How then are the elements of the first submanifold to be distinguished from those of the second? By the fact that the former have to $a$ the relation that the latter have to $b$. But how then are $a$ and $b$ themselves to be distingushed? By the fact that the two are not equal. But that is merely a relational property. If we say that the $a$s have the quantity $A$ and the $b$s the quantity $B$ we are merely returning in a circle, because the quantitative properties $A$ and $B$ were initially distinguished by means of the $a$s and $b$s.[40] Therefore, there is still no intrinsic characterization of quantity of the sort that Russell thought ought to be forthcoming.

Hitherto relations have played a very limited role in Russell's philosophy. He has not previously recognized, for example, that relations may be of different types and have different formal properties. It is surprising therefore to find him coming very close to a definition by abstraction in his attempt to break out of the circle just described. His problem is this: to find a non-circular definition of the quantity $A$ just described. Using the notion of quantitative equality, he can find a class of all elements of the manifold which are quantitatively equal to a reference element $a$. Putting his point in anachronistic modern terms, he has recognized that quantitative equality is an equivalence relation and that it partitions the manifold into a set of equivalence classes. Now he could have gone on to *define* the quantity $A$ as the class of all elements in the manifold that were quantitatively equal to $a$. This would have been a genuine definition by abstraction. Russell, however,

[40] This argument is, in fact, a special case of some contemporary puzzles about identity criteria. Consider e.g. the spatio-temporal criterion for the identity of material bodies. Body $a$ and body $b$ are said to be identical if they occupy all and only the same spatio-temporal points. Yet whether or not two spatio-temporal points are identical will depend upon whether they have the same relations to the same material bodies.

merely claims that 'the properties of equality suggest that two equal things have a common adjective' (OQ 121). Moreover, he ultimately rejects this attempt to dispel the antinomy of quantity, though, again, his reasons are interesting. It is not that such an attempt involves the use of relations, but that it needs the wrong type of relations. He seems prepared to admit that the antinomy of quantity could be resolved if the concept of a particular quantity could be introduced by means of equality only. But Russell denies that this is possible (OQ 121–2). For, if equality can be used to define an intrinsic quality of the things which are equal, the quantitative properties *A* and *B* can be defined by means of their respective equivalence classes, but the members of different equivalence classes can be distinguished only by means of the relations *greater than* or *less than*, which are not equivalence relations and therefore do not give intrinsic conceptual differences by means of which *a* and *b* (say) can be distinguished. This result, however, does not undermine Russell's claim that all that is needed for dealing with extensive quantity is the number continuum together with the idea of equality. For the number continuum itself contains the ideas of *greater than* and *less than*, or rather effective surrogates for them.

The other extant chapter of OQ is on quantity with distinction of sign. This chapter will be discussed in detail in § 8.4, since it is one of a series of attempts by Russell to treat sign. Together, they raise problems for Russell about the nature of relations which he had not previously had to face. These, in turn, formed an important part of the problematic which led Russell to abandon neo-Hegelianism. The role that sign played in this development can only be appreciated, however, when other aspects of the problematic are in place. None the less, the treatment of sign in OQ is worth a brief consideration here, because it offers a partial summing up of Russell's dialectic of the sciences.

One of the conclusions Russell draws in this chapter is that in many manifolds whose elements are capable of sign every element can be exhibited as a difference of two others. I shall call this the thesis of relative specification. It introduces what Russell calls 'a quite hopeless relativity' (OQ 133), which is unique to sign. The chapter on signed quantity ends with Russell's attempts to minimize this relativity. He does so by associating signed magnitudes with spatial or temporal quantities. Magnitudes, he notes, may be regarded not just as differences between other magnitudes, but as 'differences between terms not themselves magnitudes—e.g. positions in space—which have conceptual differences while not differing conceptually' (OQ 133). This, I think, can be seen as an attempt to reduce what might be termed the special relativity of quantities (or magnitudes) which results from the thesis of relative specification to analogues of the original antinomy of quantity, in fact to the antinomy of the point which is found in geometry.

Russell's approach is characteristically neo-Hegelian: the special relativity of quantity is to be resolved by moving outside the realm of pure quantity through the introduction of new concepts, in this case spatial and temporal concepts.

Thus some at least of the antinomies of pure mathematics can be transformed into antinomies of geometry, once the concept of space is introduced. These antinomies, in turn, require a transition to physics for resolution. We have at this point as full and as unified an account as it seems possible now to construct of Russell's dialectic of the sciences. At this stage, however, Russell's thought takes a new turn. In the first place he seems to have been convinced, largely though the arguments of G. E. Moore, that his philosophy was still not entirely free of psychologism. This led him to adopt a radical realism—'absolute realism' as Nelson (1967: 373) calls it—of the sort to be found in *POM* and in Moore's early works (especially Moore 1899*a*). At the same time, he was led to a more systematic study of the contradictions in his dialectic and the logical principles on which they depended. The first of these two developments is my concern in the next chapter.

# 7

# Logic

## 7.1 'AN ANALYSIS OF MATHEMATICAL REASONING': LOGICAL ASPECTS

Of all Russell's extant attempts to treat the fundamental concepts of pure mathematics in the period 1896–8, the most extended is 'An Analysis of Mathematical Reasoning' (AMR), written in the middle of 1898. It marks the culmination of Russell's attempts to fashion a Kantian philosophy of pure mathematics in which the concept of quantity played a central role. Russell, at least at the outset, was still quite explicitly Kantian. On 3 June 1898 he wrote to Couturat that he was 'asking the question from the *Prolegomena*, "Wie ist reine Mathematik möglich?" I am preparing a work of which this question could be the title, and in which the results will, I think be for the most part purely Kantian'. Yet the drafts of AMR which have survived show less sign of Kant's influence than this would suggest. AMR was not simply the culmination of his earlier work, for Russell's position had begun to change. In the same letter to Couturat he had said: 'To be frank, I have changed much in my philosophy since I wrote my book [*EFG*] and I no longer have any opinions of the truth of which I am certain. This scepticism makes it difficult to defend an opinion as sharply as I did in my book'. And in another letter to Couturat, written the previous month but also referring to AMR, Russell told him:

At present I am occupied in amplifying, and at several points modifying, the theory that I sketched in my article [RNQ]. I believe I can connect number and quantity . . . by using the idea of relation. In this, I would have a more continuous development of mathematical ideas. But everything I think on this subject remains at present in a tentative and provisional state.[1]

'An Analysis of Mathematical Reasoning' was obviously intended to be a substantial work, even though its exact extent is hard to determine since its table of contents and introduction are at odds on the matter, and only a few chapters and parts of others survive. According to the table of contents it was to be divided into four books dealing, respectively, with 'The Manifold', 'Number', 'Quantity', and 'The Infinitesimal Calculus'.[2] According to the

---

[1] B. R. to L. Couturat, 12 May 1898.
[2] See *Papers*, ii, 155–61, for a full account of what is known of the composition of this work. The table of contents is published in *Papers*, ii, 154. All references in this chapter will be to the

introduction these topics were to be followed by treatments of geometry and what is described as 'a kind of generalized Dynamics', both to be followed by a concluding discussion of concepts required by all mathematics and the special concepts required by its specialized branches, together with an elucidation of 'the general nature of any subject-matter which can be dealt with mathematically', which presumably amounted to an account of the a priori conditions under which mathematics is possible (p. 165). On the table of contents Russell wrote '[This MS. was finished, July 1898]', but it is not known whether he meant the manuscript as described in the table of contents or that described in the introduction. The manuscript was preceded by an earlier draft and followed by a typescript. Parts of both have survived and show a considerable amount of revision between the three versions.

It is interesting that, despite the effort that went into OQ, Russell should still have felt dissatisfied on fundamental matters. AMR was certainly an attempt to dispel his confusion. The root cause of his dissatisfaction is not hard to find. In March 1898 he had finished reading Whitehead (1898a), a work which, I suspect, gave him for the first time an overall view of the systematic unity of (a large part of) modern mathematics. The *Universal Algebra* was a work he couldn't ignore, and not just because Whitehead had been his teacher. (Russell is thanked in Whitehead's preface, 1898a: p. xi, for helping with the proofs, 'especially in the parts connected with Non-Euclidean Geometry', so Russell had read at least part of the book before publication.) The first step in Russell's dialectical treatment of a science was to identify its fundamental principles. This treatment could hardly begin, therefore, in the case of sciences that had not already achieved a considerable degree of unification, expressed through an axiomatic formulation. I use the term 'axiomatic' loosely here. It should not be taken to imply anything approaching a modern conception of rigour, but merely the expectation or hope that the entire science could be shown to depend (in some none too rigorous sense) upon some small set of postulates. (In 1898 Russell would hardly have been in a position to appreciate the sort of rigour Hilbert brought to Euclidean geometry, for example, though a year later things would be different.) None the less, some degree of axiomatization was essential to Russell's purposes, and we have already seen the difficulties he got into with projective geometry because he ignored Pasch's axiomatization. Whitehead's work on algebra probably seemed to Russell in 1898 comparable to the unification of metric geometries provided by projective geometry. Although Russell had apparently attempted to incorporate elements of Whitehead's work into OQ, it is not surprising that he abandoned this attempt and started afresh with a new work on pure mathematics.

main MS of AMR, unless otherwise noted. References to the TS will be indicated, as elsewhere, by AMR/TS.

Yet, at the same time, Whitehead's book did not itself provide everything Russell needed. It is immediately clear that Whitehead in the *Universal Algebra* had provided his system with no philosophical foundation which Russell could find acceptable. In somewhat later writings Russell made explicit a distinction between a mathematical and a philosophical approach to mathematical concepts (AOG 410–12). The mathematician is concerned to assert relationships between these concepts, the philosopher is concerned to discover what the concepts themselves mean. (This distinction also underlies his remarks on the purpose of philosophy of mathematics in the preface to *POM*.) It is clear that, from the perspective of this distinction, Whitehead had virtually nothing to say about the philosophy of mathematics in the *Universal Algebra*. Whitehead's fundamental concepts—manifold, element of a manifold, the intensity of an element, and various operations upon elements—were little more than generic names which applied to whatever kind of item might be needed if it was to be supposed that the mathematical symbols applied to anything at all. If a philosophy of mathematics is to be extracted from the *Universal Algebra* at all, it would have to be some kind of formalism. Although, this may have inclined Russell to formalism, as exhibited in his treatment of projective geometry in AOG, it cannot have done so in 1898. Russell may well have embarked on AMR thinking that his own philosophy would supply what was needed. But, in the end, as Russell's letters to Couturat indicate, it would take more than a new book along old lines to provide a philosophically satisfactory account of mathematical knowledge. The need to do justice to Whitehead's algebra strained Russell's fundamentally Kantian approach to pure mathematics to breaking point.

AMR is not exactly the first work of a new approach to the problems of mathematics, nor yet the last work of the old approach. In a sense, it is both in one. When Russell wrote it he still had not achieved the philosophical breakthrough that would provide him with a satisfactory foundation for mathematics. The key element in that breakthrough would be a new theory of relations, which he did not embrace fully until the end of 1898.

AMR starts from the point at which *EFG* left off, with what we called (above, § 4.8) the proto-relations of identity and diversity, to which he now adds a new proto-relation, unity. In AMR Russell treats identity, diversity, and unity as determinables, each with different determinate varieties. There are thus different types of identity, diversity, and unity, and various combinations of these are involved in forming the complex unities with which mathematics deals.[3] For example, the type of unity which is exemplified by many terms forming a manifold (also called a class or extension, p. 170) is

---

[3] Russell does not provide a full listing of proto-relations, nor even supply a taxonomy of them. His technique is rather to note them as they crop up in discussion. In fact, despite their fundamental nature, Russell's account of them remains underdeveloped.

recognized as 'especially fundamental in all mathematical knowledge' (p. 167).

Russell's aim in AMR is to discover the a priori foundations of mathematics, the basic concepts and propositions[4] on which mathematics depends. The results, as he told Couturat, are still in a sense Kantian, since, he claims, most[5] of the basic concepts in mathematics are those 'which express some aspect or property of space or time or both, or of whatever is in space or time' (p. 164). But appearances are misleading for the account Russell gives of the universality of these concepts and of the necessity of judgements concerning them is distinctly non-Kantian. Concepts which have this connection to space and time Russell calls *categories of intuition*, to be contrasted, on the one hand, with *pure categories*, which have no reference to space or time or spatio-temporal things, and on the other, with *empirical concepts*, which apply to the data of sense (pp. 164–5). The concepts of mathematics, therefore, have a special intermediate status between the concepts of pure logic and those of the empirical sciences.

Russell uses the term 'category' to indicate only those concepts which are fundamental, i.e. not reducible to others. (Thus quantity on the no-reduction view discussed in § 6.4 would be a category.) Russell is at pains to point out (as he was later in the preface to *POM*: p. xv) that the pure categories cannot be defined, and that, although each one of them carries 'an unanalysable and intuitively apprehended meaning', its meaning is only of heuristic importance and is 'logically irrelevant' (p. 163). It seems clear that, even this early, Russell had the view that logic was concerned only with the *form* of propositions (or the formal relations of concepts) not with their *content* or meaning (for later explanations of his view, cf. *POM* 7–8). Along with the classes of basic concepts there are classes of basic propositions, which he also calls 'axioms', 'major premisses', and 'rules of inference' (p. 163).[6] Although Russell doesn't actually present his axioms in what we have of AMR it would seem that all of them are to be of implicational form, asserting necessary connections between concepts (with a couple of exceptions this is also the case in *POM*). The basic propositions are unprovable even though their truth can be apprehended.

Russell concludes the introduction with his plan of investigation and its

---

[4] Like other neo-Hegelians, Russell still uses the term 'judgment' for what he would later call a 'proposition'. Moore, by contrast, used 'proposition' in his fellowship dissertation of 1898, although with some misgivings on account of its linguistic and psychological connotations (Moore 1898*a*: ch. 2, fo. 2). He thought 'judgment' was 'even worse' (ibid.).

[5] The exceptions are the concepts of arithmetic (p. 165).

[6] Less justifiably, Russell continued to call axioms 'rules of inference' in *POM*. The modern distinction between the two is attributed to Frege (1879), but, like most of Frege's ideas, had not passed into wide circulation. The absence of a clear terminological distinction between them in *POM* is indicative of much less confusion than is commonly thought, however.

results. These two paragraphs are worth quoting at length because many of the results he mentions do not appear in the extant manuscript:

First will come the general theory of the *extension of concepts*, dealt with by the Logical Calculus; then the more special theory of *cardinal number*, arising out of the above, and dealt with by Arithmetic; next the theory of *ordinal number*, which specializes by distinguishing between the units making up a cardinal number. From this I shall pass to *pure quantity*, which is not dealt with at all by Mathematics, but which is essential to all its spatio-temporal applications. From pure quantity I shall proceed to *extensive quantity*, discussing the application of number and the distinction of sign. This will lead to *Zero and Infinity*, and a discussion of the Differential Calculus, which will be found to depend on the *extensive continuum*. This will bring us to Geometry, in which I shall discuss first *order, dimensions*, and *distinctions of quality* in an extensive continuum—the ideas dealt with by projective Geometry. I shall proceed to a new consideration of extensive quantity, more closely related than before to the idea of the extensive continuum. This will lead to a consideration of the *thing* in space or time, and hence to the mathematical principles of a kind of generalized Dynamics. (p. 165.)

Having outlined this very substantial body of work, which apparently includes a reconsideration of the work he had published on geometry only the previous year, Russell goes on to list the (for the most part) indefinable concepts on which he finds mathematics as a whole and its various specialized branches to be based:

The Manifold and addition, which are used throughout; Number, which is first introduced in Arithmetic; Order, which is introduced with the ordinal numbers; the relations of equal, greater and less, which constitute quantity; the extensive continuum, which distinguishes extensive from intensive quantity; the idea of dimensions; and the idea of *thing*, which is vaguely present throughout, but is not explicitly introduced till we come to Dynamics. (pp. 165–6.)

Finally he mentions the 'contradiction of relativity', a generalization of the antinomy of quantity, 'to be found in almost every part of mathematics' (p. 166).

One thing that doesn't emerge clearly from what we have of AMR is what relation Russell thought there was between mathematics and symbolic logic. He did not believe that classical mathematics or even arithmetic could be derived from logic. In fact, in one respect AMR marks something of a step away from logicism, for Russell states that the concept of number itself and the concepts of individual numbers are 'incapable of analysis or derivation' (p. 196). In earlier works SDCQ and RNQ, as we have seen, there is at least some suggestion that number can be derived from an abstract notion of an instance of a concept. In AMR he is careful to note that they 'are not properties abstracted from collections of terms, but are logically independent contents . . . Numbers . . . are not qualities abstracted from sense . . . but are primarily pure conceptions' (pp. 199–200). None the less, since symbolic logic is the main topic of Book I, the table of contents, in this respect, gives the impression that the work is closer to logicism than is the case. Nor can it be claimed that symbolic logic appears in a work on mathematical *reasoning* in order simply to supply a theory of reasoning which could be used, for example, in reconstructing mathematical proofs. There is no attempt to use it in that way in AMR, nor indeed in any of Russell's works until after he had learnt of Peano's work in 1900.[7] Russell himself implies that the manuscripts he wrote before he discovered Peano's work made no contribution to what he called 'the grammar of arithmetic' (*MPD* 66). The symbolic logic to which he refers in AMR had little in common with the elaborate syntactical system of Peano. It was, in fact, good old Boolean algebra, as presented by Whitehead (1898*a*: Bk. II), and construed as a general theory of manifolds.

It seems altogether probable that Russell originally hoped to give an account somewhat along the following lines. His investigation of mathematics prior to writing AMR had shown him that the concept of a manifold was fundamental throughout mathematics (cf. VN 25–6). The logical calculus was then introduced in AMR as a theory of manifolds.[8] The logical calculus, as presented by Whitehead, offered a short-cut through the first stage of Russell's two-stroke transcendental deduction, the analysis of a theory to reveal its fundamental postulates. The second stage still needed to be accomplished, namely the transcendental deduction of those postulates as necessary conditions for some form of experience, in this case, for judgement. Thus Book I of AMR begins with chapters on 'The Elements of Judgments' and 'Subject and Predicate'. Yet Russell does not call his argument 'transcendental' and, despite the account he gave to Couturat of his work, there are no explicitly Kantian references in the manuscript or typescript outside the introduction. In this and in other respects AMR represents Russell's philosophy in a state of profound transition.

From the point of view of this plan of attack, Book I of the 'Analysis' has an agreeable symmetry. The first two chapters analyse judgements and lead to the concept of the manifold, which concerns chapter 3. The final two chapters then develop the principles of a theory of manifolds. Unfortunately, this simple scheme went rather badly astray. In the first place, in the sense in which Russell conceived manifolds, and in which he thought they were required for judgements, symbolic logic turned out not to be a theory of manifolds at all, but a theory of what Russell called 'assemblages'. In the second place, the sorts of operations which Russell's theory of judgement required on elements of judgements were not the Boolean join, meet, and

[7] B. R. to P. E. B. Jourdain, 15 Apr. 1910 (Grattan-Guinness 1977: 133).

[8] It is significant, I think, that Russell changed the title of Book I of AMR from 'The Logical Calculus' to 'The Manifold' (*Papers*, ii, 154).

complementation of the logical calculus. The root cause of both problems was one which has plagued classical logic ever since: the theory of judgement required that judgements be understood intensionally, while the symbolic logic of the day dealt only with extensions. It cannot be denied that in the analysis the philosophical base clashes disastrously with the mathematical superstructure. It was perhaps this clash, and the need it engendered for a new philosophical base (which Russell at the time could only glimpse), which led to Russell's confessions of doubt about his work to Couturat. My chief task, therefore, in this section is to explain in more detail how Russell's plans were undermined.

Although the first chapter of AMR is called 'The Elements of Judgment', it is largely taken up with a taxonomy of different kinds of judgement. This reflects no confusion on Russell's part. For Russell, it is the different types of judgement that reveal the different types of terms which compose them, rather than the other way about. The judgement (or proposition), not its constituent terms, is for Russell the basic unit.[9] The different types of element which compose judgements will in turn reveal the different specific forms of the three general proto-relations. On these, in turn, the various types of mathematical relations and operations will be based (p. 167).

The fundamental type of judgement is that of the traditional subject–predicate form. But it is certainly not the only kind. In fact, Russell claims that 'the vast majority of mathematical judgments, though sometimes capable of [subject–predicate] form, are essentially of various other kinds' (p. 167). Quite what kinds never fully emerges. Russell initially provides the following seven-fold classification: those in which a predicate is ascribed to a subject (S–P judgements); those in which two or more predicates are ascribed to a single subject (S–P–P judgements); those in which a single predicate is ascribed to two or more subjects (S–S–P judgements); judgements of intension, which assert that two or more predicates form a single predicate; judgements of extension, which assert that two or more subjects form a class; existential judgements; and pure judgements of intension, which assert necessary connections between predicates. Judgements of the first five kinds, Russell claims, are important for the theory of manifolds in Book I, while existential judgements and pure judgements of intension are not needed until later parts of the work (p. 173). But Russell's initial list is by no means complete: there are other judgements, some of importance in mathematics, which do not fall into any of his seven groups. Among the ones he mentions are those which ascribe a number to a collection, those asserting identity or

---

[9] See Pears (1967: 51–3) for a similar point made in connection with Russell's later philosophy, in particular the theory of descriptions. In this, as Pears points out, Russell's empiricism differed from Hume's, though even in 1898 it had a sizeable British tradition behind it (including Bradley 1883, Bosanquet 1888, and Mansel 1851).

difference, mathematical judgements which assert asymmetrical relations 'which are not based upon a discoverable point of difference or identity' (p. 172), and judgements of class-inclusion (p. 174).

The subject–predicate judgement introduces a number of the semantic distinctions that Russell needs. In the first place, in a subject–predicate judgement the subject occurs in a different way to the predicate which is ascribed to it. The predicate, Russell says, occurs as meaning (p. 174); the subject may be said to occur as reference or as a term. Yet the distinction between subjects and predicates is one of aspect only, for every predicate can be made a subject. Russell uses the word 'term' for '[w]hatever can be a logical subject' (p. 167; cf. *POM* 43). Thus subjects and predicates alike are terms, and terms take on the aspect of subject or predicate according to how they occur in a judgement, though only predicates are capable of taking on both aspects (p. 168; *POM* 45). An immediate consequence of this is that the subject of an S–P judgement does not have to be a thing, although things are terms which can only be subjects (p. 176). Indeed, Russell claims that '[e]very possible idea, everything that can be thought of, or represented by a word, may be a logical subject' (p. 168). A corollary is that not all terms exist,[10] but all of them have being: 'Being . . . belongs to whatever may be the subject in true judgments; and every possible idea, i.e. every idea which does not involve a contradiction, may be a logical subject' (p. 168). Terms which don't exist Russell calls 'contents'; these include all predicates but also such terms as 'any point', 'any moment', and 'thing',[11] which Russell (misleadingly) refers to as 'names for unspecified terms of specified classes' (pp. 176–7). In fact, they cannot be names since terms in general are not names. At the same time, however, they cannot be the unspecified terms themselves, for in that case, if the specified class were a class of existents, the unspecified member of the class would be an existent. Knowing how Russell's thought on the topic developed, we can suggest that what he ought

---

[10]   All things exist (cf. p. 171), but not all existents are things, for attributes (pp. 170–1) and some relations (pp. 171–2) exist and neither attributes nor relations are things. The important point is that there are no nonexistent things. (On p. 176 Russell, however, says that *existents* can only be subjects. It is not clear to me that this is a position he would want to defend for it conflicts with his claim that attributes can be predicated of a subject (p. 171). Though he does have the difficult view that a term has being only when it occurs as subject. See below.)

[11]   By the latter Russell apparently means either 'any thing' or 'a thing'. The distinctions Russell wishes to draw between the various locutions are not clear, but it seems that all of them would be better formalized by a Hilbert choice operator than by a particular quantifier. The use of quotation marks is unfortunate, since judgements are not sentences and predicates and subjects are not words. Russell, himself, does not supply any systematic notation which permits the mention of such non-linguistic items. In what follows I shall enclose mentioned judgements and mentioned predicates within slashes (as in Griffin 1980). Thus 'human' and 'Socrates' are words and 'Socrates is human' is a sentence: by contrast, /human/ and /Socrates/ are terms and /Socrates is human/ is a judgement (or proposition). In practice, the slashes in /Socrates/ are superfluous and will be omitted.

to have said was that such contents were *concepts* which denoted unspecified terms of specified classes. Russell's account of contents which are not predicates in AMR is the precursor of his theory of denoting concepts in *POM*. It may seem, especially to those who have read the very similar account of terms in *POM* in the light of Meinong's theory of objects, that Russell is countenancing nonexistent objects as logical subjects (though endowing them, as Meinong did not, with being, an *ersatz* existence). Certainly it is easy to read the remarks just quoted in this way. Yet I am inclined to regard this interpretation as a mistake (cf. Cocchiarella 1982). We need to know a little more about Russell's 1898 theory before my reasons will become fully apparent. But two preliminary points can be made. The first is that Russell at the time he wrote AMR had not read Meinong; indeed Meinong's theory of objects did not exist in any recognizable form in 1898. The second is that if Russell did countenance nonexistent objects as logical subjects his position was outrightly, unavoidably, and above all obviously, inconsistent—and, moreover, remained so until 1903. Charity would suggest that a different interpretation is called for, and the textual basis for one exists. Its details, however, will have to wait until we have examined rather more of the text.

When a term occurs in a judgement as a predicate it occurs as meaning. Yet any attempt to focus attention on, and say something about, meanings as such turns them into subjects. Each meaning is different from all the others, yet to say this is also to treat meanings as subjects. 'That there are different meanings, expresses difference of being between meanings, not difference of meaning as such' (pp. 174–5). Even to talk of 'meanings' in the plural is misleading (p. 175). Meanings as such 'are destitute of being, and incapable of plurality' (p. 174). Thus /human/ as it occurs in the judgement /Socrates is human/ does not have being and is not a subject; while in /human is different from animal/ it occurs as a subject and has being. Russell uses the word 'predicate' 'to denote whatever is meaning, whether used as subject or as predicate', and confines 'meaning' to meanings as such, i.e. to predicates occurring as meaning.[12] It is this distinction between subjects and meanings which enables Russell to overcome Bradley's famous regress argument against relations (p. 175).

The point Russell is trying to get at is fairly clear, though his terminology is somewhat awkward. In summary: 'predicates, which are meanings, may occur as subjects or as predicates. When they occur as predicates they are meanings as such, although it is a mistake to say so since referring to them in the plural treats them as subjects. Predicates are terms, since they can occur as subjects. So some terms are capable of occurring as subjects and as

[12] We might call these 'predicating predicates' on analogy with Russell's better-known use of 'relating relations' (cf. *POM* 49).

predicates, though some (e.g. things) can only occur as subjects. Meanings as such, however, cannot occur as subjects and are not terms. The situation is not entirely translucent. It might be thought, however, to involve a rather serious mistake.

Russell has asserted all the following. The distinction between occurrence as subject and occurrence as predicate is a distinction of aspect. Subjects and predicates are all terms. All terms have being. Predicates which occur as predicates in a judgement are not terms and are devoid of being. Now it is not entirely clear what he means by saying that the distinction between subject and predicate is a distinction of aspect, but, whatever it means, it must mean at least this: that the distinction between subject and predicate is not an ontological distinction. Yet it is also Russell's claim that whether a predicate has being or not depends upon whether it occurs as a predicate or as a subject. Thus it would seem that predicates gain or lose being according to how they occur in judgements—surely in itself an implausible doctrine, but at any rate one incompatible with the view that how a predicate occurs in a proposition is merely a matter of aspect. There is something in this criticism, but it is not clear that it should be couched in ontological terms, for it seems doubtful whether being for Russell is an ontological category at all. Russell's primary specification of terms is that they can occur as logical subjects and that each term is one. The claim that each term has being is arrived at only later, in efforts to characterize the way in which different terms differ. That each term has being amounts to no more than the claim that each term can be counted as one (p. 168). This may or may not have ontological significance for Russell, but I think it is premature to assume that it does just because Russell used the word 'being'.

What remains of the original objection, however, is still serious. For whether or not an item can be counted as one, which depends upon how it occurs in a judgement, is surely no more a matter of aspect than its ontological status. It is true that in order to count $X$ or to assert that it is one, it is necessary that $X$ be a term—similarly, if we are to assert that $X$ has being. But this provides no ground for the view that a predicating predicate lacks being. Admittedly, we cannot *say* of a predicating predicate that it has or lacks being, because in saying so what we speak of is not the predicating predicate but the same predicate as subject. But this is not to say that a term which is functioning as a predicate suddenly loses the being (or unity) which it had as subject. It is merely that in trying to assert that the predicating predicate has (or lacks) being we turn it back into a subject and thus cease to speak of what we had originally intended, the meaning as such.[13] It is

[13] This difficulty formed part of the problematic out of which the theory of descriptions emerged: see OF and OD. It occurs also in various guises in *POM*: e.g. in Russell's account of a

possible that it was this difficulty which led Russell to abandon his claim that predicating predicates (or meanings) lacked being, thereby treating them as fully fledged terms (*POM* 44–5). This opened the way for the relational account of predication with which he toyed for a number of years (COR, *POM* 47; *TK* 80–1) and, incidentally, for a return of Bradley's infinite regress argument (cf. COR 146; *POM* 50).[14]

In such a labyrinth it is easy to lose sight of Russell's main purpose, namely to lay the philosophical foundations of a theory of manifolds. Yet the connections are, in outline, quite easy to make, even though the details become extremely messy. The collection of all terms forms a manifold and some (but not all) of its subcollections also form manifolds. Among the submanifolds of the manifold of terms, two may be singled out for special attention: the manifold of predicates and the manifold of things.

Consider, first, the terms themselves. Each term is one, which presupposes that it forms a unity. Each term is identical with itself and different from all other terms. Russell calls the type of difference which terms have *inter se* 'difference of being' (p. 168). It is the kind of difference that numeration depends upon, and it is in virtue of their difference of being that all terms can be counted. We may call the type of unity and identity appropriate to terms 'unity of being' and 'identity of being' or 'numerical identity', although Russell does not use these expressions in AMR.[15] Predicates, considered as terms, share in these proto-relations, but they have also to be considered in their aspect as meanings. Here we have different proto-relations, namely unity, identity, and diversity of meaning or content (pp. 169, 175). This gives us six different proto-relations.[16] The manifold of existents gives us a further three: material identity, material diversity, and material unity (pp. 170–1).

These proto-relations are of crucial importance in specifying the operations which can be defined on the various manifolds. The point is to find modes of combination by which elements from a given manifold can be combined to form new elements of the same manifold. Russell specifies two such methods of combination, an extensive operation of addition and an intensive operation of synthesis. Predicates as terms can be added and the result 'is simply two

proposition as asserted and a propositional concept (pp. 34–5), in his distinction between verbs and verbal nouns (p. 48), and of course in his distinction between relations as terms and relating relations (pp. 49–50). It also troubled Frege, whose solution was different: see Frege (1892).

[14] As late as 1924 Russell cites Bradley's regress argument as evidence against the view that relations can occur as terms (cf. LA 171). By this time Russell had reversed himself again.

[15] The close connection between termhood and numerability makes 'numerical identity' particularly appropriate. Russell uses it in FIAM 280, and its companion 'numerical diversity' in COR 143.

[16] I may be guilty of some misrepresentation here, because Russell provides separate treatments of the proto-relations appropriate to terms, subjects, and predicates. Thus giving a nine-fold division of proto-relations. My simplification results from the fact that to consider a term *qua* term is to consider it as a subject.

predicates forming a class'. Predicates as meanings can be synthesized and the result is 'a new predicate taken as meaning' (p. 176). Though all terms can be added, only predicates taken as meanings can be synthesized. The new predicate which results from synthesis can be taken as a term, but its relation to the two predicates which were synthesized to form it is not that of a class to its constituent members. 'It may be said to *imply* both the predicates synthesized, but they cannot be said to be its parts. For qua meaning it is neither one nor many, neither whole nor part; while qua term it is one and only one' (p. 176). This account, though still far from complete, has already taken us considerably beyond the basis supplied so far by Russell's theory of judgement. For Russell has to show how these operations can be based upon particular forms of judgement if he is to remain consistent in his methods. How this is to be done is revealed by a study of judgements which are not subject–predicate in form.

In starting with subject–predicate judgements Russell's approach was entirely conventional. He departs from convention, however, when he distinguishes as separate categories judgements in which two or more predicates are ascribed to a single subject (e.g. /Socrates is animal and rational/) and judgements in which a single predicate is ascribed to two or more subjects (e.g. /2 and 3 are prime/). It might be thought that such judgements are rather uninteresting variants on the original S–P form. Yet for Russell they mark a crucial new development. In S–P–P judgements we have a synthesis of two predicates into a single predicate. For example, the predicate /human/ is optimistically supposed to result from the synthesis of the predicates /animal/ and /rational/. In S–S–P judgements, on the other hand, we have the combination of two terms or subjects into a single subject. The first kind of synthesis, synthesis of content or meaning, results in a term with the sort of unity appropriate to predicates, unity of meaning; the second kind results in a term (namely, a class) with the sort of unity appropriate to subjects, unity of being. But the fact that all the subjects in an S–S–P judgement share a single predicate indicates that in addition to their diversity of being they have an identity of content (p. 169). Similarly, though Russell doesn't emphasize this, the fact that in an S–P–P judgement the several predicates are ascribed to a single subject indicates that in addition to their diversity of content they have, in one sense, an identity of being— although, of course, considered as terms they have diversity of being *inter se*. It is perhaps less misleading to say that in S–S–P judgements subject terms with diversity of being exhibit identity of content *through* their common predicate, while in S–P–P judgements predicates with diverse content exhibit identity of being *through* their common subject.

S–P–P and S–S–P judgements give rise to two further classes of judgement, respectively judgements of intension and judgements of extension. The former (e.g. /Winged horse is a predicate/) asserts that 'two or more predicates have that kind of unity which is found when both are predicates of one subject', namely unity of meaning, although (as the example shows) it is not necessary that there actually be a subject to which both apply. Judgements of extension (e.g. /2 and 3 form a class/) assert that 'two or more subjects have that kind of unity which is found where subjects have a common pedicate', namely unity of being (p. 173). Unity of being is of special importance in mathematics since, according to Russell, it is the sort of unity which characterizes classes.

At first sight it might appear as if judgements of intension and extension merely make explicit what is implicit in S–P–P and S–S–P judgements. But this is not quite right. In an S–S–P judgement a common predicate is asserted of a plurality of subjects, but this is not sufficient to ensure that they form a class. For Russell a class requires that there be a predicate common *and peculiar* to all members. Thus we may not assume that the collection of subjects in an S–S–P judgement forms a class. Russell apparently ignores this difficulty. He seems to assume, though he doesn't actually state as much, that such collections always form classes. A similar problem might be thought to arise with S–P–P judgements because Russell denies that contradictory predicates can be synthesized to form a single predicate (p. 169). Thus it might be thought that S–P–P judgements where the two predicates are inconsistent pose a problem, since we seem there to have a case in which two predicates which cannot be synthesized into a third are applied to the same subject. It seems more likely, however, that Russell holds that such a case never arises. His reason for denying that contradictory predicates can be synthesized into a new predicate is presumably that what is contradictory is meaningless. For suppose it were not, then there would be a meaning (i.e. a predicate) which resulted from the combination of the original two, and it would be hard to resist the conclusion that this meaning was the synthesis of the original meanings. But if what is contradictory is meaningless then contradictory S–P–P judgements would be meaningless, and thus not really judgements at all. Thus, while there is a need in Russell's system for a manner of combination of subjects which falls short of their combination into a class, there is no comparable need in the case of predicates. If predicates can be combined at all they form a predicate. This is a further aspect of the asymmetry between subjects and predicates. We shall have to return to it later, for things are not quite as simple as they seem.

It is more than a little surprising that Russell does not regard existential judgements as merely a special case of subject–predicate judgements, for he regards existence as a predicate, even though it is a 'radically new idea' (p. 170). We need not concern ourselves much with existential judgements, since they play no role in those parts of AMR which have survived: they would have been of relevance only to the parts on rational dynamics. Russell subdivides the class of existential judgements according to the kind of relation that the term whose existence is asserted has to space and time. This, again, is a rather puzzling move, since Russell does not regard it as a necessary feature of existents that they have a relation to some part of space or time; he notes it merely as an apparently inexplicable fact that all existents have some such relation (p. 170).

Russell's seventh and last category of judgements are those which assert a necessary connection between predicates (e.g. /human implies animal/). The essential feature of such judgements is that the connection between the predicates is *necessary*. For this to be the case it is essential that both predicates occur *as meaning*. For it is in virtue of their meanings that the necessary connections hold, and it seems to be Russell's position that when a term occurs as subject in a proposition *only* its reference contributes to the proposition and, similarly, when it occurs as predicate only its meaning contributes.[17] Thus the judgements of Russell's final class are unique in that they have no subject (p. 172). Such judgements are of two types. There are those, like /human implies animal/, in which the contents are predicates of the same subject. Russell calls these pure judgements of intension. There are also those in which the contents must be asserted of different subjects. Russell says that this second group includes 'most of the axioms of mathematics' as well as necessary arithmetical judgements, e.g. /2 + 3 = 5/ (p. 173).

The pure judgements of intension in AMR were the precursors of the formal implications in *POM* (pp. 5–9). The main difference stems from the complete absence of any theory of the variable in Russell's logic of 1898. Despite the inadequacies of his treatment of variables and quantification in *POM*, his use of unrestricted variables in that work did permit him to handle mathematical propositions by means of formal implication (*POM* 6). It is interesting to note that in his *POL* Russell treats such judgements as a type of subject–predicate judgement, in which a predicate is asserted of a concept. He considers attempts to reduce them to the more usual type of subject–predicate judgement, exemplified by /Socrates is mortal/, but not surprisingly finds them wanting (*POL* 17–18). However, in the course of his discussion, he does consider analysing them in the form, /If $x$ is human then $x$ is mortal/. He rejects this on the ground that it presupposes a necessary connection between predicates (*POL* 18). His account in *POL* seems less adequate than that in AMR. For /human is mortal/ is a strange subject–predicate judgement by anyone's standards, for, if it has a subject, it is not the subject (viz. the concept /human/) to which the predicate applies.

---

[17] This, of course, raises special problems, not considered in AMR, for what Russell later called denoting concepts which seem to occur both as reference and as meaning (cf. *POM* 53–4, and OF).

Judgements of class-inclusion, which Russell somewhat inexplicably leaves out of his main classification, cannot be ignored. Judgements of class-inclusion appear to some extent as the dual of judgements of pure intension. The latter contain 'nothing but synthesized diversity of meaning'. The former contain 'nothing but diverse subjects with a relation' (p. 179). The dualism, however, is not complete, for the relation which relates the two subjects in judgements of class-inclusion occurs as meaning. Judgements of class-inclusion are thus not pure judgements of extension—indeed, there can be no such thing, since any judgement requires at least one term to occur as meaning.

The concept of a class or manifold is central to Book I of AMR and Russell devotes chapter 3 to it. Classes are logical subjects and, like things, are incapable of occurring as predicates. They have, therefore, the sort of unity appropriate to subjects, 'the unity which makes every subject *one*' (p. 179). The class differs from its members not in respect of the type of unity each exemplifies, but in the fact that the class also exemplifies diversity, while its members might be simple (p. 180). On Russell's initial account, any terms may be combined to form a class. The process by which they are combined is called addition. Unless two terms are added they remain merely different terms and cannot be counted as two. Thus classes are essential for numeration. In fact, of classes as so far conceived there can only be two types of judgement, according to Russell, existential judgements of number (e.g. /Tom, Dick, and Harry are three/) and judgements of extension (e.g. /Tom, Dick, and Harry form a class/). Yet what gives classes their importance is that the idea of *all* can be applied to them and this idea can be applied only when there is a predicate common to all members of the class. Russell doesn't need the quantifier for judgements such as /All men are mortal/, since these are handled as pure judgements of intension, e.g. /human implies mortal/, but for such judgements as /Tom, Dick, and Harry are all the members of a certain class/. The latter I will call 'judgements of class-totality'. A related category of judgements also requires a property common to all class members, or so Russell thinks. These are judgements of class-membership, which he does not at this stage differentiate from judgements of class-inclusion (p. 180).[18]

Russell's ground for thinking that judgements of class-totality and judgements of class-membership require that all the members of the class in question have a common predicate is that without such a common predicate such judgements will not be significant (AMR 180). Russell's thought here is

---

[18] The distinction was one he ultimately got from Peano (1891: 156), although Frege (1879, 1893) also had it. In later writings Russell insisted strongly on its importance (*POM* 19, 78–9). Lack of the distinction helped produce some important confusions in Russell's work in 1898 (cf. OQ 117–20).

that when the class is given by an enumeration of its members, a judgement that some item is a member is trivial, and in that sense non-significant. In this he follows Bradley's view that tautologies are meaningless (Bradley 1883: i, 141 ff.). It is easy now to see that this is just a mistake. Russell's thinking about quantification in 1898 was rudimentary in the extreme, and remained so for several years. Yet, although the mistake was simple, its consequences affect the adequacy of the whole of Book I of AMR. For Russell started by claiming that any terms could be added to form a manifold (this, indeed, is a requirement on manifolds as conceived by Whitehead). He further admits that number can be applied to any collection formed by addition. Yet such collections are excluded from some of the most important judgements which can be made about manifolds.

Russell's difficulty would be eased considerably if he required only that the members of all classes about which judgements of class-membership and class-totality can significantly be made have some common predicate. For all members of any class are terms and thus have the predicate /termhood/ in common (p. 187). On occasion, it seems as though this is all Russell requires. He talks repeatedly of the need for a 'common predicate' (e.g. pp. 179: 30, 181: 1), but it seems clear that what he really needs is a predicate which is both common *and peculiar* (cf. pp. 177, 184). Only by such a predicate could a class be defined otherwise than by an enumeration of its members as Russell requires (p. 180). And elsewhere Russell talks unequivocally of 'defining predicates' (pp. 179, 180), and on one occasion of 'common predicates by which the class is defined' (p. 181).

It is clear that wherever a group of terms share some predicate they form a class, and that the class they form has some greater degree of unity than that provided by mere addition. The unity which such classes have Russell calls 'identity of content' (p. 179). That a collection of terms have, *inter se*, identity of content does not mean that they cannot be conceptually distinguished, but merely that they have some point of conceptual identity which results from their all having some predicate in common.[19] It is clear, therefore, that some classes have a defining predicate. (Indeed, every predicate defines a class, even when no term exemplifies the predicate, p. 187.) It is much less clear that all classes have defining predicates, on account of the fact that classes can be formed quite generally by addition. At this stage, Russell introduces an awkward change in terminology. Since he plainly regards those classes

---

[19] It follows, of course, that *qua* members of the class they cannot be conceptually distinguished. Yet each one is distinct. It is for this reason, among others, that the contradiction of relativity is so prevalent in mathematics. Compare the situation with quantities, earlier investigated. *Qua* quantity of a given kind, each quantity is conceptually identical with, but numerically distinct from all other quantities of the same kind. The same situation is now revealed in connection with the members of a given class. Indeed quantities of a given kind are merely special cases of classes, namely the class of attributes of a given kind (pp. 177–8).

which have a defining predicate as the important ones (not surprisingly, since they are the only ones which permit quantification), he proposes to use the words 'class' and 'manifold' only for these cases. He uses 'assemblage' as a more general word which covers not only classes (as now defined) but collections of terms for which there is no defining predicate, if such there be (p. 180). The question of whether all classes have defining predicates becomes now the question of whether there are any assemblages which are not classes.

Before discussing this question in general terms, Russell notes two important kinds of putative exception to the claim that all assemblages are classes: namely, assemblages of attributes[20] of a given kind and assemblages of predicates of a given kind. In both cases there are strong prima facie grounds for thinking that there is a defining predicate but great difficulty in identifying it. In the case of attributes Russell's position seems to be that attributes do not have predicates at all (apart from relational predicates, p. 183). This, of course, was what Russell had long been maintaining in the special case of quantities, that all quantitative judgements are essentially comparative. To consider a non-quantitative example, the attribute of redness itself does not have the property of redness, nor the predicate /red/, for it is the thing which is red and has redness. To say that the attribute has the property of being redness, Russell says, 'merely repeats the problem' (pp. 177–8). Thus, it would seem that there is no defining predicate for the assemblage of attributes of redness. Since quantities are attributes, this raises mathematically important difficulties about assemblages of quantities.

Against this conclusion, however, Russell notes two things. First, all attributes have relations to parts of space and time. If such relations imply a corresponding predicate of each term of the relation, then there will be predicates properly predicable of attributes (p. 178). Russell is not optimistic about this response. He doesn't take issue with its fundamental assumption, namely that such relations imply predicates. Instead he points out that such relations will be insufficient to distinguish two attributes of the same thing. (p. 178). We may also note that, unless disjunctive predicates are admitted, the predicates implied by spatio-temporal relations will not provide a defining predicate for all attributes of a given kind. Second, Russell is inclined to attribute the problems of finding a defining predicate to 'the paucity of language' (p. 178). He notes that if things have thinghood in common, attributes will have attributehood (p. 178). Beyond this he postpones further discussion until he treats quantity (in a part of the manuscript now lost). The result to be shown there is that all attributes are quantities

[20] Russell introduces the term 'attribute' as the name of the particular occurrence of a quality at some part of space or time. A quality is a predicate which is capable of such particularized occurrence (p. 171). A thing can now be defined as whatever has an attribute (p. 171).

and that, contrary to what was claimed in RNQ they have the predicate /quantitative/ in common. But neither /attributehood/ nor /quantitative/ will serve to define an assemblage of attributes of a given kind. Russell offers no further reflection on the matter, but it seems he is not willing to countenance assemblages of attributes as genuine counter-examples to the thesis that all assemblages are classes.

This is not the case with numbers, nor in general with other assemblages of predicates (e.g. colour predicates) taken as terms. The problems here are so similar to those which arose in connection with attributes that it is somewhat surprising Russell did not come to the same conclusion, namely that the difficulty arose from the paucity of language. Of course, we can say of /2/ and /3/ that they are numbers or that /red/ and /blue/ are colours but these are judgements of class-inclusion and do not involve predicates. Russell considers the judgement /3 is numerical/, but rejects this on the ground the /numerical/ is a predicate which applies only to subjects of which numbers can be predicated, not to the numbers themselves (p. 178). Alternatives, such as /3 has the predicate of being a number/, are dismissed as 'mere artifice' (p. 178). Russell's difficulty is apt to look merely linguistic. There would seem to be no objection to inventing some new expression to give the required predicate. Though 'numerical' is of no use and 'numerous' is worse, we still have the adjectival sense of 'numeral'. Indeed, it is a little odd that Russell didn't consider this. If /attributehood/ is a satisfactory defining property for the assemblage of attributes, there seems no reason why the adjective /numeral/ should not be a satisfactory defining property of the assemblage of numbers. Russell's conclusion is that all numbers have in common the property of being predicable of assemblages as such (p. 182). But this, as he notes, is a relational property, it 'consists in a relation to terms which are not numbers' (p. 182). This is a different aspect of the fundamental relativity Russell remarked on in earlier writings, which arose out of the fact that all ascriptions of number were relative to the unit. But Russell's new use of relations to define the class of numbers, and (perhaps) to define individual numbers themselves (for /3/ surely forms a class with a defining property), points in a new direction which Russell would subsequently exploit once his initial qualms about relations were laid to rest. It remains, now, to discuss the principle that all assemblages are classes in more general terms.

It can be shown that all assemblages are classes if the following two assumptions are granted:

If /P/ and /Q/ are both predicates then their disjunction /P or Q/ and their conjuction /P and Q/ are also predicates. (1)

No two terms have exactly the same predicates.[21] (2)

---

[21] In fact, Russell states (2) for existents and not for terms. This, however, would give him a narrower conclusion that the one he claims.

*Proof*: Suppose we have an assemblage {*a, b, c,* . . . } of terms. By (2) and the conjunctive part of (1), every term has some predicate common and peculiar to it. Let /A/ be the predicate common and peculiar to *a*, /B/ that common and peculiar to *b*, etc. Then by the disjunctive part of (1) /A or B or C or . . . / is the predicate common and peculiar to the members of the assemblage. Thus the arbitrarily chosen assemblage has a defining predicate and is a class (AMR 185–6; cf. *PM*, i, 67).

Russell, however, rejects (2). He argues that there must, at some point, be 'material diversity without diversity of content' (p. 186) in order to break out of the circle that the relativity of position seems to impose. Existents, for Russell, fall into various groups, e.g. things, parts of space or time, attributes, etc., but all of them have the characteristic of either being or occupying a part of space or time. Now, as was established in *EFG*, two parts of space or time have, themselves, 'no intrinsic difference of predicate' (p. 186) and must be differentiated by their relations to the existents which occupy them. But the existents which ocupy them are differentiated ultimately only by their relations to parts of space and time, for they are individuated by their attributes, and attributes are differentiated by their spatio-temporal relations. To break out of the circle it is necessary to suppose that existents can be materially diverse even though they don't differ in content, i.e. in the predicates which apply to them. Thus (2) is false, and an assemblage which includes such existents among its members will not be a class. 'Any assemblage containing some, but not all, of a class of terms which do not differ in content, will be incapable of a defining predicate, and will be a mere assemblage' (p. 186).

Russell also rejects (1). He suspends judgement on the disjunctive part but definitely rejects its conjunctive part (though not in such a way as to undermine the argument that all assemblages are classes, so long as no term can have inconsistent predicates). The conjunctive part has to be rejected because Russell denies that two predicates can be synthesized into a new predicate where the synthesized result would be inconsistent (p. 186). Russell is here operating with the unstated assumption that what is inconsistent has no meaning, and thus two mutually inconsistent predicates cannot be synthesized to form a meaning. The situation is a bit more complicated than it seems, since Russell denies that the negation of a predicate is a predicate (p. 186). Thus he cannot explain contradictory predicates as a pair of predicates in which one is the denial of the other. Russell explains that two predicates are incompatible when one implies the denial of the other (p. 186).[22] This explains the basic cases, e.g. the incompatibility between /square/ and /round/,

[22] It follows, therefore, that implication is not a relation which holds only between two predicates considered as meaning, since it holds also between a predicate and the denial of a predicate, which is not another predicate.

but the case of incompatible predicates such as /red/ and /blue/ is not quite so direct. It follows from the fact that /red/ and /blue/ apply only to things which occupy parts of space and time, and are such that they can never both occur at the same part of space and time (pp. 186–7).

The discussion of classes has introduced two operations on manifolds: addition of terms and synthesis of predicates. Rather misleadingly Russell refers to both as forms of addition (p. 187). Addition of terms differs from synthesis of predicates in that it is *always* possible: any two terms may be added to form an assemblage which is itself a fresh term in the manifold of terms. Two predicates, by contrast, can be synthesized only if they are not incompatible. Only two manifolds, the manifold of terms and the manifold of numbers, are such as always to permit addition in Russell's sense. Two further manifolds might seem to warrant inclusion, the manifold of extensive magnitudes and the manifold of classes. However, extensive magnitudes are always added as numbers, so they don't really provide a new example; and classes can always be added only if disjunctive predicates are admitted as predicates, something which Russell is not prepared to affirm (p. 187). In the case of all other manifolds, addition of any kind can take place only when special conditions are satisfied. Thus, for example, there is the consistency requirement on the synthesis of predicates, and there are contiguity requirements on the synthesis of extensive quantities and things. Intensive quantities can never be added at all (p. 187).

It is at this late stage in the discussion that the difficulties in Russell's approach to the logical calculus really become apparent. As already noted, the calculus he intends to establish is Whitehead's Boolean algebra of symbolic logic. His difficulties stem from the fact that his philosophical preamble has left him with both intensions and extensions to take care of. Towards the end of chapter 4 of Book I of AMR Russell struggles valiantly to bring the two into alignment. From the point of view of Whitehead's calculus it would have been natural to deal with assemblages. But this would have left no room for predicates. Russell's best hope is to exploit the dualism of predicates and *classes*, relying on the common predicate requirement on class formation. The dualism gives little trouble, though getting the resulting structure to mesh with the Boolean requirements of the logical calculus causes major difficulties. The basic requirements are as follows. If /a/ or /b/ are two predicates then we can combine them in two different ways to form new predicates; we can form the predicate /a and b/ which implies them both and we can form the predicate /a or b/ which both imply. Similarly if $A$ and $B$ are two classes, we can combine them to form the class /A and B/ which is contained in both and the class /A or B/ in which both are contained (p. 188). Neither of these conditions is met by the structures which emerge from Russell's analysis of judgements. Russell denies that incompatible predicates can be combined to form a meet and is unwilling to admit that any two predicates form a third which is their join. In consequence, there is no guarantee that /A or B/ or /A and B/ will be a class (rather than an assemblage). None the less, the dualism holds: for /a or b/ and /a and b/ will be predicates just in case /A or B/ and /A and B/ are classes. Russell links intensions and extensions by means of the following axiom:

> *Axiom.* Let A and B be the classes defined by /a/ and /b/.
>   (i) If /a/ implies /b/ then A is part of, or coextensive with, B.
>   (ii) If A is part of, or coextensive with, B then /a/ implies /b/.

Russell goes on to show how (parts of) the syllogism can be interpreted through this system, but runs, quite naturally, into difficulties over negation since he has excluded negative predicates (p. 189). None the less, as far as classes are concerned, he notes that if we admit the assemblage of terms as a class—to be called the Universe—then we can obtain an analogue of negation in class terms. For given any class A we can define its complement as that class B such that A and B together constitute the class of terms. He then proposes to introduce a corresponding notion of a negative predicate. Given a predicate /a/ its negative is that predicate which implies the denial of /a/ synthesized with the defining predicate of the Universe. At this stage, Russell either has to admit (what he has just previously denied) that the denial of a predicate is a predicate (as by p. 193 he does), or else he has to extend the notion of synthesis (as he has implicitly extended the notion of implication) to include not just the synthesis of predicates but the synthesis of predicates with the denials of predicates.

Book I of AMR fails essentially on this point and others like it. Russell wants to be able to treat the logical calculus as a Boolean lattice, as Whitehead had done in Book II of his 1898a. This requires a set of elements with operations, meet and join, satisfying commutativity, associativity, absorption, and distribution, and with a greatest and a least element satisfying complementation. Russell is trying to mesh this formal structure with a philosophically perspicuous analysis of judgements. The aim, though it is never made quite explicit, is to underwrite the logical calculus with a philosophical account of judgement, in much the same way as Russell had earlier attempted to underwrite projective geometry with a philosophical account of externality. Russell's failure is readily apparent, and most of the problems that we have so far considered can be related to this fundamental failure. What we have in Book I of AMR is an unsatisfactory trade-off between philosophical insight and formal elegance.

Admitting negative predicates does help to ensure that a Boolean calculus of assemblages can be mapped onto a calculus of Russellian classes. However, it does not show that the assemblage of predicates taken as meanings will conform to Boolean requirements. For to consider predicates as forming a class is to treat them as terms and not as meanings. Russell concludes, therefore, that predicates taken as meanings do not form a manifold (p. 190). It might seem that this conclusion is premature. For, in implication and predicate synthesis, we have two operations on predicates as meanings. The addition of negation as an operation on meanings to either of these will enable us to define a disjunction or Boolean join operation on meanings. The effectiveness of such devices is blocked for Russell. In the first place, the philosophically (ill-) motivated consistency restriction on synthesis prevents a Boolean outcome and blocks the definition of a null-predicate through the synthesis of incompatible predicates. Moreover, for predicates as meaning to form a class requires that they have some defining predicate. Any such predicate, however, would involve treating predicates as terms and not as meanings. Given his philosophical position, Russell is right in denying that predicates form a manifold. The fundamental dualism of subjects and predicates cannot be regarded as producing two parallel Boolean lattices, and his best hope of bringing his system into line with Whitehead's logical calculus is by exploiting the duality principle stated in his axiom.

In the final chapter of Book I, on the logical calculus itself, the duality axiom helps remove some of the more superficial difficulties in his earlier presentation (especially those resulting from his inconsistent terminology). He notes explicitly that the logical calculus deals both with a collection of assemblages (of predicates) and a collection of classes (of terms) (p. 193). It is clear, however, from what has already been said, that the second part of this claim will fail given Russell's common property requirement and his qualms about the principles of predicate formation. It is best for present purposes to bracket off these qualms[23] and assume that Russell has the predicates he needs for his account. Among predicates and among classes, therefore, we have two dual operations, which Russell now calls multiplication and addition. Thus we can multiply predicates to form a new (synthesized) predicate which implies all the original ones, and we can add predicates to form a new (disjunctive) predicate which all the original ones imply. Dually, we can multiply classes to form a new class which is contained in all the original ones, and we can add classes to form a new class in which all the original ones are contained (p. 192). The two operations are linked via Russell's duality axiom. The defining predicate of the class formed by multiplication is that which results from the multiplication of the defining predicates of the original classes. The defining predicate of the class formed

[23] It seems clear that Russell will abandon his restrictions on predicate formation. He has already tacitly admitted disjunctive predicates (p. 192) and negated predicates (p. 193). The one point on which he has so far given no evidence of giving ground is the consistency requirement on predicate synthesis.

by addition is that which results from the addition of the defining predicates of the original classes (pp. 192–3). For the first time notation is introduced for the two operations: if *a* and *b* are classes, the class formed by multiplication is represented by '*ab*' and that formed by addition by '*a + b*' (p. 192). Russell doesn't supply notation for the case of predicates, but the same notation will do there. Since this account fits well with his purposes, we may assume that this account supplants the earlier ones. The fact that, in the course of his discussion, he uses 'addition' in three different ways (pp. 187, 192), indicates the uncertainty with which he picked his way.

The duality axiom, however, does not remove all Russell's difficulties. What he says about equivalence in the chapter on the logical calculus, for example, contradicts the axiom. He notes that there are many different forms of equivalence, appropriate to manifolds, numbers, orders, and quantities (equivalence in the last case he calls 'equality') (p. 191). In the case of equivalence of predicates, however, he detects a further ambiguity. Equivalence of predicates 'may mean that each of our predicates implies the other, or it may mean that each defines the same class' (p. 191). Russell's subsequent claim that the latter definition 'is wider' contradicts the duality axiom which implies that both are equivalent. Again, it is intensions which create the difficulty. Russell takes it that the predicates /man/ and /featherless biped/ define the same class, yet denies that /featherless biped/ implies /man/, since it is merely a contingent fact that there are no non-human featherless bipeds. Obviously, Russell's notion of implication, that involved in pure judgements of intension, is too strong if his linkage of predicates with classes via the duality axiom is to be preserved.

The extensive definition of predicate equivalence is important in ensuring the uniqueness of Russell's null and universal classes. A null class is defined as the common part (product) of any two mutually exclusive assemblages, while a universe is defined as the union (sum) of any two mutually exclusive classes. Given the extensional account of class equivalence all null classes and all universes will be equivalent. Thus, for the purposes of the logical calculus, we get the unique least and unique greatest element that we need for a complemented lattice. The properties of the null class and the universe are given by the following four laws (taken from Whitehead 1898*a*: 37):

$$a.\bar{a}b = a.\bar{a} = 0 \qquad a + \bar{a} = i$$
$$a.0 = 0 \qquad\qquad a + 0 = a$$

where $\bar{a}$ is, Russell now admits it, 'the predicate not-*a*' (p. 193), *i* is the defining predicate of the universe, and 0 is the denial of *i*. (Multiplication of *a* by *b* is marked indifferently by either '*ab*' or '*a.b*'.) By now the conditions which Russell earlier imposed on the treatment of predicates have been completely lost. Not only are negative predicates admitted, but they are permitted to be synthesized with their opposites, as in '$a.\bar{a}$', to yield a fresh predicate, 0 or $\bar{\imath}$.

Russell begins his chapter on the logical calculus with some brief remarks on the scope of the calculus. He wants to regard the logical calculus as the science of manifolds as such (p. 190). This gives it, he notes, a 'very high degree of generality', but not so high a degree as arithmetic. For arithmetic judgements are possible of assemblages as well as manifolds.[24] Russell attempts to minimize this result by noting that all assemblages consist of terms, and all terms form a manifold (p. 191). In fact, at the beginning of the next chapter, he retracts it altogether, claiming that judgements which ascribe number can only be about manifolds since they presuppose the concept *all*, which is applicable only to manifolds (pp. 196–7). Russell's idea there is that in ascribing a number to an assemblage a judgement of class-totality has been presupposed, since one needs to know that *all* the members of the assemblage have been counted.[25] Judgements of class-totality apply only to classes because an assemblage for which there is no defining concept can be defined only by enumerating its members. (Russell apparently forgets the possibility of disjunctively defined assemblages. Or, perhaps, he now recognizes that genuine disjunctive predicates must be admitted.) Thus judgements of totality (as well as existential judgements of number) applied to mere assemblages will be tautologous and so, in Bradley's terms, unmeaning, and therefore not genuine judgements of all. In general, the demarcation of logic and arithmetic which Russell draws in the final chapter of Book I is at odds with his account of arithmetic in Book II. The latter must be taken as Russell's more considered opinion, even though to claim that only classes are numerable is surely just wrong. The error clearly stems from Russell's adherence to Bradley's theory of judgement.

Even with allowance made for these considerations, Russell's position is

---

[24] It does not follow from this that the logical calculus could be specified as that branch of arithmetic which deals with classes. For the logical calculus includes judgements which are not arithmetical. Nor, apparently, can we assume that the subject-matter of the logical calculus is contained within the subject-matter of arithmetic. For while the logical calculus can handle infinite classes, arithmetic (so Russell seems to imply) can only deal with finite assemblages. Russell's idea seems to be that arithmetic is concerned with the assignation of numbers to assemblages and classes. Infinite numbers cannot be so assigned because they are larger than any assignable number (p. 191). Russell's position here is not fully explicit, since the chapter on infinite number (ch. 2 of Book IV) has not survived.

[25] He also claims that applying a number to an assemblage presupposes the concept *one* (p. 197), since it is necessary to know what is to count as a single element of the assemblage. Even assuming that this presupposes some concept which covers the entire assemblage (a claim made by theories which relativize identity to some covering concept), the concept required is not necessarily a defining concept for the assemblage. On Russell's theory, for any assemblage, the concept *term* will provide the requisite covering concept. Consequently, this requirement alone is insufficient to entail Russell's claim that number is applicable only to classes.

not clear of difficulty. Numbers have still to be applied to assemblages formed by addition, and, unless Russell relaxes his conditions on predicate-formation, such assemblages will not in general have a defining predicate. There are other problems, too. Russell claims that numbers themselves form a manifold (p. 191), but this seems to be in direct contradiction of his earlier conclusion that assemblages of numbers have no defining predicate (pp. 178, 181–2). It is important to notice, however, that the logical calculus does not deal with *all* judgements concerning manifolds. For arithmetic judgements in which a number is assigned to a manifold do not belong to logic. Russell had read Cantor (1878) in which the use of one-to-one correlations to establish that two manifolds have the same cardinality is fully developed, but, even had he accepted the method, he would still have had no way of obtaining by purely logical means the cardinal number itself from the notion of equal cardinality. Thus Russell concludes that the logical calculus 'supplies, together with arithmetic, the type of all possible judgments concerning manifolds as such' (p. 191).

There remains one question which must be taken up before our considera-tion of the logical aspects of AMR is complete. This is the vexed question, already adverted to, of whether Russell's theory of terms is a theory of (existent and nonexistent) possible objects.[26] If it is, then Russell's position is unavoidably inconsistent. Let /P/ be a predicate which does not apply to any term. Since /P/ is a predicate it must be consistent and thus it must be possible that there is some object to which it applies, i.e. that there be some possible object to which it actually does apply. If all possible objects were terms, it would follow that there is a term, and thus a subject, to which the predicate applies, contrary to Russell's claim that there are some predicates which do not apply to any subject. Moreover, Russell gives, as examples of such predicates, predicates which are clearly consistent (e.g. /winged horse/, p. 169). If possible objects, such as Pegasus, were admitted as terms, it would be clearly false to say that there was no subject to which /winged horse/ applies.

The most reasonable solution is to reject the common view that Russell's early theory of terms is a theory of possible objects. Actual objects, or things, are terms, and so are predicates when considered as subjects, so too are classes and assemblages. But non-actual objects are not. This interpretation, however, has to be squared with Russell's assertion that '[e]very possible idea, everything that can be thought of, or represented by a word, may be a logical subject', i.e. a term (p. 168). One interpretation of this remark would ensure that Pegasus was an object that could be thought of and represented

---

[26] It is pretty clear that Russell will not countenance impossible objects. Given his consistency requirements on predicate formation, even the predicational resources required for describing impossible objects are not available.

by a word and thus was a term. But this interpretation can be accommodated to Russell's claim that /winged horse/ does not apply to any term only by assuming that even though Pegasus is a genuine logical subject it cannot take the predicate /winged horse/. This is plainly implausible, for if Pegasus is a subject it must take some predicate, and which could it possibly take if not /winged horse/?

In fact, however, such implausible subtleties are unnecessary, for the passage just quoted is capable of a different interpretation. What Russell says does not commit him admitting Pegasus as a subject. Only if Pegasus is some*thing* which can be thought of or represented by a word must it be a term. But Pegasus is not a thing, for things exist. There is not anything which is Pegasus, and so there is no term with which Pegasus can be identified. Could Pegasus be admitted as a term because it is a possible idea? The answer is plainly, No. Because Pegasus, if it is anything, is a winged horse and not an idea. Of course, there is an idea *of* Pegasus, and this is a possible idea (in fact, an actual one) and thus the idea is a term. But this idea is not to be confused with Pegasus. What, then, are we to make of judgements in which Pegasus is the apparent subject? Russell hardly goes into details, but it would seem likely that he would regard all such judgements as false on the grounds that they lacked a subject. (Remember that terms are 'whatever may be the subject in a *true* judgment', p. 168; my emphasis.) Alternatively, it may be that some such judgements are to be regarded as judgements about the predicate /winged horse/, e.g. in the judgement / The winged horse is not impossible/ or /The winged horse does not exist/. In this case, /winged horse/ will be a term which does not exist, but it will not be a nonexistent object. It will be what Russell later called a concept (*POM* 44), but which he now construes (rather unsatisfactorily) as a predicate considered as a term.

The reason Russell cannot restrict the class of terms to existents (i.e. things) is not because he needs to take account of nonexistent objects, but primarily because he needs to take account of the occurrence of predicates as subjects. It is significant that, on p. 168, immediately after he has characterized his use of the word 'term', he goes on to give the following examples of judgements in which the subject is not an existent: /2 is numerical/, /number is categorical/, and /before is relative to after/. None of these involve nonexistent objects, for /2/ is a predicate. It is hardly likely that he would have chosen such an unbalanced collection of examples had he intended to include nonexistent objects as terms. Subsequently Russell developed this theory: first, by introducing the word 'concept' to stand for a predicate occurring as subject (p. 197) and then by a recognition of the special role of denoting concepts. This, in turn, gave rise to the sequence of theories of denoting that Russell held between 1902 and 1905. While the concept of denotation does not figure in AMR, there are traces of this development in Russell's theory of contents. Contents are those terms which do not exist; they include predicates but also such terms as /thing/, /any point/, and /any moment/ (pp. 176–7). The latter two are among the denoting concepts of *POM* 55, although Russell in AMR does not recognize the other forms of denoting concept included in *POM*—in particular, he pays no attention to denoting concepts expressed by means of the definite article. There is no indication that contents in AMR should include nonexistent objects. In fact, such an inclusion would seem to constitute an abuse of terminology and to run strongly against the illustrative examples Russell gives.

My interpretation of Russell's theory of terms is supported by a number of things Russell says. For example, he repeatedly mentions predicates which cannot be applied to any subject (e.g. pp. 170, 187). Elsewhere, Russell mentions that syllogisms about Amazons or chimeras must be interpreted intensively because there are no such terms (p. 189). The usual interpretation of Russell's theory of terms must construe such remarks as inadvertent errors.

Most importantly, my interpretation is required by Russell's account of the null class. Since all classes have defining predicates, if nonexistent objects were terms it would follow that there could be no empty class of terms. Since Russell explicitly recognizes that there are classes with no elements (pp. 187, 193), he cannot have intended to include nonexistent objects as terms. Of course, it could be maintained that Russell was simply mistaken and had not realized that the account he gave of empty classes conflicted with his theory of terms. This would perhaps be plausible if the error had only occurred in an unpublished manuscript. (Already enough fundamental inconsistencies in AMR have been noted to indicate that an error on this scale was possible.) But the same inconsistency occurs in *POM*, where the theory of terms as usually interpreted is similarly inconsistent with the definition of the null class (*POM* 43, 73–4). It is hard to imagine that so obvious an error went undetected for so long. It seems most reasonable, therefore, to abandon the usual interpretation of the theory of terms as a theory of possible objects.

## 7.2 INFLUENCES: MOORE

The theory of logic that Russell put forward in AMR is clearly an important new development. In its main features it was also a relatively enduring one, for much the same general approach is taken in *POM*, though many of the details change. It marks the first big step in Russell's break from neo-Hegelianism and, as a harbinger of things to come, it is hard to overestimate its importance. But, in itself, it does not mark the end of Russell's neo-

Hegelianism. It is as well to remind ourselves of what remains. First of all, nothing is said in AMR that suggests that Russell had abandoned his view that reality is ultimately mental. Moreover, he retained (at least as he began AMR) his Kantian methodology. Above all he retained the dialectic of the sciences. There is plenty of evidence in AMR of contradictions being piled up for future resolution. AMR, therefore, perhaps rather surprisingly for a book with such obvious similarities to *POM*, remains clearly part of Russell's neo-Hegelian programme.

In later writings, Russell gave generous acknowledgement to Moore for the ideas which make AMR a new departure. He was led to his new views on logic, he says, 'largely under Moore's guidance' (*Auto*. i, 135). 'Moore led the way, and I followed closely in his footsteps' (*MPD* 54). Moore's own account is characteristically more modest, but not necessarily inconsistent: 'I do not know that Russell has ever owed to me anything except mistakes' (Moore 1942: 15). In the preface to *POM* Russell is more explicit about what that work owed to Moore:

On fundamental questions of philosophy, my position, in all its chief features, is derived from Mr. G. E. Moore. I have accepted from him the non-existential nature of propositions (except such as happen to assert existence) and their independence of any knowing mind; also the pluralism which regards the world, both that of existents and that of entities, as composed of an infinite number of mutually independent entities, with relations which are ultimate, and not reducible to adjectives of their terms or of the whole which these compose. Before learning these views from him, I found myself completely unable to construct any philosophy of arithmetic, whereas their acceptance brought about an immediate liberation from a large number of difficulties which I believe to be otherwise insuperable. (*POM*: p. xviii.)

The text of the book reemphasizes some of these debts (e.g. the irreducibility of relations, pp. 24, 446) and adds others (e.g. Russell's eccentric understanding of modal concepts, p. 454,[27] and Russell's 'first perception of the difficulties in the relational theory of space and time', p. 446 n.).[28] As regards Russell's theory of terms in *POM*, he admits that his notion of a term is derived from Moore's notion of a concept (Moore 1899a), but notes that the two differ in some respects. It is difficult to be sure, but it seems to be the case that Moore is to be credited specifically with Russell's view that terms are immutable

[27] This was a minor matter. Moore's account didn't satisfy Russell for long, cf. N&P. The approach Russell uses in *POM* is to be found in Moore 1900a, it differs from the more usual, omnitemporal account Moore gave in 1899a: 186, of which Russell's later account (e.g. PLA 218) is a generalization.
[28] This last remark is open to misinterpretation. Russell's 'first perception of the difficulties in the relational theory of space and time' is plausibly attributed to the antinomy of absolute motion and it is quite clear that Moore had nothing to do with this. What Russell most likely means is that Moore was responsible for bringing him to see that this was a problem for the relational theory of space (rather than for physics) and, perhaps, for the realization that the absolute theory might be preferable to the relational theory as a result.

and eternally self-identical and are the constituents of propositions (*POM* 44, 448).

There are, however, problems in tracing Moore's influence in greater detail. For Moore's main account of his position is to be found in his article 'The Nature of Judgment' published in *Mind* in 1899 (Moore 1899*a*). This article itself, even if Russell saw it before publication, cannot have been the main source of Moore's influence, for Russell by mid–1898 already had many of the doctrines he says he came to with Moore's aid. Although Moore had published a number of papers and reviews before 'The Nature of Judgment', none of them can be regarded as the source of his influence on Russell. Moore's main writings before 1899, however, were his fellowship dissertations.[29] Moore's dissertations were ostensibly concerned with Kant's ethics. In the first he was concerned, characteristically, with making clear what Kant meant by 'freedom'; for the second he added to this an attempt to make clear what Kant meant by 'reason'. The latter topic took him a long way from ethics, and even from what could reasonably be called the metaphysical basis of ethics. (As one reader, possibly Ward, commented on the verso of the last sheet of chapter 2 of the 1898 version: '20½ pages Logic/ 6½ pages Ethics'.) It also took him a long way from Kant. His interpretation of Kant was itself highly idiosyncratic, as his examiners (Caird and Sidgwick in 1897; Bosanquet and Ward in 1898) complained and as Moore himself later admitted (1942: 21). But Moore was charmingly open about this in the introduction to the 1898 version: 'No meaning can be proved to have been [Kant's] by a mere citation of his words in one or even in several passages' (p. 4) for 'beyond somewhat narrow limits, there seems no ground for determining what a philosopher actually thought except a judgment of what it is right to think' (p. 2). Since '[i]t is impossible . . . to give an account of any man's ideas, without a knowledge of the facts to which his ideas can refer' (p. xv),[30] Moore in the 1898 version followed his two chapters on the meaning of 'reason' and 'freedom' in Kant with chapters giving his own account of these concepts. Despite its ostensible topic, therefore, Moore's second dissertation gave him plenty of scope for developing his own ideas in what would now be called the philosophy of logic.

None the less, there is little in the surviving text of either dissertation

---

[29] Moore wrote two fellowship dissertations. The first was submitted in the autumn of 1897 and rejected by his examiners. He was successful with the second version, submitted in the autumn of 1898. Both versions are titled 'The Metaphysical Basis of Ethics', and the second contains most of the material in the first, with comparatively minor changes, together with a great deal of new material. The final texts are not extant, but drafts of both are held in the Wren Library of Trinity College, Add. MSS. A247.

[30] Moore's pagination in his dissertations is as eccentric as his Kant scholarship. For the introduction to the 1898 version we have a sequence of typed pages paginated in Roman numerals, followed by a sequence of manuscript pages paginated in arabic numerals.

which would be of a great deal of help to Russell. But this gives a misleading impression, because only fragments of Moore's chapter on reason in the 1898 version exist. Many pages have been removed and others exist only in part, having been cut up and parts removed. It was the 'substance' of this chapter that was subsequently published as 'The Nature of Judgment' (Moore 1942: 22). And, indeed, the material that survives in the dissertation is very similar to that in 'The Nature of Judgment'. It seems very likely that the missing material from chapter 2 of the dissertation was taken to form the draft of 'The Nature of Judgment'.[31] None the less, Moore's dissertations cannot have been a direct influence on Russell's views. For Russell did not read the 1898 version until November 1898, after Moore's fellowship had been awarded, and after AMR had been written.[32]

Moore's main influence on Russell must have come through conversations. That this is so is hinted at by Russell (LA 162) and confirmed by Moore:

Russell left Cambridge in June 1894 . . . But . . . I used, for some six or eight years after that date, to see him frequently and discuss philosophical questions with him. These discussions took place either when I visited him at his house in the country or when he visited Cambridge. For several years in succession he and his wife took a house in Cambridge for the whole of the Lent term, and I had much discussion with him during these visits. In these discussions there was, of course, mutual influence. It is to ideas which he thought he owed to me as a result of them that Russell was referring in the Preface to his *Principles*. (Moore 1942: 15.)

In fact we can be quite a bit more specific than this. For Russell had at least two long discussions with Moore while he was writing AMR. The two men found themselves in considerable agreement, and the meetings left Russell optimistic that he would get his ideas 'considerably polished up'.[33] Of the first Russell reported: 'Moore . . . seemed on the whole inclined to assent to what I had to say', although he had pointed out one error 'which, fortunately, is very easy to set right' (ibid.). It seems clear from Russell's account at any rate that on this occasion it was Russell's ideas that were the main focus of discussion. Moore's work is only mentioned in connection with the second discussion. Again Moore is reported to have been 'not at all discouraging, and seemed to approve my subject' but this time Russell adds: 'We talked also about his work a great deal, and as usual I was pleased with his remarks'.[34] Unfortunately, he gives no further details, nor is there any indication that Moore's opinions appeared to Russell to involve any dramatic

---

[31] Moore had already used the chapter on freedom, written for the 1897 version of the dissertation, as the basis for an article 'Freedom' (1898c).

[32] It seems that Russell did not read the 1897 version. In any case, the earlier version, which is more or less complete, contains none of the doctrines we are looking for. The development of Moore's new philosophy seems to have taken place in 1897–8.

[33] B. R. to A. Russell, 10 May 1898.          [34] B. R. to A. Russell, 28 June 1898.

change in philosophical position. There is no hint of a sudden revelation. It is, of course, possible that the revelation had come earlier, that Moore had already let Russell know the direction his thought was taking. If so, the occasion seems not to have been recorded, unless it was the occasion in March 1898 when Russell read an unknown paper which resulted in a long debate with Moore about existence (see *Papers*, ii, 483–4). Alternatively, it is possible that the revelation took some time to sink in. But there is no denying that the impression Russell gives in these two letters is of two men whose thoughts were developing in very much the same direction, and that Moore's claim of 'mutual influence' is probably closer to the truth than the view Russell implies, that it was mainly he who learnt from Moore.

Russell's letters do not give any idea of the content of his discussions with Moore in the summer of 1898, nor is there any correspondence with Moore while AMR was being written. The best clue we get is from a letter of Moore's written on 11 September 1898, just after his second dissertation had been submitted. It tells us, however, more about what had not been discussed the previous summer. Moore begins by explaining how the second dissertation differed from the first and then continues:

My chief discovery which shocked me a good deal when I made it, is expressed in the form that an existent is a proposition.[35] I see now that I might have put this more mildly. Of course, by an existent must be understood an existent existent—not what exists, but that + its existence. I carefully state that a proposition is not to be understood as any thought or words, but the concepts + their relation of which we think. It is only propositions in this sense, which can be true, and from which inference can be made. Truth therefore does not depend upon any relation between ideas and reality, nor even between concepts and reality, but is an inherent property of the whole formed by certain concepts and their relations; falsehood similarly.[36] True existential propositions are those in which certain concepts stand in a specific relation to the concept existence; and I see no way of distinguishing such from what are commonly called 'existents', i.e. what exists + its existence. This explains how it should commonly be thought that a proposition can be inferred from an existent. Existents are in reality only one kind of proposition. The ultimate elements of everything that is are concepts, and a part of these, when compounded in a special way, form the existent world. With regard to the special method of composition I said nothing. There would need, I think, to be several kinds of ultimate relation between concepts—each, of course, necessary. (I shall read on this to the Aristotelian on Dec. 9th.)[37]

Russell replied enthusiastically on 13 September. On Moore's thesis that an existent is a proposition, Russell said: 'I think your expression needlessly

---

[35] This claim does not appear explicitly in what survives of the 1898 draft, but it is made in slightly less paradoxical language in 1899*a*.

[36] Russell adopted this theory of truth in *POM*, 35–48 and in MTCA 71–6.

[37] The paper to be read was 1899*a*.

paradoxical, but I imagine I agree with what you mean'. On the kinds of ultimate relations between concepts, he said: 'I agree emphatically with what you say about the several kinds of necessary relations among concepts, and I think their discovery is the true business of Logic (or Met[aphysi]cs if you like)'. He went on to explain his own classification of relations (see § 8.2).

It is clear from this brief exchange of letters that Moore had not read Russell's AMR, even though Russell had arranged in July for Moore to be sent a copy of the typescript of Book I.[38] Had he done so he would have realized that Russell had already gone quite some way towards identifying the different methods by which terms could be compounded to form propositions. Knowing this would, I think, have been a help to him, although Moore's insistence that all judgements involved relations was rejected in AMR. Russell took it up briefly in COR, written early in 1899, which fulfils the programme Moore set out for his paper to the Aristotelian Society far more directly than 'The Nature of Judgment' does. It is clear also from Moore's letter that Russell had not yet seen Moore's dissertation, and that he had not previously been told of Moore's view of the propositional nature of reality. On the other hand, it does seem reasonable to infer from Moore's letter that Russell would be familiar with Moore's use of 'concept'.

If we are to try and determine what Russell might have learnt from Moore in the summer of 1898, our main source will have to be Moore's paper (1899*a*) which Russell may have heard when it was read to the Aristotelian Society in December 1898. (Moore also read the paper to the Moral Sciences Club on 21 October 1898, but Russell was away in Italy at the time.) Assuming, as seems likely,[39] that Moore's paper followed closely chapter 2 of his 1898 dissertation, Russell would have learnt of its contents when he read the dissertation in November. How much of Moore's position was already worked out in May and June is an open question. But it seems unlikely that in May and June Moore's thinking on what Russell regarded as 'the true business of Logic' would have been more developed or more complete than the account he gave of it in the paper. The content of the paper, therefore, may safely be taken as an upper bound on what Russell could have learnt from Moore while he was writing AMR. In any case, whether or not the views Moore expressed in (1899*a*) influenced Russell in

---

[38] B. R. to G. E. Moore, 20 July 1898.

[39] Moore was a slow writer, whose views, even in this early period, did not change with the lightning rapidity of Russell's. Moreover, in Oct. Moore started giving a series of lectures on ethics in London. He took considerable pains over these lectures which were only loosely connected with the material in his fellowship dissertation (cf. Moore 1898*b*). While Moore probably did a fair amount of detailed rewriting of ch. 2 of the dissertation in preparing his paper, it seems unlikely that he would have had sufficient time radically to alter its contents.

writing AMR, they did influence Russell's subsequent thought. A detailed account of them is therefore in order.

Moore's paper was described by Russell (sixty years after its publication) as 'the first published account of the new philosophy' (*MPD* 54).[40] Moreover, Russell thought more highly of that paper than of Moore's subsequent writings.[41] None the less, other commentators have dealt less kindly with the paper, J. O. Nelson (1967: 373) refers to its 'bizarre metaphysics' and comments that: 'it is . . . with some justice that Moore's writings before 1903 have been generally ignored by succeeding generations of philosophers, as they were ignored by Moore himself in his subsequent summations and compilations of his work'. Jager (1972: 89) speaks of Moore's 'very curious paper'. Ayer's account is very similar: he calls Moore's views 'remarkable', 'very strange', and 'so extraordinary . . . that it may seem hardly worth while exhuming them' (1971: 188, 190).

Moore's characteristic starting-point is an attack on Bradley's theory of judgement. Bradley had been concerned to attack the psychologistic account of judgement to be found in the work of the British empiricists. Moore's complaint was that Bradley had not taken the elimination of psychology from logic far enough (in this, it was similar in focus to his main criticism of Russell's *EFG* in his review of the following year).[42] The most obvious symptom of this critique of Bradley is Moore's rejection of Bradley's term 'logical idea', as having too psychological a connotation, in favour of his own term 'concept'.

Moore's position is that propositions are 'composed not of words, nor yet of thoughts, but of concepts . . . In [propositions] concepts stand in specific relations with one another' (1899a: 179). 'A proposition is a synthesis of concepts . . . A proposition is constituted by a number of concepts, together with a specific relation between them' (p. 180). And 'a proposition is nothing other than a complex concept. The difference between a concept and a proposition, in virtue of which the latter alone can be called true or false, would seem to lie merely in the simplicity of the former' (p. 180). The import of Moore's theory (if not its truth) will become clear once we understand his central notion of concept. Concepts are fundamental for Moore's theory both in the sense that they are 'irreducible to anything else' (pp. 178–9) and in the sense that everything is a concept (p. 182).

[40] See also 1958, 1959a: 755, for similar statements. Russell's estimate of its importance is shared by Braithwaite (1970: 20) and Ryle (1970) who called it 'the De Interpretatione of early 20th-century Cambridge Logic' (p. 90).
[41] 1959a: 755. See also the report of a conversation in 1924 with Virginia Woolf in Woolf (1977: ii. 294).
[42] For a detailed account of Moore's criticisms of Bradley see J. McFarland (1971: 132–62) who comes to the fashionable conclusion that Moore did not provide an adequate refutation of idealism.

Moore characterizes concepts as 'possible objects of thought' (p. 179).[43] According to him 'the world [is] formed of concepts' (p. 182); as a result they are 'the only objects of knowledge' (p. 182), or 'the data of knowledge' (p. 183). As objects of thought and knowledge

> they may come into relation with a thinker . . . [But] it is indifferent to their nature whether anybody thinks them or not. They are incapable of change; and the relation into which they enter with the knowing subject implies no action or reaction. It is a unique relation which can begin or cease with a change in the subject; but the concept is neither cause nor effect of such a change.[44]

The passage just quoted makes it clear that, since concepts are unchanged by entering into a relation with a thinker, concepts are not mental items, and (although they are possible objects of thought) do not depend upon thought for their existence.

What Moore says concepts are *not* is more helpful than what he says they *are*. This is so in two important respects. Firstly, they are neither words nor thoughts (p. 179), and thus the propositions which are composed of them are neither linguistic nor mental. Moore says explicitly: 'a proposition is here to be understood, not as anything subjective—an assertion or affirmation of something—but as the combination of concepts which is affirmed' (p. 183). 'The concept is not a mental fact, nor any part of a mental fact' (p. 179). Nor are they even abstractions from ideas (p. 177) or things (p. 182); nor are they produced by the mind (p. 177).

Secondly, a concept is 'neither . . . an existent, nor . . . part of an existent, since it is presupposed in the conception of an existent' (p. 181). 'All that exists', he says, 'is . . . composed of concepts necessarily related to one another in specific manners, and likewise to the concept of existence' (p. 181). And nonexistent concepts can enter into propositional combinations with other concepts just as well as existent concepts can. '[W]hen I say "The chimera has three heads," the chimera is not an idea in my mind, nor any part of such idea. What I mean to assert is nothing about my mental states,

---

[43] Unfortunately, this doesn't make it clear whether he meant that they are items about which it is possible to think (in which case impossible items such as the round square would be concepts), or whether he means that they are possible items which can be thought about (in which case the round square would not be a concept).

[44] Ibid. 179. This passage would seem to provide solid evidence against McFarland's claim (1971: 135; see also pp. 155–6) that the 'concept . . . of something involves (a) a psychological process of cognition; (b) the objectively existent object of that process'. In any case, this thesis doesn't follow from the principles McFarland claims entail it. It seems from certain passages that McFarland thinks that Moore's concepts are possible items which actually are thought about—but it seems hard to reconcile this view with either Moore's radical rejection of psychologism or his claim that 'the world [is] formed of concepts' (p. 182): there are, pretty plainly, more things in heaven and earth than have been thought of in everyone's philosophies put together.

but a specific connexion of concepts' (p. 179). Existence itself is a concept which can be combined with other concepts to form an existential judgement.

Moore makes it no clearer than Russell did, whether nonexistent concepts are to be regarded as nonexistent objects as in Meinong's theory or as nonexistent 'contents' as I suggested was the most plausible interpretation of Russell's nonexistent terms. But, like Russell, Moore attributes 'being' to all concepts: 'in order that they *may* do anything, they must already *be* something' (p. 179).

The similarities between Moore's position in (1899*a*) and Russell's in AMR are clear enough. Terms for Russell, like concepts for Moore, are the ultimate constituents of the world and of propositions; they all have being, though only some of them exist. Some differences between Moore's concept of a concept and Russell's concept of term are more apparent than real. Russell, for example, characterizes a term as whatever may be a logical subject (AMR 167), whereas Moore characterizes a concept as a possible object of thought (1899*a*: 179). There is no substantive difference here, however, since for Russell to make a term a logical subject is to make it an object of thought. Moore's definition reflects the fact that his starting-point is in epistemology, while Russell's is in logic.

Two more important differences are worth noting, however. In AMR Russell gives no indication that terms are immutable, though he does not assert that they admit of change either. In *POM*, however, he adopted Moore's view that they were immutable (*POM* 44, 448). Secondly, Moore claims that every judgement involves a relation, but he leaves the status of the relation unclear. He does not state whether it is a constituent of the judgement (and thus a concept) or whether it is an item of an altogether different type. There was wisdom in this evasion, since if the relation which related the concepts in a judgement were itself a concept in the judgement, Moore's theory would be open to Bradley's famous regress arument. Russell, by contrast, makes it clear that *if* a relation occurred in a proposition it would be among the terms which constitute the proposition. And he makes it clear that not all propositions involve relations.

One way in which Moore very likely influenced the writing of AMR itself was in encouraging Russell to take a more critical view of Kant. There is a refreshing quality about Moore's criticism of Kant, in both versions of his dissertation. Most English criticism of Kant at the end of the nineteenth century was from a Hegelian point of view. It had the tendency to embed Kantian doctrines firmly and deeply within Hegelian categories and terminology. The result was often an impenetrable thicket of jargon and dialectic. Moore's attack was typical of his entire approach to philosophy. He found Kant's theories of freedom and reason baffling, and sought in his dissertations 'to make sense of these extremely mysterious assertions' (Moore 1942:

21). The results were hardly responsible Kantian scholarship, but they do show a philosopher trying to get to grips with the issues that exercised Kant. Russell had never been entirely uncritical of Kant, but Moore's much more forthright approach seems to have led him to reconsider the respects in which his own position depended on Kant. This had its effect mainly in epistemology. Russell credits Moore with leading him to the belief that the objects of knowledge were entirely independent of any knowing mind (*POM*: p. xviii; *MPD* 54). The doctrine that 'fact is in general independent of experience' was, he said (*MPD* 54), the one point in (1899*a*) with which he still agreed (and he thought Moore would do so too). The doctrine is readily apparent in (1899*a*: 179). Its importance is equally obvious. It marks the culmination of a developing trend in British philosophy in the late nineteenth century, namely the rejection of psychologism. Moore's anti-psychologism is to be found in his earliest published writings (e.g. 1897*b*). But it was also to be found in Bradley. Moore, however, found Bradley's practice in this respect less satisfactory than his principles. His (1899*a*) starts from a text of Bradley's about ideas, which Moore criticizes for failing to eliminate psychology sufficiently. Not surprisingly, Kant also is criticized for his psychologism throughout both dissertations and again in (1899*a*). Although Russell had been critical of psychologism in his first publication (1895*a*) and sought to frame a transcendental account of geometry which made no appeal to psychology, he, too, as we have seen, was subject to Moore's strictures for not going far enough.

Russell's acceptance of Moore's radical anti-psychologism entailed a reconsideration of the transcendental arguments that Russell had hitherto used in establishing his dialectic of the sciences. We have seen that, by the time Moore published his criticism of Russell's transcendental arguments, Russell agreed with him. In AMR we see an intermediate stage in Russell's development. The argument there concerning the logical calculus is set up in the form of a transcendental argument—the logical calculus is necessary if judgement is to be possible. That, at least, is what the argument looks like, especially to one who comes upon the argument after studying Russell's earlier efforts along similar lines. But Russell doesn't label the argument as transcendental. Moreover, if we take judgments or propositions as they were intended to be taken, as complexes of (non-mental) terms, then the sort of argument Russell seems to be advancing in Book I of AMR does not involve him in psychologism in any way whatsoever.

Moore himself was not entirely dismissive of Kant's arguments. He claimed that an argument from the possibility of experience 'does not . . . really represent the nature of Kant's argument . . . What Kant really shows is that space and time and the categories are involved in particular propositions; and this work is of greater value than a deduction from the possibility of experience would have been' (1899*a*: 190). Thus the *analysis* of propositions, the discovery of their fundamental constituents and the necessary propositions which are 'involved' in them (pp. 186–9), seems to be passed off as the true form of transcendental arguments. Moore understates the radicalism of his break with Kant, but if such arguments were to be counted as transcendental then Russell's arguments from the analysis of propositions to the calculus of symbolic logic are clearly also transcendental. This uncertainty implies no unclarity of thought. Arguments showing that certain concepts and proposi-tions were involved in the analysis of complexes of terms might be regarded as a new, non-psychologistic form of transcendental argument, or alternatively as a type of argument which was not transcendental at all, but analytical (in the very literal sense that Moore and Russell came to use when talking of their new philosophy).

Moore's criticism of transcendental arguments as traditionally understood may help explain Russell's remark in July 1898[45] that he had just discovered the question he had been asking himself for the last month. This announcement, coming shortly after discussions with Moore, may well have marked his realization that 'How is pure mathematics possible?' was the wrong question to be asking, and that the right question (in keeping with Moore's views as later expressed in 1899*a*) was 'What are the fundamental ideas and axioms of mathematics?' This was the problem he posed in a later letter to Couturat (18 July 1898) where he characterizes the purpose of his book as 'the discovery of the fundamental ideas of mathematics and the necessary judgments (axioms) which one must accept on the basis of these ideas'. It also supplied the title of a new attempt at a book on the foundations of mathematics, started the following year, 'The Fundamental Ideas and Axioms of Mathematics' (FIAM). This shift in problem was crucial, both for understanding his new approach of logical analysis, and for liberating his philosophy of mathematics from its previous Kantian foundations. It was very likely Russell's most important debt to Moore.

Russell's other main acknowledgement to Moore, however, is problematic. Russell's remark that he owes to Moore that 'pluralism which regards the world, both that of existents and that of entities, as composed of an infinite number of mutually independent entities' (*POM*: p. xviii), is both obscure and misleading. It is not the case, to begin with, that Moore converted Russell to pluralism. For Russell was always a pluralist. Nor is it immediately obvious what Russell means by 'mutually independent', for some concepts, on Moore's view, imply other concepts, and concepts may be causally related to one another. It seems, however, that Russell is referring to fundamental concepts, those concepts which may compose other concepts

---

[45] In a letter to A. Russell, 5 July 1898.

but are not themselves composed of other concepts, and that he is rejecting causality (at least by the time he wrote *POM*) as a relation in which one simple concept may depend upon another.[46] But while Moore clearly admitted concepts that were simple, and thus fundamental in the sense Russell had in mind, it is not clear from Moore's writings whether he would have regarded these as mutually independent. The one part of Russell's comprehensive attribution that can be found in Moore is the view that the world is composed of an infinite number of entities, not all of which exist. This may be the crucial debt that Russell owed to his discussion with Moore. If so, then it seems almost certain that either Russell incurred this debt in discussions prior to those he had while writing AMR or else that the manuscript of Book I of AMR was written quite late in the process of composition. For in the manuscript of Book I Russell comes so close to this view, though it is not explicitly stated,[47] that had he written it before learning of Moore's views he could hardly, I believe, have felt at all indebted to Moore on the issue of pluralism. The possibility that Russell learnt of Moore's position at an earlier meeting cannot be excluded. The problem in this case is determining when Moore arrived at his own pluralist position. So far as I know, there is no written reference to it before his second fellowship dissertation, which was almost certainly written in the summer of 1898. Nor can we exclude the other possibility, that the manuscript of Book I was written late in the composition of AMR. We do have evidence that it was preceded by an earlier draft of Book I (cf. *Papers*, ii, 239–42). Moreover, Russell reported that Moore had advised him to start with 'a dogmatic definition, instead of indulging my scepticism'.[48] The extant manuscript of Book I hardly indulges Russell's scepticism, in fact a series of dogmatic definitions is not a bad description of the first chapter. It is likely that an earlier draft of Book I, now largely lost, was the focus of Russell's discussions with Moore. In the earlier draft, indeed, Russell contrasts the pluralism necessary for mathematics with the possibility that, as Bradley had maintained, there is only one ultimate logical subject. Russell does not entirely reject this possibility (*Papers*, ii, 239). The safest, though not very specific, conclusion seems to be that Russell, sometime before the manuscript of Book I of AMR was written, accepted from Moore the basic doctrine of terms: that terms are the sole constituents of both the world and propositions.

[46] Cf. *POM*: ch. 45, for his later theory of causality. How he treated causality in AMR cannot be determined from the surviving manuscript.

[47] In AMR Russell states the *logical* doctrine that every proposition is composed entirely of terms. What is missing is the corresponding *metaphysical* doctrine that the world is composed entirely of terms. Had Russell intended to assert the former but not the latter, he would have been committed to the view (which surely he never held) that there were ineffable constituents of the world.

[48] B. R. to A. Russell, 28 June 1898.

What becomes clear from a comparison of Russell's AMR and Moore (1899*a*) is how much further Russell had taken this basic doctrine. In Russell's version of the theory we find, for example, categorical distinctions drawn between different kinds of terms, an attempt at a genuine taxonomy of judgements, an account of the roles that different types of term play in a proposition, some attempt to expound the logical relations between different judgements, and the beginning (however flawed) of an attempt to represent the theory of terms by means of a logical calculus. None of this is to be found in Moore. This, of course, at least partly reflects the differing interests of the two men. Moore's primary concern was with ethics, and this did not require him to press much beyond the basic doctrine, although he did elaborate a theory of truth (something which is missing in Russell's early works of 1898). Russell's desire to apply the theory in mathematics required a much fuller account of the fundamental logical apparatus. It also reflects, however, the speed with which Russell worked, and his penchant, already noted, for taking the development of an idea a long way before he was satisfied with it. Ironically, it may also help to explain the acknowledgements he made to Moore, which must appear excessive. It is clear that Moore's ideas at best formed the starting-point for Russell's own work, which developed in ways which cannot, in general, be traced back to Moore's influence. It is possible that Russell was concerned lest Moore's role in the development be altogether forgotten.

It is also possible that he feared that Moore might think his work had been plagiarized. This situation is not unique in Russell's career. Lowe (1985: 229) records a similar episode in Russell's use of Whitehead's method of extensive abstraction. In this case, also, Russell learnt of the method while Whitehead was still developing it. Russell rushed into print with applications of it that Whitehead had never contemplated, and abandoned it in favour of an alternative method of his own, all before Whitehead had got a full-fledged version of the method into print. Notwithstanding the fact that Russell's acknowledgements were excessive (see Miah 1987), Whitehead not surprisingly felt that, simultaneously, his thunder had been stolen and his position misrepresented. Russell was both an omnivorous devourer of other people's ideas and a highly original thinker. As a result, the ideas he got from others were often transmuted into parts of his system. Whether he realized they had been transmuted is often disputed, but I think he was more aware of it than he is usually given credit for. He was also an astonishingly fast worker and a prolific publisher, which meant that it was often his version which reached print first. Finally, he was a generous man who tried to be fair, a trait which expressed itself in exaggerated acknowledgements which often ended up associating someone else's name with whole blocks of his philosophy of which they had very little idea and quite possibly even less sympathy. It was a method of proceeding that has led to Russell's career being strewn with exegetical problems and irritated friends. Russell's earliest debts to Moore seem in part, to have been of this kind. There may be irony, as well as modesty, in Moore's reference to 'ideas which [Russell] thought he owed to me' (Moore 1942: 15).

## 7.3 'AN ANALYSIS OF MATHEMATICAL REASONING': ARITHMETICAL ASPECTS

In Book II of AMR Russell divides arithmetic judgements into two classes, those which assert numbers of collections of terms, and those which assert necessary connections between numbers. Logically, the second group is more fundamental since such necessary connections as there are must derive directly from the meanings of the number-predicates. None the less Russell starts with the first group, which he calls 'existential judgments of number', since these are more closely related to the logical calculus (p. 196). Number in AMR is adjectival, it gives a series of qualities, the natural numbers which may be applied to the extensions of concepts. Russell's account of number in AMR should not be confused with that of SDCQ and RNQ, where numbers were to be obtained by abstraction from instances of a concept via a synthesis of the resulting units. This remains, for Russell, an account of how numbers are applied to classes, as we shall see, but it doesn't give the essence of number itself. Numbers are no longer created by the mind through a process of counting, as they seem to have been on Russell's earlier Kantian theory (protestations of anti-psychologism notwithstanding). In AMR number is said to be 'incapable of analysis or derivation' (p. 196). Numbers 'are not properties abstracted from collections of terms, but are logically independent contents. . . . Numbers . . . are not qualities abstracted from sense . . . but are primarily pure conceptions' (pp. 199–200). They express a relation between the single instance of the concept, which functions as a unit, and the 'whole collection of instances' (p. 197).

The cardinal number of a class is thus like a ratio, and it presupposes a unit. The unit cannot be defined numerically, since it is presupposed by number. But it must be either a thing or a predicate taken as a term (which Russell now calls a concept), for classes are formed either of things or of concepts. In the case of classes of things, the unit, i.e. a single thing, can be defined 'as that of which one conception can be predicated' (p. 197). Thus the choice of a unit in the case of things is thrown back on the identification of individual concepts. The identification of the unit in the case of classes of concepts is possible owing to the brute fact that there are differences of content (or differences of meaning) which, Russell says, 'appears to be an ultimate truth concerning which . . ., there is nothing more to be said' (p. 197).

None the less, what are enumerated in counting the members of a class of concepts are materially diverse contents, not differences of content (p. 198).[49]

The mutual relations between things as units and concepts as units are thus rather complicated. On the one hand, a thing can only be individuated by means of a concept under which it falls. On the other, while concepts can be individuated by means of their diversity of meaning, the diversity among concepts which is relevant for their enumeration is not diversity of meaning, but the diversity of being which results from it. In this way, Russell maintains, 'it comes about that number applies in exactly the same way to things . . . or to whatever has material diversity, as to different contents' (p. 198). Finally, since in order to be a member of class a term must fall under the defining predicate of the class, a collection of terms (things or concepts) which is capable of numeration must have some 'point of agreement'. This point of agreement is identity of content. Thus, in the case of any enumeration, '[t]he diversity must be material diversity, but the identity must be identity of content' (p. 198). Russell, however, hopes that symmetry will be restored by the fact that 'the diversity is constituted by diversity of content, and that the identity constitutes all the terms into one thing [i.e. a single class]' (p. 198). Russell's continual anxiety to ensure a symmetry between terms and meanings is apt to appear quaint, unless it is remembered that, if his system is to fit together as it should extensions and intensions must appear as duals.

It would seem, from what Russell has just said, that diversity of content is fundamental for all kinds of diversity. Yet earlier he has given an argument which purported to show that at some point there must be material diversity without conceptual diversity (p. 186), which would appear to make material diversity fundamental. It is not easy to see how these two strands of thought can be reconciled. Russell does not draw attention to the problem, but it would seem to be connected to the fundamental antinomies: material diversity without conceptual diversity being a case of a conception of difference without a difference of conception, and conceptual diversity without material diversity being a case of a difference of conception without a conception of difference.

One feature of Russell's account, which figures also in more recent accounts of enumeration and identity (e.g. Geach 1962, but see also Frege 1884: 40, 1893: ii, 254), is what Russell calls the relativity of the unit. In making number apply to instances of a concept the number we will want to apply to a collection will depend upon which concept we choose to cover the collection. For example, given an army in mobilization we will get different answers to the question 'How many?' depending whether we count troops or divisions. Which means, of course, that it depends upon what we choose as

[49] Once again Russell's terminology has changed. Originally, material diversity was the kind of diversity appropriate to things. What would seem to be involved in the present case is what Russell has earlier called diversity of being.

our unit. As Russell says, 'three things are just as much as one thing, and the number to be applied to any actual object depends . . . upon the manner in which we introduce conceptual differentiation in the object' (p. 200). Just as 3 cannot be regarded as an intrinsic property of the collection, so 1 cannot be regarded as an intrinsic property of the unit: '1 means "one of the collection"' (p. 206), and thus presupposes some concept of which the unit is an instance.

Russell discusses whether the 'relativity of the unit' has any limitations, i.e. whether there are any absolute units. He finds them at either end of the spectrum of terms. At one end are the terms which are simple, in the sense of having no parts. He gives the positive integers, points of space and time, and men[50] as examples. At the other extreme there is the term to which nothing could be added, namely the universe or the set of all terms (pp. 210–11). Where we have an absolute unit in the first sense, i.e. where the unit is indivisible, the ratio theory of number can be avoided. Any collection of indivisible units has an absolute number. Contrary to his earlier view (SDCQ, RNQ) he now says that 'ratio, *per se*, does not demand divisibility; consequently two indivisible terms may have to each other a numerical ratio' (p. 211). What he has in mind is perhaps that the one term forms a certain fraction of some whole and the other some other fraction of a different whole. Thus one person may form half a given family, while a different person forms one-third of another family. Thus the two persons are brought into an indirect numerical ratio without divisibility. This would not seem to be a fundamental difficulty for Russell's ratio theory of number. The cases considered are cases where ratio *may* be avoided, not cases where it has to be. But Russell treats them as a limitation of the ratio theory which coincides with a limitation 'to the application of number itself' (p. 211). It is difficult to see why he should think this is so, and, unfortunately, the pages on which he might have explained it are the ones which are missing. We have only the remark that he has already shown that 'ratio gives the very meaning of number' (p. 211). Given Russell's distrust of infinite numbers we might easily expect him to deny that the class of all terms had a number—indeed, assigning a number to it, as it is presently characterized, would be paradoxical. But it is hard to see why Russell might think the application of number to finite sets of simple, indivisible terms should be problematic.

The second type of judgement concerning number comprises judgements which assert necessary connection between cardinals, e.g. the judgement that $2 + 3 = 5$. Russell first disposes of a number of views he regards as mistaken. For example, the view that numbers are made up as a sum of parts. On such a view 3 might be regarded as the sum of 2 and 1, but then,

---

[50] Regarded presumably as (simple) centres of consciousness. Russell thus belongs to the long tradition, the history of which is narrated by Mijuskovich (1974), which treated the self as simple. Russell seems to have held this position until he became a neutral monist 1918. See Wittgenstein's criticism (1921: 5.5421).

Russell says, '3 = 2 + 1 would have no meaning' (i.e. would be a tautology) and arithmetic addition would be impossible (p. 200). This shows that '=' as used in arithmetic does not express absolute identity but 'necessary connexions of contents' (p. 200). Nor does the number 1 express indivisibility or unity; whatever is is one but is not necessarily indivisible, and every item to which number can be applied is a unity of some kind. '[A]nything which has unity is one in some sense, though not necessarily for the purposes of arithmetic.' (p. 200). This gives two senses of 'one' which Russell now distinguishes notationally: using '1' for the arithmetic sense and *one* for the other, in which whatever has some kind of unity is *one*.

The relation of the class concept /number/ to particular numbers such as /3/, is like that of species to particular, except (1) that particular numbers are not arrived by giving further specifications under the general conception, and (2) that the general concept not only involves all the particular instances, but each particular instance involves all the others. The latter point Russell expresses in a way that still owes much to Hegel: 'Not only is the conception of number a self-determining universal, but the numbers are mutually determining particulars' (p. 201). In this, the relation would seem to be unique. But the way in which the particular numbers determine each other gives rise to difficulties, having to do with the interpretation of addition among pure numbers (for it is by addition that all particular numbers are related to each other). In the case of numbers applied to classes, the understanding of addition is quite clear, depending as it does upon addition of classes in the logical calculus. But in the case of pure numbers this account is blocked, since existential numerical judgements depend upon the necessary judgements (pp. 196, 201), and judgements such as /3 = 2 + 1/ should be understood as necessary connections between the concepts /3/, /2/, and /1/ (p. 201). Certainly in such a judgement /1/ and /2/ cannot be added as terms, for that would result in an assemblage of two numbers.

Yet it is addition in the logical calculus which Russell uses to obtain the explanation he desires. The relevant feature of logical addition is that any two terms may be combined in such a way as to form a third single term. According to Russell, 'This seems to depend upon a certain kind of relativity, developed fully in space and time,[51] according to which, if there is a relation between two terms, we may combine them to form a single term of which the relation is an adjective' (p. 202). Applying this to number, '1 + 1 = 2 would mean: If any term has a relation to another term, they can be combined to form a single subject: the operation of combining them is denoted by 1 + 1, while the property acquired by the whole solely in virtue of their being so

[51] It is not clear to me why Russell thinks space and time are specially privileged here. The point would seem to apply equally (and more basically), to the manifold of terms. Russell's remark probably indicates the lingering influence of Kant.

combined, and without reference to the particular nature of the relation, is that which we call 2,' (p. 202). The necessity of the judgement is then held to reside in the fact that the features of the particular relation which combines the two are not involved. The trouble with this account seems to be that it doesn't overcome Russell's own problem about the combination of /1/ and /2/ as terms. For, suppose we combine /2/ and /1/, why shouldn't the property acquired by the whole as a result of the combination be also /2/? Obviously the content of the terms combined has to be taken into account. Yet it cannot be the case that /2/ and /1/ are combined as meanings in addition, for that would give only the property of being both /2/ and /1/, which would, for Russell, be no real property because it is contradictory. I shall call this the problem of combination. It is the analogue for necessary arithmetical judgements of the one–many problem (mentioned in § 6.1) for existential judgements of number. Obviously what is needed is some form of combination which will take only the numerical content of /2/ and /1/ into account in addition.

This is to be done, according to Russell, by breaking up the collection into its units:

> [T]he addition of numbers other than unity demands their analysis into 1's before they are added. Take, for example, 2 + 3 = 5. If we added the term which has the property 2 to the term which has the property 3, we should merely get two terms. We must break the terms up into their respective units, and substitute 1 + 1 for 2 and 1 + 1 + 1 for 3. We must then combine all the units so obtained, to form a new subject which has the property 5. Generally speaking, it is not numbers, but the terms numbered which are added. (p. 204.)

One problem here is that we are supposed to be dealing with a necessary connection between the numbers /2/, /3/, and /5/. But these terms are simple and indivisible, so it cannot be the numbers themselves which have to be broken up into their units. It is, Russell says, the terms which have these numbers as properties that have to be broken up. But, considered simply as a judgement of a necessary connection between terms, /2 + 3 = 5/ makes no reference to such collections. It would seem, therefore, that Russell's account of /2 + 3 = 5/ does not capture the meaning of the original. A more fundamental problem, however, arises from the fact that Russell's assertion that a term has the property /2/ brings back the original form of the one–many problem. For the term which has the property /2/ is one. As was noted earlier, the one–many problem does not arise on the ratio theory of number, and it might be hoped that Russell's present theory successfully avoids it. This, however, is not the case, for reasons which depend upon Russell's neo-Hegelian theory of relations. We shall, therefore, return to the one–many problems in § 8.3, after Russell's treatment of relations has been examined.

# 8

# Relations
# The End of Russell's Apprenticeship

## 8.1 ANTINOMIES

It is no cause for surprise that antinomies played a major role in structuring Russell's dialectic of the sciences. It is more surprising that he never attempted a general theory of antinomies. Although individual antinomies clearly took up a good deal of his time, there is no discussion of antinomies in general in any of his surviving works from the 1890s, and even brief remarks and asides on the topic are few and far between. To modern readers this is both surprising and irritating, because by modern standards Russell's use of 'antinomy' and 'contradiction' seems loose and even chaotic. Russell used the words interchangeably of a wide range of puzzles including infinite regresses, vicious circles, false abstractions, contradictions, and paralogisms of all kinds. Some distinctions were essential to his dialectic; for example, that between those antinomies which can be resolved within a science and those which force a transition to a new science. But even this distinction is tackled by trial and error: a contradiction belongs to the former class, it seems, just in case Russell has a way of eliminating it within the science. But even this distinction raises fresh questions about what is to count as an elimination within the science; i.e. which concepts count as part of the science in question? For if the science is inconsistent without the addition of some further concept then, at least for sciences closed under standard consequence relations, the additional concept must be part of the science.[1] This suggests the further question of how the addition of further propositions to an inconsistent set of propositions could resolve the inconsistency.[2] Clearly Russell is using 'contradiction' in a way not readily recognizable today.

One of Russell's few general remarks on contradictions is relevant to this last point. In a note written in 1896 he distinguishes two kinds of dialectical transition: that from an incomplete idea to its supplement, and that from a self-contradictory idea to an idea which does not contain the contradiction

---

[1] Suppose, to consider a properly propositional case, that a science $S$ implies $p$ & $\sim p$, unless $q$ (for some $p$ and $q$). Then $S$ & $\sim(p$ & $\sim p) \supset . q$. So $S \supset q$. This suggests that sciences conceived within a dialectical framework should be closed under some other implication relation than the usual ones. Russellian implication was in any case non-standard; his talk of implication holding between concepts was clearly intentional, cf. AMR 172; FIAM 293.

[2] For if $S \supset . p$ & $\sim p$, $S$ & $q \supset . p$ & $\sim p$, at least in the usual (monotonic) logics.

(VN 17). He gives the transitions from number to things numerable and from space to matter as instances of the former, and the transitions from continua to discreta and from force to conation as instances of the latter. Certainly this is an improvement on much neo-Hegelian material where, typically, no such distinction between incompleteness and inconsistency is made.[3] None the less, it does not take us much further forward. For it leaves unaddressed the questions just raised. If, to adapt my earlier argument to Russell's switch from inconsistency to incompleteness, a concept $C$ belonging to a science $S$ is (say) meaningless or unintelligible unless another concept $C'$ is added, then surely this is as good a reason as we could wish to find for concluding that $C'$ is itself part of $S$. We have already seen that Russell was disturbed by exactly this problem in discussing the demarcation between geometry and kinematics, though he offered no meta-dialectical reflections upon it. It is not necessarily a very deep problem, however. For it is surely open to a good neo-Hegelian to maintain that under dialectical conditions the conventional divisions between the sciences will whither away, leaving a single harmonious science of the Absolute.

Nor does the distinction in itself help much with the second problem raised above. For if a science is genuinely self-contradictory it is not at all clear how adding anything more to it will resolve its contradictions. What is required here, as Russell notes, is not the addition of fresh concepts, but a replacement of the old ones by new. But this does not suggest a dialectical synthesis in which old and new are combined. If force is to be *replaced* by conation then physics is to be *replaced* by psychology: we do not get a dialectical union of physics with psychology. This is quite possibly what Russell had in mind. His remarks on the transition from force to conation are far too brief to help us decide. But his longer writings on continuity in 1896, when he was clearly searching for ways to avoid assuming continuity in any science, suggest that he thought the notion in need of complete replacement (cf. SDCQ 58). The result, of course, is not a true dialectical transition at all. But fidelity to Hegel was never a major concern for the neo-Hegelians, least of all for Russell.

It has to be admitted that in those of Russell's writings of the 1890s which have survived there is hardly even the beginnings of a theory of contradiction. There are probably three reasons for this. In the first place, the notion of

---

[3] In Bradley, at any rate, it seems a holistic justification for the absence of this distinction might be given. For if every science is deductively closed and if, from any truth, all others could be inferred, it would follow that an incomplete science is necessarily inconsistent. Since for each such science, there would necessarily be a truth that the science would both entail (since the science is deductively closed) and not entail (since the science was incomplete). It is the abstraction, upon which each individual science depends, that renders the science incomplete, i.e which ensures (contrary to the demands of holism) that there are truths which it does not contain.

contradiction was pretty much taken for granted by the neo-Hegelians in general, and bandied about by them with at least as much confusion as by Russell himself. Russell, who after all was still a very young man in 1896, might be pardoned for assuming that his elders and betters knew what they were talking about, and that it would make sense if he talked the same way. Secondly, it was entirely in keeping with his policy of beginning in the middle with a fully formed science (rather than at either extreme of brute emprical data or abstract a priori principle) that he should work first on the logical analysis of particular sciences. To have laid down an a priori theory of contradiction in advance of a detailed discussion of the individual sciences would have been to make the same mistake as Hegel, and to have produced (in all likelihood) a dialectic at variance with the best scientific results of the day. It is not so surprising, therefore, that he should have let his investigation into the individual sciences go where it would, expecting no doubt that the meta-theoretical aspects of the investigation would be clearer at the end than they were en route. Thirdly, there seems little doubt that in at least one respect the meta-theory did clarify as Russell worked, even though he did not make it a direct object of investigation. As his work progressed certain types of contradiction began to dominate his thinking, so that other contradictions were either ignored or reformulated to make them fit with the dominant types.

Russell's neo-Hegelian paradoxes are essentially of two different kinds: there are paradoxes of relativity and paradoxes of parts and wholes. The latter occurred, for example, in geometry where points were taken to be parts of space, but parts which, when combined together, did not form any whole. Conversely, they arose when a whole was given but no parts (in the sense of ultimate constituents) could be found because the whole was infinitely divisible. (Russell often referred to paradoxes of this type as paradoxes of infinite divisibility.) It is not hard to see connections between these paradoxes and some of the paradoxes which Russell was soon to make famous. The Cantor cardinality paradox, for example, can without too much difficulty be given a neo-Hegelian gloss as a part–whole paradox. If $C$ is the set of all cardinals, then the cardinality of $C$, it might naturally be assumed, must be the greatest cardinal. But Cantor had proved that for finite and infinite sets alike the cardinality of a set was always less than the cardinality of its power-set. Accordingly, the cardinality of the power-set of $C$ is greater than that of $C$ itself. Thus there is a cardinal greater than the greatest cardinal. Now it would not be hard to diagnose this from a neo-Hegelian point of view as a part–whole paradox, derived from falsely hypostatizing an infinite whole. The cardinal numbers, because there are infinitely many of them, are merely so many elements which together have no tendency to form a whole, and thus no basis for talking of the power-set of the whole. Yet since we can talk of all of them, there must be a whole which they form. On the one hand, there can be no set of all cardinals and talk of its cardinality is a mistake. On the other, there is such a set and it must have a cardinal. In 1899 Russell formulated an antinomy of infinite number along these lines. He argues that if there is a set of all numbers then there must be a number of numbers. Let $N$ be that number. But $N + 1$ is a larger number. So no number is the number of numbers (FIAM 265). He missed a genuine antinomy, however, by falsely supposing that $N + 1 > N$, for all $N$.

The part–whole paradoxes emerged, as we have seen, in two (related) areas of Russell's dialectic, namely geometry and those parts of pure mathematics (viz. analysis) which took continuous quantity as their subject matter. They were especially troublesome because they were not, as Russell eventually recognized, the sort of contradictions which could be removed simply by a transition to a more comprehensive science. They arose, Russell maintained, from a false hypostatization of relations (cf. § 4.8). For, on Russell's account, it was relations holding between elements which enabled a multiplicity of items to compose a whole of any kind. In this, Russell's diagnosis did not conflict with the more orthodox Hegelian view which saw them as resulting from a false hypostatization of infinite wholes—the traditional 'false infinites' of the Hegelians and other philosophers. None the less, it is significant that Russell should have focused on relations as the root of these antinomies. In 1896, in the heyday of Russell's point-atomism it seemed that the antinomies might be definitively eliminated by showing that the supposedly fundamental concepts which apparently gave rise to them were not, after all, necessary to the sciences in question; in short, by showing that there was no need to hypostatize relations and no such thing as continuous quantity. Russell's adoption of plenal physics in 1897 made this resolution untenable and other measures against part–whole paradoxes were necessary by 1898.

The other group of paradoxes were what I shall call paradoxes of relativity, although a common form for them did not emerge in Russell's writings until 1898. These were of continuous concern to Russell from 1896 to 1899 when he finally abandoned the hidden premiss on which they were based. These were paradoxes which offered some promise of elimination through a dialectical transition to a wider science, although by 1898 Russell's hopes that they could be entirely eliminated in this way must have been growing thin, since, with each dialectical transition, new contradictions exactly like the old emerged. Russell's first step towards a recognition of the paradoxes of relativity as an identifiable subgroup of paradoxes came with his identification of the antinomy of quantity in 1897.

The pattern common to Russell's paradoxes of relativity can be seen by comparing a number of different antinomies located in the various sciences of Russell's dialectic. In each case relations are crucially involved. We have the following:

1. *Pure mathematics: the antinomy of the quantity*. Different quantities are alike, yet each is distinct. What distinguishes them are their relations to other quantities (e.g. the extent to which they differ from standard measures). But such differences are *purely* relational, they have no basis in the intrinsic qualities of the various quantities. We have, therefore, a conception of difference without a difference of conception.

2. *Logic: the antinomy of quality*. Different qualities are distinguished by the fact that each has a different content from the others. But the difference of content cannot itself be a distinct quality, for it would have to be distinct from every quality. In this case, we have a difference of conception without a conception of difference.

3. *Geometry: the antinomy of free mobility*. The possibility of distinguishing different extended experiential contents depends upon geometry, which in turn depends upon the axiom of free mobility. But, since space is purely relational, spatial figures cannot be moved. The possibility of free mobility, therefore, requires extended contents (e.g. extended portions of kinematic matter) which occupy space and which can be moved to different positions without loss of identity. Yet, since figures of kinematic matter lack intrinsic (dynamical) properties, they can be distinguished only by their relative positions. The attempt at a relational specification results in a circularity.

4. *Geometry: the antinomy of the point*. All points are alike, yet each is distinct. Distinctions among points can only be made by means of their relations to other points. Here, as in the antinomy of quantity, these are differences which are not based upon any intrinsic difference, but are purely relational.

5. *Dynamics: the antinomy of absolute motion*. Different material objects can be distinguished (in the absence of absolute space) only by means of their dynamical relations to other material objects. But differences of dynamical relations can only be determined (in the absence of absolute space) if different material bodies can be distinguished. Differences of mass, for example, can be determined only by differences of acceleration which must be determined with respect to some material body. Again, we have differences which, although apparently based upon intrinsic qualities such as mass, turn out to be purely relational (since mass turns out, on analysis, to be relational).

6. *Kinematics: the antinomy of absolute position*.[4] Different portions of kinematical matter can be distinguished by their positions but (in the absence of absolute position) different positions can be distinguished only in

---

[4] Russell provides little explicit discussion of this antinomy. It is very similar to the antinomy of the point.

relation to kinematical matter. As before, the differences turn out to be purely relational.

The similarities between these six antinomies are perhaps clear enough. In each case, there is an implicit or explicit circularity. In each case we have a need to distinguish items of some kind, and in each case we can provide the necessary distinctions only by reference either to other items of the same kind (which presupposes that at least some items of that kind are already distinguished) or else to items of some other kind—which items, so it turns out on further analysis, can only be distinguished by reference to items of the first kind. It is not difficult to see similarities between these paradoxes of relativity and Russell's later paradoxes which violate the vicious circle principle (cf. *PM* i, 37–8). The two are not the same, however, otherwise Russell's moves against the paradoxes of relativity would suffice to block the vicious circle paradoxes. In particular, the vicious circle paradoxes are those in which items can be defined only by reference to a totality which contains the items in question. The paradoxes of relativity do not depend upon totalities (unlike the part–whole paradoxes). Nor do they depend directly upon definition. Russell in 1898, of course, had two notions of definition, mathematical and philosophical. He would have maintained that individual points (e.g.) could be mathematically defined by means of their relations to other points, but that no philosophical definition of any point could be given, because points were simple. A philosophical definition of any item was possible only when the item was complex and could be analysed into its constituents and when these constituents served to distinguish it from all other items. Philosophical definition, therefore, depends upon an item having intrinsic, differentiating constituents.

In the early stages of the dialectic, Russell's hope was to break out of the circularities created by the antinomies of relativity by means of transitions to new sciences which would provide fresh conceptual resources. On this diagnosis the antinomies were held to be the result of undue abstraction on the part of the individual sciences. But, as we have seen in individual cases, at each stage the new concepts merely widened the circle, they did not remove it. In the earlier stages of the dialectic this result could be tolerated, but with the transition to psychology the dialectic was running short of places to go, and yet the circularities remained (see § 5.3).

The first step in Russell's recognition of what was wrong came with his codification in AMR of the various antinomies in a way which revealed their dependence on relations. He identified an antinomy, closely modelled on the antinomy of quantity, which he called 'the contradiction of relativity', namely 'the contradiction of a difference between two terms, without a difference in the conceptions applicable to them'. He thought this antinomy so pervasive in mathematics as to provide a partial definition of its subject-matter (AMR 166). It seems likely that in AMR he reformulated, or intended to reformulate, all of the antinomies listed above (except that of quality, about which he says little) as specific forms of the contradiction of relativity.[5]

The most important advantage of formulating the antinomies as instances of the contradiction of relativity was that doing so made it *less* clear why they were antinomies. Indeed, to modern eyes there seems no contradiction whatsoever in there being a '[relational] difference between two terms, without a difference in the [intrinsic] conceptions applicable to them'. The contradiction, for Russell, came from his interpretation of the doctrine of internal relations. For Russell, as (at least in part) a good Bradleian, all relations must be internal. Russell took this to be the requirement that all relations must be based upon intrinsic adjectives of their relata (cf. MTT 139). Russell is often criticized for subsequently attacking this view as if it were Bradley's, and there is some justice in the charge. On occasion he writes as if the view were held by all neo-Hegelians (MTT 141). In slightly earlier writings, however, he does distinguish the doctrine of internal relations just stated (which he calls the 'monadistic view' of relations) with an alternative (monistic) view, which treats relations as dependent upon an adjective of the whole constituted by their terms (*POM* 221).[6] But this was not exactly Bradley's position either (Sprigge 1979). For, on this view, relational propositions with different terms will be reduced to adjectival propositions with different subjects. As Russell was very well aware, Bradley held that all propositions have the same subject (cf. WDWR 95; *Papers*, ii, 239). In *POM* Russell argues that a monistic theory of relations is driven to the conclusion that 'the only true whole, the Absolute, has no parts at all', a position which he regards as self-contradictory (*POM* 226). Russell, even as a neo-Hegelian, had never been seriously attracted to this position. His argument, however, is valid only if it is assumed that the monistic view of relations holds for all relational propositions, and this (as already noted) may be denied. None the less, Russell's use of this argument helps explain why he does not direct his attack against Bradley's theory itself.

Moreover, it is hardly surprising that when Russell, later in his career, attacks neo-Hegelianism it is his own version of neo-Hegelianism he has most firmly in mind. Though that version was hardly the most popular or

---

[5] He gives the antinomy of the point as an instance of the contradiction of relativity in EAE 328 n.

[6] This suggests that the two views should be regarded as exclusive alternatives, although it would seem prima facie that one could consistently urge that some relations be eliminated by the first method and others by the second. Elsewhere, Russell gave the impression that the monadistic analysis was a sort of preliminary stage, prior to the monistic analysis which held 'in ultimate analysis' (AMR/TS 224; *MPD* 54).

well-known one, it was (trivially) the version which, by Russell's lights, had most to commend it. At the turn of the century Russell had more important philosophical concerns than Bradleian exegesis or historical scholarship. It will not suffice to undermine his arguments to point out that the position he attacks is not Bradley's and it is simply false to claim that he was unaware of what Bradley's position was. If one is to attack Russell's critique of neo-Hegelianism for not taking Bradley's position seriously enough one must do it on the grounds that he never mounts a serious argument against Bradley's doctrine of degrees of truth, not that he ignores Bradley's theory of relations. For what Russell shows is that the latter is self-contradictory without the former.

In his attack on relational reduction in *POM*, Russell, quite understandably, gives pride of place to the monadistic view. Although he does on occasion appeal to the monistic theory, as when he talks of distance as a 'measurable intrinsic relation' of two point-atoms (VN 12). But the monadistic theory is not a position that Russell foists on Bradley, nor was it a position he invented for himself. The theory, pretty much as Russell presents it, is to be found in Lotze (1879: i, 191). Lotze, it is true, favours an idealist reduction of relations according to which relations are supplied entirely by the mind. Russell's anti-psychologism would have left him unsympathetic to this suggestion, but Lotze's alternative, the only view he regards as possible if relations are to be considered mind-independent, is the monadistic theory.

It was Russell's version of the doctrine of internal relations which made the contradiction of relativity genuinely contradictory. For two quantities or two points to be genuinely different, it was necessary, if the claims of Russell's doctrine of internal relations were to be met, that the quantities or points differ, not merely in their relations, but in their intrinsic qualities. Yet in their intrinsic qualities it is admitted that points and quantities are all alike. Formulating the contradiction of relativity explicitly made it easier to see that the doctrine of internal relations was chiefly responsible for the antinomies found in the individual sciences, though Russell's recognition of this fact was not immediate. We must make allowances here for the fact that Russell was now beginning to examine the hitherto unexpressed assumption on which his neo-Hegelian system was based.

The antinomy of quality stands outside this account, and it is of some importance to appreciate its peculiarity. The antinomy of quality is the converse of the contradiction of relativity. In the antinomy of quality we have different intrinsic conceptions with no concept of the difference between them. The antinomy of quality, therefore, does not depend upon the doctrine of internal relations as do the other antinomies, but upon its converse; that is, upon the doctrine that given any two conceptually different items there is a relation (or proto-relation) which conceptualizes their difference. Quite what status (if any) this proposition had in Russell's thought is hard to determine, since it seems to be logically independent of the rest of his system. But it is clear that the antinomy of quality will not be resolved by dropping the doctrine of internal relations. The antinomy of quality does not explicitly appear in Russell's writings outside 'Various Notes' and seems to have played a comparatively minor role in the development of his dialectic. In part, this might be merely a matter of emphasis: the antinomy of quality belongs to logic and Russell, until the very end of his neo-Hegelian period, paid very little attention to purely logical matters. It seems more likely, however, that the antinomy was recognized as illusory on account of the reductive theory of relations. It would seem that, once difference of content is recognized as a proto-relation, the difference between two concepts will be expressible without antinomy. Russell's love of symmetries may well have played him false here. For the duality of the antinomies of quantity and quality is more apparent than real, since, owing to the reductive theory of relations, qualities and relations play asymmetrical roles in Russell's philosophy.

The doctrine of internal relations also provided a link with the part–whole paradoxes. Russell's diagnosis of the part–whole paradoxes as involving the false hypostatization of relations does not adequately reveal the relevant connections. The part–whole paradoxes arise in connection with continuous quantity, where it proves impossible to combine any number of parts into a single whole, and conversely to analyse any whole into parts. The point was not, as Russell sometimes made it appear (see above Ch. 6, p. 249), a merely verbal one: that in calling something a whole one presupposes that it has parts, and in calling something a part one presupposes that there is a whole of which it is a part. The pre-eminent example is that of space where points are typically taken to stand to space itself as parts stand to whole. Yet no analysis of a finite spatial extent will yield spatial points, and no combination of points will result in a finite spatial extent. But this familiar view on infinite divisibility is not the whole story. For the part–whole paradoxes remain even if infinite divisibility is eschewed and continuity rejected. Indeed, when Russell denies that points can form wholes his claim is more radical than the familiar (if false) one that no finite extent may be composed of points. For a set of points is a whole of which the points are parts, yet, since the set may have only finitely many members, this is not a whole which can be ruled out by considerations against infinite totalities.

Ultimately, it is not the large size of the collections, nor the small size of the points, which creates Russell's difficulties about parts and wholes, but the homogeneity of the points: each point is exactly like all the others. It is the homogeneity of the parts in, say, a continuum which makes them incapable of cohering into a whole (*EFG* 166; cf. Bradley 1883: i, 289 n., Bosanquet 1888: 197). Russell's argument here depends, once again, on the doctrine of internal relations. If a number of elements form a whole, they must in some way be related. But, by Russell's doctrine of internal relations, two items can be related only if the relation can be founded upon their intrinsic qualities. Combining the parts of a continuum into a whole, therefore, would destroy the homogeneity of the parts which was necessary if they were to form a continuum. Putting the argument into reverse: since the parts of a continuum are homogeneous they lack the intrinsic qualities which alone would make it possible to combine them into a whole.

It can be seen, therefore, that the doctrine of internal relations is responsible for both kinds of antinomy in Russell's dialectic of the sciences. The rejection of the doctrine of internal relations was the means by which Russell was able to escape from the antinomies in which he was enmeshed. This move, which entailed the abandonment of neo-Hegelianism, was not, however, one which he embraced immediately.

## 8.1 THE THEORY OF RELATIONS

At this point it is desirable to be somewhat more precise in our terminology, and to make distinctions which Russell sometimes ignored. With the advantages of hindsight we can make clear at the outset certain things which Russell had to struggle hard to get clear (and some where clarity seemed always to elude him). In doing this, we run the risk of misinterpreting Russell's struggle with the problems of his neo-Hegelian system, but the danger of not doing it is that we become confused ourselves about the various distinct issues that were involved.

In the first place, Russell's doctrine of internal relations was the thesis that relations hold between terms only in virtue of the intrinsic properties of those terms. The first need is to distinguish those properties which are intrinsic from those which are not. The distinction is not to be drawn in terms of the number of argument places involved. For some genuinely one-place properties are clearly not intrinsic properties, e.g. $(\lambda x)xRb$. The aim is to capture what Russell meant when he spoke of a property having an external reference (e.g. VN 12). The following gives what is needed (cf. EAE 334): a property $\phi$ *has an external reference* or is *extrinsic* if there is a $\psi$ and a $b$ distinct from $a$ such that $\phi(a) \vdash \psi(b)$. If $\phi$ does not have an external reference, it is *intrinsic*.[7]

We can now define a relation $R$ as *internal* when, given $aRb$, there are intrinsic properties $\phi$ and $\psi$ such that $\phi(a)$ and $\psi(b)$. If a relation is not

---

[7] It will be noted that this cuts across the usual syntactic distinction between relations and properties drawn in terms of adicity. For some monadic properties are extrinsic, and some dyadic relations (e.g. identity) are intrinsic. In what follows, property and relation will be distinguished in terms of adicity: properties are monadic, relations $n$-adic ($n > 1$).

internal, it is *external*. Russell's doctrine of internal relations is the thesis that all relations are internal, and, furthermore, that distinct relations are always 'grounded' upon distinct intrinsic properties. This second condition is needed to capture Russell's claim that, since all spatial points (e.g.) have different (spatial) relations to all other spatial points, they must each have different intrinsic properties. More precisely, the second condition ensures that if $cSd$ is grounded upon $\chi(c)$ and $\theta(d)$ and $cSd$ is distinct from $aRb$, $\chi$ and $\theta$ are distinct from $\phi$ and $\psi$.

It is to be noted that Russell's doctrine of internal relations is a different thesis from his reductive theory of relations. Trivially, any relation can be reduced to a property. For given any relation $R$, we can specify a property, $(\lambda x)xRb$, such that $a$ having the relation to a term $b$ is equivalent to $a$ having the property $(\lambda x)xRb$. That such an account is always available is a trivial truth which need not concern us further. It is tempting, nowadays, to regard an extrinsic property like $(\lambda x)xRb$ as 'merely a cumbrous way of describing a relation', to use Russell's later phrase (*POM* 222). None the less, Russell seems in 1898 to have regarded such devices as affording a genuine elimination of relations. This I shall call 'the weak reductive theory of relations'. The strong reductive theory, by contrast, is the thesis that any relation can be reduced to *intrinsic* properties either of its terms singly (monadistic reduction) or of the whole which they both compose (monistic reduction) in conjuction with proto-relations. While the doctrine of internal relations asserts that all relations are grounded upon intrinsic properties, the reduction theory of relations asserts that every relational proposition may be replaced by an equivalent proposition (or conjunction of propositions) not involving relations.[8]

The doctrine of internal relations and the strong reductive theory are logically distinct. It is clear that the monadistic form of the strong reductive theory (but not the monistic version) implies the doctrine of internal relations. But the converse does not hold. For it is plainly possible that relations require intrinsic properties in their terms, even though they are not reducible to such properties.

Both the doctrine of internal relations and the reductive theory of relations (in both forms) are to be distinguished from a third doctrine with which they are likely to be confused, the traditional view that all judgements are of subject–predicate form. Now the claim that all propositions are of subject–predicate form does entail an eliminative theory of relations. But it is normally assumed, I think, that the reductive theory of relations, in forms

---

[8] The sense in which the two propositions are 'equivalent' can be left open. It apparently varies from context to context. In discussing Leibniz, Russell usually takes it to satisfy the *salve veritate* requirement. Modern commentators usually modalize this to the requirement that the propositions have the same truth-conditions. Russell may very well have wanted something stronger still, propositional identity.

in which the equivalence relation is propositional (or judgement) identity, is equivalent to the doctrine that all propositions (or judgements) are of subject–predicate form. For it is assumed that if relations are to be eliminated they must be eliminated in favour of predicates, and consequently that relational propositions are identical to subject–predicate propositions and thus that all propositions are subject–predicate in form. But this holds only if relational propositions are the only cases to be considered as putative exceptions to the claim that all propositions are of subject–predicate form. As we have seen (§ 7.1), Russell admitted many propositions which were neither relational nor subject–predicate in form. Moreover, it ignores the role of proto-relations. Thus while the doctrine that all propositions are subject–predicate entails a reductive theory of relations, the converse is not the case. Rescher (1967: 78) raises a further, rather trivial, objection against the claim that all propositions are of subject–predicate form. He claims that Russell's attribution of this view to Leibniz involves a 'gross blunder', since Leibniz clearly recognized logically complex propositions and admitted that relational propositions may not be reduced to a single subject–predicate proposition but to a conjunction of such.[9] This, of course, was just the doctrine in the monadistic theory that Russell was attacking. It seems *obvious* that when Russell said that previous logicians had held that all propositions were of subject–predicate form, he did not mean that they denied that there were conjunctive, disjunctive, or implicational propositions, but that they maintained that all atomic propositions were of subject–predicate form.

Having made these distinctions, it needs to be pointed out that Russell does not always adhere to them. He is clear about the distinction between the doctrine of the subject–predicate form of propositions and the doctrines about relations. The distinction is quite evident in AMR and Russell says nothing in this period which indicates he was inclined to forget it. This is not the case with the distinction between the doctrine of internal relations and the reductive theory of relations. He never draws this distinction explicitly, though what he says sometimes implies it. But in places he writes in such a way as to obscure it. The distinction is important, for it is Russell's doctrine of internal relations which is necessary to generate the antinomies of relativity. It follows, therefore, that it is not sufficient to abandon the reductive theory of relations in order to block the antinomies. Relations have to be not merely admitted but admitted to be (in at least some cases) external.

Finally, it should be re-emphasized that Russell's doctrine of internal relations was not the same as Bradley's doctrine of internal relations. For

[9] Rescher's further claim (1967: 78 n.) that this position of Leibniz's 'is not far removed' from Wittgenstein's doctrine (1921) of atomic facts, from which Russell did not demur, is little short of incredible.

Bradley, the distinctions just made between the doctrines of internal relations, relational reduction, and subject–predicate judgements are otiose. According to Bradley, all judgements (atomic or molecular) assign a property to the Absolute. And such properties are necessarily intrinsic: if the subject is the Absolute, there can be no external reference. Thus relational judgements were eliminated in favour of subject–predicate judgements. And relations were internal because they could be so eliminated. But Bradley's reduction of relations to intrinsic properties of the Absolute was not at all the same as Russell's reduction of them to intrinsic properties of their terms (or combinations of their terms).

It might seem obvious that the logical question of whether there are relations and the metaphysical question of whether the world consists of one thing (monism) or many (pluralism) are linked in the way that Russell, later in his career, frequently asserted that they were: namely, that pluralism must admit relations and monism must deny them (cf. *HWP* 703–4; *POM* 44; *MTT* 141–2). In fact, neither part of this assertion is as simple as it seems.

Two issues have to be distinguished. On the one hand, there is the question of relational realism, the view that relations are real, subsistent entities. Relational realism is itself a form of pluralism, and one which Russell embraced from 1902 onwards (cf. Reply 684; *IMT* 325–8).[10] On the other hand, there is the question of whether there are irreducibly relational propositions. These two positions are equivalent within the absolute realist framework of *POM*, in which every propositional constituent is a term. But outside that framework they may be readily distinguished. In particular, the view that there are irreducibly relational propositions does not, on its own, entail pluralism, as the Pelletier–King-Farlow models, as well as more reasonable noneist models, show.

Nor does the reductive theory of relations on its own entail monism. In later writings, Russell argued that since pluralism entailed that there were at least two distinct objects in the universe, and since distinctness is a relation, the elimination of relations is incompatible with pluralism (*HWP* 703). As a neo-Hegelian, however, Russell would have rejected this argument, on the grounds that distinctness is not a genuine relation. Even with this assumption, however, the doctrine that all propositions are of subject–predicate form entails monism. For, since 'There exist many things' is not a subject–predicate proposition, pluralism cannot be stated unless there are propositions which are not of subject–predicate form (*POL* 12; *MTT* 141–2; *HWP* 575,

---

[10] Relational realism circumvents the claims of Pelletier and King-Farlow (1975), where it is argued that monism is compatible with relations since first-order $n$-adic logic (including identity) can be given a monistic model. Russell's relational realism, however, is essentially higher order (though it is not, of course, explicitly labelled as such) and thus resists the Pelletier–King-Farlow modelling.

703). Russell seems to have been aware of these distinctions from the beginning. For the consistency of his pluralism with his reductive theory of relations was protected by his doctrine of proto-relations, and he seems never to have tried to add the view that all propositions were of subject–predicate form.

Russell's assertion that he became aware of the importance of relations in the course of his study of Leibniz in 1898–9 and that this was crucial in breaking away from neo-Hegelianism (*MPD* 48), coupled with his remark that in reacting against neo-Hegelianism he was concerned mainly with the rejection of monism (*MPD* 54), have made it natural to suppose that Russell's own form of neo-Hegelianism was monistic. This, we have seen, is a mistake. *An Essay on the Foundations of Geometry* is an explicitly pluralist work, and Russell remained a pluralist (apart from two brief periods of doubt), throughout his idealist phase. Moreover, Russell also rejects relations in *EFG*. The hypostatization of relations is responsible for some of the main geometric antinomies. In fact, in *EFG* Russell rejects relational realism, irreducibly relational propositions, and monism—a combination which his later accounts would have us believe was impossible.

The trick for reconciling all three is his little noticed theory of proto-relations. What the analysis of geometry shows is that geometry requires pure relativity, 'the bare possibility of a relation' (*EFG* 138). Pure relativity is not itself a relation, but a proto-relation, a necessary condition for relations. Russell was not proposing, as is usually supposed, to eliminate relations simply by replacing them with adjectives of their terms or of the whole which their terms compose. He believed that the elimination could be achieved only by these adjectives in conjunction with proto-relations. To take an easy example, we might suppose that the relational proposition '*A* is the same height as *B*' would be analysed in terms of an intrinsic adjective (a certain height) common to both *A* and *B*, together with the proto-relation *difference*. So the proposition, when analysed, becomes '*A* and *B* are different but they share a common adjective, namely their height'. Adjective sharing appears to reintroduce a relation, but in fact involves only another proto-relation, identity of content. It is obvious to modern eyes that asymmetrical relations will not be so tractable. But early in his neo-Hegelian period Russell did not have the distinction between symmetrical and asymmetrical relations. Later, after he had drawn the distinction, he did give an account of how his reductive theory was to apply to asymmetrical relations, in the typescript version of AMR. This account does point up, in a particularly revealing way, the difficulties that asymmetrical relations posed for the reductive theory. This coincided with his recognition of the importance of asymmetrical relations for mathematics. And the twin impossibilities of either doing without asymmetrical relations or properly reducing them was crucial to his admission of irreducibly relational propositions in 1898 (cf. VN 27; *POL* 12; NOO 358; ONO 32–3; *POM* 221–6). Prior to the summer of 1898, however, Russell didn't even have a classification of relations which would enable him to isolate asymmetrical relations. So in early versions of the reductive theory no special treatment for asymmetrical relations would have been possible.[11]

None the less, when Russell said that it was his study of Leibniz that led him to recognize the importance of relations and that his main concern as a critic of neo-Hegelianism was the rejection of monism, he was not necessarily mistaken. Although he never accepted monism, in a paper of 1897, 'Why Do We Regard Time, But Not Space, as Necessarily a Plenum?' (WDWR), he did reconsider the case for monism and leave its validity an open question. Quite how serious this development was is hard to ascertain, since we have only the one paper to go on. But maybe the paper represents a more settled trend in his thinking (associated, in particular, with his plenal theory of matter) which Russell had in mind in his later autobiographical remarks. The paper on space and time, in any case, is well worth our attention, not least because in it Russell, for the first time, distinguishes between relations and adjectives.

Previously Russell used the word 'adjective' to cover both relations and properties (cf. e.g. VN 12, 14). Unfortunately, Russell doesn't pause to define 'adjective' and 'relation' in WDWR, though his whole paper is based on the distinction between them. It seems clear, however, that he draws the distinction in terms of adicity; anything with a single argument place is an adjective, anything with more than one is a relation. The main issue dealt with in WDWR was whether there are any grounds for treating time in a different way from space—in particular, whether there are grounds for an adjectival treatment of time and a relational treatment of space. He comes to the conclusion that there is not. But the real interest of the paper lies, first, in the distinction between adjectives and relations and, second, in the contrasting metaphysical implications Russell draws from an adjectival treatment of space and time as compared with a relational treatment. He claims that an adjectival treatment of space and time would imply both that

[11] The first sign of the emerging distinction between asymmetrical and symmetrical relations occurs early in 1898 when Russell draws a distinction between a wide and narrow sense of 'relation' (COS 316 n.). In the wide sense, relations are expressible by means of a common property. But in the narrow sense (to which he proposed to restrict the word 'relation'), a relation can only be expressed in terms of extrinsic adjectives: 'Nothing can be said, as to one alone of the points whose distance is considered, from which the distance could possibly be inferred. The other point must be mentioned in any statement about distance'. In this paper, he preserved his doctrine of internal relations by assuming intrinsic properties of points, namely positions, 'to rationalize these relations', though 'nothing can be said about position *per se*, only about differences of position' (COS 316 n.). For a slightly later view, after internal relations had been rejected, see FIAM 290.

space and time were plena and that monism was true. On the other hand, a relational treatment would entail that space and time were punctual and that pluralism was true. Russell does not decide which treatment is correct, but obviously his stacking the issues in this way resulted in a very considerable simplification in the problems he faced in metaphysics, physics, and the philosophy of space and time.

Russell's essay does not make it clear why he embarked upon such an investigation at this time. The most likely explanation is that his plenal theory of matter called for an adjectival theory of space, rather than the relational theory of *EFG*. To see this, it is important to realize that Russell's contrast between a relational and an adjectival theory of space and time is not the same as the contrast betweeen the relational and the absolute theory (cf. § 4.8). Keeping Russell's grammatical nomenclature, we might call the absolute theory a substantival theory, in contrast to both the relational and the adjectival theories. Russell continues to reject the substantival theory. As he puts it: 'time and space are not solid things' (WDWR 92). This is the assumption from which his paper takes off. For, if substantival theories can be rejected, 'the only available alternatives' are to regard time or space or both as either a relation (or series of relations) between different things or as an adjective (or series of adjectives) of a single thing (WDWR 92).[12] Russell assumes, though it is hard to be sure with what justification, that the conventional wisdom would have it that time is adjectival, while whether space should be regarded as adjectival or relational is an open question. Several pages of the article are taken up with disposing of arguments for this (or any) differential treatment of time and space. All this puts the metaphysical conclusions of *EFG* up for reconsideration in a remarkably open-ended way. It is worth noting that Russell didn't wait for external criticism of *EFG* before reviewing its foundations. This was typical of the major changes in Russell's philosophical position over the next few years. The criticisms which led him to change position were usually his own, and were rarely published. One untoward result of this was that Russell and the secondary literature on him went their separate ways. His willingness to reconsider fundamental doctrines so swiftly indicates an unusual degree of open-mindedness.It also tends to undermine the view that Russell's published books represent his (relatively) fixed opinions.

For Russell, to regard space or time as adjectival is to regard them as plena, 'for both . . . will be adjectives of some thing, which thing, therefore,

---

[12] It is interesting that Russell says that the two views are 'perhaps not wholly incompatible' (WDWR 92), although he makes no attempt to combine them. The reductive theory of relations would, of course, rule out the relational theory, but a theory of internal relations (without relational reduction) would perhaps offer the sort of combination Russell had in mind here.

will be at that point of space and time'. To regard them as relational is to regard them as empty, 'for the relata cannot themselves, on this view, be spatial or temporal, so that space and time will fall between things and be empty' (WDWR 92). Neither argument is very compelling. If space is an adjective of the Absolute it seems doubtful whether it makes any sense to say that the Absolute is at some or at every point of space (see Ch. 5, pp. 217–18). The second argument is also familiar. If space consists entirely of relations then the relata of those relations are not among the constituents of space. When Russell says that the relata are not 'spatial' he must, it seems, be using 'spatial' in this rather unusual sense—for it would hardly follow that the relata are not spatial in the more usual sense of having a spatial location. But it hardly follows either that space is empty or that it 'fall[s] between things'. It is hard to make sense of the last claim, for it makes no sense to talk as if space were positioned between non-spatial things. Nor, for that matter, does it make much sense, on a purely relational theory, to speak of 'empty space' for that harks back to the container metaphor of the substantivalist position. There seems little reason, in fact, to accept the grounds Russell gives for thinking either that an adjectival theory of space entails that space is a plenum, or that a relational theory of space entails that space is punctual.

The theoretical underpinnings of Russell's account are, therefore, extremely weak. But the conclusions he comes to seem not to depend essentially upon the confusions just discussed. The most important consequence is that, if relations are admitted as distinct from adjectives, 'a monadistic view of the Universe' is required (WDWR 95). And conversely: 'There . . . remains, on a monadistic hypothesis, an irreducible difference between adjectives and relations' (WDWR 95). Here, as in some other writings, Russell includes proto-relations among relations.

Of course, if the world is comprised of monads there will be a prima facie distinction between those states of a monad which refer only to the monad whose states they are, and those which refer also to other monads. But why should this distinction now suddenly become an 'irreducible' one? Russell's comment is brief, obscure, and unhelpful: 'Even if all their states refer to other monads, still the manner of such reference will be determined by their intrinsic natures. In such a case, every monad would have an essence *consisting* of adjectives, but *exhibited* only in relations' (WDWR 95). This passage implies a distinction between Russell's doctrine of internal relations and the strong reductive theory of relations. In the first sentence, Russell claims that a monad's relations to other monads will be 'determined' by its intrinsic nature. Thus the relations will be grounded upon intrinsic properties as required of internal relations. (Russell's remark that the relation will be 'determined' by the intrinsic properties suggests, perhaps, a stronger connection—perhaps, even, that the relation can be inferred from the intrinsic properties.) In the second sentence he concedes that even in this case, relations cannot be eliminated because they are necessary to 'exhibit' the intrinsic nature (or properties) of the monad. This blocks the idea that the relation can be inferred from the properties—even if the properties 'determine', in some quite indeterminate sense, the relation. It seems that what is known (exhibited) is always the relation, from which the intrinsic properties have to be inferred (if possible). We have here a reprise of William Hamilton's theme that to think is to condition,[13] and a reaffirmation of the view of *EFG* that relations are essential for knowledge.

Conversely, the distinction between relations and adjectives is untenable in conjunction with monism: 'Everything is really an adjective of the One, an intrinsic property of the Universe. . . . [W]hatever appears as a relation between two reals is, properly speaking, *only* an adjective of the whole which embraces both. (It is this *also*, even on a monadistic view, but it is not this *only*.)' (WDWR 95). Thus the question of whether space and time are relational or adjectival will decide the issue of monism versus pluralism. Russell, at this stage, does not want to make the choice but, as he says, 'to state the alternatives may surely be not unimportant' (WDWR 97).

WDWR is in many ways an enigmatic little paper. In the first place, it reopens questions which had been resolved in *EFG* within two weeks of the latter's publication. For another it seems to throw doubt on Russell's pluralism, which was well-established in *EFG* and which, only a year later, was to be re-established on a radically different foundation in AMR. Russell's doubts about his treatment of space in *EFG* were real enough, though what he says on the topic in WDWR bears little resemblance to his later views (1900). Plenal physics was probably an influence here, although there is little explicit sign of it in WDWR. The paper was written at the time Russell first took up the plenal theory of matter, and we know that he considered metaphysical monism as a possible consequence of the theory (VN 22). Given this, he would have had little option but to consider space, like everything else, as an adjective of the Absolute.

One consequence of Russell's distinguishing between relations and adjectives in WDWR was that it enabled him to consider the properties of relations. This was hardly possible while relations were lumped together with properties as adjectives. Even this development didn't take place immediately. The first sign of it occurs at AMR 191:

What all cases of equivalence have in common, is mainly the mark of a *symmetrical* relation, namely, the two axioms: If $A = B$, then $B = A$; if $A = B$ and $B = C$, then $A = C$. These two together allow us to prove that $A = A$. . . . Relations which fulfil these conditions will be called symmetrical; all other relations will be called asymmetrical.

[13] Cf. Hamilton 1829. This central doctrine of Hamilton's seems to have been a major influence on Bradley.

These elementary considerations seem to have been prompted by a discussion of the part–whole relation in the previous chapter (AMR 188). The division of symmetrical and asymmetrical relations on the same grounds is repeated in October 1898 in the outline of 'An Inquiry into the Mathematical Categories' (VN 26). Its reappearance here indicates that Russell was aware of its importance, for it is the only point to be developed at any length in the entire outline. None the less, on its own, it hardly takes Russell very far towards a theory of relations. However, the two axioms which he uses for defining symmetrical relations do provide him with the basis for a better classification system which emerges later the same year in another outline, 'Notes for "The A Priori Concepts of Mathematics" ' (VN 27)

Relations are of four kinds, according as they satisfy one, both or neither of the following two axioms: (a) If $A \frown B$, and $B \frown A$; (b) If $A \frown B$, and $B \frown C$, then $A \frown C$. Those which satisfy the first axiom [but not the second] I call *reciprocal*; those which satisfy the second [but not the first], I call *transitive*; those which satisfy both are *symmetrical*, and those which satisfy neither are *one-sided*.[14]

This classification is followed by a paragraph in which Russell asserts the irreducibility of relations:

Only symmetrical relations can be regarded as resulting from adjectives of both terms. *Other*, e.g. is not an adjective of what is other, for if it were, all terms which are other would on that ground have identity of content, which is absurd. Even with symmetrical relations, the analysis is not valid. Equality, for example, involves no common content beyond capacity for quantitative relations—whatever this capacity may be. A pleasure may be equal, and so may a foot: but they agree only in being quantities. Relations must be regarded as concepts which, if the relation be an ultimate one, are as simple and unanalyzable as their terms. (VN 27–8.)

The classification found in 'Notes for "The A Priori Concepts of Mathematics" ' became the basis for Russell's paper 'The Classification of Relations' (COR), early the following year. The later paper is very largely concerned with the irreducibility of relations.

The irreducibility of relations, however, takes us rather ahead of our story, and can only be appreciated when some details from the intervening year and a half have been supplied. The classification of relations itself is worth some further examination. It is hard now to appreciate how significant an advance it was for Russell, though it still falls short of the modern theory of relations to be found in elementary logic books. In the first place, it is worth noting that Russell did not use relational variables to formulate his two axioms until 1899 (COR 138). The constant symbol he used before this, '$\frown$', was taken from Whitehead (1898*a*: 19)—who in turn took it from Grassmann

---

[14] The conditions in square brackets are supplied from the slightly later paper (COR 138–9). This is the classification which Russell included in his letter to Moore of 13 Sept. 1898.

(1844)—where it is used to represent the synthesis of two elements of a manifold to form a third. Using a particular relation in this way was hardly a satisfactory way of setting out to formulate a general theory of relations.

An important defect in Russell's classification is that it does not permit him to draw the usual three-fold distinction between, e.g. symmetrical, nonsymmetrical, and asymmetrical relations. Relations, for Russell at this time, were either symmetrical or asymmetrical. Nor does Russell's classification admit a category of reflexive relations—due to the traditional dogma, unchallenged in the absence of any adequate logic of relations, that every genuine relation requires a plurality of terms (COR 142). This is somewhat surprising since he recognized early on that $A \cap A$ can be derived from his two axioms (AMR/TS 223). Moreover, as will have been noted, Russell's classification does not correspond to the modern one in other ways as well, although some of the names he uses are found with different senses in the modern classification. On the one hand, this exposes some theoretical limitations of Russell's account. On the other, it opens the way for considerable terminological confusion unless we are clear whether words are being used in Russell's sense or the modern one. Consider again Russell's two axioms in modern notation:

If $xRy$ then $yRx$, (1)
If $xRy$ and $yRz$ then $xRz$. (2)

In modern terms, (1) expresses symmetry and (2) transitivity. Relations which satisfy (1) are nowadays said to be symmetrical, whether or not they satisfy (2); relations which satisfy (2) are said to be transitive, whether or not they satisfy (1). Now the problem with Russell's classification is not just the trivial one that he uses a different terminology, but that he has no means of classifying a relation which satisfies one or other condition without taking into account whether or not it satisfies the other. For example, his use of 'transitive' comes as close to the modern use as that of any of the terms he employs. Yet a relation which is transitive in the modern sense is not necessarily transitive in Russell's. For in Russell's sense a relation is transitive if it satisfies (2) but *fails to satisfy* (1).[15] Thus identity, which is transitive in modern terms, is not transitive in Russell's since it satisfies both (1) and (2). Such relations Russell calls 'symmetrical'. Confusion will certainly result unless these notions are kept terminologically distinct. In what follows I shall prefix 'symmetrical', 'reciprocal', 'transitive', and 'one-sided' with the letter 'R' when they are used in Russell's sense in VN. Thus a transitive relation will be one which satisfies (2), but an R-transitive relation will be

[15] Confusion is compounded by the fact that Russell sometimes calls these relations asymmetrical' (AMR 216–20) and by the fact that in COR Russell requires not merely that (1) fails for a transitive relation, but that from $xRy$ it can be inferred that $yRx$ is false.

one which satisfies (2) *but not* (1), i.e. a transitive asymmetrical relation. Similarly, a symmetrical relation will be one which satisfies (1), but an R-symmetrical relation will be one which satisfies (1) and (2), i.e. an equivalence relation. An R-reciprocal relation is a relation which satisfies (1) but not (2). It is thus different from a symmetrical relation, which satisfies (1) but may or may not satisfy (2). An R-one-sided relation satisfies neither (1) nor (2). It is a relation which is neither symmetrical nor transitive.

Before moving on, it is worth summarizing some of the distinctions drawn in the first half of this section. Three commonly confused, but logically distinct, theses should be noted: (*a*) the doctrine of internal relations, (*b*) the strong monadistic reductive theory of relations, and (*c*) the claim that all propositions are of subject–predicate form. Among these, (*c*) entails (*b*) and (*b*) entails (*a*). But neither converse entailment holds. There is no evidence that Russell ever held (*c*), and there is good evidence that he never seriously held the metaphysical monism which it entails (as he plainly saw, at least by 1899). As he abandoned neo-Hegelianism, Russell first gave up (*b*) and then the doctrine of internal relations. Only when (*a*) had been abandoned was it possible for him to resolve the antinomies and dismantle his dialectic. When this was done, his neo-Hegelian apprenticeship ended.

## 8.3 RELATIONS IN THE 'ANALYSIS'

Russell's distinction between adjectives and relations, and his reflections on the logical properties of relations, were important and necessary steps in the development of his appreciation of relations. But neither of them amounted to a recognition of the irreducible nature of relational propositions, though the latter could hardly have been achieved without them. Although the irreducibility of relations was a concern in the typescript of AMR the doctrine is not clearly and firmly stated for all non-equivalence relations until the very end of 1898 (VN 27–8). It is found in full force in COR early in 1899. In the mean time, Russell seems generally to have assumed a reductive theory in AMR, although with increasingly apparent reservations.

For the most part, AMR follows Russell's earlier treatment of relations, analysing them away in favour of adjectival contents and proto-relations. Relations are referred to as adjectives 'referring to another thing' (AMR 163; cf. p. 202) and as predicated (AMR 175, 177). '[A]ll ideas of relation and connection' are said to 'presuppose the three fundamental ideas of identity, diversity and unity' (AMR 167). On the other hand, as a result of his new classification of relations, Russell does recognize that not all relations can be so easily treated. Early in AMR he admits the need for judgements 'asserting the various types of mathematical relations, as greater and less, before and after, etc., *which are not based upon a discoverable point of difference or identity*' (AMR 172; my italics). Such asymmetrical, transitive relations, as we shall see more fully in § 8.5, were brought into prominence through Russell's attempts to develop a theory of sign. They clearly pose problems for the strong reductive theory. Consider, for example, the judgements /2 < 3/ and /2 > 1/. It is easy to see that the terms /1/, /2/, and /3/ all differ, but if adjectives with external reference are eschewed, it is impossible to find an adjectival content which could be added to each in order to reconstitute the original judgements. Any such addition would seem inevitably to ascribe inconsistent adjectives to /2/, as Plato long ago noted in the *Parmenides*.[16] Moreover, we need to be able to infer /1 < 3/ from the two judgements given, and this will clearly be impossible on an adjectival reduction if extrinsic references are avoided. Symmetrical relations do not pose such problems as these.

There is a good deal of evidence of Russell's changing position in AMR but little sign yet of a clear position emerging. The distinction between monistic and monadistic reduction plays a role for the first time. Russell clearly now rejects the strong monadistic reduction as regards transitive, asymmetrical (i.e. R-transitive) relations. But there is some evidence that he holds instead a strong monistic reduction for all relations, and he clearly continues to cling tenaciously to the doctrine of internal relations. An asymmetrical relation, he writes, 'cannot be inferred from any intrinsic adjectives of the terms between which it holds, and it confers on the terms adjectives which differ from each other, and can only be expressed, for either term, by reference to the other term' (AMR 207). This is clearly a view that Russell was groping towards in WDWR where, in a passage quoted in § 8.2, he spoke hypothetically of each monad having an essence consisting of adjectives but exhibited only in relations determined by the intrinsic nature of the monads (WDWR 95).[17] The two remarks are quite consistent. For Russell's suggestion in the earlier paper that the intrinsic adjectival nature of the monad determines the relations cannot be understood as the claim that the relations can be inferred from the adjectives. The advance in AMR over his former position is, first, that he is now prepared to assert what previously he put forward only hypothetically, and, second, that in 1898 the feature in question is explicitly associated with asymmetrical relations.

The notion that there are intrinsic adjectives which can only be expressed in terms of relations appears also in Russell's final attempts to dismantle the

---

[16] It is interesting to find Russell shortly afterwards reading a good deal of Plato, especially those dialogues concerned with logical matters. Thus between January and April 1899 he read *Parmenides, Gorgias, Protagoras, Theaetetus, Sophist, Timaeus*, and *Phaedrus* (all in Jowett's translation).

[17] The remark in AMR is also rather murkily anticipated in an intermediate work (OQ 133) where Russell confusedly talks of 'intrinsic adjectives' with 'external reference'.

antinomy of the point without giving up the doctrine of internal relations. 'Every point', he says, 'has a quality peculiar to itself, called its *position*. This quality is intrinsic, and is that by which points differ. But, regarded as intrinsic, absolutely nothing can be said about it. It is only the mutual relations of positions concerning which we can say anything.' (COS 311). In the same way direction is an intrinsic property of distances though 'nothing be said about direction *per se*, but only concerning mutual relations of directions' (COR 312). In retrospect it is clear that such an account was hardly satisfactory, and within the year Russell was complaining that it 'does not destroy the fundamental nature of the relation . . . but merely cloaks it under a roundabout phrase' (COR 144). Russell's doctrine of internal relations had forced him to introduce intrinsic qualities of points, which qualities were completely ineffable. Such theoretical elements, about which nothing whatever could be said, were plainly undesirable, yet, equally plainly, were demanded by the doctrine of internal relations.

A very similar problem arises in basic arithmetic. In various places in the 'Analysis' when dealing with the application of number to classes, Russell refers to the class as a term having a numerical property, e.g. a class with two members has the property /2/. Yet the term which has the property /2/ is one. This is the one–many problem mentioned in § 6.1. As was noted there, the one–many problem does not arise on the ratio theory of number. And since Russell adheres to the ratio theory in AMR it might be thought that the difficulty was safely avoided. The situation, however, is not quite so simple when the doctrine of internal relations and the reductive theory of relations are taken into account. The ratio theory makes it necessary to treat number as a relation between a collection and its members. But the doctrine of internal relations requires that every relation be grounded in intrinsic properties either of its terms individually or of the whole which they both comprise, and a strong reductive theory of relations requires that all judgements apparently involving relations can be eliminated in favour of judgements involving only intrinsic properties.

Now it is tempting to suppose that, on Russell's version of the ratio theory, in a judgement that a given collection has two members (which is putatively a judgement about the relation between the collection and its members), the intrinsic property which grounds the relation is the numerical property /2/ applied to the collection. On this interpretation, however, the one–many problem remains unsolved. For the collection also has the property /1/. None the less, the doctrine of internal relations offers sufficient latitude to avoid this interpretation. It is not essential, if the demands of the doctrine are to be met, that the intrinsic property be a numerical property. We might suppose, therefore, that the intrinsic properties which ground the ratio are not numerical properties at all. This approach has all the implausibility of assigning intrinsic positions to points. The intrinsic properties of collections, likewise, serve no useful purpose beyond that of satisfying the requirements of internal relations.

If the strong reductive theory of relations is added to doctrine of internal relations, however, even this solution is blocked. For the reductive theory requires that the original judgement, that the collection has two members, should be capable of reformulation in terms of intrinsic properties only. There seems no way in which the content of the original judgement can be captured, however, unless the intrinsic properties are numerical. In which case, the one–many problem remains. It remains, equally, on the monadistic and monistic versions of the reductive theory. Although Russell refers to /2/ as a property of a collection with two members it is not clear that this is really his considered position. Elsewhere he claims that number is not an adjective of the whole collection (nor of its members) 'but of all the units and the whole to which they are related' (AMR 203). Thus, although the class does have the property of being the sum of $n$ units, it does not have the property /$n$/. But this does not help with the one–many problem, given Russell's theory of terms. For the (higher-order) whole, which consists of all the units and the whole of which they are members, is itself a term and thus one, and so cannot be that of which /$n$/ is predicated.

The one–many problem cannot, in fact, be evaded on Russell's theory in any way at all, *unless* he either gives up his strong reductive theory of relations (in both versions), thus permitting him to treat numbers as irreducibly relational, or is prepared to admit an order hierarchy among terms, so that the conditions he imposes on terms do not hold of higher-order terms. Later on, Russell preferred the second solution. In *POM* he avoided the problem by a distinction between terms and objects; the latter (among which classes are included) do not satisfy the unity requirements imposed on terms (*POM* 55). In AMR however, his apparent failure to reject the monistic reduction theory, even in the case of relations which express ratios, will prevent any solution whatever. Indeed, even without the reductive theory, the solutions consistent with the doctrine of internal relations are unsatisfactory, for the reasons noted.

There are further problems in AMR in the concept of a class itself, although these will turn out to be more apparent than real. For a class itself is a term composed of other terms. By the doctrine of internal relations, homogeneous terms, i.e. terms lacking differentiating intrinsic properties, cannot be related, and thus cannot combine to form a whole. This would impose unacceptable limits on the formation of classes. The theory of internal relations would also apparently render Russell's earlier account of numeration (in SDCQ and RNQ) untenable. For number, on that account, resulted from the synthesis into a manifold of 'things whose qualitative and quantitative differences are disregarded' (SDCQ 46). In other words, in applying number to a collection we have to abstract out the very qualities which would make a collection (considered as a whole of related parts) possible on the theory of internal relations.

The short answer to this problem is that classes are not wholes. For their members are not, strictly speaking, related at all. Russell had previously called the unit of such collections purely abstract and formal. In AMR, however, he makes it clear that what he means by this is that the unity of a class is produced by proto-relations rather than by relations. This is what distinguishes classes from genuine wholes; the parts of a whole are related by a bona fide relation. Thus the unity of a class does not depend upon the intrinsic properties of its members. (Traces of this view are to be found in *POM* 72–3.) This resolves the problem of class unity. And a more resolute use of this idea would solve the one–many problem also. For this it would be necessary for Russell to deny that classes are unities in any sense, and thus to deny that they are terms. He does not adopt this position, however.

Russell's most thorough discussion of relations in AMR is frustratingly incomplete. It occurs in Book III, chapter 2, 'Equality and Inequality', (AMR/TS 223–6), only fragments of which have survived. In what remains of the discussion, however, we see Russell developing a new classification of relations, this one based on the adjectives on which they are grounded, rather than their formal characteristics.

Russell starts the discussion by combining both the doctrine of internal relations and the reductive theory of relations in a single statement: 'any relation implies, and is equivalent to, (1) an adjective of each of the related terms (2) an adjective of the whole into which any two related terms can be collected' (AMR/TS 224). Thus every relation implies adjectives in its terms (as required by the doctrine of internal relations) and every relational proposition is equivalent to some combination of subject–predicate propositions (as required by the reductive theory of relations).

It is clear from the passage quoted that the monadistic and the monist theory of relations are to be combined as aspects of a single position. This had been suggested earlier (in WDWR 95), although in later works they were presented as alternatives (*POM* 221). In AMR/TS Russell ignores the monistic theory as 'not relevant to this discussion' (the purpose of which was to locate the source of the contradiction of relativity) (p. 224). One suspects that the monistic theory was introduced out of deference to the demand for intrinsic properties. For it will turn out that the properties ascribed by the monadistic theory to a relation's terms considered individually will, in some cases at least, inevitably involve an external reference to the other term of the relation. By ascribing the properties instead to the compound term composed of all the terms of the relation, as is done on the monistic theory, there is hope that the relation might be expressible by means of intrinsic properties only. In short, it seems that all relations imply adjectives (which may or may not be intrinsic) in their terms, but all relations are implied by intrinsic adjectives of a compound term (the term composed of the terms of the relation). There are large elements of speculation in this, for Russell does not explain why he brings in the monistic theory. But the speculation is supported by the fact that only a strong reductive theory of relations is worthy of the name. It is hardly possible that Russell could have abandoned the strong reductive theory entirely and contented himself, even briefly, with regarding the weak theory as a genuine elimination of relations. Instead, it seems that he retained a strongly reductive monistic theory coupled with a weakly reductive monadistic theory.

In the main part of the extant discussion, Russell brings the monadistic theory to bear on the classification of relations. He draws four distinctions, three of them intended to be coextensive, which together will provide a four-fold classification:

(i) The distinction between relations which can be inferred from adjectives of their terms and relations from which the adjectives can be inferred (AMR/TS 223–4). I shall refer to the former as *logically subsequent* and the latter as *logically prior* relations.

(ii) The distinction between relations which can be regarded as relations between adjectives and relations which cannot be so regarded (AMR/TS 224). Russell claims that in a relational proposition /aRb/, where R is a logically subsequent relation inferred from adjectives /φ/ and /ψ/ of a and b, a relation between /φ/ and /ψ/ 'in some respect constitutes the relation between the terms [a and b]' (AMR/TS 223). Thus (i) and (ii) are supposed to be coextensive.

(iii) The distinction between relations for which the adjectives of either term can be expressed without reference to the other term and relations for which this is impossible. Russell refers to the former as 'relations of adjectives' and to the latter as 'adjectives of relation' (AMR/TS 224). This distinction depends on a somewhat tighter version of the distinction (drawn in § 8.2) between intrinsic and extrinsic adjectives. On the latter, an extrinsic adjective involves a reference to *any* distinct term, in an adjective of relation the distinct term must be the other term of the two-place relation. Russell holds that (iii) is coextensive with (i) and (ii).

(iv) Finally, there is the distinction between relations which are correlated with adjectives which are the same for both terms and those for which the adjectives are different for each term (AMR/TS 224).

Given Russell's assertion that the first three distinctions are coextensive, they cut across the fourth to produce four classes of relations:

Relations (e.g. identity of content) in which the relation is inferred from adjectives which are the same for both terms;                                    (I)

Relations (e.g. difference of content) in which the relation is inferred from adjectives which are different for each term;                                    (II)

Relations (e.g. equality) from which adjectives, the same for both terms, are inferred;                                    (III)

Relations (e.g. inequality) from which adjectives, different for each term, are inferred.                                    (IV)

It is clear that this classification cuts across Russell's earlier syntactic classification. For example, inequality and diversity of content belong to the same formal class of relations, namely R-reciprocal relations. Similarly, equality and identity of content are assigned to the class of R-symmetrical relations on the formal classification.

The main purpose behind this classification is to isolate the source of the contradiction of relativity. Russell goes on, in an argument to be considered in § 8.6, to show that the contradiction of relativity is produced only by relations of type IV, and that it is produced by all such relations. Indeed, Russell regards relations of both type IV and type III as anomalous, as indeed they were from the point of view of the reductive theory. In types I and II, the relation could be inferred from the adjectives. 'Now this analysis', Russell complains, 'ought, no doubt, to apply to all relations: they ought all to be relations of adjectives. But it would seem, to put the distinction a different way, that at least some relations can *only* be regarded as relations of things: in such a case we have, in both terms, adjectives of relation, but we have not a relation of adjectives' (AMR/TS 224). In other words, the strongly reductive monistic theory of relations fails.

Russell's account of the failure of the strong reductive theory suggests that the key issue was whether a relation between two terms could be reduced to a relation between adjectives of those terms or not. Yet it seems strange to think of a theory which reduces relations between terms of one type to relations between terms of a different type as a genuinely reductive theory of relations. Of course, Russell's view that all logically subsequent relations were relations of adjectives, i.e. that distinctions (i) and (iii) were coextensive, shows that, by Russell's account, the theory that all relations are relations of adjectives was equivalent to the theory that all relations could be inferred from adjectives. But, even so, his choice of wording is strange. Why didn't he say directly that all relations ought to be capable of being inferred from adjectives?

The reason may well have to do with the theory of proto-relations. For Russell may have had in mind that the relations which hold between adjectives were really proto-relations. The basis for this idea is that genuine relations involve a unity among diverse terms, which would have to be, in some sense, self-subsistent, genuinely substantial entities. However, given a substance–attribute ontology of the kind to which Russell adhered as a neo-Hegelian, it is clear that adjectives fall on the attribute side of the ontology and thus fail to provide the substantiality necessary for the components of a relational unity. Thus adjectives, if related at all, could only be related by proto-relations. All this makes perfectly good sense in the context of Russell's earlier neo-Hegelian theory, though he says little enough about the substance–attribute ontology. The trouble is that the substance–attribute ontology makes little sense within the context of Russell's new theory of terms, where predicates (considered as terms of relations) were every bit as self-subsistent as entities. It was in this area, I believe, that he was helped by his study of Leibniz which began while AMR was underway.

## 8.4 INFLUENCES: LEIBNIZ

The occasion for Russell's study of Leibniz, which occupied him from the summer of 1898 through to 1900, was his being invited to give a series of lectures at Trinity College, Cambridge, in the Lent Term of 1899 as a replacement for McTaggart, who normally lectured on Leibniz but who, on that occasion, was away in New Zealand on affairs of the heart. This fortuitous circumstance turned out to be of special importance to Russell's thinking about relations:

I first realized the importance of the question of relations when I was working on Leibniz. I found—what books on Leibniz failed to make clear—that his metaphysic was explicitly based upon the doctrine that every proposition attributes a predicate to a subject and (what seemed to him almost the same thing) that every fact consists of a substance having a property. I found that this same doctrine underlies the systems of Spinoza, Hegel and Bradley, who, in fact, all developed the doctrine with more logical rigour than is shown by Leibniz. (*MPD* 61.)

To be sure *exactly* what he learnt in this way, we would need to have a more exact chronology of his study of Leibniz. His reading on Leibniz seems to have been done from the summer of 1898 to the spring of 1899, when his lectures ended. He records no Leibniz titles in his reading list after March 1899. None the less, the preface of his book on Leibniz is dated September 1900. It would seem, therefore, that he obtained the documentation he needed in the nine months prior to March 1899 and spent the next eighteen months interpreting and organizing it in the intervals of his work on the foundations of mathematics. By Russell's standard, this was a very long delay indeed, indicating that it needed a lot of work over and above what he had done for the lectures. This impression is confirmed by the preface, in which he says that he read 'most of the standard commentators and most of Leibniz's connected treatises', but still found Leibniz's philosophy largely mysterious until he read the *Discours de métaphysique* and the correspondence with Arnauld, which threw 'a flood of light . . . on all the inmost recesses of Leibniz's philosophical edifice' (*POL*: pp. xiii-xiv).[18]

That we do not know when this flood of light was thrown limits our ability to know what exactly it was that Russell learnt from studying Leibniz. His claim that he 'realized the importance of the question of relations' while working on Leibniz cannot be correct. For there is abundant evidence of his concern about relations before any of his reading on Leibniz was undertaken, though it is possible that the important chapter on equality and inequality from AMR/TS was conceived after his study of Leibniz had begun and was influenced by his reading of Leibniz. It is difficult to believe, however, that it could have been written after his discovery of the *Discourse* and Arnauld correspondence, unless he read these early in his study of Leibniz. For similar reasons, the idea must be rejected that Russell came to abandon his reductive theory of relations as a result of seeing the consequences Leibniz drew from it. He had clearly abandoned the monadistic reductive theory by the second half of 1898. In this case, it seems to me that the influence of Moore's second dissertation was more powerful and probably earlier. It is also false that it was while studying Leibniz that he came to appreciate that not all propositions were of subject–predicate form, for if he had ever held this doctrine (which is doubtful) he had rejected it by mid–1898. The (negative) influence of Leibniz on Russell's theory of relations can be seen for the first time in COR, where Russell rejects any kind of reductive account for any relations, asserts that all relations are external, and affirms that predication is a relation. The most important lesson Russell seems to have learnt from Leibniz was that the substance–attribute ontology was closely linked with the question of the reducibility of relations. We have already seen (§ 8.3) how Russell probably made an implicit appeal to the substance–attribute ontology in an attempt to convince himself that a theory which could eliminate relations between things in favour of relations between

---

[18] Unfortunately, we can't be sure when exactly this was. His reading list includes Leibniz's *New Essays* and *Theodicée* and two editions of selected writings (Duncan 1890 and Latta 1898). None of these would have given him the two works he considered crucial. He found these in vols. ii and iv of Gerhardt's 7-vol. *Philosophischen Schriften von G. W. Leibniz* (Leibniz 1875). It is clear from the marginalia in his copy that he read very nearly all of this edition. It is in his reading list for Feb. 1899. But this presumably records when he finished reading it, and gives us no clue as to when he reached the correspondence with Arnauld and the *Discourse*. Our uncertainties are compounded by the fact that we can't be entirely sure when Russell wrote Bk. I of AMR, our main source for his views. The arguments of the next paragraph assume that it was written with the rest of the MS, and therefore completed by July 1898, before he had read much Leibniz.

adjectives was a genuinely reductive theory of relations. Yet the substance–attribute ontology was already undermined (though Russell might not have been fully aware of it) by the theory of terms which Russell developed in AMR.

This suggestion fits well with Russell's saying that it was the *Discourse on Metaphysics* and the correspondence with Arnauld which were of special importance for him, since the topic of substance and attribute is prominent in both. One of the major concerns of the *Discourse* is to examine the consequences of Leibniz's doctrine that in every true proposition the concept of the predicate is contained in the concept of the subject. The suggestion also fits well with what Russell identifies as the central argument of Leibniz's philosophy, to which he devotes chapters 2–5 of his *POL*. This argument is entirely concerned with the relations between substance and attribute and (correlatively) the relation of subject and predicate. 'That all sound philosophy should begin with an analysis of propositions', Russell writes in a famous passage, 'is a truth too evident, perhaps, to demand a proof. That Leibniz's philosophy began with such an analysis, is less evident, but seems to be no less true' (*POL* 8). It is this latter proposition that Russell is primarily concerned to prove in *POL*.

This is not the place for a detailed discussion and evaluation of Russell's treatment of Leibniz's philosophy (on which there is already a substantial literature), since we are concerned with Russell's own philosophy rather than his interpretation of Leibniz. Moreover, his *POL* is a less adequate source than might be expected for Russell's opinions during the period with which we are concerned. During the period of his work on Leibniz his thinking underwent substantial changes. He began reading Leibniz when he was still very largely a neo-Hegelian; he completed his book when he already had the outlines (and much of the detail) of the philosophy with which he proposed to replace neo-Hegelianism. The opinions expressed in the book, therefore, give no very reliable guide to the development of his thought as he abandoned neo-Hegelianism.

There are two specific doctrines of relevance to Russell's own philosophy that Russell puts at the centre of Leibniz's philosophy:

> All propositions are (ultimately) of subject–predicate form.         (1)
> In any true proposition the predicate is contained in the subject.    (2)

The second of these is stated so clearly by Leibniz on several occasions (e.g. Leibniz 1875: ii, 46; 1686: § 8) that even philosophers have apparently been unable to effect a revisionary interpretation. The first, however, seems not to have been stated in so many words by Leibniz, and this has left some ground for exegetical dispute. None the less, that all propositions are ultimately of subject–predicate form follows from (2) (with minor assumptions), if the latter is taken as a complete theory of truth (as Leibniz apparently intended it to be).

Against the claim that all propositions are of subject–predicate form Russell raises two classes of counter-examples in his *POL*. The first consists of such judgements as 'There are three men'. Such judgements cannot be reduced to any set of judgements of subject–predicate form (*POL* 12–13). He notes that Leibniz had not ignored such judgements, but had argued that the aggregates to which number applies were merely phenomenal, having a unity which was supplied by the mind (Leibniz 1875: ii, 517). Ishiguro, who denies that Leibniz held (1), points out that this was not the end of Leibniz's treatment of the topic (Ishiguro 1972: 72–3; also Parkinson 1965: 37–8). There is a passage which suggests that Leibniz may have proposed analysing 'There are three men' as '*A* is a man and *B* is a man and *C* is a man and *A, B* and *C* are disparate'.[19] Now it is obviously to Leibniz's credit that he got as far as this, but Ishiguro goes too far when she says that this account 'is quite close to that which Russell was to produce later' (Ishiguro 1972: 73), and for reasons she notes, though she glosses over them. In the first place, Leibniz's analysis mentions three individual men who were not mentioned in the original proposition. If *A, B,* and *C* do not represent men but are variables ranging over men, then the 'propositions' are not of subject–predicate form (indeed, are not properly propositions at all). Secondly, Leibniz's analysis does not capture what is essential to the original proposition, that there are no other men. This last cannot be expressed by adding another proposition of subject–predicate form. It requires a quantifier. Leibniz's account cannot, therefore, be held to be an adequate analysis of the original proposition, and cannot be turned into one without adding propositions which are not of subject–predicate form.

Russell's second class of counter-examples to (1) are relational propositions. Ishiguro argues that Leibniz treated (at least some) relations as predicates with two subjects, even while he attempted monadic reformulations of others. Russell's favourite passage in support of his interpretation is the following from the correspondence with Clarke:

The ratio or proportion between two lines *L* and *M* may be conceived three several ways; as a ratio of the greater *L* to the lesser *M*; as a ratio of the lesser *M* to the greater *L*; and lastly, as something abstracted from both, that is, as the ratio between *L* and

---

[19] The passage in question was not available to Russell. It was published by Couturat (Leibniz 1903: 240). Gerhardt's transcription of the same MS breaks off just before the relevant passage with a note that the rest of the document is more in the nature of an exploratory study (Leibniz 1875: vii. 221). Russell recognized the importance of the passages Gerhardt omitted in his review of Couturat (1901), where he cites, not the passage noticed by Ishiguro and Parkinson, but an adjacent passage in which Leibniz comes rather closer to the Frege–Schröder–Russell definition of the cardinals. (Russell 1903: 188).

*M*, without considering which is the antecedent, or which the consequent; which the subject, and which the object . . . . In the first way of considering them, *L* the greater is the subject, in the second *M* the lesser is the subject of that accident which philosophers call *relation* or *ratio*. But which of them will be the subject, in the third way of considering them? It cannot be said that both of them, *L* and *M* together, are the subject of such an accident; for if so, we should have an accident in two subjects, with one leg in one, and the other in the other; which is contrary to the notion of accidents. Therefore we must say that this relation, in this third way of considering it, is indeed *out of* the subjects; but being neither a substance, nor an accident, it must be a mere ideal thing, the consideration of which is nevertheless useful.[20]

It is easy to see why Russell liked this particular passage. It is especially close to his own interests in ratio and the direction of relations (see § 8.5). It also brings out the connection between the subject–predicate doctrine and the substance–attribute ontology. None the less, there are other passages which are equally apposite for Russell's purpose (e.g. Leibniz 1956: 609).[21]

Now Russell had a case against (1) before he embarked on his study of Leibniz. We have seen that already in AMR Russell had recognized that not all propositions are of subject–predicate form. His study of Leibniz brought to his attention the close connection between the traditional view that all propositions are of subject–predicate form and the traditional substance–attribute ontology. He remarks on the connection between the two in COR (p. 141). What he hadn't previously seen, I believe, was the extent to which his radical pluralism required an unconventional account of predication. Traditional views, which construed predication in terms of the inherence of attributes in substances, were plainly untenable if both subject and predicate alike were to be regarded as terms. Russell's theory of terms makes a relational account of predication all but essential. Yet it was not until COR that Russell admitted predication as a relation and used this as the basis for a general argument to show that relational propositions could neither presuppose nor be replaced by subject–predicate ones (pp. 143–4). This simple argument managed to achieve what many earlier, more complex arguments had failed to do: refute the reductive theory of relations, in both monadistic and monistic forms, for all relations. What it could not do was refute the doctrine of internal relations. For, even if predication is a relation, there would be neither inconsistency nor a *vicious* regress in supposing that from

[20] As cited by Russell, *POL* 12–13. The passage is from the 5th letter to Clarke, § 47 (Leibniz 1875: vii. 401 = 1956: 704). Russell quotes the entire passage again in *POM* 222. Ishiguro quotes it too (1972: 104) and finds it 'rather muddled'.
[21] Ishiguro finds different passages to support her interpretation (e.g. Leibniz 1704: ii, xxv, 10). This is not the place to pursue a detailed exegesis, though I'm inclined to think that Ishiguro's evidence is less substantial than Russell's. It seems safe to say that Leibniz's position is not consistent (as Loemker points out in his annotations, cf. Leibniz 1956: 247, 271). This, on a grander scale, is also Russell's conclusion (*POM* 130)—and perhaps Ishiguro's too, since she finds the passage from the 5th letter to Clarke 'muddled'.

any relational proposition /*aRb*/ a pair of subject–predicate propositions, /$\phi a$/ and /$\psi b$/, could be inferred, neither of which involve a reference to the other term. Obviously, an infinite regress would result on these assumptions, but one which Russell later called a harmless regress of implications (*POM* 50). A relatively hard argument against the reductive theory was, I think, the most immediate reward from Russell's study of Leibniz. It stemmed from Russell's criticism of Leibniz's subject–predicate logic and the substance–attribute ontology on which it was based. Russell long afterwards castigated the substance–attribute ontology with the sort of scorn he typically reserved for doctrines he had once accepted.

At this stage, two further details are required before the account of the collapse of Russell's neo-Hegelian philosophy is complete. We need to know why Russell thought relations were so important, and why he came to reject the doctrine of internal relations. As regards the first, with the exception of one or two isolated remarks, little has been done so far to suggest that Russell's new views about relations had much bearing upon his philosophy of mathematics. The discussion so far in this chapter has been almost entirely concerned with logic and has done little to suggest that results obtained in logic or the philosophy of language should have had so much importance for the analysis of mathematics. On the second point, I have already anticipated Russell somewhat by showing how the antinomies, upon which his entire dialectic of the sciences hinged, depended in their turn upon the doctrine of internal relations. We have yet to see how Russell came to realize this fact, and the steps he took to extricate himself from the last of his major neo-Hegelian doctrines.

## 8.5 SIGN, ORDER, AND ASYMMETRICAL RELATIONS

Russell was obviously well on the way to rejecting neo-Hegelianism by the time the manuscript of AMR was completed. The main impetus up to this point had been his strenuous attempt to eliminate, much more thoroughly than hitherto, all trace of psychologism from his position. This resulted in his radically realist account of terms and propositions. But key features of his neo-Hegelian position still remained in place when the manuscript was complete. In particular, his neo-Hegelian theory of relations was essentially untouched by his work on the manuscript of AMR. The typescript is a different matter and this chapter has chronicled the gradual erosion of this theory of relations up to the point where only the doctrine of internal relations is left.

Another key feature of Russell's neo-Hegelian philosophy of mathematics was his espousal of the quantity view of mathematics, albeit in a somewhat weakened form which excluded geometry. His study of Whitehead (1898*a*) added other branches of mathematics outside the scope of the quantity view, in particular the algebra of symbolic logic. But within the central areas of arithmetic and analysis the quantity view still held sway. It would be natural to suppose that Russell abandoned the quantity view because it would yield no satisfactory account of infinite numbers and continuity. After all, the discovery of the irrationals posed a major problem for the quantity view, and the long-standing mathematical antinomies associated with the infinite might have been expected to be high on Russell's agenda. Moreover, real analysis had been an area of major advance by pure mathematicians in the second half of the nineteenth century, and one might naturally expect Russell to have been somehow caught up in the general excitement. Finally, Russell's own retrospective assessment of his work during this period, and of the gains made once the quantity view had been abandoned, gives pride of place to the analysis of the real numbers—work which solved 'a puzzle which had perplexed mathematicians ever since the time of Pythagoras' (*MPD* 72).

A more detailed examination, however, reveals that these assumptions are erroneous. After his initial investigations in 1896 Russell seems to have ignored the problems of mathematical continuity for the best part of two years. Even his adoption of a plenal physics in 1897 does not seem to have led him immediately into any detailed reconsideration of continuity in pure mathematics. His occasional references to the number continuum in 1897 and 1898 show less advance on his opinions in 1896 than might have been expected. And he remained critical of Cantor's transfinite arithmetic through the 1899–1900 draft of *POM*. The reason for this absence of special interest in mathematical continuity in 1897 and 1898 was no doubt largely due to the fact that the antinomies which the quantity view engendered in pure mathematics did not specifically depend upon continuity.

In fact, the topic on which Russell's quantity view foundered was far less abstruse. It was the elementary and apparently uncontroversial topic of negative numbers. This led him to consider how he could treat the ordinal numbers, a matter that he had not broached before 1898. And this led, in turn, to a consideration of the concept of order and of the transitive asymmetrical relations which generate order. These were the very relations which were responsible for the contradiction of relativity. So at this stage the matter of replacing the quantity view becomes entangled with the matter of replacing the dialectic, and both turn, rather surprisingly, on the humble subject of negative numbers and, more generally, of the concept of sign in mathematics.

Russell's treatment of the distinction of sign during 1898 is particularly well documented, with three more or less complete chapters still extant (from OQ, AMR, and AMR/TS). This is no accident, for during the period

of work which led up to the completion of *POM* Russell composed his
various drafts of a book on the philosophy of mathematics by shifting
satisfactory material bodily from one draft to the next. Ultimately most of
the early material either dropped out or was transformed beyond easy
recognition. But at each stage in this complex compositional process,
material which he found unsatisfactory was left behind. It is probably the
material left behind in this way that for the most part constitutes what
survives of Russell's book drafts from this period. The fact that three drafts
on the distinction of sign have survived from one year indicates the difficulty
the topic was giving him. The fact that the third draft was included in FIAM
in 1899 (p. 268) and ended up in the 1899–1900 draft of *POM*, indicates that
his final treatment in 1898 was relatively stable, although the material was
rewritten again before being published (cf. *POM*: ch. xxvii). A comparison
of the three drafts from 1898 shows Russell's laborious attempts to clarify his
thoughts on the topic.

Before 1898, Russell devoted little attention to signed numbers. In 1896 and
1897 he included them among 'qualified numbers', that is, among numbers
which can be applied only to certain kinds of subject-matter, in this case to
subject-matter that admits of an opposite. For when two terms of opposite
sign are synthesized they neutralize one another (SDCQ 47 = RNQ 71).
Russell soon abandoned this distinction between pure and qualified numbers,
and replaced the account of sign based upon it. In other respects, though,
these early remarks bear fruit later. There is, in his remark on neutralization,
an implicit distinction between quantity and magnitude (cf. *POM* 159). In
OQ this distinction is made explicit: when two quantities of equal magnitude
and opposite sign are added 'they neutralize each other'. The result is not the
mere quantitative zero, 'which is the limit of infinite division', but absolute
zero 'which is no longer, like the quantitative zero, a quantity of the same
kind as those added' (OQ 124). The account he gives here of the quantitative
zero is reminiscent of his earlier dimensional account of the differential (see
above Ch. 6 n. 12), though he does seem to have got over finite indivisibles.[22]

The idea that sign can only be applied when certain conditions are met
also appears in OQ where Russell develops the idea a good deal more
systematically than before. First, sign cannot be applied to things—'for two
things cannot be opposites in any proper sense' (OQ 124)—and thus must
apply either to relations or to adjectives. Second, Russell confines himself to
those cases where addition is possible, for, without addition, 'the distinction
of sign is barren, and leads to no results of any value' (OQ 125). Within this
restriction, it seems that sign is always relational, that it applies to quantities

---

[22] As regards zero of one type and another, things seem to have got worse before they got
better. There is evidence in AMR/TS 235–8 that he distinguished no less than five kinds of zero.
Perhaps fortunately, most of these distinctions have been lost.

which are 'of the nature of differences, though not necessarily differences of magnitude', i.e. to extensive quantities (OQ 125).

In a manifold of extensive quantities, every term can be regarded as a difference between two terms (OQ 125; AMR/TS 231). For example, given two terms $A$ and $C$ there is a term $B$ such that $A + B = C$. $B$ is the difference between $A$ and $C$, but it is also a quantity and, by Russell's account of extensive quantities, a quantity of the same type as $A$ and $B$. Thus it is a term of the manifold of extensive quantities of that type. Moreover, for every element $B$ of the manifold there are elements $A$ and $C$ such that $A + B = C$. For brevity I shall call this last claim 'the thesis of relative specification'. The thesis holds for a continuous manifold of extensive quantities (where 'extensive' is used in Russell's sense, RNQ 75, and 'continuous' in Whitehead's 1898*a*: 17). Regarded as a difference $B$ is susceptible of sign, since we have the difference of $A$ from $C$ and the difference of $C$ from $A$, two differences of equal magnitude but opposite sign. Abstracting the sign out gives a signless magnitude, the difference between $A$ and $C$ (OQ 133).

Sign is directly applicable to extensive quantity, where the differences between quantities are themselves quantities. But it is not directly applicable to numbers. Russell explains signed numbers as follows:

the difference between two things and five things is not simply three things, but + three things; where + means that it is not the three things themselves, but the operation of adding them, which is denoted. Similarly the difference between five things and two things is – three things, where – denotes the operation of taking away. With this distinction of sign arises in pure number. (OQ 128.)

It seems that if sign brings in a relational element signed numbers are really relational, like quantities (OQ 128–9). What is essential to the distinction of sign 'is, that we . . . have a sense in which the numbers added to or subtracted from the population may be truly regarded as differences, as relations of adjectives' (OQ 130). Thus signed numbers behave exactly like extensive quantities. In fact, on Russell's view, number is transformed into quantity in this way: 'If we regard numbers as the sums of more or fewer 1's, we may transform them into quantities: and their differences in respect of this property will be positive or negative quantities' (AMR 218–9).

Sign, however, is not restricted to extensive quantity as this account might suggest. At least by the time he started his third account of sign, Russell was quite clear that sign applies wherever there are asymmetrical relations (AMR/TS 226; cf. *POM* 227). Thus sign arises wherever there are paired relations—such as before/after, left/right, east/west—and not just from the pair greater/smaller whereby quantities are ordered. Sign exists, Russell explains, wherever 'we have a difference which is not a difference of adjectives, though giving to each term an adjective of difference' (AMR/TS 227). To show that this is so for all instances of sign, Russell deals with the various cases, starting with number (AMR/TS 227–8). In the case of the cardinal numbers, there is no distinction of sign. But once addition and subtraction are introduced 'we must . . . refer to the terms added and subtracted, though these terms may be any we please'. In this case 'the distinction of sign begins to emerge', though still in an elementary form, 'in which positive and negative are distinguished by intrinsic qualities' (AMR/TS 227).

That signed numbers express differences is explained via the concept of addition. That to which number is ascribed must be defined non-numerically[23] and thus may increase or decrease in number without loss of identity. In such a case, the difference between the first and second numbers will be a signed number (AMR/TS 227). This perhaps explains Russell's earlier remark about the elementary form of sign in which positive and negative 'are distinguished by intrinsic qualities'. Consider the population of a country, a class not defined by enumerating its members. The numerical difference between the population of a country at two different times is a signed number. But whether that number is positive or negative depends upon whether the population is increasing or decreasing, which are intrinsic properties of the population. Though this does seem to be Russell's argument it hardly seems satisfactory. For increases or decreases in population can only be regarded as intrinsic properties of the population because the temporal order is taken for granted. Considering the population of the country at two different times we cannot infer that the population is increasing or decreasing unless we know which time is the earlier one. Russell's failure to consider this is not due to mere inadvertence, however. He provides no account of space and time in the extant parts of AMR. But in other pieces written around the same time he makes it clear that he regards spatial position as an intrinsic feature of points of space (COS 311). Bearing in mind the lessons of WDWR, the same account may presumably be applied to instants of time. Though he says little in *COS* about spatial order, it is not implausible to suppose that spatial and temporal order might be inferred from the intrinsic positions of points and instants. Indeed, at a slightly later date, he does indicate that this was his position (though we have no detailed account of it): 'the order of a set of numerable terms is always more or less at our disposition, except where that which distinguishes the terms is position in space or time' (PA 251). Given an absolute temporal order conferred by intrinsic temporal positions, the supposition that /increasing/ and /decreasing/ are intrinsic properties of a population at a particular time seems less perverse.

Russell distinguishes numerical cases in which a unit is introduced from

---

[23] Russell appeals here once more to Bradley's view that tautologies are unmeaning (cf. PA 257). The ascription of a number to a collection defined by an enumeration of its terms would be either self-contradictory or tautologous. Either way, it would be unmeaning.

those in which it is not. Similar considerations apply to both, however (AMR/TS 228). With the unit we can express the difference between two numbers as more or fewer 1's. But there is in this case, as in the non-numerical comparison of populations, 'a difference of intrinsic properties between $+1$ and $-1$' (AMR/TS 228). In these two cases—and, it turns out, in these cases only—the distinction of sign does not give rise to the contradiction of relativity.

In the case of quantities, sign arises wherever addition is possible. All extensive quantities, therefore, admit sign. Given two extensive quantities, $A$ and $C$, we can always identify two new quantities, $+B$ and $-B$, both of which express the difference between $A$ and $C$, since $C = A + B$ and $A = C - B$. The unsigned quantity $B$ is of the same type as $A$ and $C$. But $+B$ is a relation which expresses the difference of $A$ from $C$ and $-B$ a relation which expresses the difference of $C$ from $A$. An interesting problem, bearing on the question of relational reduction, arises from this account. Since $+B$ and $-B$ are particular relations relating particular quantities, Russell calls them '*existent* differences' (AMR/TS 228). Yet, unless $A$ is an actual part of $C$, there is no *actual* quantity by which they differ and, by the same token, it is difficult to regard their relations of difference as *existent* relations. 'And yet', Russell says, 'we must hold, I think, that a relation between two existents, when not reducible to a relation of adjectives, is itself a particular existent' (AMR/TS 228). We see here that Russell has explicitly committed himself to at least some form of relational realism. But such a position is, in any case, implicit in his theory of terms once the reductive theory of relations is rejected. More interesting is the fact that Russell maintains that the relation must be regarded as a particular existent whenever its terms are particular existents and it cannot be reduced to a relation of adjectives. In other words, it would not be sufficient to disqualify a relation as an existent to show that it could be reduced to an adjective of relation. This does confirm the entirely reasonable view that adjectives of relation are simply relations under a new name, while relations of adjectives are not.

Russell's third case concerns quantities which cannot be added, namely, intensive quantities. Here also signed quantities result from the difference of two intensive quantities. But whereas in the case of extensive quantities the signed quantities which are their differences form a manifold of terms whose differences are also signed and so on *ad infinitum*, in the case of intensive quantities it will not, in general, be possible to compare their differences. That is, given that $B$ is the difference between $A$ and $C$, and $E$ the difference between $D$ and $F$, it will not in general be possible to find a quantity which is the difference between $B$ and $E$ (AMR/TS 229). The fourth and final case concerns quantitative difference between terms which are not quantities. In this case, also, Russell maintains that distinction of sign exists, though 'it is wholly arbitrary which we call positive and which negative' (AMR/TS 229). Examples that Russell has in mind are differences between clockwise and anti-clockwise and between left and right. All such cases, he suggests, depend upon a difference of order (AMR/TS 230).

There remain two further matters to discuss in connection with Russell's treatment of sign. The first is the way contradictions emerge in connection with sign, for sign turns out to be an important source of antinomies; and the second is the dependence of sign (and the antinomies of sign) upon relations. This will reveal why Russell's attempts to understand sign led (in part) to a change in his views on relations, and why sign caused him so much difficulty—for it required a new view of relations which Russell was extremely reluctant to adopt.

Russell initially tried to use the distinction between magnitude and quantity to resolve the antinomy of quantity. For magnitude expresses the relation between two quantities of the same kind. At the same time, magnitude is an intrinsic property of quantities, which was necessary to explain the equality and inequality of quantities, but which could only be expressed 'by means of quantitative relations' (OQ 126).[24] Yet, by the same considerations mentioned above when dealing with extensive quantities, unless $A$ be part of $C$, their difference $B$ is a magnitude which expresses the difference between the magnitudes of $A$ and $C$. Thus magnitude is itself relational, and equality and inequality, which hold between magnitudes, become 'relations at two removes' (OQ 126). This was obviously a perplexing result for Russell, since he was not prepared, at this time, to admit any relations as independent terms between which a further relation could hold. The difficulty was compounded by the emergence of an infinite regress. For $A$ and $C$ could themselves be regarded as differences between the further quantities, and so on indefinitely. 'This', Russell concludes, 'is another form of the relativity which perpetually appears in Mathematics' (OQ 126; also AMR/TS 231). Far from helping to resolve the antinomy of quantity, the concept of magnitude introduces a 'more thorough-going relativity' (OQ 127). Let us call the new antinomy, 'the antinomy of relative specification'.

It is surprising that Russell should describe the thesis of relative specification, that every quantity may be regarded as the difference between two other quantities of the same kind, as a 'result' of the infinite regress just described (AMR/TS 231). For the infinite regress shows only that there must be infinitely many quantities in the manifold. It does not show that every element in the manifold is the difference between two others. Indeed, a simple model shows that the regress may hold when the thesis of relative

---

[24] Russell cites the missing chapter on equality and inequality for these conclusions (OQ 126). Again, we have the notion of an intrinsic property which yet can only be expressed relationally. Cf. WDWR 95; COS 311. See § 8.3.

specification fails. Consider two elements $A$ and $B$ of a manifold $M$. We have, by the regress argument, a third element $C \in M$, the difference of $A$ and $B$; thence elements $D$, $E \in M$, where $D$ is the difference of $C$ from $A$ and $E$ that of $C$ from $B$; and so on. But we have no pair of elements, $X$ and $Y$, such that $A$ is the difference of $X$ from $Y$. In general, the thesis of relative specification will not hold for manifolds of quantities with a least or greatest member. Nor can I see why Russell thinks the infinite regress shows that the thesis of relative specification holds for 'every quantity which has sign' (AMR/TS 231). This claim, in any case, seems to contradict his earlier admission of the case in which 'we have quantitative differences between terms which are not quantities' (AMR/TS 229). It is conceded, moreover, that the thesis of relative specification holds only for manifolds in which addition is possible (OQ 127; AMR 217); and thus not for manifolds of intensive quantities. It seems that Russell must have manifolds of extensive quantities exclusively in mind, for in these cases there is no least member, on account of the infinite divisibility of extensive quantities (RNQ 75). Equally, there is no greatest member, since any two members may be added to form a third. (We must assume, therefore, that Russell intends to exclude bounded finite submanifolds of extensive quantities.)

None the less, Russell's account of the antinomy of relative specification in AMR typescript is interesting because it links his work on sign with his work on physics and geometry. The thesis of relative specification, he says, introduces a new form of relativity, of which the relativity of motion is the most prominent example. Every motion is a difference of motions, every length a difference of lengths, every angle a difference of angles, etc. Thus not only is there an undue relativity as regards differences of magnitude, but, where quantities have signs, every quantity is itself a difference between terms like itself, and these in turn are differences. Thus we see that no manifold of quantities with sign can be self-subsistent, but the quantities with sign must always be differences between terms, which may be quantitative or not, but in any case can have no sign. It is the difficulty of finding such terms for motions which leads to the contradiction of relative and absolute motion (AMR/TS 231; cf. OQ 126).

Even where the thesis of relative specification fails, antinomies arise in connection with sign. For in these cases it is wholly arbitrary which term we call positive and which negative (AMR/TS 229).[25] In this case, there is nothing which conceptually distinguishes the positive from the negative. 'Like magnitude, [positive and negative] are conceptions indicated by relations, and invented, as intrinsic conceptions, to rationalize the relations.

---

[25] In the MS version of AMR Russell claimed that this was the case with all distinctions of sign (AMR 216), although, as we have seen in discussing Russell's treatment of sign in connection with number, it is not clear that his subsequent account bears him out.

354      *Relations*

What is fundamental and not arbitrary is the sign-relation, the being of the same or different sign . . .. Thus the relation comes first, and the assumed intrinsic adjectives positive and negative are mere inferences, and cannot be freed from extrinsic reference' (OQ 133; AMR 219; AMR/TS 230). We may call this 'the antinomy of arbitrary sign'.

Quite apart from the antinomies of relative specification and arbitrary sign, which affect particular cases, all cases of sign on Russell's account involve the antinomy of quantity (OQ 133). This is not surprising, for his account of the distinction of sign as depending upon 'a difference which is not a difference of adjectives, though giving to each term an adjective of difference' (AMR/TS 227) is virtually a paraphrase of the antinomy of quantity.

The degree to which Russell's theory of sign is infested with antinomies is one reason why it is of special importance for his dialectic of the sciences. But it is even more important in another way, for it focuses attention on relations as the source of these antinomies. The concept of sign is itself relational, but this is something it shared with quantity and is not of special importance. The special importance of sign in Russell's dialectic is due to the fact that it is always associated with a certain kind of relation. Russell called these relations 'asymmetrical' (OQ 132; AMR 216; AMR/TS 226), but what he had in mind were those relations which would nowadays be called asymmetrical and transitive, for he associates them with the relations which generate order (AMR 216; AMR/TS 230). It is notable that this association of sign with order, which figures even more prominently in *POM*: ch. 27, is not made in OQ.

The significant feature of asymmetrical, transitive relations is that they cannot be reduced to intrinsic properties (cf. *POM* 221–6). If *A* is greater than *B*, we may regard this as conferring on *A* the property of being greater than *B*, but this, as Russell notes, is a property with 'an extrinsic reference' (OQ 123, 133). If, *per impossibile*, the extrinsic reference could be eliminated, the transitivity of the relation would then be lost. It is therefore impossible to eliminate asymmetrical, transitive relations in favour of intrinsic properties. Russell's work on sign convinced him that it would be impossible to construct an adequate theory of sign without such relations and that such relations could not be eliminated.

Relations give rise to sign on account of what Russell later called their 'sense'. In *POM* Russell explains that a two-place relation *R* has sense in that it 'proceeds, so to speak, *from* one [term] *to* the other'. More formally, *R* has sense when, if $a \neq b$, '*aRb*' expresses a different proposition from '*bRa*'. The fact that relations have sense, Russell says, is 'the source of order and series' (*POM* 95; cf. Winslade 1970: 86–9). Now difference of sense, in itself, is a respect in which relations differ from properties, for it makes no sense to talk of the sense of a property.[26] In *POM* difference of sign and difference of sense of asymmetrical relations are 'closely connected (though not identical)' (*POM* 227).

Although Russell did not use the phrase 'sense of a relations' in OQ very much the same idea is expressed there. Sign makes its first appearance in OQ in the lost chapter on equality and inequality. There, as he reports at the beginning of the chapter on sign, a certain kind of difference was found to be a difference of sign. It arose from 'a relation between two terms *A* and *B*, of that kind which cannot be analysed into a relation of adjectives, but confers adjectives with an external reference' (OQ 123). These relations are differences and yield sign because they can be regarded either as the difference of *A* and *B* or that of *B* from *A* (OQ 123, 132–3). Russell did not connect sign with order until he came to write AMR. In the manuscript material he notes that the distinction of sign has 'an intimate relation to order, being deduced from precisely the same kind of asymmetrical relations'. In all cases where quantities can be ordered, their differences are signed on account of 'the two senses in which a series may be ordered' (AMR 216). In the typescript, sign is said to be more fundamental than order, since sign arises wherever there is a pair of terms related by an asymmetrical transitive relation, whereas order requires a series of such terms. None the less, wherever there is such a series, the differences between the elements of the series will be signed, even where the elements themselves are signless. Conversely, wherever we have a collection of signed differences the terms between which they are the differences may be ordered (AMR/TS 230).

Neither of these claims are made in OQ. There, only certain examples of sign result from asymmetrical, transitive relations; and only certain asymmetrical, transitive relations yield the distinction of sign. Moreover Russell still denies that difference is a genuine relation: 'the relation of difference . . . is not primarily a relation at all, but an independent magnitude of the same kind as those between which it holds' (OQ 126). There is a tension between this remark and Russell's claim at the end of the chapter on sign that signs are 'conceptions indicated by relations, and invented, as intrinsic conceptions,

[26] It is disputed whether Russell held that all relations have sense (as he maintained in *POP* 73), or only asymmetrical ones. In the case of a symmetrical relation it is at least arguable that '*aRb*' and '*bRa*' express the same proposition (cf. FIAM 278). This seems not to have been Russell's view in *POM*, however, where he adopts a very strong account of propositional identity such that mutually entailing propositions need not be identical (pp. 96, 228). The problem seems to have arisen because in *POM* he does use 'sense' ('in the present discussion at least') in a more restrictive sense to mark the distinction between an asymmetrical relation and its converse (*POM* 228). In Russell's earlier writings, COR, this second sense of 'sense' coincides with the first, for in COR only asymmetrical relations are recognized as genuine relations. The appearance of the second sense in *POM* illustrates the way in which the final MS of the work was put together from a variety of earlier MSS, inconsistency being avoided, adequately though hardly prominently, by the unobtrusive qualification 'in the present discussion at least'.

to rationalize the relations', the relations come first and the 'assumed intrinsic adjectives . . . cannot be freed from extrinsic reference' (OQ 133). There is further confusion in that the supposed *intrinsic* adjectives have an ineliminable *extrinsic* reference. It seems clear that Russell is here being forced to reject the strong reductive theory of relations, though (not surprisingly) he still finds it difficult to admit as much explicitly.

Though clearly linked with sign, the concept of order was of independent interest to Russell. His concern stemmed originally from his work in projective geometry where a four-place relation was required to define a projectively invariant ordering. His thoughts returned to this topic in 1898 when he wrote the 'Note on Order' (NOO) and thereafter it assumed a very prominent role in his philosophy of mathematics (see e.g. ONO; *POM* 199). Significantly no chapter was devoted to order in AMR, though there was a chapter on ordinal numbers (now lost), placed at the end of Book II, on number. However, when Russell laid out plans for FIAM he allocated the whole of Part III to a discussion of order, immediately following Part II on whole and part and preceding Part IV on quantity. Although AMR did not contain a chapter on order, the notion was discussed, as a couple of backwards references show (AMR 216; AMR/TS 226), presumably in connection with the ordinal numbers, but perhaps also in the chapter on equality and inequality. But the main source for Russell's thinking on the topic in 1898 is NOO which, though it begins with a consideration of issues in projective geometry, encompasses much wider concerns. The account of relations in NOO is characterized by Russell's earlier classification of relations, the use of relational variables for the first time, and the distinction between the different senses of a relation.

NOO makes it clear that Russell was already reconsidering his treatment of projective geometry several months before he received Poincaré's criticism of his efforts in *EFG*. In NOO he is concerned both with the axiom sets required for various projective constructions and (more relevantly for present purposes) with the ordering principles underlying the projective notion of cross ratio. He distinguishes between open and closed series (represented by points on a line and points on a circle, respectively) and finds, in the fact that the latter requires at least four points to define an order, a connection (somewhat obscurely realized) with the fact that four points are required to define a projective invariant. The details of all this need not concern us. Russell, it seems, is still pursuing his view of projective geometry as the purely qualitative science of any form of externality. The new development is that he has started to pay attention to the order relations which hold between the contents whose simultaneous presentation is made possible by the form of externality. Assuming that these contents are ordered, the principles which express their order ought, in some way, to be naturally expressed by means of projective geometry. Russell's attempts to formulate the necessary principles are not, in this respect, successful. He gives an axiom for the pairwise separation of points (NOO 341) which links this notion to projective invariance (NOO 342). But it is hard to regard this axiom as an a priori principle presupposed by any form of externality, since it does not hold for open series. In this respect, Russell's knowledge of projective geometry was still inadequate to the task he set himself. What he needed was Vailati's set of conditions guaranteeing pairwise separation of *five* terms. (cf. Vailati 1895; *POM* 214–16). These conditions apply equally to closed and open series; as Russell later put it, they show that the distinction between the two is 'somewhat superficial' (*POM* 215). Russell did not read Vailati until his study of the Peano school in 1900.

None the less, the efforts of 1898 led to a considerable advance in Russell's treatment of ordering relations. Several useful concepts and an even more useful notation emerge in the course of NOO. They are summed up in the following passage:

Let there be a number of terms $A$, $B$, $C$, . . . Let every pair have an asymmetrical relation $R$, and let the two senses of the relation be $r_1$, $r_2$. Then $Ar_1B$ expresses a relation with one sense, $Ar_2B$ a relation with the opposite sense. The proposition $Ar_1B$ implies $Br_2A$ and $Ar_2B$ implies $Br_1A$. Since the relation is transitive, $Ar_1B$ and $Br_1C$ imply $Ar_1C$. This suffices to decide the order of $A$, $B$, $C$. (NOO 353.)

Elsewhere the notation $R_{AB}$ and $R_{BA}$ is introduced to express, for example in the case where '$r_1$' is to be read 'before' and '$r_2$' 'after', '$A$'s priority to $B$' and '$B$'s priority to $A$', respectively (NOO 358). (Russell's advances in treating series and relations in NOO are summed up in a series of definitions at the end of the paper.)

Alongside this relatively clear conceptualization, there is a very much more murky discussion of the relation between order and quantity. The problem arises from the need to define harmonic range, an apparently quantitative concept, in projective geometry, a purely qualitative science. Now Russell had shown in *EFG* (pp. 125–6) how this could be done without presupposing quantitative notions. The definition of harmonic range, however, could be seen as introducing quantity into projective geometry, by means of the co-ordinatization of projective space. In NOO Russell is concerned to link the quantities thus introduced with the concepts of order and relation underlying projective geometry. He states his approach as follows:

We ought to be able to exhibit the relation [of forming an harmonic range] intrinsically in some manner intermediate between the projective and metrical methods. I think the following is the fact: If, to the points on a line, quantities be assigned on *any* principle, however arbitrary, provided it give a unique point for each quantity, and vice versa, then we can give the construction for a harmonic range, and show it to be unique. (NOO 344.)

What Russell intended by the phrase 'intermediate between the projective and metrical methods' is hinted at later in his paper, where he notes that the projective principle of duality 'cannot be stated without reference to the whole of space, and therefore to metrical consideration' (NOO 344). To 'metrical' he adds a footnote explaining: 'Not in the sense of implying quantity, but only as implying whole and part'. Later on he writes 'Projective Geometry seems to demand *whole* and *part*, but not *quantity*. By whole and part, the point in space can be defined' (NOO 352). It would seem that the part/whole relation occupies this intermediate position between the qualitative and the quantitative. It was, in fact, for a brief period, a key concept in Russell's semantics, underlying his new notion of philosophical analysis, of implication, and of order in general.[27] Russell's philosophy of logic, as a result, showed inevitable signs of tension between mereological and set theoretic approaches. (An example of the type of problem that emerged can be seen at *Papers*, ii, A117: 27.)

In NOO, series are connected to the part/whole relation by means of the concept of distance. The link between series and quantities is introduced in the following passage: 'A series is constituted by a single property which the terms possess in varying magnitudes. If, then, we have two terms belonging to a series, they must be completely identical in all properties except one, and in that one, they must differ as to magnitude' (NOO 343). This idea provides the basis for a new analysis of the concept of dimension. Given a collection of terms, qualitatively identical except in one property wherein each differs only in magnitude from all the others, we can form a one-dimensional series by means of an ordering relation. But given a collection of terms which differ as to the magnitude of two of their properties, we can form them into a two-dimensional series; and so on, for higher dimensions (NOO 343). Thus: 'All space [i.e. actual three-space] consists of a collection of points, and three qualities may be found, which are all possessed, though in different magnitudes, by different points. When the magnitude of each of the three qualities is given, the point is determined uniquely' (NOO 347). It seems clear enough that Russell would want to ensure that the series of magnitudes was continuous (in Russell's sense, i.e. dense), although he never states such a requirement explicitly. Russell's account of dimension—as his more technical description of a coordinate system reveals (NOO 349–51)—is influenced by Whitehead's account of a positional manifold. It does not

[27] Cf. FIAM 291–5. Implication, as we've seen, was a relation which could hold between non-propositional terms, and even between things (POM/D, Pt. II, fo. 3), as well as between propositions. It was one among ordering relations (though the one of special interest to logic) which were all, it seems, to be understood in terms of part and whole. It is historically interesting to note a rather similar treatment in McTaggart's later work, especially his use of inclosure series for the treatment of temporal relations (McTaggart 1921).

represent an abandonment of the coordinate view, and thus is still subject to the difficulties posed for that view by Cantor's mappings.

Since each term in a series possesses a property common to all the terms in a magnitude unique to each, it might be thought that each term is (or is associated with) a unique quantity. This, however, is not the case: 'Every point', we are told, 'has a unique quality, which cannot be expressed as a quantity' (NOO 351). It is the differences between these qualities (the 'positions' of COS 311) which can be expressed as quantities. This does seem to be Russell's considered view in this paper, although some passages seem to undermine it. For example: 'Thus anharmonic ratio is independent of the actual distance and depends only upon our assigning some quantity which has a one-to-one correspondence with the points, and has infinitesimal differences for infinitesimal changes of position. . . . [A] quantity such as is required for anharmonic ratio can be inferred from order and intensive continuity, without the use of distance' (NOO 344). If these quantities can be correlated one-to-one with the points of projective space, then surely the unique quality of every point can be quantitatively expressed. If the one–one correspondence between points and quantities holds, the unique quality of each point can be correlated with, and therefore expressed by, the quantity correlated with the point.[28]

The idea that it is the *differences* between the unique qualities of points, rather than the unique qualities themselves, which are quantities is confirmed by the account Russell gives of distance. As might be expected, given the role that anharmonic ratio plays in the co-ordinatization of projective space, distance is to be defined by means of differences between the unique (non-quantitative) qualities of points. Russell, however, gives a definition directly in terms of ordering relations which extends the concept of distance well beyond its applicability to space: 'A series of terms is a collection in which, by means of [transitive asymmetrical] relations . . . the terms acquire an order. Order involves, between any term of this series and one fixed term, a relation which is constant in quality but variable in magnitude' (NOO 353).[29] Russell goes on to call this relation a quantity, since 'it may be greater or less', in particular it is a 'distance, or difference of position' (NOO 354). (This very general definition of 'distance' produces some strange results, as when Russell applies it to chains of implications in POM/D, Pt. IV, fo. 45.) It

---

[28] The notion of a quantity expressing a quality is admittedly vague, and is not explicated by Russell—although he refers to it frequently enough in connection with the antinomies of quantity and quality. None the less, I think the notion does not involve the idea of meaning, and that a series *S* can be expressed by a series *S'* when the two can be brought into one–one correlation. (Cf. also, Whitehead's frequent use of 'express' in just this way in 1898*a*, and his remarks on 'substitutive symbols', pp. 3–4).

[29] Note that here it is the relations between terms, rather than the terms themselves, which are said to be constant in quality and variable in magnitude.

would seem that Russell's identification of distance with an asymmetrical transitive relation is a development of his earlier view (*EFG* 170) that the relation between two points is the line which joins them. Like the earlier view it is problematic, and Russell might have been warned against such identifications by the antinomies which resulted from the reification of relations which they involved. As things stand Russell has to admit that differences so defined are 'subject to the contradiction of relativity' (NOO 343).

## 8.6 THE CONTRADICTION OF RELATIVITY

As an account of series, NOO leaves much to be desired. Russell's further advance on this topic depended upon the acquisition of further information, much of which was in place in time for *POM*. By contrast, NOO is relatively clear about the relations which are responsible for series. Given a series of terms, there is between any two members a two-place, asymmetrical, transitive relation which, while it does not itself constitute order, is a necessary (and, provided sufficiently many terms are given, a sufficient) condition for the terms being ordered in a series. Moreover, the two senses of such relations are clearly recognized. If $R$ is an asymmetrical, transitive relation, Russell represents its two senses by $r_1$ and $r_2$ and notes that $Ar_1B$ implies $Br_2A$ and $Ar_2B$ implies $Br_1A$ and that $Ar_1B$ and $Br_1C$ together imply $Ar_1C$ (NOO 353).

The new ideas were immediately put to use in the treatment of ordinal numbers (PA 251–60), which had hitherto been almost entirely neglected by Russell. The considerations adduced there make it clear that, despite the advances he had made in the treatment of relations, the contradiction of relativity was still a serious problem. Russell, however, is far clearer now about where and how it arises. In an ordered series of terms, any two terms, $A$ and $B$, are related by an asymmetrical transitive relation $R$ which confers one adjective on $A$ and a different adjective on $B$. Each adjective involves an essential reference to the other term. Thus the adjective assigned to $A$ may be represented by $R_{1B}$ and that assigned to $B$ may be represented by $R_{2A}$ (PA 252–3). Although these adjectives cannot be regarded as intrinsic, Russell does maintain that *additional* intrinsic adjectives, namely positions, are assigned to the terms, provided the series has a first and a last member. In the case of the alphabet, Russell explains, B is intrinsically the second letter, because A is intrinsically the first (PA 254). Thus the contradiction of relativity does not arise, for the position of each letter in the alphabet, though it can only be expressed as a relation, is none the less an intrinsic property of that letter (PA 258). In other cases of order, however, the contradiction does arise, as Russell explains:

It is plain, however, that unless there be an absolutely first and an absolutely last term, [ordering] relations cannot be regarded as giving intrinsic adjectives to their terms. In any case, a term not at either end of the series is before some terms and after others—thus before and after express only relations which cannot be analyzed validly into intrinsic adjectives. They are relations which express a difference, but make no difference to their terms. (PA 253–4.)

He goes on to use this point to explain why order may be arbitrarily imposed on certain collections of terms (since the relation between them 'in no way affects the intrinsic nature of the terms'), though not in others (e.g. the letters of the alphabet).

The contrasting case of the alphabet illustrates exactly how the contradiction of relativity is avoided there. The intrinsic adjectives assigned to the individual letters by the ordering relation make an implicit reference to the whole alphabet, thus 'A is not merely the letter which preceeds B, C, . . . Z, but is also the first letter *of the alphabet*' (PA 254). It is essential for this explanation that the alphabet can be identified apart from an enumeration of its members. Considered without reference to the whole, the individual letters can be identified only by their mutual relations. If the whole can be identified only by reference to its members, the attempt to assign individuating intrinsic adjectives to the members would be circular.

Just as points are distinguished by intrinsic spatial positions, so all terms in a bounded series can be distinguished by their intrinsic position within the series. It might seem that Russell should require that the series be finite as well as bounded. But Russell, at this stage, was possibly unclear about the distinction. Intrinsic position, however, can only be expressed by means of a relation. If the series is bounded then the position is absolute and can be expressed by means of the relation of the term to the whole series. If the series is not bounded then the position is merely relative and is expressed by the ordering relation. Even in a bounded series the ordering relation itself cannot express absolute position. More surprisingly, even where position is relative it

cannot *be* only a relation: for there must be some property in virtue of which a term is before some terms and after others. . . . [B]ut it is a property which can only be described by its relations or differences, and which appears to be actually created by these relations. We have thus, where order has full scope [i.e. where the series is expressed entirely by its terms and their ordering relation], the contradiction of relativity: A conception of difference without a difference of conception. (PA 258–9.)

Such differences are of two kinds and the difference between them may be represented by a distinction of sign (PA 259). Specifying the relation, the terms which intervene between the terms related, and the sign, allows any order to be specified. '[P]osition, though it is a unique content of the term of which it is predicable, is wholly relative in the sense that it can never be expressed except as a congeries of relations to terms whose positions are defined by similar relations' (PA 259–60). What makes bounded finite series different is not that positions in such series can be expressed without relations (they cannot) nor that positions are intrinsic only in such series (they are intrinsic in all series), but that in bounded finite series the position of a term can be expressed by means of a relation to a term (viz. the series as a whole) which is *not* defined in the same way as the original term.

It is clear that the relations which generate the contradiction of relativity are, formally, those which are asymmetrical and transitive. These are the only examples that Russell discusses in detail in connection with the various forms of the contradiction, and were certainly the relations that were at the forefront of his mind as those responsible for the mathematically important concept of order. Moreover, such a view can be justified independently of Russell's use of examples. For the fact that a relation is asymmetrical ensures that the adjectives required by its terms are different for each, and thus that the relation cannot be reconstituted as the joint possession of a single adjective. At the same time, the fact that the relation is transitive ensures that the adjective of each term must have an ineliminable external reference to the other.

As far as the source of the contradiction is concerned, however, this formal classification is of less interest to Russell than the semantical classification he developed in the typescript of AMR (see § 8.3). There he has an argument to show that it is always and only relations of semantical type IV, i.e. those in which adjectives, different for each term, are inferred from the relation, which generate the contradiction. It is reasonable to suppose that all relations of class IV are asymmetrical and transitive, and conversely. But Russell's only statement of the semantic classification pre-dates his syntactic classification and this makes it difficult to be quite sure about either part of this assertion. We can be sure however, that all class IV relations must be asymmetrical. For class IV relations confer different adjectives on each term, whereas symmetrical relations confer the same adjective on both terms. Equally, it seems clear that no transitive relation can be inferred from intrinsic adjectives of its terms, and thus that all transitive relations must be logically prior to the adjectives of their terms. Whether Russell thought that only transitive relations were logically prior is impossible to determine.

It is easy to see that relations of types I and III do not give rise to the contradiction of relativity. For in these two classes the adjectives of the terms of the relation are the same for each term, so no conception of difference arises. The case with relations of type II is rather different. There the adjectives are different for each term. But in this case we have what Russell calls a relation of adjectives. The relation is said to be inferred from the adjectives, although Russell gives no help in recognizing when a relation has this property. In this case, there is a conception of difference but the contradiction of relativity is blocked because there is also a difference of conception. For the adjectives from which the relation is inferred are different for each term. This shows that only relations of type IV generate the contradiction (AMR/TS 224).

To show that *all* such relations generate the contradiction Russell considers two terms $A$ and $B$ related by a relation $R$ of type IV. The relation $R$, Russell says, 'transforms them into $A\beta$ *and* $B\alpha2$, where $\alpha$ is an adjective with an extrinsic reference to $A$ and $\beta$ is an adjective with an extrinsic reference to $B$. The adjectives differ in content, for, by the condition of type IV relations, the adjectives of each term must be different and different adjectives differ in content. On the other hand, since the adjectives are inferred from the relation, '$A$ and $B$, considered without reference to the relation $R$, have no difference of conception corresponding to the differences $\alpha$, $\beta$' (AMR/TS 225). Thus with any relation of type IV we have a conception of difference among its terms, but no difference in the conceptions applicable to each.

Now it may be that $A$ and $B$ have no differences *corresponding* to the differences $\alpha$, $\beta$ apart from the relation $R$, but this is not to say that $A$ and $B$ might not have other intrinsic differences. If they do, the contradiction will be blocked. This is a more general version of a problem with Russell's account in connection with quantities and other items which produce the contradiction. Quantitative things may well have intrinsic differences which enable them to be distinguished. It is only the abstracted quantities which yield the contradiction. This, of course, would be bad enough. But it is a mistake to say that the contradiction arises wherever relations of the fourth type (such as inequality) hold. For relations of inequality may hold between quantitative things, as well as quantities, and when they do so the contradiction does not arise. What Russell's argument proves is that the contradiction is always possible with relations of class IV. Indeed, the contradiction becomes a possibility as soon as it is recognized that not all relations confer intrinsic adjectives on their terms, while, at the same time, it is insisted that all relations must be grounded in intrinsic adjectives of their terms. The contradictions actually arise, however, only when terms (such as spatial points or quantities) are admitted which do not differ except in their relations to other terms of the same kind.

With the advantages of hindsight it is now clear that this constitutes a *reductio ad absurdum* argument against the doctrine of internal relations. For the contradiction of relativity is simply as follows. Certain terms do not differ in virtue of their intrinsic properties. These terms may be related to each other by relations of class IV. But, by the doctrine of internal relations, relations of class IV presuppose that their terms differ in their intrinsic properties. In this formulation it is immediately clear that the doctrine of internal relations has to go. Yet Russell did not immediately draw the right conclusion.

As we have seen, the contradiction of relativity continued to appear in PA, which was written after AMR. The contradiction, however, had disappeared by the time Russell came to write FIAM in 1899. In that year also, in the draft of *POM*, he turned the argument from the typescript of AMR on its head and uses it to refute the doctrine of internal relations (POM/D, Pt. IV, fos. 33, 42), taking the very sheets from AMR/TS and incorporating them in the manuscript of the draft of *POM*. What, in 1898, had been an argument for the contradiction from the doctrine of internal relations became, in 1899, a *reductio* argument against the doctrine of internal relations from the contradiction.

There is a certain irony in the fact that the only reason why Russell's general argument in favour of the contradiction has survived is because he used the very pages on which he stated it as part of his later argument against its main premiss. The derivation of the contradiction from the doctrine of internal relations remains essentially the same in the two sources. Only the surrounding argument changed. Russell kept the *reductio* argument through the various changes which preceded the publication of *POM*. It appears again, much compressed, as its interest for Russell had waned, in the published version of *POM* (pp. 222–3). There is a certain beauty, too, in the fact that, although the trend in Russell's thought against neo-Hegelianism pre-dated the draft of *POM*, the actual point of change in his philosophy should have been what can most accurately be described as a gestalt switch in the way he viewed the argument from the doctrine of internal relations to the contradiction of relativity. Russell himself, in the draft of *POM*, left a nicely matter-of-fact statement of the advances which followed once the gestalt switch was made: 'We cannot hope . . . so long as we adhere to the view that no relation can be "purely external", to obtain anything like a satisfactory philosophy of mathematics. As soon, however, as we adopt a different theory, the logical puzzles, which have obstructed our advances, are seen to be artificial' (POM/D, Pt. IV, fo. 42).

It is not known exactly when Russell made the switch, but it was certainly well before he came to write the draft of *POM*. The main consequences that he draws there from his rejection of internal relations (POM/D, Pt. IV, fos. 42–3) were already clearly stated in COR, written right at the beginning of 1899. There he defends the view that not all relations are reducible to identity and difference of content by means of six propositions. Together they indicate how far he had moved from his neo-Hegelian theory of relations, which is now rejected at every point:

(1) That identity of content may have one of two meanings, and in neither case expresses a relation. (2) That the second of these meanings presupposes the notion of predication. (3) That predication is a relation. (4) that diversity of content is the precondition of *all* relations, but cannot be the type of all relations. (5) That no relation is equivalent to a pair of predicates of the related terms. (6) That relations are concepts just as ultimate and fundamental as predicates. (COR 139–40.)

I shall consider these claims one by one.

(1) In the first sense Russell distinguishes, 'identity of content' means 'the same concept in two different connections' (COR 140). In this sense, Russell claims, identity of content, though it implies relations, is not itself a relation, 'being mere self-sameness, the mere fact that one and the same term is dealt with in both instances' (COR 140). For Russell, relations require plurality of terms.[30] In its second sense, 'identity of content' means that two subjects have one and the same predicate. This, again, is not itself a relation. 'We have the same relation, i.e. predication, to the same predicate' (COR 140). Russell argues that this does not give us a relation between two subjects but a compound of identity of content in the first sense together with the relation of predication.

(2) Russell's second proposition now follows trivially. But from it he immediately infers another of greater importance: namely that identity of content cannot be presupposed in all relations, since it presupposes a relation itself, namely predication.

(3) What is more difficult is to prove that predication is a relation. Russell rests his case on three considerations. The first, at least, is hardly convincing. Russell notes the fact that the word 'predication' means something and declares that if it does not mean something relational he is at a loss to know what it means (COR 140). The second point is more useful. In a synthetic subject–predicate judgement, the subject and predicate must be admitted as distinct. Since the judgement cannot be split into two judgements, one about the subject and the other about the predicate, what is asserted in the judgement of subject and predicate together is that they have a relation, the relation of predication (COR 140). Russell speculates that the doctrine that all judgements are analytic—he was obviously thinking of Leibniz—may have been designed to avoid treating predication as a relation. If so, it is unsuccessful—and this is Russell's third point—for in analytic judgements as usually conceived the relation of subject to predicate is one of whole to part and is thus relational.

(4) Part of Russell's fourth proposition, that diversity of content is a precondition of all relations, follows immediately from the assumption 'that

---

[30] Equivalence relations, for which *ara* holds, are not, on this account, to be admitted as genuine relations.

every term which can be used in a proposition means something, and that any other term, in order to be other, must mean something different' (COR 141). That diversity is presupposed by all relations can, of course, be shown without Russell's assumption, since all relations involve diversity of their terms. But that conclusion is not enough to establish that diversity *of content* is also presupposed.

Russell follows this argument with a long discussion of the nature of diversity. The first point established is that diversity is itself a relation (COR 141–2). This, of course, represents the end of the theory of proto-relations. What remains of the earlier theory as far as diversity is concerned is the view that diversity is 'the precondition of all other relations' (COR 142). What is obviously lacking by now is any trace of the neo-Hegelian view that all relations presuppose identity-in-difference.

Next Russell considers whether there is a fundamental distinction between diversity of content and material diversity. Such a distinction, he claims, would follow either from the assumption that 'there are terms which are fundamentally subjects and other terms which are fundamentally predicates' or from the assumption that there is a fundamental distinction between existents and concepts (COR 142). Both these assumptions are controverted on grounds familiar from AMR, for neither is compatible with the theory of terms propounded there. By contrast, if, as Russell believed, every term has both being and meaning and if different terms mean different things, it follows that every instance of diversity of terms is accompanied by diversity of meaning and conversely (COR 143). Russell's conclusion from this, though he is not prepared to state it 'dogmatically', is that

The assertion of diversity involves taking our concepts as terms, and not merely adjectivally. Hence diversity is always diversity of terms, i.e. numerical diversity . . . But the terms which are diverse are always concepts, and the diversity is therefore diversity between meanings. Thus, on the whole, there would seem to be only one kind of diversity, which may be described as material diversity of contents. (COR 143.)

(5) The fifth proposition is the crux of Russell's case, yet the argument he gives for it does not at first sight seem very strong. It looks, indeed, as if Russell argues in detail that *some* relations are not equivalent to a pair of predicates in the related terms and then jumps to the conclusion that *no* relation is equivalent to such a pair. In fact, however, his argument is considerably more subtle than this and the way he presents it hardly does it justice.

Proposition (5) appears not merely as the rejection of the (monadistic) reduction theory, but as the claim that *no* relation is capable of such a reduction. Now Russell has already argued that the reduction theory will not work for the relation of diversity. Moreover, he has also argued that predication is a relation. This last claim enables him to develop (5) into a rejection of the doctrine of internal relations, as well as of the reductive theory of relations. Now, as Bradley claimed, all relations must be grounded upon predication, and if predication is itself a relation, an infinite regress will ensue. Once predication is admitted as a relation, 'the ground of Mr. Bradley's view is gone' (COR 143). It is to no avail, against this argument, to point out differences between Bradley's reductive theory of relations and Russell's: the argument will apply to both. Nor does it help to point out that Bradley admits that an infinite regress results from relations. Bradley's famous regress (which Russell admits, COR 146) is not the one Russell complains of here.

Having granted Russell's conclusions so far in the paper, his case against both the reductive theory and the doctrine of internal relations is assured. What are not assured are his much more radical claims: that *no* relation can be eliminated in favour of predication and that '*all* relations are external' (COR 143). 'Wherever there really is a relation,' he writes, 'the attempt to find a corresponding predicate of each term will, at best, force us to admit a corresponding relation between the two predicates' (COR 144). To think that a relation consists in a 'pair of predicates' or 'in internal states' of the related terms is 'to overlook entirely the nature of relations' (COR 144–5). It appears, at first sight, as if Russell argues for these conclusions merely by dealing with examples. He deals, at some length, with temporal relations (both relations of temporal order and relations of temporal occupancy) and then notes that other relations of the same formal type can be treated similarly. But a treatment of these cases, however successful, is clearly not sufficient to establish his conclusion.

In reality, however, his treatment by cases is far more subtle than his presentation suggests. In the first place, his qualification 'wherever there really is a relation' is designed to draw attention to the fact that he does not regard equivalence relations as genuine relations. This leaves us to deal with only those relations which fail symmetry or transitivity or both. His treatment of predication and temporal occupancy deals with the only cases he knows of relations which fail both conditions (COR 139). His treatment of relations of temporal order and its generalization to all other relations of the same formal type deals with relations which are transitive but asymmetrical. The cases still to be dealt with, therefore, are those relations which are symmetrical but not transitive and those which are transitive and non-symmetrical. Russell's classification of relations is not yet sophisticated enough to recognize the latter as a distinct group. I will ignore them for the moment, therefore, though, as we shall see, Russell already has an argument general and powerful enough to deal with them, as soon as he is in a position to recognize their existence. Turning, therefore, to the one remaining class that Russell recognizes, relations which are symmetrical but not transitive, we find that these relations are of the same type as diversity. Russell has already argued at length that diversity is a relation which is not equivalent to any pair of adjectives of its terms. Though Russell doesn't say so, it seems evident that he thought that his account of diversity would apply to all relations of the same formal kind.

Be that as it may, there is a further argument in COR which Russell does not explicitly apply in arguing for (5), but which is powerful enough to deal with all cases—including those of transitive non-symmetrical relations, which slip through his classification system. It is clear, as Russell points out early in his paper (COR 139; an argument repeated much later in PLA 183–4), that if relations are to be reduced to anything else, that to which they are reduced must preserve their formal properties. For the original relation and that to which it is reduced must be equivalent, and the equivalence will be broken if the two have different formal properties. It follows, therefore, if we consider the specific case in which relations are to be reduced to predications, that only those relations which have the same formal properties as predication can be so reduced. That is, at best only relations which are neither symmetrical nor transitive can be eliminated in favour of predication. Since Russell only recognizes two examples of such relations (predication and occupancy of space and time), and gives an explicit treatment of each to show that it cannot be eliminated in favour of predication, he can justifiably consider his case for (5) complete.

(6) As stated, Russell's final claim, that relations are concepts as ultimate and fundamental as predicates, has already been established. But Russell adds to it the new claim that every proposition involves at least one relation. For every proposition involves at least two terms and the proposition says about the pair of them something which cannot be said of either alone. The proposition thus asserts a relation between the terms. Since all propositions involve relations, the 'classification of relations is . . . the classification of the types of proposition' (COR 145).

COR indicates how far Russell has moved, by the beginning of 1899, from the neo-Hegelian view of relations which had embroiled him in all the difficulties of the dialectic only a few months before. It is not unduly surprising that he didn't immediately recognize the general argument on the contradiction of relativity in the typescript of AMR for what it was. The doctrine of internal relations was the deepest of his neo-Hegelian assumptions and one that he had not discussed in detail or even found himself forced to formulate exactly. Nor could he count on his neo-Hegelian contemporaries to provide him with a clear formulation of the doctrine, in a form relevant to his work. The dialectical framework of Russell's system also helped obscure the problem. For, as a neo-Hegelian, contradictions did not show that something had to be rejected, but that a wider synthesis was needed. Only with the development of his dialectic of the sciences did it become clear that, however much the system was widened, the contradiction of relativity would not be eliminated. We saw signs of this in Chapter 5, but at that stage virtually nothing had been revealed of the source of the contradictions. The pervasiveness of these contradictions in mathematics led Russell to a more abstract formulation of the contradictions and this, in turn, helped him to uncover the principles which gave rise to them.

Russell's work as an idealist was not the farrago of muddles and confusions that he subsequently presented it as being. Nor was it a superficial patchwork of guesses and dogma. A good deal of it was extremely detailed. In general, it was well up to the standards of the best British philosophical work of the day, and in rigour and detail was far better than most. Despite some logical lapses, it had a good deal of internal coherence, and the points on which it was incoherent turned out, as we have seen, to depend logically on a small number of unstated, mutually inconsistent claims. It is hard not to admire the way Russell unearths a single set of principles as responsible for problems which emerged in such a wide range of work, encompassing geometry, physics, psychology, and pure mathematics. Few philosophers have had such a good eye for fundamental unifying principles while conducting detailed investigations over such a wide range.

# Bibliography

The bibliography lists only those works cited in the text. The date used in citations is usually the year in which the work was written or first published. Where a second date is given with the publication details, it is the date of the edition or printing actually used. Wherever possible I have used easily available reprints and translations, although on some occasions it has been necessary to cite editions that were used by, or available to, Russell. With the exception of Russell's own works, no great bibliographical effort has gone into determining dates of composition and publication, or into tracing editions. The information given is sufficient, I hope, to enable the reader to track down my references with no more difficulty than is inevitable, given the obscurity of some of the material. Where a work was published over more than one year I have cited it by the first year of publication only. Russell's own works are listed separately. Unpublished material is in the Bertrand Russell Archives, McMaster University, unless otherwise stated.

## I. Works by Russell

*Papers*      *The Collected Papers of Bertrand Russell.*
  i. *Cambridge Essays. 1888–99*, ed. by Kenneth Blackwell, *et al.* (London: Allen and Unwin, 1983).
  ii. *Philosophical Papers: 1896–99*, ed. Nicholas Griffin and Albert C. Lewis (London: Hyman Unwin, 1990).
  vii. *Theory of Knowledge: The 1913 Manuscript*, ed. Elizabeth Eames and Kenneth Blackwell (London: Allen and Unwin, 1984).
  viii. *The Philosophy of Logical Atomism and Other Essays: 1914–19*, ed. John Slater (London: Allen and Unwin, 1986).
  ix. *Essays on Language, Mind and Matter: 1919–26*, ed. John Slater (London: Allen and Unwin, 1988).
  xii. *Contemplation and Action: 1902–1914*, ed. Richard Rempel *et al.* (London: Allen and Unwin, 1985).

*Amp.P.*      *The Amberley Papers* 2 vols. (London: Allen and Unwin, 2nd edn., 1966; 1st edn., 1937).

AMR      'An Analysis of Mathematical Reasoning' (1898), *Papers*, ii. 163–222.

AMR/TS      'An Analysis of Mathematical Reasoning', TS (1898), *Papers*, ii. 223–38.

*A.Matter*      *The Analysis of Matter* (New York: Dover, 1954, 1st edn., 1927).

*A.Mind*      *The Analysis of Mind* (London: Allen and Unwin, 1971; 1st edn., 1921).

AOG      'On the Axioms of Geometry' (1899), *Papers*, ii. 394–415.

*Auto.*      *The Autobiography of Bertrand Russell*, 3 vols. (London: Allen and Unwin, 1967–9).

COR      'The Classification of Relations' (1899) *Papers*, ii. 138–46.

COS      'On the Constituents of Space and Their Mutual Relations' (1898), *Papers*, ii. 311–21.

*EA*      *Essays in Analysis*, ed. D. Lackey (London: Allen and Unwin, 1974).

EAE    'Are Euclid's Axioms Empirical?' (1898) *Papers*, ii. 325–38.

*EFG*    *An Essay on the Foundations of Geometry* (New York: Dover, 1956; 1st edn., 1897).

*EFG/F*    *Essai sur les fondements de la géométrie*, tr. A. Cadenat (Paris: Villars, 1899).

EPI    'Paper on Epistemology. I', *Papers*, i. 121–3.

EPII    'Paper on Epistemology. II' (1893), *Papers*, i. 125–30.

EPIII    'Paper on Epistemology. III' (1894), *Papers*, i. 147–50.

FIAM    'The Fundamental Ideas and Axioms of Mathematics' (1899) *Papers*, ii. 265–305.

*FF*    *Fact and Fiction* (London: Allen and Unwin, 1961).

GE    'Greek Exercises' (1888–9), *Papers*, i. 3–21.

*GSD*    *German Social Democracy* (London: Allen and Unwin, 1965; 1st edn., 1896).

*HK*    *Human Knowledge: Its Scope and Limits* (New York: Simon and Schuster, 1948).

*HWP*    *A History of Western Philosophy* (London: Allen and Unwin, 1965; 1st edn., 1946).

*IMP*    *An Introduction to Mathematical Philosophy* (London: Allen and Unwin, 1919).

*IMT*    *An Inquiry into Meaning and Truth* (Harmondsworth: Penguin, 1962; 1st edn., 1940).

LA    'Logical Atomism' (1924), *Papers*, ix, 162–79.

LD    'A Locked Diary' (1890–4), *Papers*, i. 41–67.

*LK*    *Logic and Knowledge*, ed. R. C. Marsh (London: Allen and Unwin, 1956).

LOR    'The Logic of Relations: With Some Applications to the Theory of Series' (1901), *LK* 3–38.

*ML*    *Mysticism and Logic* (London: Allen and Unwin, 1963; 1st edn., 1918).

MMD    'My Mental Development' (1944), in P. A. Schilpp (1944: 3–20).

*MPD*    *My Philosophical Development* (London: Allen and Unwin, 1959).

MTCA    'Meinong's Theory of Complexes and Assumptions' (1904), *EA* 21–76.

MTT    'The Monistic Theory of Truth' (1906), *PE* 131–46.

N&P    'Necessity and Possibility' (1903), unpubl. MS, RA220.010860.

NOG    'Notes on Geometry' (1899), *Papers*, ii. 362–89.

NOO    'Note on Order' (1898), *Papers*, ii. 341–58.

OD    'On Denoting' (1905), *LK* 41–56.

*OE*    *On Education* (London: Allen and Unwin, 1926).

OF    'On Fundamentals' (1905), unpubl. MS, RA230.030710.

*OKEW*    *Our Knowledge of the External World* (London: Allen and Unwin, 1972; 1st edn., 1914).

ONC    'On the Notion of Cause' (1912), *ML* 132–51.

ONO    'On the Notion of Order', *Mind*, NS., 10 (1901), 30–51.

OQ    'On Quantity and Allied Conceptions' (1898), *Papers*, ii. 117–35.

OSG    'Observations on Space and Geometry' (1895), unpubl. notebook, RA210.006551.

OSG/P    'Observations on Space and Geometry' (1895), extracts publ. in *Papers*,
         i. 258–65.
PA       'On the Principles of Arithmetic (1899), *Papers*, ii. 247–60.
PE       *Philosophical Essays* (New York: Simon and Schuster, 1910).
PFM      *Portraits from Memory* (London: Allen and Unwin, 1958; 1st edn.,
         1956).
PLA      'The Philosophy of Logical Atomism' (1918), *Papers*, viii. 160–244.
PM       *Principia Mathematica*, with A. N. Whitehead, 3 vols. (Cambridge:
         CUP, 1925–7; 1st edn., 1910–13).
POL      *A Critical Exposition of the Philosophy of Leibniz* (London: Allen and
         Unwin, 1975; 1st edn., 1900).
POM      *The Principles of Mathematics* (London: Allen and Unwin, 1964; 1st
         edn., 1903).
POM/D    *The Principles of Mathematics*, 1899–1900 draft, unpubl. MS, RA230.
         030320.
POP      *The Problems of Philosophy* (Oxford: OUP, 1974; 1st edn., 1912).
Reply    'Reply to Criticisms' (1944), in Schilpp (1944: 681–741).
RNQ      'On the Relations of Number and Quantity' (1897), *Papers*, ii. 70–82.
RMDP     'The Regressive Method of Discovering the Premisses of Mathematics'
         (1911), *EA* 272–83.
SDCQ     'On Some Difficulties of Continuous Quantity' (1896), *Papers*, ii. 46–
         58.
SE       *Sceptical Essays* (London: Allen and Unwin, 1962; 1st edn., 1928).
SP       *Selected Papers of Bertrand Russell* (New York: Modern Library Pub-
         lishers, 1927).
TK       *Theory of Knowledge* (1913), *Papers*, vii. 5–178.
UE       *Unpopular Essays* (London: Allen and Unwin, 1950).
VN       'Various Notes on Mathematical Philosophy' (1896–8), *Papers*, ii. 11–
         28.
WDWR     'Why Do We Regard Time, But Not Space, as Necessarily a Plenum?'
         (1897), *Papers*, ii. 92–7.
WNC      *Why I am Not a Christian*, ed. P. Edwards (London: Allen and Unwin,
         1967; 1st edn., 1957).
1893a    'Can We Be Statesmen?', *Papers*, i. 79–82.
1893b    'On the Foundations of Ethics', *Papers*, i. 208–11.
1893c    'Die Ehe', *Papers*, i. 69–71.
1894a    'On the Distinction between the Psychological and Metaphysical Points
         of View', *Papers*, i. 196–8.
1894b    'Lövberg or Hedda', *Papers*, i. 84–9.
1894c    'Cleopatra or Maggie Tulliver', *Papers*, i. 92–8.
1894d    'Paper on Descartes, II', *Papers*, i. 179–84.
1895a    Review of Heymans (1890), *Papers*, i. 251–5.
1895b    'The Free Will Problem from the Idealist Standpoint', *Papers*, i. 230–9.
1896a    Review of Hannequin (1895), *Papers*, ii. 36–43.
1896b    'The Logic of Geometry', *Papers*, i. 267–86.
1896c    'The *A Priori* in Geometry', *Papers*, i. 291–304.

1896*d*   'Oscillations of Four Particles under Attraction and Repulsion', *Papers*, ii. 454–8.

1896*e*   'Four Notes on Dynamics', *Papers*, ii. 30–4.

1896*f*   'Note on the Logic of the Sciences', *Papers*, ii. 5.

1896*g*   'German Social Democracy, as a Lesson in Political Tactics', *Papers*, i. 312–18.

1897*a*   'Is Ethics a Branch of Empirical Psychology?', *Papers*, i. 100–4.

1897*b*   'Seems, Madam? Nay, it is', *Papers*, i. 106–11.

1897*c*   'On the Conception of Matter in Mixed Mathematics', *Papers*, ii. 86–7.

1897*d*   'The Philosophy of Matter', *Papers*, ii. 84.

1897*e*   'Motion in a Plenum', *Papers*, ii. 89–90.

1897*f*   Review of Couturat (1896), *Papers*, ii. 60–7.

1898*a*   Review of Love (1897), *Papers*, ii. 99–106.

1898*b*   'On Causality as Used in Dynamics', *Papers*, ii. 108–10.

1899   'Was the World Good Before the Sixth Day?', *Papers*, i. 112–17.

1900   'Is Position in Space and Time Absolute or Relative?', *Mind*, NS., 10, pp. 293–317.

1903   'Recent Work on the Philosophy of Leibniz', *Mind*, NS., 12, pp. 177–201.

1912   Review of Ward (1911), *The Nation*, 10 Feb., p. 788.

1914   Preface to Poincaré's *Science and Method*, *Papers*, viii. 52–4.

1922   'Is There an Absolute Good?', *Russell: The Journal of the Bertrand Russell Archives*, NS, 6/2 (1986–7), 148–9.

1927   'Things that have Moulded Me', *The Dial*, 83, pp. 181–6.

1930*a*   'How I was Educated', *John O'London's Weekly*, 19 July, pp. 525–6.

1930*b*   *The Conquest of Happiness* (New York: Bantam, 1968).

1935   *Religion and Science* (London: Butterworth).

1938   'My Religious Reminiscences', in *The Basic Writings of Bertrand Russell*, ed. R. E. Egner and L. E. Dennon (New York: Simon and Schuster, 1961), 31–6.

1945   Preface to Clifford (1885), pp. v-x.

1946   *My Own Philosophy* (Hamilton, Ont.: McMaster University Library Press, 1972).

1948*a*   'A Turning Point in My Life', in L. Russell (ed.), *The Saturday Book* (London: Hutchinson), 142–6.

1948*a*   'Reminiscences of McTaggart', *Trinity Magazine*, Easter term, pp. 1–2.

1955   'My Debt to German Learning', unpubl. TS, RA220.021380.

1958   'Prof. G. E. Moore', *The Times* (London), 28 Oct., p. 14.

1959*a*   'The Influence and Thought of G. E. Moore', *The Listener*, 6, pp. 755–6.

1959*b*   'Family, Friends and Others', in *The Collected Stories of Bertrand Russell*, ed. B. Feinberg (London: Allen and Unwin, 1972).

## II. Works by Other Authors

Abbott, E. A. 1884. *Flatland* (Oxford: Blackwell; 6th edn., 1950).

Allen, Peter. 1979. *The Cambridge Apostles: The Early Years* (Cambridge: CUP).

Allison, Henry E. 1983. *Kant's Transcendental Idealism: An Interpretation and Defense* (New Haven and London: Yale University Press).

Amberley, Viscount. 1876. *Analysis of Religious Belief* (London: Trubner).

Ambrose, Alice, and Lazerowitz, Morris, eds. 1970. *G. E. Moore, Essays in Retrospect* (London: Allen and Unwin).

Anon. 1937. 'Obituary: R. R. Webb', *The Eagle* (St John's College, Cambridge), 49, pp. 272–3.

Argyll, Duke of. 1866. *The Reign of Law* (London: Strahan).

—— 1906. *Autobiography and Memoirs*, ed. the Dowager Duchess of Argyll, 2 vols. (London: Murray),.

Armstrong, William M. 1969. 'Bertrand Russell Comes to America 1896', *Studies in History and Society*, 2 (1969–70), 29–37.

Ayer, A. J. 1971. *Russell and Moore: The Analytical Heritage* (London: Macmillan).

—— 1972. *Russell* (London: Fontana).

Bacon, Francis. 1620. *Novum Organum*, in *Works*, ed. J. Spedding, R. L. Ellis, and D. D. Heath (London: Longmans; 1860), iv. 39–248.

Bain, Alexander. 1886. Review of Ward (1886), *Mind*, os., 11, pp. 457–77.

Ball, Robert S. 1887. 'On The Theory of the Content', *The Transactions of the Royal Irish Academy*, 29 (1889), 123–82.

Ball, W. W. Rouse. 1889. *History of the Study of Mathematics at Cambridge* (Cambridge: CUP).

—— 1921. *Cambridge Notes, Chiefly Concerning Trinity College and the University* (Cambridge: Heffer).

Barker, S. F. 1964. *Philosophy of Mathematics* (Englewood Cliffs: Prentice-Hall).

Bartlett, F. C. 1925. 'James Ward 1843–1925', *American Journal of Psychology*, 36, pp. 449–53.

Barnes, B. and Shapin, S., eds. 1979. *Natural Order: Historical Studies of Scientific Culture* (Beverly Hills: Sage Publications).

Becher, Harvey W. 1980. 'William Whewell and Cambridge Mathematics', *Historical Studies in the Physical Sciences*, 11, pp. 1–48.

Beck, L. W. 1967. 'Neo-Kantianism', in Edwards (1967: v. 468–73).

Beltrami, Eugenio. 1868a. 'Saggio di interpretazione della geometria non-euclidea', *Giornale di Matematiche*, 6, pp. 284–312; repr. in Beltrami (1902: i. 374–405).

—— 1868b. 'Teoria fondamentale degli Spazii di Curratura Costante', *Annali di Matematica Pura ed Applicata*, ser. 2, ii. 232–55; repr. in Beltrami (1902: i. 406–29).

—— 1868c. 'Sulla teorica generale dei parametri differenziali' *Memorie dell' Accademia delle Scienze dell' Instituto di Bologna*, ser. 2, viii. 551–90; repr. in Beltrami (1902 ii. 74–118).

—— 1902. *Opere matematiche*, 3 vols. (Milan: Ulrico Hoepli, 1902–11).

Berkeley, George. 1734. *The Analyst*, in *The Works of George Berkeley*, ed. G. N. Wright (London: Tegg, 1843), iv. 107–42.

BESANT, W. H. 1893. 'The Mathematical Tripos', in Cambridge (1893).

BIANCHI, LUIGI. 1896. *Vorlesungen über Differentialgeometrie* (Leipzig and Berlin: Teubner, 1910).

BINET, ALFRED. 1888. *Étude de psychologie experimentale: La Vie psychique des micro-organismes* (Paris: Doin).

BLACKWELL, KENNETH. 1972. 'An Essay on the Foundations of Geometry', *Russell: The Journal of the Bertrand Russell Archives*, 6, pp. 3–4.

—— 1981. 'The *Cambridge Observer* Question', *Russell: The Journal of the Bertrand Russell Archives*, NS 1/2, pp. 174–88.

BLANSHARD, BRAND. 1969. 'Bertrand Russell in Retrospect', *Dialogue*, 7, pp. 584–607.

—— 1984. *Four Reasonable Men* (Middletown, Conn.: Wesleyan University Press).

BOLYAI, JANOS. 1832. *The Science of Absolute Space*, tr. G. B. Halsted, in Bonola (1906).

BONOLA, ROBERTO. 1906. *Non-Euclidean Geometry: A Critical and Historical Study of its Development*, tr. H. S. Carslaw (New York: Dover, 1955).

BONTAFINI, M. A. 1970. 'Il primo Russell o il canto del cigno della geometria "Kantiana"', *Acme*, 23, pp. 359–433.

BOOLE, GEORGE. 1854. *An Investigation of the Laws of Thought* (New York: Dover, 1951).

BORING, E. G. 1929. *A History of Experimental Psychology* (New York: Appleton-Century-Crofts; 2nd edn., 1950.

BOSANQUET, BERNARD. 1888. *Logic, or The Morphology of Knowledge*, 2 vols. (Oxford: Clarendon Press; 2nd edn., 1911).

BOSCOVICH, R. J. 1745. *De Viribus Vivis* (dissertatio, Rome). Extracts in Boscovich (1758).

—— 1755. *De Lege Vivium in Natura Existentium*. Extracts in Boscovich (1758).

—— 1758. *A Theory of Natural Philosophy*, tr. J. M. Child, 1922 (Cambridge, Mass.: M.I.T. Press, 1966).

BOWNE, G. D. 1966. *The Philosophy of Logic 1880–1908* (The Hague: Mouton).

BOYER, CARL B. 1949. *The History of the Calculus and its Conceptual Development* (New York: Dover, 1959).

BRADLEY, F. H. 1883. *The Principles of Logic*, 2 vols. (Oxford: OUP; 2nd edn., 1967).

—— 1887. 'Association and Thought', *Mind*, 12, pp. 354–81.

—— 1893a. *Appearance and Reality* (Oxford: OUP; 2nd edn., 1969).

—— 1893b. 'Consciousness and Experience', *Mind*, NS, 2, pp. 211–16.

BRADLEY, JAMES. 1979. 'Hegel in Britain: A Brief History of British Commentary and Attitudes', *Heythrop Journal*, 20, pp. 1–24.

BRAITHWAITE, RICHARD. 1970. 'George Edward Moore 1873–1958', in Ambrose and Lazerowitz (1970: 17–33).

BRINK, ANDREW. 1979. 'Love and Conflict in Bertrand Russell's Letters', *Queen's Quarterly*, 86, pp. 1–15.

—— 1989. *Bertrand Russell: The Psychobiography of a Moralist* (Atlantic Highlands, NJ: Humanities Press).

BROAD, C. D. 1930. *Five Types of Ethical Theory* (London: Routledge and Kegan Paul).

BROAD, C. D. 1957. 'The Local Historical Background of Contemporary Cambridge Philosophy', in C. A. Mace (ed.) *British Philosophy in the Mid-Century* (London: Allen and Unwin; 2nd edn., 1966), 13–61.

—— 1967. 'Some Personal Impressions of Russell as a Philosopher', in Schoenman (1967: 100–8).

BROOKFIELD, FRANCIS M. 1906. *The Cambridge 'Apostles'* (New York: Scribners).

BROUWER, L. E. J. 1911. 'Beweis der Invarianz der Dimensionenzahl', *Mathematische Annalen*, 70, pp. 161–5; repr. in Brouwer (1975: ii. 430–4).

—— 1913. 'Über den natürlichen Dimensionsbegriff', *Journal für die reine und angewandte mathematik*, 142, pp. 146–52; repr. in Brouwer (1975: ii. 540–6).

—— 1975. *Collected Works*, ed. A. Heyting and H. Freudenthal, 2 vols. (Amsterdam: North-Holland, 1975–6).

BROWNE, B. D. 1893. 'Introduction', Cambridge (1893).

BUCHDAHL, GERD. 1969. *Metaphysics and the Philosophy of Science* (Oxford: Blackwell).

BUCHWALD, JED Z. 1985. *From Maxwell to Microphysics: Aspects of Electromagnetic Theory in the Last Quarter of the Nineteenth Century* (Chicago: University of Chicago Press).

BUCKLE, HENRY THOMAS. 1857. *History of Civilization in England*, 2 vols. (London: J. W. Parker, 1857–61).

BUCKLEY, J. H. 1951. *The Victorian Temper, a Study in Literary Culture* (Cambridge, Mass.: Harvard University Press).

BURNET, JOHN. 1892. *Early Greek Philosophy* (London: A. and C. Black).

CAIRD, EDWARD. 1892. *Essays on Literature* (Glasgow: Maclehose).

CALINON, A. 1889. 'Les Espaces géométriques', *Revue philosophique*, 27, pp. 588–95.

—— 1891. 'Les Espaces géométriques', *Revue philosophique*, 32, pp. 368–75.

—— 1893. 'Étude sur l'indétermination géométrique de l'univers', *Revue philosophique*, 36, pp. 595–607.

CAMBRIDGE, UNIVERSITY OF. 1890. *The Cambridge University Calendar* (Cambridge: CUP).

—— 1893. *The Student's Guide to the University of Cambridge* (Cambridge: Deighton, Bell; 5th edn.).

CAMPBELL, OLWEN WARD. 1927. 'Memoir', in Ward (1927: 3–96).

CANNON, SUSAN. 1978. *Science in Culture: the Early Victorian Period* (New York: Dawson).

CANTOR, GEORG. 1871. 'Über trigonometrische Reihen', *Mathematische Annalen*, 4, pp. 139–43; French tr. in Cantor (1883*b*: 329–35).

—— 1872. 'Über die Ausdehnung eines Satzes aus der Theorie der trigonometrischen Reihen', *Mathematische Annalen*, 5, pp. 123–32; French tr. in Cantor (1883*b*: 336–48).

—— 1874. 'Über eine Eigenschaft des Inbegriffes aller reellen algebraischen Zahlen', *Journal für die reine und angewandte Mathematik*, 77, pp. 258–62; French tr. in Cantor (1883*b*: 305–10).

—— 1878. 'Ein Beitrag zur Mannigfaltigkeitslehre', *Journal für die reine und angewandte Mathematik*, 84, pp. 242–58; French tr. in Cantor (1883*b*: 311–28).

—— 1879. 'Über unendliche, lineare Punktmannigfaltigkeiten, I', *Mathematische Annalen*, 15, pp. 1–7; French tr. in Cantor (1883*b*: 349–56).

—— 1880. 'Über unendliche, lineare Punktmannigfaltigkeiten, II', *Mathematische Annalen*, 17, pp. 355–8; French tr. in Cantor (1883*b*: 357–60).

—— 1882. 'Über unendliche, lineare Punkmannigfaltigkeiten, III', *Mathematische Annalen*, 20, pp. 113–21; French tr. in Cantor (1883*b*: 361–71).

—— 1883*a*. *Grundlagen einer Allgemeinen Mannichfaltigkeitslehre* (Leipzig: Teubner); partial French tr. in Cantor (1883*b*: 381–408).

—— 1883*b*. Special issue of *Acta Mathematica*, 2, pp. 305–408, devoted to French translations of Cantor's work.

—— 1883*c*. 'Über unendliche, lineare Punkmannigfaltigkeiten, IV', *Mathematische Annalen*, 21, pp. 51–8; French tr. in Cantor (1883*b*: 372–80).

—— 1883*d*. 'Sur divers théorèmes de la théorie des ensembles de points situés dans un espace continue à *n* dimensions: Première communication.' *Acta Mathematica*, 2, pp. 409–14.

—— 1884. 'Über unendliche, lineare Punkmannigfaltigkeiten, VI', *Mathematische Annalen*, 23, pp. 453–88.

—— and DEDEKIND, RICHARD. 1937. *Briefwechsel Cantor-Dedekind*, ed. E. Noether and J. Cavaillès (Paris: Hermann).

CARNAP, RUDOLF. 1937. *The Logical Syntax of Language*, tr. A. Smeaton (London: Routledge and Kegan Paul, 1967).

CAYLEY, ARTHUR. 1859. 'A Sixth Memoir upon Quantics', *Philosophical Transactions of the Royal Society*, 9, pp. 61–90.

—— 1883. 'Presidential Address', *Report of the British Association for the Advancement of Science*, pp. 3–37.

CHRISTIE, W. D. 1894. 'The Cambridge "Apostles"', *Macmillan's Magazine*, 11, pp. 18–25.

CHRISTOFFEL, E. B. 1869. 'Ueber die Transformation der homogenen Differentialausdrücke Grades betreffendes Theorem', *Jahresberichte de Deutschen Mathematiker Vereinigung*, 70, pp. 46–70.

CLARK, RONALD W. 1975. *The Life of Bertrand Russell* (London: Cape and Weidenfeld and Nicolson).

CLIFFORD, W. K. 1870. 'On the Space Theory of Matter', *Cambridge Philosophical Society Proceedings*; repr. in Clifford (1882: 21–2).

—— 1873. 'The Philosophy of the Pure Sciences', in Clifford (1879: i. 254–340).

—— 1877. 'The Ethics of Belief', *Contemporary Review*; repr. in Clifford (1879: ii. 177–211).

—— 1878. 'On the Nature of Things-in-Themselves', *Mind*; repr. in Clifford (1879: ii. 274–86).

—— 1879. *Lectures and Essays*, ed. L. Stephen and F. Pollock, 2 vols. (London: Macmillan; 2nd edn., 1886).

—— 1882. *Mathematical Papers* (London: Macmillan).

—— 1885. *The Common Sense of the Exact Sciences*, ed. Karl Pearson, new edn. by J. R. Newman (New York: Knopf; 1946).

COCCHIARELLA, NINO B. 1982. 'Meinong Reconstructed Versus Early Russell Reconstructed', *Journal of Philosophical Logic*, 11, pp. 183–214.

COCK, A. A. 1918. 'The Ontological Argument for the Existence of God', *Proceedings of the Aristotelian Society*, 18, pp. 263–84.

COHEN, HERMANN. 1883. *Das Prinzip de Infinitesimal-methode und seine Geschichte* (Berlin: Dümmler).

COHEN, P. J. 1963. 'The Independence of the Continuum Hypothesis; I, II', *Proceedings of the National Academy of Sciences* (USA), 50, pp. 1143–8; 51, pp. 105–10.

COPLESTON, FREDERICK. 1964. *A History of Philosophy*, vi/2. *Kant* (New York: Image).

—— 1966. *A History of Philosophy*, viii. *Bentham to Russell* (London: Burns and Oates).

COUTURAT, LOUIS. 1896. *De l'infini mathématique* (Paris: Alcan).

—— 1898a. Review of *EFG*, *Revue de métaphysique et de morale*, 6, pp. 354–80.

—— 1898b. 'Sur les rapports du nombre et de la grandeur', *Revue de métaphysique et de morale*, 6, pp. 422–47.

—— 1901. *La Logique de Leibniz d'après des documents inédits* (Paris: Alcan).

COXETER, H. M. S. 1942. *Non-Euclidean Geometry* (Toronto: University of Toronto Press; 5th edn.).

CREMONA, LUIGI. 1893. *Elements of Projective Geometry* (Oxford: Clarendon Press, 2nd edn.).

DAMBSKA, IZYDORA. 1974. '*An Essay on the Foundations of Geometry* de B. Russell et la critique de le livre en France dans le années 1896–1900', *Organon*, 10, pp. 245–53.

DANIELS, NORMAN. 1972. 'Thomas Reid's Discovery of a Non-Euclidean Geometry'. *Philosophy of Science*, 39, pp. 219–34.

DAUBEN, JOSEPH. 1979. *Georg Cantor: His Mathematics and Philosophy of the Infinite* (Cambridge, Mass.: Harvard University Press).

DEDEKIND, RICHARD. 1872. *Stetigkeit und Irrationale Zahlen*; English tr. in Dedekind (1963: 1–27).

—— 1878. *Was sind und was sollen die Zahlen?* English tr. in Dedekind (1963: 31–115).

—— 1963. *Essays on the Theory of Numbers*, tr. W. W. Beman (New York: Dover).

DELBŒUF, JOSEPH. 1893. 'L'Ancienne et les nouvelles géométries I', *Revue philosophique*, 36, pp. 449–84.

—— 1894. 'L'Ancienne et les nouvelles géométries II', *Revue philosophique*, 37, pp. 353–84.

DE MORGAN, AUGUSTUS. 1837. *Elements of Algebra* (London: Taylor and Walton).

—— 1842. *The Differential and Integral Calculus* (London: Baldwin and Craddock).

DESCARTES, RENÉ. 1640. 'Meditations', in *The Philosophical Works of Descartes*, tr. E. S. Haldane and G. R. T. Ross (Cambridge: CUP; 1967), i. 133–99.

DEWEY, JOHN. 1886. 'The Psychological Standpoint', *Mind* (1886), repr. in Dewey, *The Early Works*, ed. J. A. Boydston (Carbondale: Southern Illinois University Press, 1969), i. 122–43.

—— and MCLELLAN, J. A. 1895. *The Psychology of Number* (New York: Appleton).

DICKINSON, G. LOWES. 1931. *J. McT. E. McTaggart* (Cambridge: CUP).

—— 1973. *The Autobiography of Goldsworthy Lowes Dickinson*, ed. Dennis Proctor (London: Duckworth).

DIXON, EDWARD T. 1898. *A Paper on the Foundations of Projective Geometry* (Cambridge: Bell).

DRAPER, J. W. 1875. *The Intellectual Development of Europe* (London: Bell).

DUNCAN, G. M. 1890. *The Philosophical Works of Leibniz* (New Haven: Tuttle, Morehouse and Taylor).

EDWARDS, PAUL, ed. 1967. *The Encyclopedia of Philosophy* 8 vols. (New York: Macmillan).

EHRENFELS, CHRISTIAN. 1891. 'Zur Philosophie der Mathematik', *Vierteljahrsschrift für wissenshaftlichen Philosophie*, 15, pp. 285–347.

ERDMANN, BENNO. 1877. *Die Axiome der Geometrie: Eine philosophische Unter-suchung der Riemann-Helmholtzschen Raumtheorie* (Leipzig: Voss).

ERDMANN, J. E. 1878. *Grundriss der Geschichte der Philosophie*, 2 vols. (Berlin: Herts).

ERHARDT, FRANZ. 1894. *Metaphysik*, i. *Erkenntnistheorie* (Leipzig: Reisland).

EULER, LEONHARD. 1774. *Elements of Algebra*, tr. J. Hewlett (London: Longman, Rees, Orme; 4th edn., 1828).

EVES, H., and NEWSOM, C. V. 1965. *An Introduction to the Foundations and Fundamental Concepts of Mathematics* (New York: Holt, Rinehart and Winston).

FARADAY, MICHAEL. 1839. *Experimental Researches in Electricity*, 3 vols. (London: Richard Taylor, 1839–55).

—— 1844. 'A Speculation Touching Electrical Conduction and the Nature of Matter', in Faraday (1839: ii. 284–93).

—— 1846. 'Thoughts on Ray Vibrations', in Faraday (1839: iii. 447–52).

—— 1852. 'On the Physical Character of the Lines of Magnetic Force', in Faraday (1839: iii. 407–37).

FEINBERG, BARRY, and KASRILS, RONALD. 1973. *Bertrand Russell's America: His Transatlantic Travels and Writings*, i. *1896–1945* (London: Allen and Unwin).

FERRIER, J. F. 1866. *Lectures on Early Greek Philosophy and Other Philosophical Remains*, ed. A. Grant and E. L. Lushington, 2 vols. (Edinburgh: Blackwood).

FINCH, EDITH. 1947. *Carey Thomas of Bryn Mawr* (New York: Harper).

FORSTER, E. M. 1934. *Goldsworthy Lowes Dickinson* (London: Arnold).

FORSYTH, A. R. 1906. 'Edward John Routh', *Proceedings of the London Mathematical Society*, 5, pp. xiv–xx.

—— 1935. 'Old Tripos Days at Cambridge', *The Mathematical Gazette*, 19, pp. 162–79.

FOWLER, THOMAS. 1866. *The Elements of Deductive Logic* (Oxford: Clarendon Press; 10th edn., 1892).

FRASER, A. C., ed. 1894. John Locke, *An Essay Concerning Human Understanding* (Oxford: Clarendon Press).

FRÉCHET, MAURICE. 1910. 'Les Dimensions d'un ensemble abstrait', *Mathematische Annalen*, 68, pp. 145–68.

FREGE, GOTTLOB. 1879. *Begriffsschrift, eine der arithmetischen nachgebildete Formel-sprache* (Halle: Nebert), English tr. S. Bauer-Mengelberg in van Heijenoort (1967: 1–82).

—— 1884. *The Foundations of Arithmetic*, tr. J. L. Austin (Oxford: Blackwell; 2nd edn., 1953).

FREGE, GOTTLOB. 1892. 'On Concept and Object', tr. P. T. Geach in P. T. Geach and
	M. Black, *Translations from the Philosophical Writings of Gottlob Frege* (Oxford:
	Blackwell; 2nd edn., 1977), 42–55.

—— 1893. *Grundgesetze der Arithmetik*, 2 vols. (Jena: Pohle, 1893–1903).

FRENCH, R. E. 1987. *The Geometry of Vision and the Mind Body Problem* (New
	York: Peter Lang).

FREUDENTHAL, HANS. 1962. 'The Main Trends in the Foundations of Geometry in
	the 19th Century', in E. Nagel, P. Suppes, and A. Tarski (eds.), *Logic, Methodology
	and Philosophy of Science* (Stanford: Stanford University Press), 613–21.

FRISCHAUF, JOHANNES, ed. 1872. *Absolute Geometrie nach Johann Bolyai* (Leipzig:
	Teubner).

FROST, PERCIVAL. 1883. *Newton's Principia, First Book, Sections I, II, III* (London:
	Macmillan).

GALTON, FRANCIS. 1889. *Natural Inheritance* (London: Macmillan).

—— 1892. *Hereditary Genius* (London: Macmillan).

GARCIADIEGO, ALEJANDRO. 1987. 'Russell's Precise Language', paper presented to
	the Canadian Society for the History and Philosophy of Science, McMaster
	University, Hamilton, Ont.

GAUSS, C. F. 1828. *General Investigations of Curved Surfaces*, tr. A. Hittebeitel and
	J. Morehead (New York: Raven Press, 1965).

—— 1860. *Briefwechsel zwischen C. F. Gauss und H. C. Schumacher*, ed. C. A. F.
	Peters, 6 vols. (Altona: Esch, 1860–5).

GEACH, P. T. 1962. *Reference and Generality* (Ithaca: Cornell University Press; 2nd
	edn., 1968).

GILL, H. V. 1941. *Roger Boscovich S.J. (1711–1787)* (Dublin: M. McGill).

GILLESPIE, NEAL C. 1977. 'The Duke of Argyll, Evolutionary Anthropology and the
	Art of Scientific Controversy', *Isis*, 68, pp. 40–54.

GLAS, E. 1982. 'Mathematics between Logic and Society in the Work of Felix Klein
	(1849–1925)', *Nieuw Archif voor Wiskunde*, 3rd ser., 30, pp. 124–38.

GLAZEBROOK, R. T., and SHAW, W. N. 1894. *Practical Physics* (London: Longmans
	Green).

GRASSMANN, H. G. 1844. *Die Ausdehnungslehre von 1844* (Leipzig: Wigand, 1878).

GRATTAN-GUINNESS, IVOR. 1972a. 'University Mathematics at the Turn of the Century:
	Unpublished Recollections of W. H. Young', *Annals of Science*, 28, pp. 369–
	84.

—— 1972b. 'A Mathematical Union: William Henry and Grace Chisholm Young',
	*Annals of Science*, 29, pp. 105–82.

—— 1977. *Dear Russell—Dear Jourdain* (London: Duckworth).

—— ed. 1980. *From the Calculus to Set Theory: 1630–1910: An Introductory History*
	(London: Duckworth).

GREEN, T. H. 1883. *Prolegomena to Ethics* (Oxford: Clarendon Press; 2nd edn., 1884).

GRIFFIN, NICHOLAS. 1980. 'Russell on the Nature of Logic (1903–1913)', *Synthese*,
	45, pp. 117–88.

—— 1981a. 'The Acts of the Apostles', *Russell: The Journal of the Bertrand Russell
	Archives*, NS, 1/1, pp. 71–82.

—— 1981b. Review of Torretti (1978), *Philosophical Quarterly*, 31, pp. 374–6.

—— 1984. 'Bertrand Russell's Crisis of Faith', in Moran and Spadoni (1984: 101–22).

—— 1988. 'Joachim's Early Advice to Russell on Studying Philosophy', *Russell: The Journal of the Bertrand Russell Archives*, NS, 7/2, pp. 119–23.

—— 1989. 'Russell and Sidgwick', *Russell: The Journal of the Bertrand Russell Archives*, NS, 9/1, pp. 12–25.

HAGER, PAUL 1986. 'Continuity and Change in the Development of Russell's Philosophy', Ph.D. thesis (University of Sydney).

HAHN, HANS. 1933. 'The Crisis in Intuition', in J. R. Newman (ed.), *The World of Mathematics* (London: Allen and Unwin, 1961), iii. 1956–76.

HALL, ROLAND. 1964. 'The Term "Sense-Datum"', *Mind*, 73, pp. 130–1.

HAMILTON, WILLIAM. 1829. Review of Cousin's *Course of Philosophy*, *Edinburgh Review*, 50, pp. 194–221.

—— 1859. *Lectures on Metaphysics and Logic*, ed. H. L. Mansel and J. Veitch, 4 vols. (Edinburgh: Blackwood).

HANKINS, T. L. 1965. 'Eighteenth-Century Attempts to Resolve the *vis viva* Controversy', *Isis*, 56, pp. 281–97.

HANNEQUIN, ARTHUR. 1895. *Essai critique sur l'hypothèse des atomes dans la science contemporaine* (Paris: Masson).

HARKNESS, JAMES, and MORLEY, FRANK. 1898. *Introduction to the Theory of Analytic Functions* (London: Macmillan).

HARMAN, P. M. 1982. *Metaphysics and Natural Philosophy: The Problem of Substance in Classical Physics* (Sussex: Harvester).

—— 1982b. *Energy, Force, and Matter: The Conceptual Development of Nineteenth-Century Physics* (Cambridge: CUP).

HARRIS, KENNETH. 1971. *Kenneth Harris Talking To . . .* (London: Weidenfield and Nicolson).

HARROD, R. F. 1952. *The Life of John Maynard Keynes* (London: Macmillan).

HAWTREY, S. 1874. *An Introduction to the Elements of Euclid* (London: Longman, Green; 3rd edn., 1880).

HAYEK, F. A. 1953. 'Unfinished Draft of a Sketch of a Biography of Ludwig Wittgenstein', TS RA.710.050883.

HEATH, T. L. ed. 1908. *The Thirteen Books of Euclid's Elements*, 3 vols. (Cambridge: CUP).

HEGEL, G. W. F. 1812. *The Science of Logic*, tr. W. H. Johnson and L. G. Struthers (London: Allen and Unwin, 1929).

—— 1817. *Encyclopedia of Philosophy*, tr. G. E. Mueller (New York: Philosophical Library, 1959).

—— 1832. *Werke*, 18 vols. (Berlin: Dundar und Humblot; 1832–40).

—— 1836. *Lectures on the History of Philosophy*, tr. E. S. Haldane and F. W. Simson, 3 vols. (New York: Humanities Press, 1955).

HELMHOLTZ, HERMANN VON. 1866. 'Ueber die thatsächlichen Grundlagen der Geometrie', rep. in Helmholtz (1882: ii. 610–17).

—— 1868. 'Ueber die thatsächlichen, die der Geometrie zum Grunde liegen', in Helmholtz (1882: ii. 618–39).

—— 1876. 'On the Origin and Significance of Geometrical Axioms', *Mind*, OS, 1, pp. 301–21.

—— 1878. 'The Origin and Meaning of Geometrical Axioms (II)', *Mind*, OS, 3, pp. 212–25.

HELMHOLTZ, HERMANN VON 1882. *Wissenschaftliche Abhandlungen*, 3 vols. (Leipzig: Barth, 1882–95).

—— 1887. 'An Epistemological Analysis of Counting and Measurement', tr. R. Kahl in Helmholtz, *Selected Writings*, ed. R. Kahl (Middletown: Wesleyan University Press), 437–65.

HESSE, MARY B. 1961. *Forces and Fields: The Concept of Action at a Distance in the History of Physics* (London: Nelson).

HEYMANS, G. 1890. *Die Gesetze und Elemente des Wissenschaftlichen Denkens*, 2 vols. (Leiden: van Doesburgh, 1890–4).

HICK, JOHN. 1967. 'Ontological Argument for the Existence of God', in Edwards (1967: v. 538–42).

HILBERT, DAVID. 1899. *Foundations of Geometry*, tr. L. Unger (LaSalle, Ill.: Open Court; 10th edn., 1987).

HINTIKKA, JAAKKO. 1969. 'On Kant's Notion of Intuition (*Anschauung*)', in T. Penelhum and J. J. MacIntosh (eds.), *The First Critique* (Belmont: Wadsworth), 38–53).

—— 1972. 'Kantian Intuitions', *Inquiry*, 15, pp. 351–5.

HOLROYD, MICHAEL. 1967. *Lytton Strachey: A Critical Biography*, 2 vols. (London: Heinemann, 1967–8).

HOWE, MARK DEWOLFE. 1942. *The Pollock-Holmes Letters: Correspondence of Sir Frederick Pollock and Mr. Justice Holmes, 1874–1932*, 2 vols. (Cambridge: CUP).

HUME, DAVID. 1874. *Hume's Philosophical Works*, ed. T. H. Green and T. M. Grose, 4 vols. (London: Longmans, Green, 1874–5).

HUXLEY, T. H. 1874. 'Of the Hypothesis that All Animals are Automata', *Fortnightly Review*, NS, 16, pp. 555–80.

ISHIGURO, HIDÉ. 1972. *Leibniz's Philosophy of Logic and Language* (London: Duckworth).

JAGER, RONALD. 1972. *The Development of Bertrand Russell's Philosophy* (London: Allen and Unwin).

JAMES, D. G. 1970. *Henry Sidgwick: Science and Faith in Victorian England* (Oxford: OUP).

JAMES, WILLIAM. 1890. *The Principles of Psychology*, 2 vols. (London: Macmillan).

JEVONS, W. S. 1870. *Elementary Lessons in Logic* (London: Macmillan).

—— 1871. 'Helmholtz on the Axioms of Geometry', *Nature*, 4, pp. 481–2.

—— 1874. *The Principles of Science* (London: Macmillan; 2nd edn., 1879).

JOHNSON, D. M. 1979. The Problem of the Invariance of Dimension in the Growth of Modern Topology, I', *Archive for History of Exact Science*, 20, pp. 97–188.

—— 1981. 'The Problem of the Invariance of Dimension in the Growth of Modern Topology II', *Archive for History of Exact Science*, 25, pp. 85–267.

JONES, P. C. 1946. 'Kant, Euclid and the Non-Euclideans', *Philosophy of Science*, 13, pp. 137–43.

KANT, IMMANUEL. 1746. *Gedanken von der wahren Schätzung der lebendigen Kräfte*, in Kant (1902: 1–181).

—— 1756. *Monadologia Physica*, in Kant (1902: i. 485–500).

—— 1770. *De Mundi Sensibilis atque Intelligibilis Forma et Principiis Dissertatio*, in Kant (1902: ii. 385–419).

—— 1781. *Critique of Pure Reason*, tr. N. Kemp Smith (London: Macmillan, 1929).

—— 1783. *Prolegomena to Any Future Metaphysics*, tr. P. Carus, revised J. W. Ellington (Indianapolis: Hackett, 1977).

—— 1785. *Foundations of the Metaphysics of Morals*, tr. L. W. Beck (Indianapolis: Bobbs-Merrill, 1969).

—— 1786. *Metaphysical Foundations of Natural Science*, tr. J. W. Ellington (Indianapolis: Bobbs-Merrill, 1970).

—— 1902. *Kants gesammelte Schriften*, 23 vols. (Berlin: Preussischen Akademie der Wissenschaften, 1902–55).

KEEN, C. N. 1971. 'The Interaction of Russell and Bradley', *Russell: The Journal of the Bertrand Russell Archives*, 3, pp. 7–11.

KEMP SMITH, NORMAN. 1923. *A Commentary to Kant's 'Critique of Pure Reason'* (Atlantic Highlands: Humanities Press; 2nd edn., 1962).

KERRY, BENNO. 1885. 'Ueber G. Cantor's Mannigfaltigkeitsuntersuchungen', *Vierteljahrsschrift für wissenschaftliche Philosophie*, 9, pp. 191–232.

KEYNES, J. M. 1949. *Two Memoirs* (London: Hart-Davies).

KEYNES, J. N. 1884. *Studies and Exercises in Formal Logic* (London: Macmillan).

KILLING, W. K. J. 1885. *Die Nicht-Euklidischen Raumformen in Analytischer Behandlung* (Leipzig: Teubner).

KILMISTER, C. W. 1984. *Russell* (London: Harvester).

KITCHER, PHILIP. 1983. *The Nature of Mathematical Knowledge* (Oxford: OUP).

KLEIN, FELIX. 1871. 'Ueber die sogenannte Nicht-Euklidische Geometrie, I, II', *Mathematische Annalen*, 4 (1871), 573–625; 6 (1873), 112–31.

—— 1890. *Nicht-Euklidische Geometrie*, transcribed by F. Schilling, 2 vols. (Göttingen: collotype edn., 1893).

—— 1925. *Elementarmathematik von höheren Standpunkte* (Berlin: Springer; 3rd edn.).

—— 1928. *Vorlesungen über Nicht-Euklidische Geometrie* (Berlin: Springer).

KLINE, MORRIS. 1985. *Mathematics and the Search for Knowledge* (Oxford: OUP).

KÖRNER, S. 1967. 'The Impossibility of Transcendental Deductions', *The Monist*, 51, pp. 317–31.

LAMBERT, J. H. 1766. *Theorie der Parallellinien*, in P. Stäckel and F. Engel (eds.), *Die Theorie der Parallellinien von Euklid bis Gauss* (Leipzig: Teubner, 1895), 152–207.

LAND, J. P. N. 1877. 'Kant's Space and Modern Mathematics', *Mind*, os, 2, pp. 38–46.

—— 1878. Review of Erdmann (1877), *Mind*, os, 3, pp. 551–5.

LARMOR, JOSEPH. 1893. 'A Dynamical Theory of the Electric and Luminiferous Medium', *Proceedings of the Royal Society*, 54 (1893), 438–61; pt. ii, 'Theory of Electrions', 58 (1895), 222–8; pt. iii, 'Relations with Material Media', 61 (1897), 272–85.

—— 1900. *Aether and Matter* (Cambridge: CUP).

LASSWITZ, KURD. 1878. *Atomistik und Kriticismus* (Braumschweig: Vieweg und Sohn).

LATTA, ROBERT. 1898. *Leibniz: The Monadology and Other Philosophical Writings* (Oxford: Clarendon Press).

LECHALAS, GEORGES. 1890a. 'La Géométrie générale et les jugements synthétique a priori', *Revue philosophique*, 30, pp. 157–69.

LECHALAS, GEORGES. 1890*b*. 'Les Bases expérimentales de la géométrie', *Revue philosophique*, 30, pp. 639–41.

—— 1898*a*. 'Les Fondements de la géométrie, d'après M. Russell', *Annales de philosophie chrétienne*, 38 (1898), 646–60; 39 (1899), 75–93, 179–97, 317–34.

—— 1898*b*. 'L'Axiome de libre mobilité, d'après M. Russell', *Revue de métaphysique et de morale*, 6, pp. 746–58.

LEHR, MARGUERITE. 1971. 'Scott, Charlotte Angas' in E. T. James (ed.), *Notable American Women, 1607–1950* (Cambridge, Mass: Harvard University Press), iii. 249–50.

LEIBNIZ, G. W. 1686. 'Discourse on Metaphysics', tr. L. E. Loemker, in Leibniz (1976: 303–28).

—— 1695. 'Système nouveau de la nature et de la communication des substances', in Leibniz (1875: iv. 471–87).

—— 1698. 'De ipsce natura sive de vi insita actionibusque Creaturarum, pro Dynamicis suis confirmandis illustrandisque', in Leibniz (1875: iv. 504–16).

—— 1704. *New Essays Concerning Human Understanding*, tr. P. Remnant and J. Bennett (Cambridge: CUP, 1981).

—— 1714. 'Monadology', tr. L. E. Loemker, in Leibniz (1956: 643–52).

—— 1875. *Die philosophischen Schriften von G. W. Leibniz*, ed. C. J. Gerhardt, 7 vols. (Berlin: Weidmannsche Buchhandlung, 1875–90).

—— 1903. *Opuscules et fragments inédits de Leibniz*, ed. L. Couturat (Paris: Alcan).

—— 1956. *Philosophical Papers and Letters*, ed. L. E. Loemker (Dordrecht Reidel; 2nd edn., 1976).

LEITHAUSER, GLADYS. 1984. 'The Romantic Russell and the Legacy of Shelley', in Moran and Spadoni (1984: 31–48).

LESTER, JOHN A. 1968. *Journey through Despair 1880–1914: Transformation in British Literary Culture* (Princeton: Princeton University Press).

LEVY, PAUL. 1979. *Moore: G. E. Moore and the Cambridge Apostles* (London: Weidenfeld and Nicolson).

LEWIS, ALBERT C. 1989. 'The Influence of Roger Boscovich on Bertrand Russell's Early Philosophy of Physics', *Synthesis Philosophica* 4, pp. 649–58.

—— and GRIFFIN, NICHOLAS. 1990. 'Russell's Mathematical Education', *Notes and Records of the Royal Society* 44, pp. 51–71.

LIE, SOPHUS. 1888. *Theorie der Transformationsgruppen*, 3 vols. (New York: Chelsea, 1970).

—— 1890. *Ueber die Grundlagen der Geometrie* (Darmstadt: Wissenschaftliche Buchgesellschaft, 1967).

LITTLEWOOD, J. E. 1953. *A Mathematician's Miscellany* (London: Methuen).

LOBACHEVSKI, NIKOLAI. 1829. 'O nachalakh geometrii', *Kasanski Vestnik*; German tr. F. Engel, in Lobachevski, *Zwei Geometrische Abhandlungen* (Leipzig: Teubner, 1898–9), i. 1–66.

—— 1840. 'Geometrical Researches on the Theory of Parallels', tr. G. B. Halsted, in Bonola (1906).

LOCKE, JOHN. 1690. *An Essay Concerning Human Understanding*, ed. P. H. Nidditch (Oxford: Clarendon Press, 1975).

LOTZE, HERMANN. 1874. *Logic*, tr. B. Bosanquet, 2 vols. (Oxford: Clarendon Press, 1888).

—— 1879. *Metaphysic*, tr. B. Bosanquet, 2 vols. (Oxford: Clarendon Press, 1887).

LOVE, A. E. H. 1892. *A Treatise on the Mathematical Theory of Elasticity*, 2 vols. (Cambridge: CUP, 1892–3).

—— 1897. *Theoretical Mechanics: An Introductory Treatise on the Principles of Dynamics* (Cambridge: CUP).

LOWE, VICTOR. 1975. 'A. N. Whitehead on his Mathematical Goals: A Letter of 1912', *Annals of Science*, 32, pp. 85–101.

—— 1985. *Alfred North Whitehead: The Man and His Work*. i. *1861–1910* (Baltimore: The Johns Hopkins University Press).

MACE, C. A. 1945. 'George Frederick Stout: 1860–1944, *Proceedings of the British Academy*, 31, pp. 307–16.

—— 1946. 'George Frederick Stout, 1860–1944', *British Journal of Psychology*, 36, pp. 51–4.

—— 1954. 'The Permanent Contributions to Psychology of George Frederick Stout', *British Journal of Educational Psychology*, 24, pp. 64–75.

—— 1967. 'Stout, George Frederick', in Edwards (1967: viii. 22–4).

McFARLAND, J. 1971. 'Moore's and Russell's Critiques of F. H. Bradley' (Ph.D. thesis, Brandeis University).

MacKENZIE, J. S. 1894. 'Mr. Bradley's View of the Self', *Mind*, NS, 3, pp. 305–35.

McMAHON, MARTIN. 1972. 'Bertrand Russell's Two Ontologies' (Ph.D. thesis, University of Wisconsin).

McTAGGART, J. M. E. 1893*a*. 'A Further Determination of the Absolute', repr. in McTaggart (1934: 210–72).

—— 1893*b*. 'Time and the Hegelian Dialectic', *Mind*, NS, 2, pp. 490–504.

—— 1899. 'Introduction to the Study of Philosophy', in McTaggart (1934: 183–209).

—— 1901. *Studies in Hegelian Cosmology* (Cambridge: CUP).

—— 1907. 'The Relation of Time and Eternity', rep. in McTaggart (1934: 132–55).

—— 1921. *The Nature of Existence*, 2 vols. (Cambridge: CUP, 1921–7).

—— 1934. *Philosophical Studies*, ed. S. V. Keeling (Freeport, NY: Books for Libraries, 1968).

MANDELBROT, BENOIT. 1975. *Fractals: Form, Chance and Dimension* (San Francisco: Freeman, 1977).

MANSEL, HENRY. 1851. *Prolegomena Logica: An Inquiry into the Psychological Character of Logical Processes* (Oxford: Graham).

MARSH, EDWARD. 1939. *A Number of People* (London: Heinemann)

MARTIN, E. N. 1897. 'The Russell Lectures', *The Lantern* (Bryn Mawr), 6; repr. in Russell, *Papers*, i. 343.

MARTIN, GOTTFRIED. 1955. *Kant's Metaphysics and Theory of Science* (Manchester: MUP).

MASON, JOHN W. 1978. 'The Duke of Argyll and the Land Question in Late Nineteenth-Century Britain', *Victorian Studies*, 21, pp. 149–70.

MAXWELL, J. C. 1856. 'On Faraday's Lines of Force', in Maxwell (1890: 155–229).

—— 1861. 'On Physical Lines of Force', in Maxwell (1890: i. 451–513).

MAXWELL, J. C. 1865. 'A Dynamical Theory of the Electromagnetic Field', in Maxwell (1890: i. 526–97).

—— 1873a. *A Treatise on Electricity and Magnetism*, 2 vols. (Oxford: Clarendon Press).

—— 1873b. *Matter and Motion* (London: SPCK).

—— 1875. 'Atom', *Encyclopedia Britannica*, 9th edn., iii, 36–49.

—— 1890. *The Scientific Papers of James Clerk Maxwell*, ed. W. D. Niven, 2 vols. (Cambridge: CUP).

MEINECKE, W. 1906. 'Die Bedeutung der Nichteuklidische Geometrie', *Kantstudien*, 11, pp. 209–32.

MEINONG, ALEXIUS. 1877. *Hume Studien*, i. *Zur Geschichte und Kritik des modernen Nominalismus*, repr. in Meinong (1969: i. 1–72).

—— 1896. *Ueber die Bedeutung des Weberschen Gesetzes* (Hamburg: Voss).

—— 1899. 'Ueber Gegenstände höherer Ordnung und deren Verhältnis zur inneren Wahrnehmung', in Meinong (1969: ii. 379–469).

—— 1969. *Gesamtausgabe*, ed. R. Haller and R. Kindinger, 7 vols. (Graz: Akademischedruk u. Verlagsanstalt, 1969–78).

MIAH, SAJAHAN. 1987. 'The Emergence of Russell's Logical Construction of Physical Objects', *Russell: The Journal of the Bertrand Russell Archives*, NS, 7/1, pp. 11–24.

MIJUSKOVICH, BEN. 1974. *The Achilles of Rationalist Arguments: The Simplicity, Unity, and Identity of Thought and the Soul from the Cambridge Platonists to Kant* (The Hague: Nijhoff).

MILL, J. S. 1843. *A System of Logic*, in Mill (1963: vii, viii).

—— 1865. *An Examination of Sir William Hamilton's Philosophy*, in Mill (1963: ix).

—— 1873. *The Autobiography of John Stuart Mill*, in Mill (1963: i. 1–290).

—— 1963. *The Collected Works of John Stuart Mill*, ed. J. M. Robson and J. Stillinger, (Toronto: University of Toronto Press, 1963– ).

MILLER, ARTHUR I. 1972. 'The Myth of Gauss' Experiment on the Euclidean Nature of Physical Space', *Isis*, 63, pp. 345–8.

MILNE, E. A. 1941. 'Augustus Edward Hough Love: 1863–1940', *Journal of the London Mathematical Society*, 16, pp. 69–80.

—— 1952. *Sir James Jeans* (Cambridge: CUP).

MOORE, G. E. 1894. 'What End?', unpubl. paper, read to the Cambridge Apostles, 12 May 1894 (Moore Papers, Cambridge University Library).

—— 1897a. 'The Metaphysical Basis of Ethics', fellowship dissertation of 1897 (Moore Papers, Cambridge University Library, Add. Mss. A247).

—— 1897b. Review of L. Brunschvicg, *La Modalité du jugement*, *Mind*, NS, 6, pp. 554–9.

—— 1898a. 'The Metaphysical Basis of Ethics', fellowship dissertation of 1898 (Moore Papers, Cambridge University Library, Add. Mss. A247).

—— 1898b. 'The Elements of Ethics', TS in RA. Rec. Acq. 5.

—— 1898c. 'Freedom', *Mind*, NS, 7, pp. 179–204.

—— 1899a. 'The Nature of Judgment', *Mind*, NS, 8, pp. 176–93.

—— 1899b. Review of Russell, *EFG*, *Mind*, NS, 8, pp. 397–405.

—— 1899c. 'Vanity of Vanities', unpubl. paper, read to the Cambridge Apostles, 29 Apr. 1899 (Moore Papers, Cambridge University Library).

—— 1900*a*. 'Necessity', *Mind*, NS, 9, pp. 289–304.

—— 1900*b*. 'Is Conversion Possible?' unpubl. paper, read to the Cambridge Apostles, 24 May 1900 (Moore Papers, Cambridge University Library).

—— 1903. *Principia Ethica* (Cambridge: CUP, 1971).

—— 1912. *Ethics* (London: Williams and Norgate).

—— 1942. 'An Autobiography', in P. A. Schilpp (ed.), *The Philosophy of G. E. Moore* (La Salle, Ill.: Open Court, 1968), 3–39.

MORAN, MARGARET, and SPADONI, CARL, eds. 1984. *Intellect and Social Conscience: Essays on Bertrand Russell's Early Work* (Hamilton: McMaster University Library Press).

MURRAY, A. H. 1937. *The Philosophy of James Ward* (Cambridge: CUP).

NAGEL, ERNEST. 1939. 'The Formation of Modern Conceptions of Formal Logic in the Development of Geometry', *Osiris*, 7, pp. 142–224.

—— 1961. *The Structure of Science* (London: Routledge and Kegan Paul, 1979).

NELSON, J. O. 1967. 'Moore, George Edward', in Edwards (1967: v. 372–81).

NELSON, LEONARD. 1927. 'Critical Philosophy and Mathematical Axiomatics', tr. T. K. Brown, in Nelson, *Socratic Method and Critical Philosophy: Selected Essays* (New York: Dover, 1965).

OAKESHOTT, MICHAEL. 1933. *Experience and its Modes* (Cambridge: CUP).

PARKER, RICHARD. 1973. 'The Theory of Relations in Russell's Metaphysics' (Ph.D. thesis, University of Washington).

PARKER, ROBERT ALLERTON. 1959. *The Transatlantic Smiths* (New York: Random House).

PARKINSON, G. H. R. 1965. *Logic and Reality in Leibniz's Metaphysics* (Oxford: Clarendon Press).

PASCH, MORITZ. 1882. *Vorlesungen über neuere Geometrie* (Leipzig: Teubner).

PASSMORE, J. A. 1952. 'Memoir: George Frederick Stout, 1860–1944' in Stout (1952: pp. xxv–liv).

—— 1957. *A Hundred Years of Philosophy* (Harmondsworth: Penguin, 1968).

—— 1976. 'G. F. Stout's Editorship of *Mind* (1892–1920)', *Mind*, 85, pp. 17–36.

PEANO, GUISEPPE. 1888. *Calcolo geometrico secondo l'Ausdehnungslehre di M. Grassmann* (Turin: Bocca).

—— 1889. *I principii di geometria logicamente esposti* (Turin: Bocca).

—— 1890. 'On a Curve which Completely Fills a Planar Region', tr. H. C. Kennedy, in Peano (1973: 143–8).

—— 1891. 'The Principles of Mathematical Logic', tr. H. C. Kennedy, in Peano (1973: 153 61).

—— 1900. 'Formules de logique mathématique', *Rivista di matematica*, 7, pp. 1–41.

—— 1973. *Selected Works of Guiseppe Peano*, ed. H. C. Kennedy (Toronto: Univesity of Toronto Press).

PEARS, D. F. 1967. *Bertrand Russell and the British Tradition in Philosophy* (London: Collins).

PEARSON, KARL. 1936. 'Old Tripos Days at Cambridge, as Seen from Another Viewpoint', *Mathematical Gazette*, 20, pp. 27–36.

PELLETIER, F. J. and KING-FARLOW, J. 1975. 'Relations: Turning Russell's Other Flank', *Southern Journal of Philosophy*, 13, pp. 359–67.

PIERPONT, JAMES. 1899. 'On the Arithmetization of Mathematics', *Bulletin of the American Mathematical Society*, 5, pp. 394–406.

PITT, JACK. 1981. 'Russell and the Cambridge Moral Sciences Club', *Russell: The Journal of the Bertrand Russell Archives*, NS, 1/2, pp. 103–18.

POINCARÉ, HENRI. 1891. 'Non-Euclidean Geometry', *Nature*, 45, pp. 404–7.

—— 1893. 'Le Continu mathématique', *Revue de métaphysique et de morale*, 1, pp. 26–34.

—— 1898. 'On the Foundations of Geometry', *The Monist*, 9, pp. 1–43.

—— 1899. 'Des fondements de la géométrie: A propos d'un livre de M. Russell', *Revue de métaphysique et de morale*, 7, pp. 251–79.

—— 1900. 'Sur les principes de la géométrie: Réponse à M. Russell', *Revue de métaphysique et de morale*, 8, pp. 73–86.

—— 1903. 'L'Espace et ses trois dimensions', *Revue de métaphysique et de morale*, 11, pp. 281–301, 407–29.

—— 1912. 'Pourquoi l'espace a trois dimensions?' *Revue de métaphysique et de morale*, 20; English tr. J. W. Bolduc, in Poincaré (1913: 25–44).

—— 1913. *Mathematics and Science: Last Essays*, tr. J. W. Bolduc (New York: Dover, 1963).

—— 1986. 'La Correspondance d'Henri Poincaré avec des mathématiciens de A à H', *Cahiers du Séminaire d'Histoire des mathématiques*, 7, pp. 59–219.

POLLOCK, FREDERICK. 1933. 'For My Grandson: Cambridge and the "Apostles"; Oxford Scholars and Historians', *Cornhill Magazine*, NS, 74, pp. 1–15.

POOTS, ROBERT. 1950. ' "Great Scott"—and Other Descriptions', *The Philosopher*, 2, pp. 16–23.

POTTS, ROBERT. 1845. *Euclid's Elements of Geometry* (London: John Parker).

PREST, JOHN. 1972. *Lord John Russell* (London: Macmillan).

PRIOR, A. N. 1960. 'The Runabout Inference Ticket', *Analysis*, 21; repr. in P. F. Strawson (ed.) *Philosophical Logic* (Oxford: OUP, 1967), 129–31.

—— 1964. 'Conjunction and Contonktion Revisited', *Analysis*, 24, pp. 191–5.

PUJIA, ROBERTO. 1977. *Bertrand Russell e l'eredità idealista inglese* (Messina: La Libra).

PUTNAM, HILARY. 1957. 'Three-Valued Logic', *Philosophical Studies*, 8, repr. in Putnam, *Philosophical Papers* (Cambridge: CUP, 1979), i. 166–73.

—— 1969. 'Is Logic Empirical?', in R. S. Cohen and M. R. Wartofsky (eds.), *Boston Studies in the Philosophy of Science* (Dordrecht: Reidel), v. 216–41.

PYÇIOR, HELENA M. 1981. 'George Peacock and the British Origins of Abstract Algebra', *Historia Mathematica*, 8, pp. 23–45.

RADNER, MICHAEL. 1972. 'Index of Names to *An Essay on the Foundations of Geometry*', *Russell: The Journal of the Bertrand Russell Archives*, 8; p. 20.

REGAN, TOM. 1986. *Bloomsbury's Prophet: G. E. Moore and the Development of His Moral Philosophy* (Philadelphia: Temple University Press).

REICHENBACH, HANS. 1928. *The Philosophy of Space and Time*, tr. M. Reichenbach and J. Freund (New York: Dover, 1957).

REID, THOMAS. 1764. *Inquiry into the Human Mind*, in Reid, *Philosophical Works*, ed. W. Hamilton (Edinburgh: MacLachlan & Stewart, 1895), i.

RENOUVIER, CHARLES. 1891. 'La Philosophie de la règle et du compas: Théorie logique du jugement dans ses applications aux idées géometrique et à la méthode des géométres', *L'Année philosophique*, 2, pp. 1–66.

RESCHER, NICHOLAS. 1967. *The Philosophy of Leibniz* (Englewood Cliffs: Prentice-Hall).

RICCI, G. 1884. 'Principii di una teoria delle forme differenziali quadratiche', *Annali di matematice*, ser. 2/12, pp. 135–68.

—— 1888. 'Delle derivazioni covarianti e contravariante e del loro uso vella analisi applicata', *Studi . . . a commemorara . . . della origine della Università di Bologna* (Padua: Tipografic del Seminario), iii.

RICHARDS, JOAN. 1979. 'The Reception of a Mathematical Theory: Non-Euclidean Geometry in England, 1868–1883', in Barnes and Shapin (1979: 143–66).

—— 1980. 'The Art and Science of British Algebra: A Study in the Perception of Mathematical Truth', *Historia Mathematica*, 7, pp. 343–65.

—— 1984. 'Bertrand Russell's *Essay on the Foundations of Geometry* and the Cambridge Mathematical Tradition', paper given at the Conference on Russell's Early Philosophy, University of Toronto; printed in Richards (1988).

—— 1986. 'Projective Geometry and Mathematical Progress in Mid-Victorian Britain', *Studies in the History and Philosophy of Science*, 17, pp. 297–325.

—— 1987. 'Augustus de Morgan, the History of Mathematics, and the Foundations of Algebra', *Isis*, 78, pp. 7–30.

—— 1988. *Mathematical Visions: The Pursuit of Geometry in Victorian England* (London: Academic Press).

RIEMANN, BERNARD. 1854. 'On the Hypotheses Which Lie at the Bases of Geometry', tr. W. K. Clifford, *Nature*, 8, (1873); repr. in Clifford (1882: 55–71).

RITCHIE, DAVID G. 1889. *Darwinism and Politics* (London: Swan Sonnensheim).

RIVERSO, E. 1972. *Il pensiero di Bertrand Russell* (Naples: Libreria Scientifica Editrice).

ROBERTS, GEORGE W., ed. 1979. *Bertrand Russell Memorial Volume* (London: Allen and Unwin).

ROBERTSON, G. CROOM. 1883. 'Psychology and Philosophy', *Mind*, 8, pp. 1–21.

ROBSON, ANN. 1972. 'Bertrand Russell and His Godless Parents', *Russell: The Journal of the Bertrand Russell Archives*, 7, pp. 3–9.

ROSENBAUM, S. P. 1969. 'G. E. Moore's "The Elements of Ethics" ', *University of Toronto Quarterly*, 38, pp. 214–32.

—— 1987. *The Early Literary History of the Bloomsbury Group*, i. *Victorian Bloomsbury* (London: Macmillan).

ROSENBERGER, F. 1887. *Die Geschichte der Physik*, 3 vols. (Brunswick: Vieweg, 1887–90).

ROTHBLATT, SHELDON. 1968. *The Revolution of the Dons* (London: Faber).

—— 1974. 'The Student Sub-culture and the Examination System in Early Nineteenth-Century Oxbridge', in L. Stone (ed.), *The University in Society* (Princeton: Princeton University Press), i. 247–303.

—— 1976. *Tradition and Change in English Liberal Education* (London: Faber).

ROUTH, E. J. 1882. *The Elementary Part of a Treatise on the Dynamics of a System of Rigid Bodies* (London: Macmillan).

ROUTH, E. J. 1884. *The Advanced Part of a Treatise on the Dynamics of a System of Rigid Bodies* (London: Macmillan).

ROUTLEY, RICHARD. 1980. *Exploring Meinong's Jungle and Beyond.* (Canberra: Australian National University).

—— 1981. 'Necessary Limits to Knowledge: Unknowable Truths', in E. Morscher *et al.* (eds.), *Essays in Scientific Philosophy* (Bad Reichenhall: Comes-Verlag), 93–115.

ROYCE, JOSIAH. 1885. *The Religious Aspect of Philosophy* (Boston: Houghton, Mifflin; 2nd edn., 1887).

RUSSELL, FRANK. 1923. *My Life and Adventures* (London: Cassell).

RUSSELL, ROLLO. 1892. *Epidemics, Plagues and Fevers: Their Causes and Prevention* (London: Stanford).

RYAN, ALAN. 1986. 'Introduction' to Russell (1922), *Russell: The Journal of the Bertrand Russell Archives*, NS, 6/2, pp. 144–8.

RYLE, GILBERT. 1970. 'G. E. Moore's "The Nature of Judgement" ', in Ambrose and Lazerowitz (1970: 89–101).

SACCHERI, GIROLAMO. 1733. *Euclides Vindicatus*, ed. and tr. G. B. Halsted (Chicago: Open Court, 1920).

SAMS, RICHARD. 1979. 'Bertrand Russell's Spiritual Development and the Victorian Crisis of Faith, 1888–1914, (MA thesis, McMaster University).

SCARROW, DAVID. 1962. 'Bradley's Influence upon Modern Logic', *Philosophy and Phenomenological Research*, 22, pp. 380–2.

SCHILPP, P. A., ed. 1944. *The Philosophy of Bertrand Russell*, 2 vols. (New York: Harper and Row, 1963).

SCHNEEWIND, J. B. 1977. *Sidgwick's Ethics and Victorian Moral Philosophy* (Oxford: Clarendon Press).

SCHOENMAN, RALPH, ed. 1967. *Bertrand Russell: Philosopher of the Century* (London: Allen and Unwin).

SCHRÖDER, ERNST. 1890. *Vorlesungen über die Algebra der Logik (exacte Logik)*, 3 vols. (New York: Chelsea, 1966).

SCOTT, C. A. 1894. *An Introductory Account of Certain Modern Ideas in Plane Analytical Geometry* (London: Macmillan).

SCOTT, WILSON L. 1970. *The Conflict between Atomism and Conservation Theory 1644 to 1860* (London: Macdonald).

SIDGWICK, A., and SIDGWICK, E. M. 1906. *Henry Sidgwick: A Memoir* (London: Macmillan).

SIDGWICK, HENRY. 1870. *The Ethics of Conformity and Subscription* (London: Williams and Norgate).

—— 1871. 'The Verification of Beliefs', *Contemporary Review*, pp. 582–90.

—— 1874. *The Methods of Ethics* (London: Macmillan; 7th edn., 1907).

—— 1902a. *Lectures on the Ethics of T. H. Green, H. Spencer and J. Martineau*, ed. E. E. C. Jones (London: Macmillan).

—— 1902b. *Philosophy, Its Scope and Relations*, ed. J. Ward (London: Macmillan).

—— 1905. *Lectures on the Philosophy of Kant and Other Philosophical Lectures and Essays*, ed. J. Ward (London: Macmillan).

SIGWART, CHRISTOPH. 1873. *Logic*, 2 vols., tr. H. Dendy (London: Sonnenschein; 2nd edn., 1895).

SINCLAIR, ANDREW. 1986. *The Red and the Blue: Intelligence, Treason and the Universities* (London: Weidenfeld and Nicolson).

SKIDELSKY, ROBERT. 1983. *John Maynard Keynes*, i. *Hopes Betrayed 1883–1920* (London: Macmillan).

SMOKLER, HOWARD. 1959. 'Scientific Concepts and Philosophical Theory: An Essay in the Philosophy of W. K. Clifford' (Ph.D. thesis, Columbia University).

—— 1966. 'W. K. Clifford's Conception of Geometry', *Philosophical Quarterly*, 16, pp. 244–57.

SPADONI, CARL. 1976. 'Great God in Boots!—The Ontological Argument is Sound', *Russell: The Journal of the Bertrand Russell Archives*, 23–4, pp. 37–41.

—— 1977. 'Russell's Rebellion against Neo-Hegelianism' (Ph.D. thesis, University of Waterloo).

—— 1978. 'Philosophy in Russell's Letters to Alys', *Russell: The Journal of the Bertrand Russell Archives*, 29–32, pp. 17–31.

—— 1979. 'Russell and the English Idealist Heritage', *Russell: The Journal of the Bertrand Russell Archives*, 35–6, pp. 50–4.

—— 1984. 'Bertrand Russell on Aesthetics' in Moran and Spadoni (1984: 49–82).

SPATER, G., and PARSONS, I. 1977. *A Marriage of True Minds: An Intimate Portrait of Leonard and Virginia Woolf* (New York: Harcourt, Brace, Jovanovich).

SPENCER, HERBERT. 1884. *The Man vs. The State* (London: Williams and Norgate).

SPRIGGE, T. L. S. 1979. 'Russell and Bradley on Relations', in Roberts (1979: 150–70).

STALLO, J. B. 1881. *The Concepts and Theories of Modern Physics*, ed. P. W. Bridgman (Cambridge, Mass.: Harvard University Press, 1960).

STAUDT, G. K. C. VON. 1847. *Geometrie der Lage* (Nuremberg: Korn).

STEPHEN, LESLIE. 1865. *Sketches from Cambridge by a Don* (Oxford: OUP, 1932).

STEWART, J. A. 1876. 'Is Psychology a Science or a Method?', *Mind*, os, 1, pp. 445–71.

STIRLING, J. H. 1865. *The Secret of Hegel* (Edinburgh: Oliver and Boyd, 1898).

STOUT, G. F. 1896. *Analytical Psychology* (London: Sonnenschein).

—— 1899. *A Manual of Psychology* (London: University Correspondence College Press).

—— 1914. 'Mr. Russell's Theory of Judgment', *Proceedings of the Aristotelian Society*, 15, pp. 332–52.

—— 1926. 'Ward as a Psychologist', *The Monist*, 36, pp. 19–55.

—— 1952. *God and Nature*, ed. A. K. Stout (Cambridge: CUP).

STRACHEY, BARBARA. 1980. *Remarkable Relations: The Story of the Pearsall Smith Family* (London: Gollancz).

STRAWSON, P. F. 1959. *Individuals* (London: Methuen).

STUMPF, KARL. 1873. *Ueber den psychologische Ursprung der Raumvorstellung* (Leipzig: Hirzel).

SULLY, JAMES. 1878. 'The Question of Visual Perception in Germany', *Mind*, os, 3, pp. 1–23, 167–95.

SYLVAN, RICHARD, and GRIFFIN, NICHOLAS. 1989. *Tentative Answers to Ultimate Questions* (forthcoming).

TENNYSON, ALFRED. 1850. *In Memoriam* (London: Macmillan, 1899).

THOMPSON, S. P. 1910. *The Life of William Thomson*, 2 vols. (London: Macmillan).

THOMSON, J. J. 1893. *Notes on Recent Researches in Electricity and Magnetism* (Oxford: Clarendon Press).

—— 1897. 'Cathode Rays', *Philosophical Magazine*, 5th ser., 44, pp. 293–316.

THOMSON, WILLIAM. 1867. 'On Vortex Atoms', *Proceedings of the Royal Society of Edinburgh*, 6, pp. 94–105.

—— 1884. *Baltimore Lectures on Molecular Dynamics and the Wave Theory of Light* (Baltimore: The Johns Hopkins University Press, 1904).

—— 1891. 'Steps Toward a Kinetic Theory of Matter', in Thomson, *Popular Lectures and Addresses* (London: Macmillan), i. 225–59.

—— 1902. 'Aepinus Atomized', *Philosophical Magazine*, ser. 6, 3, pp. 257–83.

—— 1904. 'Plan of a Combination of Atoms having the Properties of Polonium or Radium', *Philosophical Magazine*, ser. 6, 8, pp. 528–34.

—— 1905. 'Plan of an Atom to be Capable of Storing an Electrion with Enormous Energy for Radio-Activity', *Philosophical Magazine*, ser. 6, 10, pp. 695–8.

—— and TAIT, P. G., 1867. *Treatise on Natural Philosophy*, 2 vols. (Cambridge: CUP, 1890).

TOBIAS, WILHELM. 1875. *Grenzen der Philosophie, constatirt gegen Riemann und Helmholtz* (Berlin: Müller).

TODHUNTER, ISAAC. 1858. *Algebra for the Use of Colleges and Schools* (Cambridge: Macmillan).

TORRETTI, ROBERTO. 1978. *Philosophy of Geometry from Riemann to Poincaré* (Dordrecht: Reidel).

TOTH, IMRÉ. 1982. 'Gott und Geometrie: Eine Viktorianische Kontroverse', in D. Henrich (ed.), *Evolutions theorie und ihre Evolution* (Schriffenreihe der Universitat Regensburg, 7), 161–204.

TOULMIN, STEPHEN. 1980. Review of Levy (1979), *New Republic*, 183 (Aug. 1980), 29–32.

TRENT, CHRISTOPHER. 1966. *The Russells* (London: Muller).

TREVELYAN, G. M. 1949. *An Autobiography and Other Essays* (London: Longmans).

TURCON, SHEILA. 1983. 'A Quaker Wedding: The Marriage of Bertrand Russell and Alys Pearsall Smith', *Russell: The Journal of the Bertrand Russell Archives*, NS, 3, pp. 103–28.

TWARDOWSKI, K. 1894. *On the Content and Object of Presentations*, tr. R. Grossmann (The Hague: Nijhoff, 1977).

TYNDALL, JOHN. 1878. *The Forms of Water* (London: Kegan Paul).

VAIHINGER, HANS. 1881. *Kommentar zu Kants Kritik der reinen Vernunft*, 2 vols. (Stuttgart: Spemann, 1881–92).

VAILATI, GIOVANNI. 1895. 'Sulle relizioni di posizione tra punti d'una linea chiusa', *Rivista di Matematica*, 5, pp. 75–8.

VANDER VEER, G. L. 1970. *Bradley's Metaphysics and the Self* (New Haven: Yale University Press).

VAN HEIJENOORT, JEAN, ed. 1967. *From Frege to Gödel* (Cambridge, Mass.: Harvard University Press).

VENN, J. A. 1954. *Alumni Cantabrigienses*, pt. ii (Cambridge: CUP).

VENN, JOHN. 1866. *The Logic of Chance* (London: Macmillan; 3rd edn., 1888).

—— 1881. *Symbolic Logic* (London: Macmillan).

—— 1889. *The Principles of Empirical or Inductive Logic* (London: Macmillan, 1907).

VERONESE, GIUSEPPE. 1891. *Grundzüge der Geometrie von mehreren Dimensionen und mehreren Arten gradliniger Einheiten in elementar Form entwickelt*, tr. A. Schepp (Leipzig: Teubner, 1894).

VOLKERT, K. T. 1986. *Die Krise der Auschauung* (Gottingen: Vandenhoek und Ruprecht).

VUILLEMEN, JULES. 1969. 'The Kantian Theory of Space in the Light of Groups of Transformations', in L. W. Beck (ed.), *Kant Studies Today* (La Salle: Open Court), 141–59.

WARD, JAMES. 1886. 'Psychology', *Encyclopedia Britannica*, 9th edn., xx 37–85.

—— 1887. 'Mr. F. H. Bradley's Analysis of Mind', *Mind*, OS, 12, pp. 564–75.

—— 1893a. 'The Moral Sciences Tripos', in Cambridge (1893).

—— 1893b. '"Modern" Psychology: A Reflexion', *Mind*, NS, 2, pp. 54–82.

—— 1894. Critical notice of Bradley (1893), *Mind*, NS, 3, pp. 109–25.

—— 1899. *Naturalism and Agnosticism*, 2 vols. (London: Black; 3rd edn., 1906).

—— 1911. *The Realm of Ends* (Cambridge: CUP).

—— 1918. *Psychological Principles* (Cambridge: CUP).

—— 1922a. *A Study of Kant* (Cambridge: CUP).

—— 1922b. 'Immanuel Kant', in Ward (1927: 320–48).

—— 1925. 'Bradley's Doctrine of Experience', *Mind*, NS, 34, pp. 13–38.

—— 1927. *Essays in Philosophy* (Cambridge: CUP).

WEIERSTRASS, KARL. 1872. 'Ueber Continuirliche Functionen eines reellen Arguments, die für Keinen Werth des letzteren einen bestimmten Differential-quotienten besitzen', in *Werke* (Berlin: Mayer und Miller, 1895), ii. 71–4.

WHEWELL, WILLIAM. 1840. *The Philosophy of the Inductive Sciences* (2nd edn., New York: Johnson Reprint).

—— 1845. *Of a Liberal Education in general and with Particular Reference to the Leading Studies of the University of Cambridge* (London: J. W. Parker).

—— 1858. *Novum Organum Renovatum* (London: Parker).

WHITEHEAD, A. N. 1898a. *A Treatise on Universal Algebra* (Cambridge: CUP).

—— 1898b. 'The Geodesic Geometry of Surfaces in Non-Euclidean Space', *Proceedings of the London Mathematical Society*, 29, pp. 275–324.

WHYTE, L. L., ed. 1961. *Roger Joseph Boscovich* (New York: Fordham University Press).

WILLEY, BASIL. 1952. *Christianity, Past and Present* (Cambridge: CUP).

WILLEY, THOMAS E. 1978. *Back to Kant* (Detroit: Wayne State University Press).

WILLIAMSON, COLLWYN. 1968. 'Kant and the Synthetic Nature of Geometry', *Dialogue*, 6, pp. 497–515.

WILLIS, KIRK. 1982. 'Bertrand Russell: An Intellectual Biography' (Ph.D. thesis, University of Wisconsin).

WINCHESTER, IAN. 1984. 'The Antinomy of Dynamical Causation in *Leibniz* and the *Principles* and Russell's Early Picture of Physics', *Russell: The Journal of the Bertrand Russell Archives*, 8, (1988), 35–45.

WINDELBAND, WILHELM. 1892. *A History of Philosophy*, tr. J. Tufts (New York: Macmillan, 1893).

WINSLADE, WILLIAM, J. 1970. 'Russell's Theory of Relations', in E. D. Klemke (ed.), *Essays on Bertrand Russell* (Urbana: University of Illinois Press), 81–101.

WINSTANLEY, D. A. 1947. *Later Victorian Cambridge* (Cambridge: CUP).

WIREDU, J. E. 1970. 'Kant's Synthetic A Priori in Geometry and the Rise of Non-Euclidean Geometries', *Kantstudien*, 61, pp. 5–27.

WITTGENSTEIN, LUDWIG. 1914. 'Notes Dictated to G. E. Moore in Norway', in Wittgenstein, *Notebooks 1914–1916*, ed. G. H. von Wright and G. E. M. Anscombe, tr. G. E. M. Anscombe (Chicago: University of Chicago Press; 2nd edn., 1979), 108–19.

—— 1921. *Tractatus Logico-Philosophicus*, tr. D. F. Pears and B. F. McGuinness (London: Routledge and Kegan Paul).

—— 1974. *Letters to Russell, Moore, and Keynes*, ed. G. H. von Wright, tr. B. F. McGuinness (Oxford: Blackwell).

WOLLHEIM, RICHARD. 1959. *F. H. Bradley* (Harmondsworth: Penguin, 1969).

WOOD, ALAN. 1957. *Bertrand Russell: The Passionate Sceptic* (London: Allen and Unwin).

WOOLF, LEONARD. 1960. *Sowing* (London: Hogarth Press).

WOOLF, VIRGINIA. 1977. *The Diary of Virginia Woolf*, ed. A. O. Bell and A. McNellie, 5 vols. (New York: Harcourt, Brace, Jovanovich, 1977–84).

WUNDT, WILHELM. 1889. *System der Philosophie* (Leipzig: Englemann).

WYNNE, BRIAN. 1979. 'Physics and Psychics: Science, Symbolic Action, and Social Control in Late Victorian Britain', in Barnes and Shapin (1979).

# INDEX

Concepts are indexed under the word that Russell normally used for them during the 1890s. Thus property is indexed under 'adjectives', class under 'manifolds', cross ratio under 'anharmonic ratio', etc.

396                                 *Index*

analysis, mathematical 88–9, 92, 96, 159, 197,
    234–43 (*passim*), 263–4, 317, 347; in
    Cambridge 16–17, 22, 236; non-standard
    236 n.; Russell and 67–8, 69–70, 89, 236–
    43, 253, 263; Weierstrass 89, 96, 236, 237,
    238 n.; *see also* calculus; continuity;
    infinitesimals
analysis/synthesis: in Euclid 81; in Whewell
    91
analytic: geometry 111–12; method, Russell's
    81, 111, 128, 152, 243, 261, 271, 275;
    propositions 72, 91, 101, 115, 134, 365; in
    Kant 105–7, *and see* modality; tautologies
Analytical Society 16
anharmonic ratio 137 n., 138–9, 142, 359; as
    identity condition 151–2
Anselm, St 72, 75, 78
antinomy 84, 314–23, 346, 369; of absolute
    motion 86, 165, 194, 205–10, 222, 223, 224,
    225–8, 297 n., 318, 353; of absolute
    position 318–19, *and see* antinomy,
    kinematic circle; and abstraction *see*
    abstraction, and antinomies; of arbitrary
    sign 353–4; Bradley on 84, 182–4, 186, 188;
    of composition of forces 221–3, 256; and
    continuity 181, 247–54 (*passim*), 262–3; of
    the 'divisible indivisible' 198, 201, 203,
    246–7; of the 'elasticity of hard atoms' 197–
    8, 201, 203; of free mobility 86, 191, 194,
    318; in geometry 85, 164–5, 181–93, 317,
    and geometrical matter 189–95, 217 n.; of
    the greatest cardinal 316–17; and
    hypostatization *see* hypostatization, and
    antinomies; and incompleteness 84–5,
    314–15; and infinite divisibility 146, 185–6,
    188–9, 246–7, 316, 322; kinematic circle 86,
    203–5, 210; of lines and planes 186, 188,
    189–90; of parts and wholes 146, 185–9,
    249–50, 316–17, 319, 322–3; in physics 204,
    210, 217 n.; of the point 149, 164, 183, 185–
    90, 191, 252, 260, 268–9, 318, 336; of pure
    relativity 188–9, 191, 195; of quality 260–2,
    310, 318, 321–2, 359 n; of quantities 254,
    256–8; of quantity 259–63, 267–9, 285 n.,
    317–18, 352, 354, 359 n., 363; and relations
    87, 146, 164, 182–90 (*passim*), 249–50,
    257–60, 267–8, 319–23, 325, 346, 350–4; of
    relative specification 352–4; and relativity
    181–2, 184–5, 187–90, 203–10 (*passim*),
    225–7, 268–9, 316, 317; of relativity *see*
    contradiction of relativity; Russell's class
    paradox 33; in the special sciences 84–5,
    181, 243, 317; and sign 268, 349, 352–4
anti-psychologism 96, 131–4; Bradley's 302,
    305; and Kant *see* Kant, and psychologism;
    Moore's 82, 96 n., 98–9, 131–4, 173, 269,

297, 300, 302–6; and neo-Kantians 132;
    Russell's 98–9, 131–4, 168 n., 173–4, 300,
    305–6, 309, 321, 346; and transcendental
    arguments 96, 131–4, 305–6; *see also*
    intuition
Apostles (Cambridge) 50–8; members of
    51 n.; and neo-Hegelianism 52–5; and
    Strachey 52; and Whitehead 18 n.; *see also*
    *entries under* McTaggart; Moore; Russell,
    B.
apriori vs. empirical 12, 40, 80–3, 91, 95–6,
    98, 100–5, 110, 115, 130–4, 135, 142–3,
    156 n., 159–62, 273–5
apriority: and Kant 95, 100–3; Russell's
    concept(s) of 130–2, 153; and the sciences
    80–4, *and see entries for individual sciences*;
    *see also* intuition; transcendental
    arguments
Argyll, Duke of 4 n.
arithmetic 297; and the apriori 96–9, 131;
    fundamental concepts of 85, 261, 273, 274;
    'grammar' of 275; and manifolds 262, 293–
    4, 336; its place in the dialectic 85, 252–3,
    261, 269, 274, 293–4; and quantity 90–1,
    94, 229, 234, 265, 347; transfinite 12, 240–3,
    265, 293; *see also* antinomy, of the greatest
    cardinal; antinomy, of quality; antinomy,
    of quantity; antinomy, and sign; numbers;
    sign
arithmetization of mathematics 96–7
Aristotle 26
Arnauld, A. 342–3
Arnold, M. 8
assemblages 275, 286–9, 292; application of
    numbers to 293–4; of attributes 286–7; in
    contrast to classes 286–90, 293–4; of
    numbers 287, 294; of predicates 286–7,
    290; of quantities 286–7
associationism 36
atomism *see* continuity vs. atomism
atoms: elastic 197–8; extended 195–8, 201,
    203, 204, 211–13; geometrical 187–90, 192,
    194, 216; hard 197–8, 201, 203; internal
    structure of 195–7; as relata of spatial
    relations 187–9, 193–5, 200–1, 216, 223,
    225–6; relative motion of 199–201, 205–10,
    216, 219; and spatial points 187–90;
    unextended 187–9, 192–4, 198, 201; vortex
    *see* vortex atom theory; *see also* kinematics,
    matter in; point-atom theory
attributes 277 n., 285 n., 286–8; defined
    286 n.
axiomatics 91–2, 100, 107, 111–12; Euclid 10,
    91, 93, 111; Hilbert 91, 112
axiomatization 98, 136, 141, 271
axioms 107, 273; for adding quantities

of projective line 138 n., 252; Russell's writings on 229–30, 253–4; *see also* calculus; divisibility, infinite

continuum hypothesis (Cantor) 242–3

continuum mechanics 212–16, 219–21

contradiction *see* antinomy

contradiction of relativity 274, 285 n., 310, 316, 317–23, 338, 340, 349, 351–3, 360–4, 369; its place in mathematics 274, 285 n., 320, 352; and relations 320–3, 325, 338, 340, 347, 354, 360–4

convention 44, 138–9

conventionalism 115, 176–81

co-ordinates: Cartesian 143–4; choice of 176; and dimensionality 149–51, 358–9; in projective geometry 137–9, 141 n., 143–4, 357, 359

Copleston, F. 48

Costelloe, F. 25, 63

Costelloe, M. 63

counting 12, 231–3, 234–5, 242, 251, 264, 266, 280, 284, 309–10; *see also* cardinality

Couturat, L.: on continuity 234, 263; on *EFG* 129 n., 173–6, Russell's reply 172–6, 179–80; on Leibniz 344 n.; on quantity 255–6, Russell's reply 255–8; on RNQ 253; Russell's letters to 270, 272, 273, 275, 276; Russell's review of 230, 234, 253, 255, 263

Craig, T. 126

Cremona, L. 137, 139 n.

cross ratio *see* anharmonic ratio

Currey, W. E. 29

curvature: Gaussian *see* curvature, measure of; measure of 119, 161, 171–3, 177, 179, 180–1; radii of 158; *see also* space, curvature of

curve 96; Peano 96, 149; *see also* line

Dante 2

Darwin, C. 8, 12

Darwinism *see* evolution

Dedekind, R. 70, 150 n., 236, 237, 240, 253

Dedekind cuts 234

definition 12; by abstraction 155, 267–8; and analysis 273–4, 319; mathematical vs. philosophical 155, 272, 319

Delbœuf, J. 129, 149 n., 175 n.

Delbœuf-homogeneity 175–6

De Morgan, A. 89, 90, 91, 93, 237–8, 253

denotation 295–6

density (physics) 162, 199, 203, 218, 220

Descartes, R. 26, 28, 31 n., 35, 77 n., 100; ontological argument 74–6; physics 193, 205

descriptions, theory of 33, 279 n.

desire 43

Dewey, J. 132 n., 232 n.

dialectic 49, 54–5, 252–3; *see also* antinomy

dialectic of the sciences 43–4, 69, 79–80, 84–7, 181, 204, 217 n., 261, 269, 297, 314–16, 368–9; demarcation of the sciences in 192–3, 314–15; transitions in 84–6, 130, 154, 204, 269, 315, 317–19, *and see under individual sciences*; *see also* transcendental arguments

Dickinson, G. L. 30, 49 n., 51 n., 53, 56

difference: adjectival/conceptual 142, 168–70, 185, 187, 219, 224, 227, 231, 244, 259–60, 268, 285 n., 338, 349, 354, 359, 362–3, 365–6; of angles 353; of being *see* difference, substantial; of content *see* difference, of meanings; existent 351; finite *see under* calculus; and form of externality *see* externality, form of, and diversity; and judgement 167–71, 223–4, 277; of lengths 353; of magnitudes 349; of meanings 278, 280, 281, 288, 309–10, 322, 340, 365; of motions 353; of numbers 349–50; a proto-relation 185, 272, 327; quantitative 231, 247, 255, 257, 259–60, 267–8, 338, 349, 355; a relation 366; and sign 268–9, 349–53, 355; substantial 144–5, 219, 223–4, 278, 280, 281, 284, 285 n., 288, 310, 327, 366; *see also* adjectives, of difference; identity-in-difference

differential 235, 237 n., 238, 348, coefficient 235, 236, 263

differentiation *see* calculus

differentiation of parts or contents: and form of externality 144–5, 147; in a plenum 185–7, 218–19, 311; *see also* continua, elements of

Digby, E. 31 n., 35

dimension/dimensionality 129 n., 141, 149–51, 158, 274, 358–9; of form of externality 169, 170–1; of physical space 108, 109, 110, 172, 173, 177 n.; in projective geometry 171

direction 353

distance: and conventionalism 178–9; and force 193, 208; and metrical geometry 154–66 (*passim*); and projective geometry 120, 135, 138–9, 178 n., 359; and series 328 n., 358–60; and spherical geometry 165; *see also* quantity, spatial

diversity *see* difference

divisibility: infinite 43, 141, 146, 147–9, 155 n., 188–9, 196, 202, 234, 246–7, 250, 252, 266, 322, 348, 353; of quantity 233–4, 246–7, 249–51, 254, 256, 259, 311, 312, 353

Dixon, E. T. 129 n.

'Dover Beach' (Arnold) 8

Draper, J. W. 2 n.